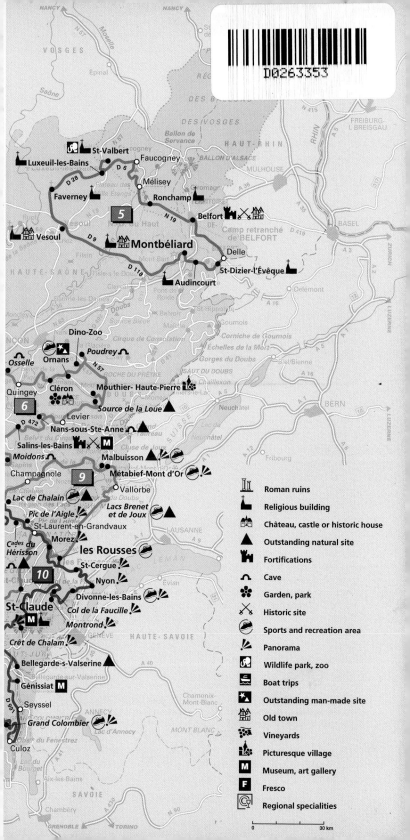

D0263353

VOSGES

St-Valbert
Luxeuil-les-Bains
Faucogney
Faverney
Mélisey
Ronchamp
5
Belfort
Vesoul
Montbéliard
Delle
St-Dizier-l'Évêque
Audincourt

Dino-Zoo
Poudrey
Osselle
Ornans
Quingey
Cléron
Mouthier- Haute-Pierre
6
Source de la Loue
Levier
Nans-sous-Ste-Anne
Salins-les-Bains
Moidons
Malbuisson
Métabief-Mont d'Or
Champagnole
9
Vallorbe
Lac de Chalain
Pic de l'Aigle
St-Laurent-en-Grandvaux
Lacs Brenet et de Joux
Cades du Hérisson
Morez
les Rousses
10
St-Cergue
Nyon
St-Claude
Divonne-les-Bains
Col de la Faucille
Montrond
Crêt de Chalam
Bellegarde-s-Valserine
Génissiat
Seyssel
Grand Colombier
Culoz

HAUTE-SAVOIE

Roman ruins	
Religious building	
Château, castle or historic house	
Outstanding natural site	
Fortifications	
Cave	
Garden, park	
Historic site	
Sports and recreation area	
Panorama	
Wildlife park, zoo	
Boat trips	
Outstanding man-made site	
Old town	
Vineyards	
Picturesque village	
M	Museum, art gallery
F	Fresco
Regional specialities	

0   30 km

BURGUNDY JURA

S. Sauvignier/MICHELIN

Editorial Director   Cynthia Clayton Ochterbeck

THE GREEN GUIDE BURGUNDY JURA

Editor   Jonathan P. Gilbert
Contributing Writer   Claire Gervat
Production Coordinator   Natasha G. George
Cartography   Alain Baldet, Michèle Cana, Peter Wrenn
Photo Editor   Lydia Strong
Proofreader   Gwen Cannon
Layout & Design   Alison Rayner and Isabelle Carbonel
Cover Design   Laurent Muller and Frank Ladd

Contact Us: The Green Guide
                                Michelin Maps and Guides
                                One Parkway South
                                Greenville, SC 29615
                                USA
                                www.michelintravel.com
                                michelin.guides@us.michelin.com

                                Michelin Maps and Guides
                                Hannay House
                                39 Clarendon Road
                                Watford, Herts WD17 1JA
                                UK
                                ☎ (01923) 205 240
                                www.ViaMichelin.com
                                travelpubsales@uk.michelin.com

Special Sales: For information regarding bulk sales,
                                customized editions and premium sales,
                                please contact our Customer Service
                                Departments:
                                USA   1-800-432-6277
                                UK   (01923) 205 240
                                Canada 1-800-361-8236

Note to the reader

One Team …
A Commitment to Quality

There's just one reason our team is dedicated to producing quality travel publications—you, our reader.

Throughout our guides we offer **practical information**, **touring tips** and **suggestions** for finding the best places for a break.

Michelin driving tours help you hit the highlights and quickly absorb the best of the region. Our descriptive **walking tours** make you your own guide, armed with directions, maps and expert information.

We scout out the attractions, classify them with **star ratings**, and describe in detail what you will find when you visit them.

Michelin maps featured throughout the guide offer vibrant, detailed and easy-to-follow outlines of everything from close-up museum plans to international maps.

Places to stay and eat are always a big part of travel, so we research **hotels and restaurants** that we think convey the essence of the destination, and arrange them by geographic area and price. We walk you through the best shopping districts and point you towards the host of entertainment and recreation possibilities available.

We **test, retest, check and recheck** to make sure that our guidebooks are truly just that: a personalized guide to help you make the most of your visit. And if you still want a speaking guide, we list local tour guides who will lead you on all the boat, bus, guided, historical, culinary, and other tours you shouldn't miss.

In short, we remove the guesswork involved with travel. After all, we want you to enjoy traveling with Michelin as much as we do.

The Michelin Green Guide Team

PLANNING YOUR TRIP

INTRODUCTION TO BURGUNDY JURA

SYMBOLS

🛈	**Tourist Information**
🕒	**Hours of Operation**
🕓	**Periods of Closure**
🙂	**A Bit of Advice**
🙂	**Details to Consider**
💰	**Entry Fees**
Kids	**Especially for Children**
🚶	**Tours**
♿	**Wheelchair Accessible**

CONTENTS

DISCOVERING BURGUNDY JURA

HOW TO USE THIS GUIDE

Orientation

To help you grasp the "lay of the land" quickly and easily, so you'll feel confident and comfortable finding your way around the region, we offer the following tools in this guide:

- Detailed table of contents for an overview of what you'll find in the guide, and how the guide is organized.
- Map of the Burgundy Jura region, with the Principal Sights highlighted for easy reference.
- Detailed maps for major cities and villages, including driving tour maps and larger-scale maps for walking tours.
- Map of Burgundy Jura Regional Driving Tours, each one numbered and color coded.
- Principal Sights organized alphabetically for quick reference.

Practicalities

At the front of the guide, you'll see a section called "Planning Your Trip" that contains information about planning your trip, the best time to go, different ways of getting to the region and getting around, and basic facts and tips for making the most of your visit. You'll find driving and themed tours, and suggestions for outdoor fun. There's also a calendar of popular annual events. Information on shopping, sight-seeing, kids' activities and sports and recreational opportunities is included as well.

LODGINGS

We've made a selection of hotels and arranged them within the cities by price category to fit all budgets (*see the Legend on the cover flap for an explanation of the price categories*). For the most part, we've selected accommodations based on their unique regional quality, their Burgundy Jura feel, as it were. So, unless the individual hotel embodies local ambience, it's rare that we include chain properties, which typically have their own imprint. If you want a more comprehensive selection of accommodations, see the red-cover **Michelin Guide France**.

RESTAURANTS

We thought you'd like to know the popular eating spots in France. So we selected restaurants that capture the Burgundy Jura experience—those that have a unique regional flavor and local atmosphere. We're not rating the quality of the food per se. As we did with the hotels, we selected restaurants for many towns and villages, categorized by price to appeal to all wallets (*see the Legend on the cover flap for an explanation of the price categories*). If you want a more comprehensive selection of dining recommendations, see the red-cover **Michelin Guide France**.

Attractions

Principal Sights are arranged alphabetically. Within each Principal Sight, attractions for each town, village, or geographical area are divided into local Sights or Walking Tours, nearby Excursions to sights outside the town, or detailed Driving Tours—suggested itineraries for seeing several attractions around a major town. Contact information, admission charges and hours of operation are given for the majority of attractions. Unless otherwise noted, admission prices shown are for a single adult only. Discounts for children, seniors, students, teachers, etc. may be available; be sure to ask. If no admission charge is shown, entrance to the attraction is free.

If you're pressed for time, we recommend you visit the three- and two-star sights first: the stars are your guide.

STAR RATINGS

Michelin has used stars as a rating tool for more than 100 years:

★★★	Highly recommended
★★	Recommended
★	Interesting

SYMBOLS IN THE TEXT

Besides the stars, other symbols in the text indicate sights that are closed to the public ⚿; on-site eating facilities ✕; also see ⚉; breakfast included in the nightly rate ⊇; on-site parking 🅿; spa facilities Spa; camping facilities △; swimming pool ☒; and beaches ⚍.

See the box appearing on the Contents page and the Legend on the cover flap for other symbols used in the text.

See the Maps explanation below for symbols appearing on the maps.

Throughout the guide you will find peach-coloured text boxes or sidebars containing anecdotal or background information. Green-coloured boxes contain information to help you save time or money.

Maps

All maps in this guide are oriented north, unless otherwise indicated by a directional arrow. The term "Local Map" refers to a map within the chapter or Tourism Region. See the map Legend at the back of the guide for an explanation of other map symbols. A complete list of the maps found in the guide appears at the back of this book.

Addresses, phone numbers, opening hours and prices published in this guide are accurate at press time. We welcome corrections and suggestions that may assist us in preparing the next edition. Please send your comments to:

Michelin Maps and Guides
Hannay House
39 Clarendon Road
Watford, Herts WD17 1JA
UK
travelpubsales@uk.michelin.com
www.michelin.co.uk

Michelin Maps and Guides
Editorial Department
P.O. Box 19001
Greenville, SC 29602-9001
USA
michelin.guides@us.michelin.com
www.michelintravel.com

Vineyards near Mercurey, Burgundy
©iStockphoto/Thomas Lambelin

PLANNING YOUR TRIP

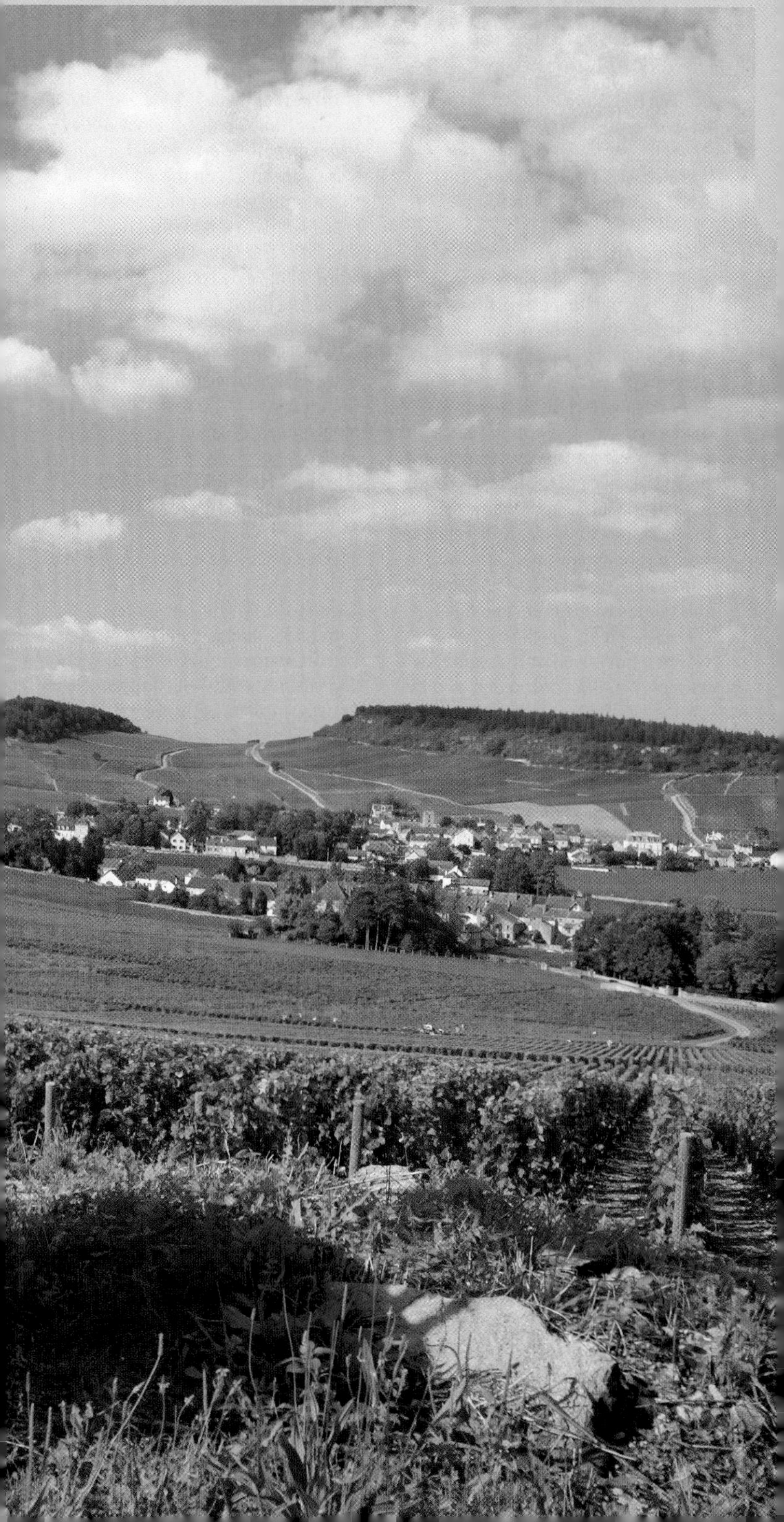

MICHELIN DRIVING TOURS

*Read on to explore the areas highlighted
on the map on the cover flap.*

1 GREAT CHÂTEAUX AND PLEASANT WINES

140km/87mi starting from Auxerre

Having visited Auxerre – its fine Gothic
cathedral, its old boatmen's district –
and admired the view from the Paul-
Bert bridge, you will enjoy a tour of
the vineyards east of the town via
Irancy and Noyers. Continue east as far
as Ancy-le-Franc then turn northwest
down the valley of the River Armance,
with the Canal de Bourgogne
meandering alongside, with its lines of
poplars and enormous locks. Two
Renaissance jewels await you along
this section of the tour: the Château
d'Ancy-le-Franc, which is being
restored but is well worth seeing for
its superb interior decoration, and the
Château de Tanlay with its bridge
flanked by two obelisks. At Tonnere,
turn west back towards Auxerre
through the Chablis vineyards which
produce a wide choice of famous
wines from the modest *petits chablis*
to the exclusive *grands crus*.

2 ROMANESQUE ART: SIMPLICITY, LIGHT AND JOY

200km/124mi starting from Vézelay

The starting point of this unusual tour
is Ste-Madeleine Basilica, which is the
embodiment of Romanesque art. The
nave conveys an immediate impression
of simplicity and light, whereas the
carvings on the tympanum and the
capitals are radiant with joy and light,
rendering to perfection the serenity of
Romanesque art. You can stop in
several places along the twisting road
to Saulieu—in Bazoches, for instance,
or in St-Léger-Vauban, where the
memory of the great 17C military
architect lives on. The Abbaye de la
Pierre-qui-Vire a little further on offers

a striking contrast. Beyond Saulieu,
head north towards Fontenay Abbey,
stopping at the Butte de Thil and in
Semur-en-Auxois on the way. The fact
that it is tucked away in a remote
valley seems to emphasise the
simplicity and lack of ornamentation
of the Abbaye de Fontenay, making it
one of the finest expressions of the
spirit of Romanesque art. Return to
Vézelay via Montbard, the native town
of the 18C naturalist Buffon (*see La
Grande Forge*), the Château de
Montjalin and Avallon.

3 OFF THE BEATEN TRACK THROUGH MORVAN COUNTRY

145km/90mi from Château-Chinon

The Morvan will delight sports
enthusiasts, ramblers and nature lovers,
with its abundance of lakes, forests
and villages. Haut-Folin and Mont
Beuvray (the site of the Gaulish city of
Bibracte) tower above the southern
part of the Morvan, offering panoramic
views over vast areas.

4 DIJON AND THE GREAT BURGUNDY WINES

130km/81mi starting from Dijon

Dijon, Beaune, Clos de Vougeot,
Pommard, Meursault: these names
symbolise what is most prestigious in
Burgundy. First of all Dijon with its two
claims to fame: gastronomy and history.
The order of the Golden Fleece and
the tombs of the dukes of Burgundy in
the Musée des Beaux-Arts attract
history buffs; St-Bénigne Cathedral
and the Chartreuse de Champmol
delight those keen on architecture
and sculpture. However, Dijon is first
and foremost a fine town with a
pleasant way of life, where tourists like
to stop for a day or two and stroll
through the streets. South of Dijon, N
74 goes through a succession of villages
which produce world-famous wines.

Visits of cellars and tasting sessions are a must. Take time to admire the vineyards looked after with loving care by generations of wine-growers. Beaune is as attractive as ever with its Hôtel-Dieu containing the famous polyptych of the Last Judgement and its shopping district offering the thousand and one regional specialities. The wine tour ends with Meursault and Pommard and the itinerary takes the long way back to Dijon, via three amazing castles: La Rochepot, Châteauneuf and Commarin.

5 TREASURES OF SACRED ART

215km/134mi starting from Montbéliard

The contrast between the simplicity of the Temple St-Georges and the elaborate ornamentation of the nearby Église St-Maimboeuf, is a perfect example of religious rivalry from the Reformation onwards. Strong beliefs and traditions are expressed in the attractive religious buildings and places of pilgrimage, some of which, dotted along this route, are truly amazing, such as the baptistery in Audincourt or Ronchamp's Chapelle Notre-Dame-du-Haut.

6 MYSTERIOUS CAVES AND SPRINGS

270km/168mi starting from Dole

Rain, more rain, nothing but rain… How many holidaymakers have cursed the rain that seems to fall for days on end; yet it is the rain that makes the Jura landscape what it is by swelling the streams which dig their way through deep gorges, feed vast lakes and keep pastures green year-round. In any case nature kindly provides sumptuous caves as shelter when the weather is bad.

7 CHAROLAIS AND BRIONNAIS COUNTRY

142km/88mi starting from Charolles

Charolais is the name of a famous breed of cattle characterised by the pale colour of their coat. If you enjoy eating meat, you will want to savour a succulent piece of Charolais beef (tastings are organised by the Charolais Institute). The surrounding area is dotted with castles, beginning with Digoine. Nearby is Paray-le-Monial and its basilica modelled, albeit on a smaller scale, on the famous Cluny Abbey. Further south, the route enters Brionnais country; churches in this area are renowned for their bell-towers and fine sculptures (Anzy-le-Duc, Semur-en-Brionnais). St-Christophe, lying in the heart of the cattle-breeding region, bustles with activity on Thursday mornings when the cattle market takes place. Go south to Charlieu, its fine abbey and nearby Couvent des Cordeliers (Gothic cloisters). Turn northwards back to Charolles via the Château de Drée (its interior is being beautifully restored) and Mont des Carges which offers a last glimpse of the Charolais countryside.

8 FROM CLUNY TO TAIZÉ: SOUTH OF BURGUNDY IN ALL ITS SPLENDOUR

120km/75mi starting from Mâcon

South Burgundy seems to stand apart from the rest of the region, an impression which is underlined by the widening Saône Valley and the use of curved tiles on the roofs of houses. Starting from Mâcon, drive across the famous vineyards of St-Vérand and Pouilly-Fuissé on the way to the Roche de Solutré. The climb is not too hard and the view is well worth the effort. Stop by the museum of prehistory partly dug out of the rock. Continue to Milly, where Lamartine spent his childhood and visit the nearby Château de St-Point where he received all his famous friends: Victor Hugo, Franz Liszt and so on. Further on lies Cluny and its abbey, once the "light of the world" but unfortunately badly damaged… Beyond the 17C Château de Cormatin, Burgundian Romanesque art is once more expressed in Chapaize, Brancion and above all Tournus. Take time to appreciate the city's architectural beauty and gastronomic delights before returning to Mâcon via the Bresse region and enjoying a boat trip on the River Seille.

⑨ ROUND TOUR OF THE LAKES

240km/149mi starting from St-Claude

Beautiful scenery is the theme of this tour of the Jura lakes. Artificial and natural lakes are very popular in summer. Their considerable number and great diversity ensure a wide choice of leisure activities. The largest of them all is the Vouglans Lake; it offers cruises aboard an elegant paddle-boat, often including a gastronomic meal. The most beautiful is probably the Chalain Lake which attracts water sports and sailing enthusiasts. The St-Point Lake, which freezes over in winter, is famous in summer for its shimmering clear waters whereas the Abbaye lake is the paradise of anglers.

⑩ ROUTE DES BELVÉDÈRES

270km/168mi starting from Les Rousses

A moderately high mountain, plateaux dotted with lakes, forests as far as the eye can see and numerous water-falls… it takes time to discover the wealth of natural beauty the region has to offer and it is sometimes necessary to get an overall view of the Jura's varied scenery from one of the many viewpoints dotted along this route. For instance, the Pic de l'Aigle offers an unforgettable panorama of the lake region and the Col de la Faucille ovelooks the Gex area, Lake Geneva with the Alps in the distance.

⑪ ROUND TOUR OF THE WILD BUGEY AREA

250km/155mi starting from Nantua

The A 40 motorway wends its way across this once-remote area through tunnels and over viaducts. Nantua and its lake now welcome visitors who enjoy its gastronomic speciality, the *quenelle de Nantua*. As the Bonnet silk works in Jujurieux testify, the area has traditionally been under the economic influence of the nearby Lyon region. The generally moderate altitude, the purity of the air and unspoilt nature are an inducement to relaxation even if one is reminded that this was not always so as the Maison d'Izieu testifies.

WHEN AND WHERE TO GO

When to Go

Burgundy enjoys a semi-continental climate with marked contrasts between the seasons. The air is sharp in spite of frequent periods of bright weather except in the south of the region where the Mediterranean influence can already be felt.
Other than at the height of summer, the mountainous Jura receives a fair amount of rain which is responsible for the lush pastures, rushing streams and rivers, and numerous cascades and waterfalls.
In **winter**, it can be very cold in Burgundy even when the sun is out. The Jura summits and plateaux are covered with snow and many resorts offer very good skiing conditions. When the weather turns extremely cold, it is even possible to skate on the many ponds and small lakes.
In **spring**, nights in Burgundy are fresh, even frosty, until late May. As for the Jura mountains, they are still white in late April, but when the snow starts to melt, the landscapes come to life with a multitude of cascading streams and rushing waterfalls.
Summer in Burgundy can be hot, although tempered by cool showers; glorious sunsets light up the façades of churches and old mansions. On the other hand, it is never too hot on the high plateaux and in the mountains

of the Jura region; even down in the valleys, woods provide shade and keep the heat out.

Early **autumn** is the ideal season to enjoy Burgundian landscapes and gastronomy; the sun shines generously as the Morvan heights act as a screen against Atlantic weather. Later on fog invades river valleys and frost settles in the region's forests. In the Jura, deciduous trees put on warm golden hues which contrast with the dark green colour of fir trees; the inevitable heavy rainfall turns mountain streams into gushing torrents.

WEATHER FORECAST

Météo-France offers detailed information at national, regional and local level. This information is updated three times a day and is valid for five days. www.meteofrance.com.

Seven-day forecast: ☎32501; towns only ☎32502; mountains ☎32504; roads ☎32505.

Local forecast: ☎08 92 68 02 followed by the number of the département (Ain: 01; Côte-d'Or: 21; Doubs: 25; Jura: 39; Nièvre: 58; Haute-Saône: 70; Saône et Loire: 71; Yonne: 89; Territoire de Belfort: 90).

Themed Tours

Travel itineraries on specific themes have been mapped out to help you discover the regional architectural heritage and the traditions which make up the cultural heritage of the region. You will find brochures in tourist offices, and the routes are generally well marked and easy to follow (signs along the roads).

HISTORY

To allow tourists to discover France's architectural heritage in a historical context, the **Fédération nationale des Routes historiques** (www.routes-historiques.com) has set the following itineraries for the region described in this guide. Brochures and maps are available from the local contacts listed, or from La Demeure Historique, Hôtel de Nesmond, 57 quai de la Tournelle, 75005 Paris. ☎01 55 42 60 00. www.demeure-historique.org.

Route Historique des Ducs de Bourgogne
Information is available from Château de Sully, 71360 Sully. ☎03 85 82 09 86. www.routedesducs.com, or from the Office de Tourisme de Pouilly-en-Auxois. ☎03 80 90 74 24. www.pouilly-auxois.com.

Route Historique des Monts et Merveilles de Franche-Comté
The route includes the châteaux of Arlay, Belvoir, Joux, Gy, Filain and the Saline royale d'Arc-et-Senans. Contact Christian Jouffroy, BP 233, 25204 Montbéliard. ☎03 81 91 45 12. www.chateaux-france.com.

TRADITIONS AND CULTURAL HERITAGE

These routes cover a selection of themes of regional interest from cheese and wine to art and famous figures of the past.

Route des Châteaux de Bourgogne du Sud
The itinerary includes, among others, the châteaux of Sully, Couches, Cormatin, La Ferté Abbey… Contact Maison de la Saône-et-Loire, 389 av. de Lattre-de-Tassigny, 71000 Mâcon. ☎03 85 21 02 20.

Route des Trésors de Puisaye
Contact the Maison de la Puisaye-Forterre. ☎03 86 74 19 27. www.puisaye-forterre.com.

Route de Madame de Sévigné
From Châtillon-sur-Seine to Saulieu. ☎03 80 92 18 87.

Route de la Bresse
Two signposted loops (200km/124mi) explore the landscape, traditions, heritage and gastronomy of the Bresse region. Free guidebook: enquire at the Fédération Départementale des Routes

Touristiques, 34 r. Général-Delestraint, BP 78, 01002 Bourg-en-Bresse Cedex. ☎04 74 32 31 30. www.ain-tourisme. com. Other guides available: Route des Étangs de la Dombes, Route du Bugey.

Route des Vins du Jura

80km/50mi tour from Salins-les-Bains to St-Amour through the great vineyards of the Jura region; visit of the wine museum in Arbois. Contact the Comité Interprofessionnel des Vins du Jura, Château Pécauld, BP 41, 39602 Arbois Cedex. ☎03 84 66 26 14. www. laroutedesvinsdejura.com.

Route des Retables

This route enables visitors to discover more than 80 splendid altarpieces mostly made after the Reformation. Information is available from the SEM Destination 70, BP 57, 70001 Vesoul Cedex. ☎03 84 97 10 70. hautesaone retables.free.fr.

Routes du Comté

The famous Comté cheese represents one of the strongest traditions of the Jura region. Several itineraries have been mapped out to include visits to farms and maturing cellars as well as meetings with local people willing to share with visitors their knowledge and enthusiasm. Information from the Maison du Comté in Poligny. ☎03 84 37 23 51. www.lesroutesducomte.com.

Route Pasteur

In the footsteps of Louis Pasteur via Dole, Arbois and Salins-les-Bains. Contact:
Office de Tourisme de Dole, pl. Grévy, 39100 Dole. ☎03 84 72 11 22.
Office de Tourisme d'Arbois, Hôtel de Ville, 39600 Arbois. ☎03 84 66 55 50.
Office de Tourisme de Salins, pl. des Salines, 39110 Salins. ☎03 84 73 01 34.

A TASTE OF THE REGION

Several sites in the region (among them production facilities, fairs, markets, demonstrations) have been labelled *Sites Remarquables du Goût* (Noteworthy sites for taste). In Burgundy, these

include Beaune (vente des Hospices), Bourg-en-Bresse (Glorieuses), Chablis, Charolles, Flavigny (aniseed sweets), Louhans (poultry market), St-Christophe-en-Brionnais (beef market), Saulieu, Villargoix (Fête du Charolais) and Vougeot (Château du Clos de Vougeot). For more information on these and other sites, visit www.legout.com.

NATURE

The routes below focus on areas of exceptional natural beauty.
Route des Mille Étangs – 61km/38mi tour of the southern part of the Vosges: Melisey, Servance, Beulotte-St-Laurent, Faucogney, Écromagny… Contact the Parc Régional des Ballons des Vosges, Maison du Parc, 1 cour de l'Abbaye, 68140 Munster. ☎03 89 77 90 20. www.parc-ballons-vosges.fr.
Route des Sapins and Route des Lacs – *see Route des SAPINS* and *Région des LACS DU JURA* in the Sights section of the guide. Further information is available from the Office de Tourisme de Champagnole. ☎03 84 52 43 67.

LOCAL INDUSTRY AND HANDICRAFT

Burgundy and Jura have a wealth of traditional industries which perpetuate ancestral skills and contribute to technical innovation. Furthermore, the development of technical tourism has become a reality.
This has prompted the Chamber of Commerce and Industry in Dijon to publish a regularly updated guide to help visitors in their economic discovery of the *Côte-d'Or département*.
Interesting technical visits mentioned in the Sights section include:
- The **Grande Forge de Buffon** near Montbard
- **La Mine et les Hommes** in Blanzy, near Le Creusot-Montceau
- The **Museum of Man and Industry** in Le Creusot
- The **underground quarry** in Aubigny

- The **Musée Nicéphore-Niepce** in Châlon-sur-Saône
- The **Musée Frédéric-Japy** in Beaucourt
- The **Forge-Musée** in Étueffont, near Belfort
- The **Écomusée du Pays de la Cerise** in Fougerolles
- The **Musée du Jouet** in Moirans-en-Montagne
- The **Taillanderie** in Nans-sous-Ste-Anne
- The **Musée de la Mine** in Ronchamp
- The **Salines** in Salins-les-Bains
- The **Forges de Syam**

WINE COUNTRY

The art of drinking wine – To identify and describe the qualities or defects of a particular wine, both wine buffs and wine experts use an extremely wide yet precise vocabulary. Assessing a wine involves three successive stages, each associated with a particular sense and a certain number of technical terms:

The eye – General impression: crystalline (good clarity), limpid (perfectly transparent, no particles in suspension), still (no bubbles), sparkling (effervescent wine) or *mousseux* (lots of fine, Champagne-type bubbles).

Colour and hues: a wine is said to have a nice robe when the colour is sharp and clean; the main terms used to describe the different hues are pale red, ruby, onionskin, garnet (red wine), salmon, amber, partridge-eye pink (rosé wine) and golden-green, golden-yellow and straw (white wine).

The nose – Pleasant smells: floral, fruity, balsamic, spicy, flinty. Unpleasant smells: corked, woody, hydrogen sulphide, cask.

The mouth – Once it has passed the visual and olfactory tests, the wine undergoes a final test in the mouth. It can be described as agreeable (pleasant), aggressive (unpleasant, with a high acidity), full-flavoured (rich and well-balanced), structured (well-constructed, with a high alcohol content), heady (intoxicating), fleshy (producing a strong impact on taste

KIR

Kir is a friendly little before-dinner drink made of cool white wine and a touch of cassis, blackcurrant liqueur, a Dijon speciality. Its rosy colour and sweet aroma make you feel better just looking at it. Start with champagne and it becomes a *kir royal*, or innovate with other flavoured liqueurs (peach, blackberry). While the origins of the concoction itself are lost in time, the name is that of Dijon's mayor (from 1945 until his death in 1968), who tirelessly served this drink to his guests at the town hall.

buds), fruity (flavour evoking the freshness and natural taste of grapes), easy to drink, jolly (inducing merriness), round (supple, mellow), lively (light, fresh, with a lowish alcohol content) etc.

Quality control – French wines fall into various official categories indicating the area of production and therefore the probable quality of the wine. AOC *(appellation d'origine contrôlée)* denotes a wine produced in a strictly delimited area, stated on the label, made with the grape varieties specified for that wine in accordance with local traditional methodology. VDQS *(vin délimité de qualité supérieure)* is also produced in a legally controlled area, slightly less highly rated than AOC. *Vin de pays* denotes the highest ranking table wine after AOC and VDQS.

Wine cellar visits – The **Bureau interprofessionnel des vins de Bourgogne (BIVB)**, *(12 bd. Bretonnière, BP 150, 21024 Beaune Cedex. ☎03 80 25 04 80, www.vins-bourgogne. fr)*, provides information and publishes brochures about wines including a repertory of wine cellars selling bottled wine with the names of the different estates, cooperatives and wine-producers/merchants.

Wine-tasting courses lasting from two hours to several days are organised by the **École des vins de Bourgogne** *(BIVB, ☎03 80 25 04 95)*.

In addition, 250 wine-producers/ merchants, cooperatives and municipal cellars have formed an association known as the **De Vignes en Caves**. Members display a sign at the entrance

Address Book

Below are the addresses of main wine centres and large cooperatives:

Côte de Beaune

Beaune	**Maison des Vins à Beaune (BIVB)** – *See address above.*
	Denis Perret – 40 pl. Carnot, 21200 Beaune. ☎03 80 22 35 47. www.denisperret.fr. The most important wine-merchant in Beaune; extensive choice of great vintage wines.
	L'Athenaeum – 7 r. de l'Hôtel-Dieu, 21200 Beaune. ☎03 80 25 08 30. www.athenaeumfr.com. All you need to know about wine… books, information, video films, specialised tools, glassware, various objects.

Hautes-Côtes

Nuits-Saint-Georges	**Maison des Hautes-Côtes** – rte. de Villars, 21700 Marey-lès-Fussey. ☎03 80 62 91 29.

Chablis, Auxerrois

Chablis	**Maison des Vins à Chablis (BIVB)** – Le Petit-Pontigny, 1 r. de Chichée, BP 31, 89800 Chablis. ☎03 86 42 42 22.
	Coopérative la Chablisienne – 8 bd. Pasteur, 89800 Chablis. ☎03 86 42 89 89. www.chablisienne.com.
Saint-Bris-le-Vineux	**Maison du Vignoble Auxerrois** – 14 rte. de Champs, 89530 Saint-Bris-le-Vineux. ☎03 86 53 66 76. www.maisonduvignoble.com.

Côte Chalonnaise

Chalon-sur-Saône	**Maison des Vins de la Côte Chalonnaise** – Promenade Sainte-Marie, 71100 Chalon-sur-Saône. ☎03 85 41 64 00.

Mâconnais

Mâcon	**Maison Mâconnaise des Vins** – 484 av. de Lattre-de-Tassigny, 71000 Mâcon, (along N 6). ☎03 85 22 91 11. www.maisons-des-vins.com.

of their estate and a list of all members with their location is offered to visitors in tourist information centres.

Wine Museums

These are described in the guide:

- **Beaune**
  Musée du Vin de Bourgogne
- **Chenôve**
  Cuverie des Ducs de Bourgogne
- **Vougeot**
  Château du Clos de Vougeot
- **Reulle-Vergy** Musée des Arts et Traditions des Hautes-Côtes
- **Cuiseaux** Maison de la Vigne et du Vigneron
- **Romanèche-Thorins**
  Hameau du Vin
- **Coulanges-la-Vineuse** Musée de la Vigne et du Vieux Pressoir

Internet

Many wine-makers maintain websites and sell their wine via the Internet; others have chosen to be included on the portal of their merchants.

- **www.bourgogne.net**
  This portal includes numerous informative websites on the themes of economy, tourism, wine, wine-growing estates etc and is a good introduction to the region.
- **www.frenchwines.com**
  Linked to the previous portal, this website offers a repertory of French wines with maps, a list of wine-growing villages, of events concerning wine, of wine-growers and merchants, an explanation of the *appellations* system and a vintage table with ratings.
- **www.louisjadot.com**
  The geographical specificity of this wine-growing estate is explained in detail. Wide list of appellations.
- **www.louislatour.com**
  Map of the various plots of land which make up this estate and the

wines produced are described with tasting tips.

Beaune Wine Auction Sale

Find out all about this famous wine auction sale (the world's most important charity sale) on the website at www.hospices-de-beaune.com.

Buying Wine Online:

- **www.denisperret.fr** – *see chart.*
- **www.vins-du-beaujolais.com**
  This elaborate website includes a great number of wine-growers and is one of the best for buying wine.
- **www.vintime.com**
  This site offers a wide selection of great Burgundy wines; the company is also renowned for its collection of old vintages.

Wine and Music

Each summer, the Festival Musical des Grands Crus de Bourgogne offers a programme linking wine tastings with musical performances. Several concerts a piano competition, and a programme of flute music are among the offerings located in intriguing locations: the cellars of the Château de Meursault, the Château du Clos-Vougeot, the Église de Noyers, the Farinier de Cluny, the Collégiale de Chablis and the Proche Chapelle de Préhy. Courses in music and enology are also offered. Contact ☎03 80 34 38 40.

COURSES IN LOCAL COOKING

The art of living well is also the art of eating well and Burgundy is, among other things, synonymous with fine food. The region boasts numerous renowned restaurants which form a sort of a triumphal path to Saulieu, the gourmet capital of Burgundy. But proceed carefully: each village possesses its little auberge, small establishments offering carefully prepared meals using the area's wealth of fresh products.

Maison Régionale des Arts de la Table

Lovers of fine cuisine will not want to miss this annual themed exhibition of gastronomy and the culinary arts, as well as a boutique and tearoom for tasting.
15 r. St-Jacques, 21230 Arnay-le-Duc. b03 80 90 11 59. www.arnay-le-duc.com.

Terroir de l'Yonne

Information and sales for regional products.
7 pl. de l'Hôtel-de-Ville, 89000 Auxerre. ☎03 86 48 22 22. www.terroir-yonne.com.

If your favourite recreation takes place with pots and pans for equipment, why not spend a few days in a prestigious French kitchen for a holiday? These courses take place mainly in winter.

À la découverte de la truffe et des vins de Bourgogne

Saturday mornings from mid-September to mid-December: all about truffles with Chef Jean-Luc Barnabet and a truffle-grower, ending with a tasting session.
Service Loisirs Accueil Yonne, 1-2 quai de la République, 89000 Auxerre.
☎03 86 72 92 10.
www.tourisme-yonne.com.

Visit Bourgogne (Charrecey)

Cooking lessons (1 to 5 days).
M. Carpentier, ☎03 85 45 38 97.

ABC de la Cuisine (Joigny)

Contemporary cooking presented by Jean-Michel Lorain; the course includes accommodation; cost, programme and calendar on request.
☎03 86 62 09 70.
www.cotesaintjacques.com.

Les Toques Nivernaises (Moulins-Engilbert),

Courses on a theme which can be chosen by the participants (from 6 to 12 persons).
M. Jean-François Boschetti, Restaurant Le Bon Laboureur.
☎03 86 84 20 55.

Le cellier du Goût (La Charité-sur-Loire)

This association organises meals with a commentary, attended by famous chefs, as well as tasting sessions during the summer.
☎03 86 70 36 21.

KNOW BEFORE YOU GO

Useful Websites

www.franceguide.com
The French Government Tourist Office/ Maison de la France site is packed with practical information and tips for those travelling to France. The home page has a number of links to more specific guidance, for American or Canadian travellers for example, or to the FGTO's London pages.

www.FranceKeys.com
This site has plenty of practical information for visiting France. It covers all the regions, with links to tourist offices and related sites. Very useful for planning the details of your tour in France.

www.visiteurope.com
The European Travel Commission provides useful information on travelling to and around 36 European countries, and includes links to some commercial booking services (such as vehicle hire), railway timetables, weather reports and more.

www.ambafrance-uk.org
The French Embassy in the UK provides useful information on France in general, pages about visiting the country, and links to other useful sites.

www.bourgogne.net
General information about culture, accommodation, restaurants and tourism in Burgundy.

www.massifdujura.com
A good selection of interesting places to stay and things to do throughout the Jura region.

Tourist Offices Abroad

For information, brochures, maps and assistance in planning a trip to France, travellers should apply to the official French Tourist Office in their own country:

AUSTRALIA – NEW ZEALAND

Sydney
Level 13, 25 Bligh Street,
Sydney, New South Wales 2000.
☎ (02) 9231 5244.
info.au@franceguide.com.

CANADA

Montreal
1800 Avenue McGill College,
Suite 1010, Montreal H3A 2W9.
☎ (514) 288 2026.
Fax (514) 845 4868
canada@franceguide.com

EIRE

Dublin
30 Merrion Street, Dublin 4.
☎ (01) 672 6172.
Fax (01) 679 0814.
info.ei@franceguide.com.

SOUTH AFRICA

P.O. Box 41022, 2024 Craig Hall.
☎ (11) 523 8292.
info.za@franceguide.com.

UNITED KINGDOM

178 Piccadilly, London W1J 9AL.
☎ (09068) 244 123.
Fax: (020) 7493 6594.
info.uk@franceguide.com.

UNITED STATES

East Coast – New York
825 Third Avenue,
29th Floor, NY 10022.
☎ (514) 288 1904.
info.us@franceguide.com.

West Coast – Los Angeles
9454 Wilshire Boulevard,
Suite 210, 90212 Beverly Hills, CA.
☎ (514) 288 1904.
info.losangeles@franceguide.com.

Tourist Offices

Visitors may also contact local tourist offices for more precise information, or to receive brochures and maps. The addresses and telephone numbers of tourist offices in the larger towns are listed after the symbol 🄸 in the town's description. Below, the addresses are given for local tourist offices of the *départements* and *régions* covered in this guide.

Regional Offices
Address enquiries to:

Comité Régional du Tourisme de Franche-Comté (Ain, Territoire de Belfort, Doubs, Haute-Saône, Jura), La City, 4 r. Gabriel-Plançon, 25044 Besançon Cedex. ☎03 81 25 08 08; www.franche-comte.org.
Comité Régional du Tourisme de Bourgogne (Côte-d'Or, Nièvre, Saône-et-Loire, Yonne), BP 1602, 21035 Dijon Cedex. ☎03 80 28 02 80. www.bourgogne-tourisme.com.

Département Offices
Address enquiries to the Comité Départemental du Tourisme (CDT), unless otherwise stated:

Ain – 34 r. du Général-Delestraint, BP 78, 01002 Bourg-en-Bresse Cedex, ☎04 74 32 31 30; www.ain-tourisme.com.
Côte-d'Or – 19 r. Ferdinand-de-Lesseps, BP 1601, 21035 Dijon Cedex. ☎03 80 63 69 49; www.cotedor-tourisme.com.
Doubs – 13 r. de la Préfecture, 25000 Besançon. ☎0825 003 265. www.doubs.com.
Jura – 8 r. Louis-Rousseau, BP 458, 39006 Lons-le-Saunier Cedex. ☎03 84 87 08 88; www.jura-tourism.com.
Nièvre – 3 av. Saint-Just, BP10318, 58003 Nevers Cedex. ☎03 86 36 39 80; www.nievre-tourisme.com.
Haute-Saône – SEM Destination 70, BP 57, 70001 Vesoul Cedex. ☎03 84 97 10 70. www.destination70.com.
Saône-et-Loire – 389 av. de Lattre-de-Tassigny, 71000 Mâcon.

☎03 85 21 02 20. www.bourgogne-du-sud.com.
Yonne – 1-2 quai de la République, 89000 Auxerre. ☎03 86 72 92 00. www.tourisme-yonne.com.
Maison du tourisme du Territoire de Belfort – 2 bis r. Clemenceau, 90000 Belfort. ☎03 84 55 90 90. www.ot-belfort.fr.

🄸Tourist Information Centres
See the individual descriptions of major sights for the addresses and telephone numbers of the local tourist offices *(syndicats d'initiative)*; they provide information on craft courses and itineraries with special themes – wine tours, history tours, artistic tours. Ten towns and areas, labelled Villes et Pays d'Art et d'Histoire by the Ministry of Culture, are mentioned in this guide (Autun, Auxerre, Beaune, Besançon, Chalon-sur-Saône, Dijon, Dole, Joigny, Nevers and Paray-le-Monial). They are particularly active in promoting their architectural and cultural heritage and offer guided tours by highly qualified guides as well as activities for 6- to 12-year-olds. More information is available from local tourist offices and from www.vpah.culture.fr.

International Visitors

DOCUMENTS

Passports
Nationals of countries within the European Union entering France need only a national identity card. Nationals of other countries must be in possession of a valid national **passport**. In case of loss or theft, report to your embassy or consulate and the local police.

Visas
No **entry visa** is required for Canadian, US or Australian citizens travelling as tourists and staying less than 90 days, except for students planning to study in France. If you think you may need a visa, apply to your local French consulate.

US citizens can obtain useful booklets on travelling abroad from the Government Printing Office, either by phone (☎(202) 512 1800) or online (www.access.gpo.gov). General passport information is available by phone toll-free from the Federal Information Center, ☎800-688-9889. US passport application forms can be downloaded from http://travel.state.gov.

CUSTOMS REGULATIONS

Apply to HM Revenue and Customs (UK) for a leaflet on customs regulations and the full range of duty-free allowances; ☎08450 109 000, www.hmrc.gov.uk. The US Customs Service offers a publication *Know before you go* for US citizens – for the office nearest you, consult the phone book, federal government, US Treasury (www.customs.ustreas.gov).
There are no customs formalities for holidaymakers bringing their caravans into France for a stay of less than six months. No customs document is necessary for pleasure boats and outboard motors for a stay of less than six months but the registration certificate should be kept on board. Americans can bring home, tax-free, up to US$ 800 worth of goods (limited quantities of alcohol and tobacco products); Canadians up to CND$ 300;

Duty-Free Allowances	
Spirits (whisky, gin, vodka etc)	10 litres
Fortified wines (vermouth, port etc)	20 litres
Wine (not more than 60 sparkling)	90 litres
Beer	110 litres
Cigarettes	800
Cigarillos	400
Cigars	200
Smoking tobacco	1 kg

Australians up to AUS$ 400 and New Zealanders up to NZ$ 700.
Persons living in a member state of the European Union are not restricted with regard to purchasing goods for private use, but the recommended allowances for alcoholic beverages and tobacco are as shown in the chart:

HEALTH

First aid, medical advice and chemists' night-service rotas are available from chemists *(pharmacie)* identified by the green-cross sign. All prescription drugs should be clearly labelled; it is recommended that you carry a copy of the prescription.
It is advisable to take out compre-hensive insurance coverage as the recipient of medical treatment in French hospitals or clinics must pay the bill.
Nationals of non-EU countries should check with their insurance companies about policy limitations. Reimburse-ment can then be negotiated with the insurance company according to the policy held.

✚ **British and Irish citizens** should apply to the Department of Health and Social Security before travelling for a European Health Insurance Card (EHIC), the replacement for Form E111, which entitles the holder to urgent treatment for accident or illness in EU countries. A refund of part of the costs of treatment can be obtained on application in person or by post to the local Social Security Offices *(Caisse Primaire d'Assurance Maladie).*

✚ **Americans** concerned about travel and health can contact the International Association for Medical Assistance to Travelers, which can also provide details of English-speaking doctors in different parts of France: ☎(716) 754-4883.

Embassies and Consulates in France		
Australia	Embassy	4 rue Jean-Rey, 75015 Paris ☎01 40 59 33 00 www.france.embassy.gov.au
Canada	Embassy	35 avenue Montaigne, 75008 Paris ☎01 44 43 29 00 www.amb-canada.fr
Eire	Embassy	4 rue Rude, 75016 Paris ☎01 44 17 67 00 www.embassyofireland.fr
New Zealand	Embassy	7 ter rue Léonard-de-Vinci, 75016 Paris ☎01 45 01 43 43 www.nzembassy.com
South Africa	Embassy	59 quai d'Orsay, 75007 Paris ☎01 53 59 23 23 www.afriquesud.net
UK	Embassy	35 rue du Faubourg St-Honoré, 75008 Paris ☎01 44 51 31 00 www.britishembassy.gov.uk
	Consulate	18 bis rue d'Anjou, 75008 Paris ☎01 44 51 31 00
USA	Embassy	2 avenue Gabriel, 75008 Paris ☎01 43 12 22 22 www.amb-usa.fr
	Consulate	2 rue St-Florentin, 75001 Paris ☎01 42 96 14 88
	Consulate	15 avenue d'Alsace, 67082 Strasbourg ☎03 88 35 31 04

✚ **The American Hospital of Paris** is open 24hr for emergencies as well as consultations, with English-speaking staff, at 63 bd. Victor-Hugo, 92200 Neuilly-sur-Seine. ☎01 46 41 25 25. Accredited by major insurance companies.

✚ **The British Hospital** is just outside Paris in Levallois-Perret, 3 r. Barbès, ☎01 46 39 22 22.

Accessibility

The sights described in this guide which are easily accessible to people of reduced mobility are indicated by the symbol ♿.
On TGV and Corail trains, operated by the national railway (SNCF), there are special wheelchair slots in 1st class carriages available to holders of 2nd-class tickets. On Eurostar and Thalys, special rates are available for accompanying adults. All airports are equipped to receive physically disabled passengers.

Web-surfers can find information for slow walkers, mature travellers and others with special needs at www.access-able.com. For information on museum access for the disabled consult http://museofile.culture.fr.

The **Michelin Guide France** and the **Michelin Camping France** indicate hotels and campsites with facilities suitable for physically handicapped people.

GETTING THERE AND GETTING AROUND

By Plane

The various international and other independent airlines operate services to **Paris** (Roissy-Charles de Gaulle and Orly airports) and **Dijon** in the heart of Burgundy. The Jura has only one regional airport, **Dole**, and therefore the international airports of **Mulhouse-Basle** to the north-east and **Geneva** to the south-east are useful alternatives. Check with your travel agent, however, before booking direct flights, as it is sometimes cheaper to travel via Paris. Air France (☎0870 142 4343; www.airfrance.co.uk), the national airline, links Paris to Dijon several times a day.

Contact airline companies and travel agents for details of package tour flights with a rail or coach link-up as well as fly-drive schemes.

By Ship
From the UK or Ireland

There are numerous **cross-Channel services** (passenger and car ferries, hovercraft) from the United Kingdom and Ireland, as well as the rail shuttle through the Channel Tunnel (Eurotunnel, ☎08705 35 35 35, www.eurotunnel.com). For details apply to travel agencies or to:

P & O Ferries
Channel House, Channel View Road, Dover CT17 9JT.
☎08705 980333. www.poferries.com.

Brittany Ferries
Millbay Docks; Plymouth, Devon. PL1 3EW.
☎0870 9 076 103. www.brittany-ferries.co.uk.

Portsmouth Commercial Port
(and ferry information)

George Byng Way, Portsmouth PO2 8SP.
☎023 9229 7391. www.portsmouth-port.co.uk.

Irish Ferries
P.O. Box 19, Alexandra Road, Ferryport, Dublin 1.
☎08705 171717.
www.irishferries.com.

Seafrance
Eastern Docks, Dover, Kent, CT16 1JA.
☎0871 663 2546.
www.seafrance.com.

By Train

Eurostar runs via the Channel Tunnel between **London** (Kings Cross-St Pancras from Nov 2007) and **Paris** (Gare du Nord) in 2hr 15min (bookings and information ☎08705 186 186 in the UK; www.eurostar.com). In Paris it links to the high-speed rail network (TGV) which covers most of France. There is fast inter-city service on the TGV from **Paris** (Gare de Lyon) to **Montbard** *(1hr 5min)*, **Le Creusot** *(1hr 20min)*, **Dijon** *(1hr 40min)*, **Mâcon** *(1hr 40min)*, **Bourg-en-Bresse** *(2hr)*, **Beaune** *(2hr 5min)*, **Dole** *(2hr 5min)*, **Châlon-sur-Saône** *(2hr 20min)* and **Besançon** *(2hr 30min)*, with connections to other towns via the Trains Express Régionaux (TER).

Eurailpass, Flexipass, Eurailpass Youth, EurailDrive Pass and **Saverpass** are five of the travel passes which may be purchased by residents of countries outside the European Union. In the US, contact your travel agent or **Rail Europe,** 44 S. Broadway, White Plains, NY 10601 (☎914-682-2999 or 800-4-EURAIL, www.raileurope.com) or **Europrail International** (☎1 888 667 9734, www.europrail.net). If you are a European resident, you can buy an individual country pass, if you are not a resident of the country where you plan to use it. In the UK, contact Europrail at 179 Piccadilly, London W1J 9BA; ☎08705 848848, www.europrail.eu. Information on timetables can be obtained on websites for these agencies and the **SNCF**, www.sncf.fr. At the SNCF site, you can book ahead, pay with a credit card, and receive your ticket in the mail at home. There are numerous **discounts** available when you purchase your tickets in France, from 25-50% below the regular rate. These include discounts for using senior cards and youth cards (the cards, with a photograph, must be purchased), and lower rates for 2-9 people travelling together (no card required, advance purchase necessary). There are a limited number of discount seats available during peak travel times, and the best discounts are available for travel during off-peak periods. Tickets bought in France must be validated (composter) by using the orange automatic date-stamping machines at the platform entrance (failure to do so may result in a fine).

By Coach/Bus

Eurolines (UK), ☎08705 143219. **Eurolines (Paris)**, 22 r. Malmaison, 93177 Bagnolet. ☎01 49 72 57 80. www.eurolines.com is the international website with information about travelling all over Europe by coach (bus).

By Car

The area covered in this guide is easily reached by main motorways and national roads. **Michelin map 726** indicates the main itineraries as well as alternate routes for avoiding heavy traffic during busy holiday periods, and gives estimated travel times. The latest Michelin route-planning service is available on the internet, **www.ViaMichelin.com.** Travellers can calculate a precise route using such options as shortest route, route avoiding toll roads or the Michelin-recommended route. In addition to

tourist information (hotels, restaurants, attractions), you will find a magazine featuring articles with the up-to-the-minute reports on holiday destinations. The roads are very busy during the holiday period (particularly weekends in July and August) and to avoid traffic congestion it is advisable to follow the recommended secondary routes (signposted as *Bison Futé – itinéraires bis*). The motorway network includes rest areas *(aires)* and petrol stations, usually with restaurant and shopping complexes attached, about every 40km/25mi, so that long-distance drivers have no excuse not to stop for a rest every now and then.

DOCUMENTS

Travellers from other European Union countries and North America can drive in France with a valid national or home-state **driving licence**. An **international driving licence** is useful because the information on it appears in nine languages (keep in mind that traffic officers are empowered to fine motorists). Permits are available from your local motoring organisations (or from the Post Office in the UK). For the vehicle, it is necessary to have the registration papers (logbook) and a nationality plate of the approved size. Certain motoring organisations (AAA, AA, RAC) offer accident **insurance** and breakdown service schemes for members. Check with your current insurance company in regard to coverage while abroad. If you plan to hire a car using your credit card, check with the company, which may provide liability insurance automatically (and thus save you having to pay the cost for optimum coverage).

ROAD REGULATIONS

The minimum driving age is 18. Traffic drives on the right. All passengers must wear **seat belts**. Children under the age of 10 must ride in the back seat. Headlights must be switched on in poor visibility and at night;

use sidelights only when the vehicle is stationary.

In the case of a **breakdown**, a red warning triangle or hazard warning lights are obligatory. In the absence of stop signs at intersections, cars must **yield to the right**. Traffic on main roads outside built-up areas (priority indicated by a yellow diamond sign) and on **roundabouts** has right of way. There are many roundabouts (traffic circles) located just on the edge of towns; they are designed to reduce the speed of the traffic entering the built-up area and you must slow down when you approach one and yield to the cars in the circle. Vehicles must stop when the lights turn red at road junctions and may filter to the right only when indicated by an amber arrow. The regulations on **drinking and driving** (limited to 0.50g/l) and **speeding** are strictly enforced – usually by an on-the-spot fine and/or confiscation of the vehicle.

SPEED LIMITS

Although liable to modification, these are as follows:
- toll motorways (autoroutes) 130kph/80mph (110kph/68mph when raining);
- dual carriageways and motorways without tolls 110kph/68mph (100kph/62mph when raining);
- other roads 90kph/56mph (80kph/50mph when raining) and in towns 50kph/31mph;
- outside lane on motorways during daylight, on level ground and with good visibility – minimum speed limit of 80kph/50mph.

PARKING REGULATIONS

In town there are zones where parking is either restricted or subject to a fee; tickets should be obtained from the ticket machines (*horodateurs* – small change necessary) and displayed inside the windscreen on the driver's side; failure to display may result in a fine, or towing and impoundment. Other parking areas in town may require you to take a ticket when passing through a barrier. To exit, you must pay the parking fee (usually there is a machine located by the exit – *sortie*) and insert the paid-up card in another machine which will lift the exit gate.

TOLLS

In France, most motorway sections are subject to a toll (*péage*). You can pay in cash or with a credit card (Visa, Mastercard).

CAR HIRE

There are car hire agencies at airports, railway stations and in all large towns throughout France. Automatic cars are available in larger cities only if an advance reservation is made. Drivers must be over 21; between ages 21-25, drivers are required to pay an extra daily fee; some companies allow drivers under 23 only if the reservation has been made through a travel agent. It is relatively expensive to hire a car in France; Americans in particular will notice the difference and should make arrangements before leaving, take advantage of fly-drive offers when you buy your ticket, or seek advice from a travel agent, specifying requirements. There are many online services that will look for the best prices on car rental around the globe. Nova can be contacted at www.rentacar-worldwide.com or ☎0800 018 6682 (freephone UK) or ☎44 28 4272 8189 (calling from outside the UK). All of the firms listed below have internet sites for reservations and information.

MOTORHOME RENTAL

- **Worldwide Motorhome Rentals** Offers fully equipped camper vans for rent.
  ☎888- 519-8969 *US toll-free.*
  ☎530-389-8316 *outside the US.*
  www.mhrww.com.
- **Overseas Motorhome Tours Inc.** Organises escorted tours and individual rental of recreational vehicles.

☎800-322-2127 *US*.
☎1-310-543-2590 *outside the US*.
www.omtinc.com.

PETROL

French service stations dispense:
- 🚗 *sans plomb 98* (super unleaded 98)
- 🚗 *sans plomb 95* (super unleaded 95)
- 🚗 *diesel/gazole* (diesel)
- 🚗 *GPL* (LPG).

Prices are listed on signboards on the motorways; it is usually cheaper to fill up after leaving the motorway; check the large hypermarkets on the outskirts of town.

Rental Cars – Central Reservation in France	
Avis:	☎ 08 20 05 05 05 www.avis.com
Europcar:	☎ 08 25 82 54 57 www.europcar.com
Budget France:	☎ 08 25 00 35 64 www.budget.com
Hertz France:	☎ 01 47 03 49 12 www.hertz.com
SIXT-Eurorent	☎ 08 20 00 74 98 www.e-sixt.com
National-CITER	☎ 01 45 22 77 91 www.citer.fr

WHERE TO STAY AND EAT

Hotel and restaurant listings fall within the description of each region.

Where to Stay

The map on the following pages illustrates a selection of holiday destinations which are particularly recommended for the accommodation and leisure facilities they offer, and for their pleasant setting. It shows **overnight stops:** fairly large towns which should be visited and which have good accommodation facilities; as well as traditional destinations for a **short holiday**, which combine accommodation, charm and a peaceful setting. As for Dijon and Besançon, the influence they exert in the region and the wealth of monuments, museums and other sights to which they are home make them the ideal setting for at least a **weekend break.**

FINDING A HOTEL

The Green Guide is pleased to offer lists of selected hotels and restaurants for this region. Turn to the Address Books (shaded in green) for descriptions and prices of typical places to stay and eat with local flair. The legend at the back of the guide explains the symbols and abbreviations used in these sections. We have reported the prices and conditions as we observed them, but of course changes in management and other factors may mean that you will find some discrepancies. Please feel free to keep us informed of any major differences you encounter.

Use the **Map of places to stay** to identify recommended places for overnight stops. For an even greater selection, use The **Michelin Guide France**, with its famously reliable star-rating system and hundreds of establishments all over France. Book ahead to ensure that you get the accommodation you want, not only in tourist season but year-round, as many towns fill up during trade fairs, arts festivals and so on. Some places require a deposit or a reconfirmation. Reconfirming is especially important if you plan to arrive after 6pm.

For a selection of reasonably priced small hotels, see Michelin's publication **1000 Charming Hotels and Guesthouses**; the guide covers all of France, with individual chapters on Burgundy and Franche-Comté.

For further assistance, **Loisirs Accueil** is a booking service that has offices in

Places to stay

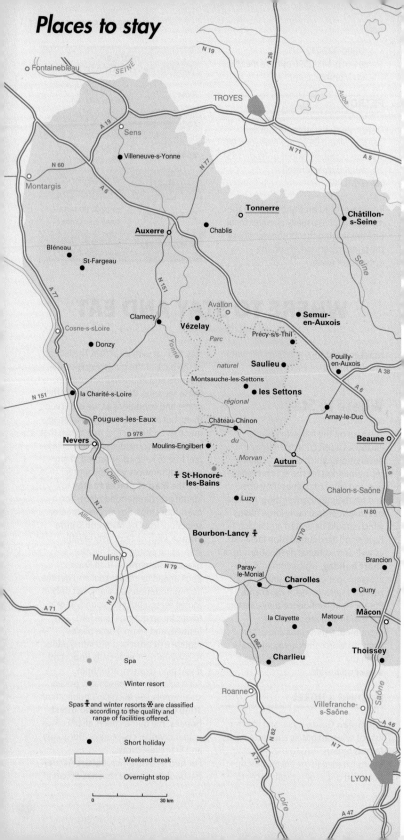

Fontainebleau

SEINE

TROYES

N 19

A 26

Sens

Villeneuve-s-Yonne

N 60

Montargis

A 19

A 8

N 77

A 5

Tonnerre

Châtillon-
s-Seine

Auxerre

Chablis

Bléneau

St-Fargeau

N 151

A 7

Seine

Avallon

Clamecy

Vézelay

Semur-
en-Auxois

Cosne-s-sLoire

Parc

Précy-s/s-Thil

Donzy

Yonne

naturel

Saulieu

Pouilly-
en-Auxois

Montsauche-les-Settons

A 38

la Charité-s-Loire

N 151

régional

les Settons

A 6

Pougues-les-Eaux

Château-Chinon

Arnay-le-Duc

Nevers

D 978

du

Beaune

Moulins-Engilbert

Morvan

Autun

A 6

LOIRE

Chalon-s-Saône

N 7

✝ St-Honoré-
les-Bains

Allier

Luzy

N 80

Bourbon-Lancy ✝

N 70

Moulins

N 79

Brancion

Paray-
le-Monial

Charolles

Cluny

A 71

N 9

la Clayette

Matour

Màcon

Saône

D 982

Thoissey

Charlieu

Roanne

Villefranche-
s-Saône

A 46

LYON

N 82

N 7

A 72

Loire

A 47

●   Spa

●   Winter resort

Spas ✝ and winter resorts �֍ are classified
according to the quality and
range of facilities offered.

●   Short holiday

▭   Weekend break

—   Overnight stop

0   30 km

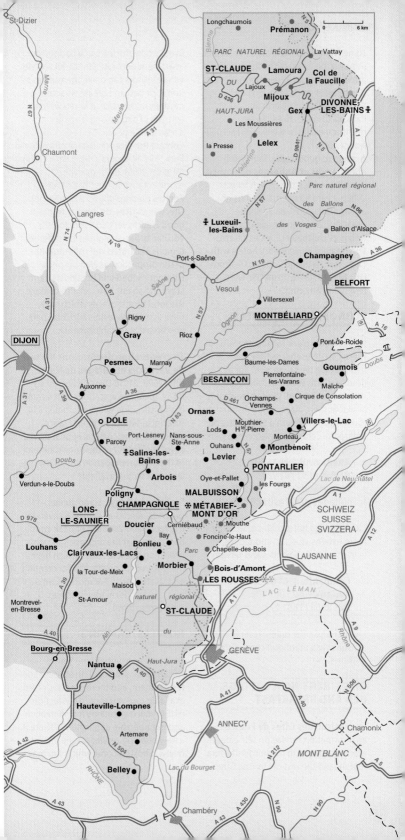

some French *départements* – for further information, contact the tourist offices listed above or the Fédération nationale des services de réservation Loisirs-Accueil, 280 bd. St-Germain, 75007 Paris, ☎01 44 11 10 44; www.resinfrance.com or www.loisirsaccueil-france.com.

A guide to good-value, family-run hotels, **Logis et Auberges de France,** is available from the French Tourist Office, as are lists of other kinds of accommodation such as hotel-châteaux, bed-and-breakfasts etc. **Relais et châteaux** provides information on booking in luxury hotels with character: ☎00800 2000 00 02 (from UK), 800 735 2478 (from US); www.relaischateaux.com.

ECONOMY CHAIN HOTELS

If you need a place to stop en route, these can be useful, as they are inexpensive (less than 38€ for a double room) and generally located near the main road. While breakfast is available, there may not be a restaurant; rooms are small, with a television and bathroom. Central reservation numbers:

- 🛏 **Akena** ☎01 69 84 85 17.
- 🛏 **B&B** ☎0892 782 929.
- 🛏 **Etap Hôtel** ☎0892 688 900.
- 🛏 **Villages Hôtel** ☎03 80 60 92 70.

The following hotel chains offer slightly more expensive accommodations, with a few more amenties and services.

- △ **Campanile** ☎01 64 62 46 46.
- △ **Kyriad** ☎0825 003 003.
- △ **Ibis** ☎0825 882 222.

Many chains offer online reservations; consult www.etaphotel.com or www.ibishotel.com.

GÎTES, RENTING A COTTAGE, BED AND BREAKFAST

The **Maison des Gîtes de France** is an information service on self-catering accommodation in the Burgundy-Jura region (and the rest of France). Gîtes

usually take the form of a cottage or apartment decorated in the local style where visitors can make themselves at home, or bed and breakfast accommodation (*chambres d'hôtes*) which consists of a room and breakfast at a reasonable price.

Contact the Gîtes de France office in Paris: 59 r. St-Lazare, 75439 Paris Cedex 09, ☎01 49 70 75 75, or their representative in the UK, **Brittany Ferries** (*address above*). The Internet site, **www.gites-de-france.fr**, has a good English version. From the site, you can order catalogues for different regions illustrated with photographs of the properties, as well as specialised catalogues (bed and breakfasts, farm stays and so on). You can also contact the local tourist offices which may have lists of properties and local bed and breakfast establishments.

The **Fédération des Stations Vertes de Vacances et Villages de Neige** (BP 71698, 21016 Dijon Cedex, ☎ 03 80 54 10 50, www.stationsvertes.com) is an association which promotes 854 rural localities throughout France, selected for their natural appeal as well as for the quality of their environment, of their accommodation and of the leisure activities available.

For **farm holidays,** three guides – *Guide des fermes-auberges, Bienvenue à la ferme* and *Vacances et week-ends à la ferme* – list the addresses of farms providing guest facilities which have been vetted for quality and for meeting official standards. For more information, apply to local tourist offices (*addresses above*).

HOSTELS, CAMPING

To obtain an International Youth Hostel Federation card (there is no age requirement, and there is a senior card available too) you should contact the IYHF in your own country for information and membership applications. There is a new booking service on the internet (www.hihostels.com), which you may use to reserve rooms as far as six months in advance.

The two main youth hostel associations (*auberges de jeunesse*) in France are:

Ligue Française pour les Auberges de la Jeunesse
67 r. Vergniaud, Bâtiment K, 75013 Paris, ☎01 44 16 78 78, www.auberges-de-jeunesse.com

Fédération Unie des Auberges de Jeunesse
27 r. Pajol, 75018 Paris, ☎01 44 89 87 27; www.fuaj.org.

There are numerous officially graded camp sites with varying standards of facilities throughout the Burgundy-Jura region. The **Michelin Camping France** guide lists a selection of camp sites. The area is very popular with campers in the summer months, so it is wise to reserve in advance.

ACCOMMODATION FOR RAMBLERS

Ramblers and those who enjoy ski touring, bike touring, mountaineering, canoeing etc, will find the guide *Gîtes d'étapes, refuges* by A. and S. Mouraret most useful. It is published by Rando Éditions La Cadole, 74 R. A. Perdreaux, 78140 Vélizy, ☎01 34 65 11 89; www.gites-refuges.com (order the catalogue online, consult the list of properties, or pay to consult the entire catalogue and book).

Where to Eat

Consult the green-shaded Address Books in the sight descriptions for listings and prices of selected places to eat in the different locations covered in this guide. The key on the back flap explains the symbols and abbreviations used in these sections. For an even greater choice, use the **Michelin Guide France**, with its famously reliable star-rating system and hundreds of establishments all over France. If you would like to experience a meal in a highly rated restaurant from the *Michelin Guide*, be sure to book ahead. In the countryside, restaurants usually serve lunch between noon and 2pm and dinner between 7.30-10pm. It is not always easy to find something between those two meal times, as the non-stop restaurant is still a rarity in the provinces. However, a hungry traveller can usually get a sandwich in a café, and ordinary hot dishes may be available in a *brasserie*.

For information on local specialities, see the chapter on Gastronomy in the Introduction.

In French restaurants and cafés, a service charge is included. Tipping is not necessary, but French people often leave the small change from their bill on their table, or about 5% for the waiter in a nice restaurant.

WHAT TO SEE AND DO

Outdoor Fun

Information and brochures outlining the sports and outdoor facilities available in the region can be obtained from the French Government Tourist Office or from the organisations listed in this section.

CANOEING AND KAYAKING

This method of exploring local water-ways need not be exclusively reserved for seasoned canoeing experts. Sometimes this sport can be a pleasant way to discover secluded spots inaccessible by any other means. The main difference between a canoe and a kayak is that the former is propelled by a single-bladed paddle and the latter by a double-bladed paddle. Besides the Morvan where streams and small rivers offer exciting possibilities to canoeists looking for a challenge, the Yonne, the Canal de Bourgogne, the Saône and the Loire lend them-

selves to canoeing trips and competitions organised by the numerous sport centres of the **Fédération française de canoë-kayak** (*87 quai de la Marne, 94344 Joinville-le-Pont, ☎01 45 11 08 50; www.ffcanoe.asso.fr).*
A guide entitled *Vacances en canoë-kayak* is published annually by the **Canoë-kayak magazine** (*1 r. des Rivières, CP 421, 69338 Lyon Cedex 9. ☎04 72 19 87 97. www.canoekayakmagazine.com*).

🔲 For additional information, contact:

Comité Régional de Franche-Comté
6 av. des Montboucons, 25000 Besançon. ☎03 81 48 29 19; www.crck.org/franchecomte.

Comités Départementaux
Ain: Canoë-kayak 01,
01500 Ambronay. ☎04 74 39 14 17. www.canoe-kayak01.com.
Doubs: Actions Loisirs Eaux Vives, 8 r. des Cantons, 25400 Audincourt, ☎03 81 30 62 14 or 06 10 16 38 29. www.audincourt-ev-canoe.com.
Jura: 1 r. de Cressey, BP 302, 39104 Dole Cedex. ☎03 84 79 26 33. www.cdck39.org.

FISHING

Trout, perch, tench and pike abound in the region's lakes, rivers and canals; carp and bream are less commonly found. Some of the rivers of the Jura *département* are considered to be among the best French rivers for trout fishing.

Angling

Regulations – They differ according to whether the water is classified as first category (contains trout) or second category (coarse fish). Generally speaking, in the case of first category rivers, the fishing season starts on the second Saturday in March and ends on the third Sunday in September. For second category rivers, fishing is authorised throughout the year. Stricter rules apply to fish needing special protection.
Anglers will need either to buy a special holiday fishing permit, valid for two weeks between June and September, or take out annual membership in an officially approved angling association. National regulations state that anglers must return to the water any fish they catch below the minimum permitted length (50cm/20in for pike, 40cm/16in for pike-perch, 23cm/9in for trout, 9cm/4in for crayfish).

Useful Addresses:
🐟 **Maison nationale de l'eau et de la pêche,** 36 r. St-Laurent, 25290 Ornans. ☎03 81 57 14 49.
🐟 **École française de pêche** – BP Courses year-round (1-15 days) for youth and adults.
25, 33112 St-Laurent-Médoc.
☎05 56 59 31 74. www.ecolede peche.com.
🐟 **Étang du Châtelet (Fédération départementale de la pêche),** Fly-fishing from March to October, daily except Tuesday.
7 quai de Mantoue, 58000 Nevers.
☎03 86 61 18 98.
🐟 **Domaine de Tarperon,** rte. de St-Marc, 21510 Aignay-le-Duc. ☎03 80 93 83 74.
🐟 **Château de Thenissey,** r. Pont, 21150 Thenissey. ☎03 80 35 85 55.
🐟 **Au fil de l'eau,** 26 r. de Lyon, 89200 Avallon. ☎03 86 34 50 41.
🐟 **Centre Pêche au Gros,**
An introduction to fishing for the carnivorous sheath-fish (up to 3m/10ft long and 150kg/331lb in weight).
4 r. de la Liberté, 71000 Mâcon.
☎03 85 39 07 50. www.peche-au-silure.com.

Lakes and Reservoirs

They are the ideal setting for windsurfing, water-skiing, fishing, rambling and so on.

Burgundy has fewer lakes; however, the following (non-exhaustive list) are suitable for the practice of various watersports (mainly windsurfing and water-skiing): the Lac de Bourdon (near St-Fargeau), the Lac du Pont and the Lac de Panthier (Côte-d'Or), the Lac Kir (Dijon) and the Lac de la Sorme (near Montceau-les-Mines). Some sections of the Saône, the Yonne and even the Loire are also sought after by watersports enthusiasts. In addition, the watersports centre in Arc-sur-Tille, used for competitions, can seat up to 3 000 spectators.

Further information is available from the **Fédération française de ski**
nautique,** 27 r. d'Athènes, 75009 Paris. ☏01 53 20 19 19. www.ffsn.fr.

HIKING

Short, medium and long distance footpath *Topo-Guides* are published by the **Fédération Française de Randonnée Pédestre** (FFRP). These give detailed maps of the paths and offer valuable information to the rambler; they are on sale at the information centre: 64 r. du Dessous des Berges, 75013 Paris. ☏01 44 89 93 90. www.ffrandonnee.fr.

Several long-distance foot-paths *(sentiers de grande randonnée – GR – marked red and white)* cover the Jura:

Two of them cross the region from north the south, **GR 5** which skirts the Swiss border and the **GR 59**

Lake / Reservoir	Dépt	Surface area (in hectares)	Swimming	Leisure park	Fishing
Abbaye (Lac)	39	100	–	–	yes
Allement (Barrage)	01	225	yes	yes	yes
Antre (Lac)	39	16	–	–	yes
Barterand (Lac)	01	19	yes	–	yes
Bonlieu (Lac)	39	17	–	–	yes
Chalain (Lac)	39	240	yes	yes	yes
Champagney (Bassin)	70	103	–	yes	yes
Clairvaux (Grand Lac)	39	64	yes	yes	yes
Divonne-les-Bains (Lac)	01	45	yes	yes	yes
Etival (Grand Lac)	39	17	–	–	yes
Genin (Lac)	01	8	yes	yes	yes
Ilay (Lac)	39	70	yes	–	yes
Lamoura (Lac)	39	4	yes	–	yes
Malsaucy (Lac))	90	66	yes	yes	–
Nantua (Lac)	01	141	yes	yes	yes
Narlay (Lac)	39	42	–	–	yes
Rousses (Lac)	39	100	yes	yes	yes
St-Point (Lac)	25	450	yes	yes	yes
Sylans (Lac)	01	50	–	–	yes
Val (Lac)	39	60	–	–	yes
Vouglans (Barrage)	39	1600	yes	yes	yes

To convert hectares to acres, mulitply by 2.47.

which follows the western edge of the region.

- Another two explore the Doubs area, **GR 590** which runs through the Loue and Lison valleys starting from Ornans and **GR 595** which links GR 59 and GR 5 from Montfaucon (near Besançon) to Maison-du-Bois (near Pontarlier).
- **GR 559** crosses the Jura from Lons-le-Saunier to Les Rousses via Ilay and Bonlieu.
- **GR 9** crosses the Jura from St-Amour in the west to Les Rousses in the east then turns south.

There are also a number of regional GR *(GR de pays – red and yellow markings)*; some of them link up with the main GR. The extensive network (6 000km/ 3 728mi) of footpaths crisscrossing Burgundy offers ramblers the possibility of visiting lesser known areas: the Loire islands with their remarkable fauna, Cîteaux or Vauluisant forests, the Puisaye countryside, the ochre-coloured villages of the Mâconnais area or the vineyards of South Burgundy dotted with Romanesque churches.

Other useful addresses:

- **Comité régional de la randonnée pédestre de Bourgogne,** 2 r. des Corroyeurs, Boîte Y1, 21068 Dijon Cedex. ☎03 80 43 15 64. crrpbourgogne@wanadoo.fr.
- **Côte-d'Or:** 1 r. de Ferdinand Lesseps, BP 1601, 21035 Dijon Cedex. ☎03 80 63 64 60.
- **Nièvre:** 31 bis r. Roger Salengro, 58640 Varennes-Vauzelles. ☎03 86 59 09 44.

S. Sauvignier-MICHELIN

Ready to roam

- **Saône-et-Loire:** Centre de loisirs, Vieille Route d'Ozenay, 71700 Tournus. ☎03 85 51 06 15.
- **Yonne:** Maison des Sports, 12 bd. Galliéni, 89000 Auxerre. ☎03 86 41 22 26, www.randopedestre89.com.

CYCLING

The **Fédération Française de Cyclo-tourisme** (12 r. Louis-Bertrand, 94207 Ivry-sur-Seine Cedex; ☎01 56 20 88 88; www.ffct.org) and its local committees recommend a number of cycling tours of various lengths. The **Fédération Française de Cyclisme** (5 Rue de Rome, 93561 Rosny-sous-Bois; ☎01 49 35 69 00; www.ffc.fr) publishes a guide which describes 36 000km/22 370mi of marked trails suitable for mountain biking.

Cycling holidays in Burgundy are organised by the following:
- **Bourgogne randonnée** 7 av. du 8-Septembre, 21200 Beaune. ☎03 80 22 06 03. www.terroirs-b.com/br or www. bourgogne-randonnees.com.
- **Dili Voyages,** 10 av. de la République, 21200 Beaune. ☎03 80 24 24 82; dilivoyage@wanadoo.fr.
- **France randonnée,** 9 r. des Portes-Mordelaises, 35000 Rennes. ☎02 99 67 42 21. www.france-randonnee.fr.
- **Cycling for Softies** (*2/4 Birch Polygon, Manchester M14 5HX; ☎0161 248 8282; www.cycling-for-softies.co.uk*) offers three to 14 night bike tours in Burgundy. Stops along the way include famous wine cellars and châteaux, monuments, local markets and restaurants rated in the *Michelin Guide France.*

Burgundy has several mountain-bike (VTT) centres recognised by the Fédération française de Cyclisme:
- **Morvan:** *see Parc naturel régional du Morvan.*
- **La Croix Messire Jean**, 71190 Uchon. ☎03 85 54 42 06. Alt 680m/2231ft – 230km/143mi

Mountain Safety

Choosing the right equipment for a rambling, cross-country ski or snow-shoe expedition is essential. If walking in the summer, choose flexible hiking shoes with non-slip soles, bring a rain jacket or poncho, an extra sweater, sun protection (hat, glasses and lotion), drinking water (1-2l per person), high energy snacks (chocolate, cereal bars, bananas), and a first aid kit. Of course, you'll need a good map (and a compass if you plan to leave the main trails). Plan your itinerary well, keeping in mind that while the average walking speed for an adult is 4kph/2.5mph, you will need time to eat and rest, and children will not keep up the same pace.

For winter expeditions, plan your itinerary carefully. Even if it is beautiful and sunny when you set out, take warm, waterproof clothing in case of a sudden storm or if you are surprised by nightfall. Always have some food and water with you. Do not leave the groomed trails unless you are with an experienced guide. Read the notices at trail entrances in regard to avalanche alerts and weather reports. Protect exposed skin from the sun with an effective lotion.

Always leave your itinerary and expected time of return with someone before setting out (innkeeper, fellow camper or friend).

If you are caught in an electrical storm, avoid high ground, and do not move along a ridge top; do not seek shelter under overhanging rocks, isolated trees in otherwise open areas, at the entrance to caves or other openings in the rocks, or in the proximity of metal fences or gates. Do not use a metallic survival blanket. If possible, position yourself at least 15m/16.5yd from the highest point around you (rock or tree); crouch with your knees up and without touching the rock face with your hands or any exposed part of your body.

of trails among rocks and ponds. Here you can learn to read maps and to find your bearings; the centre also organises night tours.

🚲 **Centre VTT Les Granges,** 71960 Serrières; 226km/140mi of trails running across an undulating landscape of vineyards and châteaux. The centre also has a mountain-biking school.

🚲 **Centre VTT de St-Saulge,** (*Syndicat d'initiative, 58330 St-Saulge.*☎*03 86 58 25 74*); 16 loops totalling 550km/342mi of trails through the Nièvre region.

In view of the fact that the Jura is a mountainous region, it is necessary to establish cycling itineraries according to the level of difficulty required. Information and advice can be obtained from:

🚲 **Ligue de cyclotourisme de Franche-Comté (FFCT)**
14 r. de la Pépinière, 70000 Vesoul. ☎03 84 76 75 53.

🚲 **Comité régional de cyclisme de Franche-Comté,**
3 av. des Montboucons, 25000 Besançon. ☎03 81 52 17 13; www.franchecomtecyclisme.fr.

There are excellent possibilities for downhill or cross-country mountain biking, the most famous site being Métabief where the world, European and French championships take place. One of the possibilities is to follow the 300km/186mi trail of the **Grande Traversée du Jura** (🚲*see cross-country skiing*).

HORSEBACK RIDING 🐎

There are many riding centres in Burgundy and in the Jura. They offer courses, excursions, forest rides and riding holidays. In addition, a visit to the **Cluny stud farm**, one of the most renowned in France, is not to be missed (*Haras nationaux de Cluny, 2 r. Porte-des-Prés, 71250 Cluny;* ☎*03 85 59 85 00; www.haras-nationaux.fr*).

Comité National de Tourisme Équestre

9 bd. Macdonald, 75019 Paris. ☎01 53 26 15 50; www.ffe.com. The Comité publishes an annual brochure entitled *Tourisme et loisirs équestres en France.* Information on riding in Burgundy and the Jura is available from the **Comités départementaux** (list of local centres, activities, accommodation, riding tours lasting from 2 to 8 days):

- 🐎 **Côte-d'Or:** La Houblonnière, 21250 Pouilly-sur-Saône. ☎03 80 20 45 81.
- 🐎 **Nièvre:** Marie-Pierre Lauprêtre, 58700 Nolay. ☎03 86 68 08 15.
- 🐎 **Saône-et-Loire:** Pierre Jalabert, 71460 St-Gengoux-le-National. ☎03 85 50 77 80.
- 🐎 **Yonne:** M. Bruneau, 89740 Cruzy-le-Châtel. ☎03 86 75 23 16. www.yonneacheval.com.
- 🐎 **Doubs:** M. Patrick David, Les Attelages des deux lacs, 109 r. des Grangettes, 25160 Malpas. ☎03 81 69 68 69.
- 🐎 **Jura:** Alain Robert, 39600 St-Cyr Montmalin. ☎03 84 66 21 60.
- 🐎 **Haute-Saône:** Pascal Chatriot, Écurie de la Borde, 70100 Bouhans et Feurg. ☎03 84 32 31 98.
- 🐎 **Territoire de Belfort:** Ferdinand Ziegler, La Madeleine, Cedex 14 Les Errues. ☎03 84 23 04 90, or 06 20 17 25 39.

Other regional addresses:

- 🐎 **Liberté** (association), Mairie, 58800 Corbigny. ☎03 86 20 08 04. www.bourgogneacheval.com.

Cooling off

- 🐎 **Ligue équestre de Bourgogne,** 6 r. du Palais, 21000 Dijon. ☎03 80 30 05 08.
- 🐎 **Comité régionale de tourisme équestre de Franche-Comté,** 52 r. de Dole, 25000 Besançon. ☎03 81 52 67 40.
- 🐎 **Jura du Grand Huit,** 8 r. Louis-Rousseau, BP 458, 39006 Lons-le-Saunier Cedex. ☎03 84 87 08 88. www.jura-tourism.com.

GOLF

The popularity of golf, which took off in the early 1980s, is steadily increasing. In 1998, more than 260 000 golf players were officially registered in France, indulging in their favourite sport on around 500 golf links.

The map *Golfs, les Parcours Français,* published by Éditions Plein Sud and based on **Michelin map no 721**, provides useful information on the location, address and type of golf course open to players throughout the country.

Fédération Française de Golf, 68 r. Anatole-France, 92309 Levallois-Perret. ☎01 41 49 77 00. www.ffgolf.org. There are 19 golf courses in Burgundy's four *départements*; the website of the **Comité régional de tourisme** (www.crt-bourgogne.fr) provides all the relevant information: list of courses with detailed address, description, prices, accommodation and so on.

SKIING

Cross-Country Skiing

The Jura region is ideal for **cross-country skiing**, because of the variety of relief to be found here. There are more than 2 000km/1 245mi of clearly marked, well-groomed trails.

A big event for lovers of this strenuous, yet peaceful sport is the **Transjurassienne**, a 76km/47mi race from Lamoura to Mouthe. Since 1984, the course has been included in the Nordic World Cup series, a set of races held in different countries over the season. Contact Trans'Organisation, Espace Lamartine, BP 20126, 39404 Morez; ☎03 84 33 45 13. A visit to the

Ph. Gajic-MICHELIN

website (*www.transjurassienne.com*), with photographs and advice, will make you long to grab your poles and join this ski celebration.

Grande Traversée du Jura

Known as the GTJ to familiars, this cross-country ski route of over 300km/124mi, with a main trail and five intermediate trails crossing through several French *départements*, along the contours of the Haut-Doubs and through evergreen forests. The national cross-country training school is at Prémanon, near Les Rousses. If you plan on skiing along this route, **Jura Randonnées** (*39370 Les Bouchoux; ☎03 84 42 73 17; www.jura-rando.com*), will help organise your tour (accommodation, transport of luggage, guides, maps etc).

🛈For more information about courses and ski tours, contact:
Accueil Montagnard (*25240 Chapelle-des-Bois; ☎03 81 69 26 19; accueil.montagnard.free.fr*).
To plan a ski adventure, contact the **Espace Nordique Jurassien** (*BP 132, 390304 Champagnole Cedex; ☎03 84 52 58 10; www.espacenordiquejurassien.com*).

Alpine Skiing

The Jura cannot compete with the Alps in terms of snow cover, steepness of downhill runs and equipment, yet the three ski resorts of Les Rousses, Métabief-Mont d'Or and Monts-Jura are expanding owing to the quality of their equipment including snow cannons which make up for the irregularity of the snow cover. The various activities they offer are suitable for those who seek a real change of scenery and lifestyle.

Dog Sledging

Races are organised at La Pesse (Jura) and Les Fourgs (Doubs). Sledge racing began in 1979 with the creation of the first dog-sledging club and this sport has grown in popularity ever since. Four different breeds of dogs are used: Siberian huskies (the fastest), Alaskan malamutes (the strongest), wolf-like Eskimo dogs from Greenland and white Arctic Samoyeds. These breeds are better suited either for touring or racing and are trained accordingly. The driver or musher either stands at the back of a sledge pulled by a team of dogs or skis beside the team harnessed to a kind of Scandinavian sledge known as a *pulka*.
The following organises sledge tours for beginners or specialists:

Parc du chien polaire

Le Cernois Veuillet, 25240 Chaux-Neuve. ☎03 81 69 20 20 www.parcduchienpolaire.com. Here you can visit the husky park, take sledge-driving treks (three or four dogs) and even sleep in tepees.

HANG-GLIDING AND PARAGLIDING

The Jura region is ideally suited to these airborne sports. Hang-gliding is the more complicated of the two, requiring a degree of technical understanding of aerodynamics. Beginners should only attempt under properly qualified supervision.
École de vol libre du Poupet, 9 r. du Poupet, 39110 St-Thiébaud, ☎03 84 73 04 56; www.poupetvollibre.com.
Club des sports des Rousses (maiden flights on a paraglider for two), 495 r. Pasteur, 39220 Les Rousses. ☎03 84 60 35 14.

ROCK-CLIMBING

Burgundy offers valuable experience to would-be mountaineers at the following sites:
Saussois rocks (Yonne) and their overhangs; these overlook D 100 between Mailly-la-Ville and Châtel-Censoir;
Saffres (Côte-d'Or), 6km/3.7mi from Vitteaux, a rock-climbing school and site particularly sought after at weekends.
Other sites: Bouilland, Hauteroche and Vieux-Château (for experienced climbers), Chambolle-Musigny and Talant (for learning and practising);
Clamecy area (Nièvre): Surgy and Basseville rocks.

GO-KARTING

There is a karting track (1 110m/1 214yd long, forming two loops) for the over-12s beside the Nevers-Magny-Cours Grand-Prix race track.

Laffite Système Karting
Complexe Automobile de Pouilly-en-Auxois, 21320 Meilly-sur-Rouvres, ☎03 80 90 60 77. Quadbikes for guided forest trail rides.

Spas   `Spa`

The benefits of spa treatments, known to the Romans and probably the Gauls, were rediscovered in the 18C-19C. At that time, taking the waters was reserved for wealthy clients with time to spare. Today, the French national health system recognises the therapeutic value of many cures, and patients' stays are provided for, all or in part, by the social security. Treatment occupies only part of the day, so the spas offer their guests many other activities to pass the time pleasantly: sports and recreation, various forms of entertainment. The beautiful natural settings provide the opportunity for outdoor excursions. In addition to traditional treatment courses, which usually last three weeks, many resorts offer shorter stays for clients with a specific goal in mind: stress relief and relaxation, fitness, quitting smoking, weight loss and more. Go to www.tourisme.fr and search the category "Spas and Fitness" for precise information (in French in most cases) on accommodation, short-stay treatments, entertainment etc. If you would like to make a spa treatment part of your holiday, be sure to plan in advance. Reservations may be scarce at certain times of the year, and special conditions, including a prior medical examination, may apply.

- **Spa** **Union nationale des établissements thermaux** – 1 r. Cels, 75014 Paris. ☎01 53 91 05 75. www.france-thermale.org.
- **Spa** **Bourbon-Lancy** – *quartier thermal* (slightly radioactive waters), 5 pl. Aligre, 71140 Bourbon-Lancy. ☎03 85 89 18 84. www.bourbon-lancy.com.
- **Spa** **Divonne-les-Bains** – Thermes de Divonne, av. des Thermes, 01220 Divonne-les-Bains. ☎04 50 20 05 70 (fitness centre); www.valvital.fr.
- **Spa** **Lons-le-Saunier** – Valvital Thermes de Lons-Le-Saunier – Parc des Bains. ☎03 84 24 20 34. www.valvital.fr.
- **Spa** **Luxeuil-les-Bains** – Chaîne Thermale du Soleil – 3 r. des Thermes. ☎03 84 40 44 22. www.luxeuil.fr.
- **Spa** **Saint-Honoré-les-Bains** – *Établissement thermal* (the waters contain sulphur), BP 8, 58360 St-Honoré-les-Bains. ☎03 86 30 73 27. www.saint-honore-les-bains.com
- **Spa** **Salins-les-Bains – Les Thermes** (salt waters), pl. des Alliés, 39110, Salins-les-Bains. ☎03 84 73 04 63. www.thermes-salins.com.

Activities for Children

The region abounds in parks, zoos, museums and various attractive sites and features as well as leisure activities which will appeal to children; in the Sights section, the reader's attention is drawn to them by the symbol `Kids`.
Museums – The Heads of State Limousines Museum in Montjalin, the

St-Honoré-les-Bains

J.-M. Klein-CRT Bourgogne

Motorbike Collection in Savigny-lès-Beaune Castle, the Old Toys Collection in the Musée Rural des Arts Populaires in Laduz.

Sites – The Briare Canal-bridge, Le Creusot mining and industrial site, the Guédelon medieval building site.

Parks and zoos – Parc de l'Auxois, 21350 Arnay-sous-Vitteaux; Parc naturel de Boutissaint, 89520 Treigny; Parc zoologique et d'attractions Touroparc, 71570 Romanèche-Thorins. Towns designated by the Ministry of Culture as **Villes d'Art et d'Histoire** organise discovery tours and cultural-heritage workshops for children. Fun books and specially designed tools are provided, and the activities on offer are supervised by various professionals such as architects, stonemasons, storytellers, actors. This programme, called **l'été des 6-12 ans** (summer activities for 6- to 12-year-olds) operates during school holidays. The towns concerned are: Autun, Auxerre, Beaune, Besançon, Chalon-sur-Saône, Dijon, Joigny, Nevers and Paray-le-Monial.

Calendar of Events

The list below is a selection of the many events which take place in this region. Visitors are advised to contact local tourist offices for fuller details of musical events, son et lumière shows, arts and crafts fairs etc., especially during July and August.

Festivals

MARCH

Dijon, Beaune, Auxerre, Nevers, Le Creusot, Mâcon, Montceau-les-Mines, Quetigny –
Contemporary Dance Festival; www.art-danse.com.

WHITSUN WEEKEND

Belfort – International university student music festival, ☎03 84 54 24 43.

MAY – SEPTEMBER

Pontigny – Saison musicale des amis de Pontigny (music festival), ☎03 86 47 54 99.

MAY

Auxerre – Jazz in Auxerre, ☎03 86 94 08 12.
Semur-en-Auxois – Medieval festival; www.ville-semur-en-auxois.fr.

JUNE

Divonne-les-Bains –
Chamber music festival. ☎04 50 40 34 16. www.domaine-de-divonne.com.
St-Claude –
Haut-Jura Music Festival. ☎06 08 47 12 23. www.festivalmusiquehautjura.com.
Audincourt – Rencontres et Racines (music, crafts, food), ☎03 81 30 42 08.
Vauluisant – Festival de Vauluisant; www.vauluisant.com.
Le Creusot – Festival national de blues. ☎03 85 55 68 99; www.festival-du-blues.com.
Auxerre – Les Nuits métisses (world music).

JUNE – JULY

Belfort – Nuits d'été au Château (theatre, concerts). ☎03 84 55 90 90.
Dijon – L'Estivade, ☎03 80 74 53 33.

JUNE – SEPTEMBER

Tournus – Tournus Passion (various events). ☎03 85 27 00 20.

LATE JUNE – EARLY JULY

Sens – Festival "Quinte et sens" (music, theatre, dance). ☎03 86 65 19 49.

EARLY JULY

Selongey, Seurre – International Bell-ringing Festival. ☎03 80 21 15 92. www.selongey.com.

JULY

Beaune – International Baroque music festival. ☎03 80 22 97 20. www.festivalbeaune.com.
Belfort – Les Eurockéennes rock festival. ☎03 84 22 46 58.
Moirans-en-Montagne – Idéklic (International children's festival). ☎03 84 42 31 57.
Tonnere and environs – Music festival. ☎03 86 54 45 26.
Saint-Bris-le-Vineux – Fête de peintres de vignes en caves. ☎03 86 53 31 79. www.saint-bris.com.

3RD WEEK IN JULY

Chalon-sur-Saône – "Chalon dans la rue" street artists festival. www.chalondanslarue.com.

2ND HALF OF JULY

Autun – Musique en Morvan (sacred choral music festival). www.musique-en-morvan.com.
Lormes – French song festival. ☎03 86 22 87 38.

JULY – AUGUST

Semur-en-Auxois and environs – Musicales en Auxois Festival. ☎03 80 96 20 24.
Château de Joux – Festival des Nuits de Joux (theatre). ☎03 81 46 48 33 (mid-July to mid-August).
Belfort – Wednesdays at the château. ☎03 84 28 08 28.
Nantua – Haut-Bugey international music festival. ☎04 74 75 24 94.

JULY – SEPTEMBER

Sens – International Organ Festival in the cathedral, ☎03 86 83 97 70.

JULY – NOVEMBER

Noyers, Cluny, Chablis, Mersault, Gevrey-Chambertin – Festival des Grands Crus de Bourgogne, Noyers-sur-Serein Music Festival. ☎03 80 34 38 40.

FIRST FORTNIGHT IN AUGUST

Besançon – Les Nuits de la citadelle (outdoor film festival). ☎03 81 87 83 33.
Trévillers – French country festival (American folk music). ☎03 81 44 45 39.
Semur-en-Auxois – Musicales en Auxois (9 concerts, various locations). ☎03 80 96 20 24.
Abbaye de Corbigny – Fêtes musicales de Corbigny. ☎03 86 20 27 90.
Saulieu – Cajun Nights. ☎06 08 53 88 75.

LATE AUGUST

Cluny – Jazz in Cluny. ☎03 85 59 04 04.
Vézelay – Rencontres musicales (vocal arts festival). ☎03 86 32 39 78. www.rencontresmusicalesdevezelay.com.

SEPTEMBER

Besançon – International music festival and young conductors competition. ☎03 81 25 05 85. www.festival-besancon.com.
Delle – Jazz festival. ☎03 84 36 68 50. www.delle-animation.com.
Various locations – "Musiques en voûtes" concert series in area churches. ☎03 80 67 11 22. www.musiquesenvoutes.com.

MID-SEPTEMBER – MID-OCTOBER

Ambronay – Festival de l'Abbaye. ☎04 74 38 74 00.

LATE OCTOBER

Beaune – Cinema Festival. ☎03 80 24 50 24.

NOVEMBER

Auxerre – International music and film festival. ☎03 86 72 89 47. www.festivalmusiquecinema.com.

LATE NOVEMBER – EARLY DECEMBER

Belfort – Entrevues
(young filmmakers festival).
☎03 84 54 24 43.
www.festival-entrevues.com.

Traditional and Religious Feasts, Fairs and Pageants

JANUARY

Arlay, Champlitte – Feast of St Vincent,
patron of wine-growers, dating back
to 1719. ☎03 84 85 01 37 (Arlay).

LATE JANUARY – EARLY FEBRUARY

Villy – Feast of St Vincent procession
(location changes yearly; consult
www.cotedor-tourisme.com, or
www.tastevin-bourgogne.com).

LATE FEBRUARY – EARLY MARCH

Chalon-sur-Saône – Carnival: musical
parade and Grand Jour des Goniots;
parade and costume ball for
children; fun fair. Information:
www.carnavaldechalon.com.

MARCH – APRIL

Auxonne – Carnival. ☎03 80 37 34 46.
Vesoul – Carnival.
Nuits-St-Georges – Wine auction sale.
☎03 80 62 11 77.
Tonnerre – Les Vinées tonnerroises.
☎03 86 55 14 48.
www.vignerons-tonnerrois.com.
Bassou – Festival de l'escargot.
☎03 86 73 23 73.

MAY – JUNE

Arlay – Medieval feast at the château.
Poligny – Les Épicuriennes
(Ascension weekend).
Dole – Pilgrimage to Notre-Dame-de-
Mont-Roland (2nd Sunday in May
and 2 August). ☎03 84 79 88 00.
Saulieu – Gourmet days.
☎03 80 64 00 21.
Besançon – Fair (week of Ascension).
☎03 81 41 08 09.

Mâcon – National Wine Fair. ☎03 85
21 07 07. www.leparcmacon.com.

3RD SUNDAY AFTER WHITSUN

Paray-le-Monial – Sacré-Cœur
pilgrimage. www.paray.org.

JUNE

Semur-en-Auxois – Fête de la Bague:
horse race whose origins date back
to 1639. ☎03 80 97 05 96.
Nozeroy – Medieval pageant.
☎03 84 51 19 15.
Le Russey – Fête des Gentianes.
☎03 81 43 72 35.
Levier – Fête des Sapins.
Gex – Fête de l'Oiseau (bird festival):
parade. ☎04 50 42 63 00.
St-Jean-de-Losne – Grand Pardon des
mariniers (Blessing of river boats).
☎03 80 29 05 48.
Escolives-Ste-Camille – Cherry festival.
☎03 86 53 34 24.

MID-JULY

Fondremand – Arts and crafts days.
☎03 84 78 98 89.
Pouilly-sur-Loire – Vintage fair
(auction sale of great vintage
wines). www.pouillysurloire.fr

JULY

Lons-le-Saunier – Fête de la St-Désiré
(last Sun).
Haut-Jura – Fête du Haut-Jura, local
crafts and products (location
changes yearly). ☎03 84 41 27 81.
www.parc-haut-jura.fr
St-Saveur-en-Puisaye – Pottery fair.
☎03 86 45 69 12.

LATE JULY

Pontailler-sur-Saône – Fête de
l'Oignon. ☎03 80 36 12 86.

AUGUST

Glux-en-Glenne – Fête des myrtilles
(Bilberry Festival). ☎03 86 36 39 80.
Maîche – Fête du cheval (horse and cow
competitions). ☎03 81 64 11 88.

St-Honoré-les-Bains – Fête des Fleurs (flower festival, 1st Sunday after 15 Aug). ☏03 86 30 71 70.

Cluny – Burgundy pottery market. ☏03 85 59 05 34.

Cluny – Harness and stallion show (last weekend).

15 AUGUST

Boutissaint – Festival of nature and wild animals. ☏03 86 74 07 08. www.boutissaint.com.

St. Léger-sous-Beauvray – Accordion festival. ☏03 85 86 15 75.

2ND HALF OF AUGUST

Anost – Fête de la Vielle (Hurdy-gurdy Festival). ☏03 85 82 72 50. perso.wanadoo.fr/ugmm.

Saulieu – Fête du Charollais. ☏03 80 64 17 60.

Métabief-Mont d'Or – Descent of the cows.

1ST SUNDAY IN SEPTEMBER

Arbois – Fête du Biou (wine festival). ☏03 84 66 55 50.

EARLY SEPTEMBER

Alise-Ste-Reine – Pilgrimage and Ste-Reine mystery play. ☏03 80 96 86 55.

Ronchamp – Pilgrimage to Notre-Dame-du-Haut (8th). ☏03 84 20 65 13.

Belfort – Wine and fine food fair. ☏03 84 55 90 90.

2ND HALF OF SEPTEMBER

Arc-et-Senans – Fête des montgolfières (hot-air balloon event).

Pierre-de-Bresse – Burgundy pottery fair.

3RD SUNDAY IN SEPTEMBER

Pupillin – Fête du Biou (wine festival). ☏03 84 37 49 16.

3RD WEEKEND IN SEPTEMBER

Maîche – Horse Festival. ☏03 81 64 11 88.

4TH SUNDAY IN SEPTEMBER

Vadans – Fête du Biou (wine festival). ☏03 84 66 22 01.

OCTOBER

Audincourt – Fête de la BD (cartoons). ☏03 81 30 42 08.

St-Léger-sous-Beuvray – Chestnut fair. ☏03 85 82 53 00.

Paray-le-Monial – Feast of Ste Marguerite-Marie.

LATE OCTOBER – NOVEMBER

Chablis, Joigny, St-Bris-le-Vineux – Yonne Wine Festival. ☏03 86 42 42 22 (Chablis). ☏03 86 62 11 05 (Joigny). ☏03 86 53 66 76 (St-Bris).

1ST HALF OF NOVEMBER

Dijon – International gastronomic fair. ☏03 80 77 39 00.

2ND HALF OF NOVEMBER

Clos Vougeot, Beaune and Meursault – The Trois Glorieuses: Brotherhood of the Chevaliers du Tastevin; auction of wines from the Hospices de Beaune. www.hospices-de-beaune.tm.fr.

Vesoul – St Catherine's Day fair. ☏03 84 97 10 85.

DECEMBER

Montbéliard – Christmas lights.

2ND WEEK IN DECEMBER

Marcigny – Turkey and goose fair. ☏03 85 25 39 06.

3RD SATURDAY IN DECEMBER

Bourg-en-Bresse – Bresse poultry show.

Son et Lumière Shows

JUNE – LATE SEPTEMBER

Auxerre – Son et lumière at the cathedral. ☎03 86 52 23 29.
Autun – La cathédrale en lumière. ☎03 85 86 80 38.

FRIDAYS AND SATURDAYS FROM MID-JULY – END OF AUGUST

St-Fargeau – Son et lumière (historical show). ☎03 86 74 05 67.

JULY – AUGUST

La Clayette –
Son et lumière at the château. ☎03 85 28 16 35.
Auxonne – Son et lumière. www.ot-auxonne.fr.
Semur-en-Auxois – Fireworks with sound over the ramparts. ☎03 80 97 01 11.

FIRST THREE WEEKENDS IN AUGUST

Autun – Son et lumière on a historical theme: "Il était une fois Augustodunum". ☎03 85 86 80 38 (town hall).

Sporting Events

FEBRUARY

Lamoura-Mouthe – Transjurassienne cross-country ski race (3rd weekend). ☎03 84 33 45 13.
Les Fourgs –
International dog-sledge race. ☎03 81 69 44 91.

MARCH

Les Fourgs – Le Marabouri, cross-country ski event. ☎03 81 69 44 91.

EARLY JULY

Nevers-Magny-Cours – Grand Prix de France de Formule 1. ☎03 86 21 80 00.

SEPTEMBER

Lamoura-Arbent – Forestière (100km mountainbike race). ☎04 74 77 20 98.
Nevers-Magny-Cours – Bol d'Or motorcycle race, information: ☎01 41 40 32 32/☎03 86 21 80 00.

Shopping

Most of the larger shops are open Mondays to Saturdays from 9am to 6.30pm or 7.30pm. Smaller, individual shops may close during the lunch hour. Food shops – grocers, wine merchants and bakeries – are generally open from 7am to 6.30pm or 7.30pm; some open on Sunday mornings. Many food shops close between noon and 2pm and on Monday. Bakery and pastry shops sometimes close on Wednesday. Hypermarkets usually stay open non-stop until 9pm or later.
People travelling to the USA cannot import plant products or fresh food, including fruit, cheeses and nuts. It is acceptable to carry tinned products or preserves.

RECOVERING VALUE ADDED TAX (VAT)

There is a Value Added Tax in France (*known as TVA*) of 19.6% on almost every purchase (books and some foods are subject to a lower rate). However, non-European visitors who spend more than 175€ (amount subject to change) in any one participating store can get the VAT amount refunded. Usually, you fill out a form at the store and have to present your passport. Upon leaving the country, you submit all forms to customs for approval (they may want to see the goods, so if possible don't pack them in checked luggage). The refund is usually paid directly into your bank or credit card account, or it can be sent by mail. Big department stores that cater to tourists provide special services to help you; be sure to mention that you plan to seek a refund before you pay for goods (no refund is possible for tax on services).

S. Sauvignier-MICHELIN

If you are visiting two or more countries within the European Union, you submit the forms only on departure from the last EU country. The refund is worth while for those visitors who would like to buy fashions, furniture or other fairly expensive items, but remember, the minimum amount must be spent in a single shop on a single day.

MARKETS AND LOCAL SPECIALITIES

Markets – All the towns and nearly all the villages hold traditional markets on at least one day of the week. Below are some of the most important:

Monday mornings –
Bresse chicken market in Louhans
Sheep market in Moulins-Englibert
Tuesday mornings –
Cattle market in Moulins-Engilbert
Wednesday mornings –
Cattle market in Charolles
Thursday mornings – Cattle market in St-Christophe-en-Brionnais
Saturday mornings –
Covered market in Beaune
Sunday mornings –
Burgundy market in Chablis

Local Specialities – The name Burgundy has been synonymous with great **wine** ever since the 12C when the monks of Cîteaux Abbey developed the famous

Clos Vougeot. Burgundy is fairly expensive, starting at around 12€ a bottle; grands crus can cost around 23€; and special bottles can easily cost 75€, even higher for collectibles. You can find good wine in all the wine-growing cellars throughout the region and in specialised shops in large towns such as Beaune, where a famous wine sale is held during the second half of November (see Calendar of Events). If you wish to learn about wine and vineyards, try **L'Athenaeum**, 5 r. de l'Hôtel-Dieu, 21200 Beaune. ☏03 80 25 08 30. www.athenaeumfr.com.

If you happen to be visiting Arbois or Château-Chalon, a bottle or two of the Jura region's unique *vin jaune* is a must; it goes well with **comté cheese**, another of the region's specialities.

Handicraft – **Nevers earthenware** is renowned worldwide and you will find a wide choice of dishes, vases and other objects in the town's specialised shops.

Pottery is the speciality of the Puisaye and several workshops are open to visitors; the list can be obtained from the **Syndicat d'initiative intercommunal de la Puisaye nivernaise,** Square de Castellamonte, 58310 St-Amand-en-Puisaye; ☏03 86 39 63 15; www.ot-puisaye-nivernaise.fr. You can also enquire at the Association de potiers-créateurs de Puisaye, La Maison du Chanoine, Le Chaîneau, 89520 Treigny; ☏03 86 39 81 26.

Handicraft is so varied in the Jura region that it is difficult to list all the specialities: in St-Claude, the capital of pipe-making, local craftsmen sell a wide choice of **pipes** beautifully carved from briar root; in Moirans-en-Montagne, you will find all kinds of high-quality wooden and plastic **toys; lace** is the speciality of Luxeuil and **clocks** abound in the Morteau area.

Sightseeing

TOURIST TRAINS

A number of charming old steam trains, often running off the beaten track, enable visitors to discover sites otherwise inaccessible.

Petit train de la Côte-d'Or (*Gare de Plombières-Canal, 21370 Plombières-lès-Dijon;* ☎03 80 45 88 51), runs along the Ouche and the Canal de Bourgogne. Departure from Lac Kir.

Train touristique des Lavières (*21120 Isle-sur-Tille;* ☎03 80 95 36 36), runs through the pine forest near Isle-sur-Tille.

Chemin de fer de la vallée de l'Ouche (*1 r. de la Gare, 21360 Bligny-sur-Ouche;* ☎06 30 01 48 29; *www. lepetittraindebligny.com*), takes steam or diesel trains along the old track between Dijon and Épinac, leaving from Bligny-sur-Ouche Station and running to Pont-d'Ouche; July and August: daily; early May to the end of September: Sundays and holidays.

Chemin de fer des Combes (*r. des Pyrénées, 71200 Le Creusot;* ☎03 85 55 26 23), offers a good view of Le Creusot and the Morvan heights; 10km/6mi journey through a wooded park; steam engine dating from 1917.

Chemin de fer touristique de Puisaye (*av. de la Gare, 89130 Toucy;* ☎03 86 44 05 58), runs small trucks and steam-powered tractors along the old track; railway museum open weekends and holidays from May to the last Sunday in September.

Coni'fer – Between Les Hôpitaux-Neufs and Fontaine Ronde (◔ *description and information, see MÉTABIEF-MONT D'OR*).

Saint-Claude to Morez (*1 Grande-Rue, 39170 St-Lupicin.* ☎03 84 42 85 96), is an old 25km/15mi line running along part of the Bienne gorge, with unfolding beautiful landscapes. It is dotted with tunnels and various engineering structures. The journey is often combined with thematic visits.

FROM ABOVE

Weather permitting, there are various ways of getting a bird's-eye view of the Burgundy-Jura region, from microlights (ULM, standing for *ultra-légers motorisés*), light aircraft or hot-air balloons (*montgolfières*).

Microlights – École professionnelle Alizé, Route de Lons, 39130 Doucier. ☎03 84 25 71 93.

Light aircraft – Aéroclub de promotion de l'aviation comtoise, Aérodrome de la Vèze, 25660 La Vèze. ☎03 81 81 50 82.

Aéroclub de Gray, r. St-Adrien, 70100 Gray. ☎03 84 65 00 84.

Hot-air balloons - It is also possible to take a trip in a hot-air balloon (generally allow about half a day for 1hr-1hr 30min in the air). Balloons fly over the Côte de Beaune vineyards during the fine season; flights last from 1hr to 3hr from April to November and take place either early in the morning or towards the end of the day to take advantage of the most favourable weather conditions.

Air Adventures, 21320 Commarin. ☎03 80 90 74 23.

Air Escargot, 71150 Remigny. ☎03 85 87 12 30. www.air-escargot.com.

France Montgolfières, ☎02 54 32 20 48. www.franceballoons.com.

Club aérostatique de Franche-Comté, 90150 Foussemagne. ☎03 84 90 20 20.

BAROUCHE RIDES

Horse-drawn carriages make an interesting way to explore the countryside at a gentle pace, whether for a few hours or several days.

Ferme équestre de l'Étang Fourchu, Les Écarts de la Chapelle, 90100 Florimont. ☎03 84 29 61 59.

Association Picheval, 39230 Darbonnay, ☎03 84 85 53 00 (wagon rides from 1hr to several days).

RIVER CRUISING

Three rivers – the Yonne, the Saône and its tributary the Seille – together with several canals or stretches of canal provide about 1 200km/1 931mi of navigable waterway for those who would like to visit Burgundy by boat. The Jura region offers its fair share of rivers (the Saône and the Doubs), canals (Canal de l'Est and Canal Rhin-Rhône) and lakes (Lac de Vouglans) – all in all, over 320km/200mi of waterways – to boating enthusiasts, who can either opt for a cruise or hire their own craft.

Houseboats

No licence is required to hire a boat but the helmsman must be an adult; a practical and theoretical lesson is given at the beginning of the hire period. To pilot such a boat successfully one must observe the speed limits and heed the advice of the rental company instructor, particularly when mooring or passing through locks. Canals are usually closed to navigation from mid-November to mid-March. Before leaving it is advisable to obtain suitable maps and guides (Collection Navicarte or Éditions du Breil or Collection Vagnon). The main embarkation ports are Digoin, St-Jean-de-Losne and Tournus (Burgundy), Gray, Joigny and Montbéliard.

For information and a list of useful addresses apply to:

The **Comité régional de tourisme de Bourgogne** (🖝 *see address above*) publishes a brochure entitled *Tourisme fluvial en Bourgogne*, listing the names and addresses of all the boat-hire companies.

Groupement pour le tourisme fluvial, (*6 r. de Chalezeule, 25000 Besançon.* ☏*03 81 88 71 38*), offers free brochures on request.

Boat trips

These can last for 1hr, half a day or a day; in this case a meal is often served on board.

Les Bateaux du Saut du Doubs, Compagnie Droz-Bartholet,

Les Terres Rouges, 25130 Villers-le-Lac. ☏03 81 68 13 25. www.sautdudoubs.fr. Trips to Besançon and the Saut du Doubs from Easter to 1 November.

CNFS – Vedettes panoramiques, BP 30, 25130 Villers-le-Lac. ☏03 81 68 05 34. www.vedettes-panoramiques. com. Cruises from Besançon and Villers-le-Lac with or without meal.

Le Vagabondo – departure from Quai Mavia, 70100 Gray. ☏06 07 42 75 54. www.bateauvagabondo.com. Guided trips along the Saône; also cruises with meal included.

Barge-hotels

There are about a dozen of these in Burgundy; cruises lasting from two to seven days provide full board and offer a fine chance to discover and appreciate Burgundian gastronomy. Barges can accommodate 6 to 24 passengers and prices vary from 760€ to 2 300€ per person per week, including transfer from the airport, excursions, evening entertainment and wine-cellar visits.

NATURE AND THE ENVIRONMENT

Nature lovers will find a wealth of information about nature trails, hiking and outdoor activities, exhibitions concerning nature and the environment and ongoing projects in the brochure *La Bourgogne Loisirs nature* (available from tourist offices) and by contacting the following:

Houseboat on a canal in Burgundy

S. Sauvignier-MICHELIN

Maison de la nature des Vosges saônoises,
Le Belmont, 70440 Haut-du-Them.
☎ 03 84 63 89 41. www.mnvs.fr.
Maison départementale de l'environnement,
Étang de Malsaucy,
90350 Évette-Salbert.
☎03 84 29 18 12.
DPIE Atelier de l'environnement du Haut-Jura,
1 Grande-Rue, 39170 St-Lupicin.
☎03 84 42 85 96.

PARC NATUREL RÉGIONAL DU MORVAN

There are three Regional Nature Parks covered in this guide; one in Burgundy and two in the Jura.

With its forests, deep valleys, numerous waterways and lakes, the Morvan lends itself to a wide range of nature-friendly activities (rambling, themed walks, cycle tours, riding tours, sailing, swimming, white-water sports, rock-climbing…). For full information about the Regional Nature Parks and the leisure activities available, apply to the **Maison du Parc**, 58230 St-Brisson; ☎03 86 78 79 00; www.parcdumorvan.org.

Guided Hikes
Guides en Morvan, 71320 Charbonnat, guidesenmorvan@parcdumorvan.org.
Morvan Découverte,
La Peurtantaine, École du Bourg, 71550 Anost.
☎03 85 82 77 74.
France Randonnée,
9 r. des Portes-Mordelaises, 35000 Rennes.
☎02 99 67 42 21.
Association Morvan VTT, Maison du Parc.
☎03 86 78 71 77.
Base de plein air,
Plan d'eau du Vallon, 71400 Autun.
☎03 85 86 95 80.

Riding Tours
Association pour la randonnée équestre en Morvan (AREM),

same address as the Maison du Parc, www.morvanacheval.com; additional information available from the Maison du Parc.

On the Water
Base nautique des Settons,
58230 Montsauche-les-Settons.
☎03 86 84 51 98.
www.activital.ne.
Base Activital de loisirs,
Baye, 58110 Bazolles.
☎03 86 38 97 39
White-water sports – AN rafting,
Auberge du lac, 58140 Plainefas.
☎03 86 22 65 28.
www.an-rafting.com.
Centre Sport nature de Chaumeçon,
58140 St-Martin-du-Puy.
☎03 86 22 61 35.
Ab Loisirs,
Route du camping, 89450 St-Père-sous-Vézelay.
☎03 86 33 38 38.

Rock-Climbing
Loisirs en Morvan,
105 r. des Mignottes, 89000 Auxerre.
☎03 86 49 55 50.

For other activities, apply to the **Maison du Parc** or send an e-mail to: morvanloisirssportsnature@parcdumorvan.org.

PARC NATUREL RÉGIONAL DU HAUT-JURA

Information about activities, nature trails etc is available from:
Maison du Haut-Jura,
39310 Lajoux.
☎03 84 34 12 30.
www.parc.haut-jura.

PARC NATUREL RÉGIONAL DES BALLONS DES VOSGES

Permanent and temporary exhibitions are held in the Maison du Parc, which also provides information and welcomes visitors.
Maison du Parc,
1 cour de l'Abbaye, 68140 Munster.
☎03 89 77 90 34.
www.parc-ballons-vosges.fr.

Books

CLASSICS

Le Rouge et le Noir. Stendhal. (1830; trans. Roger Gard as *The Red and the Black*, Penguin Classics 2002. This portrait of the foibles of French society, especially Franche-Comté, under the Second Restoration (1815-30) is based on a contemporary newspaper account of a crime of passion. In the book, Sorel is the ultimate opportunist, using seduction as a means to advance his career, but is undone by love and his final realisation of the vanity of worldly success.

The Complete Claudine. Colette. (trans. A White, 2001) One of the best-loved writers of fiction from the region, Colette's *Claudine* series is full of verve and wit, and shows clearly her love of nature and her poetic childhood memories.

The Physiology of Taste, or Meditations on Transcendent Gastronomy. Jean-Anthelme Brillat-Savarin (1825, trans. MFK Fisher, Penguin Classics). Penned in the early 19C, the musings of this French judge who barely escaped death under the Reign of Terror go beyond the culinary to attain the far reaches of philosophy. This is a classic volume for lovers of fine food, good company and sensory pleasure.

The Art of Eating. MFK Fisher. (1954, reprinted 2004). One of Fisher's excellent books on the culinary arts, which includes notes from her studies in Dijon. Her award-winning prose has set a standard for food writers, as she discusses cooking with war rations, the social status of vegetables, and travelling to some wonderful places. If you love food, you will love her work, which is resonant with emotion, often surprising and joyful.

BIOGRAPHIES

A Life of Colette. Judith Thurman. (2000) A beautifully written account of the fascinating life and work of the well-known author, who spent her childhood in Saint-Sauveur-en-Puisaye, in the Yonne.

Margaret of York: Duchess of Burgundy 1446-1503. Christine Weightman. (1993). By both birth and marriage, Margaret played a pivotal role in the alliance between the dukes of Burgundy and the English crown. A patron of the arts, she was also remarkably independent and influential for a woman of her time. The book includes maps, genealogies and several other illustrations.

Alphonse de Lamartine: A Political Biography. William Fortescue. (1983). Only a little of Lamartine's work has been translated into English, but this well-researched account of the author's career in politics gives a good insight into one part of his busy life.

GASTRONOMY

A Kitchen in Burgundy. Anne Willan. (2002). An evocative and readable book, elegantly interweaving tradtional and contemporary recipes with chapters on life in the 17C Chateau de Fey in Burgandy and its surroundings.

Burgundy Stars: a Year in the Life of a Great French Restaurant. W. Echikson. (Little, Brown, 1996). Worth tracking down is this 12-month account of Bernard Loiseau's famous restaurant in Saulieu, which is fascinating in its description of the frenetic pace and flurry in the kitchen and the elegance of one of the world's finest dining rooms.

WINE

Wines of Burgundy. Serena Sutcliffe. (Mitchell Beazley Wine Guides, 2005) A comprehensive, up-to-date guide to the sought-after wines of Burgundy. An introductory section examines Burgundy's history and geography, as well as wine-growing, winemaking techniques, and the classification system. Vintage reports are also included. The second section details Burgundy's key wine regions and the most prestigious properties, as well as the lesser-known names worth seeking out. There is also an A-Z listing of over 600 producers and their wines.

Côte d'Or: A Celebration of the Great Wines of Burgundy, by Clive Coates (University of California Press, 1997). Another much-praised comprehensive book on Burgundy wine. This work seems to cover even the smallest vineyards, and takes a deeper look at 60 of the best domaines, all with wit and finely tuned British understatement.

The Great Domaines of Burgundy: A Guide to the Finest Wine Producers of the Côte d'Or. Remington Norman. (Henry Holt & Co., Inc., second edition 1996). Another good, all-encompassing book on the subject. Excellent maps and many pictures accompany the text, which concentrates on about 100 growers. Serious Burgundy lovers will lap up the historical accounts and descriptions of practices in the vineyards, as well as tasting notes on many vintages.

Burgundy and Its Wines: An Irresistible Portrait of Burgundy's Culture, History, Landscape and Wines. Nicholas Faith. (2002). A lavishly illustrated tome, with plenty of knowledgable advice about wines, for leisurely browsing before and after your trips.

Films

Burgundy and Jura sometimes catches the attention of the world's film-makers, but only a few titles a decade are worth mentioning.

Mondovino (2004) An in-depth look into the wine business around the world, with Burgundy represented by a small family vineyard.

The Messenger: the Story of Joan of Arc (1999). Milla Jovovich takes on the role of the French heroine in Luc Besson's update on the classic historical epic.

USEFUL WORDS AND PHRASES

SIGHTS

abbaye	abbey
beffroi	belfry
chapelle	chapel
château	castle
cimetière	cemetery
cloître	cloisters
cour	courtyard
couvent	convent
écluse	lock (canal)
église	church
fontaine	fountain
halle	covered market
jardin	garden
mairie	town hall
maison	house
marché	market
monastère	monastery
moulin	windmill
musée	museum
parc	park
place	square
pont	bridge
port	port/harbour
porte	gateway
quai	quay
remparts	ramparts
rue	street
statue	statue
tour	tower

NATURAL SITES

abîme	chasm
aven	swallow-hole
barrage	dam
belvédère	viewpoint
cascade	waterfall
col	pass
corniche	ledge
côte	coast, hillside
forêt	forest
grotte	cave

lac	lake
plage	beach
rivière	river
ruisseau	stream
signal	beacon
source	spring
vallée	valley

ON THE ROAD

car park	parking
driving licence	permis de conduire
east	Est
garage (for repairs)	garage
left	gauche
motorway/highway	autoroute
north	Nord
parking meter	horodateur
petrol/gas	essence
petrol/gas station	station essence
right	droite
south	Sud
toll	péage
traffic lights	feu tricolore
tyre	pneu
west	Ouest
wheel clamp	sabot
zebra crossing	passage clouté

TIME

today	aujourd'hui
tomorrow	demain
yesterday	hier
winter	hiver
spring	printemps
summer	été
autumn/fall	automne
week	semaine
Monday	lundi
Tuesday	mardi
Wednesday	mercredi
Thursday	jeudi
Friday	vendredi
Saturday	samedi
Sunday	dimanche

NUMBERS

0	zéro
1	un
2	deux
3	trois
4	quatre
5	cinq
6	six
7	sept
8	huit
9	neuf
10	dix
11	onze
12	douze
13	treize
14	quatorze
15	quinze
16	seize
17	dix-sept
18	dix-huit
19	dix-neuf
20	vingt
30	trente
40	quarante
50	cinquante
60	soixante
70	soixante-dix
80	quatre-vingt
90	quatre-vingt-dix
100	cent
1000	mille

SHOPPING

bank	banque
baker's	boulangerie
big	grand
butcher's	boucherie
chemist's	pharmacie
closed	fermé
cough mixture	sirop pour la toux
cough sweets	cachets pour la gorge
entrance	entrée
exit	sortie
fishmonger's	poissonnerie
grocer's	épicerie
newsagent, bookshop	librairie
open	ouvert
post office	poste
push	pousser
pull	tirer
shop	magasin
small	petit
stamps	timbres

FOOD AND DRINK

beef	bœuf
beer	bière
butter	beurre
bread	pain
breakfast	petit-déjeuner
cheese	fromage
chicken	poulet

dessert	dessert
dinner	dîner
fish	poisson
fork	fourchette
fruit	fruits
glass	verre
ice cream	glace
ice cubes	glaçons
ham	jambon
knife	couteau
lamb	agneau
lunch	déjeuner
lettuce salad	salade
meat	viande
mineral water	eau minérale
mixed salad	salade composée
orange juice	jus d'orange
plate	assiette
pork	porc
restaurant	restaurant
red wine	vin rouge
salt	sel
spoon	cuillère
sugar	sucre
vegetables	légumes
water	de l'eau
white wine	vin blanc
yoghurt	yaourt

PERSONAL DOCUMENTS AND TRAVEL

airport	aéroport
credit card	carte de crédit
customs	douane
passport	passeport
platform	voie
railway station	gare
shuttle	navette
suitcase	valise
train/plane ticket	billet de train/d'avion
wallet	portefeuille

CLOTHING

coat	manteau
jumper	pull
raincoat	imperméable
shirt	chemise
shoes	chaussures
socks	chaussettes
stockings	bas
suit	costume
tights	collants
trousers	pantalon

USEFUL PHRASES

goodbye	au revoir
hello/good morning	bonjour
how	comment
excuse me	excusez-moi
thank you	merci
yes/no	oui/non
I am sorry	pardon
why	pourquoi
when	quand
please	s'il vous plaît

Do you speak English? Parlez-vous anglais?

I don't understand Je ne comprends pas

Talk slowly Parlez lentement

Where's...? Où est...?

When does the... leave? A quelle heure part...?

When does the... arrive? A quelle heure arrive...?

When does the museum open? A quelle heure ouvre le musée?

When is the show? ... A quelle heure est la représentation?

When is breakfast served? A quelle heure sert-on le petit-déjeuner?

What does it cost? Combien cela coûte?

Where can I buy a newspaper in English? Où puis-je acheter un journal en anglais?

Where is the nearest petrol/gas station? Où se trouve la station essence la plus proche?

Where can I change traveller's cheques? Où puis-je échanger des traveller's cheques?

Where are the toilets? Où sont les toilettes?

Do you accept credit cards? Acceptez-vous les cartes de crédit?

BASIC INFORMATION

Discounts

Significant discounts are available for senior citizens, students, under 25s, teachers, public transport, museums, monuments, and some leisure activities such as films (at certain times of day). Bring student or senior cards with you, and bring along some extra passport-size photos for discount travel cards. The **International Student Travel Confederation** (www.istc.org), global administrator of the International Student and Teacher Identity Cards, is an association of student travel organisations around the world. ISTC members collectively negotiate benefits with airlines, governments, and providers of other goods and services for the student and teacher community, both in their own country and around the world. The non-profit association sells international ID cards for students, under-25's and teachers. The ISTC is also active in a network of international education and work exchange programmes.

Electricity

The electric current is 220 volts. Circular two-pin plugs are the rule. Adapters and converters should be bought before you leave home; they are on sale in most airports. If you have a rechargeable device (video camera, laptop, battery charger), read the instructions carefully: in some cases you must use a voltage converter as plug adaptor, or risk ruining your appliance.

Emergencies

Emergency Numbers	
Police:	17
SAMU (Paramedics):	15
Fire (Pompiers):	18

Public Holidays

Museums and other monuments may be closed or may vary their hours of admission on certain public holidays (see chart).
National museums and art galleries are closed on Tuesdays; municipal museums are generally closed on Mondays. In addition to the usual school holidays at Christmas and in the spring and summer, there are long mid-term breaks (10 days to a fortnight) in February and early November.

1 January	New Year's Day (Jour de l'An)
	Easter Day and Easter Monday (Pâques)
1 May	May Day (Fête du Travail)
8 May	VE Day (Fête de la Libération)
Thurs 40 days after Easter	Ascension Day (Ascension)
7th Sun-Mon after Easter	Whit Sunday and Monday (Pentecôte)
14 July	France's National Day (Fête de la Bastille)
15 August	Assumption (Assomption)
1 November	All Saint's Day (Toussaint)
11 November	Armistice Day (Fête de la Victoire)
25 December	Christmas Day (Noël)

Mail/Post

Post offices open Mondays to Fridays, 8am to 7pm, Saturdays, 8am to noon. Smaller branch post offices often close at lunchtime between noon and 2pm and in the afternoon at 4pm.
Postage via air mail to
✉ UK: letter (20g) 0.60€
✉ North America: letter (20g) 0.85€
✉ Australia and NZ: letter (20g) 0.85€

Stamps are also available from newsagents and tobacconists.

Stamp collectors should ask for *timbres de collection* in any post office.
Poste Restante (General Delivery) mail should be addressed as follows: Name, *Poste Restante*, *Poste Centrale*, post code of the département followed by town name, France. **The Michelin Guide France** gives local post codes.

American Express ☏ 01 47 77 72 00	
Visa ☏ 08 36 69 08 80	
MasterCard/Eurocard ☏ 01 45 67 84 84	
Diners Club ☏ 01 49 06 17 50	

Money

CURRENCY

There are no restrictions on the amount of currency visitors can take into France. Visitors carrying a lot of cash are advised to complete a currency declaration form on arrival, because there are restrictions on currency export.

NOTES AND COINS

Since 17 February 2002, the **euro** has been the only currency accepted as a means of payment in France, as in the 11 other European countries participating in the monetary union. It is divided into 100 cents or centimes. Since June 2002, it has only been possible to exchange notes and coins in French francs at the Banque de France (3 years for coins and 10 years for notes).

BANKS

Although business hours vary from branch to branch, banks are usually open from 9am to noon and 2pm to 5pm and are closed either on Mondays or Saturdays. Banks close early on the day before a bank holiday. A passport is necessary as identification when cashing travellers cheques in banks. Commission charges vary and hotels usually charge more than banks for cashing cheques.

Debit and Credit Cards

One of the most economical ways to use your money in France is by using **ATM machines** to get cash directly from your bank account (with a debit card) or to use your credit card to get a cash advance. Be sure to remember your PIN number; you will need it to use cash dispensers and to pay with your card in shops, restaurants, etc. Pin numbers have four digits in France; enquire with the issuing company or bank if the code you usually use is longer. Visa is the most widely accepted credit card, followed by Mastercard; other cards, credit and debit (Diners Club, Plus, Cirrus, etc) are also accepted in some cash machines. American Express is more often accepted in premium establishments. Most places post signs indicating which card they accept; if you don't see such a sign and want to pay with a card, ask before ordering or making a selection. Cards are widely accepted in shops, hypermarkets, hotels and restaurants, at tollbooths and in petrol stations. Before you leave home, check with the bank that issued your card for emergency replacement procedures. Carry your card number and emergency phone numbers separate from your wallet and handbag; leave a copy of this information with someone you can easily reach. If your card is lost or stolen while you are in France, call one of the 24-hour hotlines listed in the box: These numbers are also listed at most ATM machines.

You must report any loss or theft of credit cards or travellers cheques to the local police who will issue you with a certificate (useful proof to show the issuing company).

Telephones

Most public phones in France use pre-paid phone cards *(télécartes)*, rather than coins. Some telephone booths accept credit cards (Visa, Mastercard/Eurocard). *Télécartes* (50 or 120 units) can be bought in post offices, branches of France Télécom, *bureaux de tabac* (cafés that sell cigarettes) and newsagents and can be used to make calls in France and abroad. Calls can be received at phone boxes where the blue bell sign is shown; the phone will not ring, so keep your eye on the little message screen.

NATIONAL CALLS

French telephone numbers have 10 digits. Paris and Paris region numbers begin with 01; 02 in north-west France; 03 in north-east France; 04 in south-east France and Corsica; 05 in south-west France. Numbers beginning with 08 are special rate numbers, available only when dialling within France.

INTERNATIONAL CALLS

To call France from abroad, dial the country code (33) + 9-digit number (omit the initial 0). When calling abroad from France dial 00, then dial the country code followed by the area code and number of your correspondent.
International information:
    US/Canada: 00 33 12 11
International operator:
    00 33 12 + country code
Local directory assistance: 12

International Dialling Codes (00 + code)			
Australia	☎ 61	NZ	☎ 64
Canada	☎ 1	UK	☎ 44
Eire	☎ 353	USA	☎ 1

MINITEL

France Télécom's system has directory enquiries, travel and entertainment reservations, and other services. Small computer terminals can be found in some post offices, hotels and France Télécom agencies, and in many French homes. 3614 PAGES E is the code for **directory assistance in English** (turn on the unit, dial 3614, hit the *connexion* button when you get the tone, type in "PAGES E", and follow the instructions.

MOBILE PHONES

In France mobile phone numbers start with 06. Two-watt (lighter, shorter

reach) and eight-watt models are on the market, using the Orange (France Télécom) or SFR networks. *Mobicartes* are prepaid phone cards that fit into mobile units. Mobile phone rentals (delivery or airport pickup provided):

- A.L.T. Rent A Phone
    ☎ 01 48 00 06 06
- Rent a Cell Express
    ☎ 01 53 93 78 00
- Ellinas Phone Rental
    ☎ 01 47 20 70 00

Time

France is 1hr ahead of Greenwich Mean Time (GMT). France goes on daylight-saving time from the last Sunday in March to the last Sunday in October.

Prices and Tips

Since a service charge is automatically included in the price of meals and accommodation in France, any additional tipping is up to the visitor, generally small change, and generally not more than 5%. Taxi drivers and hairdressers are usually tipped 10-15%.
As a rule, the cost of staying in a hotel, eating in a restaurant or buying goods and services is significantly lower in the French regions than in Paris.
Cafés have very different prices, depending on where they are located. The price of a drink or a coffee is cheaper if you stand at the counter *(comptoir)* than if you sit down *(salle)* and sometimes it is even more expensive if you sit outdoors *(terrace)*.

When it is **noon in France**, it is	
3am	in Los Angeles
6am	in New York
11am	in Dublin
11am	in London
7pm	in Perth
9pm	in Sydney
11pm	in Auckland

CONVERSION TABLES

Weights and Measures

1 kilogram (kg) 6.35 kilograms 0.45 kilograms **1 metric ton (tn)**	**2.2 pounds (lb)** 14 pounds 16 ounces (oz) **1.1 tons**	**2.2 pounds** 1 stone (st) 16 ounces **1.1 tons**	*To convert kilograms to pounds, multiply by 2.2*
1 litre (l) 3.79 litres 4.55 litres	**2.11 pints (pt)** 1 gallon (gal) 1.20 gallon	**1.76 pints** 0.83 gallon 1 gallon	*To convert litres to gallons, multiply by 0.26 (US) or 0.22 (UK)*
1 hectare (ha) **1 sq. kilometre (km²)**	**2.47 acres** 0.38 sq. miles (sq.mi.)	**2.47 acres** 0.38 sq. miles	*To convert hectares to acres, multiply by 2.4*
1 centimetre (cm) **1 metre (m)**	**0.39 inches (in)** 3.28 feet (ft) or 39.37 inches or 1.09 yards (yd)	**0.39 inches**	*To convert metres to feet, multiply by 3.28; for kilometres to miles, multiply by 0.6*
1 kilometre (km)	**0.62 miles (mi)**	**0.62 miles**	

Clothing

Women					Men			
	35	4	2½			40	7½	7
	36	5	3½			41	8½	8
	37	6	4½			42	9½	9
Shoes	38	7	5½		Shoes	43	10½	10
	39	8	6½			44	11½	11
	40	9	7½			45	12½	12
	41	10	8½			46	13½	13
	36	6	8			46	36	36
	38	8	10			48	38	38
Dresses	40	10	12		Suits	50	40	40
& suits	42	12	14			52	42	42
	44	14	16			54	44	44
	46	16	18			56	46	48
	36	06	30			37	14½	14½
	38	08	32			38	15	15
Blouses &	40	10	34		Shirts	39	15½	15½
sweaters	42	12	36			40	15¾	15¾
	44	14	38			41	16	16
	46	16	40			42	16½	16½

Sizes often vary depending on the designer. These equivalents are given for guidance only.

Speed

KPH	10	30	50	70	80	90	100	110	120	130
MPH	6	19	31	43	50	56	62	68	75	81

Temperature

Celsius (°C)	0°	5°	10°	15°	20°	25°	30°	40°	60°	80°	100°
Fahrenheit (°F)	32°	41°	50°	59°	68°	77°	86°	104°	140°	176°	212°

To convert Celsius into Fahrenheit, multiply °C by 9, divide by 5, and add 32.
To convert Fahrenheit into Celsius, subtract 32 from °F, multiply by 5, and divide by 9.
NB: Conversion factors on this page are approximate.

Châteaux de Joux
G. Benoît á la Guillaume/ MICHELIN

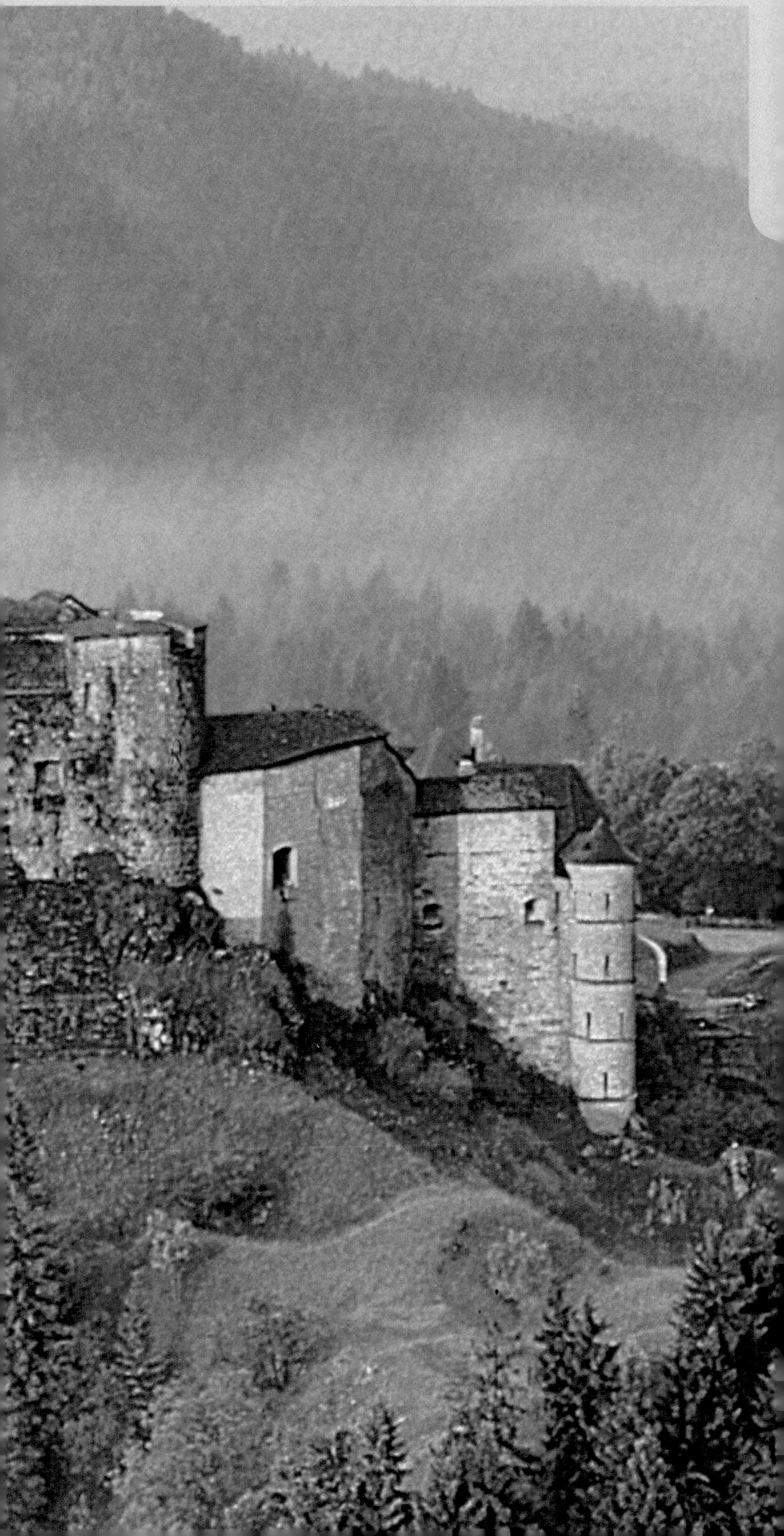

NATURE

Landscapes

POLITICAL DIVISIONS

France, exclusive of its overseas territories, is divided into administrative units: *96 départements* and *22 régions*, including **Bourgogne** and **Franche-Comté**. The région of Burgundy includes the *départements* of **Côte-d'Or, Nièvre, Saône-et-Loire** and **Yonne**; Franche-Comté encompasses **Doubs, Jura** and **Haute-Saône**. Jura is also the name of the 250km/155mi-long mountain range running from the

Rhine to the Rhone. Perhaps because the mountains cover most of the region, Jura is generally used to refer to the whole region of Franche-Comté, except for administrative or historical purposes. The region of Burgundy has several distinct geographical areas, which are commonly referred to as **Basse Bourgogne** (the Auxerre and Chablis areas), the **Arrière-Côte** and Côte and the ancient granite massifs known as the **Morvan**, the **Charollais** and the **Mâconnais** to the south.

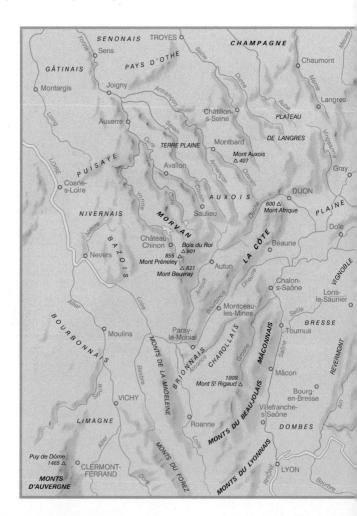

The Jura mountains reach a width of 61km/38mi; the tallest peak is the Crêt de la Neige (1 717m/5 633ft). The relief, while modest in height, is striking, characterised by long parallel ridges and valleys along a northeast-southwest axis that converge at each end. This pattern of folds steps down to an undulating plateau in the west, which rises around Montbéliard to meet the Vosges.

FORMATION OF THE LAND

Primary Era - This is believed to have begun about 600 million years ago. Modern France was entirely under water, until the movement of the earth's crust known as the **Hercynian fold** took place,

which created a number of high mountain ranges. The seas that covered the Paris and Rhône basins were linked by a strait which corresponds to the "threshold of Burgundy". Erosion wore down the highest parts of the Morvan to their rocky base, while the warm, humid climate produced lush vegetation, eventually buried under layers of alluvial deposits and pressurised into coal between the Morvan and Beaujolais massifs.

Secondary Era - This began about 200 million years ago. The Hercynian base subsided and the seas flooded the Paris basin and Jura region, covering even the highest land. They deposited strata of sedimentary rocks – marl (chalk mixed with impermeable clay) and limestone (formed from fossilised shells and fish skeletons) – on the granite seabed. The formation of such sedimentary rock strata was so prolific in Jura in particular that geologists named the middle period of the Secondary Era, which lasted about 45 million years, the Jurassic period.

Tertiary Era - This began about 60 million years ago. The parallel rock strata of the Jura region, sloping gently down to the Swiss plain, were still covered with water (the lakes of **Biel**, **Neuchâtel** and **Geneva** still remain). Then came the great Alpine folding movement, and the land was once again forced upwards and the seas pushed back.

The pressure during this Alpine-building period folded the Jura rock strata along a northeast-southwest axis into parallel ridges and valleys, curving in a giant crescent between the **Vosges** and the **Massif Central** and sloping down towards the River Saône, where all the rivers drained into the great lake of Bresse (which later vanished). Nearer the Alps, the thick layers of sedimentary rock folded under pressure, giving rise to the Jura mountains. The layers of the western edge, not so thick, split along the faults formed by the movements of the earth's crust into a series of stepped plateaux. Not far from the

Saône Valley, salt deposits were formed (later to become a local resource).

Quaternary Era - This began about 2 million years ago. Erosion continued to shape the region into its present appearance: ancient massifs (Morvan, Beaujolais); limestone plateaux (La Côte, l'Arrière Côte); sedimentary basins (Bazois, Terre-Plaine, Auxois); valleys (surrounding the Jura); and low-lying plains (Saône Valley). The era was marked by two significant events; the appearance of man, and the coming of the Ice Age with its glaciers, which invaded the valleys from the Alps. As the glaciers receded, they left in their wake a huge amount of debris, including glacial moraine, which blocked the drainage of water in many places, giving rise to the Jurassic lakes.

THE REGIONS OF BURGUNDY

From the Auxois to the Beaujolais regions, from the River Saône to the River Loire, the varied regions that make up Burgundy have preserved their own appearance, economy and way of life.

The historical links which united them in the 15C have proved strong enough, however, for several common characteristics to be apparent to this day. Administrative divisions, modern economic demands and the attraction of Paris notwithstanding, the ties holding together the constituents of this province, of which Dijon is capital in more than name, remain unbroken.

The Alluvial Plains - The **Sénonais, Gâtinais** and **Puisaye** plains are situated on the northern borders of Burgundy. These are well-watered, fertile lands, rich in alluvial deposits, where the lakes and forests provide a rich catch for hunters and anglers alike. The Sénonais is furthest to the north; agriculture there is varied and productive. The Gâtinais extends from Gien (in the Loire Valley) to just north of Montargis, and is mostly limited to dairy farming. The Puisaye, similar in landscape, also produces fodder crops. The population is widely dispersed among abundant woodlands.

The Nivernais - This region of plateaux and hills, essentially a crossroads, stretches away to the west of the Morvan Massif and slopes gently down to the Loire Valley. To the west of Château-Chinon are the verdant slopes of **Bazois**: cereal and fodder crops on the hillsides, rich pasture for stock-breeding below.

To the north, the hilly region of **Clamecy** and **Donzy** (peaks up to 450m/1 476ft high) is watered by a dense network of rivers, and used for stock-breeding and crop farming.

From Nevers to Bonny the River Loire marks the boundary between the Nivernais and the Berry region. Stock-breeding pasture alternates with wooded spurs.

The landscape of the Morvan

Pouilly lies at the heart of a well-reputed vineyard which stretches over the hillsides overlooking the Loire Valley.

The Morvan - In the aftermath of the great Alpine thrust, the edges of the great Morvan granite massif were broken up; erosion wore away at the softer limestone strata bordering the massif, scouring out a hollow on three sides. This depression is surrounded in turn by limestone plateaux which tower at its outer edges. The Morvan is distinguished by its abundant tree cover and dense network of rivers. Fields bounded by hedges form colourful patterns.

Long isolated in every sense of the word, the Morvan has recently opened up to the outside world and is popular with those seeking unspoiled landscapes.

The Auxois - To the east of the Morvan lies the Auxois region, a rich and fertile land of hard blue limestone, crisscrossed by many rivers, given over to pasture for stock-breeding. Rocky outcrops are home to fortified towns, such as Semur, Flavigny-sur-Ozerain and Mont-St-Jean, or by ancient *oppidums* from Roman times, such as Alésia on Mont Auxois.

The Charollais and Brionnais - These regions of sweeping hillsides and plateaux, with superb rich pasturage, are the home of Charollais cattle.

The Autun basin - During the Primary Era, this was a vast lake, which was gradually filled in with the coal-bearing deposits and bituminous schists.

The Dijonnais - The region around Dijon is an area of limestone plateaux, isolated outcrops, rich pastureland, wide alluvial plains and steep hillsides covered with vineyards.

The Côte - This is the edge of the last slope of the mountains (La Côte d'Or) overlooking the Saône plain. This escarpment was formed by the cracks which appeared as the Saône's alluvial plain subsided. The Arrière-Côte plateau is given over to crops and pasture, and the eastern slope is covered with vines.

The Mâconnais - This is where the mountain range formed by the Côte d'Or extends southwards. The steep faces of the escarpment are turned towards the interior, whereas along the Côte d'Or they overlook the valley of the Saône. This is a region of vine-covered hillsides and pastureland; cereal crops, beets, vegetables and poultry are also raised.

The Saône Valley - Major communications routes run through this valley which stretches along the foot of limestone cliffs. Civil engineering works have opened the river to navigation year-round. The alluvial plains of the Saône, often flooded in winter, are covered with rich pastures and arable land. In addition to wheat, beet and potato crops, there are now market gardens and fields of maize, tobacco and oilseed.

The Bresse - The Bresse plain, composed of clay and marl soil, stretches from the Saône to the foothills of the Jura, the Revermont. Numerous streams cut across the rolling countryside, which is dotted with copses. In France, the name is indissociable from the *Poulet de Bresse,* the delicious chickens raised here.

The Burgundy plateaux - From the northern edge of the Morvan to the Langres plateau and from Auxerre to Dijon is a region of limestone plateaux forming the real heartland of Burgundy. This area is known as the threshold: the point of contact between the Seine and Saône basins, and between the Vosges and the Morvan.

The plateaux rise to a relatively low altitude (400-500m/1 312-1 640ft), sloping gently to the north-west but dropping abruptly in the south-east. Their dry appearance contrasts with the much greener, richer one of the valleys of the rivers which intersect them; the Yonne, Serein and Armançon. The plateaux are, from west to east, the Auxerrois, the Tonnerrois and the Châtillonnais.

The **Auxerrois** is a rocky plateau, split by numerous valleys, in which the limestone is often dazzling white. The sunny slopes have lent themselves to vines, in the regions of Chablis, Auxerre and Irancy, and to cherry trees.

The **Tonnerrois** plateau has similar characteristics to that of Langres, but it is at a lower altitude.

The **Châtillonnais** is a series of monotonous plateaux, for the most part bare with the occasional rocky outcrop or dry river valley. These plateaux used to be covered by forests. Monks from the abbeys of Molesmes, St-Seine, Fontenay and Clairvaux cleared much of the land. In the 18C, there were foundries and nail works, thanks to the discovery of iron ore.

THE REGIONS OF JURA

The Jura range - From the Swiss plain the Jura range appears as a formidable unbroken barrier across the horizon. From the crest, however, valleys and meadows give the countryside a less harsh appearance. Each valley is a world of its own, in which the inhabitants congregate near springs, or on the banks of rivers or lakes. The meadows, where glaciers deposited a layer of clay, contrast with the bare limestone. Among the meadows, fields of barley, rye, oats and potatoes stand out. But at this altitude, winter lasts a long time, so cereals ripen late and fruit trees are few.

The Jura plateaux - These tracts of flat land look like stairs descending (900-400m/2 953-1 312ft) from Pontarlier to Besançon. To the north, they reach the Belfort Gap between the Jura and Vosges mountains. A notable feature of these plateaux is the *reculée*, a blind valley ending at the foot of a cliff.

The Vignoble - The road from Besançon to Bourg-en-Bresse, leading between the River Doubs and River Ain, runs along the continuous slope on the western rim of the Jura plateaux, part of the Revermont. The vines cultivated here for centuries have earned the region its local name, the Vignoble (vineyard).

Flora

FORESTS

In Burgundy and Jura, the forest covers an area of 1 500 000ha/3 615 000 acres, 30% and 40% of each region, respectively; well above the average for France (25%).

Vegetation – Deciduous trees give way to conifers at about 800m/ 2 624ft. Beeches dominate between 500-800m/1 640-2 624ft. Higher are the magnificent pine forests of the Joux, and above 1 000m/3 281ft, forests of spruce alternating with wooded upland pastures.

Trees – The main deciduous trees are beech and oak, and to a lesser extent ash, maple, cherry, elm and birch.
Pines, firs, cypresses and spruce make up the coniferous group, as does larch, which does lose its leaves in winter.

Spruce – It has a pointed top shaped like a spindle and a bushy appearance, with downward curving branches. The chocolate-brown bark becomes deeply cracked with age. The dark green nee-

Spruce   Fir   Beech

M. Janvier/ MICHELIN

dles are rounded and sharp and grow all the way round the branches and twigs. The cones hang below the branches, and when they are ripe their scales separate to release the seeds.

Fir – This has a broad top, flattened into a stork's nest in older trees. The bark remains a darkish grey colour, with blisters of resin here and there. The cones stand upright on the branches and scatter their seeds when ripe by disintegrating on the branch. The soft needles grow in rows along the branches, like a comb. They are a paler green colour on their undersides, which have a double white line marking (hence the name silver fir).

Beech – This tall tree is easily recognised by its trunk, cylindrical with grey and white bark, and thin, oval leaves. A beech tree can grow at an altitude of up to 1 700m/ 5 577ft and live for 150 years.

Other types of tree – The **larch** can be found on the sunnier slopes. It has small cones, and its delicate pale green foliage does not cast so much shade that grass is unable to grow. The **Norway pine,** with its tall, slender trunk, has bunches of 2-5 needles growing together, held by a scaly sheath, and cones with hard scales. The elegant **birch**, with its slender trunk, trembling leaves and white bark which comes off in shavings, thrives in moist soil. The **oak** is a beautiful tree which can grow up to 30m/98ft tall. Finally, the **durmast oak**, or white or truffle oak, can be found in dry soil above the vineyards; its thick trunk is protected by a deeply ridged bark.

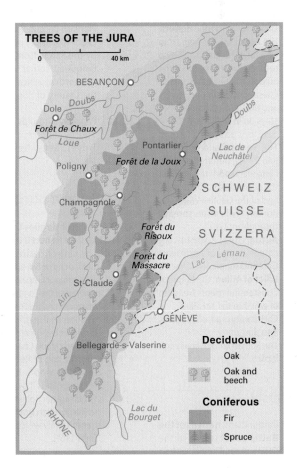

HISTORY

Prehistory

BC   Bone fragments found at Solutré show there were humans there between 18 000 and 15 000 BC.

Antiquity

6C   During the Gaulish period Burgundy is inhabited by the **Aedui**; their capital is Bibracte.

4C   The **Sequani**, from the Haute Seine, settle in Franche-Comté. They build fortified camps, including Vesontio (Besançon).

58   Under threat from the **Helvetii**, the Aedui ask for help from Caesar. The Sequani also request his help, this time against the Germanic threat. Caesar drives out the Helvetii and the Germanic tribes… but stays on in Gaul himself.

52   Gaul rises up against **Caesar**. The Sequani and the Aedui join forces, but are forced to concede victory to Caesar at the decisive battle of Alésia.

51   End of the Gaulish War.

AD   Roman civilization spreads throughout Gaul.

1-3C   **Autun**, city of Augustus, becomes capital of north-east Gaul and supplants Bibracte.

313   **Edict of Milan**: the Emperor Constantine grants freedom of worship to Christians.

Late 4C   Christianity gradually spreads into Burgundy. The Roman Empire finally collapses.

Burgundy

5C   Burgundians, **natives of the Baltic coast**, settle in the Saône plain. They give their name to their new homeland: Burgundia (which evolved in French into Bourgogne).

534   The **Franks** seize the Burgundian kingdom.

800   **Charlemagne** becomes Emperor of the West.

814   The death of Charlemagne plunges the Empire into a period of instability. The sons of Emperor Louis the Pious dispute his legacy.

841   **Charles the Bald** defeats his brother Lothar at Fontanet (Fontenoy-en-Puisaye).

843   **Treaty of Verdun**: Charlemagne's empire is divided between the three sons of Louis the Pious. Frankish Burgundy reverts to Charles the Bald. It is separated by the Saône from imperial Burgundy, Lothar's territory, the north of which becomes the County of Burgundy (or Comté).

Late 9C   Frankish Burgundy becomes a duchy and takes in Langres, Troyes, Sens, Nevers and Mâcon.

The Duchy of Burgundy

987-996   Reign of **Hugues Capet**.

996-1031   Reign of **Robert II the Pious**.

1002-1016   The King of France occupies the Duchy of Burgundy.

1032   The Germanic Emperor becomes suzerain of the Comté. But both his power and that of the count decline as the great feudal landowners gain influence, headed by the Chalons. **Henri I**, son of Robert II the Pious, to whom Burgundy returns, hands it over as a fief to his brother Robert I the Old (a Burgundian branch of the Capet family which survived until 1361).

Under the Capetian dukes, Burgundy is one of the bastions of Christianity; **Cluny**, then Cîteaux and Clairvaux reach the height of their influence.

1095 **First Crusade**.

1270 Death of **St Louis** at the siege of Tunis.

1295 **Philip the Fair** buys the Comté as an apanage for his son Philip the Long and his descendants. This is the beginning of a period of peace and prosperity.

1337-1453 Hundred Years War.

1349 The Comté is devastated by the **Black Plague**; this is *l'année de la grande mort* (the year of widespread death).

1353 Switzerland frees itself from imperial domination.

1361 Duke Philippe de Rouvres dies young without issue, bringing the line of the Capet dukes to an end. The Duchy of Burgundy passes to the King of France, John the Good, who was regent during the duke's minority.

1366 The name **Franche-Comté** appears for the first time, on an official decree proclaiming the value the inhabitants attach to their rights, as had been done in the Franche-Montagnes of the Swiss Jura.

The Comté returns to Burgundian rule

1384-1477 Philip the Bold (son of the King of France, John the Good), who had already been given the duchy in apanage, marries the heiress to the Comté and takes possession of the whole of Burgundy. He is the first of the dynasty of the "great dukes of Burgundy", whose power came to exceed that of the kings of France. He is succeeded by John the Fearless, Philip the Good and Charles the Bold. In the Comté, these rulers keep a tight rein on the feudal lords, enforce the authority of Parliament and the State

bodies and become patrons of art and literature.

1429 Orléans is saved by **Joan of Arc**.

1453 Constantinople falls to the Turks.

1461-1483 Reign of **Louis XI**.

The Great Dukes of Burgundy

Under this branch of the House of Valois, Burgundy reached the height of its power, where it remained for over a century (1364-1477).

Philip the Bold (1364-1404)

While scarcely more than a child, Philip fought bravely beside his father, King John II of France, at the battle of Poitiers (1356). He earned the nickname "the Bold" when, although wounded and a prisoner, he landed a well-aimed blow on an English lord who had insulted the French King.

By the time he became Duke of Burgundy (1364), Philip was a superb knight, who loved sport and women, and who devoted himself heart and soul to his duchy and the interests of his House. His marriage in 1369 to Margaret of Flanders, the richest heiress in Europe, made him the most powerful prince in Christendom. He lived in great splendour and kept a large and magnificent household in the palace he had built, where he employed painters and sculptors from Flanders.

Philip founded the Chartreuse de Champmol in Dijon as a mausoleum for himself and his descendants. The finest marble from Liège and alabaster from Genoa were provided for the tomb which was designed in 1384 by the sculptor **Jean de Marville**. On his death, the decoration was entrusted to **Claus Sluter.** Philip the Bold spent so much money that, when he died in 1404, his sons had to pledge the ducal silver to pay for his funeral.

John the Fearless (1404-19) – John succeeded his father, Philip the Bold. Although puny to look at, he was brave, intelligent and ambitious. No sooner had he become Duke of Burgundy than he started a quarrel with the royal council against his cousin, Louis d'Orléans, brother of the mad king, Charles VI, and in 1407 had his rival assassinated. John took control of Paris, where he was opposed by the Orleanist faction which controlled the king. When the Orleanist leader, the poet Charles d'Orléans, was captured at Agincourt (1415) and taken to England, where he was a prisoner for 25 years, his father-in-law, Count Bernard VII of Armagnac took over his leadership.

During the struggle between the Armagnacs and the Burgundians, in which the French were drawn into fighting each other, John the Fearless, realising the potential harm of the struggle for French interests, sought to negotiate an agreement with the dauphin, the future king, Charles VII. He agreed to meet him on 11 September 1419 on the bridge at Montereau, but was murdered there.

Philip the Good (1419-67)

Filled with desire for vengeance, Philip the Good, son of John the Fearless, allied himself with the English and in 1430 handed them Joan of Arc, whom he had captured at Compiègne, for the enormous sum of 10 000 livres. A few years later, however, Philip came to an understanding with Charles VII at the Treaty of Arras, which enabled him, once again, to enlarge his territory. Dijon became the capital of a powerful state which included a large part of Holland, most of Belgium,

Luxembourg, Flanders, Artois, Hainaut, Picardy and all the land between the Loire and Jura.

Philip, who had an even greater taste for magnificence than his predecessors, lived like a prince. Five great officers of state, the Marshal of Burgundy, the Admiral of Flanders, the Chamberlain, the Master of the Horse and the Chancellor, were part of the Duke's immediate entourage, in a court that was among the most sumptuous in Europe.

On the day of his marriage with Isabella of Portugal, 14 January 1429, Philip founded the sovereign Order of the Golden Fleece (⚜ see DIJON) in honour of God, the Virgin Mary and St Andrew. The Order originally had 31 members, all of whom swore allegiance to the Grand Master, Philip the Good and his successors. They met at least once every three years and were lavishly dressed: a long scarlet cloak, trimmed with squirrel fur, hung from the shoulders over a robe of the same colour, also trimmed with squirrel fur. The ducal motto, Aultre n'auray (not for others), stood out against a background of firestones, quartz, sparkling stones and fleeces. The neck chain of the Order was made of sparkling firestones and quartz. The headquarters of the Order was the ducal Holy Chapel at Dijon, destroyed during the Revolution. The Order is now one of the most prestigious and exclusive.

Charles the Bold (1467-77)

He was the last, and possibly the most famous member of the House of Valois and the dukes of Burgundy. Tall, vigorous and strongly built, Charles loved violent exercise, and in particular hunting. He was also a cultured man, however, and spent much of his time in study. Above all he was passionately interested in history. As his father had the same name as Philip of Macedonia, Charles dreamed of becoming a second Alexander and was constantly waging war in an effort to undermine Louis XI, who in turn did everything possible to break up the Burgundian state. Charles was killed during the siege of Nancy.

Musée des Beaux-Arts de Dijon-

Philip the Good by Rogier Van der Weyden; Musée des Beaux-Arts, Dijon

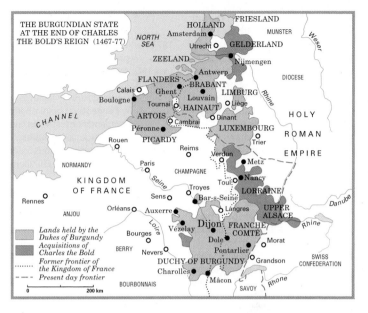

THE BURGUNDIAN STATE
AT THE END OF CHARLES
THE BOLD'S REIGN (1467-77)

Lands held by the
Dukes of Burgundy
Acquisitions of
Charles the Bold
Former frontier of
the Kingdom of France
Present day frontier
0   200 km

Return to the French Crown

1477   On the death of Charles the
Bold, **Louis XI** invades the
Comté, annexing Burgundy
and the Burgundian towns in
Picardy to the royal territory.
Mary of Burgundy, the daughter of the dead duke, deprived
of a large part of her inherit-
ance, marries Maximilian of
Habsburg who thus acquires
the rest of the old duchy.
Their union produces Philip
the Handsome whose son,
the future emperor, **Charles V**,
will continue the struggle
against the Kingdom of France
ruled by François I.

1519   The Comté enjoys a period of
prosperity under Charles V.
He includes people from the
Comté, such as the Granvelles,
in his immediate circle.

1556-98 Emperor Charles V bequeaths
the Comté to his son, **Philip II**,
King of Spain, who proves to be
far less sympathetic a ruler to
the people of the Comté.

1589-1610 Reign of **Henri IV**.

1598   On the death of Philip II, the
Comté passes to his daughter
Isabelle, who marries the
Archduke of Austria. The province of the Comté belongs to
the archdukes until it is seized
by the French in 1678.

The French Conquest

In order to understand the resistance to
French rule of a French-speaking country, one must remember that, finding
itself on the borders of the Holy Empire,
Austria and Spain, the Comté had
become used to directing its own affairs.
The independent people of the Comté
regarded the rule of a Richelieu or a
Louis XIV with trepidation.

1601   Henri IV acquires the territories of Bresse, Bugey, Valromey
and the Gex region from the
Duke of Savoy, in return for
some Italian territory of his.

1609   After 50 years of struggle against
the Spanish, the Netherlands
wins its independence.

1610   Beginning of the reign of
Louis XIII, who dies in 1643.

1618   Start of the **Thirty Years War**
between Austria and France

allied with Sweden. The war ends in 1648 with the **Treaty of Westphalia**.

1635 Richelieu gives the order to invade the Comté which gave refuge to his enemy, Gaston d'Orléans. The Ten Years War brings the country to ruin.

1643-1715 Reign of **Louis XIV**.

1648 **Mazarin** withdraws French forces from the Comté and restores it to its neutral status.

1668 Louis XIV reclaims the Comté as part of the dowry of his wife **Marie-Thérèse**, daughter of the late King of Spain. However, he is forced to abandon it and return it to Spain.

1674 Louis XIV, at war with Spain, makes a fresh attempt to take control of the province, and this time is successful. His conquest is ratified by the **Peace of Nimègue** (1678). Besançon takes over from Dole as capital. From now on, the history of the Comté follows that of the rest of France.

From the Revolution to modern times

1715-74 Reign of **Louis XV**.

1789 Fall of the **Bastille**.

1793 The Montbéliard region is annexed to France.

1804 Consecration of **Napoleon I** as Emperor of France.

1815 The battle of **Waterloo**. Heroic defence of Belfort by Lecourbe.

1822 Invention of photography by Nicéphore Niepce at St-Loup-de-Varenne.

1870 Colonel Denfert-Rochereau resists attack by 40 000 Germans during the **siege of Belfort**.

1871 General Bourbaki is defeated at Héricourt, having won victory at Villersexel, and has to fall back to Besançon.

1878 Vines devastated by the **phylloxera** aphid.

Late 19C- As industrialisation gains pace,
early 20C the Jura region is transformed. Great industrial dynasties such as **Peugeot** and Japy are born, compensating for the decline in the clockmaking industry.

1914 Joffre gives his famous order of 6 September at Châtillon-sur-Seine.

1940 Occupation of Jura by the **Germans**, who use the region to block the retreat of French forces trying to reach central France along the Swiss border.

1940-44 The **Resistance movement** is active in Burgundy: Châtillonnais forests are used as a hideout.

14 September 1944
Leclerc's division joins the army of De Lattre de Tassigny near Châtillon-sur-Seine.

November 1944
The **Allied conquest** of the northern part of the Doubs *département* completes the liberation of Jura.

1948 Génissiat reservoir is filled with water.

1970 A6-A7 motorway from Paris to Marseille opens up the west of Burgundy (Auxerre, Beaune and Mâcon).

1981 High-speed rail service (**TGV**) links Paris-Le Creusot-Mâcon-Lyon and Paris-Dijon-Besançon.

1986 Setting up of the **Haut-Jura** regional nature park.

1992 Fabrice Guy, native of Pontarlier, wins the Olympic gold medal for nordic combined.

2001 After an 85-year prohibition, production of **absinthe** is again allowed in Pontarlier.

2007 Tricentenary of the death of Burgundy-born Sebastien le Prestre de Vauban, Louis XIV's influential military engineer.

ART AND CULTURE

Religious Architecture

IN BURGUNDY

Burgundy has a rich artistic tradition. Since Antiquity, the region has been a crossroads where a wide variety of peoples and influences have met. The treasure found near Vix shows that strong currents were active in the region of Châtillon-sur-Seine in about the 6C BC. In the 15C, on the initiative of the Great Dukes, artists from Paris and Flanders settled in Dijon, which became an important artistic centre.

This penetration of foreign influences, and the enduring qualities of Roman civilization, combined with the expression of the Burgundian temperament, led to a blossoming of regional art that holds a special place in French artistic history.

Pre-Romanesque – The Carolingian epoch (8C-9C) saw architectural revival in Burgundy in particular. The religious buildings were simple. Part of the former crypt of the cathedral of **St-Bénigne** at Dijon and the crypts of **Flavigny-sur-Ozerain** and **St-Germain** of Auxerre are among the oldest examples.

Romanesque – Numerous towns, wealthy abbeys and abundant building material were favourable conditions in which the Romanesque School of Burgundy flourished, showing an extraordinary vitality in the 11C and 12C, not only in architecture, but in sculpture and painting (see below). The school's influence spread far beyond Burgundy's borders.

In the year 1000, the desire to build was given fresh impetus by the end of invasions, the strengthening of royal power and new building techniques.

Early Burgundian Romanesque churches – Among the great builders of this period, Abbot Guglielmo **da Volpiano**, of Italian origin and related to some of the greatest families of his time, built a new basilica in Dijon on the site of the tomb of St Bénigne. The building, begun in 1001, was consecrated in 1018.

Though this abbey was destroyed by fire in the 12C, the church of **St-Vorles** in Châtillon-sur-Seine – much modified in the first years of the 11C – provides an example of the features of Romanesque art at this time: slipshod building methods with badly placed flat stones; thick pillars; crude decoration of mural niches; and cornices with Lombard arcades.

The most striking example of the architecture of this time is the church of **St-Philibert in Tournus**. The narthex and the upper storey of the narthex, built at the beginning of the 11C, are the oldest extant parts to date. The most striking aspect of this solid, powerful architecture is its sober, almost austere style.

Cluny and its school – Although in the beginning Romanesque art owed much to foreign influences, the following period witnessed the triumphant emergence of a new style from Cluny, which was to spread throughout Burgundy.

In 1247 an Italian visitor noted that "Cluny is the noblest Burgundian monastery of the Benedictine Black Monk order. The buildings are so extensive that the Pope with his cardinals and entire retinue and the king and his court may be accommodated together, with-

A mermaid with a double tail on this Romanesque capital

B. Kaufmann-MICHELIN

ABC of Architecture

Ecclesiastical architecture

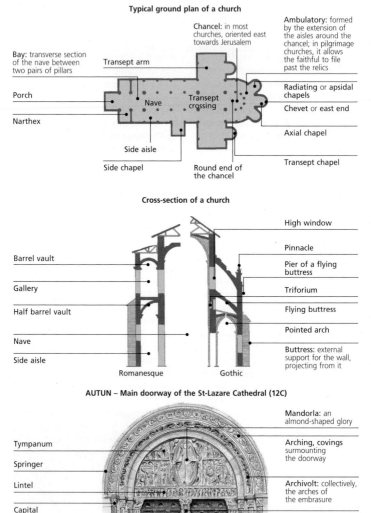

Typical ground plan of a church

Bay: transverse section of the nave between two pairs of pillars

Transept arm

Chancel: in most churches, oriented east towards Jerusalem

Ambulatory: formed by the extension of the aisles around the chancel; in pilgrimage churches, it allows the faithful to file past the relics

Porch

Narthex

Nave

Transept crossing

Radiating or apsidal chapels

Chevet or east end

Axial chapel

Side aisle

Side chapel

Round end of the chancel

Transept chapel

Cross-section of a church

Barrel vault

Gallery

Half barrel vault

Nave

Side aisle

Romanesque

High window

Pinnacle

Pier of a flying buttress

Triforium

Flying buttress

Pointed arch

Buttress: external support for the wall, projecting from it

Gothic

AUTUN – Main doorway of the St-Lazare Cathedral (12C)

Tympanum

Springer

Lintel

Capital

Shaft

Archshaft

Mandorla: an almond-shaped glory

Arching, covings surmounting the doorway

Archivolt: collectively, the arches of the embrasure

Pier: often adorned by a statue

Jamb shaft: vertical member forming part of the jamb of a door, supporting the arches

R. Corbel/MICHELIN

VÉZELAY – Nave of the Ste-Madeleine Basilica

High window

Pier: a kind of pilaster supporting the column

Groined vaulting: two ribs meet at a right angle

Abacus

Wall arch or **stringer:** lateral arch of a vault

Cornice with frieze

Archstone (here, dark and light cut stone blocks alternate)

Historiated capital decorated with scenes or characters

Triumphant arch: a large arcade separating the central nave from the transept or the chancel

Triforium: a gallery and passageway hollowed from the thickness of the wall. At the end of the Gothic period, this feature became purely decorative

Engaged half-columns: set around the four faces of a cruciform pillar

Transverse arch: reinforces the vault

Cross-ribbed vault

Chancel

R. Corbel/MICHELIN

INTRODUCTION TO BURGUNDY JURA

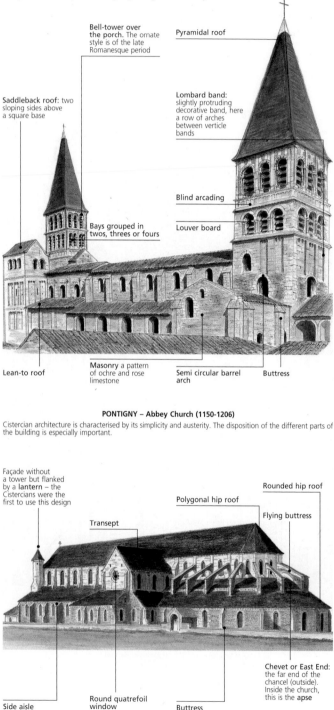

TOURNUS – St-Philibert Abbey Church (11-12C)

The fortress-like appearance of the front wall, which was a defensive feature of the abbey, is one of the first examples of Romanesque art in Burgundy, dating to around the year 1000.

Bell-tower over the porch. The ornate style is of the late Romanesque period

Pyramidal roof

Saddleback roof: two sloping sides above a square base

Lombard band: slightly protruding decorative band, here a row of arches between verticle bands

Blind arcading

Bays grouped in twos, threes or fours

Louver board

Lean-to roof

Masonry a pattern of ochre and rose limestone

Semi circular barrel arch

Buttress

PONTIGNY – Abbey Church (1150-1206)

Cistercian architecture is characterised by its simplicity and austerity. The disposition of the different parts of the building is especially important.

Façade without a tower but flanked by a **lantern** – the Cistercians were the first to use this design

Rounded hip roof

Polygonal hip roof

Flying buttress

Transept

Side aisle

Round quatrefoil window

Buttress

Chevet or East End: the far end of the chancel (outside). Inside the church, this is the **apse**

R. Corbel/MICHELIN

CLÉRON – Castle (14C)

This old feudal castle stands on the banks of the River Loue, which makes an excellent natural moat.

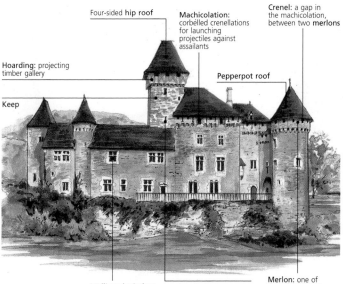

Four-sided **hip roof**

Machicolation: corbelled crenellations for launching projectiles against assailants

Crenel: a gap in the machicolation, between two **merlons**

Hoarding: projecting timber gallery

Pepperpot roof

Keep

Mullioned window

Loophole or **arrow slit**

Merlon: one of the solid intervals between two **crenels** of a battlement

BESANÇON – The citadel

An impressive sight: the fortifications hang 118m/387ft above the River Doubs. Vauban designed the citadel in the 17C.

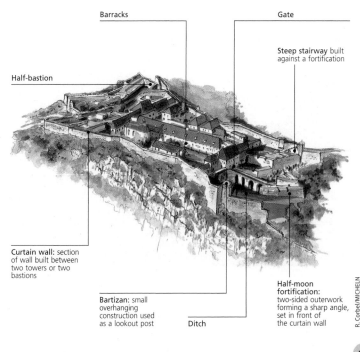

Barracks

Gate

Steep stairway built against a fortification

Half-bastion

Curtain wall: section of wall built between two towers or two bastions

Bartizan: small overhanging construction used as a lookout post

Ditch

Half-moon fortification: two-sided outerwork forming a sharp angle, set in front of the curtain wall

R. Corbel/MICHELIN

NEVERS – Palais Ducal (16C)

The former home of the Dukes of Nevers was a precursor to the famous châteaux of the Loire Valley. Note the Renaissance harmony of the structure, and the great towers revealing medieval influence.

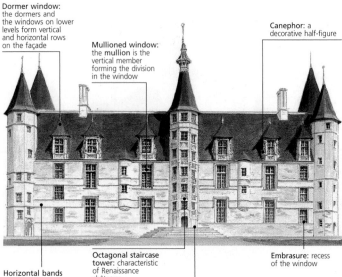

Dormer window: the dormers and the windows on lower levels form vertical and horizontal rows on the façade

Mullioned window: the **mullion** is the vertical member forming the division in the window

Canephor: a decorative half-figure

Horizontal bands mark the façade

Octagonal staircase tower: characteristic of Renaissance châteaux

Perron: the front steps and entrance platform

Embrasure: recess of the window

ANCY-LE-FRANC – Inner courtyard of the château (begun in 1544)

The square courtyard with four identical wings is an example of the architectural rhythm created by the use of alternating bays, pilasters and niches, invented by Bramante

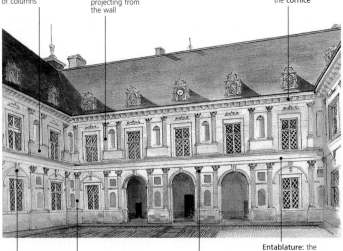

Stylobate: a continuous flat coping supporting a row of columns

Pilaster: engaged pillar sl ightly projecting from the wall

Modillions: small brackets supporting the **cornice**

Agrafe, clasp: an ornamental piece on the keystone of a bay

Fluting: grooves giving texture to the columns or pillars

Corinthian capital: embellished with two rows of **acanthus** leaves

Entablature: the horizontal part in classical architecture that rests on the column and consists of the architrave, frieze and cornice

R. Corbel/MICHELN

SYAM – Palladian Villa

One of the forge masters, Mr. Jobez, had this villa built in 1818. He drew inspiration from the Italian villas designed by Palladio (16C)

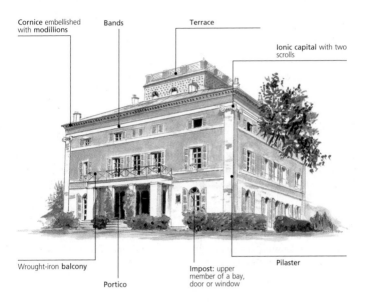

Cornice embellished with **modillions**

Bands

Terrace

Ionic capital with two scrolls

Wrought-iron **balcony**

Portico

Impost: upper member of a bay, door or window

Pilaster

VOUGLANS – Dam

Flooding part of the Ain Valley, the Vouglans DJam forms France's third largest reservoir.

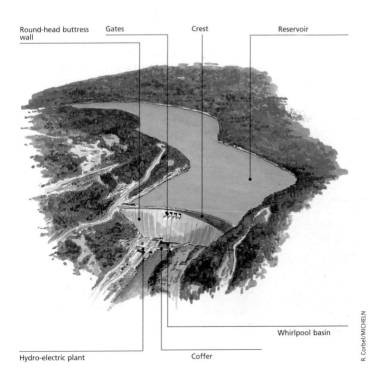

Round-head buttress wall

Gates

Crest

Reservoir

Hydro-electric plant

Coffer

Whirlpool basin

out upsetting the monks' routine or putting them out of their cells".

The extent and exceptional size of the remains of the abbey, which was started by St Hugh in 1088 and completed about 1130 (see CLUNY), are still impressive and allow one to recognise the general characteristics of the School of Cluny. Burgundian architects avoided semicircular vaulting and substituted broken-barrel vaulting which was far more efficient at withstanding the strains and stresses of the building. This style of vaulting consists of each bay having a transverse arch; the use of broken arches reduces stress and thereby the weight on the walls, thus making it possible to raise the vaulting to a far greater height. The pillars are flanked by fluted pilasters in the Antique style; a false triforium of alternating bays and pilasters, surmounted by a clerestory, runs above the narrow arches. This arrangement of three storeys rising to a pointed vault is found in many churches in the region. The priory church of **Paray-le-Monial** is a smaller replica of the great abbey church at Cluny. At **Semur-en-Brionnais**, home of the family of St Hugh, the church is almost as high as Cluny. On the interior of the west front, the gallery is similar to one in St-Michel in Cluny.

Vézelay and its influence – The Cluny School was repudiated by a whole family of churches, the purest example of which is the basilica of **Ste-Madeleine in Vézelay**, although there are others that display characteristics even further removed from Cluny. Built at the beginning of the 12C, Vézelay constitutes the synthesis of true Burgundian Romanesque architecture.The essential difference between this church and earlier Romanesque buildings is that the nave has groined vaulting whereas up to that time only the side aisles had this feature, their small size mitigating the risk of the vaulting subsiding as a result of lateral pressure.

This design, originally without the support of flying buttresses which were added in the Gothic period, required the incorporation of iron bars to prevent the walls of the nave from bulging outwards.

Clerestory windows placed directly above the main arches opened onto the axis of each bay, shedding light into the nave. Columns projecting slightly from the walls replace the rectangular pilasters of Cluny style. The vaulting is supported by semicircular transverse arches.

The church in **Anzy-le-Duc** appears to have served as a model for the building in Vézelay; it is probable that Renaud **de Semur**, who came from the Brionnais region, wished to rebel against the all-powerful influence of Cluny and took as his model the church in Anzy-le-Duc, which at that time was the most perfect piece of architecture of the region. There is no shortage of points of comparison: the elevation of the storeys is the same; both have a solitary window above the main arches; both share the same style of semicircular vaulting and cruciform pillars flanked by engaged columns. This style, created in Anzy-le-Duc and perfected in Vézelay, has been copied in **St-Lazare in Avallon** and **St-Philibert in Dijon**.

Fontenay and the Cistercian School – Cistercian architecture first appeared in Burgundy in the first half of the 12C (Cistercium was the Latin name for the town of Cîteaux). It is characterised by a spirit of simplicity in keeping with the teaching of **St Bernard**. He objected bitterly to the luxury displayed in some monastic churches, opposing the theories of some of the great builders of the 11C and 12C with extraordinary passion.

Tympanum above the central doorway, Ste-Madeleine

Ph. Gajic-MICHELIN

His argument against the belief of abbots such as St Hugh, Peter the Venerable and Suger, who believed that nothing could be too rich for the glory of God, was expressed for example in the letter he wrote to William, Abbot of St-Thierry, in which he asks, "Why this excessive height in the churches, this enormous length, this unnecessary width, these sumptuous ornaments and curious paintings that draw the eye and distract attention and meditation? ...We the monks, who have forsaken ordinary life and renounced worldly wealth and ostentation for the love of Christ, ...in whom do we hope to awaken devotion with these ornaments?".

There is nonetheless a certain grandeur even in the sobriety and austerity that he advocated. The uncluttered style and severe appearance reflected the principles of Cistercian rule, which regarded everything that was not indispensable to the development and spread of the monastic way of life as harmful.

The Cistercians almost always insisted on the identical plan of construction for all the buildings of their order and themselves directed the work on new abbeys. The abbey of Fontenay is a good example of the standard plan (© see photograph). This design is found throughout Europe from Sicily to Sweden. Every new monastery was another link with France, and craftsmen followed the monks. It was the turn of the Burgundian Cistercian monasteries to spearhead the expansion of monasticism.

In **Cistercian churches**, the blind nave is covered by broken-barrel vaulting, as at Cluny; the side aisles are generally arched with transverse barrel vaulting, and their great height enables them to take the thrust of the nave. This is found in many 12C Burgundian churches.

The transept, also of broken-barrel vaulting, juts far out and has two square chapels opening into each transept arm. The choir, of broken-barrel vaulting, is square and not very deep. It ends in a flat chevet lit through two tiers of three windows. Five windows are placed above the chancel arch, and each bay of the side aisles is also lit through a window.

The fact that most Cistercian churches have no belfry is evidence of St Bernard's

Chapter house, Fontenay Abbey

B. Kaufmann-MICHELIN

desire to adhere to poverty, humility and simplicity. Living far from their fellow men, the religious communities did not wish to attract the faithful from far and wide. Belfries, which drew attention to the existence of a church by their silhouette and shape, were thus banned.

By avoiding all decoration, be it painting or sculpture, and by eliminating every kind of superfluous ornamentation (such as stained-glass windows, or illuminated paving stones), Cistercian art achieved a remarkable purity of execution.

Gothic – About the middle of the 12C and perhaps even earlier, pointed vaulting made its appearance in Burgundy, the prelude to a new development in architecture. The Gothic style, which originated in the Parisian region (Ile-de-France), penetrated slowly into Burgundy, where it was adapted according to circumstances and trends.

Period of transition – In 1140, the gallery of the narthex at Vézelay was given pointed vaulting. The Cistercians were among the first to adopt this style of architecture and used it at Pontigny in about 1150. The choir of **Ste-Madeleine at Vézelay**, the work of Abbot Gérard **d'Arcy**, was started in the last years of the 12C; the flying buttresses were not added until the 13C. It was in the 13C that a Burgundian Gothic style emerged in religious buildings.

First half of the 13C – The church of **Notre-Dame in Dijon**, built between 1230 and 1251, is the most perfect and best-known example of this style. Its characteristics are found in many religious buildings of the period in Burgundy; beyond the transept, the fairly deep choir is flanked by apsidal chapels (there are generally two) and ends with a high apse. The use of sexpartite vaulting permitted the replacing of the uniformly sized pillars with alternating thick and thin pillars. A triforium runs above the great arches; at the clerestory level, the nave wall is set back slightly allowing for a gallery above that of the triforium. In the external decoration, the presence of a cornice goes round the choir, the nave, the apse, or the belfry and is a typically Burgundian mode of decoration. Among the buildings constructed in this style, the most important are: **Auxerre Cathedral**, the collegiate church of **St-Martin in Clamecy** and the church of **Notre-Dame in Semur-en-Auxois**. In the latter, the absence of a triforium further enhances the effect of dizzying height created by the narrow nave.

End of the 13C – Architecture now became much lighter and developed a boldness, seeming to defy the laws of gravity. The choir of the church of **St-Thibault** in Auxois is in such a style, with its keystone at a height of 27m/89ft. The five-sided, four-storey apse is amazingly light. Below the highest windows is a clerestory composed of three tiers reaching to the ground: the top tier is a gallery, the middle one is composed of pairs of radiant windows and the bottom tier consists of blind arcades. The church of **St-Père** shares certain similarities with Notre-Dame in Dijon, but it differs in its height, being of two storeys with a gallery in front of the windows.

14C – The Flamboyant Gothic style, characterised by the pointed, S-shaped ogee arch, appeared; the number of ribs multiplied and the capitals were reduced to a simple decorative role or were sometimes even dispensed with completely. This period did not produce any really fine buildings in Burgundy.

Renaissance – Under Italian influence, Burgundian art took a new turn in the 16C with a revival of Antique styles.

In architecture the transition from Gothic to Italian art met with some resistance. The church of **St-Michel in Dijon** shows evidence of this: whereas the nave (started at the beginning of the 16C) is an imitation of Gothic art, the façade (built between 1537 and 1570) is a perfect example of the Renaissance style, with two towers divided into four storeys, on which Ionic and Corinthian orders are superimposed alternately, three semicircular doorways and the porch with its richly sculpted coffered vaulting all reflecting a strong Italian influence.

IN JURA

The religious architectural heritage of the region of Franche-Comté is indebted to the numerous monastic communities in the region during the Middle Ages. The monks played a vital role in the development of this rugged, primitive country. By the Merovingian period, two abbeys were already making waves throughout the region: Luxeuil in the north and Condat (later St-Claude) in the south. The former rapidly became an intellectual centre exerting an influence on the whole of Gaul – in particular in Lure – whereas the latter devoted its energies to spreading the Christian message and to the enormous task of clearing space in the forests of Jura.

Unfortunately, the anarchy which greeted the end of Carolingian rule sounded a death knell for both these abbeys. In the 10C, the Benedictines thus faced the task of winning back territory in Burgundy. They were followed by the Cluny order, which soon dominated the province. However, in the 12C the Cluny order itself had to give way to the innumerable Cistercian communities which were springing up. At the same time, communities were being set up by the Premonstratensians, the Augustinians and the Carthusians who all threw themselves into clearing the forest and draining the soil, thus attracting their share of local residents, who set up communities round their abbeys. The churches, which are now used as parish churches, were originally monastery churches usually built according to the rules of the religious order which was to use them: thus, the Benedictine order introduced a primitive architectural style influenced by early Italian basilicas; the Cluny order preferred Burgundian style churches; and the Cistercians built churches with a flat chevet, like that at Cîteaux, and generally paved the way for Gothic art.

Romanesque – There is no Romanesque art specific to the region of Franche-Comté; the primitive churches built there during the Romanesque period drew on Burgundian and Lombard architecture for their inspiration. They generally have a basilical floor plan with a transept hardly wider than the nave itself. The chancel ends in a semicircular apse, flanked by two apsidal chapels opening into the transept, or it ends in a flat chevet (as in the church at Courtefontaine). Large arcades are supported by heavy pillars, which can be square, round or octagonal, with no capitals. The buildings and pillars are often made of small quarry stones. The nave and side aisles were originally covered by a timber roof, which was later replaced by ogival vaulting. The roofs over the side aisles are sometimes groined vaulting. The apse and apsidal chapels are closed off by half domes. The roof above the transept crossing is either a dome or a bell-tower, which never features as part of the façade.

The churches of Jura are typically understated, and the absence of almost any decoration further underlines their austerity. The churches of **St-Hymetière** and **St-Lupicin** (early 12C), **Boussières**, the crypt of **St-Denis at Lons-le-Saunier** are the best preserved examples. The cathedral of **St-Jean at Besançon** is almost the only remaining trace of Rhenish Carolingian influence in Franche-Comté; it has an apse at either end of its nave. Inside, square sturdy pillars alternate with round slender ones, creating a regular division of space.

Gothic – Romanesque art continued to exert its influence in Franche-Comté for some time. Thus, at the end of the 13C, which marked the culmination of the great period of creativity in Gothic art elsewhere, there were still numerous Romanesque features evident in buildings in Franche-Comté which had adopted

St-Hymetière

the new style. The most typical and best-preserved example of this period of transition is the church of St-Anatoile at Salins. This has a semicircular arched doorway, large pointed arches in the nave and a triforium with Romanesque arcades. It is in fact this long-lasting preference for semicircular arches that gives the churches of Franche-Comté their distinctive character. The Gothic style did not really become widespread in Franche-Comté until the middle of the 15C, when Flamboyant Gothic features were adopted. It did not reach its apogee there until the following century, even surviving into the middle of the 17C, when the Renaissance style was already starting to decline in other parts of France.

Flamboyant Gothic churches in Franche-Comté typically have three tall blind naves separated by elegant pointed arches supported on round pillars. The ribs from the vaulting and the moulding from the arches run down these pillars. The church is topped by an enormous bell-tower. Large windows shed light into the deep, five-sided choir (St-Claude Cathedral, Poligny Collegiate Church), which is flanked by two chapels. These open onto the transept, which is a little wider than the nave. However, vaulting is generally uncluttered and only seigneurial chapels, such as the Chalon family chapel at Mièges, have ornate features.

Renaissance – The Italian Renaissance had little effect on the religious architecture of Franche-Comté, which adhered to Flamboyant Gothic until quite late on. The new style was applied, once it began to make its influence felt, for the most part to church annexes, such as chapels (Pesmes) or entrance doorways (Collège de l'Arc at Dole).

Classical to modern periods – Classical art was slow to catch on in Franche-Comté; it only really began to make its mark from 1674 onwards, when the churches destroyed during the Ten Years War (1633-43) and the destructive campaigns of Louis XIV were being re-built. The small size and run-down nature of the churches which had survived from the Middle Ages, coupled with a huge rise in population figures from the middle of the 18C, may explain the great number of construction projects undertaken up until the Revolution.

The most characteristic feature from this period, which typifies the religious architecture of the region as a whole, is the way the porch is incorporated in a bell-tower, which is surmounted by an imperial style pointed dome, formed of four reversed curve sides covered with glazed tiles. There are three common layouts: a church with a single nave, with or without a transept; a church with a centralised floor plan, either octagonal or in the shape of a Greek cross; or a hall-church with three naves of equal height, generally without a transept. The naves are covered by pointed vaulting, and need buttresses outside to counteract the outward pressure which might otherwise make the walls bulge at the top. The interior is often painted white, apart from the columns, pillars and ribs, which are picked out in grey. The façade is enlivened by frontons, pilasters and columns.

In the late 18C and early 19C, the neo-Classical style took over, with consciously simple, almost austere ornamentation. As in the Antique temples, the straight line replaced the curve, and side aisles with ceilings took the place of the side naves with pointed vaulting of the hall-churches. The central nave was covered with a barrel vault.

After 1850, the neo-Gothic style reintroduced pointed arches.

During the **contemporary** period, Jura is proud of the fact that it has been the setting for a revival of religious art. Since the 1950s and 1960s, some important architectural projects have been undertaken, for example, at Audincourt, Ronchamp and Dole. A desire to emphasize the spirituality of such places is often evident in the powerful movement of the line of the building and in the way the decorative effects of light have been employed. Many artists, such as Manessier, Gabriel Saury, Bazaine, Le Moal and Fernand Léger, have contributed in the same spirit, giving a new or renewed vitality to religious buildings with their stained-glass windows, sculptures, mosaics or tapestries.

Civil and Military Architecture

IN BURGUNDY

Gallo-Roman art – The Romans were responsible for many monuments in Burgundy. To this day the town of **Autun**, built by order of Emperor Augustus to replace Bibracte, capital of the Aedui tribe, recalls Roman civilization with its monumental gateways and vast theatre.

Excavations at **Alésia**, the possible site of the camp where Vercingetorix made his last stand in 52 BC, have led to the discovery of a complete town built a little later, including paved streets, the foundations of temples and a forum, and many dwellings. Other excavations out at the source of the Seine have revealed the ruins of a temple and a number of bronze statuettes and wooden sculptures. Pottery dating from Gallo-Roman times as well as examples of gold and silver work of great value were found more than 50 years ago at **Vertault**, not far from **Châtillon-sur-Seine**.

At **Dijon**, the remains of an entrenched camp (Castrum Divionense), built about AD 273, have been uncovered. Excavations at **Fontaines-Salées** near St-Père-sous-Vézelay have revealed very extensive Gallo-Roman baths.

Gothic – Fine mansions and houses built by wealthy merchants in the 15C have survived in Dijon and some other towns, such as **Flavigny-sur-Ozerain** and **Châteauneuf**. Part of the palace of the dukes of Burgundy in Dijon, the synodal palace in **Sens** and the hospital in **Beaune** all date from this period. Among the fortified castles of the 13C, those of Châteauneuf, built by Philippe Pot the Seneschal of Burgundy, Posanges and the ducal palace at Nevers are particularly interesting.

Renaissance – There was no blossoming of Renaissance châteaux in Burgundy, however, towns such as **Ancy-le-Franc**, **Tanlay** and **Sully** boast some magnificent mansions.

Classical – The reunion of Burgundy with the crown of France marked the end of the duchy's political independence, but its artistic expression survived. Classical art, initially imitated from Paris and later Versailles, is to be seen in **Dijon** in the layout of the **Place Royale**, the alterations to the old **Palais des Ducs** and in the building of the new Palais des Ducs. Many fine mansions were built by the families of parliamentarians who were in favour at Court at the time and who held high positions.

Although retaining the characteristics of the Renaissance period, the Hôtel de Vogüé (built 1607-14) features the new design where the living quarters are set back behind a courtyard with access to the street only through the coach gateway, with the opposite façade of the house opening onto the gardens.

Among the numerous châteaux built in the 17C and 18C, those of **Bussy-Rabutin**, **Commarin**, **Grancey**, **Beaumont-sur-Vingeanne**, **Menou** and **Talmay** deserve a special mention. The sculptors – **Dubois** in the 17C and **Bouchardon** and **Attiret** in the 18C – were very influential, as were painters and draughtsmen such as Greuze and François Devosge and above all **Mignard**, master painter at the court of Louis XIV.

Burgundy prides itself on its contribution to the musical world, **Jean-Philippe Rameau**, born in Dijon at the end of the 17C. He was a contemporary of Bach and Handel and ranks as one of the great French classical composers. Besides many pieces for the harpsichord, he composed some operas, of which one, *Les Indes Galantes*, is still included in the contemporary repertoire.

Ancy-le-Franc

19C and 20C – In architecture, **Gustave Eiffel** (1832-1923), an engineer from Dijon, specialised in metal construction: bridges, viaducts etc. The mention of his name conjures up the tower he erected in Paris for the universal exhibition in 1889; its structure is based on a web of girders.

IN JURA

The architectural heritage of Franche-Comté reflects its turbulent history. The region was regularly subjected to the ravages of war and invasion, and it spent most of its rare periods of peace rebuilding its ruins. For this reason, there are relatively few real architectural masterpieces. However, the restrained style of the buildings has its own charm. During the **Gallo-Roman** period, Sequania was wealthy, but little trace of this glorious past remains after the invasions of the 9C and 10C. The Roman triumphal arch which the inhabitants of **Besançon** call Porte Noir (the black gate), the Roman road at Boujailles, the remains of a theatre at Mandeure near Montbéliard are about all that is left from this period.

The Middle Ages – After the Carolingian invasions and the subsequent disintegration of Carolingian rule, power devolved into the hands of local lords. These felt the need to protect themselves and their property, and turned to the Scandinavians for a design of fairly crude castle: the **keep** or **castle mound** (11C). This consisted of an earth mound surrounded by a moat, and surmounted by a square wooden tower, which was later replaced by a stone tower.

At the same time, **stone fortresses** (Pesmes, Champlitte) made their appearance, generally on existing hills. The surrounding fortified wall – a stone embankment with a moat around its outer edge – enclosed the living quarters and outbuildings, whereas the keep remained the stronghold. This kind of fortress reached its apogee in the late 12C and the 13C. At this point, a new kind of seigneurial dwelling evolved with the rise of the middle-ranking class of knights: the **fortified house** (especially after 1250). This would be located just outside the village near a stream or river, and be constructed on a man-made platform surrounded by a water-filled moat. The residential wings and outbuildings are arranged around a central courtyard.

Fortresses did not fare well during the 14C and 15C, as first the Hundred Years War, then the guns of Louis XI's troops wreaked devastation. However, the Château du Pin (15C), which is very well preserved, is an interesting example of medieval military architecture.

At the end of the Gothic period, town houses began to feature much more prominently, and were decorated with mullioned windows surmounted by ogee arches.

Renaissance – The return of peace and prosperity to Franche-Comté during the 16C was marked by numerous castles being modified to reflect the new style, while at the same time having their defences reinforced to withstand the new metal cannon balls, which were much more destructive than the old stone ones. But the aristocracy tended to prefer their mansions in town where Renaissance art really came into its own.

Unlike religious architecture, civil architecture drew very little inspiration from Gothic art, while it was wide open to the graceful, attractive lines and forms which arrived from Italy. Emperor Charles V's Chancellor, Perrenot de Granvelle, set the example by building himself a mansion in Besançon in 1534. On the façades of Franch-Comté, different styles were superimposed on columns (Hôtel de Ville at Gray), moulded bands were added between storeys, ogee arches above windows gave way to simpler geometric forms. On the ground floor, the basket-handle arch was used for doorways or open arcades, introducing a regular movement clearly Spanish in inspiration (the interior courtyard of the Palais Granvelle at Besançon). Architectural renewal was apparent in floral decoration. The decorative artist and architect **Hugues Sambin** (1518-1601), born near Gray, left a magnificent example of his energetic artistic creativity on the polychrome façade of the Palais de Justice at Besançon (1581), his finest piece of work in Jura.

Classical – In the 17C, Franche-Comté was crushed by the Ten Years War. It was not until after 1674, when the province was incorporated into France, that a new architectural impetus came to life. The strategic position of the region compelled the French to consider implementing a comprehensive project of fortification without further ado. The task was entrusted to **Vauban**, who paid particular attention to the defence of the points along the routes leading to Switzerland. Although part of it has been destroyed, Vauban's monumental work has left an indelible impression on parts of the Jura countryside. The royal architect's greatest achievement is to have developed the concept of bastion layout (adopted during the 16C) to its maximum potential. This idea had been developed before Vauban, but he not only refined it to its definitive form but was able to adapt it to suit the terrain of any site, whether it be a fortified town wall (Belfort, Besançon) or an isolated fortress (Fort St-André near Salins-les-Bains).

Civil architecture flourished in its turn in the 18C, which was a richly productive period for art in Franche-Comté. The most original work of this period is the royal salt works at Arc-et-Senans, designed as an ideal town by visionary architect Ledoux (👈 see Arc-et-Senans). Châteaux (typically on a horseshoe layout, as at Moncley), private houses and civil buildings display perfectly symmetrical façades, pierced with large windows surmounted by triangular or rounded pediments. Another characteristic of these monuments, which some consider to be on a level of perfection with the Louis XVI style, is their traditional high roof.

19C and 20C – In the region of Franche-Comté, military architecture continued to evolve throughout the 19C and 20C. In the 19C, a number of fortresses were built (including the large fort at Les Rousses) to improve sites vulnerable to gun warfare. Most of these constructions have survived. The invention of the torpedo shell in 1885, then of the double-action fuse meant that forts were abandoned in favour of semi-underground concrete bunkers. During the Second World War, the French High Command even went so far as to build 30 or so blockhouses to protect Swiss neutrality. Modern architecture has produced some great works of civil engineering in the region; in the 19C, impressive viaducts (Morez) were built to span some of the Jura gorges. Since the war, engineers have been concerned mainly with constructing dams; the Génissiat dam (1948) on the Rhône and the Vouglans dam (1968) in the Ain Valley are two impressive examples.

Rural Architecture

The wine-growers of Burgundy have large, comfortable houses; the vats and storerooms are on the ground floor, with living quarters on the first floor reached by a covered outside staircase. Often the houses are built into the hillside. The storage rooms may be partly underground, but are protected from fluctuations in temperature by thick stone walls.

The farmhouses of the **Bresse plain** look much as they always have, although cob walls and thatched roofs have gradually given way to bricks and tiles. The houses are low, with a wide overhanging roof for drying maize. Inside, there is the traditional stove room. A few 17C and 18C houses have a **Saracen chimney,** high on the roof like a belfry.

In **Jura**, besides the traditional **chalets** (wooden buildings on a stone foundation), there are **mountain houses** which consist of living quarters, stable and barn under the same roof. They are compact, built close to the ground to shut out the wind. The thick stone walls have tiny

Farmhouse in Saint-Trivier-de-Courtes

Ph. Gajic-MICHELIN

windows; those on the sides exposed to wind and snow are protected by wooden slats known as *tavaillons*. Roofing materials are the tiles typical of Jura or, more commonly, steel sheeting. The living quarters occupy the ground floor: the *houteau*, or kitchen, in which there is almost always a huge fireplace, and the *poêle*, a big heated room used as a bedroom or a dining room. The stable next door is joined to the house. The barn is on the first floor and has an opening through which fodder can be thrown down into the stable below.

The typical dwelling of the plateaux shares traits with that of the mountains, not least having man and beast under the same roof. However, they are taller, with a rectangular roof with edges that slope steeply downwards, covered in typical Jura tiles. Walls divide the ground floor lengthwise to separate the living quarters from the stable. The main rooms are as above, but the first floor is often also given over to bedrooms.

THE ROOFTOPS OF BURGUNDY

The colourful rooftpss of the Hôtel-Dieu in Beaune and the Hôtel de Vogüe in Dijon are classic images of Burgundy. **Glazed polychrome tiles**, laid out in geometrical designs, may have arrived in Burgundy from Central Europe via Flanders. The patterns carry symbolic messages, signifying status or reputation.

Finials in glazed earthenware, ornate weathervanes and crockets are all decorative features of the pinnacles and crests of the distinctive roofs of Burgundy, especially in the Côte d'Or region. Upland, the broad, slanted roofs are covered in flat dark-brown tiles known as **tuiles de Bourgogne**, much used on Cistercian abbeys.

The tiles called **laves** are by-products of quarrying. An upper layer was removed from the surface of building stones. Roofers used these leftover pieces, interspersed with small rocks (as in the church at Ozenay in the Mâconnais region) as an aerated and frost-proof covering. The weight (600-800kg/1 320-1 760lb per m2) of the tiles required heavy-duty framework. In the Morvan, thatch has slowly replaced tile and slate.

The area around Tournus is a transitional zone where flat tiles are used on the main house, and rounded tiles, **tuile canal**, on the outbuildings or porch roof. Rounded tiles are more prevalent in the southern reaches of Burgundy; the pitch of the roofs decreases (less than 35°), framing is different. In Beaujolais, the style already shows Mediterranean influence.

Painting and Sculpture

IN BURGUNDY

Pre-Romanesque – During this period, sculpture was clumsily executed: the crypt of **Flavigny-sur-Ozerain**, all that remains of an 8C basilica, contains four shafts of columns, of which three appear to be Roman and the fourth Carolingian. The capitals are of great interest: they carry a decoration of fairly crudely exe-

Capital illustrating the flight from Egypt, Autun

cuted flat foliage. Two of the capitals in the crypt of the cathedral of St-Bénigne at Dijon are decorated on each face by a man with his arms raised in prayer. During the same period, frescoes and glazed surfaces were used to decorate the walls of religious buildings. In 1927, frescoes of the stoning of St Stephen (among other scenes) were discovered in the crypt of St-Germain in Auxerre.

Romanesque sculpture – The Cluny School of sculpture is the most significant in the Romanesque period.

Artists reveal-ed a new interest in nature in the variety of vegetation and keenly observed poses of the human figures they carved on the capitals in the choir (only rare examples survive). The influence of Cluny's sculpture was at first apparent in the church of **Ste-Madeleine at Vézelay** – both in the carved capitals and in the tympanum of the doorway in the narthex, which shows Christ sending out his Apostles before his ascension into heaven. This sculpture (1120) has much in common with the doorway of the church of St-Lazare in Autun.

The two doorways of the church of St-Lazare in **Avallon**, which date from the mid-12C, reveal a desire for a new style: luxuriant decoration including wreathed columns, an expression of the Baroque tendency of Burgundian Romanesque art, is depicted side by side with a column statue which recalls Chartres. The gravity of the round bosses on the tomb of St Lazarus in **Autun** (1170-84) already point forward to the Gothic style.

The Brionnais, where there is an unusual profusion of sculpted doorways, seems to have been the oldest centre for Romanesque sculpture in Burgundy. From the mid-11C to the great projects of **Cluny** this region produced a slightly crude and gauche style. After working in Cluny, the Brionnais artists has a new grace to their work. These trends appeared beside traditional elements, and evolved towards a mannerist decorative style (tympanum of St-Julien-de-Jonzy).

Romanesque painting – The crypt of the cathedral in **Auxerre** contains some 11C frescoes depicting Christ on horseback. At Anzy-le-Duc, restoration work in the choir in the mid-19C uncovered a large collection of murals with different characteristics from those at Auxerre: subdued, dull tints with dark outlines on a background of parallel bands.

Another style (blue backgrounds) appears at Cluny and at **Berzé-la-Ville**, in the chapel of the Château des Moines, where one can see a fine collection of Romanesque mural paintings. These frescoes, uncovered at the end of the 19C, were painted in the early years of the 12C. The use of glossy, bright paints is the distinctive feature of this innovative technique. As Berzé-la-Ville was one of the residences of the abbots of Cluny, it appears certain that these frescoes were painted by the same artists employed in the building of the great abbey.

Gothic sculpture – This concedes nothing in quality to Romanesque art.

13C – The influence of the Paris and Champagne regions is evident in the composition and presentation of subjects, but the Burgundian temperament appears in the interpretation of some scenes, where local artists have given free rein to their fantasy and earthy realism.

Much of the statuary of this period was destroyed or damaged during the Revolution; some examples survive in Vézelay, St-Père, Semur-en-Auxois, St-Thibault, Notre-Dame in Dijon and Auxerre.

At **St-Père** the sculpted decoration of the gable on the west front is repeated in a floral decoration on the capitals. It is probable that the gable of the Vézelay basilica was inspired by St-Père, but the statutes in St-Père are of a much finer workmanship than those in Vézelay.

The tympanum of the Porte des Bleds in **Semur-en-Auxois** depicts the legend of St Thomas: the figures are heavy and the draperies lack grace – characteristics of the Burgundian style. This style was modified at the end of the 13C: the bas-relief sculptures on the base of the doorways on the western side of Auxerre Cathedral are of a delicacy and grace never achieved before.

14C – The advent of the Great Dukes of Burgundy in 1364 coincided with a period of political expansion and the spread of artistic influence.

Fresco in the crypt of the Auxerre Cathedral museum

In 1377, Philip the Bold began the construction of the **Chartreuse de Champmol** at the gates of Dijon. The Duke spared no expense in the decoration of this monastery, bringing in a large number of artists from elsewhere. A new trend in sculpture emerged: statues ceased to be part of pillars and doorways; facial expressions were treated with realism, and the artist, searching for authentic representation first and foremost, did not hesitate to portray ugliness or suffering.

15C – The tomb of Philip the Bold has given rise to many imitations: the mausoleum of John the Fearless and Margaret of Bavaria is a faithful replica; the tomb of Philippe Pot, Seneschal of Burgundy, shows more originality, since it is the mourners who support the flagstone bearing the recumbent figure.

Sculpture now turned to a different style from that of the 13C; proportions were more harmonious and the draperies simpler. The Virgin Mary in the Musée Rolin at **Autun** is a good example of this particular Burgundian style.

Gothic painting – The Valois dukes surrounded themselves with painters and illuminators whom they brought from Paris or from their possessions in Flanders. In Dijon, **Jean Malouel**, Jean de Beaumetz and **André Bellechose**, natives of the north, created an artistic style remarkable for its richness of colour and detail of design, a synthesis of Flemish and Burgundian styles.

Among the best-known works, the polyptych in the Hôtel-Dieu at Beaune by Roger van der Weyden and the paintings in the Dijon museum are of great interest. During the Gothic period, frescoes came into favour again. Apart from the frescoes in the church of Notre-Dame in Beaune by Pierre Spicre, a painter of Dijon, the curious Dance of Death in the little church at La Ferté-Loupière is also noteworthy. Pierre Spicre created the designs for the remarkably bright tapestries in the church of Notre-Dame at Beaune.

The tapestries in the Hôtel-Dieu at Beaune, commissioned by Chancellor Nicolas Rolin in the 15C, are among the most beautiful of this period.

Renaissance sculpture – While Burgundian Renaissance architecture was characterised by the triumph of horizontal lines and semicircular arches, sculpture of this style used the antique form of medallions and busts in high relief, and gradually replaced sacred subjects with the profane.

In the second half of the 16C, ornamental decoration such as that conceived by **Hugues Sambin**, artist of the gateway of the Palais de Justice in Dijon and probably also of a large number of mansions, was much in vogue in the city.

In the 16C, decorative woodwork – door panels, coffered ceilings, church stalls – was prevalent. The 26 stalls in the church of Montréal, carved in 1522, are a work of local inspiration in which the Burgundian spirit is plain for all to see.

Classical to modern – The transition from the 18C to the 19C is marked by **Girodet**, the famous citizen of Montargis. Proud'hon and Rude, both pupils of **Devosges** and attached to the academic tradition, were producing paintings and sculpture at the beginning of the 19C; the work of the former is characterised by muted tones and dreamy, sensual figures; that of the latter recalls his Neoclassical debut, and the force of his subsequent expression of his romantic temperament in the Marseillaise on the Arc de Triomphe in Paris. They were followed by Cabet, Jouffroy, and the contemporary sculptor François

Pompon, all of whom contributed to the artistic reputation of Burgundy.

IN JURA

Jura cannot pride itself on having been home to a regional school of painting or sculpture. However, despite having been under the influence mainly of Burgundian and Flemish artists, local artists produced numerous works of art which reflect their talent.

Unlike painting, sculpture was overlooked by local artists as a way of expressing their ideas during the Romanesque period.

Romanesque painting – The art of painting underwent significant development during the 12C and 13C, while sculpture was making little progress. During the Romanesque and Gothic periods, artists turned to frescoes in particular to decorate the interiors of churches.

Gothic sculpture – During the 13C, craftsmen produced emotive wooden statues in a naïve style, mainly Virgins. It was not until the 14C that a real surge of creativity burst onto the scene, inspired by Burgundian art and in particular the work of **Claus Sluter**. The production and decoration of religious furniture also developed during this period; the magnificent choir stalls at St-Claude (15C) and the ones at Montbenoît (16C) are some interesting examples.

Gothic painting – In the 14C and 15C, the art of painting altarpieces spread at the same time as the fresco technique. Painters of altarpieces were primarily inspired by Flemish artists. Unfortunately, in the 16C, the initial impetus of the primitive artists of Franche-Comté petered out. **Jacques Prévost**, trained in Italy, was the only artist to produce works of any quality (triptych at Pesmes). The aristocracy and merchant classes took advantage of their travels abroad to buy Flemish and Italian paintings, some of which are still part of the artistic heritage of Jura (church at Baumes-les-Messieurs, cathedral and Musée des Beaux-Arts at Besançon).

Renaissance sculpture – In the 16C, sculptural forms became less tortured, and Italian sculptors were brought in to work on projects in Franche-Comté. The Gothic tradition was dropped as artists such as **Claude Arnoux**, known as Lullier (altarpiece of the Chapelle d'Andelot in the church at Pesmes), and **Denis le Rupt** (pulpit and organ loft in Notre-Dame at Dole) adopted the new style.

Classical to modern sculpture – During the Classical period, religious statuary became bogged down in academism. Only furniture showed signs of the originality and good taste of the local artists (Fauconnet woodwork at Goux-les-Usiers). Later, some sculptors achieved a certain degree of fame, such as Clésinger, Luc Breton and Perraud (1819-76), who were inspired by the Romantic movement to produce sensitive works.

At the end of the century, **Bartholdi** immortalised the resistance of the city of Belfort in 1870, by sculpting an enormous lion out of rock.

Classical to modern painting – From the 17C, French art became less regionalised. Famous artists from Jura include **Jacques Courtois** (1621-76), who specialised in painting battle scenes, Donat Nonotte (1708-85), a portrait painter from Besançon, and above all **Courbet** (1819-77), an ardent defender of realism.

Religious Orders

After the fall of Charlemagne's empire, the Church used its considerable influence to resume a leading role in society; there was a renewal of fervour for the monastic life throughout Europe, but especially in Burgundy.

St Benedict and his Rule – In 529 Benedict, who was born in Italy, moved to Monte Cassino where he worked out his Constitution, soon to be adopted by many monasteries. His advice was moderate: fasting, silence and abstinence were recommended, but mortification was strongly condemned. Relations with the outside world were to be avoided, and Benedictine communities were to be self-sufficient through their own work.

The rise of Cluny – In 910 the founding of a monastery in the Mâcon region by the Duke of Aquitaine marked the start of an important religious reform associated with the name of Cluny. The spirit of the Benedictine Rule was marked by the observance of the three cardinal rules of obedience, chastity and fasting, but there was a much heavier emphasis on prayer, which almost eliminated the time for manual labour and other work. Another innovation was that Cluny was directly attached to the Holy See in Rome, effectively making it autonomous. The Order grew rapidly; by the 12C there were 1 450 monasteries throughout Europe.

Cîteaux and St Bernard – When a young French nobleman from near Dijon spoke out about the lazy ways and luxury among the monks of Cluny, he could not have known that it was the start of a new Order. St Bernard, having entered the monastic life at Cîteaux, embarked on a new and more austere interpretation of Benedictine Rule: plain woollen tunics, frugal meals, the simplest of beds, early rising and hard physical work.

Like St Bernard, the Cistercians had an impact on society that went beyond issues of faith. Well organised and hardworking, the monks were able to bring prosperity to the harshest and most isolated places by clearing and draining land and setting up irrigation systems.

The contemporary order – After the turmoil and physical destruction of the Revolution, monastic life has found a place in the modern world. Today there are about 3 000 Trappist Cistercians (the name is derived from the abbey of Notre-Dame-de-la-Trappe, reformed in the 17C), in 92 establishments worldwide, 15 of which are in France.

Traditional Crafts

The Comtoise Clock – Cabinetmakers craft the traditional long-case clocks known in France as *horloges comtoises*. The early models were usually made of oak wood, and embellished with ornaments and moulding. Beginning in 1850, pine wood became the material of choice and simple painted motifs were used to decorate the case. Enamel artists worked to create stylised clock faces.

Smaller and smaller – The first French watch was made towards the end of the 15C, and there were many models by the second half of the 16C.

At the courts of Henri II and Henri III, women would wear watches as pendants and men had them set into the handles of their daggers as decoration. These timepieces only had one hand, the hour hand.

In 1694, the Dumont brothers, master watchmakers, brought out the first watches manufactured in Besançon, entirely handmade. In 1767, Frédéric Japy of the village of Beaucourt mechanically manufactured some rough models of watches, using machines he had invented. This was an immediate success,

and his production was soon turning out 3 000 to 3 500 watches per month.

In 1793, a Swiss watchmaker, Mégevand, and 80 master watchmakers immigrated to Besançon. The *Convention* (national assembly) took them under its wing and advanced them some money to enable them to set up a factory and a national school of clock and watchmaking. They were to take in 200 apprentices per year, funded by the *Convention*.

A matter of time – From then on, sales grew rapidly. In 1835, 80 000 watches were made in Besançon and 240 000 in 1878. The industry spread to many Jura towns. Today, clock and watchmaking are of little economic importance, yet a certain reputation for craftsmanship has been maintained. Morez and Morbier still make grandfather clocks, as they have since the 17C.

THE REGION TODAY

Economy

France's largely prosperous postwar period has seen farming and industry slowly being replaced as main wealth generators by service businesses. This shift has been accompanied by a movement of people away from the urbanised north and north-east of the country towards parts of the south and west. Burgundy and Jura remain sparsely populated, although the northernmost parts of Burgundy have seen a rise in the number of inhabitants caused by new arrivals from the Paris region.

Both regions remain largely agricultural, with beef and dairy cattle, cereal crops, fruit, timber and wine among the main crops. Many people work in the service industries and there is a healthy tourist trade. Otherwise, people work in various industries, from pharmaceuticals and metallurgy to clocks and toy-making.

France's postwar economic growth has brought about a substantial rise in living standards. The working week is fixed at 35 hours and income tax and indirect

taxes are relatively high, helping to pay for a generous welfare system.

Recent years, however, have seen growing worries over unemployment and sluggish economic growth. On 6 May 2007, centre-right Nicolas Sarkozy defeated his Socialist rival Segolene Royal in the presidential elections with promises of reforms to boost the economy, such as incentives to encourage overtime and social security reforms.

Gastronomy

IN BURGUNDY

Burgundy's reputation as a gastronomic paradise has been established for a long time. Dijon has been a city of fine food since Gallo-Roman times. In the 6C, Gregory of Tours praised the quality of Burgundian wines, and King Charles VI lauded the gastronomic delights of Dijon, both good wines and local dishes. The historic États Généraux de Bourgogne and the gastronomic fair at Dijon perpetuate this tradition of good food and wine in the region.

The raw materials – Burgundy is home to first-class beef cattle in the regions of Auxois, Bazois and Charollais, as well as some of the tastiest game in France. It produces incomparable vegetables, many varieties of fish (white fish from the Saône and Loire and trout and crayfish from the rivers of the Morvan), delicious mushrooms *(cèpes, girolles, morilles* and *mousserons)*, snails and mouthwatering fruit (cherries from the Auxerre region, for example). And of course, Dijon is forever associated with the **mustards** produced there.

Burgundian cuisine is both rich and substantial, reflecting the Burgundian temperament and robust appetite; people here expect both quality and quantity at the table. Wine, the glory of the province, naturally plays an important part: the *meurette* sauces made from wine thickened with butter and flour with flavourings and spices added are the pride of Burgundian cuisine. These sauces work well with fish – carp, tench and eel – brains, poached eggs and **bœuf bourguignon** (Burgundian beef casserole). Cream is used in many dishes: **jambon à la crème** (cooked ham in a cream sauce) and **champignons à la crème** (mushrooms in a cream sauce). **Saupiquet** is a spicy wine and cream sauce that dates back to the 15C.

Burgundian specialities – Beyond the long-simmering *bœuf bourguignon*, the cuisine of this region is renowned for **escargots** (snails cooked in their shells with garlic, butter and parsley), **jambon persillé** (ham seasoned with parsley), **andouillette** (small sausages made from chitterlings), **coq au vin** (chicken in a wine sauce), **pauchouse** (stew of various fish cooked in white wine) and **poulet en sauce** (chicken cooked in a cream and white wine sauce).In the Nivernais and Morvan regions, home-cured ham and sausage, ham and eggs, calf's head *(sansiot)*, eggs cooked in wine *(en meurette)*, roast veal and pullet fried with bacon and pearl onions *(jau au sang)* figure among the traditional dishes.

Perhaps the greatest moment in the meal comes with the **cheese** course. A good vintage wine enhances the experience of eating **Soumaintrain, Saint-Florentin, Époisses, Bouton-de-culotte**, or **Citeaux**, all produced locally. A traditional preparation that honours a great vintage is **gougère**, cheese pastry.

IN JURA

Poultry and freshwater fish go particularly well with Jura wines, and **coq au vin jaune** or **truite au vin jaune** are classic local specialities.

Game is abundant and there are many traditional recipes for hare, wild boar, venison, woodcock etc. Wild hare in white wine sauce, venison casserole with cream and roast thrush flambéed in Marc d'Arbois are just a few dishes.

Potée is made with a variety of vegetables cooked slowly in a casserole with Morteau sausage, a speciality of this region, as is sausage from Montbéliard. Local *charcuterie*, such as Jésus from Morteau and the many smoked hams (Luxeuil-les-Bains), is also appreciated. For centuries, pork and bacon were the only meat eaten in the mountain regions. Pigs were therefore very important on the farms, and careful calculation went into the diet on which they were fattened. On pig-killing day, an occasion for great celebration in the family, a pig feast was prepared consisting of black pudding *(boudin)*, sausages made from tripe *(andouilles)*, head-cheese *(fromage de tête)*, chops and various other bits.

In Jura, there are as many types of fish as there are rivers and lakes for them to thrive in: char and trout from the Loue; carp and pike from the Doubs; tench and perch from the Ain. In the lakes there are fish from the salmon family (Coregonidae), white fish and small fry. *Meurette* sauces and *pauchouse* stew are as popular here for fish dishes as they are in Burgundy.

Mushrooms from the forests – *morilles, chanterelles* and *cèpes* – add their delicate flavour to aromatic sauces.

The local cheeses are excellent: **Comté**, with its hazelnut flavour, can be used to make a fondue. Try a mild and delicate **Emmenthal**, rich and creamy **Morbier**, or **Mont d'Or**, a subtly flavoured cheese made from milk from cows that have been kept on mountain pastures. **Gex Septmoncel** is a blue cheese with a delicate parsley flavour; **Cancoillotte**, a soft fermented cheese, is one of the region's oldest specialities.

To top off your meal in style, all the local vineyards produce good quality **marc** spirits, but the **kirsch** from the Loue Valley (Mouthier-Haute-Pierre, Ornans) is particularly well regarded. Pontarlier, generally acknowledged as the capital of absinthe, produces an apéritif based on green aniseed, **Pontarlier Anis**. Liqueurs made from gentian and pine in the Haut-Jura plateaux are also popular.

WINEMAKING

Burgundy

Burgundy wines are so well known that the name itself is synonymous with the deep red colour of some of the great vintages; yet the fine white wines are certainly not to be neglected!

The history of Burgundy wine – The cultivation of vines was introduced to the region by the Romans and spread rapidly. Wine from Burgundy was quick to win accolades, a historical fact confirmed by the names of certain vineyards (Vosne-Romanée) which recall the popularity of the wines with the Roman prefects of the province of Maxima Sequanorum.

In the 12C, Cistercian monks built up the vineyards, in particular the famous Clos-Vougeot. In the 15C the dukes of Burgundy took to styling themselves "lords of the best wines in Christendom" and supplying their wine to royalty. Louis XIV is known to have contributed to the fame of Côte de Nuits, whereas Madame de Pompadour favoured Romanée Conti and Napoleon preferred Chambertin.

In the 18C the first commercial warehouses opened at Beaune, Nuits-St-Georges and Dijon, sending representatives all over France and Europe to find new markets for Burgundy wines.

One of the enemies of the vine is a small aphid from America, phylloxera, which made its appearance in the Gard *département* in 1863. In 1878, it was found at Meursault and within a short time it had completely ravaged the Burgundy vineyards. Luckily, disaster was checked by grafting French vines onto resistant American root stock, enabling the slow restoration of the Burgundy vineyards.

Distribution of vineyards – There are 25 000ha/ 62 500 acres of vineyards producing officially registered vintages in the Yonne, Nièvre, Côte-d'Or, Saône-et-Loire and Rhône *départements*. Average annual production of high quality wines is about 1 400 000hl/36 400 000 gal. In the Yonne, the region of **Chablis** produces some excellent crisp, dry white wines, and the hillsides of the Auxerrois some pleasant rosés and reds (**Irancy, Coulanges-la-Vineuse**). Well-known wines such as **Pouilly-Fumé** come from Pouilly-sur-Loire in Nièvre. In the **Côte-d'Or** highly reputed vineyards stretch from Dijon to Santenay. The **Côte de Nuits** produces almost exclusively top vintage reds, some of the most famous of which are **Gevrey-Chambertin, Vougeot, Vosne-Romanée** and **Nuits-St-Georges.** The **Côte de Beaune** wines include reds such as **Volnay, Savigny-lès-Beaune** and **Pommard** and whites such as **Meursault, Puligny-Montrachet** and **Chassagne-Montrachet.**

In Saône-et-Loire, the Mercurey region (Côte Chalonnaise) produces high quality reds (**Givry, Rully**) and whites (**Rully-Montagny**), whereas the Mâconnais is justly proud of its **Pouilly-Fuissé**, widely considered one of the best white wines in France.

Grape varieties – All the great red Burgundy wines are made from the **Pinot Noir,** the aristocrat of grapes. It was already highly prized at the time of the Great Dukes. The Pinot Noir is native to Burgundy but has been successfully elsewhere. The juice of the Pinot Noir grape is colourless, and a special vinification process produces Champagne.

The **Chardonnay** grape is to white wines what the Pinot Noir is to red. It makes all the great white wines of the Côte d'Or (Montrachet-Meursault), the famous vintages of the Côte Chalonnaise (Rully), of the Mâconnais where it grows best (Pouilly-Fuissé) and the wines of Chablis (where it is known as the Beaunois grape).

Other grape varieties include the **Aligoté**, which has been cultivated for centuries in Burgundy, as it grows in the areas where the Pinot Noir and Chardonnay grapes do not thrive, and which produces white wines which are popular, even if they do not have quite the same reputation for character and quality as those from the more famous vineyards. These are the wines that are combined with blackcurrant liqueur *(cassis)* to make the popular French apéritif known as Kir after the man who is credited with its invention, a mayor of Dijon, Canon Kir.

Soil – The soil type plays an important role in allowing the particular characteristics of the vines to develop. Vines grow best in dry, stony soils, which are well-drained and easily warmed by the sun. Limestone soils produce wines with rich bouquets and a high alcohol content, which can be aged for many years (Côte de Nuits, Côte de Beaune), whereas mixed soils of silicas, limestone and clay yield lighter wines (Chablis).

Climate – The prevailing climate in Burgundy is temperate, but frosts do occur and must be taken into consideration. Burgundy vineyards are usually laid out in terraces on the hillsides at altitudes of between 200-500m/656-1 640ft. They seem to thrive best when facing between south and east (south-west for Pouilly-sur-Loire). In each village, the vineyards are divided into *climats*, as determined by the soil content and exposure of the plot. The name of an individual vineyard with excellent conditions for producing fine wine, often known as a *clos*, may be added to the name of the village on the label. Some of the *climats* have earned such a reputation over the years that their name alone suffices to identify them: Chambertin, Musigny, Clos de Vougeot and Richebourg.

Millésime and aging – When selecting a Burgundy wine, it is important to take into account the year in which it was bottled, as the weather conditions have a big impact on quality. Although they do not enjoy the exceptional longevity of the famous *vin jaune du Jura*, Burgundy wines mature well. Generally,

they are best kept for five to seven years, but some white wines can age eight to ten years and exceptional reds can be stored for up to 15 years. Wines mature best in a dark, well-ventilated area at a constant cool temperature and about 70% humidity.

Serving Burgundy wines – Certain dishes enhance the pleasure of drinking Burgundy wines:
– with oysters, shellfish, fish: Chablis, Meursault, Pouilly-Fuissé, Mâcon, or other dry white wines, chilled;
– with fowl, veal, pork and light dishes: Côte de Beaune, Mercurey, Beaujolais or other light red wines served at the storage temperature;
– with game, red meat, wild mushrooms and cheese: Chambertin, Côte de Nuits, Pommard and other hearty reds served at room temperature.

Beaujolais wine – The Beaujolais vineyards cover an area 60km/37mi long and 12km/7.5mi wide from the Mâcon escarpment to the north to the Azergues Valley to the south. This area occupies about 22 500ha/55 595 acres and yields an average of 1 250 000hl/27 375 000 gallons of wine a year. The majority of these (99%) are red, exclusively from the Gamay grape. There are three categories of Beaujolais wine, starting with the crus, the best vintages, followed by **Beaujolais Villages** and **Beaujolais supérieurs.**
The 10 leading *crus* are **Moulin-à-Vent,** an elegant wine with lots of substance, which can be kept for 5-10 years, closely followed by **Morgon** with its fine bouquet, which has often been described as the "Beaujolais most like a Burgundy". Firm and fruity **Juliénas**, well-rounded **Chénas**, classy **Fleurie** and **Côte de Brouilly** all have a keen following, whereas the fresh and lively **Saint-Amour, Chiroubles** (which the French consider to be a feminine wine), **Brouilly** and **Régnié-Durette** (the baby of the crus, having been promoted in 1988) are best enjoyed young.
Fruity Beaujolais-Villages is at its best after about a year in the bottle. Beaujolais or Beaujolais *supérieurs* do not age well and are best served slightly chilled (unlike most red wines).

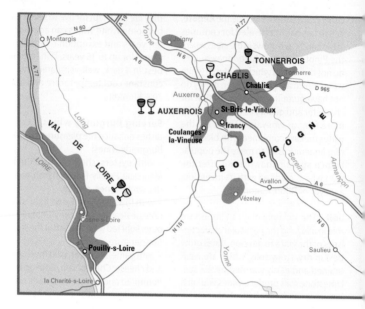

Jura

The vineyards of the Franche-Comté extend south-west of Salins, along a narrow strip of land 5km/3mi wide, covering the limestone and mixed clay and limestone slopes of the western edge of Jura. Four vintages are produced from these vineyards: **Arbois**, the most famous, **Château-Chalon, Étoile** and those of the **Côtes du Jura** appellation, which includes local wines such as Poligny and Arlay. A Jura wine festival is held each September in Arbois.

The grape varieties cultivated in Jura include Trousseau for red wines, Poulsard for rosé, Chardonnay for white wines and Savagnin, used to create the celebrated *vin jaune du Jura*.

Red wines are produced in small quantities and are fresh and fruity when young, developing a subtle, characteristic bouquet with age. The most famous **rosé wines** come from Arbois and Pupillin. These lively but not overpowering wines have a pleasant fruity flavour. Local **white wines ,** mainly from the Arbois and Étoile regions, are dry, yet supple, and fairly heady. Not only do these wines accompany local dishes, they are also excellent apéritif wines. The region also produces **sparkling wines**, both white (Étoile, Arbois and Côtes du Jura) and rosé (Arbois and Côtes du Jura).

Vin jaune is a speciality of the Jura region (Château-Chalon and Arbois), made from the Savagnin grape. The wine is left to age in barrels for 6-10 years, where it begins to oxidise and acquires its characteristic deep yellow colour and distinctive bouquet beneath a film of yeasts (similar to the production of sherry). A good vintage can be kept for over a century. It is relatively rare and expensive, with a strong flavour. .

Vin de paille, straw wine, also particular to the Jura region, is made from almost over-ripe grapes dried on a bed of straw for a couple of months before being pressed. This produces a strong, sweet dessert wine.

Macvin is another Jura dessert wine, made from grape must blended with Franche-Comté eau-de-vie, and can reach up to 16-20% alcohol content. It is usually drunk chilled as an apéritif.

Red and rosé **Bugey wines** are light and fruity, but the white Bugey wines are the best. Particularly good examples are Roussette and Seyssel, followed by rarer wines such as Virieu or Montagnieu. This region also produces some sparkling wines, **Seyssel** and **Cerdon**.

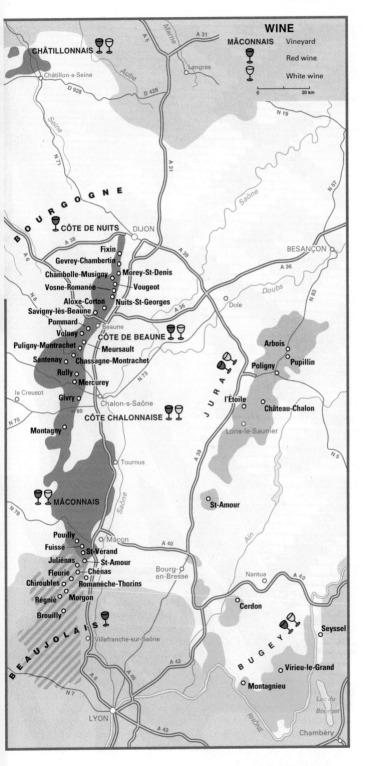

WINE

CHÂTILLONNAIS

MÂCONNAIS — Vineyard

Red wine

White wine

0   20 km

Châtillon-s-Seine

Langres

BOURGOGNE

CÔTE DE NUITS — DIJON

BESANÇON

Fixin
Gevrey-Chambertin
Chambolle-Musigny — Morey-St-Denis
Vosne-Romanée — Vougeot
Aloxe-Corton — Nuits-St-Georges
Savigny-lès-Beaune
Pommard — Beaune
Volnay — CÔTE DE BEAUNE
Puligny-Montrachet — Meursault
Santenay — Chassagne-Montrachet
Rully
Givry — Mercurey
— Chalon-s-Saône
Montagny — CÔTE CHALONNAISE

Dole

JURA

Arbois
Poligny — Pupillin
l'Étoile — Château-Chalon
Lons-le-Saunier

Tournus

MÂCONNAIS

St-Amour

Pouilly
Fuissé — St-Vérand
Juliénas — St-Amour
Fleurie — Chénas
Chiroubles — Romanèche-Thorins
Régnié — Morgon
Brouilly

Mâcon

Bourg-en-Bresse

Nantua

Cerdon

BUGEY

Seyssel

BEAUJOLAIS

Villefranche-sur-Saône

Virieu-le-Grand
Montagnieu

Lac du Bourget

LYON

Chambéry

le Creusot

*Glazed tiles on the roof
of the Hôtel-Dieu in Beaune*
Ph. Gajic-MICHELIN

ALISE-STE-REINE
16KM/10MI NORTH-EAST OF SEMUR-EN-AUXOIS
POPULATION 674
MICHELIN MAP 320: G-4

Alise-Ste-Reine is on the slopes of Mont Auxois (407m/1 335ft) between the Oze and Ozerain valleys overlooking the Les Laumes plain. The first part of its name comes from Alésia, a Gaulish, then Gallo-Roman settlement on the plateau. The second recalls a Christian woman, Reina, who was martyred locally in the 3C.

- **Information:** pl. Bingerbrück, 21150 Venarey-Les-Laumes. ☎03 80 96 89 13. www.alesia-tourisme.net.
- ▶ **Orient Yourself:** There is an excellent overview of the site from the panorama on Mont Auxois.

A Bit of History

Siege of Alésia
After his defeat at Gergovie in the spring of 52 BC, **Caesar** retreated northwards to join forces with his lieutenant near Sens. Once united they made for the Roman base camps, but on route they were attacked near Alésia by the Gauls under **Vercingétorix**. Despite the surprise of their attack and superior numbers, the Gauls suffered a crushing defeat, and Vercingétorix retreated to the camp at Alésia.

Caesar's legions surrounded the camp with a double line of fortified earthworks, such as trenches, walls, palisades of stakes and towers. For six weeks, Vercingétorix tried and failed to break out. A rescue army of Gauls, 250 000 strong, could not relieve the besieged force and withdrew. Vercingétorix was forced to surrender to Caesar.

A battle of experts
During the 19C, some historians hotly disputed the site of Alésia as the scene of the siege. To end the controversy, Napoleon III had excavations carried out at Alise-Ste-Reine from 1861 to 1865. These revealed extensive military works, as well as the bones of men and horses and a mass of objects left behind during the siege, from silver coins to weaponry.

More recently, excavations at Chaux-des-Crotenay to the south-east of Champagnole in the Jura have revealed another site which also claims to be Alésia.

The latest excavation work (1991-98) in the area could not reconcile Caesar's account of the battle with what was found on location and, in November 1998, it was officially stated that Alise was no longer considered the site of the battle of Alésia. However, the discussions are definitely not over yet.

Mont Auxois★

Panorama★
There is a good viewpoint from beside the bronze statue of Vercingétorix. The panorama extends over the plain of Les Laumes and the site of the Roman outworks to the outskirts of Saulieu.

MuséoParc Alésia
⏰Open Jul-Aug 9am-7pm; Mar-Jun, Sep to Nov 10am-6pm. ⊘4€, 5€ museum and archeological digs (children 3€). ☎03 80 96 85 90. www.alesia.com.

The summit of the fortified settlement (oppidum) was occupied by a Gallo-Roman town. The tour (signs and numbered sites) shows the different districts grouped round the forum. The western district contained the theatre, religious buildings and a civilian basilica. The northern district had shops, the bronze-workers' guild house and a mansion, heated by a hypocaust (underfloor heating), where a statue of the mother goddess was found in the cellar, hence the name *Cave à la Mater*. The craftsmen's district to the south-east is composed of small houses. To the south-west, the ruins surrounded by a cemetery belong to a Merovingian basilica dedicated to St Reina; it was the last building constructed on the plateau before the population moved down to the site of the present village.

The museum contains objects found during excavation of the Gallo-Roman town: statues and statuettes, building fragments, the reconstructed façade of a Gallo-Roman chapel, coins, pottery and other objects.

AMBRONAY

6KM/3.7MI N OF AMBÉRIEU

POPULATION 2 146

MICHELIN MAP 328: F-4

Ambronay developed around a Benedictine abbey founded in the 9C by St Bernard, one of Charlemagne's knights (ruins of the Carolingian church have been found under the choir and chancel).

- **Information:** Les Arcades, r. Alexandre Bérard, 01500 Amberieu-en-Bugey. ☏04 74 38 1817. www.ville-amberieuenbugey.fr.
- **Don't Miss:** A renowned Baroque music festival takes place in the abbey each year from mid-September to mid-October.

Ancienne Abbaye

Open Apr-Sep 9am-6.30pm; Oct-Mar 9am-5pm.☏04 74 34 52 72. www.ambronay.org.

The church, cloister and chapter-house, as well as most of the conventual buildings, remain of the **abbey**, which has been rebuilt several times.

Church★

This dates mainly from the 13C and 15C. Many figures on the façade were destroyed during the Revolution. The lintel of the doorway on the left represents scenes from the Life of the Virgin. The Resurrection of the Dead can be seen on the lintel of the central doorway (13C, extensively restored). The **Chapelle Ste-Catherine,** north of the chancel, contains the 15C **tomb**★ of Abbot Jacques de Mauvoisin, who had the church restored.

Cloisters

Access through a door in the south side aisle.

The cloisters, a 15C construction, consist of arcades with graceful tracery, surmounted by a gallery reached by the substantially restored Louis XIV corner staircase.

R. Magnin–MICHELIN

Cloisters

CHÂTEAU D'ANCY-LE-FRANC★★
18KM/11MI SE OF TONNERRE
MICHELIN MAP 319: H-5

This **château** on the banks of the River Armançon is one of the most beautiful Renaissance mansions in Burgundy. The château was built in 1546 for Antoine III de Clermont, husband of Anne-Françoise de Poitiers (sister of François I's mistress Diane), using plans by influential architect Sebastiano Serlio. It was later sold to Louvois, Minister of War under Louis XIV, in 1684. In the mid-19C, the Clermont-Tonnerre family recovered it. In 1980, the estate and contents were sold; from 1985 to 1999 the castle was largely abandoned.

- **Information:** ☎03 86 75 14 63. www.chateau-ancy.com.
- **Orient Yourself:** Start outside in the Le Nôtre gardens. The château, with four identical wings linked by corner pavilions, is a perfect square.
- **Don't Miss:** For a special experience, book tickets for the monthly Concert Visits, where the tour is rounded off by a classical music performance. See www.musicancy.org for details.

The Château

🕐*Open Mar-Nov.* 👁*Guided tours (1hr) 10.30am, 11.30am, 2pm, 3pm and 4pm (Apr-Sep extra tour 5pm, Jul-Aug extra tour 9.30am). Closed Mon except public holidays.* 🎫*8€ (under 11 5€).*

Regional artists contributed to the sumptuous interior decoration, along with students of Primaticcio and Nicolo dell'Abbate. Some of the Renaissance murals are more intact than others, but as a whole they are remarkable. Most of the 16C furnishings were in place when the château was built.

Ground floor – Don't miss the fabulous Salle de Diane, whose Italian-style vaulted ceiling dates from 1578.

First floor – Beginning in the south wing, admire the **Chapelle Ste-Cécile**★, which, restored in 1860, is covered with barrel vaulting. The *trompe-l'œil* paintings (1596) depict the Fathers of the Desert; they are the work of André Meynassier, a Burgundian artist.

The impressive **Salle des Gardes** was decorated for Henri III, although he never lived here. Facing the monumental fireplace is a full-length portrait of Marshall Gaspard de Clermont-Tonnerre (1759)

P. Lefevre-

Chambre des Arts

by Aved. Note the varying poses of the horses along the walls of the **Galerie Pharsale**. Beyond this gallery and the Chambre des Fleurs, the **Chambre des Arts**★ contains a rare 16C Italian cabinet with decorative inlay work. The walls of the **Chambre de Judith** are hung with nine high-quality paintings from the late 16C depicting the story of Judith. Judith and Holopherne are seen as likenesses of Diane de Poitiers and François I.

The **Cabinet du Pasteur Fido**★ has carved oak panelling and a magnificent Renaissance coffered ceiling. The scenes on the upper part of the walls are based on an Arcadian oracle about a faithful shepherd, hence the room's name.

The library, which houses 3 000 volumes, and the **Galerie des Sacrifices** lead to the **Salon Louvois**★ (the former king's chamber where Louis XIV slept on 21 June 1674).

ARBOIS★

POPULATION 3 698

MICHELIN MAP 321: E-5

Arbois is at the entrance of one of the beautiful blind rift valleys known as *reculées* **in the Jura, on either bank of the Cuisance. This picturesque town surrounded by vineyards is a popular holiday centre.**

- **Information:** 10 r. de l'Hôtel de Ville, 39600 Arbois, ☎03 84 66 55 50. www.arbois.com.
- ▶ **Orient Yourself**: Arbois is on the Jura wine trail, so there are lots of wineries open for tasting. Most sights, as well as restaurants and boutiques, lie on the east bank of the river.

A Bit of History

The Fête du Biou

This is the great Jura wine festival. On the first Sunday in September, the wine-growers of Arbois parade with an enormous bunch of grapes weighing 80-100kg/176-220lb, which is made of many smaller bunches of grapes bound together. It is carried by four men, behind fiddle players, and behind these march local dignitaries and wine-growers, escorted by soldiers of the *garde-fruits* carrying halberds festooned with vine shoots. After the procession, the *Biou* is hung in the nave of the church as an offering to St Just, the patron saint of Arbois.

Pasteur In Arbois

Although Louis Pasteur was born in Dole, his true home in Jura was Arbois. The Pasteur family moved to Arbois in 1827, settling in a tannery that the scientist turned into a large residence. At the local school he was a conscientious pupil who gave the impression of being rather slow and was never considered more than a slightly above average student. His greatest interest was drawing. He drew portraits in pastels and pencil of his parents and friends, in which a certain talent is apparent. To be able to study for his baccalaureate, the young man entered the grammar school of Besançon as a teaching assistant.

With his admission to the École Normale in 1843, Pasteur embarked on the career which was to distinguish him as one of mankind's greatest minds. His study of fermentation led him to discover the pasteurisation process; his work on illnesses in silkworms were invaluable to the silk industry. He produced vaccines to cure rabies in man and anthrax in animals. He put forward theories in microbiology which were to revolutionise surgery and medicine in general, leading to the use of antiseptic, sterilisation and isolation of those with contagious diseases. Pasteur also paved the way for immunisation therapy (antiserums). Every year Pasteur returned to Arbois with his family for the holidays, where

Address Book

🪙 *For coin ranges, see the Legend on the cover flap.*

WHERE TO STAY

🛏 **Camping municipal Les Vignes** – *Near the stadium.* ☎03 84 66 14 12. *www.camping.arbois.fr. Open Apr-Sep.* 🍴 At this pleasant campground, shaded sites are arranged in terraces, offering views of the surrounding hillsides.

🛏 **Hôtel des Messageries** – *2 r. de Courcelles.* ☎03 84 66 15 45. *www.hoteldesmessageries.com. 26 rooms.* 🛏8€. This former coaching inn in the town centre offers basic comfort at low prices: some rooms have no bathrooms.

🛏🍽 **Le Prieuré (annexe of the Hôtel Jean-Paul Jeunet)** – *9 r. de l'Hôtel-de-Ville.* ☎03 84 66 05 67. *7 rooms.* 🛏16.50€. The quiet, carefully kept rooms are furnished in charming old-fashioned style.

🛏🍽 **Chambre d'Hôte Le Château de la Muyre** – *39210 Domblans, 8km/5mi W of Château-Chalon by D 5 until you reach Voiteur then D 120 to Domblans then D 57E on the left.* ☎03 84 44 66 49. *Closed Jan-Feb.* 🍴 *5 rooms.* This fine 12C and 14C residence extends a simple and unpretentious welcome to travellers. The accommodation is somewhat basic and looks out onto fields and wooded parkland. Shared bathroom facilities. Wine tastings. Wine for sale.

🛏🍽 **Chambre d'Hôte Le Jardin de Misette** – *r. Honoré-Chapuis, 39140 Arlay, 12km/7.5mi W of Château-Chalon by D 5 until you reach Voiteur then D 120.* ☎03 84 85 15 72. 🍴 *4 rooms. Meals* 🛏🍽. Misette and her husband, who used to run a restaurant, left the business to settle here near the river. Needless to say, the meals here are of the highest standard. Of the comfortable rooms, the prettiest is Chabotte, set in a separate small cottage.

🛏🍽 **Hostellerie St-Germain** – *39210 St-Germain-lès-Arlay.* ☎03 84 44 60 91. 🍴 🛏6€. *Meals* 🛏🍽. Calm, clean rooms await you in this lovely hostelry among the vineyards. Take your pick of three beamed and vaulted dining-rooms and sit back and enjoy such regional

delights as *filet de lieu au vin jaune* or rich fondue of Comté cheese.

WHERE TO EAT

🍽 **Auberge Le Grapiot** – *r. Bagier, 39600 Pupillin, 3km/1.8mi south of Arbois by D 246.* ☎03 84 37 49 44. *Closed Sun pm, Thu pm and Mon.* This charming auberge, known for franc-comtoise dishes, is in a pretty village.

🍽🍷 **La Finette Taverne d'Arbois** – *22 av. Louis-Pasteur.* ☎03 84 66 06 78. *www.finette.fr.* This friendly tavern with its rustic decor and wooden tables is a relaxed place to sample regional cuisine and country wines.

🍽🍷 **Caveau d'Arbois** – *3 rte de Besançon.* ☎03 84 66 10 70. *www.caveau-arbois.com. Closed Sun evenings and Mon.* Traditional cuisine featuring a few regional dishes accompanied by local wines is served in a bright, uncluttered dining-room.

🍽🍷 **La Balance Mets et Vins** – *47 r. de Courcelles.* ☎03 84 37 45 00. *www.labalance.fr. Closed 23 Dec-6 Mar, 24 Jun-2 Jul, Tue evenings and Wed (except public holidays).* Imaginative recipes, an inspired wine list and the freshest ingredients make for a memorable meal.

🍽🍷 **Jean-Paul Jeunet** – *9 r. de l'Hôtel-de-Ville.* ☎03 84 66 05 67. *www.jeanpauljeunet.com. Closed Dec, Jan, Tue and Wed (except Jul-Aug).* This prestigious establishment blends the traditional and modern. The dining-room offers fine regional specialities and a superb wine list. Comfortable rooms feature contemporary decor.

🍽🍷 **Les 16 Quartiers** – *pl. de l'Église.* ☎03 84 44 68 23. *Closed end Oct to end Mar, Sun evenings and Wed.* Time seems to stand still in this charming 16C village house with its pretty dining-room and shady terrace. Treat yourself to regional cooking or medieval specialities. Jura wines served by the glass.

SHOPPING

La Cave de comté – *44 Grande-Rue.* ☎03 84 66 09 53. *Open Tue and Thu-Sun 9am-6pm. Closed 28 Jun-4 Jul.* Stock up on regional cheeses include Comté, Morbier, Bleu de Gex, Mont d'Or, Époisses, chèvres and other delicacies.

Domaine Rolet Père et Fils – *11 r. de l'Hôtel-de-Ville.* ☎*03 84 66 08 89. www.rolet-arbois.com. Open 9am-noon, 2-7pm, Sun 9.30am-noon, 2.30-7pm. Closed 25 Dec and 1 Jan.* This award-winning winery produces wines with the Côtes-du-Jura, Étoile and Arbois appellations. Other treasures include *vins jaunes, vins de paille* and marc aged in oak.

Fruitière vinicole Château Béthanie – *2 r. des Fossés.* ☎*03 84 66 11 67. www.chateau-bethanie.com. Cellar visits Tue-Sun (Jul-Aug) 11am, 2:30pm, 4:30pm. Closed 1 May and 25 Dec.* Established in 1906, this cooperative is among Jura's oldest. Sparkling wines, whites, reds and *vins jaunes* are all for sale.

Overnoy-Crinquand Daniel – *Chemin des Vignes, 39600 Pupillin.* ☎*03 84 66 01 45. Mon-Sat 9am-7pm.* With a treasure of *poulsard* and *trousseau rouges, vin jaune, vin de paille* and *brut blanc* or *rosé,* it's the perfect spot to make your acquaintance with fine Jura wines.

Henri Maire – *pl. de la Liberté.* ☎*03 84 66 15 27. www.henri-maire.fr. Open 8am-7pm.* This hard-to-miss shop offers tastings and cellar tours.

Hirsinger – *38 pl. de la Liberté.* ☎*03 84 66 06 97. www.chocolat-hirsinger.com. Open 8am-7:30pm. Closed Wed and Thur except holidays.* This renowned chocolatier sells an astonishing array of delicious homemade chocolates, including some unique to them.

Fruitière de Plasne – *39800 Plasne.* ☎*03 84 37 14 03. Open 10am-noon, 4-7pm. Closed Tue.* Comté, Morbier and Tomme de Jura are among the regional cheeses produced at this local cooperative. Tastings and visits to the production workshops and aging cellars are offered in season.

he continued his work. While his Paris office and laboratory were out of bounds to visitors, in Arbois visitors flocked to ask his advice. He was also believed to be a great doctor, and the hope of a free consultation brought many a thrifty Arbois citizen to his office. He would participate enthusiastically in the parade for the Fête du Biou and the harvest celebrations. In 1895, illness prevented the great scientist from going to Arbois as usual; he died on 28 September.

Sights

Maison de Pasteur★
🕐 *Open Apr-Oct.* 🚶 *Guided tours (30min) Jun-Sep 9.45am, 10.45am, 11.45am and 2pm-6pm; Apr, May and Oct 2.15pm, 3.15pm, 4.15pm and 5.15pm.* 💶*5.80€.* ☎*03 84 66 11 72. www.academie-sciences.fr/pasteur.htm.*
Restored on the occasion of the centennial of Pasteur's death, the house on the banks of the Cuisance looks much as it did when the family lived there.
There are numerous personal mementoes on display in the billiard room. On the first floor, two early drawings show his hidden talent as an artist.

The laboratory contains Pasteur's instruments and some of the amenities were exceptional for their time: running water and a gas line, cork insulation around the warming cupboard.

Musée Sarret-de-Grozon
🕐*Open Jun-Sep.* 🚶*Guided tour (1hr) daily except Tue 3-6.30pm; early-mid Sep weekends 3-6.30pm.* ☎*03 84 66 55 50. www.arbois.com.*
This 18C mansion has original furniture and decor, which evoke the atmosphere of a well-to-do home of the time.

Excursions

L'Ermitage
2.5km/1.5mi by D 469 S on the town plan; 1.5km/0.9mi out of town, leave D 469 and turn right onto a road climbing in a series of hairpin bends to an esplanade.
From the edge of the plateau, near the chapel, there is a fine view of Arbois and the Cuisance Valley.

Pupillin
3km/1.9mi S along D 246.
One of the most famous local vineyards, specialising in one type of vine, *plous-*

Atelier M. Bevalot-

Arbois

sard. Because of the quality of its wines, Pupillin has been allowed to use the appellation **Arbois-Pupillin**, which includes several renowned wine-growing estates such as Désirée Petit et Fils.

Grottes des Moidons

10km/6.2mi S. [Kids] 🕐 *Open Apr-Sep.* 🔦 *Guided tours (45min) Jul-Aug daily 9.30am-5.30pm. Rest of the year Thu-Tue 2.15pm, 3.15pm, 4.15pm (Jun and Sep extra tours 10.15am and 11.15am).* 👁6€ *(children 3.20€).* 📞03 84 51 74 94. www.grottes-desmoidons.com.

Deep in the forest, these caves contain a wealth of **concretions**★. The visit ends with an enjoyable *son et lumière* show.

Driving Tours

Reculée des Planches★★

21km/13mi – allow one day.

▶ *Leave Arbois on D 107, then take D 247 to the right near the church in Mesnay. This road soon enters the Reculée des Planches. Go past the church on coming to Planches-près-Arbois, head past the stone bridge and take the narrow surfaced road sharply to the left, along the foot of the cliffs. Leave the car 600m/660yd further on, near a little refreshment stand.*

Grande source de la Cuisance

This is the more interesting of the two sources of the Cuisance, a tributary of the Loue. In rainy seasons the water

cascades from a cave, which is also the entrance to the cave of Les Planches.

Grotte des Planches★

[Kids] 🕐*Open Apr-Sep. Guided tours (1hr) Jul-Aug daily 10am-6pm. Rest of the year daily 10am-noon and 2-5pm.* 👁6€ *(children 3€).* 📞03 84 66 13 74.

This cave was formed by water running between rock strata. Two of the galleries have been set aside for tourists, who can trace the underground path of the water as it flows through the rock.

Petite source de la Cuisance

500m/550yd from leaving Les Planches, then 1hr there and back on foot. On reaching Arbois head for Auberge du Moulin; leave the car in the park next to the river. 🚶 *Follow the path uphill. This waterfall is formed by the young river and the spring itself in periods of heavy rain.*

▶ *Retrace your steps. Straight after the bridge over the Cuisance, turn left on D 339, a narrow surfaced road leading uphill. Then take D 469, cut into the rock face, on the left. Leave the car in the car park 30m/33yd further on.*

Retrace your steps to enjoy a view of the Fer-à-Cheval (horse-shoe) amphitheatre, which closes off the Planches reculée.

▶ *Return to the car and take D 469.*

Belvédère du cirque du Fer-à-Cheval★★

Leave the car near an inn and take the signposted path (10min) on the left.

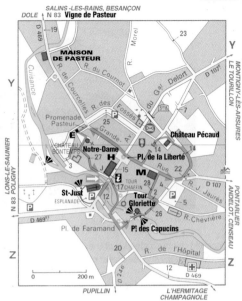

The path goes through a little wood, at the edge of which the amphitheatre opens out *(protective barrier)*. There is a superb **view** of the *reculée* from the viewpoint overlooking the valley floor from nearly 200m/656ft up.

▶ *Return to Arbois on D 469.*

The Vineyards★

90km/56mi round tour – allow one day.

The region is divided into four AOC areas (Appellation d'Origine Contrôlée): Arbois, Château-Chalon, Côtes-du-Jura and l'Étoile. For more information, see the chapter on Wine in the Introduction.

▶ *Leave Arbois on N 83 W.*

Poligny

This prosperous little medieval town, surrounded by rich farmland and vineyards, has also earned itself a reputation as the capital of Comté cheese. Learn more about how it is made at the **Maison du Comté** (○ *open Jul-Aug 10-11.30am, 2-6pm; May-Jun and Sep 2-6pm; rest of the year times vary; ⊜4€; ☎03 84 37 78 40; www.lesroutesducomte.com*); then pick up some to take home at award-winning specialist **Juraflore** (○ *open Mon-Sat 8am-noon, 2.30-7pm, Sun 9am-noon; ☎03 84 37 13 50; www. juraflore.com*).

▶ *Take N 5 towards Champagnole.*

Vaux-sur-Poligny

See the Cluniac church with an unusual roof of multicoloured varnished tiles.

Belvédère de Monts-de-Vaux★

This viewpoint *(car park)* offers a beautiful **view** all along the *reculée*.

▶ *Rejoin N 5 towards Poligny: after about 3.5km/2mi D 257 towards Chamole leads off to the right.*

Observe birds of prey in flight

The road climbs to **views**★ of the Culée de Vaux, Poligny and the Bresse region.

▶ *Return to Poligny. Leave on D 68 S.*

Plasne
A stroll around this hilltop village offers pretty **views**★ of the Bresse region.

▶ *Now take D 96, a narrow, bumpy road.*

Belvédère du Cirque de Ladoye★★
Car park above the reculée, right of the road, 40m/44yd after the D 96-D 5 junction.
The **view** is impressive.

▶ *Take D 204 at Granges-de-Ladoye. This road heads down to Ladoye-sur-Seille, before following the Seille Valley. Turn left at the junction with D 70, towards Baume-les-Messieurs.*

Baume-les-Messieurs★★★
See BAUME-LES-MESSIEURS.

▶ *Drive S to D 471 and turn right towards Lons-le-Saunier. Shortly beyond a deep bend, turn right onto a minor road towards Panessières. Follow the sign-posts to the Château du Pin.*

Château du Pin★
Open Jul-Sep 1-7pm. 4€. 03 84 25 32 95.
Built in the 13C by Jean de Chalon, Count of Burgundy and Lord of Arlay, it was destroyed by Louis XI, rebuilt in the 15C and restored in the 20C.

▶ *Continue to N 83 and turn left towards Lons-le-Saunier; 1km/0.6mi further on, turn right onto D 38 towards St-Didier and L'Étoile.*

L'Étoile
In spite of its small size, L'Étoile has no fewer than five châteaux and several wine-growing estates where tourists can take part in wine-tastings.

Château d'Arlay★
Open Jun to mid-Sep. Guided tours (30min) of the château, unaccompanied tours of the park and Jurafaune daily 2-6.30pm. 8.80€ (children 6.70€). 03 84 44 41 94. www.arlay.com.
The imposing 18C château is surrounded by a superb park. The apartments of the Prince of Arenberg, who resided here around 1830, are open to visitors. Note the library and the doll's bedroom.
Kids The park extends uphill to the medieval ruins of the original fortress, often used for demonstration flights of birds of prey (**Jurafaune**).

▶ *Follow D 120 towards Voiteur then take the D 5 to Château-Chalon.*

Château-Chalon★
This former stronghold on top of a rocky outcrop is surrounded by vineyards producing the famous **Vin Jaune**.
The village has a fortified gate and the ruins of its castle. The streets are lined with tall wine-growers' houses; some have wide rounded doorways and outside access to the cellars.

SALINE ROYALE D'ARC-ET-SENANS ★★

POPULATION 1 381
MICHELIN MAP 321: E-4

Not far from the River Loue is the old royal saltworks of Arc-et-Senans, a rare example of 18C industrial architecture, now on UNESCO's World Heritage List.

- **Information:** ☎03 81 54 45 45. www.salineroyale.com.
- ▶ **Orient Yourself:** Arc-et-Senans is arranged in concentric circles, with the most important buildings at the centre.
- **Don't Miss:** The musée Ledoux in the Coopers' building, with its fascinating collection of architectural models.
- 🕐 **Organising Your Time:** Start in the basement of the director's residence, where you can learn all about how and why the saltworks came to be here.

A Bit of History

An ideal town in the 18C

In 1773, the King's Counsel decreed that a royal saltworks should be founded at Arc-et-Senans, using the salt waters of Salins and timber from the nearby forest of Chaux for fuel. **Claude-Nicolas Ledoux** (1736-1806), inspector general of the saltworks in the Lorraine and Franche-Comté regions and already a famous architect, was commissioned to design it. Work on his masterpiece took place from 1774 to 1779, but only part of the plan was completed. However, what we see today is enough to evoke the idea of an ideal 18C city. It was an ambitious design; a whole town laid out in concentric circles with the director's residence at the centre, flanked by storehouses, offices and workshops, and extending out to include a church, a market, public baths, recreational facilities and so on. Unfortunately, the saltworks never produced as much salt as had been forecast and were eventually closed in 1895. Part of the buildings now houses a cultural centre that organises events.

Visit★★

🕐Open daily Jul-Aug 9am-7pm, Apr-Jun & Sep-Oct 9am-noon, 2-6pm. Rest of the year times vary. ☞7.50€.

Gatehouse

The road to Salins leads to the gatehouse with its peristyle of Doric columns. Arti-ficial grottoes recall the origins of salt. The building now houses the reception, bookshop and another shop.

Director's Residence

The director's residence is much restored, having been badly damaged by fire in 1918 and a late dynamite attack which wrecked the façade. The salt warehouse was in the basement, with offices on the ground and first floors. The landing of the main staircase was fitted out as a chapel and above that was the administration department. The rooms are now used for conferences and presentations.

In the basement, the **lieu du sel** contains a display explaining why this place was chosen for the royal saltworks and how the saltworks operated, with a slide show and a film on 20C saltworkers.

Courtyard

The semicircular courtyard, now a lawn, gives a good impression of the beauty and originality of the design of this complex. All the buildings around it face the director's residence, which is symbolically placed at the centre of the enterprise. They are decorated with carved motifs: petrified water flowing out of the necks of urns, evoking the source of the saltworking industry. This stylistically unified complex is all the more striking for the beauty and solidity of its masonry. The influence of Palladio, the 16C Italian architect, makes itself felt in the Antique style columns and pediments, whereas the roofs are constructed in the manner typical of the region.

Address Book

For coin ranges, see the Legend on the cover flap.

WHERE TO STAY

Chambre d'Hôte Le Val d'Amour – 29 rte. de Salins, 39380 Ounans, 13km/8.1mi SW of Arc-et-Senans by D 17 E then D32 and D472. ☎03 84 37 62 28. A warm welcome at this private residence near Arc-et-Senans. In summer, breakfast is served on the terrace, which looks out onto the meadows. Simple yet comfortable rooms.

Château de Germigney – 39600 Port-Lesney, 7.5km/4.6mi SE of Arc-et-Senans by D 17 E and D 48E. ☎03 84 73 85 85. www.chateaudegermigney.com. Closed Jan. 20 rooms. ⚓15€. Restaurant. Calm and charming old home by a pretty park. Well-appointed rooms and delicious food.

WHERE TO EAT

Le Relais – pl. de l'Église. ☎03 81 57 40 60. Closed 15 Dec-15 Jan and Sun evenings. Good-value meals are served on the terrace in summer. The dining room has stone walls, beams and old tiled floors. A few simple, tidy rooms.

Auberge de la Lavandière – 10 r. de la Lavandière, 25440 Lavans-Quincey, take the D 101 SE from Courtefontaine 12.5km/7.7mi to Byans-sur-Doubs, then the D 13 to Quingey, then to Lavans-Quingey. ☎03 81 63 69 28. la.lavandiere@wanadoo.fr. Closed 20 Dec-4 Jan, Sat afternoon, Sun evening and Mon. Enormous farmhouse with an ancient fireplace. Regional specialities served in the dining-room and the garden.

SHOPPING

Institut Claude-Nicolas-Ledoux – Saline Royale. ☎03 81 54 45 44. www.salineroyale.com. Closed 25 Dec-1 Jan. Bookstore specializing in architecture as well as the Franche-Comté region.

Coopers' Building

The cooper's building houses the **musée Ledoux**, a collection of about 60 architectural scale models which reveal his ideas about the ideal society.

The right wing contains those buildings which were only partly finished: the theatre at Besançon, of which only the façade remains; the saltworks at Arc-et-Senans; and the Château de Maupertuis. In the left wing, the ideal city of Chaux, the gun forge and the guardians' house at the source of the Loue are all projects that Ledoux never realised.

Prints and photographs complete the exhibition.

Chemin des Gabelous

As you leave the saltworks, turn left then right at the roundabout along rue des Graduations. The signposted trail begins from the camp site; 5hr 30min on foot, 2hr 30min by bike.

The 24km/15mi waymarked path follows the historic trail from the salt-extraction site in Salins to Arc-et-Senans.

Excursions

Val d'Amour

This is the delightful name of part of the Loue Valley, best-known for its legends and attractive river. A variety of crafts, mostly linked to timber, livened up the valley until the early 20C.

Chamblay

Downriver from Chissey, this village had a long-standing tradition of timber-floating. This activity developed during the 18C in order to supply timber to the navy; later on timber was used for factories and for heating.

Chaux Forest is nearby and for a long time the fast-flowing River Loue provided the best means of transport, although it was dangerous for the men guiding the large rafts when the river was in spate.

The **Confrérie St-Nicolas des radeliers de la Loue** has been reviving this traditional craft annually since 1994 through a series of events.

Port-Lesney★

This pretty village on the River Loue is popular in summer for a country holiday. On Sundays, fishermen, boating enthusiasts and lovers of trout and fried fish flock to the village.

There is a footpath *(1hr round trip)* from the Chapelle de Lorette which leads through the undergrowth to the Belvédère Edgar-Faure overlooking the village and the entire valley.

AUTUN★★

POPULATION 16 419
MICHELIN MAP 320: F-8
LOCAL MAP SEE MORVAN

The city of Autun is flanked by wooded hills overlooking the valley of the Arroux and the vast plain that extends westwards. The cathedral, the museums and the Roman remains bear witness to the city's past greatness.

- **Information:** 2 av. Charles de Gaulle, 71400 Autun. ☎03 85 86 80 38. www.autun-tourisme.com.
- **Orient Yourself:** The cathedral and several museums are close to Place du Champ de Mars. There are excellent shops in the pedestrian streets near the square, along Avenue Charles de Gaulle, Rue Guerin and by the cathedral.
- **Don't Miss:** The ruins of the Roman theatre, the largest in Gaul.
- **Organizing Your Time:** If you visit in August, stop at the cathedral in the evening for "Nocturnes de la cathédrale," a free cultural series featuring art, music and poetry.

A Bit of History

The Rome of the Gauls

Autun, from Augustodunum, was founded by Emperor Augustus with the aim both of honouring the Aedui, the local tribe, and of making them beholden to Rome. The splendour of the new town, which was known as the sister and rival of Rome, soon eclipsed the contemporary Gaulish settlement at Bibracte (*see Mont BEUVRAY*). The city's location on the great commercial and military road between Lyon and Boulogne brought it prosperity. All that remains of the fortified enclosure and the numerous public monuments are two gates and traces of the largest Roman theatre in Gaul.

The century of the Rolin family

In the Middle Ages Autun became prosperous again, largely because of two men: Nicolas Rolin and one of his sons. Born in Autun in 1376, **Nicolas Rolin** became one of the most celebrated lawyers of his time. He attracted the attention of the Duke of Burgundy, Philip the Good, who made him Chancellor. Despite rising to such heights, he never forgot his native town, helping to restore its fortunes. A son, **Cardinal Rolin**, who became Bishop of Autun, made the town a great religious centre. The completion of the cathedral of St-Lazare, the ramparts to the south of the town and many private mansions date from this time.

Upper Town Tour

- *Start from place du Champ-de-Mars (parking area, tourist office).*

Lycée Bonaparte

This was once a Jesuit college, built in 1709, and it provides a noble focal point for place du Champ-de-Mars. The wrought-iron **grille**★, dating from 1772, is adorned with gilded motifs of medallions, globes, astrolabes and lyres. On

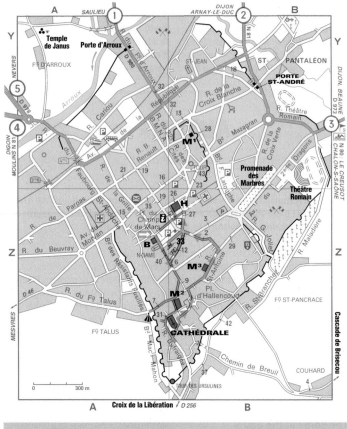

the left, the 17C **church of Notre-Dame** was once the college chapel. Notable pupils included the Bonaparte brothers, Napoleon, Joseph and Lucien.
Walk along rue St-Saulge, admiring the 17C Hôtel de Morey at no 24; continue along rue Chauchien and note the façades decorated with wrought-iron balconies.

▶ *Rue Cocand leads to the ramparts.*

Les Remparts
The walk round the ramparts begins at boulevard des Résistants Fusillés to the west of town. Follow the ramparts south as far as the Tour des Ursulines, a 12C keep.

▶ *Walk towards the cathedral along rue Notre-Dame (Hôtel de Millery at no 12), then stroll along rue Dufraigne (timber-framed houses) and impasse du jeu de Paume (Hôtel Mac-Mahon). From place d'Hallencourt, you can visit the courtyard of the bishop's residence. Continue towards rue St-Antoine. A little further on, turn left onto rue de l'Arbalète which leads to the pedestrianised rue des Cordiers.*

Cathédrale St-Lazare

Passage de la Halle

This mid-19C covered passageway opens onto place du Champ-de-Mars through an imposing Classical doorway.

▶ *Follow rue De-Lattre-de-Tassigny, lined with 18C private mansions.*

Hôtel de Ville

The town hall houses a large **library** including a rich collection of **manuscripts**★ and incunabula, displayed in rotation during summer exhibitions.
Finally, walk along rue Jeannin, situated behind the town hall, and enter one of the gardens through a porte-cochère.

Cathédrale St-Lazare★★

In the 12C the Bishop of Autun decided to supplement the existing cathedral (destroyed in the 18C) with a new church, to house the relics of St Lazarus, in the hope of creating a place of pilgrimage to rival the Basilique Ste-Madeleine in Vézelay. Construction took place from 1120 to 1146, and the cathedral was consecrated in 1130 by Pope Innocent II.
The exterior of the cathedral no longer looks particularly Romanesque because of later modifications. The belfry was destroyed by fire in 1469, and when it was rebuilt later that century, a Gothic spire was added. The upper part of the choir and the chapels in the right aisle date from the same period. Those in the left aisle are 16C. The two towers flanking the main front, which resemble those at Paray-le-Monial, were added in the 19C. The building was seriously damaged during the French Revolution; the cathedral canons demolished the rood screen, the tympanum of the north doorway and the tomb of St Lazarus which stood behind the high altar *(what remains can be seen in the Musée Rolin).*

Tympanum of the central doorway★★★

The tympanum (1130-35), one of the masterpieces of Romanesque sculpture, bears the signature of its creator, **Gislebertus**, beneath the feet of Christ. Nothing is known about him, except that his work suggests he was trained in Vézelay, and perhaps also in Cluny. Unlike his contemporaries, he did not conform to the Cluniac tradition, but produced his own distinctive style. The

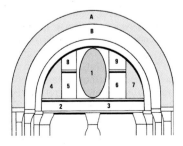

Address Book

For coin ranges, see the Legend on the cover flap.

WHERE TO STAY

Tête Noire – 3 r. de l'Arquebuse. ☎03 85 86 59 99. www.hoteltetenoire.fr. Closed 15 Dec-25 Jan. 31 rooms. 9€. Restaurant. The smartly appointed and newly soundproofed rooms in this charming property boast rustic painted wood furniture. Traditional dishes are served in the pleasant dining room.

WHERE TO EAT

Le Chalet Bleu – 3 r. Jeannin. ☎03 85 86 27 30. www.lechaletbleu.com. Closed 16 Feb-10 Mar, Sun evenings and 15 Nov-31 Mar, Mon evenings and Tue. The thoughtful cuisine successfully combines tradition with fresh regional produce. Highly affordable prices.

Le Relais des Ursulines – 2 r. Dufraigne. ☎03 85 52 26 22. www.hotelursulines.fr. Closed Sat lunch and Thu in winter. The décor is classic bistro: a wooden counter, copperware, antique pieces picked up from flea markets, tables covered with red and white checked fabric. The menu includes pizzas and meat grilled on an open fire.

SIT BACK AND RELAX

Irish Pub – 5 r. Mazagran. ☎03 85 52 73 90. Open Tue-Sun 11am-2am, Fri-Sat until 3am. Mix in with the trendy and appreciative crowd who throng here to listen to live music played by French, Celtic and Irish bands.

SHOPPING

Henriot – 29 r. Guérin. ☎03 85 52 28 56. Closed 14 Jun-4 Jul. An attractive shopfront makes it hard to miss this popular charcuterie, well-known for the quality of its wares. Try the *jambon persillé*, the *boudin*, the *pâté de campagne*, the *terrine de lièvre et de gibier en saison*, the *andouillete*, the *mousse de volaille* and other prepared dishes.

Le Pause-Café – 9 r. aux Cordiers. ☎03 85 86 34 60. Open Tue-Sat 9am-noon and 2-7pm. This pleasant purveyor of fine coffees roasts some 15 varieties of beans from Nicaragua, Kenya, Guatemala and other regions.

Au Cygne de Montjeu – 12 r. St.-Saulge. ☎03 85 52 29 61. Open Tue-Sat 8.30am-12.30pm and 2-7.15pm, Sun 8am-12.30pm; daily in summer except closed 2 weeks in Jul. This is the spot for diehard chocolate lovers, its owner being an accomplished practitioner of the art. Cakes, candies, tarts are all excellent. Try the *Croquets du Morvan*, or the *nougat tendre*, both local favourites.

---

composition of the central tympanum is a masterly solution of the problems posed by the decoration of such a large area. The theme is the Last Judgement. Despite its apparent complexity, the design is highly structured. At the centre, dominating the composition, is the tall figure of Christ in Majesty (1) surrounded by a mandorla supported by four angels. Below are the dead rising from their graves, summoned by four angels blowing trumpets (4, 7, 8, 9); in the centre of the lintel, an angel is separating the blessed (2) from the damned (3). At the left hand of Christ, the Archangel Michael confronts Satan, who is trying to upset the weighing of souls by pressing on the beams of the scales (6). Behind him yawns the mouth of Hell, which is squeezed to the extreme right

of the tympanum (7), whereas Heaven occupies the whole of the upper register with *(right)* two Apostles or Enoch, the patriarch, and Eli, the prophet, transported straight to Heaven (9) and *(left)* Mary (8) in the heavenly Jerusalem (4) and the Apostles (5) attending the weighing of souls. St Peter, with the key on his shoulder, lends a hand to one of the blessed, while a soul tries to escape by clinging to the robe of an angel.

The whole composition is crowned by three orders of rounded arches. The outer order (A) represents the passing of time, the labours of the months alternating with the signs of the zodiac in the medallions; in the centre, between Cancer and Gemini, is a small crouching figure representing the year. The middle order (B) bears a serpentine garland of leaves and flowers.

The inner order, destroyed in 1766 when the tympanum was plastered over, showed the elders of the Apocalypse.

Interior

The pillars and vaulting date from the first half of the 12C. The Cluniac Romanesque style survives in spite of much alteration: three rows of elevation (large pointed arches, false triforium and high windows), massive cruciform pillars divided by fluted pilasters, broken-barrel vaulting with transverse ribs in the nave and rib vaulting in the aisles.

The chancel conforms to the early Christian design of an apse flanked by two apsidal chapels. The over-vaulting disappeared in the 15C when the tall windows were put in by Cardinal Rolin (the glass in the pointed windows is from the 19C, in the Romanesque ones from 1939).

The use of fluted pilasters surmounted by foliated capitals, found throughout the upper gallery, gives a sense of unity to the interior of the cathedral; these elements would have been familiar to the local masons from the many ancient buildings in Autun.

The majestic effect is enlivened by the carved capitals (binoculars are useful here). The most admirable features are:

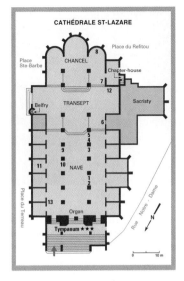

CATHÉDRALE ST-LAZARE

- ◆ **1) and 2)** Simon the Sorcerer tries to ascend to Heaven watched by St Paul and St Peter with his key. Simon falls head first under Peter's approving eye. The devil (visible from the main nave) is beautifully portrayed.
- ◆ **3)** The stoning of St Stephen.
- ◆ **4)** Symbolic representation of Samson pulling down the temple.
- ◆ **5)** The loading of the Ark, with Noah supervising from an upper window.
- ◆ **6)** 16C sacristy door.
- ◆ **7)** Statues of Pierre Jeannin, who died in 1623, President of the Burgundian Parliament and a minister of Henri IV, with his wife.
- ◆ **8)** The relics of St Lazarus are placed under the high altar.
- ◆ **9)** Jesus appearing to Mary Magdalene against a background of curled foliage.
- ◆ **10)** The second temptation of Christ. Oddly enough the devil is the only figure placed high up on the roof.

- ◆ **11)** A 16C stained-glass window representing the Tree of Jesse in the burial chapel of the bishops of Autun.
- ◆ **12)** Painting by Ingres (1834) representing the martyrdom of St Symphorian, by the Porte St-André.
- ◆ **13)** The Nativity. St Joseph meditating in a strange, arched chair.

Chapter-house – The chapter-house was built in the early 16C, using some fine **capitals**★★ made of heavily grained stone containing mica, which originally capped the pillars in the chancel.

Belfry

The belfry (80m/262ft high) was built by Bishop Jean Rolin in 1462. From the top (230 steps) there is a good **view**★ of the old roofs of the town, the bishops' palace and the hills of the Morvan.

The Gallo-Roman Town

Théâtre romain

The remains reveal the size of the largest theatre in Gaul (capacity: 12 000). Gallo-Roman stone fragments are incorporated into the wall of the porter's house.

Porte St-André★

This gate is where the roads from Langres and Besançon meet. It is the sole survivor

Detail of the Nativity

of four original gates in the Gallo-Roman fortifications, which were reinforced with 54 semicircular towers. One of the guard-houses has survived by being converted into a church in the Middle Ages. Tradition has it that St Symphorian was martyred near this gateway.

Porte d'Arroux

This gateway was the Roman Porta Senonica, leading towards Sens and the Via Agrippa which ran from Lyon to Boulogne. Smaller and not as well preserved as the Porte St-André, it has similar arches. The upper arcading, decorated with fluted pilasters topped by Corinthian capitals, dates from the time of Emperor Constantine.

Additional Sights

Musée Rolin★

○Open Apr-Sep daily except Tue 9.30am-noon, 1.30-6pm. Rest of the year daily except Tue 10am-noon, 2-5pm, Sun 10am-12pm, 2.30-5pm. ○Closed 1 Jan, 1 May, 14 Jul, 1 and 11 Nov, 25 Dec. ♒3.35€. ☎03 85 52 09 76.

TThe 20 rooms contain many noteworthy exhibits. Two rooms (8 and 9) are devoted to masterpieces of Roman **statuary**★★, mostly by the two great sculptors of the Burgundian School, Gislebertus and Martin, a monk. Gislebertus' **Temptation of Eve**★★ expresses sensuality through the curves of the body and the plants; the carving adorned the lintel of the north door of the cathedral before 1766. Martin created part of the **tomb of St Lazarus**, which took the form of a miniature church and stood behind the altarpiece in the chancel of the cathedral until it was destroyed during the changes made by the canons in 1766. The surviving figures from the main group, which depicted the Resurrection of Lazarus, are the slim and poignant figures of St Andrew and Lazarus' sisters, Martha (who is holding her nose) and Mary. The rest of the work is represented by a few fragments supplemented by a sketch.

The first floor houses 14C and 15C sculptures from the Autun workshops and works by French and Flemish Primitive painters. The room devoted to the Rolin family contains the famous 15C painting of the **Nativity**★★ by the Master of Moulins. 15C Burgundian statuary is represented by the **Virgin**★★ of Autun in polychrome stone and a St Catherine attributed to the Spanish sculptor Juan de la Huerta who worked in the region during the reign of Philip the Good.

Excursions

Croix de la Libération★

6km/4mi S.

The road climbing in a series of hairpin bends offers a fine view of the cathedral, the old town and the Morvan in the distance; 50m/55yd beyond the entrance to Montjeu Castle, a steep path on the right leads up to the granite cross put up in 1945 to commemorate the liberation of Autun; from here, there is a good **view**★ of Autun.

Château de Sully★

15km/9.3mi NE along the road to Nolay.

○Open Apr-Nov. Guided tours (45min) Jul-Aug 10am-7pm, Apr-Jun and Sep-Nov 10am-6pm. ♒7.30€. ☎03 85 82 09 86. www.chateaudesully.com.

This Renaissance mansion in a vast park is similar in its layout and decoration to Ancy-le-Franc. It was begun early in the 16C by Jean de Saulx, who had already acquired the land at Sully, and continued by his son, the Maréchal de Tavannes.

AUXERRE★★

POPULATION 37 790

MICHELIN MAP 319: E-5

Auxerre (pronounced *Oh-ssair*), the capital of Lower Burgundy (Basse Bourgogne), is on a hillside beside the River Yonne, at the start of the Nivernais canal. The town's fine monuments are highlighted in summer by a *son et lumière* show near the cathedral, while the shady boulevards, steep streets and old houses contribute to its overall interest. From the bridges and the right bank of the river, there are fine views★ of the town.

- **Information**: 1 quai de la République, 89000 Auxerre. ☎03 86 52 06 19. www.ot-auxerre.fr.
- ▶ **Orient Yourself:** Boulevard du 11 November encircles the historic downtown area, where most of the sights are located. For a self-guided walking tour of the old town, follow the markings painted on the ground (enquire at the tourist office).
- **Don't Miss:** St. Germain Abbey, home to some of the oldest frescoes in France.

A Bit of History

The Romans built Autessiodurum on the road from Lyon to Boulogne, near a simple Gaulish village, and from the 1C it thrived. By the Middle Ages, Auxerre was a spiritual centre, and was declared a Holy City by the Pope in the 12C.

Two great figures in history have visited Auxerre. In 1429 **Joan of Arc** passed through twice; and on 17 March 1815, **Napoleon** arrived on his return from Elba.

Town Walk

▶ *Start from quai de la Marine.*

Quartier de la Marine

This part of town with its narrow streets was once home to the boatmen. Take rue de la Marine *(no 37 on the town plan)* to see the remains of the north-east tower of the Gallo-Roman fortified wall. Walk across pretty place St-Nicolas *(no 45 on the town plan)*, overlooking quai de la Marine. The square is named after the patron saint of boatmen. Rue du Mont-Brenn leads to the place du Coche-d'Eau *(no 8 on the town plan)*. At no 3, a 16C house hosts temporary exhibitions as part of the **Musée du Coche-d'Eau**. Go up rue du Docteur-Labosse *(no 10 on the town plan)* to reach rue Cochois.

▶ *Walk towards the town centre via place St-Étienne, then rue Maison-fort on the left prolonged by rue Joubert.*

Town centre

There are many interesting old houses here, mostly 16C with half-timbering. **Rue Fécauderie** intersecting with rue Joubert has two half-timbered houses with a sculpted corner post; it leads to **place de l'Hôtel-de-Ville**; note nos 4, 6, 16, 17 and 18.

Tour de l'Horloge

This tower, also called the Tour Gaillarde, was built in the C15. The astrological clock (17C) has faces showing the movement of the sun and moon.

Astronomical clock

S. Sauvignier-MICHELIN

Auxerre on the banks of the River Yonne

S. Sauvignier-MICHELIN

A vaulted passageway beside the clock tower leads to place du Maréchal-Leclerc. Continue along **rue de l'Horloge**: no 6 (sculpted corner post) and the four houses opposite; then along **rue de la Draperie:** note the houses occupied by a bank and a jeweller's. It leads to **place Charles-Surugue** which has interesting houses at nos 3, 4, 5 and 18.

▸ *Strolling through the area, you will come across:*

The **Église St-Eusèbe** is all that remains of an old priory. The church has a 12C tower decorated with multifoil arches. The stone spire dates from the 15C. Inside, note the rib vaulting in the high hexagonal drum above the Renaissance

Frescoes in the Crypt of St-Étienne

S. Sauvignier/MICHELIN

chancel, the beautiful axial chapel and the 16C stained-glass windows.

The town's oldest house, from the 14C and 15C, is at no 5 **place Robillard.** Note the Renaissance mansion, Hôtel de Crole, with dormer windows and sculpted cornice at no 67 **rue de Paris**. Head towards the footbridge over the River Yonne via rue des Boucheries and rue **Sous-Murs**; this street owes its name to the walls of the Gallo-Roman city which ran alongside it; note the houses at nos 14 and 19.

Sights

Cathédrale St-Étienne★★

🕐 *Open 7.30am-6pm. Tour of the treasury and crypt available from Easter to All Saints Day daily 9am-6pm (Sun 2-6pm), rest of the year daily except Sun 10am-5pm.* ☎03 86 52 23 29.

The fine Gothic cathedral was built between the 13C and 16C to replace the existing Romanesque one. The building was practically finished by 1525.

West front – The Flamboyant style façade has four storeys of arcades surmounted by gables. The sculptures on the doorways (13C-14C) were mutilated in the 16C during the Wars of Religion, and the soft limestone has weathered badly. Among the scenes are the Last Judgement (*lintel*) and Christ between the Virgin Mary and St John (*tympanum*).

The sculptures framing the north door trace the lives of the Virgin Mary, St Joachim and St Anne. The Coronation of the Virgin is on the **tympanum**.

The sculptures round the south door are 13C. The tympanum, divided into three, and the recessed arches are dedicated to the childhood of Christ and the life of John the Baptist.

The more interesting of the side entrances is the 14C south door, which is dedicated to St Stephen; the north is dedicated to St Germanus.

Interior – The nave, built in the 14C, was vaulted in the 15C. The **choir and the ambulatory** date from the beginning of the 13C. In 1215, the cathedral's Romanesque choir was pulled down; rising above the 11C crypt is the beautiful piece

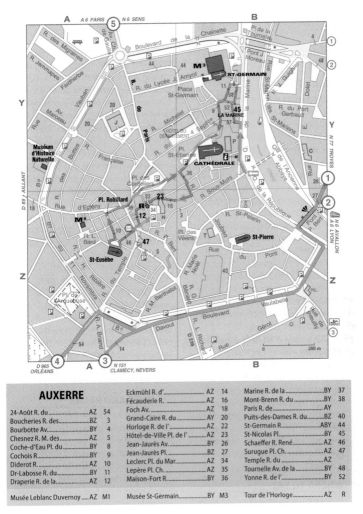

of architecture built to replace it, completed in 1234.

The ambulatory is lit by a magnificent array of **stained-glass windows**★★ composed of 13C medallions in which blue and red are the dominant colours. They represent scenes from Genesis, the stories of David, of Joseph and of the Prodigal Son and many saintly legends.

Romanesque crypt★ – The crypt, the only remaining part of the 11C Romanesque cathedral, has 11-13C frescoes.

Treasury★ – The many interesting exhibits include a collection of 12C-13C chased enamels, manuscripts, 15C-16C books of hours and miniatures.

Ancienne Abbaye St-Germain★★

Open year round. Guided tours of the crypt (45min; last tour departs 1hr before closing) Jul-Aug daily except Tue 10am-12.30pm, 2-6.30pm; Oct-May daily except Tue 10am-noon, 2-6pm. Closed 1 Jan, 1 and 8 May, 1 and 11 Nov, 25 Dec; 4.30€. 03 86 18 05 50.

This Benedictine abbey was built in the 6C by Queen Clotilda, wife of Clovis, on the site of an oratory where St Germanus, the 5C Bishop of Auxerre, was buried. In the time of Charles the Bald the abbey had a famous school; St Patrick, who converted the Irish, was a student.

Address Book

For coin ranges, see the Legend on the cover flap.

WHERE TO STAY

Chambre d'Hôte Domaine Borgnat Le Colombier – *1 r. de l'Église, 89290 Escolives-Ste-Camille, 9.5km/5.8mi S of Auxerre by D 239.* ☎03 86 53 35 28. *www.domainebornat.com. 5 rooms. Meals*. This magnificent fortified 17C farmhouse is a haven for wine buffs. Choose between the chambres d'hôtes or the self-catering formula in the dovecote. Relax by the pool on the terrace, while sipping one of the delicious wines produced on the estate.

Hôtel Le Cygne – *14 r. du 24-Aug.* ☎03 86 52 26 51. *hcygne3and1hotels.com. 30 rooms.* 6.40€. A modern hotel near the town centre offering simple, comfortable rooms. Some of the attic rooms have considerable charm and feature sloping ceilings.

Chambre d'Hôte Château de Ribourdin – *89240 Chevannes, 9km/ 5.6mi SW of Auxerre by N 151 and D 1 then a minor road.* ☎03 86 41 23 16. *www.chateauderibourdin.com.* 5 *rooms.* A sumptuous 16C château surrounded by meadows, located below the village. The cosy bedrooms and spacious breakfast room are housed in the 18C outbuildings, which give out onto the countryside.

WHERE TO EAT

La P'tite Beursaude – *55 r. Joubert.* ☎03 86 51 10 21. *auberge.beursaudiere@ wanadoo.fr.* Push open the doors of this charming eatery to discover the essence of the Burgundian countryside. The dining room opens to the kitchen, all beneath exposed beams and heavy stone.

Auberge Les Tilleuls – *89290 Vincelottes, 16km/10mi S of Auxerre by N6 and D 38.* ☎03 86 42 22 13. *lestilleulsvincelottes@wanadoo.fr. Closed 19 Dec-21 Feb, Thu Oct-Easter and Wed.* This small village inn will delight you thanks to its setting, its summer terrace along the banks of the Yonne and its succulent cuisine.

Chamaille – *89240 Chevannes, 8km/5mi SW of Auxerre by N 151 and D 1.* ☎03 86 41 24 80. *lachamaille@wanadoo.fr. Closed Feb. Reservations required.* Chamaille is surrounded by a delightful garden with a small stream meandering through fields stretching as far as the eye can see… The tastefully restored farmhouse has a pretty veranda.

Auberge du Château – *89580 Val-de-Mercy, 18km/11.2mi S of Auxerre by N 6, D 85 and D 38.* ☎03 86 41 60 00. *delfontaine.j@wanadoo.fr. Closed 15 Jan-5 Mar, Sun evenings, Tue lunch and Mon. Reservations required.* A country inn with spacious, well appointed rooms. The decoration features works by local artists. In summer the simple but tasty meals are served on the terrace, against a backdrop of flowers.

Barnabet – *14 quai de la République.* ☎03 86 51 68 88. *www. jlbarnabet.com. Closed 23 Dec-12 Jan, Sun evenings, Tue lunch and Mon.* This imposing residence tucked away from the quays flanking the Yonne is the perfect address for gourmets. Delicious, lovingly prepared meals are served in the elegant dining hall decorated in pastel hues or on the terrace inside the courtyard.

SIT BACK AND RELAX

Le Galion – *2 r. Étienne-Dolet.* ☎03 86 46 96 58. *Summer open daily 10am-2am; rest of the year noon-1am. Closed 25 Dec-1 Jan.* This small galleon lulled by the Yonne waters offers splendid views of Auxerre and the surrounding countryside. A lively ambience and the odd improvised concert make this a popular café with locals.

Pullman Bar – *20 r. d'Egleny.* ☎03 86 52 09 32. *Open Mon-Fri 4pm-1am, Sat 4pm-2am. Closed 3 weeks in Aug.* This unassuming bar has more than 110 special beers from 18 different countries and over 40 cocktails, with or without alcohol… Ask to see the cigar box.

SHOPPING

Au Fin Palais – *3 pl. St-Nicolas.* ☎03 86 51 14 03. *aufinpalais@9online.fr. Open daily 9.30am-7.30pm. Closed 15-30 Mar.* This shop offers a mouthwatering selection of the best regional produce, including liqueurs, brandies, beer from Sens, wines and the famous *nonnette* sweetmeats (iced gingerbread filled with jam). Also

on sale is the pretty sapphire-blue stoneware pottery from Puisaye. Charming welcome.
Domaine Anita, Jean-Pierre and Stéphanie Colinot – *1 r. des Chariats, 89290 Irancy. ☏03 86 42 33 25. Open Mon-Sat 8.30am-6.30pm, Sun 9.30am-noon.* The wines from the Colinot estate are matured in accordance with long-standing Burgundy tradition. Tastings are organised in the storehouse. The vaulted cellars date back to the 17C.
Roy – *89-91 r. du Pont. ☏03 86 52 35 93. Open 5am-7.30pm.* A warm welcome

awaits in this bakery and chocolate shop, where the delicacies of the house are introduced and explained with care. Confections created by the owner have won a wide audience, so sample a few!
P. Soufflard – *23 r. Joubert. ☏03 86 52 07 07. Open Tue-Sat 8am-12.30pm, 3-7pm.* You'll find an enormous array of local cheeses, all carefully selected by Monsieur Soufflard from a close group of suppliers. Try such specialties as *plaisir au chablis, brillat-savarin, pouligny-saint-pierre, vézelay* or *crottin de Chavignol.*

Abbey church – The upper part of the church was built from the 13C-15C and is Gothic in style; it replaced a Carolingian Romanesque church. The 10-sided Lady Chapel, dating from 1277, is linked to the ambulatory by a passageway and over-lies two semi-underground chapels (& see below) from the same period. In 1811, bays were demolished at the west end of the church isolating the 12C Roma-nesque **bell-tower** (51m/167ft high).
Crypt★★ – The crypt forms a semi-underground church consisting of a nave and two aisles; the barrel vaulting dates from the Carolingian period. The confessional, raised on three steps in the centre of the crypt, provides a fine view of the Carolingian, Romanesque and Gothic vaulting; four Gallo-Roman columns, with composite capitals, sup-port two millennial oak beams. The ambulatory is decorated with red and ochre **frescoes★** which date from 850 and are among the oldest in France.
The axial chapel, dedicated to St Maxime, was rebuilt in the 13C on the site of the rotunda of the Carolingian crypt. The vaulted roof is divided by ribs into 10 panels. Below is the Chapelle St-Clément, which can be reached via a narrow stair-case *(to the right on leaving the Chapelle Ste-Maxime).* The steeply sloping ground means that only part of the chapels are underground, so there are good views of the valley from some windows.

Musée St-Germain

This museum is in the old conventual buildings of the abbey, including the abbot's residence rebuilt at the begin-ning of the 18C *(entrance to abbey and museum)*, 14C cellars, 12C chapter-house (the latter's façade was found behind the cloisters - *restoration work in progress*) and sacristy. There is an archaeological collection in the monks' dormitory.

Museum

Musée Leblanc-Duvernoy

⊙*Open daily except Tue 2-6pm.* ⊙*Closed 1 Jan, 1 and 8 May, 1 and 11 Nov, 25 Dec.* ⊙*2.10€.* ☏*03 86 18 05 50.*
This museum is mainly devoted to fai-ence ware, with many exhibits from French or local ceramists. It also houses 18C Beauvais tapestries depicting scenes from the life of the Emperor of China.

Excursions

Seignelay
10km/6mi N.
Charming hillside town. Note the 17C covered market on place Colbert and the church of St-Martial. All that remains of the castle destroyed during the Revo-lution is a section of the curtain wall, a tower restored in the 19C, a 17C gate-house and the former park.

Vallée de l'Yonne from Auxerre to Clamecy
59km/38mi along D 163 and D 100.
Between Auxerre and Cravant, at the confluence of the River Yonne and River Cure, the road runs through a wide val-ley overlooked by low hills planted with

vines and cherry trees. Upriver from Cravant, the valley becomes narrower and the river flows faster.

Vallée de la Cure from Auxerre to Vézelay★

60km/38mi. The River Cure flows into the Yonne at Cravant. Beyond Cravant, the road runs close to the river through a hilly landscape of woodlands and vineyards. Upriver from Arcy-sur-Cure, the limestone cliffs towering above the west bank are riddled with caves; the Grande Grotte★ is the only one open to visitors. From there, there is a pleasant walk along the Cure.

AVALLON★

POPULATION 8 217
MICHELIN MAP 319: G-7

This pretty town, on a rocky outcrop high above the Cousin Valley, still has its old fortified town centre★. It is the ideal starting point of excursions into the surrounding area and the Morvan region.

Information: 6 r. Bocquillot, 89200 Avallon.
☎03 86 34 14 19. www.avallonais-tourisme.com.

▶ **Orient Yourself:** The old town is bounded by ancient ramparts and circular bastions, so there's no danger of getting lost.

A Bit of History

A powerful stronghold

Avallon was one of the key cities of Burgundy during the Middle Ages. In 1432, Jacques d'Espailly, known as Forte-Épice seized several castles of lower Burgundy. Protected by their fortifications, the people of Avallon felt safe, yet Forte-Épice took the guard by surprise, climbed the walls and seized the town. The Duke of Burgundy hurried back, made a breach in the city walls with a bombard and launched an attack, yet his troops were forced to withdraw. Infuriated by this delay, he immediately called on knights and cross-bowmen whereupon Forte-Épice disappeared through one of the posterns opening onto the riverside, abandoning his men.

Walled Town★

▶ *Start from the bastion of the Porte Auxerroise to the north.*

Tour of the ramparts

From the hospital, an early-18C building, follow rue Fontaine-Neuve overlooked by the Tour des Vaudois; next comes the Bastion de la Côte Gally towering over a ravine. Continue along rue du Fort Mac-Mahon (9) to the Bastion de la Petite-Porte, past the Tour du Chapitre (1454) and the Tour Gaujard.

From the **Promenade de la Petite Porte**, a terrace shaded by lime trees, there is a lovely view of the Cousin Valley 100m/109yd below, of several manor houses and of the Morvan heights in the distance.

▶ *Continue eastwards round the ramparts.*

This section of wall overlooks another ravine and runs past the well-preserved Tour de l'Escharguet and the Tour Beurdelaine, the oldest tower built in 1404 and reinforced in 1590 by a bastion.

Église St-Lazare

Built on the site of several previous sanctuaries, the church has two interesting **doorways★** on the façade. Note in particular the richly carved archivolt of the main doorway.

The carvings on the tympanum and lintel of the small doorway have been badly damaged but it is possible to see the Adoration, the Three Kings riding and visiting Herod then the Resurrection

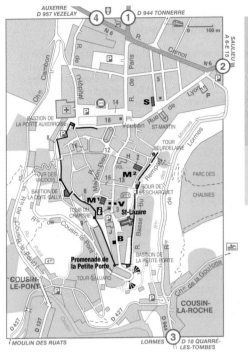

and the Descent in limbo. The archivolt is decorated with flower motifs.

To the right is the old Église St-Pierre which now houses temporary exhibitions. The interior is on different levels, the chancel being 3m/10ft lower than the west doorway. In the south aisle there are 17C statues in polychrome wood, a 15C Virgin with St Ann and a 14C stone statue of St Michael slaying the dragon. The chapel to the right of the chancel is profusely decorated with trompe-l'œil paintings dating from the 18C.

Do not miss the splendid 15C organ loft. Nearby, in rue Bocquillot, there is a salt storehouse, a former 15C winepress with its recess and mullioned windows.

Additional Sights

Musée de l'Avallonnais
Open Jul-Sep daily except Tue 2-6pm. Oct-May school holidays and weekends 2-6pm. Closed 1 Jan, 24, 25, 30 and 31 Dec. 03 86 34 03 19.
The local museum, founded in 1862, contains an eclectic collection of exhibits,

including a number of Gallo-Roman artefacts (a mosaic thought to be of Venus) and an exceptionally fine collection of Roman and medieval coins.

In the Fine Arts section, local artists are well represented; note also the famous 58-plate Expressionist series of the **Miserere**★ by Georges Rouault (1949).

Musée du Costume et de la Mode
Open mid-Apr to end Oct. Guided tours (45min) 10.30am-12.30pm, 1.30-5.30pm. 4€. 03 86 34 19 95.
Housed in the Hôtel de Condé (17C-18C) the fashion museum contains exhibitions of period costume.

Excursions

Château de Montjalin
7km/4.3mi E on D 957. Open 9am-7pm. 6€ (children 3€). 03 86 34 46 42. www.voiturespresidentielles.com.
The outbuildings of this elegant 18C castle house the **Musée des Voitures de chefs d'État**★. Among the 30 or so official cars, note De Gaulle's Citroen DS

Address Book

For coin ranges, see the Legend on the cover flap.

WHERE TO STAY

Chambre d'Hôte Haras de Kenmare – 19 rte du Morvan, Le Meix, 89630 St-Germain-des-Champs, 10km/6.5mi S of Avallon by D 944, D 10 then D 75. 03 86 34 27 63. 5 rooms. Meals. A welcoming family manor house built in the 19C. The bedrooms carry the names of local writers such as Vauban, Lamartine, Vincenot, Colette and story-teller Marie Christmas; their works can be found as bedside reading.

Avallon Vauban – 53 r. de Paris. 03 86 34 36 99. avallonvaubanhote. com. 26 rooms. 7.50€. Located near a busy intersection, this pretty building opens on to a vast, shaded park. There are cool colours and cherrywood furniture in the guest rooms (those at the back are quieter).

Relais Hôtelier du Château d'Island – 89200 Island, 7km/4.3mi SW of Avallon by D 957 then D 53. 03 86 34 22 03. disland.free.fr. Closed 10 Jan-1 Feb and 15 Nov-15 Dec. 20 rooms. Meals. Guests may choose between a bedroom and a suite in this 15C and 18C château nestling in a lovely park. Imposing beams, antique furniture and stately fireplaces await you in this prestigious hotel which affords lovely views of the leafy grounds and Franco-Vietnamese cuisine.

WHERE TO EAT

Le Grill des Madériens – 22 r. de Paris. 03 86 34 13 16. Closed winter, Sun evenings and Mon. Reservations required Sat-Sun. The owners of this restaurant, who are very fond of Madeira, have used this island as a source of inspiration for their decor. The vaulted dining rooms feature white and blue azulejo tiling on the walls, lace fabrics and traditional costumes for the waitresses. Try the delicious grilled meats on skewers served with salads, spicy fish fritters and vegetable dishes with Caribbean seasoning. Lively atmosphere.

Ferme-Auberge des Châtelaines – 3km/1.9mi S of Avallon by D 127 then a minor road. 03 86 34 16 37. Closed 15 Nov-15 Mar, Mon-Fri out of season and Mon-Wed 1 Jul-1 Sep. Reservations recommended. Pigs, rabbits and lambs are raised on this farm lying in the vicinity of the Cousin Valley... which may explain why the home-grown vegetables and produce are so delicious. Tasty cheese pies and cakes are served in the rustic-style dining room decorated with oilcloth, farming tools and waffle irons. Pretty views of Avallon.

Relais des Gourmets – 47 r. de Paris. 03 86 34 18 90. www.relaisdes-gourmets.com. Closed Jan, Sun evenings and Mon Sep-Jun. Local diners come from afar to enjoy the generous helpings of hearty cuisine served on the verandah, on the lovely flowered terrace or in the dining room with its exposed beams. Reasonable prices.

TIME FOR TEA...

Chez Dame Jeanne – 59 Grande-Rue. 03 86 34 58 71. Mon-Sat 10.30am-7pm. The pleasing décor of this tea room in a 17C home features exposed stonework, beams, a fireplace, comtemporary furnishings and a pretty terrace. Extensive menu of teas and coffees, accompanied by a selection of gourmet snacks.

---

19 with its bullet holes, Pope Paul VI's Popemobile or the extravagant Cadillac of the Emir of Abu Dhabi.

Ste-Magnance

19km/9.3mi SE towards Saulieu (N 6). The Gothic church of this small village was erected in 1514. The chancel and the apse are covered with Flamboyant vaulting. Inside, note the unusual **tomb**★ of St Magnance from the 12C; the low-relief carvings depict the legend of St Magnance and the miracles she performed.

Vallée du Cousin★

The D 427 follows the River Cousin which wends its way through verdant country-side; the itinerary is dotted with castles and picturesque watermills.

MASSIF DU **BALLON D'ALSACE** ★★★

MICHELIN MAPS 315: E-9/10 AND 314: I TO J-6

The Ballon d'Alsace is the southern peak of the rounded granite summits *(ballons)* of the Vosges range. It has beautiful forests of pines and larches, spectacular gorges and mountain pastures covered in colourful alpine flowers.

- **Information**: Parc du Paradis des Loups, Grande Rue, 90200 Giromagny. ☎03 84 29 09 00. www.parc-ballon-vosges.fr.
- ▶ **Orient Yourself:** There is a magnificent panorama of the whole area from the highest peak (1 250m/4 101ft); in fine weather, you can see as far as the Alps. Unfortunately, the view is often obscured by fog.

Driving Tours

Giromagny to the Ballon D'Alsace★★★

Giromagny

Fort Dorsner at Giromagny, built between 1875 and 1879, was the link in the line of defensive fortifications between the upper Moselle Valley and the fortress at Belfort. The restored building is open to the public.

▶ *Having passed Lepuix, a small town, the road follows a narrow gorge.*

Roches du Cerf

These rocks line the end of an old glacial valley. They have deep horizontal stripes scoured out by the lateral moraine of the glacier. A rock-climbing school exploits the challenging natural features of this site.

Cascade du Rummel

15min there and back on foot.
🚶A signposted footpath leads to a bridge and then the waterfall, not far from D 465.

▶ *Continue along D 465 (leaving the Masevaux road to your right).*

The road leads upwards through pretty countryside. In the distance, you should be able to see Sewen and Alfeld lakes.

Ballon d'Alsace★★★

🚶*30min there and back on foot.*
The footpath to the summit leads off D 465, from in front of the Restaurant du Ballon d'Alsace. It leads to a statue of the Virgin Mary. Before Alsace was returned to France, this statue marked the frontier. The Ballon d'Alsace (1 250m/4 101ft high) is the most southerly peak of the Vosges range. From the viewing terrace, there is a **panorama**★★.

Ballon De Servance★★

West of the Ballon d'Alsace, the Ballon de Servance reaches 1 216m/ 3 990ft.

The pass route★★

▶ *Leave Servance by D 486 towards the Col des Croix.*

Servance

🚶On the way out of the village to the right, a path (15min there and back) leads to the Saut de l'Ognon, a picturesque waterfall gushing out of a narrow gorge.

Saut de l'Ognon

M. Paygnard/MICHELIN

Address Book

For coin categories, see the Legend on the cover flap.

WHERE TO STAY

Grand Hôtel du Sommet – 90200 Lepuix-Gy, at the summit of the Ballon d'Alsace. ☎03 84 29 30 60. Closed Mon except school holidays. 25 rooms. 6.50€. Restaurant. Waking up in the mountains, breathing in the bracing country air, surrounded by cows in their peaceful meadows... this is what awaits you in this comfortable hotel, which commands pretty views of Belfort Valley or, on a fine day, the Swiss Alps.

Auberge Le Lodge de Monthury – 70440 Servance, 4.5km/ 2.8mi N of Servance by D 263. ☎03 84 20 48 55. Closed Christmas and New Year and Sun evenings. 6 rooms. Meals. Facing the Ballon de Servance, this 18C farmhouse dominating Ognon Valley is lost in the Jura countryside. Simple, comfortable rooms. Regional cuisine. Fishing facilities in private ponds for keen anglers.

WHERE TO EAT

Le Saut de la Truite – 90200 Giromagny, 7km/4.3mi N of Giromagny by D 465 and rte du Ballon d'Alsace. ☎03 84 29 32 64. saut.de.la.truite@wanadoo. fr. Closed 15 Dec-1 Feb and Fri. In a quiet valley, this restaurant's charming garden is enhanced by a quaint wooden bridge spanning a stream. Choose a table by the window, looking out over pine trees. There are a few simple but carefully kept rooms.

SPORTS AND RECREATION

Skiing – 90200 Vescemont. ☎03 84 29 06 65. Enquire at the ski school chalet ESF à la Gentiane. In winter the Ballon is the setting for a multitude of snow sports. Downhill and cross-country trails attract novices and experts alike.

Parc Naturel Régional des Ballons des Vosges – This vast park, which straddles the boundary between Alsace and Franche-Comté, boasts an astonishing variety of natural landscapes, from alpine meadows and mountain plateaux to bogs, lakes, rivers and pine-forested hills.

Col des Croix

Alt 678m/2 225ft.

The Château-Lambert fort overlooks the border between the regions of Lorraine and Franche-Comté. This watershed is the dividing line between waters which flow to the North Sea and those which flow to the Mediterranean.

Château-Lambert

Located 1km/0.6mi beyond the Col des Croix, this charming mountain village is home to the **Musée départemental de la Montagne** (open Apr-Sep daily except Tue 9.30am-noon, 2-6pm, Sat-Sun 2-6pm (last admission 30min before closing); Oct-Mar daily except Tue 2-5pm. Closed 1 Jan, 1 May, 1 Nov, 25 Dec and public holidays. 4€ (under 16 free). ☎03 84 20 43 09).

Among the displays, you will find a rural miner's dwelling, a mill, a forge, a 17C wine-press, a sawmill, exhibits on foresters' trades and local geology. Nearby, visit the 17C chapel and the St-Antoine Oratory.

▶ *Back at the Col des Croix, take D 16 to the right; this old strategic roadway runs along a ridge top. Views of the Ognon Valley open up below, before the path winds into the trees.*

Panorama: Ballon de Servance★★

Leave your car at the entrance to the Fort de Servance army road (off-limits). Follow the blazed trail leading to the top (15min there and back on foot).

A fabulous prospect stretches out all around; to the west, the Ognon Valley, the Esmoulières glacier plateau studded with ponds and the Langres plateau, to the north-west, the Faucilles mountains and farther on, the Moselle Valley. North-east, you will see from Hohneck to Gresson, passing by the distant Grand Ballon, the outline of the Vosges mountain range. Eastward looms the rounded contour of the Ballon d'Alsace; to the south and south-east lie the foothills of the Vosges.

BAUME-LES-DAMES

POPULATION 5 284

MICHELIN MAP 321: I-2

Baume-les-Dames is set against a backdrop of greenery at a point where the valley of the River Doubs widens. The relatively small historic town centre escaped destruction during the Second World War and is being restored.

▯ **Information**: 6 r. de Provence, 25110 Baume-les-Dames.
☎03 81 84 27 98. www.baumes-les-dames.org.

▶ **Orient Yourself**: Baume-les-Dames is the starting point for several scenic excursions along the Doubs and Cusancin valleys.

A Bit of History

Caves, Abbeys and Boats

Baume-les-Dames owes its name partly to an old Celtic word meaning cave, and partly to an old abbey run by Benedictine nuns. In the 18C the canonesses of Baume-les-Dames were the cream of the aristocracy; to be admitted, they had to prove that they had 16 noble ancestors.

The physicist Jouffroy d'Abbans (1751-1832) first tested a steamboat at Baume-les-Dames in 1778; a monument near the Doubs bridge commemorates the event.

Driving Tours

The Cusancin Valley

25km/15.5mi round tour – allow 3hr 30min

▶ *Drive S out of Baume-les-Dames along D 50 to Pont-les-Moulins then turn left onto D 21.*

The picturesque road runs through the green Cusancin Valley to the source of the river at Val de Cusance.

Source Bleue★

This is where the Cusancin springs up; to the left, the Source Bleue (Blue Spring), a pool of still waters in the woods; to the right, the Source Noire (Black Spring), which flows out of a cave at the foot of a limestone cliff.

▶ *Follow the road up to Lomont-sur-Crête and turn left onto D 19E. Continue past the 2nd fork to Villers-St-Martin, turn right onto the forest road of Bois de Babre then onto the path to Fente de Babre and the cliff top.*

▯Fente de Babre

15min on foot there and back.

A pleasant path running through a wooded area leads to the Fente de Babre, a joint in the rock which overlooks the south bank of the Doubs and offers a pleasant **view**★ of Pont-les-Moulins and the Audeux Valley, Baume-les-Dames and the surrounding area.

▶ *Return to D 19E and turn right towards Baume-les-Dames.*

Valley and mountain

▶ *Drive E out of Baume-les-Dames towards Montbéliard.*

The road winds along the Doubs Valley through a pleasant rolling country landscape dotted with riverside villages.

Clerval

There are some interesting works in the **church**: two 16C statues on each side of the crucifix and a 16C wooden Pietà in a side aisle.

L'Isle-sur-le-Doubs

The Doubs divides this town into three districts: the Ile (island) in the middle of the river; the Rue (street) on the north bank; and Le Magny on the south.

▶ *Return to the entrance to the town, driving towards the A 36 interchange and continue along D 31 which runs S under the motorway to Belvoir.*

Château de Belvoir★

○*Open Easter-Oct.* ◝◟*Guided tour (1hr) Jul-Aug daily 10-11.30am, 2-5.30pm; rest of the year Sun and public holidays only.* ◟*5€.* ☎*03 81 86 30 34. www.chateau-belvoir.com.*

Built in the 12C, the castle is on a promontory overlooking the Sancey Valley south of the Lomont mountains. The visit includes the kitchen with its gleaming copper utensils, the guard-room, the former arsenal, and the weaponry in which arms and armour from the Middle Ages to the 19C are on display.

A living room and study have been attractively furnished in the Madge-Fà Tower, which owes its curious name to the strange bearded character crouching on a monster's head beneath the *cul-de-lampe* which supports the turret overlooking the road.

From the keep, there is a beautiful view of the surrounding countryside.

▶ *Continue to Sancey-le-Grand and turn right onto D 464 to Vellevans, Servin and Vaudrivillers. At the intersection with D 50, turn left to Orsans then right onto D 120 to the Grotte de la Glacière.*

Grotte de la Glacière

○*Open Mar-Oct.* ◝◟*Guided tours (1hr) daily Jun-Aug 9am-7pm; Mar-May 10am-noon, 2-6pm; Sep-Oct 10am-noon, 2-5pm.* ◟*6€.* ☎*03 81 60 44 26. www.grotteglaciere.com.*

This 66m/217ft-deep glacial cave lets in daylight through a large opening. The **Maison des minéraux**, at the entrance, displays a rich collection of minerals from various countries.

▶ *Continue along D 120 towards Aissey, then turn right onto D 492 which runs onto D 50 to Baume-les-Dames.*

BAUME-LES-MESSIEURS★★★

POPULATION 194 MICHELIN MAP 321: D-6

Baume-les-Messieurs stands in a grandiose **setting** at the convergence of three valleys, one of which is the magnificent blind valley (reculée) of the Baume amphitheatre. The village, framed by rocky cliffs, is particularly known for the picturesque ruins of its old abbey.

- **Information**: The restaurant Le Grand Jardin, pl. de l'Abbaye, ☎03 84 44 68 37, has guides to walks and hikes in the valley.
- **Orient Yourself:** Try to arrive in Baume-les-Messieurs by the D 4 via Crançot; the approach into the village is particularly lovely.

A Bit of History

Monks and Gentlemen

The abbey at Baume was founded c 870 and adopted the Benedictine Rule. One of its claims to glory is that in 909 six of its monks were among the founders of the illustrious abbey at Cluny. Monastic life, however, grew increasingly lax, as it did at St-Claude (*see ST-CLAUDE*); from the 16C onwards, the humble monks of the abbey's beginnings were replaced by canons of noble birth. These high and mighty Messieurs lost no time in modifying the name of their home, thus Baume-les-Moines became Baume-les-Messieurs. This lasted until the Revolution; in 1793 all the abbey's possessions were seized and auctioned off.

The adventurous life of Jean de Watteville

Jean de Watteville was one of the abbots of Baume in the 17C, as well as one of the most extraordinary characters of his age, if one is to believe the Memoirs of St Simon. His many adventures have almost certainly been embellished.

Soldier, Franciscan friar, Carthusian monk, Turkish Pasha...

Watteville initially followed a military career. While a minor officer in the Burgundy regiment during the Milan campaign he fought a duel with a Spanish nobleman in the service of the Queen of Spain and killed him. He fled to Paris. While there, he heard a sermon on the dangers of hell and, overcome with

Abbey of Baume-les-Messieurs

© CDT Jura

remorse, converted to Christianity. The ex-soldier became a Franciscan friar, then entered the abbey of Bonlieu as a Carthusian monk.

Watteville soon tired of monastic life. He was caught climbing the wall in his bid for freedom by the prior himself. Watteville shot the man and escaped, crossing the Pyrenees into Spain.

Leaving behind a second noble Spanish corpse, Watteville fled to Constantinople. The ex-monk converted to Islam and put his military talents to the service of the Sultan, who was so impressed with him that he promoted him first to Pasha, then to Governor of the province of Morea.

...Abbot of Baume

After several years of living the high life surrounded by a sizeable harem, Watteville made an offer to the Venetians, whom he had been engaged by the Sultan to fight: if they could promise him papal absolution for his past crimes as well as the abbey of Baume as a reward, he would surrender his troops. This outrageous deal was struck, and our opportunist ex-Pasha shaved his head for the second time and took charge of the abbey of Baume.

The abbot remained as impetuous as ever, as several anecdotes illustrate. For example, Watteville had the series of ladders, previously the only way of getting to the bottom of the valley from Crançot, replaced by steps cut into the rock (the Échelles de Crançot). Seeing his monks taking infinite pains not to break their necks on the steep, slippery steps, the abbot flew into a rage, leapt onto his long-suffering mule's back and drove it down the steps, berating the monks as he went for their cowardice.

Parliamentary Intermediary

When Louis XIV invaded Franche-Comté, Watteville, after weighing up the French chances of winning, offered his services to the French king. Thanks to his skilful use of language, he won over the last centres of resistance (Gray, Ornans, Nozeroy) to the French king's cause without a single shot being fired.

After the Nijmegen peace treaty of 1678, Watteville returned to his abbey and a life of luxury. He died in 1702, aged 84.

Abbaye

Open mid-Jun to Sep 10am-noon, 2-6pm. 3.50€. ☎03 84 44 95 45.

A vaulted passageway leads into the first courtyard, round which are the guesthouse, abbot's house, keep, tower used as a court *(tour de justice)* and church.

Church

The 15C façade has an interesting doorway: God the Father giving Blessing is depicted on the central pillar and angels enthusiastically playing musical instruments in the side niches. The nave was once paved with tombstones, of which about 40 remain; the most interesting are leaning against the wall of the north side aisle. Close by is the tomb of Abbot Jean de Watteville. The Chapelle de Chalon, the mausoleum of the aristocratic Chalon (*see NOZEROY*) family, is to the north of the chancel. It contains a 16C statue of St Catherine and a 15C stone **statue of St Paul**, as well as tombs of the Chalon family. There is a beautiful painted and sculpted 16C Flemish **altarpiece**★★ *(accessible by guided tour only).*

Cour du cloître
A door in the middle of the nave on the south side leads to what used to be the cloisters. The monks' dormitory and refectory overlooked this courtyard.

Abbey buildings
An arch on the left leads into another courtyard surrounded by buildings which once contained the apartments of the aristocratic canons.

Cirque de Baume Driving Tour ★★★

21km/13mi round tour. Leave Baume-les-Messiers on D 70E3; left on D 70E1, to the bottom of the amphitheatre along the banks of the Dard.

The tall rocky cliffs which form this amphitheatre are an awe-inspiring sight.
Leave the car near the Chalet des Grottes de Baume.

Grottes de Baume★
Open Apr–Sep. Guided tour (45min) Jul–Aug 10am–6pm, Apr–Jun and Sep 10am–noon, 2–5pm. ⊗4.50€ (children 2.20€). ☎03 84 48 23 02.
After the entrance gallery, visitors are taken through tall, narrow chambers to the **great hall**. The visit continues round a lake containing small, white blind shrimp. The **Catafalque gallery** is 80m/262ft high.

▸ *Return to D 70 and then turn right to Crançot.*

There is a view after the second hairpin bend of Baume and its abbey.

La Croix viewpoint

▸ *Stop at the D 70/ D 210 cross-roads.*

▸ *Take the path on the right which leads to the forest, following the blue trail markers (20min there and back on foot). At the end of the path, near the cross, there is a* **view**★ *over Baume-les-Messiers.*

▸ *Turn back, and if you like, head for the village of Granges-sur-Baume.*

A belvedere at the town limits *(follow the signs)* offers another remarkable **view**★.

▸ *Go back to the crossroads. Further ahead turn right on D 4, then right again at Crançot on D 471, then right once more towards the Belvédère des Roches-de-Baume, also known as the Belvédère de Crançot.*

Belvédère des Roches-de-Baume★★★
Walk along the edge of the cliff which forms the famous viewpoint. At the last minute an astounding view of the entire amphitheatre unfolds though a gap in the rocks. *Near the viewpoint furthest to the right there are steps cut into the rock.* These steps, the **Échelles de Crançot,** lead down to the amphitheatre's floor and the caves.

▸ *Return to D 471 and follow it to Crançot then take D 4 back to Baume-les-Messiers.*

BEAUNE★★
POPULATION 21 923
MICHELIN MAP 320: I-7 – LOCAL MAP SEE LA CÔTE

Right at the heart of the Burgundian vineyards lies Beaune, a name synonymous with good wine; a visit to this ancient city, which boasts a splendid architectural heritage and some fine museums, is not complete without a tour of the vineyards of La Côte.

- **Information**: rue de l'Hôtel-Dieu, 21200 Beaune.
  ☎03 80 26 21 30. www.ot-beaune.fr.
- ▶ **Orient Yourself:** Traffic moves anticlockwise along the one-way boulevard *(peripherique)* encircling the historic centre. Restaurants, cafes and shops offering regional specialities cluster around place de la Halle, the city's heart.

A Bit of History

Birth of a town
First a Gaulish centre and then an outpost of Rome, Beaune was the seat of the dukes of Burgundy to the 14C. After the death of Charles the Bold, last Duke of Burgundy, in 1477, the town refused Louis XI's efforts to annex it and gave in only after a five-week siege.

Wine auction at the Hospices de Beaune
This is the main event of the year and draws a large crowd. The Hospices de Beaune (this name includes the Hôtel-Dieu, the Hospice de la Charité and the hospital) acquired a very fine vineyard (58ha/143 acres) between Aloxe-Corton and Meursault through Chancellor Rolin. The wines from this vineyard have won international acclaim. The proceeds of the auction sales, **Les Trois Glorieuses**, known as the "greatest charity sale in the world", go to the modernisation of the medical facilities and maintenance of the Hôtel-Dieu.

Town Walks

The town centre
Enter through Porte St-Nicolas, a triumphal arch erected during the reign of Louis XV. Among the many old houses, those at nos 18, 20, 22 and 24 **Rue de Lorraine** form a fine 16C ensemble.

Hôtel de la Rochepot★
Not open to the public. This 16C building has an admirable Gothic façade.
In place Monge is a 14C belfry and a statue of **Gaspard Monge** (1746-1818), a local shopkeeper's son who became a famous mathematician.
No 4 **place Carnot** is a 16C house with attractive sculptures.

Place de la Halle
The Hôtel-Dieu with its fine slate roof overlooks the square. Avenue de la République and rue d'Enfer lead to the former mansion of the dukes of Burgundy, dating from the 15C and 16C, now the museum of Burgundy wine.

Collégiale Notre-Dame★
The daughter house of Cluny, begun about 1120, was considerably influenced by the church of St-Lazare in Autun; it is a fine example of Burgundian Roma-

Wine auction in Beaune

S. Sauvignier-MICHELIN

Address Book

⚭For coin ranges, see the Legend on the cover flap.

WHERE TO STAY

⚬**Chambre d'Hôte Le Meix des Hospices** – *r. Basse (near the church), 71150 Demigny, 10km/6.2mi S of Beaune by D 18.* ☎*03 85 49 98 49. Closed 1st wk of Jul and last wk of Aug.* ⚯ *3 rooms.* This former hospice annexe consists of several outbuildings arranged around a courtyard. The quiet, simple rooms beneath the eaves are decorated with modern furniture. The dining room features exposed beams, a worn stone floor and a fireplace.

⚬**Hôtel le Parc** – *21200 Levernois, 5km/3.1mi SW of Beaune by rte de Verdun-sur-le-Doubs, D 970 then D 111L.* ☎*03 80 24 63 00. www.hotelleparc.fr. Closed 28 Nov-27 Jan. 25 rooms.* ⚬*8€.* Covered with Virginia creeper and bursting with flowers in summertime, this hotel is charming. The two buildings are separated by a patio. The park at the back looks out over fields.

⚬⚬**Hôtel Le Cep** – *27 r. Maufoux.* ☎*03 80 22 35 48. www.hotel-cep-beaune.com. 61 rooms.* ⚬*20€.* Ravishing 16C house in the old quarter. The bedrooms, decorated in old-fashioned style, carry the names of famous vintages from the Côte-d'Or. Breakfast is served in the vaulted cellar or, weather permitting, in the courtyard with its pretty Renaissance arcades and medallions.

⚬⚬⚬**Hostellerie du Château de Bellecroix** – *rte de Chalon, 71150 Chagny, 18km/11.2mi SW of Beaune by N 74 then N 6.* ☎*03 85 87 13 86. www.chateaubellecroix.com. Closed 1 Oct-31 May and Wed out of season. 20 rooms.* ⚬*18€. Restaurant*⚬⚬⚬⚬. The two towers of this 18C château stand amid wooded parkland. Nearby lie the turrets of a former 12C Knights Templar building belonging to the Order of Malta. The bedrooms are appointed with antique furniture. There are some fine replicas of medieval wainscoting in the dining hall.

WHERE TO EAT

⚬**Le Bouchon** – *pl. de l'Hôtel-de-Ville, 21900 Meursault, 8km/5mi SW of Beaune by N 74.* ☎*03 80 21 29 56. Closed 20 Nov-28 Dec Sun evenings and Mon.* A small, popular restaurant in the centre. Regional dishes are served in a simply decorated dining room with small but pretty square tables.

⚬⚬**Le Bénaton** – *25 r. du Fg-Bretonnière.* ☎*03 80 22 00 26. www.lebenaton.com. Closed 30 Nov-8 Dec, Wed and Thu except in high season.* Small tranquil restaurant with a covered terrace for warm days. Attractive quality/price ratio for delicious meals made with fresh seasonal produce.

⚬⚬**Le P'tit Paradis** – *25 r. Paradis.* ☎*03 80 24 91 00. Closed 8-16 Mar, 9-17 Aug, 21 Nov-14 Dec, Mon and Tue.* The dining room and terrace border a flower garden. Contemporary cuisine incorporates regional flourishes and wines are from boutique producers.

⚬⚬**Ma cuisine** – *passage Ste-Hélène.* ☎*03 80 22 30 22. cave-sainte-helene@ wanadoo.fr. Closed August, Christmas holidays, Wed, Sat and Sun.* Located along a tiny street, this small dining room sports the colours of Provence. Regional wines on the wine list.

⚬⚬**Le Caveau des Arches** – *10 bd. Perpreuil.* ☎*03 80 22 10 37. www.caveau-des-arches.com. Closed 24 Jul-25 Aug, 23 Dec-17 Jan Sun and Mon.* Savour fine classic Burgundy cooking in the cosy vaulted dining rooms of this restaurant on the ramparts.

SIT BACK AND RELAX

Bouché – *1 pl. Monge.* ☎*03 80 22 10 35. Open Tue-Sun 8am-8pm, Sun 8am-1pm and 3-8pm.* Step inside this pretty tearoom and you'll find lovely gift boxes ready to fill with tantalizing house specialities, among them chocolate "snails", candied chestnuts and candied fruits. At table, you'll have to chose between *tarte vigneronne, millefeuille,* or any of the 20 or so specially created sweets.'

Palais des gourmets – *14 pl. Carnot.* ☎*03 80 22 13 39. Open daily 7am-7.30pm (7pm Oct-Apr and closed Tue).* This delightful patisserie-tea room serves many local delicacies, including cassissines (black-currant jelly flavoured with black-currant liqueur), *roulés au cointreau* (pancakes with Cointreau

Cordeliers wine cellar

B. Kaufmann/MICHELIN

filling) and chocolate medallions depicting the Hôtel-Dieu.

ON THE TOWN

Le Bistrot Bourguignon – *8 r. Monge.* ☎*03 80 22 23 24. www.restaurant-lebistrotbourguignon.com. Open Tue-Sat 11am-3pm, 6-11pm. Closed mid-Feb to mid-Mar.* Relax on the terrace or sink into one of the comfortable armchairs inside this old house as you sip a glass of wine to the mellow strains of classic jazz music.

WINELOVERS' PARADISE

L'Athenaeum de la Vigne et du Vin – *5 r. de l'Hôtel-Dieu.* ☎*03 80 25 08 30. www.athenaeumfr.com. Open daily 10am-7pm. Closed 25 Dec and 1 Jan.* This bookshop has earned a reputation as the best on the art of oenology, Burgundy and gastronomy. They stock various wine-related items from corkscrews to cellarman's knives.

Cave Patriarche Père & Fils – *5-7 r. du Collège.* ☎*03 80 24 53 79. www.patriarche.com. Open daily 9.30-11.30am, 2-5.30pm (Nov-Mar Sa-Su 5pm). Closed 24, 25, 31 Dec and 1 Jan.* Burgundy's largest cellars (15 000m2/18 000sq yd) are housed in a former convent dating from the 14C and 16C. Guided tours and tasting sessions of 13 different wines.

Caves de La Reine Pédauque – *Porte St-Nicolas.* ☎*03 80 22 23 11. www.reine-pedauque.com. Open end of Nov to Mar daily 10am-noon, 2-5pm; Apr-Nov daily 9.30am-12.30pm, 2-7pm. Closed*

Christmas and Jan. After exploring the 18C vaulted cellars, visitors may take part in a wine tasting session around an imposing round marble table.

La Cave des Cordeliers – *6 r. de l'Hôtel-Dieu.* ☎*03 80 25 08 85. Open daily Oct-Apr 10.30-11.30am, 2-5.30pm; May-Sep 9.30am-noon, 2-6pm. Closed 25 Dec and 1 Jan.* The Couvent des Cordeliers, built in 1242, provides a splendid backdrop to these wine cellars, which you can visit before tasting six fine wines.

Le Comptoir Viticole – *1 r. Samuel Legay.* ☎*03 80 22 15 73. www.comptoirviticole.com. Open daily 8am-noon (9am Mon), 2-7pm. Closed Sun and public holidays.* Wine buffs and amateur vignerons will adore this shop, which sells all manner of devices related to winemaking.

Marché aux Vins – *2 r. Nicolas Rolin.* ☎*03 80 25 08 20. www.marcheauxvins.com. Open Jul-Aug daily 9.30am-5.45pm, rest of the year daily 9.30-11.45am, 2-5.45pm. Closed 25 Dec and 1 Jan.* Housed in Beaune's oldest church (13C and 14C) opposite the famous hospice, this wine market offers 18 wines of between 3 and 15 years of age.

Vins de Bourgogne Denis-Perret – *40 r. Carnot.* ☎*03 80 22 35 47. www.denisperret.fr. Open May-Oct Mon-Sat 9am-7pm, Sun 9am-noon; rest of the year Mon-Sat 9am-noon, 2-7pm. Closed public holiday afternoons and Sun out of season.* Five wine-growers and a group of landowners have teamed up to offer you some of the most prestigious names from the Burgundy region.

nesque art despite successive additions.

Exterior – The façade is concealed by a wide 14C porch with three naves. The sculpted decoration was destroyed during the Revolution, but the 15C carved door panels have survived.

Walk clockwise round the church to get the best view of the chevet. Three different phases of construction – the pure Romanesque of the ambulatory and apsidal chapels, the 13C refurbishment of the chancel and the 14C flying buttresses – can be detected in the handsome proportions of the whole. The crossing tower, which is formed of Romanesque arcades surmounted by pointed bays, is capped by a dome and a 16C lantern.

Interior – The lofty nave of broken-barrel vaulting is flanked by narrow aisles with groined vaulting. A triforium, composed of open and blind bays, goes round the building, which is strongly reminiscent of Autun with its decoration of arcades and small fluted columns.

Besides the decoration of the small columns in the transept, it is worth noting the sculptures on certain capitals in the nave representing Noah's Ark, the Stoning of St Stephen and a Tree of Jesse and the Renaissance chapel with the fine coffered ceiling off the south aisle.

Tapestries★★ – In the choir behind the high altar are some magnificent tapestries which mark the transition from medieval to Renaissance art. Five richly coloured panels, worked in wool and silk, trace the whole life of the Virgin Mary in a series of charming scenes. They were commissioned in 1474 and offered to the church in 1500 by Canon Hugues le Coq.

▷ *Go back to the Hôtel-Dieu.*

At no 2 **rue E.-Fraysse**, the Maison du Colombier is a Renaissance house which can be seen from the square in front of the church of Notre-Dame; no 13 **place Fleury** is the Hôtel Saulx, a mansion with a quaint tower and an interior courtyard. The Maison des Vins (tastings) is on rue Rolin, beyond the Hôtel-Dieu.

▷ *Continue to place Carnot and place Ziem, opposite the Chapelle St-Éti-enne; rue de l'Enfant and rue des Tonneliers lead to place du Dr-Jorrot.*

At no 10 **rue Rousseau-Deslandes** there is a house with its first floor decorated with trefoiled arcades.

▷ *Rue Favart and rue Belin lead to the town hall.*

Hôtel de ville

The town hall is in a 17C former Ursuline convent. The right wing houses two **museums** (see Additional Sights).

The Ramparts★

The relatively well-preserved ramparts form an almost continuous wall walk (2km/1mi). They were built between the end of the 15C and the middle of the 16C, and are adorned with a few surviving towers and eight rustic bastions of various shapes – the double one, originally a castle, is known as the **Bastion St-Jean**. The encircling moat is now occupied by gardens, tennis courts etc.

Tour of the ramparts

▷ *From the Bastion St-Jean follow the outer boulevards, beginning with boulevard Joffre, counter-clockwise.*

The north tower of the Bastion St-Jean has gargoyles and a niche occupied by a Virgin and Child. Pass the Blondeau Tower to get to the **Bastion Notre-Dame,** with a charming turret covering the spur. The line of the ramparts is broken by the 18C Porte St-Nicolas at the end of rue Lorraine. Next come the Bastion des Filles, spoilt by the addition of an ugly new roof, and the now filled-in Bastion St-Martin forming a triangular terrace **(square des Lions)** overlooking a shaded garden.

The route now takes you past the Bastion des Dames, the **Rempart des Dames** and the now-abandoned Bastion de l'Hôtel-Dieu. The 15C Grosse Tour on the Rempart Madeleine is followed by the Bastion Ste-Anne with a turret overlooking the moat. The tour ends in front of the castle's **south tower**.

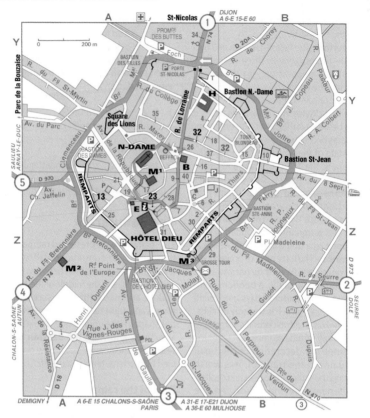

BEAUNE						
Alsace R. d'	AZ	2	Dr-Jorrot Pl. du	BY	15	Monge R. ....AZ 28
Belin R.	AZ	4	Enfant R. de l'	AY	16	Perpreuil Bd ....AZ 29
Bourgelat R.	AZ	5	Enfert R. d'	AZ	17	Poterne R. ....AZ 30
Carnot Petite-Pl.	AZ	6	Favart R.	AY	18	Rolin R. ....AZ 31
Carnot Pl.	AZ	7	Fleury Pl.	AZ	19	Rousseau-Deslandes R. ......BY 32
Carnot R.	AZ	9	Fraysse R. E.	AZ	21	St-Nicolas R. du Fg ....AY 34
Château R. du	BY	10	Halle Pl. de la	AZ	23	Ste-Marguerite R. ....AY 35
Dames Rempart des	AZ	13	Lorraine R. de	AY		Tonneliers R. des ....AY 37
			Maufoux R.	AZ	25	Ziem Pl. ....AZ 40
			Monge Pl.	AY	26	

Hôtel de Saulx	AZ E	Moutarderie Fallot	AZ M2
Hôtel de Ville (musée Étienne-Jules Marey)	AY H	Musée du Vin de Bourgogne	AZ M3
Hôtel de la Rochepot	AY B	Tour des Billes (musée des Beaux-Arts)	AZ M3

Hôtel-dieu★★★

 ♿ ⏰ *Open year round 9-11.30am, 2-5.30pm.* 👁5.60€. ☎*03 80 24 45 00. www.hospices-de-beaune.tm.fr.*
The Hôtel-Dieu in Beaune, a marvel of Burgundian-Flemish art, was founded as a hospital by Chancellor Nicolas Rolin in 1443. The building with its medieval decor has survived intact and was used as a general hospital until 1971. Today it is a very successful tourist attraction.

Exterior
Street façade – The main decorative elements of this sober façade with its tall and steeply pitched slate roof are the dormer windows, the weather vanes, the delicate pinnacles and lacework cresting of lead. The roof line is broken by the bell turret surmounted by a slim Gothic spire 30m/98ft high.
The delicate roof above the porch is composed of three slate gables terminating in worked pinnacles. Each weather vane

Ph. Gajic-MICHELIN

The Grand'Salle, Hôtel-Dieu

bears a different coat of arms. On the panelled door, note the ironwork grille and the door knocker, a magnificent piece of sculpted wrought-iron work.

Courtyard – The wings to the left and rear have magnificent roofs of coloured glazed tiles (recently restored) in geometric patterns. These roofs are punctuated by turrets and a double row of dormer windows, surmounted by weather vanes adorned with heraldic bearings and small spires of worked lead.

Interior
Grand'Salle or Chambre des Pauvres

★★★ – This immense hall (72m/236ft long, 14m/46ft wide, 16m/52ft high), used as the poor ward, has a magnificent timber roof in the shape of an upturned keel which is painted throughout; the ends of the tie-beams disappear into the gaping mouths of monsters' heads.

In earlier times on feast days the 28 four-poster beds were covered with fine tapestry bedspreads, now displayed in the Salle du Polyptyque. Even without the tapestries, the double row of beds with their red and white bedclothes, hangings and testers makes a striking impression. At the end of the room stands an arresting, larger than life-size polychrome wooden statue (15C) of **Christ seated and bound**★ carved from a single piece of oak.

The Flamboyant style screen separating the Grand'Salle from the chapel was reconstructed in the 19C together with the large stained-glass window. The chapel exhibits a copper funerary plaque in memory of Guigone de Salins, wife of Nicolas Rolin and co-founder of the Hôtel-Dieu. The Clermont-Tonnerre collection of sacred art is displayed in showcases.

Salle Ste-Anne – The linen room, visible through the windows, was originally a small bedroom reserved for the nobility. The work of the nursing nuns is illustrated by life-size models dressed in the habits worn by the staff until 1961.

Salle St-Hugues – This ward, taken out of use in 1982, has been partly refurbished with its 17C decor; the beds are those in use from the end of the 19C. The frescoes, by Isaac Moillon, depict St Hugues, as bishop and Carthusian monk, and the nine miracles of Christ.

Salle St-Nicolas – This ward now houses a permanent exhibition on the history of the Hôtel-Dieu and the healing of the body and mind which it offered to the poor and sick. A glass slab in the centre reveals the Bouzaise stream which flows beneath the hospital and which carried away the waste.

Cuisine – *Son et lumière presentation every 15min*. In the kitchen, an old-fashioned scene has been set up round the huge Gothic fireplace with its double hearth and automatic spit, which dates from 1698.

Pharmacie – The first room of the pharmacy contains pewter vessels displayed on a handsome 18C dresser; the second, which is panelled, contains a collection of 18C Nevers porcelain and a huge bronze mortar.

Salle St-Louis – The walls are hung with early-16C tapestries from Tournai depicting the parable of the Prodigal Son and a 16C series illustrating Jacob's story.

Salle du Polyptyque – This room was designed to exhibit the famous **polyptych of the Last Judgement**★★★ by Roger van der Weyden. This masterpiece of Flemish art, commissioned by Nicolas Rolin to grace the altar in the Grand'Salle and completed between 1445 and 1448, was extensively restored in the 19C and sawn in two so that both faces could be displayed simultaneously. A mobile magnifying glass enables viewers to study the smallest detail on the highly expressive faces of the subjects.

In the central panel Christ presides at the Last Judgement; he is enthroned on a rainbow surrounded by golden clouds suggestive of Paradise; four angels carrying the instruments of the Passion stand at his sides in the flanking panels. St Michael is weighing the souls, with angels sounding their trumpets on either side of him. In attendance on the central figures are the Virgin Mary and St John the Baptist appealing to the Saviour for mercy. Behind them are the Apostles and a few important people (including the donors) who are interceding on behalf of humankind.

The reverse side of the polyptych is on the wall to the right. In the past, only this face was usually visible, as the polyptych was opened only on Sundays and feast days. The fine portraits of Nicolas Rolin and his wife are accompanied by monochromes of St Sebastian and St Anthony, the first patrons of the Hôtel-Dieu, and the Annunciation. On the wall to the left hangs a beautiful early-16C *mille-fleurs* tapestry depicting the legend of St Eligius. The tapestries hanging opposite the Last Judgment belonged to Guigone de Salins; against the deep rose-coloured background, scattered with turtle doves, are the arms of the founder of the hospital, an interlaced G and N and the motto Seulle (you alone) expressing Nicolas Rolin's faithful attachment to his wife. In the centre is St Anthony the hermit, patron saint of Guigone de Salins.

Additional Sights

Musée du Vin de Bourgogne (Burgundy Wine Museum)★

🕐*Open Apr-Nov daily 9.30am-6pm; Dec-Mar daily except Tue 9.30am-5pm.* 🕐*Closed 1 Jan and 25 Dec.* ⊙*5.40€.* ☎*03 80 22 08 19.*

The museum is in the former mansion of the dukes of Burgundy, dating mainly from the 15C and 16C. The history of Burgundian vineyards and vine cultivation is explained in a comprehensive exhibit on the ground floor. Note the 16C polychrome statue known as the *Virgin Mary with a Bunch of Grapes* or *Notre-Dame de Beaune*. The large first-floor room decorated with two huge Aubusson tapestries is the headquarters of the Ambassade des Vins de France.

Driving Tour

The vineyards of La Côte★★

⚲*Beaune can be the starting point of the itineraries suggested under La Côte.*

Excursion

Château de Savigny-lès-Beaune★
5km/2mi NW.

🕐*Open Apr-Oct daily 9am-6.30pm. Rest of the year 9am-noon, 2-5.30pm.* ⊙*8€.* ☎*03 80 21 55 03. chateau-savigny.com.*

This village, known for its quality wines, has a 14C castle with some interesting collections on display. The smaller 17C château is now home to a wine-tasting and sales room and an exhibit of **Arbath endurance cars**. Visitors to the park will see 60 **jet fighter planes**, including Mirages (I to V), MIG 21 US (1962), Sikorsky helicopters and more.

The château was built by Jean de Frolois, Maréchal de Bourgogne, and restored by the Bouhier family in the 17C. The interior was restored more recently, with a view to accommodating receptions and conferences. An upper floor has been set aside for the **motorcycle collection**★, including over 500 models from around the world, which gives an overview of changes in mechanics and design over the 20C.

BELFORT ★

POPULATION 50 417
MICHELIN MAP 314: J-7

Belfort is in a strategic position on the River Savoureuse and by the 30km/19mi Belfort Gap, which provides a natural passage between the two great valleys of the Rhine and the Rhône. Its main attraction is the imposing citadel built by Vauban on the east bank of the Savoureuse.

▪ **Information**: 2 bis r. Clemenceau, 90000 Belfort.
☎03 84 55 90 90. www.ot-belfort.fr.
▸ **Orient Yourself:** Treat yourself to an intriguing view of Belfort and its citadel by arriving via the Porte de Brisache. The historic town, boutiques, restaurants and cafes are east of the river, between it and the citadel.

A Bit of History

An invasion route

The Belfort Gap has drawn successive waves of invaders: Celts, Germanic tribes and soldiers of the Holy Roman Empire among them. The French finally conquered it in 1638, and Louis XIV ordered Vauban to make Belfort impregnable. The resulting fortified town is the great military engineer's masterpiece.

The battles continue

During the 1870 Franco-Prussian War, 40 000 German troops besieged the town for several months without success. The town saw more action in November 1944, as the French army advanced towards the Rhine. Belfort was finally liberated from the Germans on 22 November after fierce street fighting.

BELFORT

Ancêtres Fg des	Y	3
Armes Pl. d'	Y	5
As-de-Carreau R. de l'	Z	6
Bourgeois Pl. des	Y	12
Carnot Bd	Z	15
Clemenceau R. G.	Y	20
Denfert-Rochereau R.	Z	21
Dr-Corbis Pl. du	Z	23
Dr-Fréry R. du	Y	24
Dreyfus-Schmidt R.	Y	25
Espérance Av. de l'	Z	28
Foch Av. Mar.	Z	29
France Fg de	Z	30
Gaulard R. du Gén	Z	31
Grande-Fontaine Pl. de la	Z	32
Grande-Fontaine R.	Y	33
Grand'Rue	Y	34
Joffre Bd du Mar.	VY	37
Lebleu R. F.	Z	40
Magasin Q. du	Y	43
Metz-Juteau R.	Y	45
Mulhouse R. de	Y	46
Pompidou R.	Y	48
République Pl. de la	Y	49
République R. de la	Z	50
Roussel R. du Gén.	Y	51
Sarrail Av. du Gén	Z	52
Vauban Q.	Y	60

Cathédrale St- Christophe	Y	B	Monument des Trois Sièges	Y	E
Donation Maurice Jardot	Y	M¹	Musée d'Art et d' Histoire	Z	M²
Fresque	Z	F	Statue " Quand même "	Y	D
Hôtel de ville	Z	H			

135

Old Town Tour★

The old town has been undergoing restoration since 1986, and the colourful façades of the houses, with pale stone decoration around the windows, lend a friendlier atmosphere to the streets and squares of the once austere garrison town. Particularly charming examples are to be found in place de l'Arsenal, place de la Grande-Fontaine, Grande Rue and place de la Petite-Fontaine.

▶ *Park the car in place de la République and walk along rue de la Porte-de-France to place d'Armes. Across the square stands the austere-looking cathedral.*

Cathédrale St-Christophe

The church, built of red sandstone, has an 18C Classical façade. A frieze of angels' heads in relief runs all around the nave. The beautiful **gilded wrought-iron grille** enclosing the choir is similar to the railings by Jean Lamour in place Stanislas in Nancy. Note in the transept paintings by the Belfort painter G Dauphin; an *En-tombment of Christ (on the right)* and *The Ecstacy of St François-Xavier (on the left)*. The 18C **organ**★, by Valtrin, has a beautifully carved and gilded wooden case.

▶ *Walk round the north side of the cathedral along rue de l'Église. Turn left onto rue du Général-Roussel which leads to the foot of the ramparts and turn right onto rue des Bons-Enfants to the Porte de Brisach.*

Porte de Brisach★

This gateway, constructed by Vauban in 1687, has been preserved in its original style. It features a pilastered façade decorated with the Bourbon coat of arms and, on the pediment, those of Louis XIV: the sun surmounted by the famous motto *Nec pluribus impar.*

▶ *Rue de la Grande-Fontaine, opposite the gate, leads to place de la Grande-Fontaine.*

Place de la Grande-Fontaine

The square owes its name to the successive fountains which have decorated it; the latest dates from 1860.

▶ *Turn right towards place de l'Arsenal and place d'Armes.*

Hôtel de Ville

🕐 *Open Mon-Fri 8.30am-6pm, Sat 8.30am-noon.* ☎*03 84 54 24 24. www.mairie-belfort.fr.*
The town hall was built in the Classical style. The beautiful Salle Kléber on the ground floor is a good example of late-18C French art (Rococo style). There are paintings of Belfort's history in the main hall *(Salle d'honneur)* on the first floor.

▶ *Rue des Nouvelles leads to place de la République with its large central monument.*

Porte de Brisach

G. Magnin-MICHELIN

Address Book

For coin ranges, see the Legend on the cover flap.

WHERE TO STAY

Hôtel Vauban – *4 r. du Magasin. ☎03 84 21 59 37. www.hotel-vauban. com. Closed Feb school holidays, 25 Dec-2 Jan and Sun. 14 rooms. ⌂8.50€. The* carefully kept rooms in this peaceful small hotel are hung with pictures painted by the owner. Relax in the pretty garden by the Savoureuse.

Hôtel Les Capucins – *20 fg de Montbéliard. ☎03 84 28 04 60. hotel-des-capucins@wanadoo.fr. Closed 21 Dec-5 Jan. ⌂7€. Restaurant.* This handsome building near the banks of the Savoureuse and the pedestrian district exudes considerable charm. The comfortable rooms are appointed with modern furniture; the best are the newly renovated ones at the back. For meals, two formulas are available: a restaurant and a brasserie.

Grand Hôtel du Tonneau d'Or – *1 r. Reiset. ☎03 84 58 57 56. www. tonneaudor.fr. 52 rooms. ⌂11€. Restaurant.* In the heart of the old quarter, this imposing turn-of-the-century house has been extensively restored and now boasts lofty ceilings, columns and fine stuccowork. Spacious rooms furnished in the 1900 style. The ambience in the restaurant is reminiscent of a Parisian brasserie. Piano-bar.

WHERE TO EAT

Auberge du Lac – *27 r. du Lac, 90350 Evette-Salbert, 3km/1.9mi N of Belfort by D 24. ☎03 84 29 14 10. Closed 2 Jan-15 Feb, 15-30 Oct, Tue lunchtime and Mon.* This former ice house on the shores of Malsaucy Lake, opposite the venue chosen for the Eurockéennes Festival, specialises in fried fish.

Le Molière – *6 r. de l'Étuve. ☎03 84 21 86 38. Closed 8-20 Feb, 25 Aug-13 Sep, Tue and Wed.* Located in a renovated area of the old town, this restaurant has a wide choice of menus. Meals are served in the cosy dining room or on the terrace, depending on the weather.

La Fontaine des Saveurs – *1 pl. de la Grande-Fontaine. ☎03 84 22 45 38. Closed 16 Aug-7 Sep, Monday out of* season and Wed. Myriad flavours await you at this restaurant. The menu changes with the seasons and there's a large selection of wines by the glass.

Le Pot au Feu – *27 bis Grande Rue. ☎03 84 28 57 84. Closed 1-12 Jan, 1-18 Aug, Sat lunchtime, Mon lunchtime and Sun. .* The cosy dining room of this small restaurant in the old town has stone vaulting and neat checked tablecloths. Sample tasty regional cuisine in an easy-going, laid-back atmosphere.

SIT BACK AND RELAX

Le Piano-Bar – *23 fg de France. ☎03 84 28 93 35. Open Mon-Sat 8.30pm-1am.* This undoubtedly the trendiest bar in town. Customers of all ages flock to this vaulted cellar in the town centre. The thematic evenings are especially popular; they include karaoke on Thursday and jazz-blues on Friday and Saturday.

SHOPPING

Marché aux Puces – *Mar-Dec 1st Sun of the month.* Don't miss the local monthly flea market in the historic centre.

Michel Perello – *4 r. Porte de France. ☎03 84 28 04 33. Open Mon-Sat 8am-12.30pm, 2.30-7.30pm. Closed 15 Aug-15 Sep.* A native of the Balearic Islands settled here in 1938 and bought one of the oldest stores in France, dating from 1825... It has remained in the family ever since, selling fine foodie produce from Spain, Italy and Algeria: rice, semolina, beans, 100 brands of tea and coffee, and an outstanding list of wines and liqueurs.

Klein – *19 av. Wilson. ☎03 84 28 06 91. Open Tue-Sun 8am-7pm.* Every resident of Belfort is acquainted with the culinary delights from the Maison Klein. Chocolates, caramels, cakes and pastries tempt all who enter; don't miss the locally prized *gâteau du Lion*.

Boucherie-Charculterie de la Roseraie – *2 bis r. Roger-Salengro. ☎03 84 21 27 52. Open Tue-Sat 9am-12.30pm and 4-7pm. Closed Aug.* The reputation of this fine butcher shop extends for miles around. It's the place to sample the *Épaule du Ballon*, a local specialty blending lamb and pork flavoured with bilberries.

G. Magnin-MICHELIN

The Belfort Lion

Monument des Trois Sièges

This work by Bartholdi shows France and the city of Belfort with three defenders (Legrand in 1814, Lecourbe in 1815 and Denfert-Rochereau in 1870).

The Belfort Lion★★

The great beast (22m/72ft long and 11m/36ft high) carved from red Vosges sandstone symbolises the spirit and strength of Belfort's defenders in 1870. It is the work of **Frédéric Bartholdi**, who here gave free rein to his patriotic fervour and creativity.

A path leads from the **viewing platform** (◔*open Jun-Sep 9am-7pm; Apr-May*

10am-noon, 2-7pm; Oct-Mar 10am-noon, 2-5pm; ◔*closed 1 Jan, 1 Nov, 25 Dec;* ✆*0.90€;* ✆*03 84 55 90 30)* at the base of the Lion to the memorial. The Lion is even more awe-inspiring when it is floodlit at night.

The Citadel★★

A Key Position

Vauban began his masterwork in 1687, surrounding the existing fortress and town with several pentagonal fortified walls anchored to the rocky cliff on which the buildings stood. The work took about 20 years, but the fortifications would play their part in the town's history for several centuries to follow.

Fortifications

◔*Open daily year round. Apr-Sep to 6.30pm, Oct-Mar to 5pm.*

The terrace of the fort

This public terrace is at the top of the barracks which houses the museum of art and history. It is an excellent view point, from which you will be able to place the fortress in its geographical context and gain a better understanding of its comprehensive system of defence.

The **panorama**★★ reveals to the south the Jura mountain chain on the horizon; to the west the old town and the Fort du Salbert; to the north the southern Vosges with the peaks of the Ballon de Servance,

Frédéric Auguste Bartholdi (1834-1904)

This sculptor was born in Colmar and showed his artistic prowess from an early age. He won a competition held by his home town in 1856 to find someone to execute a memorial statue of General Rapp. His travels in Egypt and the Far East affected his later work. After the Franco-Prussian war in 1870, he sculpted a large number of patriotic monuments, the most famous of which are the Belfort Lion and the statue of Liberty Lighting the World at the entrance to New York harbour.

the Ballon d'Alsace, the Baerenkopf and the Rossberg; to the east the fortress' curtain walls and the Belfort Gap.

You can make out the outline of the **Grand Sousterrain**, a covered moat from the reign of Louis XV, which was used to provide shelter during attacks, and further to the east the moat known as the **Grand Couronné**, with its bastions, and the moat round the intermediate curtain wall (3rd moat) and that round the outer curtain wall (4th moat).

At the foot of the barracks to the east, the **cour d'honneur** (main courtyard) is surrounded by the Haxo casemates, which have been converted into art galleries. One of them houses the 1 000-year-old **well** which reaches a depth of 67m/220ft.

The curtain walls (enceintes)

1hr. 🚶*Follow the path at the foot of the fortress through the tunnel beneath the Lion and carry on along it until you get to the 4th moat.*

Note the impressive proportions of the moats and the **glacis**, a vast area of bare land which slopes gently away. Walking along the 4th or 3rd moats is a good way to see the defences in detail. The walk ends at the Tour des Bourgeois, the old tower from the medieval curtain wall demolished by Vauban.

Musée d'Art et d'Histoire

🕐*Open Apr-Sep daily 10am-6pm. Rest of the year daily except Tue 10am-noon, 2-5pm.* 🕐*Closed 1 Jan, 1 Nov, 25 Dec.* 👁*2.85€, no charge under 18 and 2nd Sunday in the month.* ☎*03 84 54 25 51.*

The varied exhibits include items from the Neolithic, Gallo-Roman and Merovingian periods, a reproduction of Vauban's relief model of his fortifications in 1687 and numerous military artefacts. A separate wing contains a collection of paintings, engravings, sculptures and photographs.

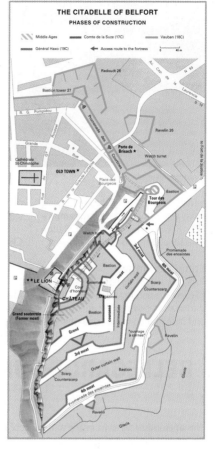

THE CITADELLE OF BELFORT
PHASES OF CONSTRUCTION

Middle Ages — Comte de la Suze (17C) — Vauban (18C)
Général Haxo (19C) — Access route to the fortress

Additional Sight

Donation Maurice Jardot★

♿🕐*Open Apr-Sep daily except Tue 10am-noon, 2-6pm. Rest of the year daily except Tue 10am-noon, 2-5pm.* 🕐*Closed 1 Jan, 25 Dec.* 👁*3.95€.* ☎*03 84 90 40 70.*

In 1997, Maurice Jardot bequeathed 110 paintings by modern artists to the city. The exceptionally fine collection includes little-known works by Picasso, Braque and, above all, Léger.

Excursions

Fort du Salbert

8km/5mi NW on D 4.

A winding forest road leads to the fort, at an altitude of 647m/2 123ft. The vast

A venerable forge

terrace *(200m/220yd to the left – viewing table)* gives a marvellous **panorama**★★ over Belfort, the Swiss Alps, Ballon d'Alsace and surrounding mountains.

Étang des Forges
Park near the sailing base.
There is a nature trail round the lake. Information boards describe the flora and fauna found in this area (the little bittern, the smallest heron in Europe, the crested grebe and the coot).

Etueffont: Forge-Musée
15km/9.3mi NE. Leave Belfort on N 83; after 10km/6.2mi, turn left on D 12.
Open Palm Sunday to All Saints. Guided tours (1hr30min) daily except Tue 2-6pm. 4€ (under 13 free). 03 84 54 60 41. forgemusee.etueffont.free.fr/.
This small museum offers a glimpse at the way of life of four generations of blacksmiths from 1844 and 1975.

Chapelle de Ronchamp★★
22km/13.7mi NW.
See RONCHAMP.

Massif du Ballon d'Alsace★★★
28km/17.4mi N.
See Massif du BALLON D'ALSACE.

BELLEGARDE-SUR-VALSERINE
POPULATION 10 846
MICHELIN MAP 328: H-4

This small industrial town, on the confluence of a gushing mountain stream with the Rhône, is at the heart of a region that offers visitors a wealth of fine excursions.

Information: 24 pl. Victor Bérard, 01202 Bellegarde-Sur-Valserine. 04 50 48 48 68. www.ot-bellegarde01.fr.

Orient Yourself: To the north lies the scenic Valserine Valley, best explored from south to north in the afternoon. There are more areas to explore by car to the south and south-west.

Excursions

The River Valserine is 50km/31mi long and drops 1 000m/3 280ft from its source to its junction with the Rhône at Bellegarde-sur-Valserine. This mountain stream runs through a charming valley known as Valmijoux bounded on both sides by mountain ranges with two high peaks almost facing each other. The **Crêt de la Neige** (1 717m/5 633ft), the highest summit of the Jura mountains, is so called because it retains a few patches of snow on its north face all year. Its 'twin' on the other side of the valley is the **Crêt de Chalam** (1 545m/4 069ft).

Berges de la Valserine★
From the town centre (tourist office), follow N 84 towards Lyon. Park just behind the railway viaduct (rue Louis-Dumont).
The Valserine skirts the town but, because of its steep banks, it was difficult to reach in the past. A path from the viaduct now enables visitors to walk all the way to the Pertes de la Valserine *(allow 2hr there and back)*.

Pertes de la Valserine★

N out of Bellegarde along N 84, pass beneath the railway line and continue for 2km/1.2mi. There is parking on the right-hand side of the road.

🚶Follow the steep path *(45min there and back)* running down through the woods *(many steps)*. It leads to a spot where the Valserine disappears from view amid a setting of rocky crevices and great cauldrons *(oulles)* scoured out in the rocks by the river. The waterfall is a little further upstream.

Driving Tours

Défilé de l'Écluse★

32km/20mi round tour. Leave Bellegarde E along N 206.

This picturesque transverse valley separates the Grand Crêt d'Eau and Montagne de Vuache ranges. The river, the N 206 Franco-Swiss highway and the scenic D 908A all run through the valley.

▶ *Beyond Longeray, just before the entrance to the tunnel, turn right towards Fort de l'Écluse.*

Fort l'Écluse★

🕐Open mid-Jun to mid-Sep daily 2-7pm (Sun from 1pm). ⎕4.50€. ☎04 50 56 73 63. www.fortlecluse.fr.
This remarkable fort was built high above the Rhône between 1820 and 1840. Owing to its strategic position, it was bitterly fought over in 1944. It is a hard climb *(800 steps, 1hr there and back)* to the top, but the view is worth it.

▶ *Go through the tunnel and continue along N 206 to the right; in Chevrier, turn right onto D 908A and return to Bellegarde via N 508.*

Haut-Bugey

136km/85mi round tour – allow 6hr. Drive South out of Bellegarde along N 508; turn right onto D 168 towards St-Germain-sur-Rhône. The road soon runs onto D 214 to the Génissiat dam.

Barrage de Génissiat★

This imposing gravity dam, started in 1937, is the area's most important hydro-electric plant.

▶ *D 72 leads to D 991; turn left.*

Seyssel

👝 *See GRAND COLOMBIER.*

▶ *Follow D 991 towards Ruffieux.*

South of Seyssel, the Rhône, joined by the Fier, spreads out and wanders through a stony marsh dotted with islets, known as the Marais de Chautagne.

▶ *As you reach Ruffieux, turn right onto D 904 which runs through marshland, crosses the Rhône and heads for Culoz.*

The river used to cut its way across the Jura mountains from east to west via a series of transverse valleys, a route now used by the Culoz-Ambérieu road, but today it continues south to Yenne.

▶ *From Culoz, climb up to the Grand Colombier.*

Grand Colombier★★★
See GRAND COLOMBIER.

▶ *A steep narrow road leads to Virieu-le-Petit on the west side of the Montagne du Grand Colombier. From Assin, just south of Virieu, D 69 leads to Don. From there take D 31 then a surfaced track on the left above the Cerveyrieu waterfall.*

Cascade de Cerveyrieu★
Impressive drop by the River Séran forming a picturesque waterfall.

▶ *Return to D 31 and turn right onto D 30B.*

Vieu
The village is on the site of the Roman capital of the Valromey region. Brillat-

Savarin (*see BELLEY*) had a country residence here.

Champagne-en-Valromey
This is now the main town of the area; it has a few old houses and hosts a festival of traditional crafts in summer.

▶ *Drive towards Lochieu (D 69F).*

Musée Rural du Valromey
Open Jun-Aug Wed-Sun 11am-7pm; Apr-May and Sep-Oct Thu-Sat 2-6pm, Sun and public holidays 10am-6pm. ⌾4€. ☎04 79 87 52 23.
Housed in a Renaissance building (1501), this local museum celebrates daily life in the valley with everthing from clothes to religious objects.

▶ *Return to D 31 and drive N towards Ruffieu then follow D 9 and D 30 to the Col de Richemont.*

Col de Richemont★
There is a **view** from the pass (alt 1 036m/3 399ft) of the Michaille region, an undulating landscape stretching at the foot of the mountain as far as the Rhône, whose course is blocked by the dams at Seyssel and Génissiat; of the Grand Crêt d'Eau mountain range (1 534m/5 062ft); the Défilé de l'Écluse, through which the Rhône flows into the Jura; and, in clear weather, the Mont Blanc mountain range.

▶ *Go back to Ruffieux, turn right and drive N via the Petit and Grand Abergement, along D 39 then D 55 and D 101 to the Retord plateau.*

Plateau de Retord
From the panorama at Le Catray, there is a view of the Alps with Mont Blanc to the south-east, the Valserine Valley, the Défilé de l'Écluse and the Lac du Bourget.

▶ *Return to Bellegarde via D 101.*

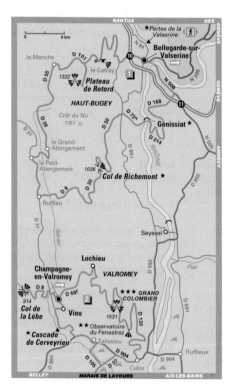

BELLEY

POPULATION 8 004

MICHELIN MAP 328: H-6

This peaceful town lies in a little valley watered by the Furan in the heart of the beautiful Bugey region. One of Belley's claims to fame is being birthplace of France's great epicure Jean-Anthelme Brillat-Savarin.

- **Information**: 34 Grande Rue, 01300 Belley.
  ☎04 79 81 29 06. www.cc-belley-bas-bugey.com.
- ▶ **Orient Yourself**: Belley is an appealing base from which to explore the surrounding attractions of the scenic Bas Bugey.

A Bit of History

The Physiology of Taste

When **Jean-Anthelme Brillat-Savarin** was born in Belley in 1755, at 62 Grande Rue (*courtyard open to the public*), he was already destined be a lawyer like his father. In 1789, he was elected deputy of the States General, but five years later he was forced to flee, first to Switzerland, then to the United States. He returned to France in 1796. In his free time he wrote, initially legal or political works, then the little masterpiece which earned him his fame: *The Physiology of Taste*. In 30 essays he examines the various aspects of and issues associated with good living and good food; philosophical principles appear side by side with reflections on gluttony, sleep and dreams.

Address Book

For coin ranges, see the Legend on the cover flap.

WHERE TO STAY

◎**Chambre d'Hôte Les Charmettes** – *La Vellaz, St-Martin-de-Bavel, 01510 Virieu-le-Grand, 11km/6.8mi N of Belley by N 504 until you reach Chazey-Bons, then D 31C.* ☎04 79 87 32 18. ⌓ *3 rooms.* This charming Bugey farmhouse has converted its stables into pretty, comfortable bedrooms, one of which has been specially equipped for the handicapped. Cooking facilities are available for guests.

◎◎**Chambre d'Hôte Ferme des Grands Hutains** – *Le Petit Brens, 01300 Brens, 3km/1.9mi S of Belley by D 31A.* ☎04 79 81 90 95. *Closed Nov and Sun.* ⌓ *4 rooms. Meals*◎. Settle under the oak tree and sip a drink at the large stone table while admiring the pretty arbour... Or take a stroll through the vegetable garden, where the owners pick their home-grown produce to prepare succulent meals. The cosy rooms beneath the eaves are appointed with family heirlooms. For non-smokers.

WHERE TO EAT

◎◎**Auberge de Contrevoz** – *01300 Contrevoz, 9km/5.6mi NW of Belley by D 69 then D 32.* ☎04 79 81 82 54. *www.auberge-de-contrevoz.com. Closed 24 Dec-30 Jan, Sun evenings except Jul-Aug and Mon.* The flowered garden planted with fruit trees is a pretty sight for diners. This old inn has retained all its country charm, with its fine fireplace, and farming tools adorning the dining-room walls. Regional cuisine.

◎◎**Auberge La Fine Fourchette** – *01300 Belley, 3km/1.9mi SE of Belley on the road to Chambéry.* ☎04 79 81 59 33. *Closed 22-31 Aug, 22-31 Dec, Sun evenings and Mon.* The open countryside and an ornamental lake can be glimpsed through the large bay windows of the dining-room. In fine weather, settle down on the terrace to enjoy the view. Traditional cooking.

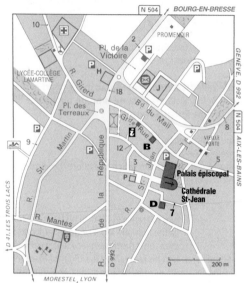

Sights

Cathédrale St-Jean-Baptiste

Open daily 9am-6pm.
Although the cathedral was almost entirely rebuilt in the 19C, it still has its original north portal, dating probably from the 14C: a door beneath a pointed arch, between two blind arcades.
Inside, the six-bayed **chancel**★ (1473) and the triforium with its pretty openwork balustrades are also original.

Palais épiscopal

A bishop was in residence in Belley from 555. The 18C palace is thought to have been built to designs by Soufflot. It now houses the library, a music school and a concert and exhibition hall.

Bas-Bugey Driving Tour

170km/106mi round tour – One day.

▶ *Leave Belley on N 504, N of the map, then turn right onto D 69, and after Billieu turn right again as far as D 37.*

Shortly after Polliou, the road brings you to the **Lac de Barterand** (*see What to See and Do: Outdoor Fun*), a lake set in peaceful, green surroundings.

▶ *Take D 992 on the left which runs alongside the canal, then take D 37 on the right. Before reaching N 504, turn right towards Chemillieu.*

The view opens up to the Yenne basin, the Dent du Chat, Mont Revard (glimpsed through the gap of the Col du Chat), and the Chartreuse mountain range (the Grand-Som and Grande Sure summits).

▶ *Leave the car near the wash-house in the hamlet of Nant. Take the tarmac path on the immediate left, which soon becomes a stone track along the rock face to the top of the gorge.*

Défilé de Pierre-Châtel

1hr 30min there and back on foot.
There is a **view**★ of the ravine from the top of a rocky outcrop left of the path. The Rhône has found a crack in the Jura mountains' armour; it cuts into the mountain range at the Col de Pierre-Châtel, forming a gorge, then flows on into a valley which it follows as far as its confluence with the Guiers. The buildings of an old Carthusian monastery tower above the ravine. The **Chartreuse de Pierre-Châtel,** founded in 1383, soon had fortifications added to it, before being fully converted into a fortress in the 17C, when it found itself situated on

the frontier, as the Bresse and Bugey regions were handed over to France.

▷ *Return to D 37 and take N 504 which runs along the bottom of the ravine. Cross the Rhône. At Virignin take D 31A on the left, then D 24 on the left to Peyrieu, where you rejoin D 992.*

The road follows the course of the river as changes its course again, this time to bypass the Izieu mountain mass. Where it meets the Guiers, it flows off north-west along a channel in the plateau.

▷ *Take D 19C on the right to the outskirts of La Bruyère then turn right to Izieu.*

Izieu

This peaceful village was the setting for one of the more tragic events of the Second World War. Forty-four Jewish children who had found refuge there, and the adults with them, were betrayed and sent to Auschwitz. The small **Musée-Mémorial** (⊙ *open Jul-Aug 10am-6.30pm except Wed. Rest of the year 9am-5pm except Wed.* ⊙*Closed mid-Dec to mid-Jan.* ⊗*4.60€.* ☎*04 79 87 20 08. www.izieu.alma.fr.)* brings to life the daily routine in this short-lived safe haven and the trials of Nazi occupation.

▷ *Return to La Bruyère and turn right onto the old D 19 through the villages of Brégnier-Cordon and Glandieu.*

Cascade de Glandieu

On weekdays the waterfall is harnessed by two hydroelectric plants at its foot.

▷ *Carry on N along D 19.*

Shortly after Flévieu the road runs past the ruins of the **château de St-André.**

▷ *At Serrières-de-Briord take D 32 to the right, then D 99 to the left which leads to the Calvaire de Portes.*

Calvaire de Portes★

The summit on which this Calvary stands (alt 1 025m/3 363ft) at the tip of a rocky spur can be seen from a long way off. From the viewing table, the view encompasses the small, pointed mountain called

St Christopher

G. Magnin-MICHELIN

Dent du Chat (cat's tooth; alt 1 390m/ 4 203ft), to the left the towering form of the Grand Colombier (alt 1 531m/5 023ft) and to the right the plain through which the Ain flows on its way to the Rhône.

▷ *Follow the D 99 down towards Lagnieu.*

St-Sorlin-en-Bugey★

This village occupies a picturesque site at the foot of a cliff which overlooks a curve in the Rhône Valley. Wander through the narrow streets and admire the carefully restored houses on the way up to the church; at the intersection with the montée des Sœurs, note the fine 16C **fresco depicting St Christopher**.

▷ *Continue to Ambérieu, take a road on the left by the church that climbs toward the Château des Allymes. Leave the car at the edge of the hamlet of Brédevent. From here you can walk to either Mont Luisandre or the Château des Allymes.*

Mont Luisandre★

🚶1hr 15min there and back on foot.
Take the steep, stone track between two houses in the village, to the left of the wash-house. A 15min walk brings you to a steep bank, where you take the path to the right which leads up through meadows to the summit.
There is a cross at the summit (alt 805m/ 2 641ft). Walk round the grove to obtain a sweeping **view**★ of the Château des Allymes on one of the spurs of the Bugey, the Dombes plateau, the confluence of

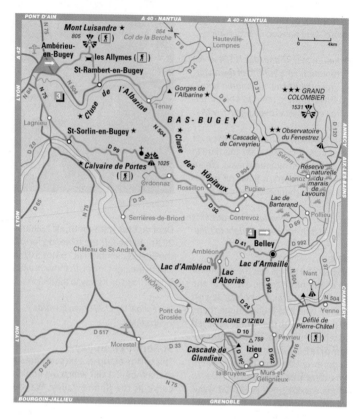

the Ain and the Rhône and the wooded summits of the Bugey region, slashed by the deep gorges of the Albarine.

Château des Allymes

🚶 *30min there and back on foot from Brédevent.*

🕐*Open Jul-Aug daily 10am-noon, 2-7pm. Rest of the year times vary.* ⚏*4€.* ☎*04 74 38 06 07. www.allymes.org.*

This fortified château was laid out as a square. The courtyard in its centre is protected by a solid, square keep in one corner, and a round tower with a lovely **timber roof**★ in the other.

Cluse de l'Albarine★

This valley cuts across from Ambérieu to Tenay. The Albarine, the railway line and the road wind along together between the steep slopes on either side. The wooded upper slopes culminate in limestone ridges in which the rock strata run diagonally and at times almost vertically between crumbling boulders.

St-Rambert-en-Bugey

This little industrial town in a green valley on the banks of the Albarine houses a **Maison de Pays** (🕐*open daily except Sun, Mon and public holidays 9am-noon, 2-5pm.* ⚏*2€* ☎*04 74 36 32 86)* in which traditional industries are on display along with a reconstruction of the inside of a house from days gone by.

The road between Argis and Tenay, at the bottom of the cluse, passes one factory after another. These used to specialise in silk by-products, but now produce nylon and its derivatives.

Cluse des Hôpitaux★

This valley opens up between Tenay and Pugieu. Its steep rocky sides, taller and craggier than those of the Cluse de l'Albarine, and its plunging gorge give the landscape a bleak and rugged air, accentuated by the almost complete absence of houses.

▶ *Return to Belley on N 504.*

BESANÇON ★★

POPULATION 117 733

MICHELIN MAP 321: G-3

The capital of the Franche-Comté lies in an almost perfect ox-bow meander of the Doubs, overlooked by a rocky outcrop with a Vauban fortress. Ever since Roman times, when it was called Vesontio, Besançon has been not just an important military centre but also an ecclesiastical and cultural one. Fine private mansions, including the famous Palais Granvelle, line the narrow pedestrianised streets, testifying to the city's rich history. Famous people born here include Victor Hugo (1802-85) and the Lumière brothers, Auguste (1862-1954) and Louis (1864-1948).

- **Information**: 2 pl. de la 1re-Armée-Française, 25000 Besançon. ☎03 81 80 92 55. www.besancon-tourisme.com.
- ▶ **Orient Yourself:** Take the tourist train from the Rivotte parking area *(enquire at the tourist office)* for an overview; a stop at the citadel is included. Shops and restaurants can be found along the Grande-Rue, near the bridges and in the vicinity of the Quartier Battant.
- Kids **Especially for Kids:** The Musée d'Histoire Naturelle has lots of creepy-crawlies, an aquarium and a full-size zoo and all within the walls of a 17C fortress.

A Bit of History

The rise of the Granvelles

The Granvelles rose from humble beginnings to become one of the most powerful families in the Holy Roman Empire in the 16C. The first to achieve high office was Nicolas Perrenot de Granvelle, Chancellor to Charles V, who placed such trust in him that he referred to him as "my bed of rest". Having made a fortune from his various offices, Granvelle had a vast palace built in Besançon and collected works of art to put in it.

His son Antoine went on to become Cardinal, Prime Minister of the Netherlands and Viceroy of Naples. As Minister for Foreign Affairs he was the only nobleman from the Franche-Comté whom Philip II of Spain would allow into his presence. Despite all these honours, Granvelle never forgot the town of his birth, return often to his magnificent mansion, which he continued to embellish with works of art and other treasures.

S. Sauvignier/ MICHELIN

Quai Vauban on the Doubs

Address Book

For coin ranges, see the Legend on the cover flap.

EATING OUT

Au Petit Polonais – *81 r. des Granges. ☎03 81 81 23 67. Closed 14 Jul-15 Aug, Sat evenings and Sun.* A simple, unpretentious setting for traditional regional cuisine. Warm, congenial atmosphere.

Le Cavalier Rouge – *3 r. Mégevand. ☎03 81 83 41 02. Closed Sun and Mon evening.* A trendy urban atmosphere and speedy service attracts plenty of local regulars, who talk shop over the specialities of the day.

Le Chaland – *Prom. Micaud, near Pont Brégille. ☎03 81 80 61 61. www. chaland.com. Closed Sat lunchtime.* Settle into the restaurant on this charming old barge moored along the Doubs, offering views of the old town and the Promenade Micaud. In fair weather, meals are served on the upper deck, from where you can see the cormorants circling above the water.

Barthod – *22 r. Bersot. ☎03 81 82 27 14. www.barthod.fr. Closed Sun and Mon.* Sit down on the terrace bursting with bushes and potted plants and admire the view of the nearby waterfall... The owner is a wine buff who proposes lovingly prepared menus (prices include wine) washed down by an interesting selection of vintages. Don't forget to drop into the shop on your way out.

WHERE TO STAY

Hôtel du Nord – *8 r. Moncey. ☎03 81 81 34 56. www.hotel-du-nord-besancon. com. 44 rooms. ⏄5.50€.* Situated in the historic quarter, this hotel is a perfect base for venturing out into the old town. The spacious, traditional rooms are equipped with all modern conveniences.

Relais des Vallières – *3 r. P.-Rubens, 4km/2.5mi from Besançon by bd. de l'O. ☎03 81 52 02 02. www.relais-vallieres. com. 49 rooms. ⏄7.50€. Restaurant.* Near the Micropolis expo park, this hotel offers clean, comfortable rooms (those at the rear are quieter); a few boast balconies. Buffet-style meals in the bistrot-style restaurant.

Hôtel Citotel Granvelle – *13 r. du Gén.-Lecourbe. ☎03 81 81 33 92. www. hotel-besancon.com. 30 rooms. ⏄7€.* This stone building has an ideal location just steps from the historic town centre. Comfortable rooms giving onto a paved interior courtyard. Buffet breakfast.

SIT BACK AND RELAX

Brasserie 1802 – *2 pl. Granvelle. ☎03 81 82 21 97. Closed 1 Jan and 25 Dec.* Since it's named after the year Victor Hugo was born, you'd think this brasserie would carry the weight of history but, no, it's as hip as they come. The menu features local products transformed in contemporary style. Wide, shady terrace.

Brasserie du Commerce – *31 r. des Granges. ☎03 81 81 33 11. Open daily 8am-1am.* This brasserie founded back in 1873 has kept its original decor and has become something of an institution. Its old-fashioned atmosphere is charming but its popularity is such that, on some evenings, it is almost impossible to find a table, or even a single seat.

Le Vin et l'Assiette – *97 r. Battant. ☎03 81 81 48 18. www.levin-et-lassiette.com. Open Tue-Sat 9am-9.30pm. Closed 1 Jan, 1 May, Ascension, 2 weeks in Aug, 1 Nov, 25 Dec, Sun and Mon.* This former wine-grower's cellar in the old quarter is in a 14C building which is an officially listed site. Wine buffs can taste wine by the glass, accompanied by a plate of *rosette* (dry pork sausage) or Comté cheese.

Baud – *4 Grande-Rue. ☎03 81 81 20 12. www.baud-traiteur.fr. Open Tue 2-7pm, Wed-Sat 7.30am-noon and 2-6.30pm.* This family business has literally become an institution in Besançon on account of the delicious food it provides: cakes and pastries, ice cream, take-away dishes. If the terrace is crowded, just grin and bear it: it is definitely worth the wait.

SHOPPING

Courbet – *71 r. de Dole. ☎03 81 52 02 16. www.courbet-traiteur.com. Open Tue-Sat 6.30am-12.30pm and 2.30-7.15pm. Closed public and Feb holidays and late Jul-mid-Aug.* You've everything to gain by stepping inside this fine gourmet shop. There's an astounding variety of fine prepared dishes including meat speciality, salads, savoury tarts and cheeses.

La Ferme Comtoise – *12 r. Battant.* ☎*03 81 81 38 78. Open Tue-Sat 9am-12.30pm and 3-7.30pm, Sun 9am-12.30pm; Jun-Sept 9am-12.30pm and 4-7.30pm. closed 1 week in Sept. Entering* this tempting shop, with its old-fashioned utensils and tools, is like stepping inside a cheese museum. *Bleu de Gex, mamirolle, comté, morbier...* the treasured cheeses of the region are all represented, along with yogurts, jams, sausages and a selection of Jura wines.

Capital of the Franche-Comté

In 1674 Louis XIV's troops, 20 000 men strong, laid seige in an attempt to take the city for France. After resisting for almost a month, Besançon finally fell. Three years later, the King named it the capital of the new French province, and the Treaty of Nijmegen (1678) annexed the Franche-Comté to France once and for all. The Parliament, treasury, university and mint were all moved from Dole to Besançon. At first the residents were delighted, but their pride soon changed to dismay when they were handed a bill of 15 000 to 30 000 livres for each transfer by royal officials, who also more than trebled their taxes.

Old Town★★

1 Lower Town Tour

Bound by the meander of the River Doubs, this part of town was once walled.

▶ *The old town should be visited on foot (much of it is pedestrian zones). Park your car either in the car park on the Promenade Chamars, or on the northwest bank of the Doubs. Cross the Battant bridge.*

Before going down the Grande-Rue, take a few steps back along the bridge to get a better view of the 17C residences with beautiful grey-blue stone **façades**★ which line the banks of the Doubs.

▶ *Head N along quai (or promenade) Vauban to passage Vauban leading to place de la Révolution; when the river is in spate, follow the road running parallel to the quai Vauban.*

Place de la Révolution

This lively square, better known as place du Marché, is at a junction with the **Musée des Beaux-Arts et d'Archéologie**★★ (📖*see description below*) on one side and old buildings along rue des Boucheries.

▶ *Follow rue des Granges (behind the covered market) and turn immediately right onto rue R.-L.-Breton leading to place Pasteur and Grande-Rue.*

Grande-Rue

This street is an old Roman highway and is still the main road through the city. The part between the Pont Battant and place du 8-Septembre is a pedestrian zone. Note the **Hôtel d'Emskerque** at no 44, a late-16C mansion and one-time residence of Gaston d'Orléans, with elegant grilles on the ground floor.
Opposite, at no 53, the interior courtyard has a remarkable stone and wrought-iron staircase. At no 67, the **Hôtel Pourcheresse de Fraisans** also has a lovely staircase in the courtyard. No 68, once the Hôtel Terrier de Santans, was built in 1770 and has a pretty interior courtyard. No 86 used to be a **convent for Carmelite nuns;** it dates from the 17C and has an arcaded courtyard. At no 88 stands the old entrance doorway to the **convent of the Great Carmelites** with a 16C fountain to the left of it. The sculptor Claude Lullier depicted the Duke of Alva, Philip II of Spain's military chief, as Neptune. No 103 has a lovely timber staircase in the courtyard.

Hôtel de Ville

The town hall dates from the 16C. Its façade is decorated with alternately blue- and ochre-coloured rustic work.

Opposite, the unusual façade of the **church of St-Pierre** is the work of Besançon architect Bertrand (late 18C).

Palais de Justice

The law courts has a pretty Renaissance façade by Hugues Sambin. The wrought-iron gates in the entrance doorway are really beautiful. The Parliament of the Franche-Comté sat in session inside, on the first floor.

Palais Granvelle★

The mansion was built from 1534 to 1542 for Chancellor Nicolas Perrenot de Granvelle. It has an imposing Renaissance façade. There is a rectangular interior **courtyard**★ surrounded by porticoes with depressed basket-handle arches.
The **Musée du Temps** (clock museum) was installed in the palace in 2002 (⊙ see Additional Sights).
The Promenade Granvelle is a pleasant shady walk through the old palace gardens. It leads past the Kursaal, a concert and meeting hall.

▶ Carry on along Grande-Rue.

Victor Hugo was born at no 140, and the Lumière brothers, inventors of the first moving-picture camera, were born at no 1 place Victor-Hugo.

Roman ruins

Rue de la Convention, the extension of Grande-Rue, offers a good view of square archéologique A-Castan, a pretty park with a row of columns which were once part of the peristyle of a nymphaeum. The channels of the aqueduct which supplied it can still be seen.
Go through the **Porte Noire,** a Roman triumphal arch built in the 2C. It would once have stood in solitary splendour. The sculpture work on it has been badly eroded by the weather.

Cathédrale St-Jean★

The cathedral, most of which was built in the 12C, has two apses, one at either end of the central nave. The bell-tower collapsed in 1729 and was rebuilt in the

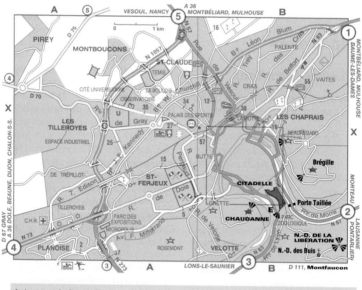

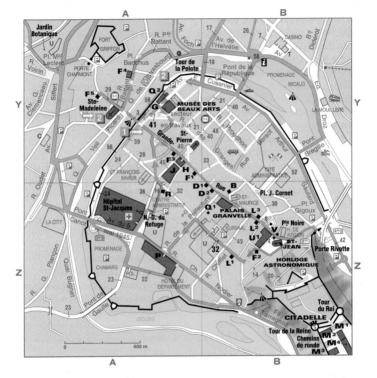

BESANÇON

18C, along with one of the apses (Saint-Suaire, *left of entrance*) which was damaged when the tower fell in. The Saint-Suaire apse is Baroque in style and contains paintings from the 18C (Van Loo, Natoire, de Troy). In the south aisle, left of the great organ loft, is the famous painting by Fra Bartolomeo, the **Virgin Mary with Saints**★, executed in 1512 in Rome for the cathedral's canon Ferry Caron-delet, abbot of Montbenoît and coun-sellor to Charles V. The prelate is depicted on his knees on the right. Elec-tric lighting *(switch located to the right below the painting)* enables viewers to appreciate fully the detail and colours of this work. The left apsidal chapel houses the marble tomb of Abbot Ferry Carondelet.

Horloge Astronomique★

Open Feb-Dec. Guided tours (20-30min) daily except Tue and Wed (Jul-Aug except Tue) at 9.50am, 10.50am, 11.50am, 2.50pm, 3.50pm, 4.50pm and 5.50pm. Closed 1 May, 1 and 11 Nov, 25 Dec. 3€. 03 81 81 12 76. horloge-besan-con.monuments-nationaux.fr.

The astronomical clock, a marvel of mechanics comprising 30 000 parts, was designed and made between 1857 and 1860 by A-L Vérité from Beauvais, and reset in 1900 by F Goudey from Besan-çon. It is connected to the clock faces on the bell-tower. The 62 dials indicate among other things the days and sea-sons, the time in 16 different places all over the world, the tides in 8 ports, the length of daylight and darkness, the times at which the sun and the moon rise and set and, below the clock, the movement of the planets around the sun. Several automata are activated on the hour.

▶ *Take the pretty rue du Chambrier down to the Porte Rivotte.*

Porte Rivotte

This gate is the remains of 16C fortifica-tions. After the French conquest, Louis XIV had the fronton decorated with a symbolic sun. The cliffs of the citadel tower above the gate. These cliffs once plunged straight into the river; the nar-row strip of land along which the road

passes was blasted out of the rock face. A 375m/1 230ft-long canal cuts through the cliffs in a tunnel, providing a short-cut past the Doubs meander.

▶ *Walk round the cathedral along rue du Chapitre and turn right onto rue du Palais. On the left is the fine Hôtel Bonvalot.*

Hôtel Bonvalot

Built between 1538 and 1544, this rather austere mansion is brightened up by its ogee-arched stained-glass windows.

▶ *Rue du Cingle leads to rue de la Vieille-Monnaie; turn right.*

Maison espagnole

10-12 rue de la Vieille-Monnaie.
Although built after the region was uni-ted to the kingdom of France, this house has clear Spanish features.

▶ *Rue de la Vieille-Monnaie is prolonged by rue Mégevand.*

Rue Mégevand

At the beginning of this street, at the junction with rue Ronchaux, there is a lovely 18C fountain representing the River Doubs. A little further on to the right, place du Théâtre offers a very appropri-ate setting to the Classical-style theatre, the work of CN Ledoux. On the left side of the street, the university is flanked by the former St Vincent Abbey (now the Église Notre-Dame) which has retained the old bell-tower and 16C doorway.

▶ *On reaching place de Granvelle, turn left onto rue de la Préfecture.*

Préfecture★

The erstwhile Palais des Intendants was built in the 18C after designs by the architect Louis.
Outside, on the corner of rue Ch.-Nodier, stands the pretty Fontaine des Dames (18C), or Ladies' Fountain, decorated with a mermaid (copy of a 16C bronze).

▶ *Return to the junction with rue de la Préfecture and follow rue Ch.-Nodier to place Saint-Jacques then turn right towards rue de l'Orme-de-Chamars.*

Hôpital St-Jacques

This hospital dates from the 17C. It has a splendid **wrought-iron gate**★ and a pretty 18C **pharmacy**. *(Contact the tourist office.)*

Chapelle Notre-Dame-du-Refuge

This chapel owes its name to an establishment founded in 1690 by the Marquis de Broissia to shelter young girls in danger of falling into vice. It was built by the architect Nicolas Nicole in 1739, and became part of the hospital in 1802. Even the building's architecture takes on a religious significance: the shape of the interior gradually changes from an oval to a circle, the symbol of perfection. Note the beautiful Louis XV woodwork.

▸ *Rue de l'Orme-de-Chamars is prolonged by rue Pasteur which leads back to the beginning of Grande-Rue.*

2 Quartier Battant Tour

This lively district on the north-west bank of the Doubs, once the vine-growers' area, is one of the oldest in the city.

Église Ste-Madeleine

This church was built in the 18C; the towers were added in 1830. The interior is vast, with elegant vaulting supported on fluted columns. The great organ (restored) is the work of Callinet.

▸ *Walk along rue de la Madeleine.*

On the corner of rue du Petit-Charmont and rue du Grand-Charmont stands the **Hôtel Jouffroy** which dates from the late 15C and early 16C.

▸ *Return to Église Ste-Madeleine and walk along the famous rue Battant.*

Hôtel de Champagney

This mansion was built in the 16C. Four gargoyles jut out over the pavement. Pass through the archway to admire the inner courtyard with its arcades. The passage leads through the **Clos Barbusier**, a garden of old roses, to Fort Griffon from where there is a good view of the rooftops of Besançon.

▸ *From the square containing the Bacchus fountain go down rue du Petit-Battant on the right.*

Tour de la Pelote

The rather curious late-15C tower was integrated into Vauban's defence system. It now houses a restaurant.

▸ *Walk across the Pont Denfert-Rochereau then turn right onto avenue E.-Cusenier to return to place de la Révolution.*

Citadel and Museums★★

ⓘ*Open Jul-Aug daily 9am-7pm; Apr-Jun and Sep-Oct daily 9am-6pm. Rest of the year daily except Tue 10am-5pm.* ⓘ*Closed 1 Jan, 25 Dec.* ⬭*7.20€ (children 4.20€; combined ticket for all citadel museums).* ☎*03 81 87 83 33. www.citadelle.com.*

▸ *Take the steep, winding rue des Fusillés-de-la-Résistance up behind the cathedral.*

During Roman times this high ground was crowned with a temple, the columns of which now feature on the town's coat of arms. Later, a church dedicated to St Stephen stood on this spot. After the French conquest in 1674, Vauban had most of the earlier buildings demolished to make way for the fortress which now overlooks the River Doubs from a height of 118m/387ft. The citadel of Besançon has played a variety of roles – barracks, military cadet academy under Louis XIV, state prison and fortress besieged in 1814 – and both its natural setting and historical interest have much to offer. The fortress was built on a gentle ridge and has a more or less rectangular ground plan. Three bastions (or *enceintes* or *fronts*) with large esplanades in between them stretch across its width one after the other on one side: Front St-Étienne towards the town, Front Royal in the centre and Front de Secours nearest the fortress. The whole site is surrounded by fortified ramparts, along which a watch-path runs. Several watchtowers (**Tour du Roi** to the east and **Tour de la Reine** to the west) and bartizans remain.

Tour de la Reine

Chemins de Ronde (Watch-paths)

The watch-path to the west, which begins at the Tour de la Reine *(on the right in the first esplanade)*, reveals a wonderful **view**★★ of Besançon, the valley of the Doubs and the Chaudanne and Les Buis hills. The watch-path which leads off towards the Bregille gives a good view of Besançon and the Doubs meander. On the side of the fortress away from the town the **Échauguette sur Tarragnoz**, reached via the **Parc Zoologique**, overlooks the valley of the Doubs.

Musée Comtois★

This museum houses a large collection of exhibits of traditional local arts, crafts and folklore from the Franche-Comté.

Espace Vauban

The Cadet's building now houses an exhibit and film which trace the history of the citadel, reviewing the civil and military context of Louis XIV's reign, in particular the brilliant engineering accomplishments of Vauban.

Muséum de Besançon★

Kids The Natural History Museum is in two wings of the old arsenal and contains clear, up-to-date exhibitions on exotic fauna, with stuffed animals and birds, skulls and skeletons, and insects, including a large butterfly collection.

The **Aquarium Georges-Besse** is in a large room on the ground floor of the Petit Arsenal. A succession of tanks

(50 000l/11 000gal) imitates the course of the River Doubs, complete with trout, perch, carp, pike and catfish. There are also ponds outside.

The **Parc Zoologique** (2.5ha/5 acres) is at the far end on the fortress on the slope known as the Glacis du Front St-Étienne and the Front de Secours moat. About 350 animals live there, including a growing number of felines and primates. The **Noctarium**, in a former powder magazine, houses creatures that are mainly active at night.

Musée de la Résistance et de la Déportation★

This museum on the French Resistance and deportation occupies 22 rooms and comprises a huge collection of photographs, objects, posters and documents on the birth and rise of Nazism, the Second World War, the invasion of France in 1940, the Vichy régime, the French Resistance, deportation and the liberation of France. Pictures, paintings and sculptures by inmates of German prison camps are also on display, along with contemporary works on this theme. An audio-visual room completes the visit.

Additional Sights

Musée des Beaux-Arts et d'Archéologie★★

&. ⊘Open daily except Tue 9.30am-noon, 2-6pm; weekends 9.30am-6pm. ⊘Closed 1 Jan, 1 May, 1 Nov, 25 Dec. ⊛5€ except Sun. ☎03 81 87 80 49. www.musee-arts-besancon.org.

The Museum of Fine Arts and Archaeology is in the old grain hall, which dates from 1835. It has been extended since the 1970s by a follower of Le Corbusier, Louis Miquel, who built an original construction of concrete in the courtyard consisting of a succession of gently sloping ramps with landings in between them.

The museum contains some rich collections of works of art, some of which come from the Granvelle family, more particularly from Nicolas de Granvelle. At the heart of the building, the ground floor houses a collection of **Egyptian antiquities (Seramon's sarcophagus**★

still containing his mummy) and statues and objects from the Middle Ages and the Renaissance. In the side galleries, there is a chronological display of local archaeological finds (**Gallo-Roman mosaic** depicting a quadriga, a bronze bull with three horns, god with a hammer).

The section of **paintings**★ includes a wide variety of works by non-French schools, signed by some of the greatest names of the 14C to the 17C. Some of the most remarkable works include: *The Drunkenness of Noah* by Giovanni Bellini (1430-1516) in Venice; **Deposition from the Cross** by Bronzino (1503-1572) in Florence; the central panel of the **Triptych of Our Lady of Seven Sorrows** by Bernard Van Orley (1488-1541) in Brussels; **Ill-Assorted Pair** and **Nymph at the Fountain** by Lucas Cranach the Elder (1472-1553) in Germany. Flemish painting is also represented by fine portraits of animals and humans (**Portrait of a Woman** by Dirck Jacobs). In the gallery of 18C works, note the two panels illustrating Scenes of *Cannibalism* by Goya.

The French collection includes some 18C and 19C French masterpieces: tapestry cartoons on a Chinese theme by Boucher; works by Fragonard and Hubert Robert; sketches by David; and, best of all, landscapes by Courbet, *The Conche Hill* and the monumental painting **Death of a Stag.** Make a point of looking at some works by artists from the Franche-Comté (J Gigoux, T Chartran, JA Meunier).

A fine relief model of Besançon shows the triumphal arch, no longer extant, which once stood on the quai Vauban, and the old bell-tower of the cathedral. The 20C has not been neglected: the Besson collection of paintings, watercolours and drawings includes some of Bonnard's best paintings, such as *Place Clichy* and *Café du Petit Poucet,* as well as the portrait of Madame Besson by Renoir, *The Seine at Grenelle* and *Two Friends* by Albert Marquet and **Yellow Sail** by Paul Signac.

The Cabinet des Dessins *(open by appointment only)* houses a comprehensive collection of over 5 000 drawings, including the famous red chalk sketches of the Villa d'Este by Fragonard. The drawings are exhibited in rotation, with only a selected few at a time on display.

Musée du Temps

♿🕐*Open Tue-Sat 9.15am-noon, 2-6pm, Sun 10am-6pm.* 🕐*Closed 1 Jan, 1 May, 1 Nov, 25 Dec.* 5€, *half-price Sat afternoon; free (with guided tour at 3pm) Sun afternoon.* ☎03 81 87 81 50.

The clockmaking industry, established in Besançon in 1793, remained the town's main activity until the 1920s. This museum in the restored Palais Granvelle has all kinds of objects connected with time: a rich collection of clocks, watches, tools and engravings from the 16C.

Excursions

Notre-Dame-de-la-Libération★
3.5km/2mi SE.

On a vast platform, located 400m/437yd from the chapel, is a statue of the Virgin Mary erected as a gesture of gratitude for the liberation of Besançon. A large Romanesque crypt houses marble slabs bearing the names of the region's war dead. From the viewing table, the **view**★ extends over Besançon and the surrounding area as far as the Vosges (weather permitting).

Nancray, Musée de Plein Air des Maisons Comtoises★
16km/10mi E.

🕐*Open Jul-Sep daily 10am-7.30pm; Apr-Jun and Oct-Nov times vary.* 🕐*Closed mid-Nov-Mar.* 7.50€ (6-16 4€, children under 6 free). ☎03 81 55 29 77. www.maisons-comtoises.org.

Kids This open-air museum of typical Franche-Comté houses stages demonstrations of ancient crafts on Sundays as well as festivals, fairs and markets throughout the year.

Boussières
17km/11mi SW along N 83 and D 104.

This village of the Doubs Valley downriver from Besançon boasts one of the few Romanesque churches in the region.
Église St-Pierre★ – The massive porch built in 1574 opens onto the splendid four-storey Romanesque **bell-tower**★ (11C), decorated with lombard bands with pilasters to the third storey.

MONT **BEUVRAY**★★
8KM/4.8MI W OF ST-LÉGER-SOUS-BEUVRAY

MICHELIN MAP 320: E-8
LOCAL MAP SEE MORVAN

A Gaulish tribe known as the Aedui established their capital in a fortified settlement *(oppidum)* on one of the highest points of the Haut-Morvan, and named it Bibracte. Dating from the early 2C BC, it was protected by a double line of fortifications – Bibracte was probably a term meaning 'twice fortified' – of wood, earth and stone. Extensive excavations have focused attention on the site and led to the opening of a museum offering an insight into Celtic history.

- **Information**: Musée de la Civilisation Celtique.
  ☎03 85 86 52 39. www.bibracte.fr.
- **Orient Yourself**: Start with a guided tour of the excavations to help make sense of what remains and hear all about the archaeologists' latest finds. You can always return later on your own.

A Bit of History

A historic site
Of the 200ha/494 acres, about 40 were built up and may have housed as many as 10 000 people.

Dumnorix, Celtic chieftain

Strategically placed at the crossroads of trade routes linking the Mediterranean to Celtic Europe, Bibracte was also a political, religious and crafts centre.
In the early Christian era, Bibracte sank in importance as Augustodunum (presently Autun) grew. However, it remained a centre for trade up to the 16C.

Sights

Musée de la Civilisation Celtique★
&🕑*Open Mar-Nov daily 10am-6pm (Jul-Aug 7pm).* ☜*5.75€.* ☎*03 85 86 52 39; www.bibracte.fr.*
The museum displays artefacts from ancient Bibracte: amphorae, ceramic vases, bronze dishes, tools, weapons, jewellery and sculpture. Video films, computer terminals, maps, photos taken during excavations, models, dioramas etc provide a wealth of information about

The Gaulish Wars

It was in Bibracte, in 52 BC, that the king of the Arverni, Vercingetorix, was chosen to lead the combined Gaulish forces in their fight against the Romans. The Aedui, originally allies of the Romans, changed sides after Caesar's defeat at Gergovia in the Auvergne. This only delayed Caesar's victory at Alesia where Vercingetorix waited in vain for reinforcements (🕮*see ALISE-STE-REINE).*

The following winter, Caesar began writing his *Commentaries on the Gaulish Wars* in which he reveals his talent as a historian as well as his huge personal ambition.

the daily life of the Celts arranged thematically (economy, religion, funeral traditions, wars…). The ticket includes use of an audioguide to the displays.

Oppidum de Bibracte

Open Jun-Oct. Guided tours (1 1/2hr) Jul-Aug daily 11am, 2pm, 3pm and 4.15pm; mid-Mar to Jun Sundays and public holidays at 2.30pm. 9€ site and museum. 03 85 86 52 39. www.bibracte.fr.
The first excavations took place in the late 19C, but it was not until 1984 that an international effort got underway to explore the area in depth. Today, the site (135ha/ 333 acres) offers a look at the organisation of the ancient city: the craftsmen's quarter, the network of streets, a section of the ramparts and one of the monumental gateways (Porte de Rebout) have been partially restored.

Panorama★★

From the platform with its orientation table, amid gnarled beech trees, there is a magnificent view over Autun, the Uchon beacon (see Le CREUSOT-MONT-CEAU) and Mont St-Vincent. On a clear day, you can see as far as the Jura range and even Mont Blanc.

BOURBON-LANCY★

POPULATION 5 634
MICHELIN MAP 320: C-10

Built on a hill overlooking the Loire Valley, Bourbon-Lancy is both an ancient town and a renowned spa.

- **Information**: Pl. d'Aligre, 71140 Bourbon-Lancy. 03 85 89 18 27. www.bourbon-lancy.com.
- **Orient Yourself**: Starting from the belfry, there's a scenic 4km/2.5mi-long trail round the ramparts.

Old Town

Maison de bois et tour de l'Horloge★

At no 3 rue de l'Horloge stands a 16C timber-framed house featuring ogee-shaped windows, a corner pillar, glazed medallions and an ancient statue.

Musée de la Machine Agricole

Open Jul-Aug daily except Tue 3-6pm. Guided tours Fri 4.15pm. 03 85 89 23 23.
This quirky museum illustrates the history of agricultural machinery produced by the Puzenat factory (1902-56), which drastically changed agricultural techniques at the start of the 20C.

Église St-Nazaire and museum

Open Jun-Sep 3-6pm. Rest of the year by request. Guided tours (1hr) available (2€). 03 85 89 23 23.
This 11C church (note the panelled ceiling) was under the authority of the Cluniac priory founded by Ancel de Bourbon. Since 1901, it has housed a museum displaying local antiquities including Gallo-Roman statues of Venus discovered in 1984, stone fragments from nearby churches as well as early-19C paintings and sculptures (Barrias's *The Abolition of Slavery by Victor Schoelcher*).

Spa District

Royal spring

In 1544, after 11 years of marriage, Catherine de' Medici had yet to produce an heir to the French throne for her royal husband. She decided to try the waters in Bourbon-Lancy, reputed to cure infertility… and subsequently bore 10 children.

Hospice d'Aligre

The chapel contains a fine pulpit, carved in 1687 and offered to the abbess of St-Cyr by King Louis XIV. To the left of the chapel, on the landing of the main staircase, stands

Address Book

⏣For coin ranges, see the Legend on the cover flap.

WHERE TO STAY

⊝⊝**Tourelle du Beffroi** – *17 pl. de la Mairie. ☎03 85 89 39 20. www.latourelle. net. 9 rooms.* ⊟*8€.* A patio overgrown with Virginia creeper and wisteria welcomes you to this modest hotel near the church tower. Small, comfortable rooms with wooden flooring, each decorated in its own style.

WHERE TO EAT

⊝⊝**Villa du vieux puits** – *7 r. Bel-Air – ☎03 85 89 04 04. Closed 15 Feb-15 Mar, Sun evenings and Mon.* This charming family-style restaurant offers a traditional French menu, with dishes such as quenelles in crayfish sauce, roasted salmon, and cream chicken.

---

the silver statue of her descendant, the Marquise d'Aligre (1776-1843), the bene-factress of the hospice.

The thermal establishment

At the foot of the fortified hill, in the cour-tyard of the thermal baths, water springs up at a temperature varying from 46°C/ 115°F to 58°C/136°F and at the rate of 400 000l/88 000gal per day. The waters are used for the treatment of rheumatism and circulatory complaints.

Excursions

Signal de Mont

7km/4.3mi NE along D 60 then 15min on foot there and back.
From the viewpoint (alt 469m/1 539ft), there is a panorama of the Val de Loire, the Morvan hills, the Signal d'Uchon, the Charolais region and sometimes the Auvergne mountains.

Ternant

20km/12.5mi N along D 973 then D 198.
Art lovers should not miss going to Ter-nant to see the two magnificent 15C Flemish triptychs in the village church.
The triptychs★★ – The triptychs were given to the church be-tween 1432 and 1435 by Baron Philippe de Ternant, Chamberlain to Philip the Good, Duke of Burgundy, and his son Charles de Ter-nant. They are made of wood – carved, painted and gilded.
The **large triptych** is devoted to the Passion of Christ. The centre panel por-trays Christ's death. Below, a fainting Virgin Mary is supported by St John and the holy women; the donor Charles de Ternant and his wife Jeanne are shown kneeling in the foreground.
The left-hand panel is a Pietà including the figures of St John, Mary Magdalene and the holy women. To the right is the Entombment. The folding panels show scenes from the Passion: the Agony in the Garden, Christ carrying the Cross, the Resurrection and the Descent into Hell.
The **small triptych**, which is older, is devoted to the Virgin Mary. In the centre of the carved panel is a scene from the Assumption: a little angel, his head cove-red by a hood, draws the Virgin's soul, depicted as a little girl at prayer, out from her head. Above this is shown the later scene of the Assumption of the Virgin, when she is carried to heaven on a crescent moon held by an angel, sym-bolising her chastity.
The last meeting of the Virgin with the Apostles is shown on the left of the cen-tral motif; on the right is her funeral procession.
The panel paintings are remarkable. Besides the scenes from the life of the Virgin Mary – the Annunciation, the Crowning of the Virgin, Christ holding the world, the Virgin's funeral – one can see the donor, Philippe de Ternant, dressed in chequered material – the arms of his house – the Order of the Golden Fleece about his neck, and his wife Isabella, in full state dress, accompanied by the crowned Virgin Mary, her patron saint.

BOURG-EN-BRESSE★★

POPULATION 57 198
MICHELIN MAP 320: L-12

Bourg is at the heart of the rich Bresse region, noted for its poultry. However, it is also known for its many cultural attractions, not least of which are the outstanding art treasures at the old monastery of Brou.

- **Information**: 6 av. Alsace-Lorraine, 01005 Bourg-en-Bresse. ☎04 74 22 49 40. www.bourg-en-bresse.org.
- ▶ **Orient Yourself:** The historic section of town lies west of the Église Notre-Dame. The famous monastery is located in a suburb south-east of the town centre.
- ⏰ **Organising Your Time:** Try to be here on a Wednesday or Saturday morning, when the Bresse farmers bring their fabulous produce to the weekly markets.
- ⏱ **Also See:** *La BRESSE.*

A Bit of History

The Vow of Margaret of Bourbon

In 1480 Philip, Count of Bresse, later Duke of Savoy, had a hunting accident. His wife Margaret of Bourbon vowed that if he recovered she would transform the priory of Brou into a monastery. The Count duly lived, but Margaret was unable to carry out her vow before her death.

Building Brou

It took 26 years for Margaret's wishes to be carried out, under the aegis of her daughter-in-law **Margaret of Austria**. This remarkable woman, well-read and artistic, who went on to become Regent of the Low Countries and the Franche-Comté, found herself a widow for the second time at the age of 24 when her husband Philibert of Savoy died of a cold after a hunting expedition. Seeing it as divine punishment, she embarked on carrying out her mother-in-law's vow. Work began in 1506. The priory church was pulled down to make way for the magnificent building which was to serve as the shrine for the three tombs of Philibert, his wife and his mother. Margaret entrusted the construction to a Flemish master mason, Loys Van Boghem, who erected the fabulous building in the record time of 19 years (1513-32). Sadly, Margaret died two years before the church was consecrated.

Town Centre

Old houses

There are two late-15C timber-framed houses: **Maison Hugon** (on the corner of rue Gambetta and rue V.-Basch) and **Maison Gorrevod** (rue du Palais). Equally attractive are the fine 17C stone façade of the Hôtel de Bohan (on the corner by the town hall) and the 18C **Hôtel de Marron de Meillonnas,** which houses the Trésorerie Générale (rue Teynière). A row of medieval half-timbered corbelled houses adjoins the Porte des Jacobins, built in 1437 (rue J.-Migonney).

Ph. Gajic-MICHELIN

Margaret of Austria

Address Book

For coin ranges, see the Legend on the cover flap.

WHERE TO STAY

Chambre d'Hôte Les Vignes – *01310 Montcet, 12km/7.5mi W of Bourg-en-Bresse by D 936 then D 45.* ☎04 74 24 23 13. *www.chambres-hotes-lesvignes.com. 4 rooms. Meals.* Lost in the country-side, this typical Bresse house made of brick and wood is surrounded by a charming garden. The cosy bedrooms are wood-panelled. Have breakfast on the terrace or the verandah or take a relaxing nap down by the pool.

Logis de Brou – *132 bd. de Brou.* ☎04 74 22 11 55. *www.logisdebrou.com. 30 rooms. 8.50€.* This pleasant hotel near Brou church offers comfortable, well-kept rooms with modern, rustic or bamboo furniture. Nice garden.

Prieuré – *49 bd. de Brou.* ☎04 74 22 44 60. *www.hotelduprieure.fr. 14 rooms. 9.50€.* Nearly all the rooms in this modern hotel boast balconies with views of the Brou abbey church. Non-smoking rooms, furnished in Louis XV, Louis XVI or Bresse style.

WHERE TO EAT

L'Amandine – *4 r. de la République.* ☎04 74 45 33 18. Relax in the almond green dining room as you sample fine regional dishes featuring locally raised produce and poultry.

Le Chalet de Brou – *168 bd. de Brou.* ☎04 74 22 26 28. *Closed 1-15 Jun, 23 Dec-23 Jan, Mon evenings, Thu evenings and Fri.* This small family restaurant opposite Brou Church offers regional cooking at moderate prices. Traditional dining room with tapestries and wood panelling. Warm welcome.

Le Français – *7 av. Alsace-Lorraine.* ☎04 74 22 55 14. *info@le-francais.fr. Closed 20-24 May, 1-24 Aug, 24 Dec-4 Jan, Sat evenings and Sun.* This turn-of-the-century brasserie in the town centre has authentic decor, complete with huge mirrors and stucco ceilings. Traditional French cuisine with emphasis on seafood. Warm, congenial hospitality.

SHOPPING

Market – *Cours de Verdun. Wed and Sat mornings.* A stroll through the market is a must to see the finest this farming region has to offer. Poultry, of course, takes centre stage.

Émaux Bressans Jeanvoine – *1 r. Thomas Riboud.* ☎04 74 22 05 25. *émauxbressans.free.fr. Open Tue-Sat 9am-noon, 2-7pm.* Designed by a Parisian craftsman who settled in Bourg-en-Bresse, Bresse enamels are hand made and embellished with gold motifs.

Église Notre-Dame

The church was begun in 1505 but not completed until the 17C. The apse and nave are in Flamboyant Gothic style, but the triple doorway is Renaissance. The belfry was erected under Louis XIV, but the dome and the lantern are modern. A carillon plays at 7.50am, 11.50am and 6.50pm. The church contains interesting works of art and furnishings, in particular the finely carved 16C **stalls**★ in the apse. The high altar, eagle-shaped lectern, the pulpit and organ loft are all fine examples of 18C woodcarving.

Excursion - Brou★★★

Once a hamlet round a Benedictine priory outside Bourg, Brou is now in the town's south-eastern suburbs. Happily, the buildings survived the Wars of Religion and Revolution fairly unscathed.

Church★★

Open Jun-Sep daily 9am-6pm. Rest of the year times vary. Closed 1 Jan, 1 May, 1 and 11 Nov, 25 Dec. 6.50€ (ticket combined with museum and cloisters). ☎04 74 22 83 83.

The church is deconsecrated. The building, in which the Flamboyant Gothic style is influenced by the Renaissance, was built at the same time as the château of Chenonceau in the Loire Valley.

Exterior

The tympanum above the fine Renaissance **doorway**★ shows Philibert the

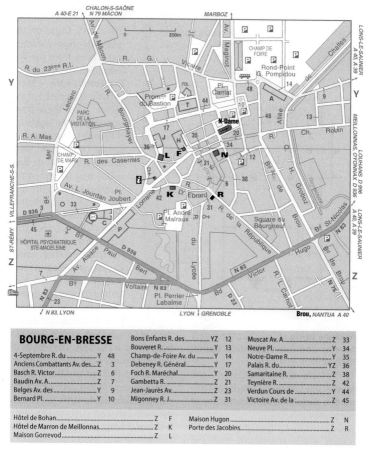

Handsome and Margaret of Austria and their patron saints at the feet of Christ Bound. On the pier is St Nicolas of Tolentino, to whom the church is dedicated (his feast falls on the day of Philibert's death). Surmounting the ornamental doorway arch is a statue of St Andrew; St Peter and St Paul flank the doorway on the arch shafts.

The decorative sculpture includes a variety of Flamboyant Gothic floral motifs (leaves and fruit), some showing a decidedly Renaissance influence (laurel, vine and acanthus), intermingled with symbolic motifs such as palms interlaced with marguerites. Other motifs include the initials of Philibert and Margaret linked by love-knots intermingled with crossed batons, the arms of Burgundy. The simpler façade of the north transept has a pinnacled gable. The five-storey belfry is on the south side of the apse.

The roof had been modified significantly in 1759, so during restoration from 1996 to 1998 it was returned to its original design; Mansard frameworks were replaced by more steeply sloping forms. Flat roof tiles laid in a diamond pattern have been glazed in typical colours.

Interior

Nave – The pillars, formed by numerous little columns, thrust upwards in an unbroken line to the vaulting and open out into a network of ribs meeting at the carved keystones. A finely sculpted balustrade runs below the windows of the nave. The overall impression is one of elegance, magnificence and good taste.

In the second bay of the nave (right) is a 16C black marble font (1) bearing Margaret's motto.

The south transept is lit through a beautiful stained-glass window (2) showing

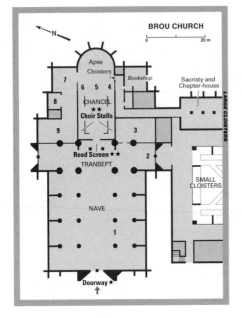

New Testament and satirical characters, those on the south side show characters and scenes from the Old Testament.

The tombs★★★ – Many artists collaborated in the decoration of these three monuments, the high point of Flemish sculpture in Burgundy. The designs were sketched by Jean de Bruxelles, who furnished the sculptors with life-size drawings. The ornamentation and the statuary, much admired by visitors, are attributed for the most part to a Flemish workshop which was set up in Brou, in collaboration with French, German and Italian sculptors. The statues of the three princely personages are the work of Conrad Meyt, born in Germany but trained in Flanders. The effigies of the prince and princess are carved in Carrara marble. Philibert and the two Margarets are represented, each lying on the tomb on a slab of black marble, their heads on embroidered cushions. A dog, emblem of fidelity, lies at the feet of the two princesses, and a lion, symbol of strength, at the feet of the prince. The tomb of Margaret of Bourbon (4) occupies a recessed niche in the south wall of the choir.

The two other tombs differ in that they have two recumbent effigies: the first depicted alive and the second dead in a shroud. That of Philibert (5), the most sober in conception but also the most moving, is in the centre. The tomb of Margaret of Austria (6), with its huge canopy of chiselled stone, is north of the chancel. On the sole of her foot can be seen the wound which supposedly caused the princess' death by blood poisoning. Princess Margaret's motto is inscribed on the canopy: **Fortune in-fortune fort une** (*Fate was very hard on one woman*).

Stained-glass windows★★ – The windows in the centre of the apse show Christ appearing to Mary Magdalene (*upper part*) and visiting Mary (*lower part*), scenes taken from engravings by

Susanna being accused by the Elders (*above*) and exonerated by Daniel (*below*).

To the right of the rood screen is the Montécuto Chapel (3) which contains models explaining the construction of the church.

Rood screen★★ – The richly decorated screen, which separates the nave and transepts from the chancel, is composed of three basket-handled arches supporting seven religious statues.

Chancel – Margaret spared no expense to make this, the most important part of the church, as resplendent as possible. Taken as a whole, the sculpted decoration might border on the excessive, but the longer and closer one examines the ornamentation, the greater its charm, since the smallest detail is treated with quite extraordinary craftsmanship.

Choir stalls★★ – The 74 stalls, which line the first two bays of the choir, were carved from oak in just two years (1530-32). The master carpenter, Pierre Berchod, known as Terrasson, had to mobilise all the local wood craftsmen. They are carved in the same manner as the sculptures on the tombs, and the designs appear to be those of the same artist, **Jean de Bruxelles**. The stalls on the north side feature scenes from the

The Seven Joys of the Virgin Mary

Albrecht Dürer. On the left and right, Philibert and Margaret kneel before their patron saints. The coats of arms of their families are above them: Savoy and Bourbon for the duke, and Imperial and Burgundian for the duchess.

Chapels and Oratories – The **chapel of Margaret**★★★ (7) opens to the north of the choir. An altar screen and a stained-glass window, both fine works of art, deserve to be admired.

The **altar screen**★★★ depicts the Seven Joys of the Virgin Mary. This white marble masterpiece of delicate workmanship is exceptionally well preserved. A scene of the Seven Joys is set in each of the niches, designed for the purpose: on the left, below, is the Annunciation; on the right, the Visitation; above, the Nativity and the Adoration of the Magi; higher still are the Assumption, framed by Christ appearing to his mother, and Pentecost. The retable is crowned by three statues: the Virgin and Child flanked by Ste Mary Magdalene and Ste Margaret. On either side of the retable note St Philip and St Andrew.

The **stained-glass window**★★★ is inspired by an Albrecht Dürer engraving of the Assumption. The glass workers have added Philibert and Margaret kneeling near their patron saints.

The oratories of Margaret were arranged for her personal use. They are next to the Chapelle de Madame (8) and are one above the other, linked by a staircase.

These two chambers were effectively little drawing rooms. An oblique window,, below a highly original arch, allowed the princess to follow the religious services. The nearby chapel (9) has a remarkable **stained-glass window**★★ and a triptych ordered by Cardinal de Granvelle.

Museum and Cloisters★

🕐*Opening hours as for church.*

The museum is housed in the monastic buildings which are ranged around two-storey cloisters, unique in France.

Small cloisters – On the ground floor the sacristy and the chapter-house, now one room, are used for temporary exhibitions. From the galleries, now a stone depository with fragments of cornice and pinnacles, enjoy the view of the south transept gable and the spire.

Great cloisters – This leads to the second chapter-house, now the museum reception. A staircase leads up to the dormer where the old monks' cells now house collections of paintings and decorative art. On the landing and in the recess in the middle of the great corridor are some fine pieces of Bresse furniture and 18C Meillonnas earthenware.

The cells on the south side are devoted to 16C-18C art, among them a fine **portrait of Margaret of Austria**★ painted by B Van Orley c 1518 and a triptych of the life of St Jerome (1518).

BRANCION★
15KM/9MI SW OF TOURNUS
MICHELIN MAP 320: I-10
LOCAL MAP SEE LE MÂCONNAIS

The old feudal market town of Brancion is perched on a spur overlooking two deep ravines, forming a picturesque and most unusual sight.

🛈 **Information**: www.brancion.fr.

▶ **Orient Yourself**: Walk through the gateway in the 14C ramparts, where you will find the imposing ruins of a fortress, narrow streets lined with medieval-style houses, the 15C covered market *(halles)* and the church.

🅿 **Parking**: Vehicles are not allowed into town, so leave them in the car park outside the walls.

Sights

Château
🕐 *Open Apr-Sep 10am-1pm, 2-6.30pm; Oct 2-6.30pm. ⊜4€. ☎03 85 51 11 41. www. brancion.fr.*

This feudal castle dates to the beginning of the 10C. It was enlarged in the 14C by Duke Philip the Bold, who added a wing to lodge the dukes of Burgundy. In the 16C it was assaulted by Catholic League militants, and finally ruined by D'Ornano's troops. The keep has been restored. From the viewing platform *(87 steps)* there is a good **view**★ of the town and its church, the Grosne Valley and, to the west and north-west, the mountains of Charollais and the Morvan.

Château and St-Pierre church

St-Pierre
The church is a squat 12C building built in the Romanesque style, surmounted by a square belfry. Inside, there are some striking 14C frescoes commissioned by Eudes IV, Duke of Burgundy, a recumbent effigy of Jocerand IV of Brancion (13C), who died on the Seventh Crusade, and many funerary stones.

💰*For coin ranges, see the Legend on the cover flap..*

AN INEXPENSIVE MEAL …
⊜**Ferme-Auberge de Malo** – *In the locality of Malo, 71240 Étrigny, 9km/ 5.6mi N of Brancion by D 159 then a minor road. ☎03 85 92 21 47. www. aubergemalo.com. Closed 10 Nov-1 Apr. ⤳ Reservations required.* This pretty medieval farmhouse offers traditional cuisine made with home-grown produce and poultry reared on the property. Delicious home-made charcuterie.

… LUXURIOUS LODGING
⊜⊜⊜**Hôtel Montagne de Brancion** – *At Col de Brancion. ☎03 85 51 12 40. www.brancion.com. Closed early Nov to mid-Mar. 19 rooms. ⊑16€. Restaurant ⊜⊜⊜.* This hotel dominating the vineyards on the Mâconnais heights is a haven of peace. The bright bedrooms are decorated with bamboo and wooden furniture painted white. The radiant dining room opens out on to the garden with its pool.

LA BRESSE ★★
MICHELIN MAP 328: D-2 TO E-3

The Bresse region is the southernmost part of Burgundy, bordered on the west by the Saône and on the east by the Revermont plateau: it is a pastoral landscape of babbling brooks and ancient hedgerows, old windmills and timber-framed farmhouses. The differing influences of Burgundy and of the Mediterranean divide the region in two. The northern part is known as *Bresse bourguignonne* and the southern as *Bresse savoyarde*, each with some unique characteristics.

- **Information**: 6 av. Alsace-Lorraine, 01005 Bourg-en-Bresse. ☎04 74 22 49 40. www.bourg-en-bresse.org; pl. St Jean, 71500 Louhans. ☎03.85.75.05.02. www.bresse-bourguignonne.com.
- ▶ **Orient Yourself:** A tour of the northern part (La Bresse Bourguignonne) begins in the town of Cuiseaux; start the southern tour (La Bresse Savoyarde) at Bourg-en-Bresse.
- **Don't Miss:** Poultry from the region is world renowned, so be sure to sample this regional delicacy while you're here.

A Bit of History

La Bresse Bourguignonne

The proximity of the powerful Duchy of Burgundy long overshadowed the modest Bresse. These lands along the Saône were often the subject of dispute and acted as a border until the southern part of the Bresse and Franche-Comté were united to France in the 17C. Left without effective local administration, the region slowly built its own identity through the excellence of its agricultural output and the eventual emergence of a bourgeois class which took the management of business and government in hand.

La Bresse Savoyarde – The southern area of the Bresse is better known than its northern neighbour. In 1272, the marriage of Sibylle de Bâgé and Amédée V Le Grand, Count of Savoy, brought the province under the House of Savoy. There it remained until the Treaty of Lyon (1601), by which Henri IV obtained its return to the kingdom of France.

Bresse Chicken – The reputation of the local poultry dates back to the 17C, since when it has made a huge contribution to the local economy and made some farmers very wealthy. As consumer awareness has grown and claims of quality come under greater scrutiny, *poulet de Bresse* has passed all the tests for standards of excellence, and has worn a special label guaranteeing its origins since 1957. The birds are raised free-range for four to five months, feeding on grains from Bresse's fertile fields. They spend their last days in a pen where they are fattened up.

Driving Tours

La Bresse Bourguignonne ★
138km/86mi round tour

Cuiseaux
This former fortified town on the border between Burgundy and Franche-Comté is in a peaceful agricultural landscape. There are traces of the 12C fortifications, which originally included 36 towers.

Maison de la Vigne et du Vigneron
🕑*Open mid-May to end Sep daily except Tue 3-7pm.* ✏*3€.* ☎*03 85 76 27 16. www.ecomusee-de-la-bresse.com.*
This wine museum has displays on Jura vineyards, along with tools and equipment and the reconstruction of a wine-grower's room (*chambre à feu*).

▶ *Drive 19km/12mi along D 972.*

Address Book

For coin ranges, see the Legend on the cover flap.

WHERE TO STAY

Au Puits Enchanté – 71620 St-Martin-en-Bresse. ☎03 85 47 71 96. www.aupuitsenchante.com. Closed 8-16 Mar. 13 rooms. ☐8€. Restaurant☐☐. In a leafy setting in the town centre, this family establishment offers small, tidy rooms. The cuisine is well prepared and the prices reasonable.

Pillebois – rte de Bourg-en-Bresse, 01340 Montrevel-en-Bresse, 2km/1.2mi S of Montrevel by D 975. ☎04 74 25 48 44. www.hotellepillebois.com. Closed Sun Oct-Apr. 30 rooms. ☐7.50€. This modern house has pastel-coloured rooms with white furniture. The dining room has a maritime theme, hence the pirogue in the centre of the room.

Georges Blanc – 01540 Vonnas. ☎04 74 50 90 90. www.georgesblanc.com. Closed Jan. 32 rooms. ☐26€. Restaurant☐☐☐☐. This elegant half-timbered mansion on the banks of the Veyle has sumptuous individually decorated rooms. The

restaurant serves delicious regional cuisine of the highest quality.

WHERE TO EAT

Vuillot – 71480 Cuiseaux. ☎03 85 72 71 79. hotel.vuillot@wanadoo.fr. Closed Jan, Sun evenings and Mon. This restaurant has two dining rooms and terraces, one glassed-in. Simple fare. Light snacks available at the bar.

Ferme-Auberge du Poirier – at Bourg de Cuet, 01340 Montrevel-en-Bresse, 1km/0.6mi SW of Montrevel by D 67. ☎04 74 30 82 97. www.fermeaubergedupoirier.fr. Closed 30 Oct-20 Mar and Sun to Fri evenings. Reservations required. Charolais cows, pigs, chickens and capons are bred on the grounds around this large farmhouse. The dining room has a fireplace, exposed beams and clogs on the walls. Naturally, all the ingredients are farm-fresh!

L'Ancienne Auberge – 01540 Vonnas. ☎04 74 50 90 50. www.georgesblanc.com. Closed Jan. Conveniently located on the main square, this restaurant has decor reminiscent of the early 20C. Tasty, unpretentious cuisine.

Louhans★
see LOUHANS.

▷ *Leave Louhans travelling N on D 13 towards St-Germain-du-Bois.*

St-Germain-du-Bois: Maison de l'Agriculture
Open mid-May to end Sep daily except Tue 3-7pm. ☐3€. ☎ 03 85 76 27 16. www.ecomusee-de-la-bresse.com. 15km/9mi N. This museum of rural life includes a collection of farm implements from the 19C to today, and exhibits on local products.

▷ *Continue on D 13.*

Pierre-de-Bresse★, Écomusée de la Bresse Bourguignonne
The Château de Pierre-de-Bresse is a handsome 17C building. The left wing houses the **Écomusée de la Bresse bourguignonne** (*open mid-May to end Sep daily 10am-7pm. Rest of the year*

daily 2-6pm. *Closed 25 Dec-1 Jan. ☐6€. ☎03 85 76 27 16. www.ecomusee-de-la-bresse.com*). The exhibits cover the environment, history, traditional way of life and present economic situation in Burgundian Bresse. It has branches at Louhans, Rancy, St-Germain-du-Bois, St-Martin-en-Bresse, Verdun-sur-le-Doubs and Cuiseaux.

▷ *Continue on D 73 towards Charette.*

Château de Terrans
The design of the château, begun in 1765, is plain. An attractive wrought-iron gate closes off the courtyard, beyond which the elegant façade rises.

▷ *Continue on D 73 to Frontenard and take D 996 left towards Louhans. At Mervans, take D 970 to the right, continue for 7km/4mi and turn left towards St-Martin-en-Bresse. From St-Martin follow D 35 to Perrigny.*

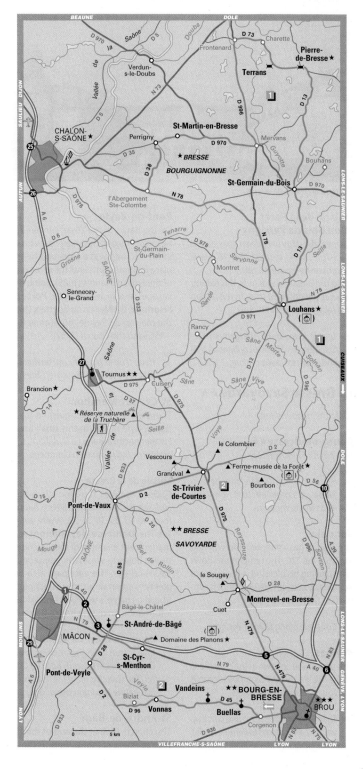

Château de Pierre-de-Bresse

Maison de la Forêt et du Bois de Perrigny

🕐 *Open mid-May to end Sep daily except Tue 3-7pm.* ∞*3€.* ☎*03 85 76 27 16. www.ecomusee-de-la-bresse.com*

Amid the Bresse woodlands, this exhibit looks at the different trees in the region and related trades and crafts.

▶ *Take D 38 towards l'Abergement-Ste-Colombe, drive back to Louhans on N 78 and return to Cuiseaux along D 972.*

La Bresse Savoyarde★★

104km/65mi round tour

Bourg-en-Bresse★★
👢*see BOURG-EN-BRESSE*

▶ *Head W towards Villefranche-sur-Saône. At Corgenon, turn right on D 45 as far as Vandeins.*

Vandeins
The **church** has a sculpted doorway dating from the 12C. The tympanum shows Christ giving his blessing; a fine piece of Romanesque sculpture, with angels supporting the central figure.

▶ *Continue along D 96 to Vonnas.*

Vonnas
This peaceful little town at the crossroads of the Bresse and the Dombes region is a favourite stop for gourmets.

▶ *Take D 96 towards Bizat and catch up with D 2, which leads to Pont-de-Veyle.*

Pont-de-Veyle
On the banks of the Veyle, surrounded by former moats, this village developed in the 13C and was a secret gathering place for Protestants until the revocation of the Edict of Nantes (1685). Some fine vestiges remain, including the **Porte de l'Horloge**, the Maison du Guetteur (16C), the Maison de Savoie (66 Grande Rue – 15C) and the church (1752).

▶ *Head N on D 28. 3km/2mi further on, take N 79 towards Bourg-en-Bresse.*

St-Cyr-sur-Menthon
There are several distinguished traditional-style homes in this small town. Further north, around La Mulatière, several farms have Saracen chimneys.

Musée de la Bresse
🕐 *Open Apr-Nov Thu-Mon 10am-6pm (Jul-Sep Wed-Mon).* ∞*4.50€ (children free).* ☎*03 85 36 31 22. www.ain.fr.*
🅺🅸🅳🆂 The **Domaine des Planons★**, a magnificent example of local architecture, is home to a fasinating museum of 18C rural life. The vast park also has plenty to entertain visitors: a duck pond, a bowling game, a woodworking exhibit, information on raising Bresse poultry.

▶ *Return to St-Cyr-sur-Menthon and take N 79 as far as the crossroads with D 28. Turn right towards Bâgé-le-Châtel. The church is off to the left, visible just before you enter the village.*

St-André-de-Bâgé
The church, built at the end of the 11C with the help of monks from Tournus,

J. Cartier –Château de Pierre-de-Bresse

Saracen chimneys

The 30 or so that survive date from the 17C and 18C. Within the house there is a vast hearth, set away from the wall and covered by a hood, under which a man can stand upright; the flue is lined with wood panels. The chimneys resemble small belfries or, more rarely, reliquaries in the Romanesque, Gothic and sometimes Byzantine style; their shapes are round, square (modelled on the belfry of St-Philibert in Tournus) or octagonal (the belfry of St-André-de-Bâgé); they have one or two bands of vents and are capped by a cone, a pyramid or a Baroque belfry.

They are unusually high (3-5m/10-16ft) and surmounted by a wrought-iron cross. In the past some may have housed a bell, a useful feature in the daily life of these traditionally isolated farms. Saracen, the adjective, does not describe the chimneys' geographical provenance but is a survival of the medieval use of the word Saracen to mean belonging to a foreign, old or unknown culture; the term was therefore quite naturally applied to these unusual chimneys.

sits in the middle of a cemetery. An elegant, octagonal **bell-tower**★ rises above the apse with its radiating chapels, topped by a graceful stone spire.

▶ *Continue on past Bâgé-le-Châtel and N on D 58 to Pont-de-Vaux.*

Pont-de-Vaux

This historic hamlet in a meander of the River Reyssouze, a tributary of the Saône, has quaint half-timbered houses and façades from the 16C and 17C.

▶ *Leave Pont-de-Vaux travelling NE on D2 towards St-Trivier-de-Courtes.*

St-Trivier-de-Courtes

The town is a good place to start a tour of Saracen chimneys, as many have been preserved in the surrounding villages:

◆ **St-Trivier** – *1.5km/1mi W via D 2.* **Grandval** *farm.*
◆ **Vescours** – *5km/3mi W of St-Trivier; on the left at the entrance to the village.*
◆ **Vernoux** – *3km/2mi NE of St-Trivier.* **Colombier** *farm.*

Ferme-Musée de la Forêt★

3km/2mi E of St-Trivier. ◐*Open Jul-Sep 10am-noon, 2-6.30pm; Apr-Jun and Oct, weekends and public holidays only.* ◎*2.50€.* ☎*04 74 30 71 89. www.fermemuseedelaforet.com.*
This attractive 16C-17C farm has been restored and turned into a museum devoted to all things agricultural, including antique implements.

▶ *Return to St-Trivier, and take D 975 S then N 479 to Bourg-en-Bresse.*

BRIARE

POPULATION 5 994

MICHELIN MAP 318: N-6

This quiet town on the banks of the Loire is the meeting point of two canals that connect the basins of the Rivers Seine and Loire. Today, commercial navigation has given way to leisure and the marina has been adapted for recreational boating.

🛈 **Information**: 1 pl. Charles-de-Gaulle, 45250 Briare.
☎02 38 31 24 51. www.briare-le-canal.com.
▶ **Orient Yourself**: There are pleasant walks along the banks of the Loire, from where there are views of the impressive canal bridge.

The canal bridge at Briare

Ph. Gajic-MICHELIN

🪙 *For coin ranges, see the Legend on the cover flap.*

WATERSIDE INN

🍽️🛏️**Auberge du Pont Canal** – *19 r. du Pont-Canal.* ☎*02 38 31 24 24. www.auberge-du-pont-canal.com. Closed Sun evenings and Mon noon (Jun-Sep).* In a sleepy setting by the Briare Canal, this small restaurant with its 1960s façade is a haven of tranquillity. The accommodation is modern.

🍽️🍽️**Mme François-Ducluzeau** – *Domaine de la Thiau, Rte de Gien, Lieu-area of La Thiau.* ☎*02 38 38 20 92. lathiau.club.fr.* 🛏️ *3 rooms plus one suite.* This lovely 18C home is in a park with cedar trees. *Toiles de Jouy* and antique furniture all add to its charm.

A Bit of History

The Briare Canal

The canal was completed in 1642, 38 years after its conception. Along its 57km/36mi path, six locks move the waters from the Loire Lateral Canal (which runs alongside that river) to the Loing Canal. It was the first canal in Europe designed to link up two different canal networks in this way. At Rogny-les-Sept-Écluses, about 15km/9mi north on the towpath, the seven original locks, no mean feat of engineering at the time, are no longer in use; they form a sort of giant's stairway, in a natural setting.

Sights

Pont-Canal★★

🧒The canal bridge (662m/2 172ft long, 11m/37ft wide) was completed in 1890 and inaugurated in 1896. The waters of the Loire ripple below while ducks glide on the calm surface of the brimming canal suspended high above. The ironwork, which can be seen from stairs down to the river, was by the Société Eiffel.

Musée de la Mosaïque et des Émaux

♿🕐*Open Jun-Sep 10am-6.30pm. Rest of the year 2-6pm.* 🕐*Closed 25 Dec, Jan.* 💶*5€.* ☎*02 38 31 20 51. www.emauxde-briare.com.*
The museum devoted to the local enamel crafts is in the still-operating factory, and houses an impressively varied collection, including work by Art Nouveau precursor Eugène Grasset.

LE BRIONNAIS★★

MICHELIN MAP 320: E-12 TO F-12

This part of south Burgundy, with Semur-en-Brionnais at its heart, is a tranquil corner with an impressive architectural heritage. The rolling countryside, dotted with churches and castles, is given over mainly to cattle rearing.

- **Information**: Place des Halles, 71110 Marcigny. ☎03 85 25 39 06.
- ▶ **Orient Yourself:** The region is bounded on the west by the Loire, with Paray-le-Monial marking its northernmost point.
- ☺ **Don't Miss:** Anzy-le-Duc and its church, among the loveliest in the area.

A Bit of History

Churches and stonemasons
At the peak of its power, the great abbey at Cluny (☺*see CLUNY*) had a great impact on the religious architecture of the Brionnais, and there are still about a dozen Romanesque churches in the area well worth seeing. Part of their beauty is down to the local materials. The medieval stonemasons found the yellowish, fine-grained limestone of the region relatively easy to work but at the same time very durable, making it ideal for decorative sculpture on façades and doorways. It gives the churches a lovely warm colour, which looks particularly striking in the rays of the setting sun.

Driving Tour

Allow one day.

- ▶ *Drive W out of Charlieu along D 487 then D 4.*

La Bénisson-Dieu
The village **church** and the imposing 15C square bell-tower in front of it are all that remains of the abbey founded in the 12C by disciples of St Bernard, which became a convent in the 17C. The early-Gothic nave is roofed with superb glazed tiles forming diamond motifs.

- ▶ *Drive back towards the Loire, cross the river and turn left onto D 482.*

Iguerande
The 12C church is at the top of a steep hill overlooking the Loire and offering an interesting view of the Loire Valley, the Forez to the left and the Madeleine hills to the right. The nave and the chancel contain some unusual capitals; note, in particular, the musician-cyclop at the top of the first pillar on the left.

Marcigny
This picturesque town close to the Loire, on the edge of the Brionnais region, has some 16C timber-framed houses (round the church) and a mansion dating from 1735 (between place du Cours and place Reverchon).

Tour du Moulin
🕐*Open mid-Jun to mid-Sep 10.30am-12.30pm, 2-7pm; Apr to mid-Jun and mid-Sep to mid-Oct 2-6pm.* ⊚*3.50€.* ☎*03 85 25 37 05.*
The 15C tower, once part of a Benedictine priory, has unusual walls decorated with stone cannon-balls. It houses a museum of local history, with everything from sculptures to chemist's jars in Nevers faience.

- ▶ *Follow D 10 towards Charolles.*

Anzy-le-Duc★
This hillside village in the Arconce Valley possesses one of the most beautiful Romanesque churches in the area. The harmonious **church**★ in golden stone was probably built in the early 11C. Its fine doorway is now in the Musée du Hiéron in Paray-le-Monial. There is a magnificent Romanesque belfry, a polygonal tower with three storeys of bays. The nave is roofed with groined vaulting and lit through the clerestory windows. The capitals have been well

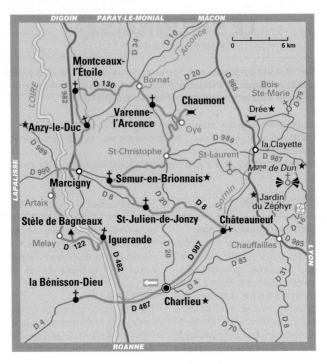

preserved; those in the nave represent biblical and allegorical scenes. The frescoes of the apse, now in poor condition, portray the lives of St John the Baptist and Hugues d'Anzy. Those in the choir show the Ascension of Christ.

If you have time, make a short detour N along D 174 then drive directly to Varenne along D 130.

Montceaux-l'Étoile

The doorway of the church features a tympanum and lintel carved out of one block of stone, illustrating the Ascension as at Anzy-le-Duc and St-Julien-de-Jonzy. The arching framing the tympanum rests on columns decorated with capitals.

▶ *In Bornat, turn right onto D 34.*

Varenne-l'Arconce

The **church** looks rather massive owing to its projecting transept and square tower. Its decoration was limited by the use of hard sandstone as building material. Note the elegant tympanum surmounting the south doorway and depicting the Agnus Dei.

Château de Chaumont

5km/3mi SE along D 158 (near Oyé).
The Renaissance façade is flanked by a round tower, the other façade in the Gothic style is modern.

▶ *Head towards Semur via St-Christophe-en-Brionnais, famous for its cattle markets held on Thursday mornings.*

Semur-en-Brionnais★

The small town is on a promontory covered with vines and fruit trees. The château, the Romanesque church, the former priory and 18C court room (now the *mairie*, or town hall) make an attractive ensemble in pinkish stone.

Église St-Hilaire★

Guided tours by request, Vieilles Pierres. ☎03 85 25 13 57.
The church, in the Cluniac style, has an elegant octagonal belfry decorated with a double band of twin Romanesque arcades; the upper band is framed by a series of recessed arches.
The west doorway is richly decorated. The lintel depicts a scene from the life of St Hilary of Poitiers: condemned by a

Address Book

WHERE TO EAT

📗📗**Le Pont** – *71110 St-Julien-de-Jonzy. ☎03 85 84 01 95 Closed Feb school holidays, Sun evening and Mon evening.* Family restaurant with a warm welcome. The owner, who also runs the nearby bar and butcher's shop, offers traditional fare. There are a few rooms for guests.

SHOPPING

Leblanc – *71340 Iguerande. ☎03 85 84 07 83. Open daily 9am-7pm.* On the shelves of this boutique you'll find hazelnut oil, pistachios, pine nuts, toasted sesame seeds and a selection of fine vinegars as well as mustards ground by hand on site. Take a look at the mustard mill, used by the family since 1878.

---

council of bishops, he sets off into exile, a begging bag on his shoulder; on the road he meets an angel who returns him to his place among the bishops; meanwhile the devil makes off with the soul of the Council President.

The nave is attractive; at the west end the triforium, which consists of an arcade with twin arch stones, forms a bowed gallery which is supported by an impressive corbel springing from the keystone of the west door. The gallery may be an imitation of the chapel of St-Michel above the west door of Cluny abbey church.

Château St-Hugues

🕔*Open mid-May to mid-Sep 10am-noon, 2-7pm, Sun and public holidays 2-7pm. Rest of the year times vary.* 🕔*Closed 3rd Sun in Jul.* ✅*2.50€.* ☎*03 85 25 13 57.*
The 9C rectangular keep was the birthplace of the famous abbot St Hugh of Cluny. The two round towers served as a prison in the 18C.

▷ *Follow D 9.*

St-Julien-de-Jonzy

From its position on top of one of the highest hills in the area, the village offers a fine panorama of the Brionnais and Beaujolais rolling countryside.
The present church has retained the square bell-tower and lovely carved **doorway**★ of its 12C Romanesque predecessor. The tympanum and lintel are carved out of a single block of sandstone. The former

shows the Last Supper; all the heads except two were damaged in 1793.

▷ *Drive E along D 8.*

Châteauneuf

The church, standing out against its wooded setting, was one of the last Romanesque buildings erected in Burgundy; the west front is massive, the south doorway has an interesting lintel featuring a naïve representation of the 12 Apostles. Inside, note the clerestory windows in the nave with their slender columns decorated with capitals and, surmounting the transept, the dome on squinches with its octagonal base and arcaded gallery.

▷ *Return to Charlieu along D 987.*

The belfry of St-Hilaire

LE BUGEY ★

MICHELIN MAP 328: G-4

This is the name by which the whole southern Jura region is known. There are two natural divisions: the Haut-Bugey and the Bas-Bugey. In the 9C it was part of the kingdom of Burgundy, before eventually coming under the rule of the Counts of Savoy.

- **Information**: 34 Grande Rue, Belley. ☎04 79 81 29 06. www.cc-belley-bas-bugey.com; and towns throughout the region.
- ▸ **Orient Yourself**: The Haut-Bugey is bounded to the north by a series of transverse valleys (*cluses*), which run from Nantua to Bellegarde, to the south by the *cluses* of Albarine and Hôpitaux, to the east by the Rhône and to the west by the Ain Valley. The Bas-Bugey is contained within the great meander of the Rhône

A Bit of History

A place of transit

It has always been easy to cross the Bugey region, thanks to its transverse valleys linking the smaller mountain chains. Over the centuries the region's geographical location has brought it many sudden changes in fortune. In the 18C Spanish troops rode roughshod through the region during the Spanish War of Succession; in the 19C, the allied nations rising against Napoleon used the Bugey as their main battleground. It was not until 1855, with the creation of the Lyon-Geneva railway line through the Cluse de l'Albarine, that the region could actually benefit from its position.

Excursions

Haut-Bugey
◔*NANTUA/ BELLEGARDE-SUR-VALSERINE.*

Bas-Bugey
◔*see BELLEY.*

Grand Colombier
◔*see GRAND COLOMBIER.*

CHÂTEAU DE BUSSY-RABUTIN ★

MICHELIN MAP 320: H-4

Halfway up a hill few miles north of Alise-Ste-Reine is the château of Bussy-Rabutin. Its highly original interior decor provides a fascinating insight into the mind of a scandalous former owner.

- **Information**: Château de Bussy-Rabutin, 21150 Bussy le Grand. ☎03 80 96 00 03. www.azurline.com/bussy/chateau.html.
- ▸ **Orient Yourself**: Take time to explore the park (34ha/84 acres), shaped like an amphitheatre with beautiful stone steps linking the levels, which makes a fine backdrop to the gardens with their statues, fountains and pools, apparently designed by Le Nôtre, Louis XIV's own gardener.

A Bit of History

The misfortunes of Roger de Bussy-Rabutin

While his cousin, Mme de Sévigné, was very successful with her pen, Roger de Rabutin, Count of Bussy, caused nothing but trouble with his. Having compromised himself, in company with other young libertines, in a famous orgy in which he improvised and sang couplets ridiculing the love affair of young Louis

Château de Bussy-Rabutin

XIV and Marie de Mancini, Bussy-Rabutin was exiled to Burgundy on the orders of the king.

Accompanied into Burgundy by his mistress, the Marquise de Montglat, he passed his time writing his *Histoire amoureuse des Gaules*, a satirical chronicle of the love affairs of the court. This libellous work earned its author a stay in the Bastille, where he languished for over a year. Then he was sent home to Bussy, where he lived in exile – alone this time, as the beautiful marquise had forgotten all about him.

Visit

🕐 *Open Tue-Sun 9.15am-noon, 2-5pm (6pm May-Sep).* 🕐 *Closed 1 Jan, 1 May, 1 and 11 Nov, 25 Dec.* ≈6.50€.

This 15C fortified castle was bought during the Renaissance by the Comtes de Rochefort, who knocked down the wall which closed in the courtyard and transformed the defensive towers into elegant living quarters. The façade is 17C. Roger de Rabutin's grandfather began works on the ground floor during the reign of Louis XIII; the upper floors, completed in 1649, show the naissant Louis XIV style.

Interior – It was Bussy-Rabutin himself who designed the interior decoration of the apartments, a gilded cage in which he spent his exile, indulging in nostalgia for army and court life and giving vent to his rancour against Louis XIV and his unfaithful mistress.

Cabinet des Devises – Numerous portraits and allegorical paintings along with pithy maxims *(devises)* by Roger de Rabutin are framed in the woodwork panels of this room. The upper panels show views of châteaux and monuments, some of which no longer exist. Over the fireplace is a portrait of Bussy-Rabutin by Lefèvre, a student of Lebrun. The furniture is Louis XIII. **Antichambre des Grands Hommes de Guerre** – Portraits of 65 great warriors, from Du Guesclin down to the master of the house, Maistre de Camp, Général de la Cavalerie Légère de France, are hung in two rows around the room. Some of the portraits are very good originals, but most of them are only copies. The woodwork and ceilings are decorated with fleurs-de-lis, trophies, standards and the interlaced ciphers of Bussy and the Marquise de Montglat.

Chambre de Bussy – Bussy's bedchamber is adorned with the portraits of 25 women. That of Louise de Rouville, second wife of Bussy-Rabutin, is included in a triptych with those of Mme de Sévigné and her daughter, Mme de Grignan. Other personalities portrayed include Gabrielle d'Estrées, Henri IV's mistress, Mme de la Sablière, Ninon de Lenclos, the famous courtesan, and Mme de Maintenon.

Tour Dorée★ – Bussy-Rabutin surpassed himself in the decoration of the circular room where he worked on the first floor of the west tower. The walls are entirely covered with paintings, on subjects taken from mythology and the gallantry of the age, accompanied by quatrains and couplets. Bussy-Rabutin is depicted as a Roman emperor. Portraits of the personalities of the courts of Louis XIII and Louis XIV complete the collection.

Chapelle – The Galerie des Rois de France leads to the south tower, which houses a small, elegantly furnished oratory.

CHABLIS

POPULATION 2 594

MICHELIN MAP 319: F-5

Chablis is the capital of the prestigious wine-growing region of lower Burgundy. Thanks to its many old buildings, harking back to its heyday in the 16C, it still has a medieval feel. The annual wine fair and the village fairs of November and late January, held in honour of St Vincent, patron of wine-growers (see Calendar of Events), recall the town's lively commercial past.

- 🛈 **Information**: 1 r. du Maréchal de Lattre de Tassigny, 89800 Chablis. ☎03 86 42 80 80. www.chablis.net.
- ▶ **Orient Yourself**: This small town, with the feel of a big village, is tucked away in the valley of the River Serein, between Auxerre and Tonnerre.

Sight

Église St-Martin

🕐Open Jul and Aug Mon-Fri 11am-1pm, 3-6pm; Fri-Sat 11am-1pm, 2.30-6pm; Sun 2.30-6pm. ☎03 86 42 80 80.
The church dates from the late 12C. It was founded by monks from St-Martin-des-Tours, who carried their saint's relics with them as they fled the Normans. On the door leaves of the Romanesque south doorway, known as the Porte aux Fers, note the early-13C strap hinges and the horseshoes, offerings made by pilgrims to St Martin. The interior is reminiscent of St-Étienne in Sens.

Excursion

Noyers

25km/15.5mi SE along D 956.
Upriver from Chablis, this charming medieval town has kept its interesting architectural heritage: timber-framed houses or gabled stone ones with quaint

White wines of Chablis

Chablis has been made in Burgundy since the 12C, when the vineyards stretched as far as the eye could see, and tending them was the population's sole occupation, the source of an enviable prosperity. Today, the land is used more selectively, and the soil is the determining factor in the appellation on the bottle, which is a reference to the silica, limestone and clay content of the soil (as in Champagne), rather than to domaines, or specific vineyards (as in Bordeaux, for example).

The best vintages are the Grand Cru, mostly grown on the steep hillsides of the east bank: Vaudésir, Valmur, Grenouilles, Les Clos, Les Preuses, Bougros and Blanchots. Rich in aroma yet dry and delicately flavoured, distinguished by their golden hue, these generally bloom after three years in the bottle, but are rarely kept more than eight. Premier Cru wines are grown on both banks of the river; lighter in colour and less full-bodied, they are best aged three years, never more than six. More than half of the production, bearing the Appellation Chablis Contrôlée label, is very dry and pale, to be aged one to three years before reaching its best.

Often described as crisp or fresh, a good Chablis made exclusively from Chardonnay grapes is delightful with oysters, freshwater fish, ham or chicken dishes with creamy sauce. Lesser vintages, including hearty Bourgogne Aligoté or fruity Petit Chablis, are best enjoyed young with local country fare (grilled sausage, crayfish) or regional cheese (Chaource, St-Florentin) and fresh bread.

Address Book

For coin ranges, see the Legend on the cover flap.

WHERE TO STAY

Chambre d'Hôte La Marmotte – *2 r. de l'École, 89700 Collan, 7.5km/ 4.8mi NE of Chablis by D 150 then D 35. ☎03 86 55 26 44. 3 rooms.* In the heart of a quaint little village, a tastefully restored house built with old stones and beams offers tidy, lovingly kept rooms each decorated with a different colour. Have breakfast in the winter garden graced by a fountain. Table d'hôte meals on request during the summer season.

Aux Lys de Chablis – *38 rte d'Auxerre. ☎03 86 42 49 20. www.hotel-lys-chablis.com. 38 rooms. 6.50€.* Convenient location along one of the main routes into Chablis. Most rooms are modern and well soundproofed.

WHERE TO EAT

Le Syracuse – *19 av. du Maréchal-de-Lattre-de-Tassigny. ☎ 03 86 42 19 45. Closed 2 weeks in Oct and 2 weeks in Mar.* This restaurant has an appealing rustic setting, lovingly prepared cuisine, thoughtful service and a wine list featuring a fine selection of Chablis.

Le Vieux Moulin – *18 r. des Moulins. ☎03 86 42 47 30. www.larochehotel.fr. Closed 24 Dec-1 Jan.* This medieval mill exudes charm and personality. The stone walls of the dining hall decorated with farming tools make a suitable backdrop to the traditional cooking. The connected shop sells all things related to wine.

Hostellerie des Clos – *☎03 86 42 10 63. www.hostellerie-des-clos.com. Closed 22 Dec-16 Jan.* The handsome dining room giving onto the garden is the setting for delicious meals, washed down with fine Chablis wines. Attractive colour schemes in the bedrooms.

SHOPPING

Château Long-Depaquit – *45 r. Auxerroise. ☎03 86 42 11 13. château-long-depaquit@wanadoo.fr. Open Mon-Sat 9am-12.30pm, 1.30-6pm. Closed 24 Dec-2 Jan,1 May and 1 Nov.* Visitors are shown round the storehouses and given a tasting of three wines accompanied by gougère (choux pastry puff flavoured with cheese and pepper).

La Maison de l'Andouillette – *3 bis pl. du Gén.-de-Gaulle. ☎03 86 42 12 82. Open Mon-Sat 9am-12h30pm, 2-7pm, Sun 9am-noon.* Michel Soulié makes andouillete (a type of small sausage) the old-fashioned way. Other regional products also for sale.

COUNTRY LIVING

Chambre d'Hôte Château d'Archambault – *Cours, 2km/1.2mi S of Noyers by D 86. ☎03 86 82 67 55. www.chateau-archambault.com. 5 rooms. Meals.* This imposing 19C mansion once belonged to Napoleon III's private chef. It has been tastefully restored with contemporary furniture. The rooms look over the park or the vegetable garden. Warm, unpretentious welcome. Self-catering accommodation available.

outside stairs, and cellar doors opening onto picturesque streets and tiny squares, form a most attractive setting enhanced at night by discreet lighting. Between June and September, the **Rencontres musicales de Noyers** provides entertainment for music lovers.

Stroll through the town, admiring the 14C and 15C timber-framed houses in **place de l'Hôtel-de-Ville**, the arcaded stone house and Renaissance mansion in **place du Marché-au-Blé**, the Renaissance façade and square tower of the **Église Notre-Dame**, and follow **rue du Poids-du-Roy** to the tiny **place de la Petite-Étape-aux-Vins**. From place du Grenier-à-Sel, a passageway leads to the river bank: here, a **promenade** planted with plane trees offers a pleasant walk and the opportunity to see the seven defensive towers still standing (out of a total of 23), which used to protect the town. Walk through the **Porte Peinte**, a square fortified gate, to return to the town centre.

CHALON-SUR-SAÔNE★

POPULATION 75 447

MICHELIN MAP 320: J-9

Chalon is Burgundy's second town, a prosperous place in the heart of an area of arable farming, stock raising and vineyards; the best wines are worthy of their great neighbours from the Côte d'Or.

Information: 29 bd. de la République, 71100 Chalon-sur-Saône. ☎03 85 48 37 97. www.chalon-sur-saone.net.

▶ **Orient Yourself**: Chalon is on the banks of the Saône where it meets the Canal du Centre. To the north are the Côte de Beaune and Côte de Nuits vineyards; to the south, those of the Mâconnais and the Beaujolais.

A Bit of History

The earliest days of photography

Joseph Nicéphore Niepce, born in Chalon in 1765, devoted himself to scientific research. After perfecting an engine on the same principles as the jet engine (the Pyreolophore), along with his brother Claude, he then devoted his time to lithography and in 1816 succeeded in obtaining a negative image with the aid of a camera obscura, or pinhole camera, and then a positive one in 1822. In 1826 Nicéphore Niepce developed a process of photoengraving: **heliogravure**. The inventor of photography died in Chalon in 1833. A statue in Quai Gambetta and a monument on the edge of the N 6 road at St-Loup-de-Varennes *(7km/4mi S of Chalon)*, where his discovery was perfected, perpetuate the memory of this great inventor.

Sights

Old houses

In the streets near the cathedral there are fine half-timbered façades overlooking place St-Vincent (note also at the corner of rue St-Vincent the statue of a saint), rue aux Fèvres and rue de l'Évêché. **Rue St-Vincent** forms a picturesque crossroads at the junction of rue du Pont and rue du Châtelet. No 37 **rue du Châtelet** has a handsome 17C façade with low-relief sculptures, medallions and gargoyles. No 39 **Grande Rue** is a fine 14C house (restored).

Cathédrale St-Vincent

The cathedral of the old bishopric of Chalon (suppressed in 1790) is not uniform in appearance. The oldest parts date from the late 11C; the chancel is 13C; and the neo-Gothic façade is from 1825.

The pillars in the nave are composed of fluted pilasters and engaged columns. A 15C font and a Flamboyant vault adorn the third chapel in the north transept. The north apsidal chapel contains a large contemporary tabernacle in bronze gilt (1986). A finely sculpted canopy adorns the chancel, and a triptych of the Crucifixion (1608) the apse.

The 15C sacristy was divided horizontally in the 16C, and the lower chamber covered with a vault supported by a central pillar. The ante-chapel is vaulted with five pendant keystones and lit through a stained-glass window of the woman with the 12 stars of the Apocalypse.

The south transept opens into the chapel of Notre-Dame-de-Pitié (15C Pietà and Renaissance tapestry) and into the 15C cloisters (restored) which contain four wooden statues. The well in the cloister garth has also been restored.

The south aisle contains many burial stones; some chapels are closed off by stone screens (claustra); the last chapel contains a 16C polychrome Pietà.

L'Ancien Hôpital St-Laurent

⊙*Open year round.* ⟶*Guided tours (1hr15min) Apr-Sep Wed and Thu 2.30pm; Oct-Mar Wed 2.30.* ⊙*Closed public holidays.* ⊛*3€.* ☎*03 85 44 65 87.*

The Flemish-style building on an island in the River Saône was started in the

Address Book

For coin ranges, see the Legend on the cover flap.

WHERE TO STAY

Hôtel St-Jean – *24 quai Gambetta.* *03 85 48 45 65. www.hotelsaintjean.fr. 25 rooms. 6€.* This 19C hôtel particulier facing the River Saône has a bright breakfast room enhanced with painted wrought-iron furniture. Access to the simple yet comfortable rooms is by an imposing stone staircase.

Hôtel St-Régis – *22 bd. de la République. 03 85 90 95 60. www. saint-regis-chalon.fr. 40 rooms. 10.20€. Restaurant .* Country charm permeates this hotel in the town centre. The carefully kept rooms are suffused with light. Relax in the lounge-bar with its wood panelling and leather armchairs. Bright, spacious dining room.

WHERE TO EAT

Le Bourgogne – *28 r. de Strasbourg. 03 85 48 89 18. Closed 4-9 Jul, 25-30 Dec, Sun evening and Mon.* Candlelight and Louis XIII-style furniture, fire-places and exposed beams all lend an air of comfort. Regional dishes include Burgundy *escargots* and *tournedos de Charolais.*

Ripert – *31 r. St-Georges. 03 85 48 89 20. Closed 12-21 May, 12-31 Aug, 1-6 Jan, Sun and Mon.* Tavern-style décor and market-style cuisine at this pleasant restaurant near the *sous-préfecture.*

Le Bistrot – *31 r. de Strasbourg. 03 85 93 22 01. Closed Sat-Sun.* Wood panelling, old posters, faded postcards and enamelled advertising plaques form the decor of this typical bistrot. Traditional cuisine with a regional touch.

Auberge des Alouettes – *rte. de Givry, 71880 Châtenoy-le-Royal, 4km/ 2.5mi W of Chalon by D 69. 03 85 48 32 15. Closed 4-19 Jan and 15 Jul-8 Aug, Sun evenings, Tue evenings and Wed.* This welcoming restaurant on the road to Givry has two rustic dining rooms and a fine fireplace. Traditional cooking at affordable prices. Meals are served on the terrace in fair weather.

Moulin de Martorey – *71100 St Remy. 03 85 48 12 98. www. moulindemartorey.com. Closed 16-31 Aug, 23 Feb-8 Mar, Sun evening, Tue lunchtime and Monday.* Peaceful 19C flour mill overlooking a canal. Charming rustic interior arranged around the antique works. Cuisine with a personal touch.

SIT BACK AND RELAX

Place St-Vincent – *Pl. St-Vincent.* Lined by colourful half-timbered houses, this square brings together most of the town's cafés, pubs and wine bars, whose terraces are prettily arranged around a fountain.

Aux Colonies des Arômes – *67 Grande-Rue. 03 85 93 99 40. Open Mon 2.30-6.30pm, Tue-Fri 8.30am-7pm, Sat 9am-noon, 2-7pm. Closed 2 weeks in Jan.* This tea shop streaming with light has an elegant blue and white decor; the wicker chairs go well with the rush floor covering. Sip scented tea or try one of the many brands of coffee.

Paddy Brophy's – *4 bd. de la République. 03 85 93 15 19. Open Mon-Sat 11-1am, Sun 5pm-1am. Closed 3 weeks in Aug.* Most of this cheery pub's decor was brought over from Ireland, including the huge fresco and the welcome stone with its inscription in Gaelic.

SHOPPING

La Maison des Vins de la Côte Chalonnaise – *2 prom. Ste-Marie. 03 85 41 64 00. Open Mon-Sat 9am-7pm. Closed public holidays.* The Maison des Vins organises tastings of around 100 vintages, among the best in the region.

Le Cellier Saint-Vincent – *14 pl. St-Vincent. 03 85 48 78 25. Open Tue-Sat 9am-noon, 2-7pm; Sun 9am-12.30pm. Closed public holidays and Mon.* The owner himself designed the barrels made of ash wood where the many wines and liqueurs have been laid down to mature, as well as the glasses for tasting wine, called Les Impitoyables, which bring out the best of each vintage. Charming welcome.

Légendes gourmandes – *4 pl. St-Vincent. 03 85 48 05 64. Open Tue-Sat 9.30am-12.30pm, 2.30-7pm; Sun 9.30am-12.30pm.* There is a gold mine of flavours in this shop, where vinegars, caramels, liqueurs, syrups and terrines all sit cheek-by-jowl with homemade *marc de Bourgogne* and sugars flavoured with rose, lilac, green apple...

16C. The first floor, the nuns' quarters, comprises several panelled rooms, including the infirmary which contains four curtained beds. The buildings were extended in the 17C, and in the 18C certain rooms were decorated with magnificent **woodwork**★. The nuns' refectory and the kitchen passage, which is furnished with dressers lined with pewter and copper vessels, are particularly interesting.

Tour du Doyenné

The 15C deanery tower originally stood near the cathedral. It was dismantled in 1907 and rebuilt at the point of the island.

Additional Sights

Musée Denon★

Open daily except Tue 9.30am-noon, 2-5.30pm. Closed public holidays. 3.10€. ☎03 85 94 74 41.

The 18C building, once part of an Ursuline convent, had the Neoclassical façade added to it when it was converted to house the museum which bears the name of one of Chalon's most illustrious citizens, Dominique Vivant **Denon** (1747-1825), a diplomat under the Ancien Régime, who was also a famous engraver and one of the first to introduce lithography to France. During Napoleon's campaign in Egypt he pioneered Egyptology and became artistic adviser to the Emperor,

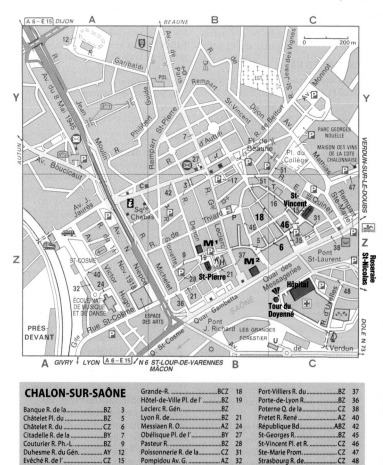

Grand Purveyor and Director of French Museums (including the Louvre), which he endowed with works of art.

The museum displays an important collection of 17C-19C paintings. The Italian School is represented by three large canvases by Giordano, as well as works by Bassano (*Plan of Venice, Adoration of the Shepherds*), Solimena and Caravaggio. The golden age of Dutch painting (17C) is represented by Hans Bollongier (*Bouquet of Tulips*) and De Heem (still-life paintings). 19C French painting is represented by Géricault (*Portrait of a Black Man*) and the pre-Impressionist landscape painter Raffort, a native of Chalon. Local history is illustrated by examples of domestic traditions, the life of the Saône boatmen and a collection of local furniture. Also on display is a collection of wood carvings dating from before the Revolution. The ground floor is devoted to the rich archaeological collections: prehistoric flint implements from Volgu (Digoin-Gueugnon region – the largest and most beautiful Stone Age relics discovered, dating from the Solutré period), many antique and medieval metal artefacts,

a magnificent Gallo-Roman group in stone of a lion bringing down a gladiator. There are also Gallo-Roman and medieval lapidary collections.

Musée Nicéphore-Niepce★

⊙*Open Jul-Aug daily except Tue 10am-6pm. Rest of the year daily except Tue 9.30-11.45am, 2-5.45pm.* ⊙*Closed public holidays.* ⊠*3.10€.* ☎*03 85 48 41 98. www. museeniepce.com.*

This museum is in the 18C Hôtel des Messageries on the banks of the Saône. The rich collection includes photographs and photographic equipment, and some of the earliest cameras ever made, used by Joseph Nicéphore Niepce, and his first **heliographs**. There are also works by well-known contemporaries of Niepce in the world of photography, including Daguerre, his associate in 1829. Note in particular Niepce's first camera (1816), the machinery for producing **daguerreotypes**, the first colour and relief photographs and the famous 19C cameras: Chevalier's Grand Photographe (c 1850), the Bertsch cameras (1860) and the Damoizeau cyclographs (1890).

CHAMPAGNOLE

POPULATION 8 616

MICHELIN MAP 321: F-6

This leafy town in the heart of the Jura makes a relaxed base for explorations into the spectacular surrounding countryside.

- **Information**: av. de la République, 39304 Champagnole. ☎03 84 52 43 67. www.tourisme.champagnole.com.
- ▸ **Orient Yourself**: Head south or east out of town for the fabulous natural sights of the Ain Valley, La Joux Forest and the lakes region (⊙*see Région des LACS DU JURA*).

Driving Tour

Upper Valley Of The Ain

84km/52mi – allow 4hr
⊙*see local map.*

▸ *Leave Champagnole heading SW on D 471. At Ney, take D 253 to the left; after 2.5km/1.5mi take the unsurfaced road, in poor condition, to the left for about 2.4km/1.4mi, until you reach a car park.*

Belvédère de Bénedegand

🚶*15min there and back on foot.*
A pretty forest path leads to this viewpoint. There is a lovely view of the Ain Valley, Champagnole, Mont Rivel and, in the distance, the forest of Fresse.

▸ *Retrace your steps to the main road (D 253), go through Loulle and Vaudioux and turn right on N 5. Take the first road on the left, D 279, and leave the car in*

*the car park at the side of the road, on
a level with the Billaude waterfall.*

There is a good view of the waterfall and
its setting from the platform below.

Cascade de la Billaude★
30min there and back on foot.
⚑ Take the path marked Saut Claude Roy
which leads down to the waterfall. Take
the steep, sharply twisting footpath down
into the ravine, keeping to the right. Then
there is quite a stiff climb uphill *(100 steps,
many of which are very high)*. At the top,
the Lemme can be seen tumbling from
a narrow crevice in a wooded setting between towering rock faces, dropping a
total of 28m/92ft in two successive cascades. Delicately perfumed cyclamens
grow near the waterfall in summer.

▶ *Return to N 5 and follow it to the left.*

River Lemme★
N 5 follows the valley of the River Lemme,
a tributary of the Ain, as far as Pont-de-
la-Chaux. The sight of this turbulent little
river gushing between pines and rocky
crags is fresh and exhilarating.

▶ *At Pont-de-la-Chaux, take D 16 on
the left.*

Chaux-des-Croteney
This town, built on a triangular rocky plateau with precipitous rock faces dropping
away at the edges, providing a natural
defence, is thought by some archaeologists to be the site of ancient Alésia.

▶ *Take D 16 and D 127E1 to Les
Planches-en-Montagne.*

Gorges de la Langouette★
⚑*30min round trip on foot. Leave the car
in the shady car park after the bridge called
La Langouette.*
There is a lovely view from this bridge
of the Gorges de la Langouette, only 4m/
13ft wide and 47m/154ft deep, cut into the
limestone by the River Saine. The three
viewpoints★ over the gorge can be reached by taking the path on the left before
the bridge *(access also possible by car,
follow the road indicated from the village
of Les Planches)*. The rather steep foot-

path is signposted and leads to where
the Saine cascades into a narrow crevice,
the beginning of the gorge.

▶ *Return to Les Planches and turn right
at the church; then just before Chaux-
des-Crotenay, turn right again onto a
forest road.*

Vallée de la Saine
The route continues along a pretty road
running through forest along the top of
the cliffs which form the sides of the narrow valley of the Saine, a small tributary
of the Lemme.

▶ *Turn right after coming out of the
gorge and cross the bridge.*

Syam
Excavations in the Syam plain, near the
confluence of the Lemme and the Saine,
have enabled a team of archaeologists to
say they believe they have located the site
of the Battle of Alésia. Having been besieged
by Caesar's troops in the oppidum of Alésia
for six weeks, the army of the Gauls is
thought to have stormed down from the
Gyts heights near Syam, where Vercingetorix had an observation post, in an attempt
to join up with the Gallic relief forces which
were attacking the Roman field camps
defending the Crans threshold. In the
ensuing battle, involving 400 000 men,
the Gauls were unable to break through the
Romans' double line of defence fortifications and suffered a crushing defeat.

Villa Palladienne★
🕐*Open mid-Apr to mid-Oct daily except
Tue 11am-6pm.* 💶*6.50€.* ☎*03 84 51 64
14. www.chateaudesyam.fr.*
This amazing Palladian villa was commissioned in 1825 by Emmanuel Jobez, a
Forge Master who admired Italian architecture. The square plan underlined by
Ionic pilasters, the central rotunda and
the Pompeiian-style decoration is reminiscent of Italian villas. The interior decoration and period furniture are very attractive. *Concerts are organised regularly.*

Forges
🕐*Open Jul-Aug daily except Tue 10am-
7pm; May-Jun and Sep Sat-Sun and public
holidays 10am-6pm.* 👣*Guided tours*

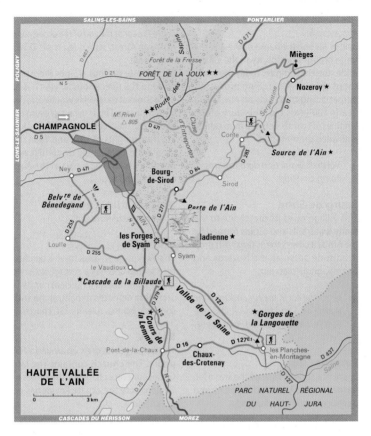

Address Book

🪙 For coin ranges, see the Legend on the cover flap.

WHERE TO STAY

🍽️🛏️**Hôtel Bois Dormant** – rte. de Pontarlier. ☎03 84 52 66 66. www.boisdormant.com. 40 rooms. 🍴10€. Restaurant🍽️🛏️. You will undoubtedly get a good night's sleep in this peaceful hotel surrounded by greenery. Functional rooms with light, pine wood panelling, many of which open onto the forest. Spacious dining room extended by a verandah.

🍽️🛏️**Grand Hôtel Ripotot** – 54 r. du Mar.-Foch. ☎03 84 52 15 45. Closed Nov-Mar. 35 rooms. 🍴7€. Restaurant🍽️🛏️. An aura of yesteryear reigns at this hostelry, operated by the same family since 1875. Spacious rooms overlook the tranquil garden. The large dining room features lovely windows in the Belle Époque style, traditional cuisine and attentive service.

WHERE TO EAT

🍽️🛏️**Auberge des Gourmets** – 8km/5mi S of Champagnole heading for Genève by N 5. ☎03 84 51 60 60. www.auberge-des-gourmets.com. Closed 20 Dec-31 Jan, Sun evenings and Mon lunchtime out of season. This country inn on the edge of the road has a very appropriate name and is popular among local residents. The owner offers carefully prepared, succulent dishes at highly affordable prices. Meals are served in the traditional dining room or on the rustic-style verandah. A few rooms available. Swimming pool.

(1hr 30min). ⌚3€. ☎03 84 51 61 00. www. forgesyam.fr.

Built in 1813 on the banks of the Ain, the forge brought prosperity to the village under the First Empire. Today the workshops specialise in rolling processes, perpetuating traditions on machinery nearly 100 years old. The story of the Smithies of Syam is detailed in an exhibit and video presentation.

▶ *North of Syam, turn right towards Bourg-de-Sirod.*

Bourg-de-Sirod

This village owes its pretty site to the many waterfalls and rapids formed by the Ain as it covers the 100m/328ft drop in altitude between the Nozeroy and Champagnole plateaux.

▶ *Leave the car in the car park near the Bourg-de-Sirod town hall (mairie). Follow the path marked Point de vue, Perte de l'Ain.*

Perte de l'Ain

There is a superb view of the waterfall formed by the Ain as it disappears into a crevice between fallen rocks.

▶ *Carry on through Sirod and Conte.*

Source de l'Ain★

Leave the car at the end of the access road (through forest) which leads off D 283 after Conte.

🚶Continue on foot *(15min there and back)* to the river's source, which is at the bottom of the thickly wooded, rocky amphitheatre. This is in fact a resurgent spring and has a very variable flow. During the droughts of 1959 and 1964 the mouth was completely dry, and it was possible to climb up a part of the Ain's underground course.

▶ *Return to D 283, turn left and continue to Nozeroy.*

Nozeroy★

This picturesque market town is perched on a hilltop and has a certain old-style charm. The traces of its ancient ramparts and other defences remain, along with some old houses near its 15C church.

Mièges

This farming town grew up around a 16C priory. The **church** contains the late Gothic funerary chapel of the dukes of Chalon; note the ornate keystones on the ceiling.

▶ *Return to Champagnole by taking D 119, then D 471 to the left, which crosses the pleasantly green Entreportes ravine.*

LA CHARITÉ-SUR-LOIRE★

POPULATION 5 686

MICHELIN MAP 319: B-8

La Charité, which is dominated by the belfries of its handsome church, rises in terraces from the majestic sweep of the Loire. La Charité was a busy port in the days when the river was active with traffic.

▯ **Information**: 5 pl. Ste-Croix, 58400 La Charité-sur-Loire.
☎03 86 70 15 06. www.ville-la-charite-sur-loire.fr.

▶ **Orient Yourself:** There is a good view of the town from the picturesque 16C stone bridge over the Loire.

A Bit of History

The Charity of the Good Fathers

The founding early in the 8C of a convent and church marked the start of a period of prosperity which was interrupted by Arab invasions and attendant destruction. By the 11C, when the present church was built, the reorganised abbey began to attract travellers and pilgrims.

The hospitality of the monks became so widely known that the poor came in droves to ask for the good fathers' charity (charité) and the town acquired a new name.

Sights

Église prieurale Notre-Dame★★

Despite the damage it has incurred over the centuries (a few bays, the transept and the chancel are all that remain), this **priory church** is still one of the most remarkable examples of Romanesque architecture in Burgundy.

Eldest daughter of Cluny – The church and its attendant Benedictine priory, a daughter house of Cluny, were built during the second half of the 11C. The church was consecrated in 1107 by Pope Paschal II. Its outline and decoration were modified in the first half of the 12C.

After Cluny the priory church of La Charité was the largest church in France; it consisted of a nave and four aisles (122m/399ft long, 37m/120ft wide, 27m/89ft high under the dome). It could hold a congregation of 5 000, carried the honorary title Eldest daughter of Cluny and had at least 50 daughter houses.

Exterior – The façade, which was separated from the rest of the church by a fire in 1559, is in place des Pêcheurs. Originally two towers framed the central

---

Address Book

For coin ranges, see the Legend on the cover flap.

WHERE TO STAY

Camping Municipal La Saulaie – *Quai de la Saulaie.* ☎03 86 70 00 83. *charite@club-internet.fr. Open 26 Apr-12 Sep.* 🖵 *100 sites.* Pitch your tent along the banks of the Loire on the small island of La Saulaie, near the beach. Numerous hiking trails for nature lovers. Swimming pool on the premises. Facilities for tennis, angling and archery nearby.

Le Bon Laboureur – *Quai Romain-Mollot (Île de la Loire).* ☎03 86 70 22 85. *www.lebonlaboureur.com. 16 rooms.* 🖵*6.50€.* A former post office and boat barn transformed as a hotel with well-maintained rooms. Breakfast served on the veranda overlooking the garden.

Relais de Pouilly – *58150 Pouilly-sur-Loire, 11km/6.8mi N of La Charité-sur-Loire by N 151 then N 7.* ☎03 86 39 03 00. *www.relaisdepouilly.com. 24 rooms.* 🖵*8.50€. Restaurant*🖵🖵. Restful in spite of its location near the new motorway, thanks to rooms fitted with double glazing that look out onto a lush setting. Cosy accommodation decorated with bamboo furniture. The dining room gives onto the garden.

EATING OUT

Le Moulin aux Crêpes – *26 r. des Hôtelleries.* ☎03 86 70 00 55. 🖵. Simple, quiet and welcoming are the watchwords for this small *creperie.* Regulars turn up for the short but well-rounded menu.

TAKE A BREAK

Confiserie du Prieuré – *11 pl. des Pêcheurs.* ☎03 86 70 01 81. *la.confiserie. du.prieure@cegetel.net. Open Tue-Sat 9.30am-12.15pm and 2.30-7pm, Sun 9.30am-12.30pm.* This magnificent stone building houses a cosy tearoom. In summer the flower-bedecked terrace is the perfect spot for an afternoon snack of housemade pastries or chocolates.

Domaine Hervé-Seguin – *3 r. Joseph-Renaud, take the Route de Donzy for 1km, 58150 Pouilly-sur-Loire.* ☎03 86 39 10 75. *www.domaineseguin.com. Open 10am-noon, 2-7pm.* Come and sample the wares of the Seguin family, winemakers for six generations. These days they specialize in three wines: two *pouilly-fumés* and a special prestige *cuvée.*

Caves de Pouilly-sur-Loire – *39 ave. des Tuileries, 58150 Pouilly-sur-Loire.* ☎03 86 39 10 99. *www.cavespouillysur-loire.com. Mon-Fri 8am-noon and 2-6pm, Sat 9am-12.30pm and 2-6pm, Sun in season 10am-12.30pm and 2.30-6.30pm.* Established in 1948, this cellar boasts 100 members and is one of the principal producers of *pouilly-fumé* and *coteaux-du-giennois.* Large tasting room within the cellars.

The town seen from the far bank of the Loire

doorway; only one *(left)*, the 12C **Tour Ste-Croix**, has survived.

The steps of the Romanesque central doorway, of which very little is left and which was replaced by a Gothic construction in the 16C, lead to place Ste-Croix, on the site of six bays of the nave destroyed in the fire of 1559.

Houses have been built into the former north aisle, which was transformed into a parish church from the 12C to the 18C. The arcades of the false triforium are still visible.

Interior – The present church consists of the first four bays of the original nave, the transept and the chancel. The nave has nothing of interest, but the transept and the chancel constitute a magnificent Romanesque ensemble.

The transept crossing is surmounted by an octagonal dome on squinches. The arms of the transept have three bays and two apsidal chapels dating from the 11C; this is the oldest part of the church. In the south transept, the second Romanesque **tympanum**★ of the Tour Ste-Croix

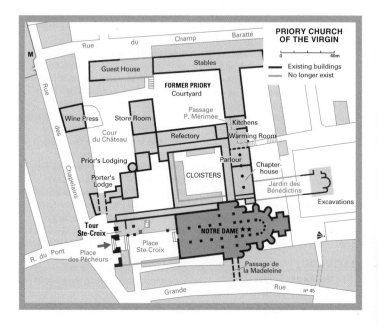

PRIORY CHURCH
OF THE VIRGIN

0   40m

━━ Existing buildings
▦ No longer exist

Rue   du   Champ   Baratté

M

Guest House   Stables

FORMER PRIORY
Courtyard

Rue   Wine Press   Store Room   Passage
P. Mérimée   Kitchens

des   Cour
du Château   Refectory   Warming Room

Prior's Lodging   Parlour   Chapter-
house

Chapelains   Porter's
Lodge   CLOISTERS   Jardin des
Bénédictins

Excavations

**Tour
Ste-Croix**   ℹ   **NOTRE DAME** ★★ ★

R. du Pont   Place
des Pêcheurs   Place
Ste-Croix

Passage de
la Madeleine

Grande   Rue   n° 45

is visible, representing the Transfiguration with the Adoration of the Magi and the Presentation in the Temple.

A bestiary of eight motifs accentuates the false triforium; its five-lobed arcades, of Arabic inspiration, are supported by ornamented pilasters. There are good modern stained-glass windows by Max Ingrand.

Ancien Prieuré

The vast ensemble formed by the old priory is gradually being restored: note in particular the 14C chapter-house, the 18C cloisters, the refectory, the prior's drawing room and dining room… The prior's lodging (early 16C) with an attractive seven-sided turret overlooks the lower courtyard (now called Cour du Château). Exhibitions relating to the history of the priory or to the restoration work are organised every summer.

Museum

🕐 *Open Jul-Aug daily except Tue 10am-noon, 3-6pm; Apr-Jun and Sep-Oct daily except Mon and Tue 3-5pm.* 🕐 *Closed Dec-Feb, 1 May.* 1€. ☎03 86 70 34 83.

Considerable space is devoted to medieval objects found during excavations behind the church: lapidary fragments and terracotta tiles, implements, pottery, keys, jewellery and so on. There are also sculptures by Pina (1885-1966), a pupil of Rodin, and a fine collection of Sèvres ceramics.

CHARLIEU ★

POPULATION 3 582
MICHELIN MAP 320: F-13

Pretty Charlieu was a bustling market town on the road linking the Saône and Loire valleys in Gallo-Roman times. These days it is a centre for the millinery and silk industries. However, it is Charlieu's archaeological treasures in particular that have won the town its renown.

- **Information**: Maison de Pays, pl. Saint-Philibert, 42190 Charlieu. ☎04 77 60 12 42. www.ville-charlieu.fr.
- ▶ **Orient Yourself**: In July and August, the tourist office offers tours of the Old Town; otherwise pick up a leaflet from them and follow the arrows set into the pavements.

Abbaye Bénédictine ★

🕐 *Open Jul-Aug daily except Mon 10am-noon, 1-7pm. Rest of the year daily except Mon 10am-12.30pm, 2-6.30pm (5.30pm in winter).* 🕐 *Closed Jan and 25 Dec.* 4.50€. ☎04 77 60 09 97.

The abbey was founded c 872, attached to Cluny c 930, converted into a priory c 1040 and then fortified on the orders of Philippe Auguste, its protector. The architects and artists from Cluny collaborated here with particularly happy results to rebuild the 11C church and add on the 12C narthex. Excavations show that a small 9C church was replaced by a 10C church, which was replaced in turn by an 11C abbey church, on a slightly different axis. This church had a nave with four bays and aisles either side, a transept with transept chapels and an ambulatory with radiating chapels opening off it. The abbey was not to escape the ravages of the Revolution, however; the Benedictine priory, which at the time still housed two monks, was secularised in March 1789. The abbey buildings and the church of St-Fortunat, one of the finest of Cluny's daughters, were largely demolished. All that remains of the church are the narthex and the first bay, in which the capitals bear a resemblance to those of the Brionnais. The warm golden glow of the stone of the abbey buildings adds to the charm of the scene.

There is a good view of the two doorways, which are the abbey's best feature, from place de l'Abbaye.

Tympanum of the great doorway on the north side of the narthex, abbey of Charlieu

Société des Amis des Arts de Charlieu-

Façade★★★

The north façade of the narthex is entered through a **great doorway**, dating from the 12C, which is decorated with some wonderful sculpture work. Christ in Majesty is depicted on the tympanum in a mandorla, supported by two angels and surrounded by the symbols of the four Evangelists. On the lintel, the Virgin Mary appears with two attendant angels and the 12 disciples. The arch mouldings and the columns which frame the doorway are decorated with geometrical and floral motifs. The abbey owed this luxuriant plant-like decoration, of Eastern inspiration, to the Crusades. The inside of the left doorpost bears a representation of Lust, depicted as a woman grappling with frightful reptilian monsters.

The **small doorway**, to the right of the great doorway, also dates from the 12C. The Wedding at Cana is depicted on its tympanum, the Transfiguration of Christ on its archivolt and an Old Testament sacrifice on the lintel.

As you enter, you will see to your left the foundations of the various churches which have stood on this site. They can be seen more clearly from the Salle du Chartrier.

Cloisters

These were built in the 15C to replace the previous ones, which were Romanesque. The east gallery contains six huge arches supported on twin colonnettes, whose capitals are richly decorated with sculpted acanthus leaves, birds and geometrical motifs.

Chapter-house

This dates from the early 16C and features pointed arches supported on a round stone pillar, into which a lectern has been carved.

Prior's chapel

This dates from the late 15C. The old terracotta floor tiling has been reconstructed based on the original. Above the chapel is a bell turret with a timber roof.

▶ *The next two rooms form the Musée Armand-Charnay.*

Parlour

This lovely vaulted room dating from the early 16C houses a **lapidary museum** in which, next to old capitals from the priory, note two bas-relief sculptures: a 10C Carolingian one depicting Daniel in the Lions' Den and a 12C one depicting the Annunciation amid interlaced arches.

Cellar

The cellar, beneath two semicircular vaults, houses a museum of sacred art including a lovely collection of polychrome wood statues from the 15C to the 18C. Note in particular a Virgin Mary with Bird, from the church in Aiguilly (near Roanne), and a Virgin with Child, both Gothic dating from the 15C.

Narthex

This rectangular building, 17m/56ft long and about 10m/33ft wide, comprises two rooms, one above the other, with ribbed vaulting.

One of these contains a **Gallo-Roman sarcophagus** (1) which was found in the crypt of the Carolingian church. The east wall of the narthex is the former west front of the 11C church of St-Fortunat, consecrated in 1094, comprising: a doorway (2), on the tympanum framed by three well-defined arch mouldings, Christ is depicted in Majesty in a mandorla held by two angels); two twin windows with arch mouldings, and above, a pair of figures facing each other.

Charter room (Salle du Chartrier)

A spiral staircase leads up to this room, which is also known as the Salle des Archives. It contains an exhibition on the history of the abbey.

The great window to the east has two small blind arcades either side of it, and beautiful arch mouldings above it which are supported on engaged columns with capitals decorated with foliage. From

here there is a good view of the site of the previous churches – the outline of each of their foundations shows up in the grass. The view also takes in the Philippe-Auguste tower, the prior's lodging (*not open to the public*) and the rooftops of the town.

Before leaving the abbey, have a quick look down into the courtyard of the prior's lodging.

Tour Philippe-Auguste

This imposing tower of ochre-coloured stone, was built c1180 on the orders of Philippe-Auguste, who considered the fortified town of Charlieu to be of great use to the French crown. It was part of the abbey's fortifications.

Old Town

Strolling through the streets near place St-Philibert, you will come across numerous picturesque houses dating from the 13C to the 18C. On the corner of place St-Philibert and rue Grenette stands a 13C stone house which has twin win-

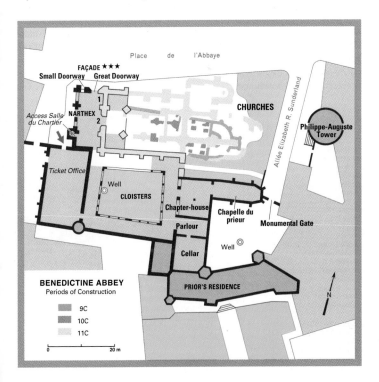

Place de l'Abbaye

FAÇADE ★★★
Small Doorway   Great Doorway

Access Salle du Chartier   NARTHEX

Ticket Office

CHURCHES

Allée Elizabeth R. Sunderland

Philippe-Auguste Tower

Well   CLOISTERS

Chapter-house

Chapelle du prieur

Monumental Gate

Parlour

Well

Cellar

PRIOR'S RESIDENCE

N

BENEDICTINE ABBEY
Periods of Construction

9C
10C
11C

0   20 m

dows with colonnettes as mullions on its upper floor.

Église St-Philibert

This 13C church, which has no transept, has a layout typical of 13C Burgundian architecture: a nave with five bays, side aisles and a rectangular chancel. It houses some beautiful works of art, such as a 15C pulpit hewn from a single block of stone and 15C and 16C stalls with pretty painted panels. One chapel contains a 16C Madonna (Notre-Dame-de-Charlieu). In the chapel of Ste-Anne on the south side of the chancel there is a 15C polychrome stone altarpiece depicting the Visitation and the Nativity. The chapel of St-Crépin on the north side of the chancel contains a 17C Pietà and a statuette of St Crispin, patron saint of shoemakers and saddlers.

Ancien Hôtel-Dieu

The 18C hospital has a beautiful façade overlooking rue Jean-Morel and consists of two huge rooms for the sick, separated by a chapel in which there is a handsome 17C gilded wood altar. The building now houses two museums.

Musée de la Soierie★

Open Jul-Aug daily except Mon 10am-1pm, 2-7pm. Rest of the year 2-6pm. Closed Jan. 4.30€. 04 77 60 28 84. www.amisdesartscharlieu.com.

This museum documents the history of the silk industry in Charlieu. The large room on the left houses the statue of Notre-Dame-de-Septembre, patron of the powerful weavers' guild, in whose honour there is an annual procession *(2nd Sunday in September)*. The exhibition includes samples of local silk production (sumptuous clothing, one-off creations commissioned by aristocratic families etc) and impressive old looms, giving a good overview of the technical developments in weaving from the 18C on. All the equipment on display is in working order, and from time to time there is a **demonstration**★. On the first floor there is a display of materials and designer clothes as well as a video on silk weaving techniques.

Musée Hospitalier

As for the Musée de la Soierie.
The Hôtel-Dieu, where for three centuries the sisters of the Order of St Martha cared for the sick, closed its doors in 1981 and reopened as a museum. It is a faithful representation of a small provincial hospital from the end of the 19C through the 1950s. The apothecary is fitted with 18C woodwork to accommodate medicinal herbs, flacons with ground-glass stoppers and ceramic urns. Past the operating and treatment rooms, the wooden linen press, the work of regional craftsmen, has room for 850 sheets. The

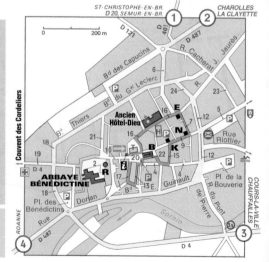

wealth of bedding was due to the infrequency of wash days, which only came around twice a year. One of the two large wards has been recreated with its rows of curtained beds.

▶ *Continue along rue Jean-Morel and stop outside no 32.*

The **Maison des Anglais** dating from the 16C, has mullioned windows on its upper storey with Gothic niches in between them. Two watch-turrets frame the façade.

▶ *Turn right onto rue André-Farinet.*

No 29: 13C stone house; no 27: 15C half-timbered house, the **Maison Disson**; on the corner opposite, no 22: old 14C salt warehouse.

▶ *Turn right again onto rue Charles-de-Gaulle.*

At no 9, the 13C-14C **Maison des Armagnacs** has two twin windows surmounted by trefoil arches. That on the left is decorated with a floral motif, and that on the right with a human face. The upper storey is half-timbered and overhangs the street.

▶ *Take rue Michon and then rue Chanteloup, a shopping street, to reach rue du Merle.*

On the corners of rue du Merle and rue des Moulins (no 11), and of rue des Moulins and place St-Philibert, stand old half-timbered houses.

Couvent des Cordeliers★

🕐*Open Jul-Aug daily except Mon 10am-1pm, 2-7pm. Rest of the year times vary.* 🕐*Closed Dec-Jan.* 🎫*4.50€.* ☎04 77 60 12 42.

This Franciscan monastery was founded in the 13C in St-Nizier-sous-Charlieu. Its unprotected site outside the town walls meant that it suffered quite a lot of damage both during the Hundred Years War and at the hands of roving bands of mercenaries. The monastery buildings have recently undergone restoration.

The **Gothic cloisters**, of pale gold stone, were sold to the United States and were to be taken down and rebuilt there, but luckily they were rescued at the last minute by the French State, which managed to buy them back in 1910. The arcades (late 14C-15C) are decorated with a fascinating variety of plant motifs. The capitals along the north arcade depict vices and virtues in an amusing series of figures and animals; one capital portrays the expressive face of a monk, another has the dance of death as its theme. The west arcade is adorned with a frieze of oak leaves with snails, rabbits and caterpillars on the capitals.

The single-nave church (late 14C), with no transept, has three side chapels on its south side (late 15C-early 16C) and has been partially restored. Originally, it was entirely decorated with paintings, but only a few mural paintings now remain in the chancel.

CHAROLLES

POPULATION 3 027

MICHELIN MAP 320: F-11

Bygone capital of the counts of Charolais, the appealing little town of Charolles draws its charm from the rivers and canals winding through the old streets and the flower-decked squares, which invite relaxation.

The distinctive white **Charolais cattle** raised on the rich pasture lands in this area are valued for their tasty beef. Regional cattle markets take place several times a year; hundreds of hardy animals are offered for sale by local breeders, valued for their ancestral know-how.

- **Information**: Ancien Couvent des Clarisses, 24 r. Baudinot, 71120 Charolles. ☎03 85 24 05 95. www.charolles.fr.
- **Orient yourself**: Sites as diverse as Cluny, La Clayette, the churches of the Brionnais region and Mont St-Vincent are all within 30km/ 18mi.

Sights

Town houses

The town is proud of the 14C vestiges of its castle: two towers known as the Tour du Téméraire and Tour des Diamants, the latter now serving as the town hall. There is a nice **view** of the landscape from the terrace gardens. The tourist office is at the bottom of rue Baudinot, in a former Poor Clare's convent house, once home to St Marguerite-Marie Alacoque (*see PARAY-LE-MONIAL*).

Le Prieuré Sainte-Madeleine

Under the authority of the abbot at Cluny, this building welcomed pilgrims on their way to Santiago de Compostela. Note the collection of capitals and the remarkable carved beams of the chapter-house.

The priory also houses a **museum** (*open Jun-Sep daily except Tue 2-6pm; rest of the year by appointment; 3€; ☎03 85 24 24 74*) where you can see a collection of **earthenware**★ using the typical bright motifs of Charolles – flowers, butterflies, dragonflies – and, in particular, works by the region's seminal ceramics artist, Hippolyte Prost (1844-92).

Maison du Charolais

Open daily 10am-6pm. Closed late Dec, 1 May and 1 Nov. 4.60€. ☎03 85 88 04 00. www.institut-charolais.com.

This attraction provides a wealth of information about the distinctive white **Charolais cattle** raised on the rich pasture lands in this area, which are highly valued for their meat.

Address Book

For coin ranges, see the Legend at the back of the guide.

LIFE ON THE FARM

Ferme-Auberge de Lavaux – *71800 Châtenay, 8.5km/5.3mi E of La Clayette by D 987 then D 300.* ☎03 85 28 08 48. *Closed 1 Nov to Easter and Tue. Reservations required. Meals*. This tastefully restored 19C farmhouse with old-fashioned turrets has a dining room under the eaves and a covered terrace. There is a charming room in the square tower, with antique furniture and a private balcony giving onto the courtyard.

Chambre d'Hôte M. et Mme Desmurs – *La Saigne, 71800 Varennes-sous-Dun, 4km/2.5mi E of La Clayette by D 987 then a minor road.* ☎03 85 28 12 79. *michelealaindesmurswanadoo.fr.* 3 *rooms. Meals*. This converted farmhouse is deep in the countryside. Two rooms are furnished in old-fashioned style and one suite has been set up under the eaves. You may want to choose the third room, quite charming with its stone walls and tiled floor.

Warm, friendly welcome. Charolais cows reared on the premises.

Ferme-Auberge des Collines – *In the hamlet of Amanzé, 9km/5.6mi NW of Clayette by D 989 then D 279.* ☎03 85 70 66 34. *www.fermeaubergedescollines. com. Closed 1 Nov to Easter.* Reservations required. Meals. The pretty square tower of this farmhouse testifies to its long-history. The sturdy beams, tiled floors and stone walls make for a strong rustic atmosphere. The quiet rooms look out onto the fields or the blossoming garden. Charolais cows and pigs are reared on the premises. Home-grown vegetables.

SHOPPING

Les Chocolats Bernard-Dufoux – *32 r. Centrale.* ☎03 85 28 08 10. *www. chocolatsdufoux.com. Open daily 9am-8pm.* Widely regarded as being one of France's finest chocolatiers, Dufoux puts 40 years of experience into the creation of such delicacies as the golden palette of chocolates, and special spiced chocolate. He also gives lessons.

Excursions

Mont des Carges★

12km/8mi E.

From the esplanade, with its monuments to the underground fighters of Beaubery and the Charolais battalion, an almost circular **view**★★ takes in the Loire country to the west, all the Charolais and Brionnais regions to the south and the mountains of Beaujolais to the east.

Ph. Gajic-MICHELIN

Charolais bull

CHÂTEAU-CHINON★

POPULATION 2 307

MICHELIN MAP 319: G-9

LOCAL MAP SEE LE MORVAN

The little town of Château-Chinon, in the heart of the Morvan regional park, occupies a picturesque site★ on the ridge that separates the Loire and Seine basins on the eastern edge of the Nivernais. Its easily defended hilltop position made this place successively a Gallic settlement, a Roman camp and a feudal castle, which gave its name to the town. More recently, a certain François Mitterand was mayor for 22 years before becoming President.

- **Information**: Maison du Morvan, pl. St-Christophe, 58120 Château-Chinon, ☎03 86 85 06 58. www.ot-chateauchinon.com.
- ▶ **Orient Yourself**: Starting at the Porte Notre-Dame, all that remains of a 15C rampart, take a stroll through the medieval streets.

Sights

Musée du Septennat★

ⓘOpen Jul-Aug 10am-1pm, 2-7pm. Rest of the year times vary. ⓘClosed Jan-Feb. ☜4€. ☎03 86 85 19 23. www.cg58.fr.

The "seven years" in this museum's name refer to the President's term of office in France (now only five years), and the displays include presidential memorabilia and gifts given to former mayor **François Mitterrand** (1916-96) during his 14-year

---

Address Book

WHERE TO STAY

🛏**Camping Municipal Les Soulins** – 58120 Corancy, 10.5km/6.5mi N of Château-Chinon by D 37, D 12 and D 161. ☎03 86 78 01 62. Open 15 Jun-15 Sep. 42 sites. ☞ Reservations recommended. This camp site near the lake enjoys a lovely view of the wooded hills nearby.

🛏**Chambre d'Hôte Les Chaumottes** – 58120 St-Hilaire-en-Morvan, 5.5km/ 3.5mi W of Château-Chinon by D 978. ☎03 86 85 22 33. Closed Dec-Feb. ☞ 3 rooms. A well restored 14C manor. Two of the large, comfortable rooms look out onto Château-Chinon. Excellent value. Self-catering accommodation is available.

🛏🛏**Vieux Morvan** – 8 pl. Gudin – ☎03 86 85 05 01. www.auvieuxmorvan.com. Closed 15 Dec to 15 Jan. 24 rooms. ☞7€. Restaurant🛏🛏. This spot was made famous by numerous visits from François Mitterrand; you can even request "his" room. The dining room has a lovely view of the Morvan.

WHERE TO EAT

🍴**Auberge de la Madonette** – 58110 St-Péreuse, 14km/8.7mi W of Château-Chinon by D 978 and then a minor road. ☎03 86 84 45 37. www.lamadonette.fr. Closed 15 Dec-1 Feb, Tue evenings and Wed. A friendly restaurant full of country charm, serving enjoyable classic cuisine.

SHOPPING

Gaudry – 25 pl. St-Romain – ☎03 86 85 13 87. Mon Sat 7am-7pm; Sundays from 1 Jun to 1 Nov 7am-7pm. Feast your eyes on the homemade pâtés, terrines, quiches and sausages in the window, but don't stop there; be sure to step inside to inhale the mouthwatering aromas.

Les Rûchers du Morvan – Port-de-L'Homme D 37. ☎ 03 86 78 02 43. No visits Oct-late Apr. The proprietor keeps 800 to 1,000 beehives depending on the season. Through a glass partition visitors can watch the bees going about their business, plus participate in honey extractions and (of course) tastings.

tenure beginning in 1981. The 18C building used to be a Poor Clare's convent. Visitors will see photographs of world leaders and international events, medals and honorific decorations. The collection includes a surprising range of art.

Panorama from the Calvaire★★
15min on foot there and back from square Aligre.
The calvary (609m/1 998ft) is built on the site of the fortified Gallic settlement and the ruins of the fortress. There is a fine panorama *(viewing table)* of Château-Chinon's slate roofs, and further off the wooded crests of the Morvan. The two summits of the Haut-Folin (901m/2 956ft) and the Mont Préneley (855m/2 805ft) are to the south-east.

Promenade du Château★
A road *(starting in faubourg de Paris and returning via rue du Château)* encircles the hill halfway up. Through the trees there are glimpses of the Yonne gorge on one side and countryside on the other.

Driving Tour

▶ *Drive N out of Château-Chinon then bear right onto D 37 and left onto D 12 to Lac de Pannesière-Chaumard.*

Lac de Pannesière-Chaumard★
The reservoir (7.5km/5mi long) forms a glorious expanse of water in an attractive **setting**★ amid wooded hills. A road

runs all round it and along the top of the dam, giving a pretty **view** with the summits of the Haut Morvan.

▶ *Before reaching the dam, make a detour to the NE along D 301 to Ouroux-en-Morvan.*

Ouroux-en-Morvan
There is a charming view from this village of the surrounding hills and a stretch of the Pannesière reservoir. Two paths *(15min round trip)* lead up to the **viewpoint**★ from the village square and the church.

▶ *Drive back towards the lake on D 12 via Courgermain.*

The last mile or so of this downhill run towards the Pannesière reservoir provides superb bird's-eye views of this stretch of water.

▶ *Before Chaumard, turn sharp right on D 303, which runs along the bank of the reservoir and across the dam.*

Barrage de Pannesière-Chaumard
This 340m/1 115ft-long and 50m/164ft-high dam is supported on numerous slender arches and flanked by massive concrete embankments on either river bank. Twelve supporting buttresses rise from the bottom of the gorge.

▶ *Beyond, turn left on D 944 then left again on D 161 and follow the west shore back to Château-Chinon.*

CHÂTILLON-SUR-SEINE★

POPULATION 6 269
MICHELIN MAP 320: H-2

The trim little town of Châtillon is set on the banks of the young Seine, which is joined here by the River Douix. For several centuries, sheep breeding has been the main source of wealth on the dry plateaux of the Châtillon region (Châtillonnais), and up to the 18C Châtillon was the centre of a flourishing wool industry.

▯ **Information**: 4 pl. Marmont, 21400 Châtillon-Sur-Seine.
☎03 80 91 13 19. www.pays-chatillonais.fr.
▶ **Orient Yourself**: Get out into the countryside on foot or even on horseback; there are plenty of footpaths and bridleways in the area.

A Bit of History

Talking peace with Bonaparte - In February 1814, while **Napoleon I** was defending the approaches to Paris, a peace congress was held in Châtillon between France and the countries allied against her (Austria, Russia, England and Prussia). Napoleon rejected the conditions laid down and fighting resumed, but his Empire soon fell.

The tide turns
In September 1914 French troops retreated in the face of a violent German attack. **Général Joffre**, Commander-in-Chief of the French armies, set up his headquarters at Châtillon-sur-Seine, where he issued his famous order of 6 September: "We are about to engage in a battle on which the fate of our country depends, and it is important to remind all ranks that the moment has passed for looking back..." The German advance was halted and the French counter-attack on the Marne was a victory.

Sights

Musée du Châtillonais★
Open Jul-Aug 10am-6pm. Rest of the year daily except Tue 9.30am-noon, 2-5pm. Closed 1 Jan, 1 May and 25 Dec. 4.50€. ☎03 80 91 24 67.
This museum is in the Maison Philandrier, an attractive Renaissance building, but scheduled to move to the old Notre-Dame abbey. There are several interesting Gallo-Roman exhibits found during excavations in the 19C and early 20C, particularly at Vertault (20km/12mi W of Châtillon). The pride of the museum is the extraordinary archaeological find of January 1953 at Mont Lassois near Vix.
The Treasure of Vix★★ – A reconstitution of the tomb is displayed behind glass. The treasures were found in a 6C BC grave containing the remains of a woman: jewellery of inestimable value, parts of a state chariot, countless gold and bronze items and a huge bronze vase. The rich decoration of the vase – sculpted frieze made of applied panels in high relief portraying a row of helmeted warriors and chariots and Gorgon's heads on the handles – reveals a highly developed art form influenced by the archaic Greek style. The showcases contain other items found in the tomb of the Gaulish princess: a massive golden diadem, bronze and silver goblets, wine jugs and jewellery.

Source de la Douix★
The source of the River Douix is in a stunningly beautiful spot at the foot of a rocky escarpment (over 30m/98ft high). The normal flow is 132gal a second but it can reach 660gal in flood periods. The promenade, laid out on a rocky platform, gives a view over the town, the valley and the swimming pool.

Excursion

Forêt de Châtillon
This vast forest, extending over 9 000ha/22 240 acres to the south-east of Châtillon-sur-Seine, offers walkers an unspoilt natural environment to enjoy.

Abbaye du Val-des-Choues
Open Jul-Aug 11am-6pm Apr-Jun and Sep daily except Tue 1-5pm. Rest of the year weekends only 1-5pm. Hunting dog feedings Jul-Aug 4pm. 4€. ☎03 80 81 01 09. www.abbayeduvaldeschoues.com.
In the heart of the forest, surrounded by lovely gardens, this small museum houses collections relating to forests, hunting and gypsum. Sound and light (son et lumière) shows in summer.

FORÊT DE **CHAUX**★

MICHELIN MAP 321: D-4 TO E-4

This 20 000ha/49 420-acre forest just east of Dole between the Rivers Doubs and Loue is one of the largest in France. It originally belonged to the sovereigns, who hunted here; the nearby population also enjoyed extensive rights to the use of the land. These rights disappeared in the 19C, when the areas at the edge of the forest were given to the community *(forêts communales)*, whereas the central part (13 000ha/32 123 acres) became State property *(forêt domaniale)*.

- **Information:** Office Nationales des Forêts, 21 r. du Muguet, 39100 Dole. ☎03 84 82 09 21. www.onf.fr.
- ▶ **Orient Yourself**: In summer and early autumn, the Association des Villages de la Forêt de Chaux (☎03 84 71 72 07) brings the forest's past to life with live demonstrations in La Vieille-Loye and the Musée Joseph-Martin at Étrepigney. Ask at the tourist office in Dole for details of their guided walks.

A Bit of History

From industry to leisure

For centuries the forest has been a vital resource for the factories at its edge: saltworks at **Salins** and **Arc-et-Senans**, forges at Fraisans, glassworks at La Vieille Loye and so on. The previous layout of the forest in coppices no longer conforms with modern needs, and it is now managed with more modern methods. Oak pre-dominates (60%), followed by beech (20%) and various deciduous (15%) and coniferous trees (5%).

A tourist zone has been established to the west of the forest to protect the plants and wildlife elsewhere. Facilities include a bridle path, footpaths, a fitness trail, car parks and part of the long-distance footpath GR 59A from Dole to Arc-et-Senans, three game enclosures in which you can see various types of

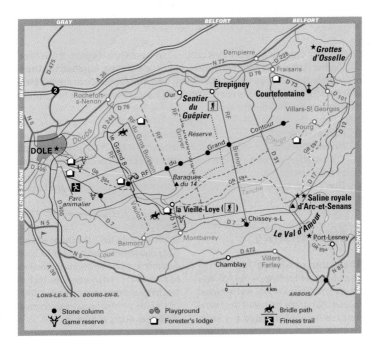

● Stone column	◉◉ Playground
⚕ Game reserve	🏠 Forester's lodge
🏇 Bridle path	🤸 Fitness trail

deer and wild boar and a nature reserve (88ha/217 acres) where deer and wild boar roam at liberty. You can observe these from one of two raised observation posts, or by strolling around the forest.

Visit

La Vieille Loye

This is the only village in the forest. It used to be inhabited by woodcutters, who lived in huts, or *baraques*, at the centre of each forest area. Some of these huts, such as the **Baraques du 14** (&🕐*open Jul-Aug daily except Fri 2.30-6.30pm. ∞2.50€. ☎03 84 71 72 07.)* have been restored.

Le sentier du Guêpier

This 4km/2.5mi-long trail offers an insight into the history of the forest. In **Etrepigney**, the starting point, a *bacul* – small woodcutter's cottage – has been reconstructed, and in **Our** a 19C bread oven has been restored.

Excursions

Grottes d'Osselle★

🕐*Open Jun-Aug 9am-7pm (Jun 6pm). Rest of the year times vary.* 🕐*Closed Nov-Mar. ∞6.50€. ☎03 81 63 62 09. grottes.osselle.free.fr.*

These caves are set in a cliff overlooking a meander in the Doubs. They were discovered in the 13C and have been visited since 1504. In the Revolution, the galleries were used as refuges and chapels by local priests; a clay altar can still be seen. A bear's skeleton has been assembled from bones found among the debris.

Out of 8km/5mi of long, regularly shaped galleries, 1.3km/0.8mi have been adapted and opened for guided tours.

Le Val d'Amour

&*See Saline royale d'ARC-ET-SENANS.*

Dole★

&*See DOLE.*

Saline royale d'Arc-et-Senans★★

&*See Saline royale d'ARC-ET-SENANS.*

ABBAYE DE CÎTEAUX

14KM/9MI E OF NUITS-ST-GEORGES

MICHELIN MAP 320: K-7

Cîteaux, like Cluny, is an important centre in western Christendom. It was here, among the cistels or reeds, that Robert, Abbot of Molesme, founded the Order of Cistercians in 1098, an off-shoot of Cluny, which under the great driving force of St Bernard (who joined the community in 1112 and later became abbot), spread its influence throughout the world.

- **Information**: ☎03 80 61 32 58. www.citeaux-abbaye.com.
- ▶ **Orient Yourself**: It is important to remember that this is not just a historical site, but also a working religious community. Expect your two-hour guided tour to reflect this.
- 😊 **Don't Miss**: A stop at the abbey shop for their homemade cheese and bags of honey sweets.

A Bit of History

The sound of silence

The abbey of La Trappe, which was attached to Cîteaux in 1147 and reformed in1664, has given its name to several monasteries which joined the Strict Observance. In 1892, the Order was officially divided into two branches: Cistercian monks who may devote themselves to a pastoral or intellectual life, such as teaching; and the more numerous Trappist monks who follow a strictly contemplative vocation, as here.

Visit

🕐 *Open May-Oct. Guided tours (2hr) Jul to mid-Sep daily except Mon 9.45am-6.30pm. Rest of the year 9.45am-12.45pm, 2.15-6pm, Sun 2.15-6pm.* 👁7.50€.

During the Revolution, Cîteaux nearly perished in its entirety. The monks were expelled and did not return until 1898. The church containing the tombs of the first dukes of Burgundy and of Philippe Pot *(now in the Louvre, Paris)* was completely destroyed. All that remains are relics of the library, faced with 15C enamelled bricks, which incorporates six arches of a Gothic cloister and a vaulted room on the first floor; a handsome 18C building still used by the 35 or so monks; and a late-17C building beside the river.

Notre-Dame de Cîteaux
A new church was built and inaugurated in 1998 to commemorate the 900th anniversary of the abbey's foundation.

S. Sauvignier-MICHELIN

From the church in Bagnot

Excursion

Église de Bagnot
9km S of the abbey. The church has interesting 15C frescoes in a naive style.

CLAMECY

POPULATION 4 806

MICHELIN MAP 319: E-7

The old town, with its narrow winding streets, is perched on a spur overlooking the confluence of the Rivers Yonne and Beuvron. It remains "the town of beautiful reflections and graceful hills" described by **Romain Rolland** (1866-1944), the French writer and philosopher, who is buried in the Nivernais not far from his native town.

- **Information**: r. du Grand-Marché, 58500 Clamecy. ☎03 86 27 02 51. www.vaux-yonne.com.
- ▶ **Orient Yourself**: The Bethlehem Bridge, on which there is a statue in memory of the loggers, provides a good overall view of the town and its quays.

A Bit of History

Log floating
This method of moving timber, which goes back to the 16C, brought wealth to the river port of Clamecy for nearly 300 years. The logs, cut in the forests of the Upper Morvan, were piled along the banks of the rivers and marked with their owners' signs. On an agreed day, the dams holding back the rivers were opened and the logs thrown into the flood which carried them to Clamecy. There, a dam stopped the wood, the timbermen dragged the logs from the water and piled them up by mark. From here, immense rafts of wood, called *trains*, were sent down the Yonne and the Seine towards Paris, where the wood was used for heating. The building of the Nivernais Canal ended this; the last *train* of wood left Clamecy in 1923.

Address Book

SLEEP UNDER THE STARS...

Camping La Plage Blanche – *39380 Ounans, 2km/1.2mi SE of Montbarrey by D 71. ☎03 84 37 69 63. www.la-plage-blanche.com. Open Apr-Oct . 220 sites. Reservations recommended. Meals available.* Relax on the shores of the river and watch brave swimmers plunge into the cool waters of the Loue, which runs alongside this camp site. Riding centre nearby. Recreational facilities for children.

...OR IN A FINE CHÂTEAU

Chambre d'hôte Le Château de Salans – *39700 Salans, 5 km/3.1mi N of Courtefontaine by a minor road. ☎03 84 71 16 55. 3 rooms.* This magnificent 17C château is situated in the middle of a sizeable landscaped park. Rooms with Louis XVI-style furnishings) feature beautiful bathrooms decorated with red and white tiles.

Sights

Église St-Martin★

The church was built between the end of the 12C and the beginning of the 16C. Episodes in the life of St Martin are illustrated on the arch stones over the door (damaged during the Revolution).

The interior reveals the rectangular plan and the square ambulatory characteristic of Burgundian churches. The rood screen was constructed by Viollet-le-Duc to counteract the bowing of certain pillars in the chancel.

Musée d'Art et d'Histoire Romain-Rolland

Open daily except Tue (Oct-May except Mon-Tue) 10am-noon, 2-6pm, Sun 2-6pm. Closed Jan, 1 Nov, 11 Nov, 25 Dec. 3€. ☎03 86 27 17 99.

There is a bust of the writer in front of the museum, which is installed in the Duc de Bellegarde's mansion. Paintings include French and Dutch works. There is Nevers and Rouen pottery and an archaeological collection. There is a display devoted to the old practice of floating of logs down the river. A room with a fine timberwork ceiling contains works by Charles Loupot (1892-1962), a famous poster designer who lived in Clamecy.

Excursions

Druyes-les-Belles-Fontaines

18km/11.2mi NW.

The hilltop ruins of the 12C **feudal castle** (*open Jul-Aug 10am-noon, 2-*

6pm; Sat-Sun 3-6pm; Sun Guided tours at 4pm. Rest of the year times vary. 5€. ☎03 86 41 51 71. www.chateau-de-druyes.com) are best seen from the south, along D 148 or D 104. From the road to Courson-les-Carrières, a 14C fortified gate gives access to the rocky outcrop occupied by the old village and the castle ruins.

Carrière souterraine d'Aubigny

6km/3.7mi N of Druyes along D 148. Open Jul- Aug 10am-6.30pm (Sun from 2.30pm. Apr-Jun and Sep-Oct 10am-noon, 2.30-6.30pm (Sun from 2.30pm). 5.50€. ☎ 03 86 52 38 79. www.carriereaubigny.org.

This underground quarry dates back to the Roman Empire. The limestone was first used for sacred funeral items, later for castles and, in the late 19C in Paris, for monuments such as the Hôtel de Ville and the Opera. In addition to an explanation of the formation and uses of this 150-million-year-old mineral, exhibits display cutting and sculpting tools plus other minerals and stones.

Vallée de l'Yonne from Clamecy to Corbigny

38km/24mi along D 951 and D 985; allow 2hr 30min.

The road runs alongside the river and the Canal du Nivernais overlooked by wooded hills. The itinerary is dotted with pleasant riverside villages such as Armes and hilltop ones such as Metz-le-Comte and Tannay offering wide views of the picturesque Yonne Valley.

CLUNY ★★

POPULATION 4 376
MICHELIN MAP 320: H-11
LOCAL MAP SEE MÂCONNAIS

Cluny is synonymous with the religious order that exercised such an immense influence on the religious, intellectual, political and artistic life of western Europe in medieval times. Until the Revolution, every century left its architectural mark here. From 1798 to 1823, this centre of civilisation was ransacked, but one can still get an idea of the majesty of the basilica from what remains. The town itself also has plenty of sights for the visitor.

- **Information**: 6 r. Mercière, 71250 Cluny.
  ☎03 85 59 05 34. www.uk.cluny-tourisme.com.
- **Orient Yourself:** A climb to the top of the Tour des Fromages will give you the best view of the town and its historic structures.
- **Organising Your Time:** If you're here between late July and late August, don't miss the Grandes Heures de Cluny, a series of classical concerts in the abbey's former Flour Store followed by wine tastings in the cellars.

A Bit of History

The rise

Cluny's influence grew rapidly from the moment it was founded in the 10C, particularly through the establishment of numerous daughter abbeys. "You are the light of the world" said Pope Urban II (himself from Cluny, as were many other popes) to **St Hugh** in 1098. When St Hugh died in 1109, having begun the construction of the magnificent abbey church which **Peter the Venerable**, abbot from 1122 to 1156, was to finish, he left the abbey in a state of great prosperity. In 1155 there were 460 monks resident in the abbey alone, and young men from all over Europe flocked here.

The decline

Rich and powerful, the monks of Cluny slipped gradually into a worldly way of life that was strongly condemned by **St Bernard.** The 14C saw the decline of Cluny's power, and by the 16C it was reduced to a quarry for spoils. It was devastated during the Wars of Religion and the library was sacked.

Destruction

In 1790 the abbey was closed. Its desecration began at the height of the Revolution. In September 1793, the local authority gave the order for the tombs to be demolished and sold for building. In 1798 the buildings were sold to a property speculator who knocked down the nave and sold off the abbey church bit by bit until by 1823 all that was left was what we see today.

Old Town

Tour Fabry and Tour Ronde

The Fabry Tower (1347) with its pepper-pot roof and the older Ronde Tower are visible from the garden near the town hall.

Hôtel de Ville

The town hall now occupies the building erected for Cluny's abbots at the end of the 15C and beginning of the 16C. The garden front has an original decoration in the Italian Renaissance style.

Romanesque houses

Cluny has several fine Romanesque dwellings: note in particular a 12C house at no 25 rue de la République and the 13C mint (restored) at no 6 rue d'Avril.

Tour des Fromages

Open Jul-Aug daily 10am-6.45pm. Rest of the year times vary. Closed 1 May, 1 and 11 Nov. ≤1.25€. ☎03 85 59 05 34. From the top (120 steps) of the curiously named 11C Cheese tower there is a good view of the abbey, Clocher d'Eau-Bénite, flour store and adjoining mill tower, belfry of St-Marcel and Notre-Dame.

Église Notre-Dame

The square in front of the church has an 18C fountain and old houses. The church, built shortly after 1100, was enlarged in the Gothic period. The 13C doorway is badly weathered. The interior is a good example of Cluniac architecture.

Église St-Marcel

⊙ Open Jun-Sep 9am-7pm. ☎03 85 59 07 18.

This church has a fine octagonal Romanesque **belfry**★ of three storeys, topped by a graceful 15C polygonal brick spire (42m/138ft high).

Ancienne Abbaye★★

⊙ Open May-Aug 9.30am-6.30pm; Sep-Apr 9.30am-noon, 1.30-5pm. ⊙ Closed 1 Jan, 1 May, 1 and 11 Nov, 25 Dec. ⊗7€ combined ticket from the Musée d'Art et d'Archéologie. 03 85 59 15 93.

Most of the abbey church of St Peter and St Paul, called Cluny III, was built between 1088 and 1130 when the Cluniac Order was at its most powerful. It was the largest Christian church (177m/ 581ft long) until the reconstruction of St Peter's in Rome (186m/610ft long). It consisted of a narthex, a nave and four aisles, two transepts, five belfries, two towers, 301 windows and 225 decorated stalls. The painted apsidal vault rested on a marble colonnade. Sadly, only the south transepts are still standing.

Narthex

The site of the narthex is now bisected by rue Kenneth-J.-Conant. During excavations in 1949 the base of the south end of the façade was uncovered, together with the footings of the doorway which was flanked by square Barabans towers (only the foundations survive). The south aisle of the narthex was uncovered later, revealing a wall with pilasters attached to semi-columns.

The long Gothic façade (restored) in place de l'Abbaye is named after Pope Gelasius who died at Cluny in 1119 (abbey entrance).

Cloisters

The 18C monastic buildings form a harmonious group enclosing the vast; two great flights of stone steps with wrought-iron railings occupy two corners.

Galilee Passage

The 11C passage, which was used by the great Benedictine processions, linked the Galilee (a covered porch) of Cluny II with the south aisle of the great church of Cluny III.

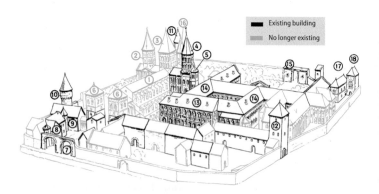

Existing building

No longer existing

Cluny Abbey at the end of the 18C

1) Abbey Church of St Peter and St Paul – **2**) Clocher des Bisans – **3**) Clocher du Chœur – **4**) Clocher de l'Eau-Bénite – **5**) Clocher de l'Horloge – **6**) The Barabans – **7**) Main Gate – **8**) Palais de Jean de Bourbon – **9**) Palais de Jacques d'Amboise – **10**) Tour Fabry – **11**) Tour Ronde – **12**) Tour des Fromages – **13**) Pope Gelasius Façade – **14**) Cloistral Ranges – **15**) Garden Gate – **16**) Clocher des Lampes – **17**) Flour store – **18**) Tour du Moulin

Address Book

🥄 *For coin ranges, see the Legend on the cover flap.*

WHERE TO STAY AND EAT

🍴**Chambre d'hôte La Courtine** – *Pont de la Levée, exit at l'E de Cluny by the D 15 rte d'Azé just after the bridge.* ☎03 85 59 05 10. *Closed Nov-Feb.* 🛏 *5 rooms.* Little by little, Virginia creeper and wisteria vines have taken over the facade of this old farmhouse on the bank of the Grosne River. Scandinavian-style interior decoration. Comfy rooms, some overlooking the river. Homemade jams at the breakfast table.

🍴🍴**Auberge du Cheval Blanc** – *1 r. de la Porte-de-Mâcon.* ☎03 85 59 01 13. *Closed 28 Nov-8 Mar, 28 Jun-10 Jul, evenings Mar and Nov, Fri-Sat.* Imposing regional auberge. Enjoy classic French dishes while admiring the fresco on the dining room wall.

🍴🍴**Hôtel Bourgogne** – *pl. de l'Abbaye.* ☎03 85 59 00 58. www.hotel-cluny.com. *Closed Dec-Jan, Tue and Wed in Feb.* 13 *rooms.* 🍽10€. *Restaurant*🍴🍴. The poet Lamartine was a regular visitor to this hotel opposite Cluny Abbey. The rooms are sober but comfortable and well-kept. Cosy dining room with fireplace. Light meals can be had in the bar at lunchtime. Terrace in the flower-filled patio.

🍴🍴**Chambre d'Hôte Le Moulin des Arbillons** – *71520 Bourgvilain, 8km/5mi S of Cluny by D 980 then D 22.* ☎03 85 50 82 83. www.arbillons.fr. *Open Apr-Oct.* 🛏 *5 rooms.* This 18C mill is next to a 19C mansion in the middle of a park, overlooking the village. The rooms are filled with family heirlooms. Breakfast is served in the colourful orangery. Wine tastings available and bottles for sale.

🍴🍴🍴**Château d'Igé** – *71960 Igé, 13km/8.1mi E of Cluny by D 134.* ☎03 85 33 33 99. www.chateaudige.com. *Closed Dec-Feb.* 8 *rooms.* 🍽14€. *Restaurant*🍴🍴. Feel like a trip back to the Middle Ages? Then this château is the perfect place for you: medieval dining hall with impressive timberwork and a huge fireplace, cosy bedrooms with personalised decor... Thoughtful cuisine made with fresh seasonal produce. Pretty garden.

SHOPPING

Dentelle Cluny – *Aymé de Réa, 15 r. Lamartine.* ☎03 85 59 31 78. brunoindiana@aol.com. *Open Apr-Sep daily 9am-8pm.* A young craftsman has set up his lacemaking studio in a small medieval building. He designs original pieces inspired by traditional motifs, including the legendary Cluny stitch.

Le Cellier de l'Abbaye – *13 r. Municipale.* ☎03 85 59 04 00. *Open Tue-Sat 9.30am-12.30pm, 2.30-7pm; Sun 10am-12.30pm (open Mon 14 Jul-15 Aug). Closed Feb.* A total of 250 Burgundy wines, 90 whiskies and a wide choice of local liqueurs are on offer in this superb store made of 13C stone.

Château de l'Aubespin – *71220 St-André-le-Désert.* ☎03 85 59 49 48. *Open daily from 9am.* This family business produces gourmet delicacies, from fruit liqueurs to jams, in a medieval chateau.

SIT BACK AND RELAX

Au Péché Mignon – *23-25 r. Lamartine.* ☎03 85 59 11 21. www.chocolateriegermain.fr. *Open daily 7.30am-8pm. Closed 2 weeks in Jan.* This patisserie-tea room sells a mouthwatering selection of cakes and delicacies of all kinds: *perle d'or* (almond paste with griotte cherries), tomato jam...

Traces of the church of St Peter and St Paul

From the size of the south transepts it is possible to work out the size of the whole basilica. Its height (30m/98ft under the barrel vaulting, 32m/105ft under the dome) is exceptional in Romanesque architecture. The church consisted of three bays; the central one, topped by an octagonal cupola on squinches, supports the handsome **Clocher de l'Eau-Bénite**★★ (Holy Water Belfry). St-Étienne (St-Stephen's Chapel) is Romanesque; St-Martial's Chapel dates from the 14C. The right arm of the smaller transept contains the Bourbon Chapel

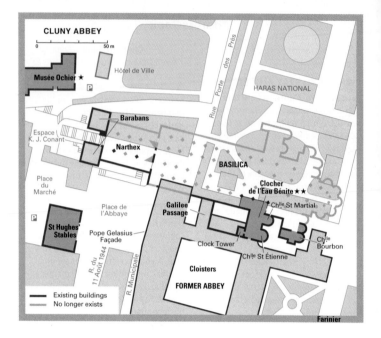

CLUNY ABBEY

0   50 m

Musée Ochier ★

Hôtel de Ville

Rue   Porte   des   Prés

HARAS NATIONAL

Barabans

Espace
K. J. Conant

Narthex

BASILICA

Place
du
Marché

Clocher
de l'Eau Bénite ★★

Ch lle St Martial

Place de
l'Abbaye

Galilee
Passage

St Hughes'
Stables

Pope Gelasius
Façade

Ch lle
Bourbon

Clock Tower

R. du
11 Août 1944

R. Municipale

Ch lle St Étienne

Cloisters

FORMER ABBEY

Existing buildings

No longer exists

Farinier

with its late-15C Gothic architecture and a Romanesque apse.

Monastic buildings

The buildings, which house the School of Arts and Crafts, were nicknamed Little Versailles owing to the elegant Classical east façade.

Flour Store

The storehouse (54m/177ft long) was built in the late 13C; in the 18C it was truncated (by about 20m/65ft) to reveal the south end of the façade of the cloister building overlooking the gardens.

The low storeroom with its two ranges of ogive vaulting houses sculptures including a doorway with recessed arches from Pope Gelasius' palace.

The **high chamber**, with its beautiful oak roof, makes an dramatic setting for pieces of sculpture from the abbey. The fine **capitals**★ and column shafts saved from the ruins of the abbey church are exhibited by means of a scale model of the chancel: the eight capitals on their columns are set in a semicircle round the old Pyrenean marble altar consecrated

by Urban II in 1095. They are the first examples of the Burgundian Romanesque sculpture which was to blossom in Vézelay, Autun and Saulieu. The two models, of the great doorway and of the apse of the basilica, were designed by Professeur Conant, the archaeologist who directed the excavations from 1928 to 1950.

Additional Sight

Musée d'Art et d'Archéologie★

🕔For opening hours see Abbaye.

Models in the entrance hall and, upstairs, an audio-visual reconstruction of Cluny III allow visitors to appreciate the greatness of the abbey. Two basement rooms contain stone fragments of the monument: part of the frieze of the narthex and arcading from the choir screen. Upstairs, sculptures and architectural elements from various façades give an insight into the decoration of medieval houses (harvest frieze, capital decorated with a shoemaker, lintel carved with a tournament scene).

CIRQUE DE **CONSOLATION**★★
13KM/8MI N OF MORTEAU
MICHELIN MAP 321: J-4

The natural amphitheatre, from which the Dessoubre and its tributary the Lançot spring, takes the shape of a double semicircle against an awe-inspiring background of partly wooded rocky crags towering majestically to over 300m/984ft.

🗐 **Information**: pl. de l'Hôtel-de-Ville, 25190 Saint-Hipplyte. ☎03 81 96 58 00.

▶ **Orient Yourself:** The drive from St-Hippolyte passes through the placid Dessoubre River valley before ascending to the craggy cirque.

🕭 **Don't Miss:** The breathtaking view from La Roche du Prêtre.

Driving Tours

1 **Vallée du Dessoubre**★

From St-Hippolyte to the park of Notre-Dame-de-Consolation – 33km/21mi.

St-Hippolyte

This town occupies a pretty **site** at the confluence of the Doubs and the Dessoubre.

▶ *Leave St-Hippolyte on D 39 heading SW.*

D 39 follows the course of the Dessoubre quite closely, going through the villages of Pont-Neuf and Rosureux. The peaceful valley runs between wooded slopes (fir, oak and ash) topped by limestone cliffs.

Gigot

The Dessoubre is joined here by a small tributary, the Reverotte, which wiggles its way west upstream of the village along a steep-sided valley known as the **Défilé des Épais Rochers**.

After Gigot, D 39 carries on along the banks of the Dessoubre, past woods and meadows with the river bubbling alongside.

Notre-Dame-de-Consolation

This former Minimist convent was a small seminary until 1981, and now serves as a religious centre. The chapel is in the Baroque style.

🝘The **park** *(allow 1hr)* is a pretty place for a walk through fields, among trees, rocks, waterfalls, springs (Source du Lançot, Source Noire and Source du Tabouret) and the Val Noir (black valley).

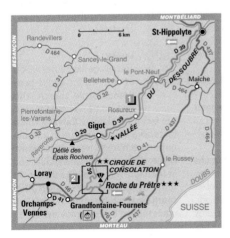

2 **La Roche du Prêtre**★★★

From La Roche du Prêtre to Loray – 14km/9mi.

La Roche du Prêtre

This famous viewpoint offers inspiring views of the Cirque de Consolation and its surroundings. The summit towers 350m/1148ft above the wooded amphitheatre in which the Dessoubre rises. Here and there rocks break through the greenery in a

Address Book

For coin ranges, see the Legend on the cover flap.

WHERE TO STAY

Chambre d'Hôte Chez Patrick Dorget – La Joux, 25380 Bretonvillers, 7km/4.3mi N of Gigot by D 125 until you reach Bretonvillers then head for Pierrefontaine and follow directions to La Joux. 03 81 44 35 78. 4 rooms. This old farmhouse in a vast leafy clearing is a haven of tranquillity. Pretty rooms adorned with beams. Fine kitchen has old-fashioned floor tiling.

Hôtel du Moulin – 25380 Cour-St-Maurice, 1km/0.6mi SW of Pont-Neuf by D 39. 03 81 44 35 18. Closed Oct-Feb. 6 rooms. 6.10€. Restaurant. This handsome 1930s residence with turrets and colonnades has a bright dining room with parquet flooring, large, cosy

rooms and a riverside garden bursting with flowers. Peace guaranteed.

WHERE TO EAT

Ferme-Auberge de Frémondans – 25380 Vaucluse, 7km/4.3mi NE of Gigot by D 39. 03 81 44 35 66. Open evenings Jul-Aug and Fri evenings to Sun evenings Nov-Sep. Closed Oct. Reservations required. Tuck into specialities such as terrine, fondue, kid, stuffed cabbage, goat's cheese and homemade pastries at this family-owned farmhouse overlooking the Dessoubre Valley.

La Truite du Moulin – In Moulin-du-Bas, 25380 Cour-St-Maurice, 0.5km/0.3mi SW of Pont-Neuf by D 39. 03 81 44 30 59. Closed Dec, Tue evenings and Wed. This former mill offers simple but tasty fare in a cosy dining room. Moderately priced menus.

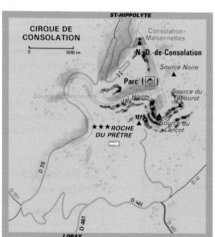

romantic scene of solitude and rugged grandeur.

Grandfontaine-Fournets
This hamlet at the heart of the Haut-Doubs is typical of the Jura region. It is home to the **Ferme du Montagnon** (open Apr-Sep 9am-noon, 2-6.30pm; Oct 2-6pm. 03 81 43 57 86. www.montagnon.com), dating from the 17C and 18C. It still has

its **smoking loft**★ (tuyé) where meat, hams, bacon and sausages are cured (locally cured products on sale).

Orchamps-Vennes
This sizeable mountain village occupies a high plateau set back from D 461 from Besançon to Morteau. Its low-roofed houses adorn a charming setting of green meadows and trees.

Loray
This village has houses typical of the region and a neo-Romanesque church with handsome 18C furnishings. Not far off stands a 12C **Calvary**, which features a life-size statue of a figure holding a human head in its hand. Higher up are the Virgin Mary, Christ and St Michael overcoming the dragon. At the centre of the village square is a 19C **fountain wash-house** with fluted columns topped by Doric capitals.

CHÂTEAU DE **CORMATIN**★★

Cormatin was built in the aftermath of the Wars of Religion between 1605 and 1616 by the Governor of Chalon, Antoine du Blé d'Huxelles.

- **Information:** Chateau de Cormatin, 71460 Cormatin.
  ☎03 85 50 16 55. www.chateaudecormatin.com.
- ▶ **Orient Yourself**: Take time to admire the understated exterior, probably designed by Jacques II Androuet du Cerceau, architect to Henri IV.

Visit

Open Apr-Nov. Guided tours (45min) Jul-Aug 10am-6.30pm. Rest of the year times vary. Grounds open. 8€.

The north wing contains a magnificent grand **staircase**★★ (1610); the straight flights of steps, flanked by balusters, open directly on to the central well. It is the oldest and largest stair of this kind (25m/82ft high).

The sumptuous Louis XIII decor in this wing is the work of Marquess Jacques du Blé and his wife Claude Phélypeaux, who were close friends of Marie de Medici and the literary salon of the Précieuses. They intended their summer house to reflect the sophistication of Parisian fashion, so they used the artists and craftsmen who had worked for the Queen at the Luxembourg Palace. The gilt, paintings and sculptures which cover the walls and ceilings are proof of an informed mannerism; each painting has an allegorical meaning re-affirmed in the symbolism of the decorative motifs and the colours used for the panelling. The **ante-chamber of the Marchioness**★ (daughter and sister of government ministers), which was created in the middle of the Protestant revolt (1627-28), is in homage to Louis XIII who is represented above the chimney-piece: the red panelling (colour of authority) celebrates the activities and virtues of the king. The **Marchioness' room**★★ has a magnificent French ceiling in gold and blue, symbol of fidelity; the great painting of Venus and Vulcan, a work of the second Fontainebleau School, symbolises love and the baskets of fruit and flowers on the woodwork represent plenty. One of the oldest heavenly ceilings, made fashionable by Marie de Medici, adorns the **Cabinet des Curiosités**★★ The sumptuous Baroque decor in Jacques du Blé's tiny study, the **Cabinet de Ste-Cécile**★★★, is dominated by blue lapis-lazuli and rich gilding; the figure of St Cecilia accompanied by the cardinal virtues represents moral harmony.

Park★★

The lovely view of the park from the aviary reveals its typical 17C symbolism: the flower beds represent paradise, with the fountain of life in the centre. Within a triangle, the apple tree recalls the forbidden fruit and paradise lost; the labyrinth symbolises mankind's errant ways. From the borders inward, the seven walkways culminate in seventh heaven at the highest point.

M. Simonet-Lenglart/Château de Cormatin

Cabinet de Sainte-Cécile

LA CÔTE★★

MICHELIN MAP 320: I-6 TO J-8

The celebrated vineyards of the Côte d'Or (Golden Hillside) stretch from Dijon to Santenay (60km/37mi). Each place bears the name of a famous wine, making it a desirable destination for connoisseurs and gourmets alike.

- **Information**: Côte d'Or Tourism. ☎03 80 63 69 49. www.cotedor-tourisme.com.
- ▶ **Orient Yourself:** Anchored by Dijon and Santenay, the wine route runs mostly north-south, paralleling the A 6 and passing through Beaune.

Burgundy's Fine Wines

Natural conditions

The Côte is formed by the eastern edge of the region known as La Montagne, whose rectangular shape is cut by transverse combes in the same way as the blind valleys of the Jura vineyards. The vineyards cover about 8 000ha/ 19 768 acres in the Côte-d'Or and 10 000ha/ 24 711 acres in the Saône-et-Loire and are planted with first-quality vines (Pinot Noir for red, Chardonnay for white). They are set in terraces overlooking the plain of the Saône at an altitude varying from 200m to 300m/686ft to 984ft.

The vineyards are planted on the south and east-facing limestone slopes, exposed to the morning sun – the best – and sheltered from cold winds. This position makes the grapes extremely sweet, which in turn gives the wine a high alcohol content. In addition, the slopes facilitate drainage; vines like dry soil and the slope is therefore an important factor in the quality of the grape. The finest wines generally come from grapes grown halfway up the slopes.

South of the Dijon vineyards the Côte d'Or is divided into two parts, the **Côte de Nuits** and the **Côte de Beaune**. The wines of both are well known; those of Nuits for their robustness; those of Beaune for their delicacy. The former extends from the village of Fixin to the southern limits of the Côte d'Or; its most famous wines are Chambertin, Musigny, Clos-Vougeot and Romanée-Conti. The Côte de Beaune stretches from north of Aloxe-Corton to Santenay and produces great smooth reds such as Cortin, Volnay, Pommard and Beaune and rich and fruity whites such as Meursault and Montrachet.

Driving Tour of the Vineyards★★

1 Côte De Nuits

The road goes along the foot of hillsides covered with vines and passes through villages with world-famous names.

Dijon★★★ ⓒSee DIJON.

▶ *Leave Dijon on D 122, known as the Route des Grands Crus.*

Chenôve

The Clos du Roi and Clos du Chapitre recall the former owners of these vineyards, the dukes of Burgundy and the canons of Autun. The dukes' wine cellar, **Cuverie des ducs de Bourgogne** (♿ⓒopen Jul-Sep 2-7pm; rest of the year by appointment; ☎03 80 51 55 00) contains two magnificent 13C presses.

Marsannay-la-Côte

Part of the Côte de Nuits, Marsannay produces popular rosé wines, obtained from the black Pinot grapes.

Fixin

This village produces wines that some consider among the best of the Côte de Nuits appellation. The small **Musée Noisot** (ⓒopen mid-Apr to mid-Oct Sat-Sun 2-6pm. ◈4.50€. ☎03 80 52 45 52) houses mementoes of Napoleon's campaigns.

Address Book

For coin ranges, see the Legend on the cover flap.

WHERE TO STAY

Chambre d'Hôte Les Sarguenotes – *r. de Dijon, 21220 Chambœuf, 6km/ 3.7mi E of Gevrey-Chambertin by D 31.* ☎*03 80 51 84 65.* *5 rooms.* Take a relaxing break in this modern house in luxuriant countryside. The bedrooms are somewhat lacking in character, but they are comfortable and each has its own terrace. Reasonable prices.

Chambre d'Hôte Les Brugères – *7 r. Jean-Jaurès, 21160 Couchey, 2km/1.2mi S of Marsannay by D 122.* ☎*03 80 52 13 05. www.francoisbrugere.com. Closed Dec-Mar. 4 rooms.* This superb 16C residence belonging to a wine-grower has pretty rooms with exposed beams decorated with furniture picked up from antique dealers. The perfect place for wine buffs...

Domaine du Moulin aux Moines – *Auxey-Duresse, 21190 Meursault.* ☎*03 80 21 60 79. www.laterrasse.fr. 6 rooms.* *15€.* This manor house in vineyards was once attached to Cluny Abbey. The spacious rooms are tastefully decorated; the ones in the mill are particularly nice. Tastings are organised in the wine cellars. Small wine museum.

Hôtel Le Hameau de Barboron – *21420 Savigny-lès-Beaune, 2km/1.2mi N of Savigny by a minor road.* ☎*03 80 21 58 35. www.hameaudebarboron.com. 9 rooms.* *15€.* Surrounded by 350ha/865 acres of private fields and forest, this old farmhouse has been admirably restored. The luxurious rooms are furnished in elegant old-fashioned style. Tastings are held in the vaulted cellar that houses the wine produced and bottled on the estate.

WHERE TO EAT

Le Bouchon – *pl. de l'Hôtel-de-Ville – 21190 Meursault, 8 km/5mi SW of Beaune by N 74.* ☎*03 8021 29 56. Closed 20 Nov-28 Dec, Sun evening and Mon.* This simple bistrot is a favourite with locals. Sober interior, with small, square tables. Classic regional cuisine with a good choice of menus.

Le Cellier Volnaysien – *pl. de l'Église, 21190 Volnay.* ☎*03 80 21 61 04.* Closed 25 Jul-8 Aug, 21-31 Dec, Wed and evenings except Sat. Walk through the pretty garden planted with rare trees and discover a fine 18C residence fronted by a perron. Vaulted cellars. One of the three dining rooms is located in the former storehouse. Unpretentious local cuisine and Château de Savigny wines at extremely reasonable prices.

La Table d'Olivier Leflaive – *1 pl. du Monument,21190 Puligny-Montrachet.* ☎*03 80 21 37 65. www. olivier-leflaive.com. Closed Dec-Feb, evenings and Sun.* Wine buffs will adore this restaurant where meals tend to focus on drink rather than food. Each different wine is commented by a sommelier. An unforgettable experience in a typical village house.

Rôtisserie du Chambertin – *21220 Gevrey-Chambertin.* ☎*03 80 34 33 20. Closed 7-28 Feb, 1-15 Aug, Sun evenings, Tue lunch and Mon.* Grilled meat is the speciality here. You may choose between regional dishes in the vaulted dining hall or light meals in the friendly setting of the Bon Bistrot and its terrace. Don't miss the small wax museum re-enacting the daily life of a cooper.

WINE TASTING...

Caveau de Chassagne – *7 r. Charles-Paquelin, 21190 Chassagne-Montrachet.* ☎*03 80 21 38 13. Open daily 8am-7pm.* The fruity white wines of this region are a delight to drink, whereas the reds are refined and robust. To quote Alexandre Dumas, these wines are to be drunk "kneeling down and bare-headed"...

Château André-Ziltener – *r. Fontaine – 21220 Chambolle-Musigny.* ☎*03 80 62 81 37. www.chateau-ziltener.com. Open daily 9.30am-6.30pm. Closed mid-Dec to end Feb.* Tourists may visit the cellars, set up as a museum devoted to Cistercian monks. Discover six wines, accompanied by bread and *gougère* (choux pastry puff flavoured with cheese).

Château de Corton-André – *21420 Aloxe-Corton.* ☎*03 80 26 44 25. www.pierre-andre.com. Open Apr-Oct daily 10am-12.30pm, 2.30-6pm; Nov-Mar Thu-Mon 10am-12.30pm, 2.30-6pm. Closed Tue-Wed in Dec-Feb.* This magnificent castle with its glazed roof tiling is the only Côte de Beaune château to boast the Grand Cru appellation. Tour of cellars and tastings of wine made on the premises. Bottles for sale.

Clos de Langres – *Domaine d'Ardhuy, Clos des Langres, 21700 Corgolin. ☎03 80 62 98 73. domaine.ardhuy@wanadoo.fr. Open Mon-Fri 8am-noon, 2-6pm, Sat 10am-noon, 2-7pm. Closed Sun and public holidays.* Clos de Langres has an 18C manor house built around a 17C press which is a listed historic site. Tour of cellars and wine tastings.

Cassissium de la Maison de Védrenne – *r. des Frères Montgolfier, 21700 Nuits-St-Georges. ☎03 80 62 49 70. www. cassissium.com. Guided visit (1hr 30min) Apr-Nov 10am-1pm, 2-7pm; early Oct to end Mar Tue-Sat 10.30am-1pm, 2-5.30pm. Closed Sun and Mon Dec-Mar. ☜6.80€.* Founded in 1919, this famed *cassisier* occupies a vast space dedicated mainly to the production of the blackcurrant liqueur cassis. Visitors can witness the various production stages, explore the aging cellars, taste, and perhaps purchase a sample or two.

The 10C church in nearby **Fixey** is thought to be the oldest in the area.

Brochon

Brochon, which is on the edge of the Côte de Nuits, produces excellent wines. The **château** was built in 1900 by the poet Stephen Liégeard who coined the phrase Côte d'Azur for the Provençal coast. The name has stuck long after the poet has faded into obscurity, together with his poem which was honoured by the French Academy.

Gevrey-Chambertin

This village is typical of the wine-growing community immortalised by the Burgundian writer **Gaston Roupnel** (1872-1946). It is situated at the open end of the gorge, Combe de Lavaux, and surrounded by vineyards. The older part lies grouped around the church and château whereas the Baraques district crossed by N 74 is altogether busier.

The famous Côte de Nuits, renowned for its great red wines, starts to the north.

Château

🕐*Open Mar-Oct.* 🚶*Guided tours (1hr) 10am-noon, 2-6pm. ☜5€. ☎03 80 34 36 77. www.chateau-de-gevrey-chambertin. com.*

In the upper village is this square-towered fortress, lacking its portcullis; it was built in the 10C by the lords of Vergy. In the 13C it was given to the monks of Cluny who enlarged the windows and installed a fine spiral staircase, wider than the simple ladders used hitherto.

The great chamber on the first floor with its uncovered beams contains a beautiful late-14C credence table. The great tower

Gevrey-Chambertin

H. Champollion/MICHELIN

Chambertin

Among the wines of the Côte de Nuits, full-bodied wines that acquire body and bouquet as they mature, Chambertin, from the two vineyards of Clos de Bèze and Chambertin, is the most famous and one of the most celebrated wines of all Burgundy. The Champ de Bertin (Field of Bertin), which became Chambertin, was the favourite wine of Napoleon I and was always to be found in his baggage-train, even on campaigns. Today there are only 28ha/69 acres producing this celebrated wine, whereas there are 500ha/1236 acres producing Gevrey-Chambertin.

has retained its watch room and bowmen's room. Beneath the basket-handle vaulting in the cellars, vintage wines are stored.

▶ *At Morey-St-Denis rejoin N 74.*

Vougeot

Its red wines are highly valued. The walled vineyard of Clos-Vougeot (50ha/124 acres), owned by the abbey of Cîteaux from the 12C up to the French Revolution, is one of the most famous of La Côte.

Château du Clos de Vougeot★

♿ ⓒ *Open daily year round.* ⬩ *Guided tours (45min) Apr-Sep 9am-6.30pm (Sat 5pm); Oct-Mar 9-11.30am, 2-5.30pm (Sat 5pm).* ⓒ *Closed 1 Jan and 24, 25 and 31 Dec.* ⬩ *3.70€.* ☎ *03 80 62 86 09. www. tastevin-bourgogne.com.*
Since 1944 the château has been owned by the **Confrérie des Chevaliers du Tastevin** (Brotherhood of the Knights of the Tastevin). Ten years earlier in 1934 a small group of Burgundians met in a cellar in Nuits-St-Georges and decided

to form a society whose aim was to promote the wines of France in general and, in particular, of Burgundy. The brotherhood was born and its renown spread throughout Europe and America.
The château was built in the Renaissance and restored in the 19C. The rooms visited include the Grand Cellier (12C cellar) where the *disnées* (banquets) and the ceremonies of the Order are held, the 12C cellar containing four huge wine-presses, the 16C kitchen with its huge chimney and ribbed vault supported by a single central pillar, and the monks' dormitory with a spectacular 14C roof.

Chambolle-Musigny

The road from Chambolle-Musigny to Curley *(north-west)* passes through a gorge, Combe Ambin, to a charming beauty spot: a small chapel stands at the foot of a rocky promontory overlooking the junction of two wooded ravines.

Clos de Vougeot

H. Champillon/MICHELIN

Reulle-Vergy

8km/5mi W of Chambolle-Musigny.
This village has a 12C church and a curious town hall, built on top of a wash-house. Opposite the town hall a barn now houses a **museum** (🕐 *open Mar-Dec Wed-Sun 10am-6pm; ⊚2€; ☎ 03 80 61 41 98*) describing the traditions associated with Hautes Côtes wines. Themes covered include day-to-day work in the vineyards, archaeology, flora and fauna, daily life in the 19C and the history of the region.

▸ *From l'Etang-Vergy take D 35 and D 25 S and E to Nuits-St-Georges.*

Nuits-St-Georges

This attractive little town is surrounded by the vineyards to which it has given its name. The fame of the wines of Nuits goes back to Louis XIV. When the royal doctor advised him to take some glasses of Nuits and Romanée with each meal as a tonic, the whole court wanted to taste it. The vast **church of St-Symphorien** was built at the end of the 13C although it is pure Romanesque in style. The flat chevet is pierced by a large rose window and three windows flanked by small columns and sculptures. A massive belfry surmounts the transept crossing. In addition, there are two fine 17C edifices: the **belfry** of the former town hall and the St-Laurent hospital.

Museum

🕐*Open May-Oct daily except Tue 10am-noon, 2-6pm. ⊚2.15€. ☎03 80 62 01 37.*
This museum, in the cellars of an old wine business shows items found in the Gallo-Roman settlement excavated at Les Bolards near Nuits-St-Georges.

Vosne-Romanée

2km/1.25mi N of Nuits-St-Georges.
These vineyards produce only red wines of the highest quality. Among the various sections (*climats*) of this vineyard, Romanée-Conti and De Richebourg have a worldwide reputation.

▸ *Beyond Nuits-St-Georges, the itinerary partly follows N 74 and also some of the picturesque roads of the Burgundian part of La Montagne.*

Comblanchien

4.5km/2.5mi S of Nuits-St-Georges.
This town is known for the limestone quarried from its surrounding cliffs.

▸ *S of Comblanchien turn right to Arcenant, 9km/5.5mi NW.*

Beyond Arcenant, raspberry and blackcurrant bushes border the road. During a fairly stiff climb, there is a good view over Arcenant, the arable land and the deep gorge of the **Combe Pertuis.**

▸ *From Bruant take D 25, D 18 and D 2 S to Bouilland.*

On the way downhill, there is a view of **Bouilland** encircled by wooded hills.

▸ *From Bouilland take D 2 S.*

Beyond the hamlet of La Forge the road is dominated on the left by the rocky escarpments crowning the hill and on the right by the rock known as the pierced rock *(roche percée)*. Soon after there is the cirque of the Combe à la Vieille on the left. The road then follows the green and narrow valley of the Rhoin. Shortly before **Savigny-lès-Beaune** (🕐 *see BEAUNE*), the valley opens out.

▸ *From Savigny take the minor road E to Aloxe-Corton (3km/2mi).*

② Côte De Beaune

Aloxe-Corton

This village (pronounced *Alosse*), the northernmost village of the Côte de Beaune, is of ancient origin. Emperor Charlemagne owned vineyards here and Corton-Charlemagne, "a white wine of great character", recalls this fact. However, red wines are produced almost exclusively at Aloxe-Corton, the firmest and most forward wines of the Côte de Beaune. The bouquet improves with age and the wine remains full-bodied and robust.

Beaune★★

🕐*See BEAUNE.*

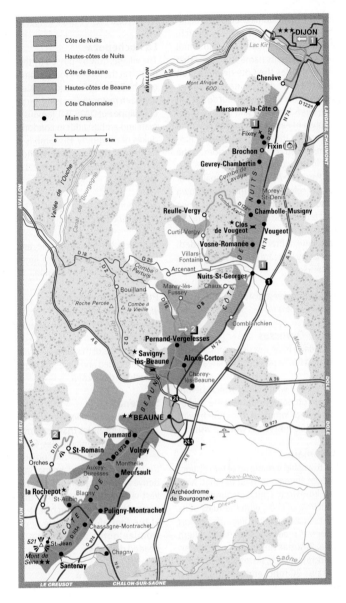

Côte de Nuits
Hautes-côtes de Nuits
Côte de Beaune
Hautes-côtes de Beaune
Côte Chalonnaise
• Main crus

0   5 km

Pommard

3km2mi SW of Beaune on N 74 and D 973.

The large village of Pommard takes its name from an ancient temple dedicated to Pomona, the goddess of fruits and gardens. These vineyards of the Côte de Beaune produce red wines that were greatly appreciated by Ronsard, Henri IV, Louis XV and Victor Hugo.

Volnay

1km/0.5mi SW of Pommard on D 973.

Its red wines have a delicate bouquet and silky taste. When he acquired the Duchy of Burgundy in 1477, Louis XI had the whole production of Volnay taken to his château at Plessis-les-Tours.

Meursault

2km/1.25mi SE of Auxey.

This little town, dominated by the beautiful Gothic stone spire of its church, produces high-quality red and white wines. It owes its name to a valley that clearly divides the Côte de Meursault from the Côte de Beaune. This valley, known as the Rat's Leap (*Saut du Rat* – in Latin *Muris Saltus*), is said to have given the present name of Meursault. Its white wines, with those of Puligny and Chassagne-Montrachet, are considered the best in the world.

The *Paulée de Meursault*, the final day of a yearly celebration of the grape known as **Les Trois Glorieuses**, is a well-known local fête. At the end of the banquet, to which each guest brings bottles of his own wine, a literary prize is awarded. The happy laureate receives 100 bottles of Meursault.

▷ *Continue west to Auxey-Duresses by way of Monthélie.*

Auxey-Duresses

This village is set in a deep *combe* leading to La Rochepot and its château. The vineyards of Auxey-Duresses produce fine red and white wines which, before the law on nomenclature, were sold as Volnay and Pommard. The church, with its fine 16C triptych, is worth a visit.

St-Romain

This township is made up of two distinct parts: St-Romain-le-Haut perched high on a limestone spur, surrounded by a semicircle of cliffs, with the ruins of its 12C-13C castle (*archaeological site, short visitor trail marked out*) on the southern edge. Right at the top stands the terraced 15C church, tastefully restored; it contains 2C fonts and a pulpit dating from 1619. Lower down in St-Romain-le-Bas stands the **town hall** (◷*open Jul to mid-Sep 2-6pm; rest of the year on request; ☎03 80 21 28 50*) which contains displays on local archaeology and ethnology.

▷ *N of St-Romain turn left on D 171 to Orches and La Rochepot.*

As the road approaches **Orches**, in its attractive rocky site, there is a fine **view**★ of St-Romain, Auxey, Meursault and the Saône Valley.

▷ *Beyond Orches, drive 4km/2.5mi S.*

La Rochepot★

The village, now by-passed by the main road, is at the foot of a rocky promontory on which stands the feudal castle which has been restored. It was the birthplace of Philippe Pot (1428-94), famous statesman and ambassador in London of the dukes of Burgundy. His tomb is a masterpiece of the Burgundian School and is now to be seen in the Louvre Museum.

▷ *From La Rochepot take D 973 NE skirting the château.*

The road follows a narrow valley and prior to Melin crosses a series of limestone escarpments worn by erosion.

Puligny-Montrachet
4km/2.5mi S of Meursault.
The white wines of Puligny-Montrachet, like those of Meursault, are excellent. The red wines of this old walled vineyard are full-bodied and have subtle qualities of taste and bouquet.

Santenay
6km/3.5mi SE of Puligny.
The three localities that go to make up Santenay – Santenay-le-Bas, Santenay-le-Haut and St-Jean – are spread along the banks of the River Dheune. Santenay derives its reputation not only from its vast vineyards but also from the local mineral water. The church of **St-Jean** is at the foot of a semicircle of cliffs; a wooden porch protects the round-headed doorway.

Mont de Sène★★
6km/3.7mi W of Santenay via D 113 to Dezize-lès-Maranges, then a minor road to the right; the road is narrow with sharp bends and steep gradients near the top.
The Mont de Sène is also known as the **Montagne des Trois-Croix** after the three crosses on the summit. The **panorama**★★ from the top reveals (north) the vineyards of the Côte beyond La Rochepot (east), the Saône Valley, the Jura and the Alps (south) and Mont St-Vincent and the Morvan (west).

LE CREUSOT-MONTCEAU

CONURBATION 100 000
MICHELIN MAP 320: G-9

Created in 1970, the conurbation of Le Creusot-Montceau is an interesting place to learn more about France's industrial heritage, thanks to its wealth of mines, foundries, factories, workshops and workers' settlements.

- **Information**: Château de la Verrerie, 71200 Le Creusot. ☎03 85 55 02 46. www.creusot.net.
- **Orient Yourself**: The Le Creusot basin, on the north-east edge of the Massif Central, is a natural depression containing the towns of Montceau-les-Mines, Blanzy, Montchanin and Le Creusot, from which it takes its name.

A Bit of History

Development of industry
Although iron ore was mined in the Middle Ages in the region of Couches, the discovery of vast coal deposits at Épinac, Le Creusot and Blanzy in the 17C marked the real origin of the industrial development of the whole area. Industrial exploitation really began in 1769 and by 1782, The Royal Foundry of Montcenis consisted of a foundry and blast-furnaces.

City of steel
In 1836 **Joseph-Eugène Schneider,** forge-master at Bazeilles, and his brother, **Adolphe Schneider**, set themselves up at Le Creusot, at that time a little township of 3 000 inhabitants. The rapid expansion of the Schneider works was to contribute to the wealth of the town, which from that date increased its population tenfold.

Sights

Le Creusot, Château de la Verrerie★
The crystal manufactory which supplied Marie-Antoinette , and later home of the Schneider family, now houses the tourist office and various exhibits on the region's industrial heritage.
In front of the **château** stand two huge conical glass-firing ovens. They were converted in 1905, one into a **miniature theatre** and the other into a chapel now used for temporary exhibitions.

Écomusée
◷Open Mon-Fri 10am-noon, 1-6pm (Oct-Jun from 2pm), weekends 3-7pm. ◷Closed 1 Jan, 25 Dec. ⊕6€. ☎03 85 73 92 00. www.ecomusee-creusot-monceau.com. The museum cover the history of Le Creusot and the life of the Schneiders, among other things, through displays of everything from crystal to tools.

Blanzy, Musée de la Mine
♿◷Open Jul-Aug daily except Tue 2-5pm; Mar-Jun and Sep-Nov Sat-Sun 2-5pm. ⊕5€. ☎03 85 68 22 85. www.ecomusee-creusot-monceau.com. A 22m/72ft-high head frame indicates the location of the former St-Claude mine shaft, worked from 1857 to 1881, which has now been refitted with its original equipment: light maintenance, machinery in working order (for operating lifts

"Le marteau pilon"

Address Book

For coin ranges, see the Legend on the cover flap.

WHERE TO STAY

La Petite Verrerie – 4 r. J. Guesde. ☎03 85 73 97 97. www.hotelfp-lecreusot.com. Closed 23 Dec-3 Jan. 43 rooms. ⌖11.50€. Restaurant⌖. Fomerly a factory pharmacy, then an employee club and finally, in its latest incarnation, a spacious hotel imbued with the history of the city. Newly renovated rooms.

Hôtel Le Moulin Rouge – 71670 Le Breuil, 3km/1.9mi E of Le Creusot by D 290. ☎03 85 55 14 11. www.le-moulin-rouge.com. Closed 20 Dec-10 Jan, Fri evenings, Sat lunchtime and Sun evenings. 31 rooms. ⌖9€. Restaurant⌖. This hotel located near a farmhouse is a haven of peace. Large, comfortable rooms decorated in the classical tradition. Meals are served in two dining rooms, one of which has a fireplace. Have a nap in the garden or down by the pool.

WHERE TO EAT

Moulin de Galuzot – In Galuzot, 71230 St-Vallier, 5km/3.1mi SW of Montceau-les-Mines by N 70 and D 974. ☎03 85 57 18 85. Closed 20 Jul-14 Aug, Tue evenings, Sun evenings and Wed. A typical country inn on the banks of the Bourbince Canal. Meals are served in two dining rooms on a raised platform: one with a colourful setting and old-fashioned chairs, the second with a more rustic touch. Traditional fare.

Le France – 7 pl. Beaubernard, 71300 Montceau-les-Mines. ☎03 85 67 95 30. www.jeromebrochot.com. Closed 6-20 Jan and 29 Jul-19 Aug, Sat lunch, Sun evening and Mon. Tucked away from the bustling town centre, this friendly restaurant is run by a charming young couple. Lovingly prepared dishes are served in an elegant dining room with fireplace. The smallish rooms are light and very quiet.

and pumping water). Former miners show visitors round galleries where extracting and pit-propping techniques are illustrated (15min audio-visual presentation).

Écuisses, Musée du Canal

Open Jun-15 Sep daily 10am-noon, 2-6pm; Apr-May and Sep-Nov 2-6pm. 2.80€. ☎03 85 78 97 04)
An annexe of the Écomusée, housed in an 18C lock-keeper's house and in a barge, *L'Armançon*, tells the history of inland water transport and *bargees*. Boat trips are organised in summer.

Excursions

Promenade des Crêtes (Le Creusot)

Follow rue Jean-Jaurès, rue de Longwy, D 28 (towards Marmagne) and a sharp right-hand turn to join this scenic road. The switch-back road overlooks the Le Creusot basin. A clearing in the woods

(viewing table) provides an overall view of the town and its surroundings. Further on another viewpoint reveals the extent of the old Schneider works and the central position, in this context, of the Château de la Verrerie.

Mont-St-Vincent★

12km/7.5mi SE of Montceau-les-Mines. The Charollais village stands on a bluff, on the watershed between the Loire and the Saône. It is one of the highest peaks (603m/1 987ft) in the Saône-et-Loire.

Church

The church, built at the end of the 11C, was once a priory of Cluny Abbey. Above the doorway is a carved tympanum, now badly damaged, showing Christ in Majesty between two figures, believed to be St Peter and St Paul. There is transverse barrel vaulting, similar to that in St-Philibert in Tournus, in the nave and groined vaulting in the aisles.

DIJON★★★

CONURBATION 236 953
MICHELIN MAP 320: K-6
LOCAL MAP SEE LA CÔTE

The capital of Burgundy is a lively city at the hub of a communications network linking northern Europe to the Mediterranean regions. Rich in history, the city has also been an influential cultural centre and its museums and architectural heritage are well worth exploring.

- **Information**: 34 r. des Forges, 21000 Dijon.
  ☎03 80 44 11 44. www.dijon-tourism.com.
- **Orient Yourself:** From the train station, avenue Maréchal Foch intersects with rue de la Liberté, leading to the core of the city around the place de la Libération. You'll find cafes and shops along the many pedestrian streets in this area. Lined with outdoor restaurants, place Emile-Zola is a good place for dining al fresco. Most museums are within walking distance of the historic centre.
- **Don't Miss:** The Musée des Beaux-Arts, one of the largest in France, founded more than 200 years ago and housed in a former ducal palace.
- **Especially for Kids:** The Musée d'Histoire Naturelle for its superbly lifelike animal habitat displays.
- **Parking:** You'll find spaces at the train station, adjacent to the ducal palace, and near many public squares.

A Bit of History

The Great Dukes of Burgundy

The dukes spent little time in Dijon (Charles the Bold was only here for a week), as they were busy establishing their authority in recalcitrant corners of their realm, but they did much to develop the city's cultural heritage. Manufacturing grew in the city and as trade prospered wealthy merchants built mansions which still stand today along rue des Forges, rue Vauban, rue Verrerie...

Capital of the Province of Burgundy

Change came when the duchy became part of the kingdom of France, with certain concessions: the *États de Bourgogne* (regional assembly) was maintained in the old ducal palace, along with various other privileges and, most importantly, the Burgundy Parliament was transferred from Beaune to Dijon. The King visited Saint-Bénigne in 1479 and solemnly swore to preserve "the freedoms, liberties, protections, rights and privileges" previously enjoyed by the duchy. All the same, he did build a fortress, repair the fortifications and appoint a governor.

A provincial town comes of age

As an administrative centre, seat of the princes of Condé, Dijon underwent significant urban development in the 17C and 18C. Jules Hardouin-Mansart (architect who designed the Versailles Palace) and later his brother-in-law Robert de Cotte rebuilt the ducal palace as the splendid Palais des États de Bourgogne on a monumental esplanade then known as the place Royale. Local officials and parliamentarians built many of the fine houses that give Dijon its character. The University was founded in 1723, the Academy in 1725 and, in 1731, Dijon became the Episcopal See. From 1851 onwards, the construction of the railway from Paris through Dijon and to the Mediterranean brought new life and new people; the population doubled between 1850 and 1892, as the industrial era took hold.

Town Walks

Around the Palais des Ducs★★

The old district around the palace of the dukes of Burgundy is charming. As you stroll along the streets, many of which are for pedestrians only, you will come across beautiful old stone mansions and half-timbered 15C-16C houses.

Place de la Libération

This is the former place Royale. In the 17C, when the town was at the height of its parliamentary power, it felt itself to be a capital and decided to transform the ducal palace, which had stood empty since the death of Charles the Bold, and to re-arrange its approaches. Plans for the fine semicircular design were drawn up by Jules Hardouin-Mansart, the architect of Versailles, and were carried out by one of his pupils from 1686 to 1701; the arcades of place de la Libération, surmounted by a stone balustrade, enhance the main courtyard.

▷ *Follow rue de la Liberté – formerly rue Condé – to the left of the palace, a pedestrianised shopping street.*

Place François-Rude

At the heart of the pedestrian zone is this irregularly shaped, lively square, with one or two half-timbered houses overlooking it. When the statue by the foun-

Place François Rude

B. Kaufmann–MICHELIN

tain (the *Bareuzai*) was erected in 1904, it provoked some raised eyebrows, but the grape-treading wine-grower, clad only in verdigris, has since been accepted as part of the scenery and is even looked on with affection by many.

Further on, on the corner of rue des Godrans and rue Bossuet, a department store now occupies the site of the former Maison du Miroir but the locals still agree to meet "on Miroir corner"!

Rue des Forges★

This is one of the most characteristic old streets of the town. Note the 15C façade of the **Hôtel Morel-Sauvegrain** at nos 52, 54 and 56. At no 40 the **Ancien Hôtel Aubriot** has a Classical doorway, which contrasts with the elegant 13C arcaded façade of the mansion built by the first bankers of Dijon. This was the birthplace of Hugues Aubriot, provost of Paris under Charles V. He was responsible for building the Bastille, several of the bridges over the Seine (notably the St-Michel Bridge), and the first vaulted sewers. (*Opposite, at no 8 rue Stephen-Liégeard, note the Renaissance façade of the Maison Chissere.*)

Further along, at no 38, note the Renaissance façade of **Maison Milsand**, lavishly decorated in the style of Hugues Sambin. Finally, in the inner courtyard of no 34, is the **Hôtel Chambellan**, a 15C house built by a rich family of drapers. It has a very fine spiral staircase; the central column rises to a flamboyant palm-tree vault supported by the statue of a wine-grower carrying a basket.

Église Notre-Dame★

This church is a good example of 13C Gothic architecture in Burgundy. With only a restricted space in which to work, the master mason showed astonishing technical prowess.

Exterior – The façade is original. Above the great porch with its three bays, closed in laterally as is the porch at Autun, two delicately arcaded galleries are underscored by three tiers of **gargoyles**. Two graceful bell-turrets top the towers hidden by the façade: that on the right carries the **Jacquemart clock** brought from Courtrai by Philip the Bold in 1382 after his victory over the Flemish.

Address Book

&For coin ranges, see the Legend on the cover flap.

WHERE TO STAY

⊜ **Jacquemart** – 32 r. Verrerie. ☎03 80 60 09 60. www.hotel-lejacquemart.fr. 31 rooms. ⊡6.50€. Simple, family-style rooms in a 17C building.

⊜⊜**Hôtel Victor Hugo** – 23 r. des Fleurs. ☎03 80 43 63 45. 23 rooms. ⊡5€. You will appreciate the thoughtful service at this traditional hotel. The rooms with their white roughcast walls are simple and quiet, despite their location near the town centre.

⊜⊜**Hôtel Wilson** – pl. Wilson. ☎03 80 66 82 50. www.wilson-hotel.com. 27 rooms. ⊡11€. This former post house has retained its traditional charm and charisma. The rooms are prettily decorated with light wood furniture. The exposed beams and luminosity make for a cosy atmosphere where one immediately feels at home.

WHERE TO EAT

⊜**Café du Vieux Marché** – 2 r. Claude-Ramey. ☎03 80 30 73 61. Closed Sun. This café opposite the covered market is fronted by a pretty terrace. Simplicity and authenticity guaranteed.

⊜⊜**La Mère Folle** – 102 r. Berbisey. ☎03 80 50 19 76. Closed Tue. This small restaurant in the town centre offers regional specialities such as escargots, œufs en meurette and sandre au Chablis. Convivial atmosphere, good service and 1930s-style décor.

⊜⊜**Les Deux Fontaines** – 16 pl. de la République. ☎03 80 60 86 45. Closed 10-25 August, Sun and Mon. Whitewashed walls, old banquettes, wood tables plastered with advertisements of yesteryear: it all makes for a nostalgic trip to bistrots past. Nostalgia reigns over the menu as well.

⊜⊜**Le Bistrot des Halles** – 10 r. Bannelier. ☎03 80 49 94 15. Closed Sun and Mon. A typical bistrot a stone's throw from the covered market. Choose one of the dishes chalked up on a slate and enjoy the warm and friendly ambience.

⊜⊜**L'Auberge de la Charme** – 21121 Prenois, 13km/8.1mi NW of Dijon by N 71 then D 104 heading towards the Circuit Automobile. ☎03 80 35 32 84. www. chateauxhotels.com/lacharme. Closed Feb school holidays, 1-14 Aug, Sun evenings, Tue lunchtime and Mon. Reservations required. Bellows and other old-fashioned tools from the smithy adorn this flower-filled country inn. Be won over by its hearty, delicious meals.

⊜⊜**La Dame d'Aquitaine** – 23 pl. Bossuet. ☎03 80 30 45 65. dame. aquitaine@wanadoo.fr. Closed 1-6 Jan, Mon lunchtime and Sun. In the town centre, a paved courtyard and a long flight of steps will take you down to a superb 13C vaulted dining hall. The décor is medieval, with tapestries and stained glass. Regional cuisine.

ON THE TOWN

Theatres and Opera – Comedians and actors regularly ply the stages of the Théâtre du Sablier (R. Berbisey), the Théâtre du Parvis-St-Jean (Pl. Bossuet), the Bistrot de la Scène (R. D'Auxonne). In May the city hosts the Rencontres Internationales du Théâtre. The Théâtre National Dijon-Bourgogne is directed by Robert Cantarella. Classical music, opera and dance productions are held at the Auditorium and at the Opéra de Dijon (Pl. du Théâtre).

L'Agora Café – 10 pl. de la Libération. ☎03 80 30 99 42. Open Tue-Sat 11.30am-2am. Piano-bar in a former 16C convent chapel. Wide selection of whiskies, beers and cocktails in a quiet, convivial atmosphere. Performances on Saturday evenings. Patio open in summer.

Le Caveau de la Porte Guillaume – pl. Darcy. ☎03 80 50 80 50. www.hotel-nord. fr. Open daily 7am-2am. Closed 20 Dec-5 Jan. Adjoining the Hotel du Nord, this wine bar is an ideal spot for discussing (and sampling) the delights of the region by the glass or the bottle.

SIT BACK AND RELAX

Comptoir des Colonies – 12 pl. François-Rude. ☎03 80 30 28 22. Open Mon-Sat 8am-7.30pm. Teas, coffees roasted in-house and hot chocolate await in this colonial-style tea shop, which also has a large sunny terrace.

Maison Millière – 10 r. de la Chouette. ☎03 80 30 99 99. www.maison-milliere.fr. Open Tue-Sun 10am-7pm. This pleasant tearoom occupies a 15C structure that began as a fabric shop behind the Église Notre-Dame.

La Causerie des Mondes – *16 r. Vauban.* ☎*03 80 49 96 59. Open 11am-7pm, Sundays Oct-Mar 3-7pm. Closed Mon.* Jute-covered walls and Asiatic-themed decor, with a backdrop of mood music, makes for an exotic atmosphere in this pleasant tearoom. More than 70 teas, 20 house-roasted coffees, chocolates and cakes to tempt you.

Mulot et Petitjean – *13 pl. Bossuet.* ☎*03 80 30 07 10. www.mulotpetitjean.fr. Open Mon 2-7pm, Tue-Sat 9am-noon, 2-7pm.* This long-standing establishment, founded in 1796, specialises in all forms of gingerbread: round biscuits filled with jam, crunchy *gimblettes* with almonds, and sweetmeats shaped as snails, fish, hens, eggs or clogs.

SHOPPING

Marché des Halles – *centre of town. Tue, Thu and Fri mornings, and Sat.*

Nicot Yves – *48 r. Jean-Jacques-Rousseau.* ☎*03 80 73 29 88. nicotvins@infonie.fr. Open Mon-Fri 8am-12.30pm, 3-8pm, Sat 8am-8pm, Sun 8am-12.30pm.* The proprietor, M Nicot, nurtures a veritable passion for wines in this shop. He also runs courses in wine tasting and oenology. Good selection of Burgundies.

Auger – *16 and 61 r. de la Liberté.* ☎*03 80 30 26 28. Open Sun-Tue 10am-noon, 2-pm, Wed-Sat 9am-7pm.* One of the last producers of traditional gingerbread in Dijon (documents indicate the beginnings of gingerbread baking here as early as the 14C). You'll also find a good selection of regional products for sale.

Boutique Amora-Maille – *32 r. de la Liberté.* ☎*03 80 30 41 02. Open Mon-Sat 9am-7pm.* Founded in 1777, this shop specialises in the mustards and vinegars of Dijon.

L'Escargotière de Marsannay-le-Bois – *rte d'Épagny, 21380 Marsannay-le-Bois.* ☎*03 80 35 76 15. sylvainmansuy@ wanadoo.fr. Open 10am-8pm.* In addition to sampling and purchasing snails, scallops and other fine prepared dishes, you can learn about how culinary snails are raised, harvested and prepared for consumption.

Interior – The overall effect is harmonious; the triforium of small tapering columns is of great delicacy. Note the height of the transept crossing beneath the lantern tower. The boldly conceived choir, ending with a polygonal chevet, is sober and graceful.

The stained-glass windows of the north transept date from the 13C. The 15C fresco has been restored. The chapel situated to the right of the choir houses the statue of Notre-Dame-de-Bon-Espoir (Our Lady of Good Hope). This 11C Virgin has been the object of particular veneration since the Swiss raised the siege of the town on 11 September 1513; the tapestry given at that time as a votive offering is now to be found in the fine arts museum. After Dijon had been liberated without damage from the German occupation on 11 September 1944, a second tapestry, made by Gobelins, commemorating the town's two liberations, was given as a new votive offering to Notre-Dame-de-Bon-Espoir. It can be seen in the south arm of the transept. Rue Musette offers an overall view of the west front and leads to the market.

Rue de la Chouette provides a good view of the east end of the church. On one of the buttresses (15C), there is a statue of the owl who gives the street its name. Legend has it that the wise bird will grant the wishes of visitors who stroke it with their left hand.

Hôtel de Vogüé

This early-17C mansion with its colourful tiled roof was one of the early meeting places of the representatives of the province. A portico richly decorated in the Renaissance style opens to a courtyard. The mansion is now occupied by the offices of the city architect and the department of cultural affairs. In July, the main courtyard is the venue of the Estivade, a dance, theatre and singing festival.

Rue Verrerie

Nos 8, 10 and 12 form an attractive group of half-timbered houses. Some of the beams have been richly carved.

▸ *If you have time to spare, continue along rue Chaudronnerie.*

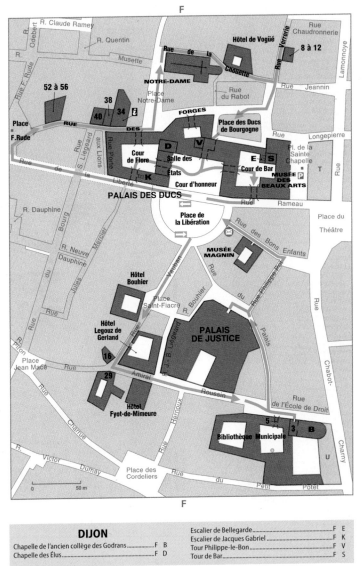

At no 28, the **Maison des Cariatides,** built in 1603, has 12 caryatids on its façade. No 66 rue Vannerie is a Renaissance house with ornamental windows flanking a watchtower by Hugues Sambin.

Place des Ducs-de-Bourgogne
From this little square, one can imagine what the palace must have looked like at the time of the dukes. The handsome Gothic façade is that of the Salle des Gardes, dominated by Philip the Good's tower.

▶ *From place des Ducs, return to the main courtyard of the palace by the vaulted passageway.*

Palais des Ducs et États de Bourgogne★★

Tour Philippe-le-Bon
🕐*Open Apr-Nov 9am-noon, 1.45-5.30pm. Rest of the year Wed 1.30-3.30pm, Sat-Sun 9-11am, 1.30-3.30pm.* ✒*2.30€.* ☎*03 80 74 52 71.*

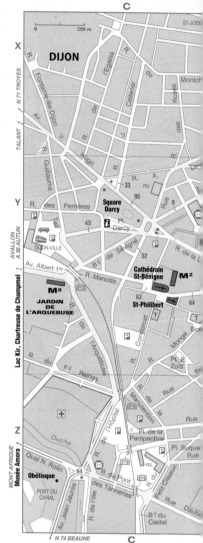

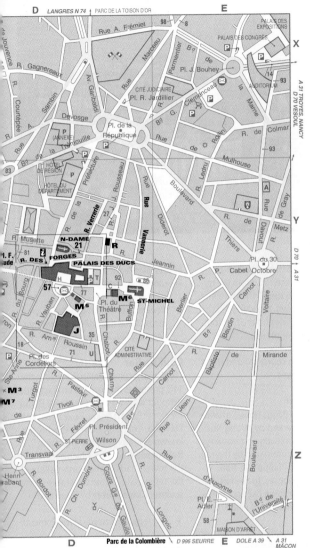

View of the city

B. Kaufmann-MICHELIN

The tower (46m/151ft high) was built by Philip the Good in the 15C. From the terrace at the top (316 steps), there is a fine **view**★ over the town, the valleys of the Ouche and the Saône and the first foothills of the Jura mountains.

▶ *Enter the main courtyard and stand near the railings.*

Cour d'honneur

The old Logis du Roi (King's House), a handsome ensemble marked by strong horizontal lines and terminating in two wings at right angles, is dominated by the tall medieval tower of Philippe-le-Bon. The ducal palace houses, to the left, the departments of the town hall and, to the right, the famous Museum of Fine Art.

▶ *The vaulted passageway to the left leads to the Flore courtyard.*

Cour de Flore

The buildings surrounding the courtyard were finished just before the Revolution in 1789. In the north-east corner is the **Chapelle des Élus**; its interior decor and the doors date from the period of Louis XV. Mass was celebrated in the chapel during the sittings of the States of Burgundy. Under the porch which gives access to rue de la Liberté (former rue Condé) a magnificent staircase (**L**), designed in 1735 by Jacques Gabriel, father of the architect who designed the Petit Trianon

at Versailles, leads to the **Salle des États** (⊶ *not open to the public*).

▶ *Return to the main courtyard, walk across it and through the vaulted passageway leading to the Cour de Bar.*

Cour de Bar

The **tower**, built by Philip the Bold in the 14C, preserves the name of an illustrious prisoner who was kept there by Philip the Good: René d'Anjou, Duke of Bar and Lorraine, Count of Provence, who was known as King René. The charming 17C **Bellegarde staircase**, which goes round the tower, leads to the north gallery of the same period. Note the statue of the sculptor **Claus Sluter** by Bouchard.

▶ *Leave by the passage to rue Rameau.*

Around the Palais de Justice★

▶ *Leave from place de la Libération by way of rue Vauban heading S.*

No 12 rue Vauban has a Classical façade adorned with pilasters and pediments, overlooking the inner courtyard.

Hôtel Legouz de Gerland

Take rue Jean-Baptiste-Liégeard to the left to skirt this mansion with its Renaissance façade pinpointed by four watch-

Jacquemart and family

The clock has quite a history. The name of Jacquemart, describing the figure of the man who strikes the bell of the clock with a hammer, first appeared in 1500.

The people of Dijon were very fond of him and in 1610 considered that his continued celibacy must be weighing very heavily on the poor man. So he was given a female companion.

In 1714 the poet Aimé Piron took pity on this brave couple, who seemed to have undertaken a vow of chastity. They were given a son, Jacquelinet, whose hammer strikes the little bell for the half-hours; in 1881, a daughter was added, Jacquelinette, who strikes the quarter-hours.

Ph. Gajic-MICHELIN

turrets. The Classical inner façade may be seen from no 21 rue Vauban.

At the corner of rue Vauban and rue Amiral-Roussin is a half-timbered house (no 16) which once belonged to a carpenter. This craftsman embellished his shutters with linenfold panelling and some of the beams with scenes of his craft. The house almost opposite, at no 29, has an elegant courtyard screened off by a curved balustrade. Note the fine door of no 27.

Hôtel Fyot-de-Mimeure

The façade in the inner courtyard of no 23 rue Amiral-Roussin is in the style of Hugues Sambin (16C).

Bibliothèque Municipale

🕐 Open Jul-Aug Wed-Fri 10am-noon, 2.30-6.30pm, Sat 10am-noon, 2.30-5.30pm. Rest of the year times vary. ☎03 80 44 94 14. www.bm-dijon.fr. Enter by no 3 rue de l'École-de-Droit.

The 17C chapel of the former college of Les Godrans, founded in the 16C by a rich Dijon family, has been transformed into a reading room. Among its 300 000 or more items, this library contains precious illuminated manuscripts, including some executed at Cîteaux in the first 30 years of the 12C.

▷ *Follow rue du Palais to reach the Palais de Justice.*

Palais de Justice (Law Courts)

This building was formerly the Burgundian Parliament. The gabled façade, in the Renaissance style, has a covered porch supported by columns. The door is a copy of a work by Sambin *(the original is in the Musée des Beaux-Arts)*. The huge Lobby *(Salle des Pas-Perdus)* is covered by a **vaulted ceiling**★ in the shape of an upturned boat. The ceiling of the Chambre Dorée, seat of the Court of Appeal, is adorned with the arms of François I (1522).

Musée Magnin★

🕐 *Open Tue-Sun 10am-noon, 2-6pm.* 🕐 *Closed 1 Jan and 25 Dec.* ✎3.50€. ☎03 80 67 07 15. www.musee-magnin.fr.

The museum is in an elegant 17C mansion, the home of art lovers Maurice Magnin (a magistrate) and his sister Jeanne, herself a painter and art critic. Their collection covers lesser-known painters, and reveals hidden talents. The more than 1 500 paintings also include works by great masters. On the ground floor are Flemish and Dutch paintings of the 16C and 17C. Italian painting has a place of honour with paintings by Cariani, Di Benvenuto, Allori, Cerano, Strozzi and Tiepolo. On the first floor, French paintings from the late 16C through 19C are on display, including works by Claude Vignon, Le Sueur, Bourdon, Girodet, Géricault, Gros and others.

The furnishings from the early 18C through the Second Empire were clearly chosen with as much care as the works of art, creating an intimate atmosphere.

▷ *Take rue des Bons-Enfants back to place de la Libération.*

Ph. Gajic-MICHELIN

Procession of mourners at the tomb of Philip the Bold

Musée des Beaux-Arts★★

The huge fine arts museum created in 1799 is in the former ducal palace.
 ♿ 🕐 *Open May-Oct daily except Tue 9.30am-6pm; Nov-Apr daily except Tue 10am-5pm.* 🕐 *Closed 1 Jan, 25 Dec.* ☎03 80 74 52 09. www.dijon.fr.

Ground floor

On the left, at the far end of the rooms devoted to temporary exhibitions, are the **ducal kitchens**, built in 1435. The six huge chimneys were scarcely sufficient for the preparation of feasts worthy of the Burgundian court.

The **chapter-house** of the former 14C ducal chapel (*ground floor of the Tour de Bar*) illustrates the evolution of religious sculpture – an art form held in high regard in Burgundy – from the 14C to the 17C. The works of art include 15C stained-glass windows, reliquaries, 16C silver gilt altarpiece together with St Robert's cross (11C) and a cup belonging to St Bernard.

On the grand staircase is a statue of the Maréchal de Saxe by **François Rude** (1784-1855).

On the landing is the old door of the Dijon law courts, carved by Hugues Sambin (16C), and some fine medieval and Renaissance pieces of religious gold- and silver-ware and carved ivory.

First floor

This floor houses Italian painting from the 14C to the 16C, with particularly

good examples of the Primitive schools of Florence (Taddeo Gaddi) and Siena (Pietro Lorenzetti) and of the Florentine Renaissance. Two galleries contain paintings by 15C and 16C German and Swiss masters, including the Master of the Darmstadt Passion (1425), Conrad Witz (*Emperor Augustus and the Tibur Sibyl*).

Of the next three galleries (*overlooking the courtyard*), the first two are devoted to Renaissance art: furniture, medals, enamels and paintings (*Lady dressing*, Fontainebleau School); the third is hung with 17C Burgundian paintings.

The wing overlooking rue Rameau is devoted to French painting, starting with 17C works by painters under Louis XIV: Philippe de Champaigne (*Presentation in the Temple*), Le Sueur, Le Brun and François Perrier. Note also the *Portrait of a Painter* by P Mignard and the *Holy Family Resting* by Sébastien Bourdon. Artists from the late 17C and 18C are represented in two galleries, in particular Burgundian painters such as JF Gilles, known as Colson (*Rest*, 1759) and JB Lallemand (Dijon 1716-Paris 1803), creator of landscapes and genre scenes. A large gallery displays paintings by Nattier (*Portrait of Marie Leszczynska*), Van Loo (*St George and the Dragon*) and others.

The **Salle des Statues,** in the corner of the west wing, which contains copies of ancient works and 19C pieces including *Hebe and the Eagle of Jupiter* by Rude, has a view of place de la Libération.

The adjacent **Salon Condé** is decorated with woodwork and stucco of the Louis

XVI period. It displays 18C French art: furniture, terracottas and paintings as well as sculptures by Coysevox (bust of Louis XIV) and Caffieri.

The **Prince's Staircase,** which is built against the Gothic façade of the old Dukes' Palace, leads down to the **Salle d'Armes** (Arms Room) on the ground floor: weapons and armour from the 13C to the 18C, cutlery and knives dating from the 16C to the 18C.

The **Salle du Maître du Flémalle**, which contains 14C-15C Flemish and Burgundian painting, including the famous *Nativity*★★ by the **Master of Flémalle** and several works of art from the Chartreuse de Champmol, provides an excellent introduction to the Salle des Gardes.

The **Salle des Gardes**★★★ overlooking place des Ducs is the most famous gallery in the museum. It was built by Philip the Good and used as the setting for the Joyous Entry of Charles the Bold in 1474; it had to be restored in the early 16C after a fire. It houses treasures from the Chartreuse de Champmol (see below), the necropolis of the dukes of Valois.

From 1385 to 1410 three men – Jean de Marville, Claus Sluter and his nephew, Claus de Werve – worked successively on the **tomb of Philip the Bold**★★★. The magnificent recumbent figure, watched over by two angels, rests on a black marble slab surrounded by alabaster arches forming a cloister to shelter the procession of mourners composed of 41 very realistic statuettes. The funeral procession consists of clergymen, Carthusians, relatives, friends and officials of the Prince, all hooded or dressed in mourning.

The **tomb of John the Fearless and Margaret of Bavaria**★★★, dating from between 1443 and 1470, is in a similar, although more Flamboyant style.

The two altarpieces in gilt wood commissioned by Philip the Bold for the Chartreuse de Champmol are very richly decorated. They were carved between 1390 and 1399 by Jacques de Baerze and painted and gilded by Melchior Broederlam. Only the **Crucifixion altarpiece**★★★ near the tomb of Philip the Bold has retained Broederlam's famous paintings on the reverse side of the wings: the *Annunciation*, the *Visitation*, the *Presentation*

Ph. Gajic-MICHELIN

Ducal kitchens

in the Temple and the *Flight into Egypt*. At the other end is the **altarpiece of the Saints and Martyrs**★★★. In the centre, note an early-16C **altarpiece of the Passion**★★ from an Antwerp workshop.

Above the central altarpiece, between two 16C wall hangings from Tournai, hangs a tapestry dedicated to Notre-Dame-de-Bon-Espoir, protector of the city since the raising of the siege of Dijon by the Swiss on 11 September 1513.

A niche contains a handsome portrait of Philip the Good wearing the collar of the Order of the Golden Fleece, painted by the Rogier Van der Weyden workshop (c 1455). A staircase leads to the tribune, from which there is a good **view**★.

The **Galerie de Bellegarde** contains some good examples of 17C and 18C Italian and Flemish painting, in particular *Moses in the Bullrushes* by Veronese and *Adam and Eve* by Guido Reni; there is an unusual panoramic landscape of the *Château de Mariemont* and its grounds by Velvet Brueghel, and a *Virgin and Child with St Francis of Assisi* by Rubens. Next comes a gallery devoted to 19C French sculpture and displaying works by Rude, Canova, Carpeaux and Mercié.

Second and third floors

These are devoted to modern and contemporary art. Works by the great animal sculptor **François Pompon** (1855-1933) are displayed in an old gallery in the Tour de Bar *(signposted)*.

The other galleries contain paintings, drawings, graphics and sculptures dating from the 16C to the present. Particularly famous names include Georges de la Tour (Le Souffleur à la lampe), Géricault, Delacroix, Victor Hugo (imaginary landscapes in wash), Daumier, Courbet, Gustave Moreau and various painters from the Barbizon School (Daubigny, Rousseau, Diaz de la Peña etc), Rodin, Maillol, Bourdelle and others.

The Impressionists and Post-Impressionists are represented by works by Manet (Portrait of Méry Laurent in pastel), Monet, Boudin, Sisley and Vuillard.

A remarkable collection of African sculpture and masks (Mali, Cameroon, Congo) gives an insight into the art forms which inspired Cubist painters and sculptors.

Among the rich collection of contemporary painting and sculpture note in particular works by artists in or linked with the Paris School and abstract artists of the 1950s to 1970s: Arpad Szenes and Vieira da Silva, his wife, Lapicque, De Staël (Footballer), Bertholle, Manessier, Messagier, Mathieu and Wols; also several lovely sculptures by Hajdu.

Additional Sights

Cathédrale St-Bénigne

The ancient abbey church, on the site of an earlier Rmanesque building, is pure Burgundian-Gothic in style. The **west front** of is supported by massive buttresses flanked by two great towers with conical roofs of multicoloured tiles. Within the porch, which is surmounted by a delicately pierced gallery, is the old 12C Romanesque doorway in the centre of the Gothic façade. The transept crossing is marked by a tall spire (93m/305ft) in the Flamboyant style.

The **interior** is quite austere; its lines are unadorned: plain capitals, simply moulded arcades in the triforium, little columns extending unbroken from the vault to the floor in the crossing and to the tops of massive round pillars in the nave. Since St-Bénigne lost its own works of art during the Revolution, it has provided a home for tombstones and pieces of sculpture from other churches in Dijon. The organ (1743) is by Riepp.

The only remaining traces of the Romanesque **crypt★** (🕐open 9am-6pm. ∞1€ donation) consist of part of the transept with four apsidal chapels on the east side and a trench in the middle containing the remains of a sarcophagus which was probably used for the burial of St Benignus, the first Burgundian martyr who died in the 3C; there is a pilgrimage to his tomb on 20 November. The sarcophagus faces a broad opening in the lower storey of the **rotunda★★** which echoes the highly symbolic architecture of the tomb of Christ in Jerusalem built in the 4C; only eight rotundas of this type are known in the world. Three circles of columns radiate from the centre; some have retained their original capitals decorated with palm leaves, interlacing, monstrous animals or praying figures, rare examples of pre-Romanesque sculpture. The eastern end of the rotunda opens into a 6C chapel which may be a cella (sanctuary).

Musée Archéologique★

🕐Open daily except Tue 9am-12.30pm, 1.30-6pm. 🕐Closed Mon (Oct-May), 1 Jan, 1 and 8 May, 14 Jul, 1 and 11 Nov, 25 Dec. ☎03 80 30 88 54. www.dijon.fr.

The museum is in the eastern wing of what used to be the cloisters of St-Bénigne. Galleries on the lower level hold Gallo-Roman sculptures, including a bronze statue of the **goddess Sequana★** found during the excavation of the sanctuary at the source of the River Seine.

The 13C Gothic monk's dormitory on the next floor is is devoted to medieval sculpture from the region of Dijon, such as a head of Christ, made by Claus Sluter for the Chartreuse de Champmol. From St-Bénigne, two Romanesque tympana frame the **Christ on the cross★★** (1410) attributed to Claus de Werve.

The top storey is home to a varied collection of items from different periods, from Paleolithic times to the Merovingian Era. Included in the collection are a **gold bracelet** which weighs 1.3kg/3lb found in **La Rochepot** (9C BC), and the **Blanot Treasure★**, a hoard of objects from the late Bronze Age (belt buckle, leggings, necklace and bracelet). In the last room, among some typical stone renderings of Gallo-Roman deities, notice the

frieze from Alésia, representing mother-goddesses, and a marble portrait of a woman found in Alise-Ste-Reine.

Église St-Michel★

The church, in Flamboyant Gothic style, was consecrated in December 1529, although its façade was eventually completed in the full Renaissance style; the four-storey towers framing it were finished in the 17C. The façade, on which the three classical orders are superimposed, is the most curious part of the building. The porch, which juts far out, is pierced by three doorways: a long frieze of ornamental foliage and grotesque decorations runs along the upper part of the porch for its whole length. Under it, in medallions, are busts of the prophets Daniel, Baruch, Isaiah and Ezekiel, as well as of David with his harp and Moses with the Tablets of the Law. The right doorway dates from 1537 and is the oldest of the three.

The interior is Gothic in style. Note the height of the choir, which like St-Bénigne lacks an ambulatory, the 18C woodwork, and four paintings by Franz Kraus (18C German): *Adoration of the Shepherds* and *The Flight into Egypt* (deteriorated) in the north transept; *Adoration of the Magi* and *Presentation in the Temple* in the chapel of the Saint-Sacrement, which also has a fine Flamboyant altar. The far north chapel contains a fragment of a 15C Entombment.

Chartreuse de Champmol★

🕐*Open daily 10am-6pm. Follow signs to the Puits de Moïse.*

This former monastery was largely destroyed in the Revolution; a psychiatric hospital now occupies the site.

The first dukes of Burgundy were buried at Cîteaux but Philip the Bold wanted an almost royal burial place for himself and his heirs and in 1383 he founded the charter house which was consecrated five years later by the Bishop of Troyes. The best artists of the period contributed to the magnificent undertaking but nothing remains except the tombs of the dukes, the retables preserved in the Musée des Beaux-Arts, and two works by Claus Sluter (late 14C), the sculptor from Haarlem who became the leader

Le puits de Moïse

of the Burgundian-Flemish School of Art: the **chapel doorway★** and the **Well of Moses★★ (Puits de Moïse)**.

The well (*walk round the buildings to reach the courtyard*) is actually the base of a polychrome Calvary made between 1395 and 1405 to decorate the font in the great cloisters (the painting is barely visible). It is named after the figure of Moses, probably the most impressive of the six huge and strikingly lifelike statues which surround the hexagonal base; the other five figures are the prophets *(going round to the right from Moses)* David, Jeremiah, Zachariah, Daniel and Isaiah. The angels beneath the cornice are the work of Claus de Werve, Sluter's nephew; with touching veracity each one through a different pose expresses his suffering before the Calvary.

The doorway, which is now inside the chapel, consists of five statues sculpted by Claus Sluter between 1389 and 1394. Duke Philip the Bold and Margaret of Flanders, his wife, are depicted kneeling, watched by their patron saints (St John the Baptist and Ste Catherine), on each side of the Virgin Mary and Child who are portrayed on the central pier.

Musée de la Vie bourguignonne★

♿🕐*Open May-Sep daily except Tue 9am-6pm; Oct-Apr daily except Tue 9am-noon, 2-6pm.* 👥*Guided tour (1hr) Sun 3pm and 4pm.* 🕐*Closed 1 Jan, 1 and 8 May, 14 Jul, 1 and 11 Nov, 25 Dec.* ☎*03 80 44 12 69. www.dijon.fr.*

The Prestigious Order of the Golden Fleece

In 1404, Philip the Bold created the Order of the Golden Tree, which John the Fearless and Philip the Good perpetuated and enhanced.

It was this second Philip who, at the time of his marriage to Isabella of Portugal in Bruges in 1429, first wore the insignia of the **Golden Fleece**: a chain encircling his neck, from which hung a sheepskin. The symbolism of the Order relates to Jason of Greek mythology as well as Gideon in the Old Testament.

There were two reasons for creating the Order: first, to draw Burgundy closer to the Church by keeping the spirit of the Crusades and chivalry alive, and second, to strengthen the duchy's position in regard to the English crown, the Holy Roman Empire and the Kingdom of France.

The Order was based in the chapel of the ducal palace in Dijon, where the young Count of Charollais, who was later to become Charles the Bold, was knighted in 1433.

The marriage of his only daughter, Marie de Bourgogne, in 1477, to Archduke Maximilian of Austria, brought the Hapsburgs into the Order.

The Order of the Golden Fleece still carries great prestige and implies a commitment to a disciplined life. It is not hereditary, and the official insignia must be returned by the heirs upon a knight's death.

The museum covers local history. Furnishings, household items, clothing and other souvenirs of times past are used to bring to life the daily habits, ceremonies and traditions of Burgundy at the end of the 19C. On the upper floor, a whole street has been re-created, complete with a beauty salon (some of the tools of the trade look more like instruments of torture) and a corner grocery.

Jardin de l'Arquebuse★

This park owes its name to the company of *harquebusiers*, who occupied the site in the 16C. All the western part is taken up by the botanical gardens (3 500 different species), which were founded in the 18C and joined to the Promenade de l'Arquebuse. In addition there is an arboretum, tropical glasshouses and a vivarium. Magnificent trees surround the colourful flower beds.

Muséum d'Histoire Naturelle★

&. ⏱Open daily 9am-noon, 2-6pm; Wed, Sat-Sun 2-6pm. ⏱Closed 1 Jan, 1 and 8 May, 14 Jul, 15 Aug, 1 and 11 Nov, 25 Dec. ☎03 80 76 82 76. www.dijon.fr.
Kids The Natural History Museum, founded in 1836 by a nature lover from Dijon, Léonard Nodot, is housed in the old crossbowmen's barracks (1608). As an introduction to the museum, visit the **ground floor**

exhibits on the origins and evolution of the world, including a magnificent **glyptodon**, a giant armadillo from the Argentinian pampas which first saw the light during the Tertiary Era.
The **first floor** is devoted to animal life, and displays include exceptionally good **reconstitutions of the natural habitat**★. Multimedia and hands-on exhibits provide a lively approach to the flora and fauna of the five continents, the Arctic and Antarctic.
On the **second floor**, there is a surprisingly diverse collection of insects, in particular the superb butterfly display.
The orangery houses temporary exhibitions, a vivarium and beehive.

Musée Amora

⏱Open year round. Guided tours mid-May to mid-Sep daily except Sun and public holidays 3pm and 4pm; Rest of the year times vary. Enquire at the tourist office. ☎03 80 44 11 41.
This museum, created by the Amora company, the world's leading mustard manufacturer, recounts the history of the condiment, its origins, and every aspect of its production. It is interesting to note that Dijon has become the "Mustard Capital of the World", although there is not a single mustard field in France.

DIVONNE-LES-BAINS ✈

POPULATION 6 171
MICHELIN MAP 328: J-2
LOCAL MAP SEE ST-CLAUDE: EXCURSION

Divonne is a well-known spa town half way between Lake Geneva and the great Jura mountain range, on the Franco-Swiss border, and has plenty of luxury hotels, a golf course, a racecourse and a 45ha/111-acre lake.

- **Information**: r. des Bains, 01220 Divonne-Les-Bains.
  ☎04 50 20 01 22. www.divonnelesbains.com.
- ▶ **Orient Yourself**: To the west, trails lead up Mont Ussy from where there are views over Lake Geneva and the Alps.

A Bit of History

The Romans enjoyed the waters at Divonne long ago, building an 11km/6.6mi aqueduct to carry them to their colonial capital Noviodunum (Nyon). In later years, the springs ran on forgotten until 1848, when Dr Paul Vidart founded a spa. It soon became famous, attracting clients like Prince Jérôme Bonaparte and Guy de Maupassant.

Sights

Thermal Baths

🕐 *Open Mon-Fri 9am-8.30pm (9.30pm Mon and Wed), Sat 9am-6pm, Sun 9am-2pm).* ☎*04 50 20 27 70. www.valvital.fr.* The spa specialises in the treatment of ailments often associated with modern living, such as stress and insomnia. However, they also organise wellness pack-

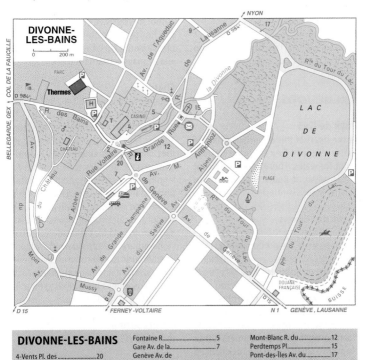

Address Book

WHERE TO EAT, STAY AND PLAY

Auberge du Vieux Bois – *1km/0.6mi W of Divonne on road to Gex.* ☎04 50 20 01 43. www.aubergeduvieuxbois.fr. *Closed Feb, 28 Jun-11 Jul, 25 Oct-3 Nov, Sun evenings and Mon. This family inn serves traditional cuisine.*

Jura – *rte Arbère.* ☎04 50 20 05 95. www.hotel-le-jura.com. *21 rooms.* 9€. *This family-run hotel offers functional, well-kept rooms (some newly renovated).*

Auberge des Chasseurs – *01170 Échenevex, 11km/6.8mi SW of Divonne by D 984C.* ☎04 50 41 54 07. *Closed 12 Nov-28 Feb, Sun evenings and Mon except Jul-Aug, Tue and Fri lunchtime. 15 rooms.* 12€.

Restaurant . *Peaceful inn offering tidy bedrooms and views over Mont Blanc.*

Joy's Club – *783 av. des Alpes.* ☎04 50 20 14 12. *Open Apr-Oct 10am-11pm. Organised activities for all ages in a leafy setting near Divonne lake.*

Les Quatre-Vents – *pl. des Quatre-Vents.* ☎04 50 20 00 08. *Open Tue-Sat 6.30am-7.30pm, Sun 6.30am-2pm. Closed Oct. Tuck into delicious home-made pastries in this tea shop and art gallery.*

Casino de Divonne-les-Bains – *av. des Thermes.* ☎04 50 40 34 34. www.domaine-de-divonne.com. *Open noon-4am (11am Sun). Roulette, blackjack, slot machines, as well as a discotheque.*

ages for those who just want to pamper themselves a little.

Racecourse

Located near the lake, the racecourse is used in summer for flat racing and also for trotting races.

Lake

This vast artificial lake has a beach, and is popular for windsurfing and sailing.

Excursions

Pays de Gex

At the heart of this mountain area, the pretty village of **Gex** is a good starting point for walks. There are magnificent views of Mont Blanc from the main square, place Gambetta.

Creux de l'Envers

2hr on foot there and back, starting from the bottom of rue du Commerce, then along rue Léone-de-Joinville, and returning via rue de Rogeland on N 5 N of Gex. This pleasant walk takes you to a wooded gash in the mountainside through which flows the River Journans. The narrowest place is known as the **Portes Sarrasines;** the mountain stream rushes through a small gap in the rock flanked

on both sides by limestone escarpments looking like a door frame.

Ferney-Voltaire

15km/ 10mi.
Ferney-Voltaire, on the border with Switzerland, was home to the famous author for nearly 20 years, and a visit to the house where he held court will please both fans of Voltaire and those less acquainted with his work.

Château★

Closed to 2008. ☎04 50 40 53 21. www.ferney-voltaire.net.
Built by Voltaire to replace a fortress too austere for his tastes, the château is in the Doric style and surrounded by a landscaped park. Voltaire took his role as landlord very seriously; he had sanitation installed in the village, part of his estate, and endowed it with a hospital, school and clockmaking workshops. He had homes built for the residents out of stone, around a church in which Voltaire – rather surprisingly – had his own pew. The house contains many mementoes of the philosopher's life, including his portrait by Quentin de La Tour.

Monts Jura❋

See MONTS JURA.

DOLE★

POPULATION 24 949
MICHELIN MAP 321: C-4
LOCAL MAP SEE FORÊT DE CHAUX

The brown-tiled roofs of Dole's old houses cluster around the church and its imposing bell-tower. The citizens of Dole are proud of their city; it was the capital of the free province of Burgundy (the Franche-Comté) for many centuries. The present city is adorned with many splendid monuments to its illstrious past.

- **Information**: pl. Grévy, 39100 Dole. ☎03 84 72 11 22. www.dole.org.
- ▶ **Orient Yourself**: The town is on a hillside overlooking the north bank of the Doubs, which is joined at this point by the Rhône-Rhine Canal.

A Bit of History

The arrival of the French

By the 15C, Dole was already playing the role of a capital city, and it was not long before the flourishing town was noticed – and coveted – by Louis XI and the French. In 1479 the king laid siege to the town; Dole eventually fell and was burned to the ground. However, Louis' son Charles VIII returned the Comté to the Hapsburgs in 1493. French attempts to annexe the Comté were renewed under **Louis XIII**. In 1636 the Prince of Condé laid siege to Dole, but after a three-month bombardment was forced to withdraw. In 1668 and 1674 Louis XIV's troops renewed the attack on Dole, which finally succumbed, and in 1678 the town and province were officially annexed to France. The Sun King did not forgive Dole for having put up such strong resistance; he made Besançon the capital of the Franche-Comté instead, stripping Dole of its Parliament, university and ramparts.

Walking Tour

The **old town★★** is clustered around the church of Notre-Dame. Its narrow, winding streets are closely packed with houses dating from the 15C to the 18C, many of which have interesting details: coats of arms above doorways, turrets, arcaded inner courtyards and so on.

▶ *Leave from place Nationale.*

Place Nationale

This charming square in the centre of the old town has been restored and is once more a busy market square.

Collégiale Notre-Dame★

For access to the top of the bell-tower, contact the tourist office; ☎03 84 72 11 22.

The size of the 16C church's interior is striking. Its sober lines are a resolute departure from the excessive ornamentation of the Late Gothic style. It contains some of the first Renaissance works

Dole on the banks of the Doubs

M. Paygnard-MICHELIN

DOLE

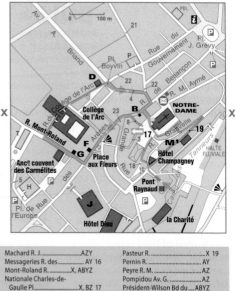

of art to manifest themselves in Dole, such as the beautiful **works in polychrome marble**★. These are characterised by motifs typical of the Dole workshops (foliage, tracery and birds) as, for example, on the façade of the Sainte-Chapelle, the organ case and the pulpit (Denis Le Rupt) and the holy-water stoup.

The marvellous carved wooden **great organ** dating from the 18C is one of the very rare examples of its type in France to have survived virtually intact. The organ builder was Karl Joseph Riepp.

▶ *To the right of the old town hall, take rue d'Enfer, rue de Besançon, place du 8-Mai-1945 and rue des Arènes.*

Place aux Fleurs
There is a pretty **view** of old Dole, dominated by Notre-Dame's bell-tower.

Rue Mont-Roland
Note the polychrome marble and stone doorway of the old Carmelite convent (17C) and the façades of some of the private mansions, for example, the Maison Odon de la Tour (16C) and the **Hôtel de Froissard** (early 17C), where you should pass through the gate to admire the double horseshoe staircase and the courtyard's loggia.

▶ *Right on rue du Collège-de-l'Arc.*

Collège de l'Arc
The Jesuits founded this school in 1582.

▶ *Go under the arch.*

The deconsecrated chapel is distinguished by its richly decorated Renaissance **porch**, surmounted by a loggia with arches supported by the figures of angels in flight. Notice the two mansions on the left, one of which dates from 1738; they still have their small inner courtyards and beautiful balustrades.

▶ *Place Boyvin; rue Boyvin, rue de la Sous-Préfecture; rue de Besançon (right).*

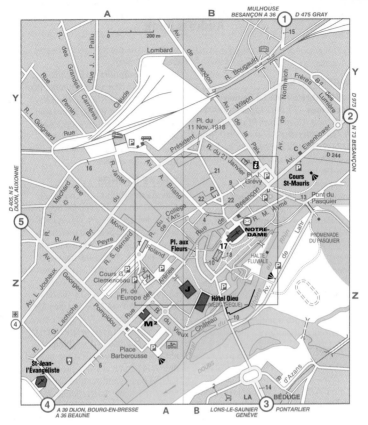

Cave d'Enfer

A plaque recalls the heroic resistance of a few Dole citizens during the attack on the town in 1479.

▷ *Turn back to reach place Nationale, then take rue Pasteur.*

Rue Pasteur

This street used to be called rue des Tanneurs, as all the houses of the hemp and leather craftsmen were here along the banks of the canal. No 43 is the birthplace of Pasteur.

▷ *Take the passage on the right of Pasteur's birthplace, follow the canal walk and take the footbridges to get to the Pont Raynaud-III.*

Pont Raynaud-III

View of a handsome architectural group: the Charité (18C hospital), the Hôtel-Dieu (17C hospice) and an 18C convent.

The Grande Fontaine, an underground spring and wash-house, can be seen under the last arch of the bridge *(to get to it, go down passage Raynaud-III off rue Pasteur).*

Hôtel Champagney

An 17C portal surmounted by a crest leads into a courtyard where two interesting staircases and a beautiful balcony on corbels can be seen.

▷ *Take rue du Parlement, to the left and then to the right, from where there is a view of Notre-Dame's bell-tower.*

Additional Sights

Maison Natale de Pasteur and Musée Pasteur

🕐Open Jul-Aug Mon-Sat 10am-6pm, Sun 2-6pm. Rest of the year times vary. 🕐Closed 1 Jan, 1 May and 25 Dec. ➔4.50. ☎03 84 72 20 61. www.musee-pasteur.com

Address Book

For coin ranges, see the Legend on the cover flap.

WHERE TO STAY

Chambre d'Hôte La Thuilerie des Fontaines – *2 r. des Fontaines, 39700 Châtenois, 7.5km/4.8mi NE of Dole by N 73 heading for Besançon then D 10 and D 79. ☎03 84 70 51 79. michel.meunier2@wanadoo.fr. 4 rooms.* The rooms in this 18C house, reached by a stone staircase, are comfortable and impeccably kept. Take a break down by the pool, near the former stables.

Hôtel La Chaumière – *346 av. du Mar-Juin. ☎03 84 70 72 40. Closed 20 Dec-4 Jan, Sun except Sun evenings 15 Jun-15-Sep, Sat lunch and Sun lunch. 18 rooms. 10€. Restaurant.* The rooms give onto the peaceful garden. The dining room is bright and comfortable with stone walls and exposed beams. Summer terrace. Family cooking with fresh regional produce.

WHERE TO EAT

La Demi Lune – *39 r. Pasteur. ☎03 84 72 82 82. la-demi.lune.dole@wanadoo.fr. Closed 7-27 Jan and Mon.* Enjoy regional delicacies, buckwheat pancakes and grilled meat on the terrace by the Canal des Tanneurs or in the vaulted dining room. Playing area for children.

La Romanée – *11-13 r. des Vieilles-Boucheries. ☎03 84 79 19 05. la-romanee.franchini@wanadoo.fr. Closed 1-8 Jul, 30 Aug-5 Sep, Sun evenings and Wed Oct-Jun.* This former butcher shop, its meat hooks still on the wall, serves hearty traditional meals.

Les Templiers – *35 Grande-Rue. ☎03 84 82 78 78.www.restaurantlestempliers.com. Closed 2-16 Feb, 10-18 Nov, Sat lunchtime, Sun evenings and Mon.* Meals from the freshest produce are served in a 13C crypt with ribbed vaulting and chandeliers illuminating the light stone walls. .

WHERE TO SHOP

Marché des Halles – *pl. Charles-de-Gaulle. Open Tue, Thu and Sat 8am-1pm.* On market days these halls explode with life as shoppers and merchants meet to trade wares. You'll find fish, meat, poultry, cheese and dairy and other high quality products: the best the region has to offer.

La Porteuse du Pain – *13-15 r. de Besançon. ☎03 84 72 00 32. Open Tue-Sat 7am-7.30pm, Sun 7am-1pm. Closed Feb holidays and 3 wks in Oct.* Open for 34 years, this bakery does things the old-fashioned way, with stone-ground flour and natural yeast, to produce a feast of breads and pastries. Try the house speciality: *galette flamande à l'orange.*

Fromagerie et Cave Comtoise – *r. d'Enfer. ☎03 84 72 24 29. Open Tue-Sat 8am-12.15pm and 2.30-7pm.* This 100-year-old cheese shop is remarkably good. Regional cheeses include Comté, morbier, raclette, bleu de Gex and marmirolle, plus several kinds of chèvre.

The house where Louis Pasteur was born still contains the evidence of his father's trade as a tanner, with old tools and the tannery in the basement. In the living quarters, documents and souvenirs relating to Pasteur are displayed in several rooms. Portraits and personal mementoes recall his family and childhood; note the Légion d'Honneur awarded to the scientist's father by Napoleon I. Among Pasteur's possessions on view are his university cape and cap, his desk and two pastels executed in his youth.

The **Musée Pasteur** is in another tanner's workshop next door and illustrates the enormous significance of the great scientist's work.

Musée des Beaux-Arts★

Open daily except Mon 10am-noon and 2-6pm. ☎03 84 79 25 85.

The Museum of Fine Art's collections include Gallo-Roman finds, Burgundian sculpture and mainly French paintings from the 15C to the 20C: Simon Vouet *(Death of Dido)*, Mignard *(Portrait of a Woman and Her Son)* and several landscapes by Courbet.

CHÂTEAU DE **FILAIN**★

POPULATION 207
MICHELIN MAP 317: F-7

Filain is one of the finest châteaux in the Franche-Comté region, with a magnificent monumental fireplace.

- **Information**: ☎03 84 78 30 66. www.filain.com.
- **Don't Miss**: The château's magnificent landscaped park and the sweet smell of the rose garden, all set in undulating countryside.

Visit

🕑*Open Easter to mid-Nov weekends only.*
Guided tour (45min) 10am-noon, 2pm-6pm. 6€.

In the 15C a stronghold flanked by four towers stood on this spur. The right wing of the château dates from this period; the windows were enlarged and mullions were added in the 16C. The central, Renaissance building was linked in the 16C to the earlier buildings. There are large mullioned windows between the two orders of superposed columns (the Roman Doric style can be seen on the ground floor, and the Ionic style on the first floor). The once open gallery on the ground floor was converted to its present state at the beginning of the 19C.

From the garden the 16C south-facing façade is seen at its best, framed by two square towers each topped by a more recent, typically Comtois roof in the Imperial style. Under the First Empire, the old drawbridge was replaced by a staircase with balustrades.

The building is entered through a beautifully sculpted Renaissance doorway, which was carved out of one of the old stronghold corner towers in the 15C.

The tour begins on the ground floor, in the kitchen where a beautiful collection of waffle irons and host moulds are displayed; then come two rooms containing an ornithological collection. On the first floor, the **Salle des Gardes** (guard-room) is embellished by a particularly ornate **Renaissance fireplace**★: the top of the composition features the château's two façades and a superb stag can be seen leaping out of the centre part. The tour now goes through the Grande Galerie and the parlours, before going down to the old kitchens, which have been converted into a library, and the barrel-vaulted passageway which was once the main entrance of the château.

FLAVIGNY-SUR-OZERAIN★

POPULATION 411
MICHELIN MAP 320: H-4

Flavigny's narrow streets flanked by old mansions, its fortified gateways and the remains of its medieval ramparts and abbey recall its past grandeur. Its setting, too, is picturesque: a rocky perch surrounded by streams.

- **Information**: pl. Bingenbrück, 21150 Venarey-les-Laumes. ☎03 80 96 89 13. www.alesia-tourisme.net.
- **Don't Miss**: Flavigny's famous aniseed sweets. This local confection, aniseed coated in snow-white sugar, has been made in the old abbey since the 9C. The pretty tins and boxes they come in are as attractive as the tiny sweets inside.

Sights

Old houses★

Many houses have been restored; they date from the late Middle Ages and the Renaissance and are decorated with turrets, spiral stairs or delicate sculptures. Note, in particular, the Maison du Donataire (15C-16C) in rue de l'Église.

Ancienne abbaye

Guided tours (10min) by appointment daily except Sat-Sun 8.30-11am. Closed in Aug, 25 Dec-1 Jan and public holidays. ☎03 80 96 20 88.

The Benedictine abbey, founded in the 8C, once consisted of a great church, the basilica of St-Pierre and the usual conventual buildings. The latter were rebuilt in the 18C and now house the aniseed sweet factory. There are interesting remains from the Carolingian period of St-Pierre.

Crypte Ste-Reine

Open Mon-Fri 8.30-11.30am, 2-5pm. 1€. ☎03 80 96 20 88.

The upper level of the double-decker Carolingian apse, reached by steps from the nave, contains the high altar. The lower chamber, built c 758, contains the tomb of St Reina (see ALISE-STE-REINE). Following her martyrdom, her remains were buried here around 866. The finely carved pillar is a good example of Carolingian decorative work.

Chapelle Notre-Dame-des-Piliers

In 1960 excavations revealed the existence of a hexagonal chapel with ambulatory beyond the crypt. The style recalls the pre-Romanesque rotundas of St-Bénigne in Dijon and Saulieu.

Église St-Genest

Open May-Oct daily except Fri 1.30-5.15pm, (Sun 6.15pm). ☎03 80 96 22 77.

This 13C church, built on the site of an even earlier religious building, was altered in the 15C and 16C. It has a stone central gallery dating from the beginning of the 16C. Other galleries run along the top of the aisles and the first two bays of the nave, something that is very rare in Gothic architecture. They are enclosed by 15C wooden screens. The stalls are early 16C.

Among the many interesting statues, note the **Angel of the Annunciation**, a masterpiece of the Burgundian School, in the last chapel on the right in the nave, and a 12C Virgin nursing the Infant Jesus, in the south transept.

Tour of the ramparts

Starting from the 15C gateway, Porte du Bourg, with its impressive machicolations, take chemin des Fossés and chemin des Perrières to reach the Porte du Val flanked by two round towers. Nearby is the Maison Lacordaire, a former Dominican monastery founded by **Father Lacordaire** (1806-61).

Excursion

Château de Frôlois

17km/10.2mi NW. Jul-Aug. Guided tours (30min) 2.30-6.30pm. 4.50€. ☎03 80 96 22 92. .

The Frolois family established its residence on this site in the 10C; the medieval fortress was often remodelled, leaving only the main building (14C-15C).

On the first floor, the family heir, Antoine de Vergy, has a room with a French-style ceiling decorated with the family coat of arms and initials. The ground floor was remodelled in the 17C and 18C, and is hung with attractive late-17C Bergamo tapestries.

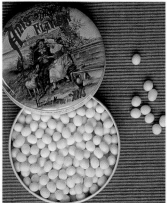

Anis de Flavigny

S. Sauvignier-MICHELIN

ABBAYE DE **FONTENAY**★★★

MICHELIN MAP 320: G-4

The abbey of Fontenay, nestling in a lonely but verdant valley, is a superb example of what a 12C Cistercian monastery was like, self-sufficient within its walls.

Information: ☎03 80 92 15 00. www.abbayedefontenay.com.

Don't Miss: The abbey makes a magical setting for summer concerts.

A Bit of History

A Second Daughter

After he became Abbot of Clairvaux, Bernard founded three religious settlements one after the other: Trois-Fontaines near St-Dizier in 1115, Fontenay in 1118 and Foigny in Thiérache in 1121. Accompanied by 12 monks, he arrived near Châtillon-sur-Seine at the end of 1118 and founded a hermitage there. After he returned to Clairvaux, Bernard found that the monks he had left under the direction of Godefroy de la Roche had attracted so many others that the hermitage had become much too small. The monks moved into the valley and established themselves where the abbey stands today.

Up to the 16C the abbey was prosperous with more than 300 monks and converts, but the regime of Commendam – abbots nominated by royal favour and interested only in revenues – and religious wars brought about a rapid decline. The abbey was sold during the French Revolution and became a paper mill.

In 1906 new owners undertook to restore Fontenay to its original appearance. They tore down the parts which had been

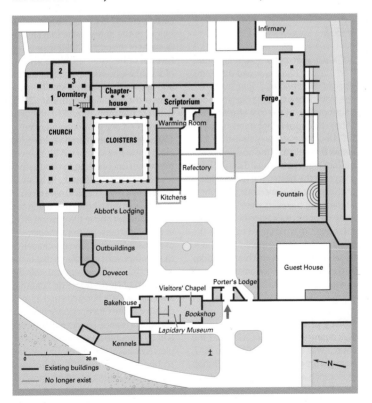

D. Delacroix-MICHELIN

Cloisters

added for the paper mill and rebuilt the abbey just as it was in the 12C. The many fountains from which the abbey takes its name are today the most beautiful ornaments of the gardens surrounding the buildings; these were added in 1981 to UNESCO's World Heritage List.

Visit

♿🕒 *Open year round.* ☞☞ *Guided tours (1hr) Apr-Oct 10am-6pm (Jul-Aug 7pm), Nov-Mar 10am-noon, 2-5pm.* ⚁ *8.50€.*
The main doorway of the porter's lodge is surmounted by the coat of arms of the abbey; the upper floor dates from the 15C. Under the archway, note the niche below the staircase: the opening at the bottom allowed the guard dog to keep an eye on the hostel, the long building on the right of the inner courtyard, where pilgrims and travellers were lodged.
After the porch, walk along beside a large 13C building, which used to house the visitors' chapel and the monks' bakehouse, remarkable for its round chimney. Today this houses the reception area and a small lapidary museum. Further on to the right is a magnificent circular dovecote.

Abbey Church

Built during the lifetime of St Bernard, the church was erected from 1139 to 1147, owing to the generosity of Ebrard, Bishop of Norwich, who took refuge at Fontenay. The church was consecrated by Pope Eugenius III in 1147. It is one of the most ancient Cistercian churches preserved in France.
The façade, stripped of all ornament, is marked by two buttresses and seven round-headed windows, symbolising the seven Sacraments of the church. The porch has disappeared but the original corbels are still in place. The leaves and hinges of the doorway are exact reproductions of the original folding doors.
Interior – The Cistercian rules and plans of design have been scrupulously observed and despite the relatively small dimensions of the building (length: 66m/217ft, width of transept: 30m/98ft), the general effect is one of striking grandeur.
The nave, of broken-barrel vaulting, has eight bays; it is supported by aisles of transverse barrel vaulting, forming a series of communicating chapels, lit by small semicircular bays. The blind nave receives its light from openings in the façade and from those set above the chancel arch.
In the huge transept, the arrangement of the barrel vaulting and the chapels in the transept arms is similar to that in the aisles. In the north transept arm, note the statue (1) of Notre-Dame de Fontenay (end of the 13C); her smile and ease of pose recall the Champagne School.
The square chancel (2) with its flat chevet, is lit by a double row of windows in triplets (symbol of the Trinity). Tombstones and the remains of the 13C paving of small squares of glazed stone, which once covered the floor of the choir and a great

part of the church, have been assembled here. On the right, there is the tomb (3) of the nobleman Mello d'Époisses and his wife (14C). The stone retable of the former Gothic high altar (13C) is damaged.

The night stair to the monks' dormitory is in the south transept.

Dormitory

The monks slept on straw mattresses on the floor and each compartment was screened by a low partition. The superb oak timberwork **roof**★ is late 15C.

Cloisters

The cloisters, on the south side of the church, are a superb example of Cistercian architecture, both elegant and robust. Each gallery has eight bays marked by fine buttresses; the semicircular archways, except for those of the doorways giving on to the garth, are divided by double arches resting on coupled columns.

The **chapter-house**, with quadripartite vaulting and water-leaf capitals, communicates with the eastern cloister by way of a splendid doorway. The monks' workroom or scriptorium is situated at the end of the east range. From the latter a doorway leads to the warming room. The two fireplaces were the only ones allowed in the abbey apart from those in the kitchen.

The prison is open to view; so too is the forge which was built beside the river to provide water power for the hammers and bellows.

The monks cultivated medicinal plants in the gardens next to the infirmary, which is set apart from the other buildings.

The new gardens laid out by an English landscape gardener were designed to moderate the austere appearance of the buildings and to ease the flow of visitors around the abbey.

FOUGEROLLES

POPULATION 3 967

MICHELIN MAP 314: G-5

The little town of Fougerolles, in the valley of the Combeauté, was ruled successively by the dukes of Lorraine and of Burgundy, until becoming French in 1704. It is best known for the kirsch made here from the local cherries.

- **Information**: 1 r. de la Gare, 70220 Fougerolles. ☎03 84 49 12 91. www.otsi-fougerolles.net.
- ▶ **Orient yourself**: Fougerolles is at the edge of the Ballon des Vosges regional park with its welath of natural beauties (*see Massif du BALLON D'ALSACE*).

Sight

Écomusée du Pays de la Cerise★

2km/1mi N on C 201. ⏱*Open Apr-Oct daily. Guided tours (1hr 30min) Jul-Aug 10am-7pm, Sun 2-7pm. Rest of the year daily except Tue 2-6pm.* ⊚*5€.* ☎*03 84 49 52 50.*

Kids This interesting museum, in the hamlet of Petit-Fahys on the premises of one of the region's first industrial distilleries (1831), aims to show visitors an authentic kirsch distillery as it would have been in the 19C and early 20C. It includes the distiller's house with all its furniture, the servants' quarters, the maturing loft, the

warehouse and the two large workshops with their rows of huge shining stills worked by boilers or steam. Local agri-

Stills

Y. Perton-Écomusée du Pays

cultural activity, and various crafts associated with the distillery (cooperage,
basket-making, textiles) are represented
by displays of tools and other equipment and reconstructions of workshops.
Next to the buildings is a conservatory
where various local varieties of cherry
are cultivated.

Excursion

Ermitage St-Valbert

5km/3mi S. ☎*03 84 49 54 97.* A hermitage
developed in the 17C near the cave
where St Valbert lived as a hermit in the
7C. Note the statue of the saint carved
in the rock.

GOUMOIS

POPULATION 196
MICHELIN MAP 321: L-3

Downstream of its spectacular waterfall, the River Doubs cuts its way through
a deep and narrow gorge before reaching Goumois on the Franco-Swiss border,
a pleasant resort much liked by anglers and canoeists.

- **Information**: Mairie, 25470 Goumois. ☎03 81 44 28 24. www.goumois.com.
- **Orient Yourself**: The municipality was divided into two by the Vienna Treaty
  in 1815, so part is in France and the other in Switzerland.

Driving Tour

- *Drive out of Goumois along D 437B
  towards Montbéliard. In Trévillers,
  turn right onto D 201 and continue to
  the intersection with D 134 leading to
  Courtefontaine and Soulce, then turn
  onto D 437C to St-Hippolyte.*

St-Hippolyte

This little town is surrounded by pretty
countryside★, where the Dessoubre
flows into the Doubs.

- *Leave St-Hippolyte on D 437
  towards Maîche.*

Les Bréseux

The parish church of this modest village
boasts a remarkable set of seven stained-
glass windows made in 1948 by the famous
glassblower Alfred Manessier.

Maîche

Situated between the Dessoubre and
Doubs valleys, Maîche occupies a pleasant site overlooked by the Mont Miroir
(alt 986m/3 235ft). The maîchards or
Comtois horse, a famous breed of draught
horses, originate from Maîche. Every
summer the village stages a competition
to ensure the survival of the breed. A
lively carnival takes place in March.

View over the Doubs from the Corniche de Goumois

Address Book

🪙 *For coin ranges, see the Legend on the cover flap.*

WHERE TO STAY AND EAT

🍴**Au Bois de la Biche** – *Aux Belvédères de la Cendrée ,25140 Charquemont.* ☏*03 81 44 01 82. www.boisdelabiche.com. Closed 2 Jan-2 Feb, Tue Oct-Mar and Mon.* This peaceful establishment serves regional cooking and offers a few sober but pleasant rooms. Choose a table by the picture window to enjoy the view of the Swiss Alps.

🍴**Moulin du Plain** – *5km/3.1mi N of Goumois by a minor road.* ☏*03 81 44 41 99. www.moulin-du-plain.com. Closed 3 Nov-21 Feb. 22 rooms.* ⎚*6.60€. Restaurant*🍴🍴*.* At the edge of the Doubs, this family inn in the heart of a forest is a favourite haunt of anglers. The simple, well-kept rooms all give onto the river. Regional specialities.

🍴🍴**Taillard** – *3 rte de la Corniche.* ☏*03 81 44 20 75. www.hoteltaillard.com. Open Mar-Nov. 18 rooms.* ⎚*12€. Restaurant*🍴🍴*.* This hostelry overlooking the village and the Doubs Valley has been in the same family since 1874. The guestrooms in the annexe are the best. The garden, pool and fitness room will ensure that your stay here is a healthy one. Carefully prepared meals.

Note the 18C church and the castle of Charles de Montalembert (1810-70).

▸ *Drive S along D 464 to Charquemont and beyond as far as the Swiss border.*

Les Échelles de la Mort★★ (The Ladders of Death)

Straight after the La Cheminée customs (*tell the official you are not going to Switzerland*) take the road on the left to the Le Refrain hydroelectric plant. This leads downhill to the bottom of the gorge, where there is an impressive **landscape**★ of tall cliffs crowned by firs and spruces. ⚠*Leave the car left of the plant gates and take the signposted path on the left (45min there and back on foot) to the foot of the Échelles de la Mort (steep climb through undergrowth).*

To reach the **viewpoint** requires climbing three steel ladders fixed into a rocky wall, which have solid reinforced steps and are equipped with hand rails. The climb leads up to a viewpoint about 100m/330ft high, overlooking the Doubs gorges.

▸ *Return to Charquemont and take D 10E to La Cendrée (car park).*

Belvédères de la Cendrée

⚠Two paths 200m/220yd further on lead to the viewpoints, from which there are beautiful views of the Doubs gorge and Switzerland. The first path (*30min there and back on foot*) comes to a rocky spur which rises sheer 450m/1 476ft above the Doubs Valley. The viewpoint at the end of the second path (*45min there and back on foot; marked with arrows*) is at the top of the La Cendrée rocks.

▸ *Back in Charquemont, take D 201 to the right; drive to Damprichard and turn right onto D 437A which leads to the Col de la Vierge (altitude of pass: 964m/3 163ft) and the beginning of the famous Corniche de Goumois overlooking the River Doubs.*

Corniche de Goumois★★

This very picturesque road runs along the steep west side of the Doubs Valley, where the river marks the border between France and Switzerland. For 3km/2mi the drive overlooks the depths of the gorge from a height of about 100m/ 330ft (*best viewpoints have protective railings*). The steep slopes are wooded or rocky, or carpeted with meadows. The landscape exudes a calm grandeur rather than wild ruggedness. The Swiss Franches Montagnes range can be seen on the other bank of the Doubs (*linked to this itinerary by the Goumois bridge and 107 road*).

GRAND COLOMBIER★★★

MICHELIN MAP 328: H-5
LOCAL MAP SEE BELLEGARDE-SUR-VALSERINE

This is the highest peak (1 531km/5 023ft) in the Bugey region, at the tip of the long mountain chain separating the Rhône from the Valromey. The arduous climb offers exceptional panoramic views.

- **Information**: 6 r. de la Mairie, 01350 Culoz. ☎04 79 87 00 30.
- ▶ **Orient Yourself:** The road climbs from Virieu to a parking area, from which the mountain is accessible on foot. From there you can drive along a ridge up to another viewpoint. After that, there is a steep descent into Culoz.
- ⊙ **Don't Miss:** The panoramas from the summit and from the Observatoir du Fenestrez are well worth the arduous climbs.

Driving Tour

29km/18mi from Virieu-le-Petit to Culoz – allow 2hr.

After leaving Virieu, the road climbs the slopes of the Grand Colombier along a series of hairpin bends. Once it reaches the forest, the road passes through stands of fir trees. The gradient becomes 12% (1:8), then 14% (1:7) and finally even 19% (1:5). After passing the Lochieu road on the left, it comes to beautiful mountain pastures at La Grange de Fromentel, from which there is a good view of the Champagne-en-Valromey Valley. Climbing about 1km/0.5mi further up through the forest, the road branches off to the left towards the Colombier

service station and hotel; the last bend up the mountain leads to the pass.

Grand Colombier★★★

From the car park, there are easy footpaths up to both Grand Colombier peaks. On the rounded northern peak there is a cross and a viewing table *(30min round trip on foot)*; the south peak ends in a steep crest on the west face of the mountain *(45min round trip on foot)*.
There are vast panoramas of the Jura, the Dombes, the Rhône Valley, the Massif Central and the Alps; in fine weather three lakes can be seen twinkling in the sun – Geneva, Bourget and Annecy.
On the east face of the mountain the road runs through mountain pastures before entering the forest.

▶ *From the hairpin bend 5km/3mi from the Fenestrez summit, take the right turn.*

Observatoire du Fenestrez★★

A footpath leads to the edge of the cliff *(benches and hang-gliding take-off strip; no parapet)* from where, at a height of about 900m/2 950ft, there is a view of the Culoz plain. The lakes of Bourget and Chambéry can be seen to the south-east and that of Annecy to the east. Beyond this, the view stretches as far as the Alps, from La Meije to the Matterhorn.

▶ *Return to the main road and turn right (15% – 1:7 gradient downhill). After 4km/2mi keep right towards*

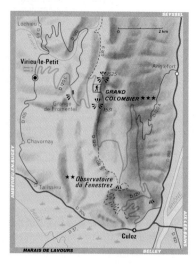

Culoz when the road forks left to Anglefort.

There are impressive views of the Bugey region, the Rhône Valley and the Culoz plain on the way downhill *(13 hairpin bends),* particularly when the road runs along the ridge of the crest.

Excursions

Réserve naturelle du marais de Lavours

From Culoz drive W on D 904 then turn left onto D 37 to Ceyzerieu and left again on a minor road to Aignoz.

Kids A 2.4km/1.5mi-long trail raised on piles enables visitors to penetrate deep into the marsh. The **Maison de la Réserve** (◔*open Apr-Sep daily; rest of the year weekends only;* ◔*closed Dec-Jan.* ☜ *5€, children 3.50€;* ☎*04 79 87 90 39)* offers an interactive study of this ecosystem.

UNDER THE OLD LINDEN TREE

☞ **Au Vieux Tilleul** – *01260 Belmont-Luthézieu – 10.5km/6.5mi W of Virieu-le-Petit by D 69F then D 54C –* ☎ *04 79 87 64 51 –* ◔ *closed Tue lunch and Mon Oct-Apr –* 🅿 *– 16 rooms –* ☐ *6€ – restaurant* ☞☞*. The beautiful interior decoration echoed by yellow and blue fabrics, the comfortable, well-kept rooms and the kind hospitality will ensure that your stay here is a most pleasant one. Pretty vistas of the forest and the Grand Colombier. The meals too are an uplifting experience.*

Seyssel

Once a major port on the River Rhône, Seyssel is now better known for its excellent white wines. The **Barrage de Seyssel** *(1.5km/0.9mi upstream)* was built to regulate the Rhône downstream of Génissiat. The reservoir lies beneath the spur on which stands **Bassy Church**.

GRAY

POPULATION 6 773
MICHELIN MAP 314: B-8

This handsome town rises up like an amphitheatre from the banks of the Saône. While it played a major role in commercial river navigation in the 19C, Gray has now found favour with recreational boaters.

🄸 **Information**: Île Sauzay, 70100 Gray. ☎03 84 65 14 24. www.ville-gray.fr.
▶ **Orient Yourself**: There is a pretty view of the town from the 18C stone bridge.

Sights

Hôtel de ville★

The town hall is an elegant building, with arcades in the Renaissance style (1568), embellished by pink marble columns and a beautiful varnished-tile roof.

Musée Baron-Martin★

◔*Open May-Sep daily except Tue 10am-noon, 2-6pm. Rest of the year daily except Tue 2-5pm.* ◔*Closed 1 Jan, 1 May, 1 Nov, 25 Dec.* ☜*3.60€.* ☎*03 84 65 69 10.*

This art museum is in the 18C château of the Count of Provence, brother of Louis XVI. The first galleries contain works by Primitive artists from various western schools: the Italian (16C-18C), Flemish (17C), Dutch (17C) – including some engravings by Rembrandt – and French (16C-19C). The first floor is devoted to contemporary art and to late-19C and early-20C works – extensive sets of prints by Albert Besnard and Aman Jean, Fantin-Latour's lithographic stones, and paintings by Tissot and Steinlen.

The 13C vaulted cellars (survivors of an earlier fortress) house, among other things, a collection of coins, fragments of Gallo-Roman earthenware found locally and a display case of Hellenic vases.

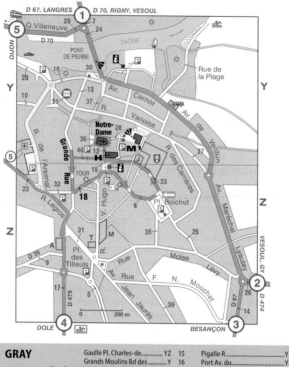

GRAY

Boichut Pl.	Y	3	Gaulle Pl. Charles-de	YZ	15	Pigalle R.	Y	28
Capucins Av.	Z	5	Grands Moulins Bd des	Y	16	Port Av. du	Y	29
Casernes R. des	Z	6	Libération Av. de la	Z	17	Quatre-Septembre Pl. du	Y	30
Couyba Av. Ch.	Y	7	Marché R. du	Z	18	Revon Av.	Z	31
Curie R. P.	Y	9	Mavia Quai	Y	20	Rossen R.	Z	32
Devosge R. F.	Y	10	Mavia R.	Y	21	Signard R. M.	Z	34
Église R. de l'	Y	12	Neuf Chemin	Z	22	Soupirs R. des	Z	35
Gambetta R.	X	13	Paris R. de	Y	24	Sous-Préfeture Pl. de la	Y	36
Gaulle Av. Général-de	Z	14	Perrières Fg des	Z	26	Terreaux R. des	Y	40
			Perrières R. des	Z	25	Thiers R.	Y	37
			Perrières R. du Fg des	Y	27	Vieille-Tuilerie R. de la	Z	39

Hôtel de ville	Y	H	Musée Baron-Martin	Y	M¹

CASCADES DU **HÉRISSON**★★★
MICHELIN MAP 321: F-7
LOCAL MAPS BELOW OR SEE RÉGION DES LACS DU JURA

The Hérisson is a magnificent spectacle during rainy periods, with water tumbling down in a mighty torrent or in a lengthy series of cascades. Although the falls are not quite so interesting after dry spells, the riverbed, especially between the Gour Bleu and the Grand Saut, features some fascinating evidence of erosion: natural stone steps, giants' cauldrons and multi-storeyed systems of caves.

- **Information**: 36 Grande-Rue, 39130 Clairvaux-les-Lacs. ☎03 84 25 27 47. www.juralacs.com.
- **Orient Yourself:** There are several possible departure points, but the most logical is Doucier. Most of this itinerary involves hiking through gorges (wear sturdy shoes). For those who don't wish to hike, the D 39 linking Doucier to Ilay crosses a vast forest; one lookout point along here offers views of the waterfall.
- **Don't Miss:** The view over the falls from the Sentier des Cascades.
- **Organising Your Time:** The hike will take a good three hours there and back.

A Bit of Geology

From the beginning
The source of the Hérisson is at an altitude of 805m/2 641ft, in the lake of Bonlieu to the south of the waterfalls. The upper course of the river takes it for barely 2km/0.5mi, before it drops down to the Doucier plateau (alt 520m/1 706ft). The Hérisson covers the 280m/920ft difference in altitude in only 3km/2mi, by cutting through narrow gorges, forming spectacular waterfalls.
The river owes its picturesque stepped course to the differing textures of the horizontal limestone strata through which it wears its way. Each shelf is formed by strata of more resistant rock. Bear in mind that the flow of small rivers in the Jura, a terrain of mostly porous limestone, is very dependent on the weather.

Hike

- *From Doucier drive 8km/5mi SE along D 326; leave the car at the end of the road.*

Lac de Chambly and Lac du Val
The D 326 road climbs the Hérisson Valley downstream of the waterfalls, giving the occasional glimpse of these two lovely lakes through the trees. The valley floor is flat and green, the slopes steep and wooded. Once it has passed through the lakes of Chambly and Le Val, the river flows into the Ain.

- *Continue on D 326 as far as the Jacquand mill (moulin) and leave the car there (fee charged).*

Cascade de l'Éventail★★★
Allow 2hr 30min there and back on foot.
After about 400m/440yd the path (*Sentier des Cascades*) brings you to the foot of this waterfall, where you will get the best view. The water tumbles a total of 65m/213ft in leaps and bounds, forming a vast pyramid of foaming water.

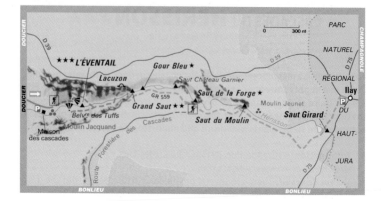

The path then leads very steeply uphill to the top of the Éventail waterfall. Take the Sarrazine footbridge across the Hérisson, and then follow the path on the right to the Belvédère des Tuffs, from where there is a beautiful view of the Hérisson gorge and the Éventail waterfall.

▶ *Return to the footbridge and continue upstream along the river course to the Lacuzon footbridge about 300m/330yd further on.*

Grotte Lacuzon
30min there and back on foot from the footbridge.
Cross the Hérisson and follow the very steep path up to this cave.

▶ *Continue upstream along the south bank, to the Grand Saut.*

Cascade de l'Éventail

Cascade du Grand Saut★★
The best view of the Grand Saut is from the foot of the waterfall. The water falls from a height of 60m/200ft in a single cascade.

▶ *The footpath, now cut into the rock face, is very steep and quite narrow (but with handrails) in places as it leads to the Gour Bleu waterfall.*

Gour Bleu★
At the foot of the little waterfall known as the Gour Bleu lies a beautiful shallow basin *(gour)* in which the water is a clear blue colour.

▶ *The path carries on to the Saut Château Garnier and the Saut de la Forge waterfalls.*

Saut de la Forge★
The river, flinging itself from the top of a curving, rocky overhang, makes a very pretty spectacle.

Saut du Moulin and Saut Girard
1hr 30min there and back on foot from Saut de la Forge.
From the path, which runs through woods at some points and meadows at others, the Saut du Moulin can be seen, near the ruins of the Jeunet mill, and, further on, the Saut Girard, falling from about 20m/66ft.

▶ *The path crosses the Hérisson at the foot of Saut Girard and leads back to* the Ilay crossroads, near the Auberge du Hérisson.

Excursion

Ferme de l'Aurochs
Le Val Dessous near the Cascades du Hérisson. ⏱Open Jun to mid-Sep 10am-7pm; Apr-May Sat-Sun and public holidays 10am-7pm. ∞5€. ☎03 84 25 72 95. www.ferme-auroch.com.

Kids A 2km/1.2mi trail along the Hérisson Valley offers the possibility of encountering some of the ancestors of domestic cattle such as aurochs, bisons and other breeds of wild ox.

JOIGNY

POPULATION 10 032

MICHELIN MAP 319: D-4

Joigny (whose townsfolk are known as Joviniens) is a busy, picturesque little town at the gateway to Burgundy on the borders of the forest of Othe. It is built in terraces on the side of a hill, the Côte St-Jacques, overlooking the River Yonne.

- **Information**: quai H.-Ragobert, 89300. ☎03 86 62 11 05. www.tourisme-joigny.fr.
- ▶ **Orient Yourself**: From the Yonne bridge, which has six 18C arches, there is a pretty view of the river, the quays, the shady promenades and the town.

A Bit of History

The Revolt of the Maillotins
In 1438 the people of Joigny rebelled against the lord of the manor, Count Guy de la Trémoille. They attacked his castle and killed the Count with blows from their mauls or mallets, tools used by wine-growers of those days. Since then the Joviniens have been known as Maillotins (Maul-bearers) and the maul figures in the town's coat of arms.

Sights

St-Thibault
This church, built in both the Gothic and Renaissance styles between 1490 and 1529, is dominated by a 17C square tower crowned by a delicate belfry. Above the door is an equestrian statue of St Theobald (1530) by the sculptor who settled in Spain and took the name Juan de Juni (Jean de Joigny). Inside the church, the chancel slants to the left; this asymmetry is emphasised by the chancel vaulting.

St-Jean
A belfry porch precedes the west front of this church which lacks transepts but has a pentagonal chevet. The Renaissance-style coffered ceiling has carved medallions framed by decorated ribs. In the south aisle is the 13C recumbent figure of the Comtesse de Joigny. The tomb is lavishly sculptured and includes the figures of the countess' children. The Louis XV woodwork and the furnishings of the sacristy came from Vézelay.

Old houses
A stroll through the narrow streets around St-Thibault and St-Jean will reveal several half-timbered houses dating from the 15C and 16C. Most were badly damaged, either during the bombardments of 1940 or a gas explosion in 1981, but have been restored. The best-known is the one on the corner, called the Arbre de Jessé (Tree of Jesse).

Excursions

View from the Côte St-Jacques★
1.5km/1mi N.
The road climbs in hairpin bends round the Côte St-Jacques. From a right-hand bend there is a semicircular **panorama**★ over the town and valley of the Yonne.

Address Book

For coin ranges, see the Legend on the cover flap.

WHERE TO STAY AND EAT

L'Orée des champs – *10 rte. de Chambéry, 89400 Épineau-les-Voves. ☎03 86 91 20 39. Closed 23 Aug-5 Sep, Feb holidays, Thu evening out of season, Mon evenings, Tue evenings and Wed*. The small veranda at the entrance is preceded by a pretty flowered terrace, which is very popular in summer. Traditional French cuisine in the sober dining room.

Hôtel La Côte St-Jacques – *14 fg de Paris. ☎03 86 62 09 70. www.cotesaintjacques.com. Closed 3 Jan-3 Feb. 27 rooms. 30€. Restaurant*. Treat yourself to a wonderful stay at this sumptuous hotel. The spacious rooms and suites giving onto the garden and the River Yonne are a haven of tranquillity. Refined cuisine in the stylish dining room. Covered pool.

Musée Rural des Arts Populaires de Laduz★

15km/10mi S on D 955; take the first left after motorway bridge. Open Jul-Aug daily 2.30-6pm; Easter-Jun and Sep weekends only 2.30-5.30pm; Nov-Mar: Wed 2-5pm. 6€ (under 14 3€). ☎03 86 73 70 08. www.art-populaire-laduz.com. This folk museum recalls rural working life before 1914; the tools and products of about 50 craftsmen are on display together with a large collection of old toys and many of the carved figures which were popular in the past.

La Ferté-Loupière

8km/11mi SW.

This old fortified market town is home to a 12C and 15C **church** with remarkable 15C-16C **mural paintings**★★ depicting the parable of the three living and three dead men and a Dance of Death. The latter represents 42 figures from all walks of life and is thus an interesting historical document as well as a moral lesson. Note also on the larger pillars the archangel St Michael Slaying the Dragon and an Annunciation.

CHÂTEAU DE **JOUX**★
4KM/2.5MI S OF PONTARLIER

MICHELIN MAP 321: I-5

This château reigns over the extreme end of the Pontarlier cluse, used since the Roman Empire as a route linking northern Italy with Flanders and Champagne.

Information: ☎03 81 69 47 95. www.chateaudejoux.com.

Don't Miss: A renowned theatre festival, Les Nuits de Joux, takes place in the castle in summer.

A Bit of History

The château was built by the lords of Joux in the 11C and enlarged under Emperor Charles V. Vauban fortified it, in view of its vulnerable position near the border, after France annexed the Franche-Comté in 1678. The last modernisations were carried out between 1879 and 1881, by the future field marshal, Joffre. The stronghold has seen many prisoners. Mirabeau was locked inside after his father obtained an order for his arrest from the king, hoping it would cool down his hot-headed son and protect him from his many creditors. In 1802, two insurgents against the Revolution escaped by sawing bars and climbing down curtains. By the time **Toussaint Louverture**, hero of Haitian independence, arrived a few months later, security had been reinforced; the freedom fighter died there on 7 April 1803.

Visit

☉Open daily Apr-15 Nov. ⟶Guided tour (1hr15min) Jul-Aug 9am-6pm. Rest of the year 10-11.30am, 2-4.30pm. ⊙5.80€.

The tour of the five successive curtain walls covering 2ha/5 acres, each separated by deep moats crossed by three drawbridges, unfolds 10 centuries of fortification. There is a beautiful view of the Doubs Valley and the Pontarlier cluse from the terrace of the gun tower.

A **Musée d'Armes Anciennes**★, comprising 650 antique weapons, is in five rooms of the old keep. The collection ranges from the first regulation flint-lock rifle (1717 model) to repeating firearms from the Third Republic (1878). There is also an exhibition of military headgear – including a beautiful collection of shakos – and uniforms.

It is possible to visit the cells of Mirabeau, with a beautiful dowelled timber roof frame; that of Toussaint Louverture; and the tiny dark cell of the legendary Berthe de Joux. A 35m/115ft-deep vertical gallery *(212 steps)* leads down to the underground section and the great well shaft, 3.70m/12ft in diameter and 120m/394ft deep.

♿*For coin ranges, see the Legend on the cover flap.*

MOUNTAIN RETREAT

⊖**Auberge Le Tillau** – *Le Mont-des-Verrières, 25300 Les Verrières-de-Joux, 7km/4.3mi E of La Cluse-et-Mijoux by D 67bis and a minor road.* ☎03 81 69 46 72. www.letillau.com. 12 rooms. ⊏7€. Restaurant⊖⊖. City dwellers will love the mountain air at this delightful inn perched at an altitude of 1 200m/ 3 937ft amid pastures and pine trees. The rooms are comfortable and suitable for a short stopover as well as for a longer stay. The traditional cuisine is good and made with fresh seasonal produce.

Excursion

Cluse de Joux★★

This is one of the most beautiful examples of a Jura cluse. The transverse valley through the Larmont mountain cuts a passage just wide enough for the road and the railway line running from Pontarlier to Neuchâtel and Berne. Two strongholds command the cliffs: that of Le Larmont Inférieur to the north and the Château de Joux to the south.

Le Frambourg

Excellent **view**★★ over the Cluse de Joux from the platform of the monument to the fallen of the First World War.

B. Kaufmann-MICHELIN

Château de Joux

RÉGION DES **LACS DU JURA**★★

MICHELIN MAP 321: E-7

The Jura Lake District is the area between Champagnole, Clairvaux-les-Lacs and St-Laurent-en-Grandvaux, which boasts a string of delightful lakes – Chalain, Chambly, Le Val, Ilay, Narlay – set in peaceful, unspoilt countryside.

> **Information**: 36 Grande-Rue, 39130 Clairvaux-les-Lacs. ☎03 84 25 27 47. www.juralacs.com.
> ▶ **Orient Yourself:** The driving tour starting at Doucier passes seven lakes. Most lookout points are accessible via short footpaths, although the hike to Pic de l'Aigle is more rigorous. Small villages with historic churches dot the area.
> ☺ **Don't Miss:** The view from Pic de l'Aigle, which covers the entire Jura region.

A Bit of History

The peace shattered

In 1635, Richelieu attacked the Comté, and in the subsequent brutal campaign the lake district was overrun by Swedish troops, allies of the French. Homes were torched, crops cut down and vines and fruit trees uprooted. The resulting famine was so great that people even resorted to cannibalism. Terrible tortures were devised to force people to reveal the whereabouts of their life savings. Entire families, discovered hidden in caves or underground passages, were walled into their refuge alive to die lingering deaths. The entire province was subjected to this appalling treatment, with the result that large numbers of Comtois fled to Savoy, Switzerland or Italy. Some 10 000 to 12 000 settled in a single district in Rome, where they had a church built, dedicated to St Claude.

Driving Tour★★

Round tour of 46km/29mi – allow 2hr 30min

▶ *Leave Doucier E on D 39 towards Songeson and Menétrux-en-Joux; after Ilay turn left on N 78; leave N 78 N of Chaux-du-Dombief, taking the-Boissière road, and park the car 250m/275yd further on.*

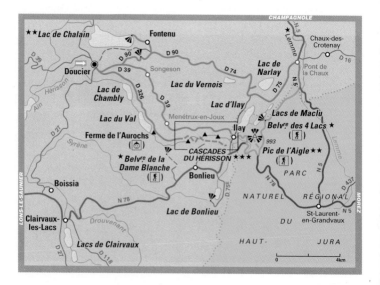

Address Book

For coin ranges, see the Legend on the cover flap.

WHERE TO STAY

Chambre d'Hôte Chez Mme Devenat – 17 r. du Vieux-Lavoir, 39130 Charezier, 13km/8.1mi SW of Lac de Chalain by D 27. ☎03 84 48 35 79. ⌸ 4 rooms. Meals. Quiet, comfortable family house in a pretty village between Clairvaux-les-Lacs and Chalain Lake. There are more rooms in the cottage near the little wood. Table d'hôte meals with new regional specialities every day.

Camping Domaine de Chalain – 39130 Doucier, 3km/1.9mi S of Lac de Chalain by D 27. ☎03 84 25 78 78. www.chalain.com. Open May-19 Sep. 804 sites. Reservation recommended. Meals available. This campsite on the lake shore is ideal for family holidays, with plenty of organised activities.

Camping La Pergola – 39130 Marigny. ☎03 84 25 70 03. www.lapergola.com. Open 10 May-21 Sep. 350 sites. Reservation recommended. Meals available. This site on the hill above the lake has heated pools and watersports facilities. Camping trailers available.

Camping Le Fayolan – 39130 Clairvaux-les-Lacs, 1.2km/0.8mi SE of Clairvaux-les-Lacs by D 118. ☎03 84 25 26 19. www.campingfayolan.com. Open 8 May-15 Sep. 516 sites. Reservations recommended. Meals available. This high quality campground has widely spaced plots by a lake with a beach. Activities for children and a fitness trail for adults.

Chambre d'Hôte Les Cinq Lacs – 66 rte des Lacs, 39130 Le Frasnois, 3.5km/2.3mi N of Ilay by D 75. ☎03 84 25 51 32. auberge.5.lacs.free.fr. ⌸ Reservations required. 5 rooms. Meals. The comfortable rooms are named afer local lakes. The half-board formula will give you a chance to enjoy the succulent regional specialities. Two self-catering gîtes. For non-smokers.

Hôtel La Chaumière du Lac – 21 r. du Sauveur, 39130 Clairvaux-les-Lacs. ☎03 84 25 81 52. Open Easter-Sep. 12 rooms. ⌸6.50€. Restaurant. The pleasing bedrooms give onto the lake or surrounding greenery. Beautiful terrace. Regional dishes.

Chambre d'Hôte M. et Mme Grillet – 12 r. de la Maison-Blanche, 39130 Bonlieu. ☎03 84 25 59 12. dominique.grillet@wanadoo.fr. ⌸ 4 rooms. A painstakingly restored old cottage with comfortable bedrooms. Breakfast is served in a dining room with beams and arched windows.

Hôtel L'Alpage – 1 chemin de la Madone, 39130 Bonlieu. ☎03 84 25 57 53. www.hotel-lesalpages.com. Closed 15 Nov-15 Dec, Sun evening and Mon except school holidays. 9 rooms. ⌸8.50€. Restaurant. The cosy rooms in this chalet have lake views. Franche-Comté specialities are served in the panoramic dining room or on the sheltered terrace. Two self-catering gîtes.

WHERE TO EAT

La Sarrazine – 39130 Doucier, 3km/1.9mi S of Lac de Chalain by D 27. ☎03 84 25 70 60. Closed early Dec to early Jan and Thu out of season. A rustic atmosphere pervades this jolly restaurant with farming scenes painted on its walls. Specialities include grilled meat and pig trotters.

La Poutre – 25 Grande-Rue, 39130 Bonlieu. ☎03 84 25 57 77. Open 4 May-31 Oct. Closed Tue. This handsome 18C building features rustic decor, with its large fireplace, Comtoise clock and Louis XIII chairs. Fine regional cuisine with regional accents.

Au chalet – rte du Lac, 39130 Bonlieu, 1.5km/0.9mi E of Bonlieu by N 78, rte. de St-Laurent-en-Grandvaux. ☎03 84 25 57 04. Closed Jan, Tue, Wed evenings out of season. Lovely chalet along the road to Bonlieu. Wooded interior. The chef makes good use of local products, and all regions of France are represented on the wine list.

Le Comtois – Le Bourg, 39130 Doucier. ☎03 84 25 71 21. restaurant.comtois@wanadoo.fr. Closed 28 Nov-11 Feb, Sun evening, Tue evening and Wed except 15 Jun-15 Sep. This restaurant has a rustic décor with exposed beams and stone fireplace. The owner is president of the local association of sommeliers.

Pic de l'Aigle★★

45min there and back on foot along a path which is indicated initially but sometimes hard to make out; it climbs steeply to the right, towards the wooded outcrop of rock called Pic de l'Aigle.

The **view** from the top of the Pic de l'Aigle (993m/3 258ft) stretches across the entire Jura region, overlooking the Ilay cluse and the Chaux-du-Dombief heights. The Jura mountain chains tower on the left, behind which the summit of Mont Blanc can be seen in fine weather; the plateaux extend to the right, as far as their rim above the Saône plain.

▸ *Leaving the road to Boissière to the right, take a narrow road uphill.*

Belvédère des Quatre-Lacs★

15min there and back on foot.

The lakes of Ilay, Narlay, the Grand Maclu and the Petit Maclu can be seen from this viewpoint.

▸ *Return to N 5 and take it to the left to Pont-de-la-Chaux, then take D 75 to Le Frasnois then D 74 to the right.*

Lac de Narlay

The lake is overlooked by wooded slopes. It has a distinctive triangular shape and, at a depth of 48m/157ft, it is the deepest lake in the area. Its waters drain into several gullies at the west end of the lake and flow underground for 10km/6mi, after which they re-emerge and feed into the Lac de Chalain.

Lac du Vernois

The lake, surrounded by woods, comes into view suddenly at a bend in the road. There is not a house in sight; the atmosphere is one of absolute peace and seclusion. The waters from this little lake spill into a gully and flow into those from the Lac de Narlay, underground.

▸ *Continue along D 74 and take D 90 towards Fontenu.*

Fontenu

The church in this village is surrounded by century-old lime trees. About 800m/880yd beyond Fontenu is the north shore of the Lac de Chalain, from which there is an excellent **view**★★.

Lac de Chalain★★

This vast stretch of water is the most impressive of all the Jura lakes. There is a path (10km/ 6.25mi) round the lake and three beaches with watersports.
In June 1904, a drop of 7m/23ft in the lake level caused by a drought revealed the remains of a 5 000-year-old village. Traces of more dwellings were found on the west and north shores. At the **Maisons néolithiques** (*guided tours Jul-Sep, days vary, ☎03 84 47 12 13)*, two Neolithic houses have been reconstructed on the shores of the lake using prehistoric techniques.

▸ *Turn back and keep right, without going down to the lakeside (one-way), taking D 90 towards Doucier.*

There is a second **view**★★ of the lake 500m/547yd after rejoining the road.

▸ *Return to Doucier on D 90 and D 39.*

Excursions

Lac de Bonlieu

4.5km/3mi SE of Bonlieu on the picturesque N 78, then D 75E to the right.

This pretty lake in the forest is overlooked by a rocky wooded ridge crisscrossed by numerous footpaths. Boat trips can be taken on the lake. A forest road runs above the east shore, leading to a viewpoint south of the lake, from where there is a beautiful view of the Pic de l'Aigle, the lakes of Ilay and Maclu, and of Mont Rivel in the distance.

Belvédère de la Dame-Blanche★

2km/1mi NW of Bonlieu, then 30min there and back on foot. Drive towards Saugeot from the N 78/D 67 crossroads, and after about 800m take the unsurfaced road to the right on leaving the forest. At the first crossroads turn left and park the car at the edge of the forest.

A rocky bank overlooks the Dessus and Dessous valleys. There is a view of the lakes of Chambly and Le Val to the left and the Pic de l'Aigle to the right.

LONS-LE-SAUNIER★

POPULATION 18 483
MICHELIN MAP 321: D-6

The capital of the Jura region, with its cultural heritage and spa facilities, is an excellent base for excursions to the vineyards or the Jura plateaux.

- **Information:** pl. du 11-Novembre, 39000 Lons-Le-Saunier. ☎ 03 84 24 65 01. www.ville-lons-le-saunier.fr.
- ▶ **Orient Yourself:** The tourist board runs fascinating themed walks through the historic centre in July and August.

A Bit of History

Rouget de Lisle

The author of the French national anthem, the *Marseillaise*, was born here in 1760. He enlisted with the army and became a captain of the Engineers, although his tastes ran more to poetry and music. He composed the war song for the Army of the Rhine, later to become known as the *Marseillaise*, in April 1792 at Strasbourg, where he was garrisoned. But the poet-musician was then imprudent enough to write a hymn dedicated to Henri IV, for which he was put into prison as a monarchist.

Town Walk

Place de la Liberté

To the east the square is closed off by the imposing Rococo façade of the theatre, with a clock which runs through two bars of the *Marseillaise* before ringing the hour. The clock tower (Tour de l'Horloge) once defended the entrance into the fortified town (the square is located on the site of the old moat).

- ▶ *If you wish, you can first walk along rue St-Désiré to the Église St-Désiré which is not in the town centre.*

Église St-Désiré

A beautiful 15C Burgundian School Entombment or Pietà is to the right of the chancel. The 11C **crypt** is one of the oldest in the Franche-Comté. The triple nave has six bays and is roofed with ribbed vaulting. The sarcophagus of St Desiderius is in one of the three apsidal chapels.

- ▶ *Return to the clock tower.*

Rue du Commerce★

The arcaded houses along this street (146 archways onto the street and under cover) make it very picturesque indeed. The houses were built in the second half of the 17C, after a terrible fire had literally cleared the space. Yet, in spite of the symmetrical balance dictated by the arcades, the people of Lons managed to

Houses along Place de la Comédie

M. Paygnard/MICHELIN

Address Book

For coin ranges, see the Legend on the cover flap.

WHERE TO STAY

Nouvel Hôtel – *50 r. Lecourbe. ☎03 84 47 20 67. www.nouvel-hotel-lons.com. Closed 17 Dec-9 Jan. 26 rooms. ⊇7.50€.* The host has a passion for warships and his hotel is decorated with beautiful miniature models of boats. The rooms on the third floor are smaller.

Parenthèse – *39570 Chille, 3km/1.9mi N of Lons-le-Saunier by D 157. ☎03 84 47 55 44. www.hotelparenthese. com. 34 rooms. ⊇11€. Restaurant.* Modern hotel close to the Jura vineyards offering comfortable rooms, many of which have a balcony overlooking wooded parkland. The restaurant provides generous cuisine with a strong regional touch.

WHERE TO EAT

Ferme-Auberge La Grange Rouge – *39570 Geruge, 9km/5.6mi SW of Lons-le-Saunier by D 117. ☎03 84 47 00 44. Closed 25 Aug-17 Sep. Reservations recommended.* In the hills south of Lons-le-Saunier, this inn is popular among locals. Phone ahead to ask about the day's menu. The cosy and quiet rooms exude warm, country-style charm.

Auberge de Chavannes – *39570 Courlans, 6km/3.7mi SW of Lons-le-Saunier by N 78. ☎03 84 47 05 52. www. auberge-de-chavannes.com. Closed Jan, 21 Jun-6 Jul, Sun evenings, Mon and Tue. Reservations required.* The meals served here are lovingly prepared and deserve their glowing reputation. On fine days, sit on the terrace to soak up the sun.

SIT BACK AND RELAX

Au Prince d'Orange – *1 r. St-Désiré. ☎03 84 24 31 39. www.pelen.fr. Open (shop) Mon-Sat 9am-12.30pm, 2-7pm, Sun 9am-12.30pm; (tearoom) 2.30-7pm.* Since 1899 the Pelen family has been making delicious pastries and sweetmeats such as *galets de Chalain* (chocolate-coated nougatine with praline). The upstairs tearoom is cosy and elegant.

Pâtisserie Rouget-de-l'Isle – *22 r. du Commerce. ☎03 84 24 51 80. Open Mon, Tu, Thu, Fri 8am-12.30pm and1.30-7pm, Sat 8am-7pm and Sun 8am-6pm (summer 8am-1pm).* This pastry shop occupies the birthplace of Rouget de Lisle. Here you'll find the famed macaroon named after him, plus 40 different kinds of chocolates. The tearoom opens onto the terrace in summer.

Brasserie de Strasbourg – *4 r. Jean-Jaurès. ☎03 84 24 36 92. Open Mon-Sat 7am-midnight.* This popular café is in a handsome late-19C building. Settle on the terrace and drink to the strains of Louis Armstrong, Billie Holiday or Miles Davis.

Grand Café du Théâtre – *2 r. Jean-Jaurès. ☎03 84 24 49 30. Open Mon-Sat 7am-1am.* This historic café has an interesting choice of menus and a nice terrace on the square.

La Maison du Vigneron – *23 r. du Commerce. ☎03 84 24 44 60. mbailly@ cguj.fr. Open Tue-Thu 10am-noon, 2-6.30pm, Fri 10am-noon, 2-7pm, Sat 9am-noon, 2-7pm.* Learn all about Jura wine at this cellar with tastings of the main regional crus. Shop with bottles for sale.

---

manifest their taste for beauty as well as the independent spirit common to all Comtois people by varying the dimensions, curve and decoration on the arches. Note the large roofs, with a dormer windows to let in the light and tall chimneys. The house in which Rouget de Lisle was born (no 24) is now a museum.

▶ *Continue to place de l'Hôtel-de-Ville.*

The Musée des Beaux-Arts and the **Hôtel-Dieu**, are both 18C.

▶ *Walk across place Perraud and along rue du Puits-Salé to the spring.*

Puits-Salé

The town developed around this saltwater spring, used as early as the Roman period.

▶ *Turn right onto rue Richebourg then right again onto place de l'Ancien-collège.*

Rue de Balerne leads to **place de la Comédie** and its wine-growers' houses.

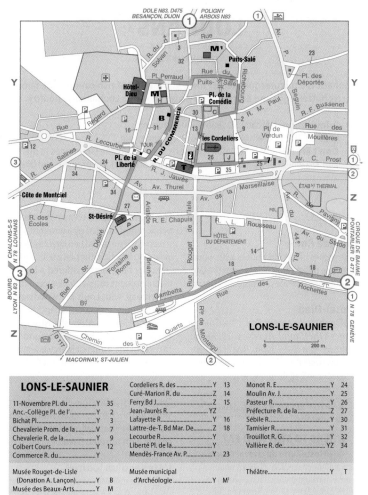

LONS-LE-SAUNIER

▷ *Follow rue du Four to rue des Cordeliers.*

Église des Cordeliers

This Franciscan church is the burial place of the Chalon-Arlays, who were Lons' feudal lords in the Middle Ages. The church was restored in the 18C. Besides the Louis XVI woodwork in the chancel, note the 1728 pulpit executed by the Lamberthoz brothers of Lons.

▷ *Continue to place du 11-Novembre.*

The square is prolonged by the **promenade de la Chevalerie**, adorned with a statue of Rouget de Lisle by Bartholdi.

Additional Sights

Theatre★

🕐*Open Jul to mid-Sep.* 👁️*Guided tours, ask at tourist office.* ☎03 84 24 65 01. Damaged by fire in 1901, the theatre, dating from 1847, had to be partially rebuilt. The architects drew their inspiration from the Opéra Garnier in Paris. The edifice was recently restored.

Musée Rouget-de-Lisle

🕐*Open 19 Jun-17 Sep.* ☎03 84 47 29 16. Rouget de Lisle's birthplace has been turned into a small museum in which mementoes, documents and a video film relate the story of the French national anthem and its composer.

LOUHANS★

POPULATION 6 327
MICHELIN MAP 320: L-10

Louhans is a picturesque market town at the heart of rich countryside famed for its butter, eggs and Bresse poultry, also known as Louhannaise poultry.

- **Information**: 1 Arcade St.-Jean, 71500 Louhans.
  ☎03 85 75 05 02. www.bresse-bourguignonne.com.
- **Don't Miss**: The Monday morning market, especially the larger ones in the 1st and 3rd weeks of the month, for a staggering array of local produce and lots of atmosphere.

Sights

Grande Rue★

The arches of the old houses with wood or stone pillars, which date from the late Middle Ages, create an impressive decor.

Hôtel-Dieu

Open daily except Tue. Guided tours (1hr15min) Apr-Nov 10.30am, 2.30pm, 4pm and 5.30pm. Rest of the year 2.30pm and 4pm. Closed 1 Jan, 1 May and 25 Dec. 4€. ☎03 85 75 54 32.

For coin ranges, see the Legend on the cover flap.

WHERE TO STAY AND EAT

Hostellerie du cheval rouge – 5 r. d'Alsace. ☎03 85 75 21 42. hotel-chevalrouge@wanadoo.fr. Closed 16-26 Jun, 22 Dec-12 Jan, Sun evening from 24 Nov-30 Mar, Tue lunchtime and Mon. Former post office building located on a shopping street in the town centre. The modern annexe offers well-lit rooms brightened by colourful fabrics. Unsurprisingly, Louhannaise poultry features prominently on the menu.

Le Moulin de Bourgchâteau – in Guidon, on the road to Chalon. ☎03 85 75 37 12. www.bourgchateau.com. Closed 1-23 Jan. 17 rooms. 9€. Restaurant. Delightful 18C mill spanning the waters of the River Seille, whose former machinery now adorns the hotel bar. Comfortable rooms, some of which are nestled under the eaves. Dining room with beams and stone walls.

The 17C-18C hospital contains two large public rooms divided by a wrought-iron screen. Each curtained bed bears a plaque indicating for whom the bed was intended – usually benefactors offered a bed to the inhabitants of a particular town. The **pharmacy**, with Louis XIV woodwork, has a beautiful collection of hand-blown glass and Hispano-Moorish lustreware. There is also an unusual Burgundian carving of the Virgin of Mercy kneeling before the dead Christ (early 16C).

Church

This building has been greatly restored with stone and brick and is roofed with glazed tiles. On the left is a belfry-porch and large chapel with turreted pavilions (14C).

L'Atelier d'un journal

Open mid-May to Sep 3-7pm. Rest of year Mon-Fri 2-6pm. 3€. ☎03 85 76 27 16. www.ecomusee-de-la-bresse.com. This annexe of the Écomusée de la Bresse Bourguignonne at the Château de Pierre-de-Bresse is housed in the old premises of *l'Indépendant*, a Bresse newspaper abandoned in 1984 after 100 years of publication. The old machines are still in place; the offices have been reconstructed.

Excursion

Chaisiers et pailleuses de Rancy

12km/8mi SW by D 971 on the outskirts of Rancy. Open mid-May to Sep: daily except Tue 3-7pm. 3€. ☎03 85 76 27 16. www.ecomusee-de-la-bresse.com. Chair making, which at the start of the 19C was a long-established part-time occupation in Rancy and Bantanges, had become a full-time job by the end of the century. This centre, now the second most important French producer of caned chairs, illustrates the development of the different stages in this manufacture from the wooden frame to the addition of the straw seat.

LUXEUIL-LES-BAINS⚓

POPULATION 8 814
MICHELIN MAP 314: G-6

This well-known spa town, with its historic red sandstone mansions, was home to a famous abbey founded by the Irish monk St Columban in the 6C. These days visitors come to enjoy the abbey remains and the spa facilities.

- **Information**: r. Victor-Genoux, 70300 Luxeuil-les-Bains. ☎03 84 40 06 41. www.luxeuil.fr.
- **Orient Yourself**: A 4km/2.5mi walk known as the Sentier des Gaulois leads from the baths past all the historical monuments of the town.

Sights

Hôtel du Cardinal Jouffroy★

The house in which Cardinal Jouffroy, Abbot of Luxeuil lived (15C) is the town's most beautiful. In addition to its Flamboyant Gothic windows and arcade, it has Renaissance features, includingan unusual corbelled turret (16C) topped by a lantern. Famous figures such as Madame de Sévigné, Lamartine and André Theuriet all lived in this house. Beneath the balcony, the third keystone from the left shows three rabbits, sculpted in such a way that each appears to have two ears, although only three in total have been carved.

Maison François-Ier★

This Renaissance mansion (west of the abbey church) is named not after the king of France, but an abbot of Luxeuil. Splendid carved faces decorate the Renaissance arcades.

Ancienne abbaye St-Colomban★

For guided tours, ask at the tourist office. ☎03 84 40 13 38.
The abbey has survived almost intact and much of it has been recently restored.
Basilica – The present building, which replaced the original 11C church of which only traces are left, dates from the 13C and 14C. Of the three original towers, only the west bell-tower remains. This

---

Address Book

For coin ranges, see the Legend on the cover flap.

NEAR THE SPA

Hôtel Beau Site – 18 r. G.-Moulimard. ☎03 84 40 14 67. www.beau-site-luxeuil.com. 33 rooms. ☐7€. Restaurant☐. In a quiet corner near the thermal baths, this imposing residence in a pretty flower garden has nicely proportioned rooms. Take a dip on the pool or enjoy breakfast on the terrace.

TAKE A BREAK...

Éric Rubichon – 31 r. Victor-Genoux. ☎03 84 40 02 62. Open Mon-Fri 9am-12.30pm, 2.30-7pm, Sat 8.30am-1pm, 2-7pm, Sun 8.30am-1pm, 3-7pm. Depending on the season, this popular pâtisserie offers up to 50 different cakes, 40 chocolates and 14 ice creams, along with several intriguing house specialties. Teas and hot chocolate are served in the tearoom.

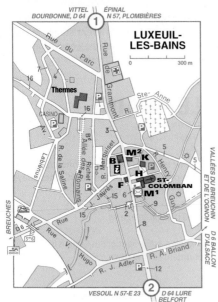

VITTEL | ÉPINAL
BOURBONNE, D 64 | N 57, PLOMBIÈRES

LUXEUIL-LES-BAINS

0   300 m

Thermes

CASINO

M² K
B
Z
F H
ST-COLOMBAN
M¹

VESOUL N 57-E 23 ② D 64 LURE
BELFORT

VALLÉES DU BREUCHIN ET DE L'OGNON

D 6 BALLON D'ALSACE

BREUCHES

was rebuilt in 1527 and the top of it dates from the 18C. The apse was rebuilt by Vauban in 1860. The north façade of the church can be seen from place St-Pierre. A Classical doorway with a pediment leads into the interior, which is in the Burgundian Gothic style. The **organ case**★ is supported by an atlas and decorated with magnificent sculpted medallions. There are interesting 16C stalls in the chancel. The south transept houses the shrine of St Columban, and the north one a 14C statue of St Peter.

Unique lacework

G. Magnin-MICHELIN

Cloisters – Three of the four red-sandstone galleries remain. One arcade with three bays surmounted by an oculus dates from the 13C; the others were rebuilt in the 15C and 16C.

Conservatoire de la dentelle – In the Salle des Moines, there is a lacemaking workshop and a display of the finest examples of the lacemakers' work.

Conventual buildings – These include, to the south of the church, the 17C-18C *Bâtiment des Moines* (monks' building) and, on place St-Pierre, the 16C-18C abbot's residence, now the town hall.

Musée de la Tour des Échevins

Open Apr-Oct Wed, Fri-Sun 2-6pm. 2.50€. 03 84 40 00 07.

The Hôtel des Échevins dates from the 15C, and has a splendid Flamboyant Gothic loggia. The museum inside houses on the ground and first floors some remarkable stone funerary monuments from the Gallo-Roman town (Luxovium), votive **steles**★, inscriptions, Gallic ex-votos, a reconstruction of a potter's kiln and so on. The second and third floors are occupied by the **Musée Adler** containing paintings by Adler, Vuillard and Pointelin. From the top of the tower *(146 steps)* there is a good **view** of the town and, in the distance, the Vosges, the Jura and the Alps.

MÂCON

POPULATION 34 469
MICHELIN MAP 320: I-12
LOCAL MAP SEE LE MÂCONNAIS

Mâcon spreads along the west bank of the Saône between the river and the Mâconnais heights with their slopes covered in vineyards. The round roof tiles mark it as a southern town. Its lively atmosphere is due partly to the busy waterfront, the marina and, not least, to the national French wine fair (see Calendar of events) held here every year.

▪ **Information**: 1 pl. St-Pierre, 71000 Mâcon.
  ☎03 85 21 07 07. www.macon-tourism.com.
▸ **Orient Yourself**: The quai Lamartine is lined with pavement cafes; from here, walk to the Pont St-Laurent from which there is a pretty view of the town.

A Bit of History

The Prince of French Romanticism

Alphonse de Lamartine (*see MÂCONNAIS*) was born in Mâcon in 1790 and took an interest in literature and religious issues from an early age. In 1816, he met a great love of his life, Julie Charles, but her premature death drove him to write the melancholy ode *Le Lac*. His *Méditations poétiques,* in which the poet extols Julie under the name of Elvira, were published in 1820, and it was these that won Lamartine fame.

Sights

Musée des Ursulines★

○*Open daily except Mon 10am-noon, 2-6pm, Sun and public holidays 2-6pm.*
○*Closed 1 Jan, 1 May, 14 Jul, 1 Nov, 25 Dec.*
2.50€. ☎03 85 39 90 38.
The museum, housed in a 17C Ursuline convent, contains sections on prehistory, Gallo-Roman and medieval archaeology, regional ethnography, painting and ceramics.
Among the displays are articles from excavations at Solutré and other regional sites, such as tools, weapons and ceramics from the Paleolithic period to the Iron Age. Other rooms are given over to the Gallo-Roman period (statuettes, tools, funerary urns from the Mâcon necropolis), medieval artefacts (Merovingian weapons and sepulchres) and sculpture

from the 12C to the 17C. Further galleries are devoted to 17C and 18C furniture, French and foreign glazed earthenware and painting: 16C Flemish works; Fontainebleau School; 17C and 18C French and Northern schools (Le Brun, De Champaigne, Greuze); 19C Romanticism (Corot), academics and Symbolists (Busière); 20C post-Cubist canvases (Gleizes, Cahn) and contemporary works (Bill, Honegger, Boussard).

Musée Lamartine

○*Open daily except Mon 10am-noon, 2-6pm, Sun and public holidays 2-6pm.*
○*Closed 1 Jan, 1 May, 14 Jul, 1 Nov, 25 Dec.*
 2.50€. ☎03 85 39 90 38.
The museum dedicated to the man is in the Hôtel Senecé (18C), an elegant,

On the banks of the Saône

H. Champollion-MICHELIN

Régence-style mansion. It contains paintings, tapestries and furniture of the period. A collection of documents recalls the life and work of Lamartine.

Excursion

Romanèche-Thorins
15km/9.5mi S Via N 6.
This, and the neighbouring village of Chénas, is the home of arguably the most famous of the Beaujolais *crus*, Moulin-à-Vent: a powerful, full-bodied wine suitable for laying down.

Le Hameau du vin★
⏱Open Apr-Oct 9am-7pm. Rest of the year 10am-6pm. ⏱Closed Jan, 25 Dec. 🎟16€. ☎03 85 35 22 22. www.hameau-enbeaujolais.com.
This interesting museum is devoted to Beaujolais wine. The various stages of winemaking, crafts linked to wine-grow-

ing and the different vintages are illustrated, and the collection includes an impressive winepress dating from 1708s. The visit ends with a tasting session.

Musée Guillon du Compagnonnage
⏱Open Jun-Sep 10am-6pm; Oct-May 2-6pm. 🎟3.50€. ☎03 85 35 22 02.
This small museum has exhibits from the days of travelling craftsman; there are some fine examples of their work.

Touroparc★
♿⏱Open daily 9.30am-7pm. 🎟15.50€. ☎03 85 35 51 53. www.touroparc.com
Kids This 10ha/25-acre zoological park and breeding centre houses 800 animals from all over the world. Most of them roam free through the park, which offers plenty of other leisure activities, including an elevated monorail train, swimming pools with water slides, a picnic area with several bars and so on…

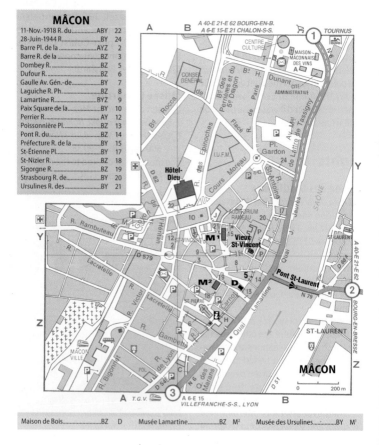

Address Book

For coin ranges, see the Legend on the cover flap.

WHERE TO STAY

Chambre d'hôte Mme Marin – *r. du Lavoir, 71960 Chevagny-les-Chevrières, 5km/3.1mi W of Mâcon by D 17 and a minor road. ☎03 85 34 78 60. marie-therese.marin@wanadoo.fr. 3 rooms.* This lovely 17C building, owned by the same family for six generations, has huge charm. Rooms open onto a terrace with views of the Roche du Solutré.

Hôtel Concorde – *73 r. Lacretelle. ☎03 85 34 21 47. hotel.concorde.71@ wanadoo.fr. Closed 20 Dec-12 Jan and Sun 15 Oct-15 Apr. 13 rooms. 8€.* Small, cheap and unpretentious hotel with simple, well-kept rooms. Breakfast is served in the rustic dining room or on the terrace in fine weather.

Chambre d'Hôte Château de Salornay – *71870 Hurigny, 6km/3.7mi W of Mâcon by D 82 then a minor road. ☎03 85 34 25 73. 4 rooms and 2 gîtes.* A splendid 11C and 15C castle at the entrance to Mâcon, complete with turrets. The peaceful bedrooms give out onto fields; the ones in the keep and the tower are more comfortable. The terrace affords a nice view of the city.

Vieille Ferme – *☎03 85 21 95 15. vieil.ferme@wanadoo.fr. Closed 20 Dec-2 Jan. 24 rooms. 6€. Restaurant.* A rural retreat on the banks of the Saône, recently renovated to include modern-style rooms. The rustic restaurant opens onto a pretty terrace.

Chambre d'Hôte Les Pasquiers – *69220 Lancié, 2km/1.2mi S of Romanèche-Thorins. ☎04 74 69 86 33. www.lespasquiers.com. 4 rooms. Reservations required. Meals.* This handsome Second Empire residence has a pretty walled garden. Relax in the lounge with its grand piano, its fireplace and its library. The spacious rooms look out onto the garden. Terrace with pool.

WHERE TO EAT

Le 88 – *39-47 pl. des Herbes. ☎03 85 38 00 06.* A pleasant dining experience and excellent value are guaranteed at this agreeable restaurant. On the menu: regional specialities prepared with care and beautifully presented.

Le Charollais – *71 r. Rambuteau. ☎03 85 38 36 23. Closed 8-23 Aug, Sun evening and Mon.* The timber-framed facade gives way to a rustic interior where the chef serves up regional cuisine featuring charolais beef.

Au p'tit Pierre – *10 r. Gambetta. ☎03 85 39 48 84. Closed 25 Jul-15 Aug, Tue evening, Wed, from Sep-Jun, Mon lunchtime and Sun Jul-Aug.* Locals flock to this recently opened bistro for well-prepared dishes at reasonable prices.

Le Poisson d'Or – *allée du Parc, 1km/0.6mi N of Mâcon by N 6 and along the banks of the Saône. ☎03 85 38 00 88. www.lepoissondor.com. Closed 15-31 Mar and 15 Oct-8 Nov, Sunday evenings Oct-May, Tue and Wed.* Not to be missed, especially if you like frogs' legs and fried fish. Shaded terrace along the banks of the Saône. Good choice of menus.

SIT BACK AND RELAX

Le Petit Monde des Douceurs – *268 r. Carnot. ☎03 85 39 17 90 – Mon-Sat 9.30am-7pm.* On cold days take refuge in this pleasant tearoom over a cup of hot chocolate flavoured with caramel, orange or hazelnut and a pastry...

SHOPPING

Maison des Vins – *484 av. de Lattre-de-Tassigny. ☎03 85 22 91 11. www.maison-des-vins.com. Open daily 11.30am-6.30pm.* An exhibition, shop and wine tastings led by connoisseurs.

Cave de Chaintré – *rte. de Juliénas, 71570 Chaintré. ☎03 85 35 61 61. www. cavedechaintre.com. Open Mon-Fri 8am-noon and 2-6pm, Sat 8am-noon.* This cellar focuses on Chardonnay varietals (Pouilly-Fuissé, Saint-Véran, Beaujolais, Mâcon), with a few reds.

Château du moulin-à-vent – *71570 Romanèche-Thorins, 15km/9.5mi S via N 6. ☎03 85 35 50 68. chateaudu-moulinavent@wanadoo.fr. Open Mon-Fri 9am-noon, 2-6pm, weekends and public holidays by appointment.* The most celebrated of Beaujolais wines, made to be kept and aged. Old vintages available. Tastings.

LE MÂCONNAIS★★

MICHELIN MAP 320: H-10 TO I-12

The delightful and varied landscape of the Mâconnais is a joy to explore, especially for wine lovers. It is at the point where the north becomes the south, with a milder climate than that of northern Burgundy, and houses with low-pitched roofs covered with rounded red tiles known as Roman or Provençal.

- **Information**: 6 r. Dufour, 71000 Mâcon. ☎03 85 38 09 99. suivezlagrappe.free.fr.
- ▶ **Orient Yourself:** The region is bounded by the Saône River to the east, and the Grosne River valley to the west. The cities of Mâcon and Tournus serve as south and north anchors.
- ☺ **Don't Miss:** The frescoes in the Chapelle des Moines at Berzé-la-Ville, a fine example of Cluniac art.

A Bit of History

A blessed crop

The monks of Cluny planted the first vines in the Mâconnais many centuries ago, of which the Chardonnay, the Pinot and the Gamay are the best-known. The whites are from the Chardonnay stock, the great white grape of Burgundy and Champagne. The most celebrated is Pouilly-Fuissé. This wine has a beautiful green-gold colour; when young it is fruity but with age acquires a bouquet. Pouilly-Loché, Saint-Vérand, Pouilly-Vinzelles, Mâcon-Lugny and Mâcon-Viré, members of the same family as Pouilly-Fuissé, are also well known. The other white wines are sold under the names of White Burgundy, White Mâcon and Mâcon-Villages. As for the reds, without pretending to equal the great wines, they are excellent value. Fairly full-bodied and fruity, they are generally produced from Gamay, a red grape with white juice.

Driving Tours

Among the Vines

79km/49mi – 3hr 30min

This drive passes through a picturesque region of fine views and wide panoramas, dotted with Romanesque churches *(signposted itinerary)*.

Tournus★
⏺*See TOURNUS.*

▶ *Leave Tournus along D 14.*

The road climbs, providing views over Tournus, the Saône Valley and the Bresse region. South-west of the Beaufer pass the countryside has many valleys with boxwood and conifers.

Ozenay
Set in a little valley, Ozenay has an impressive 13C fortified farm (castel) and a rustic 12C church.

▶ *Continue along D 14 to Brancion*

Brancion★
⏺*See BRANCION.*

▶ *Leave Brancion heading toward Tournus, then turn right on D 161.*

Fortified farm

D. Delacroix-MICHELIN

At Bissy-la-Mâconnaise, turn left on D 82 to Lugny.

Lugny

Lugny produces an excellent white wine and is on the Mâconnais Wine Route *(Route des Vins du Mâconnais)*.
Beside the ruins of a fortress stands the **church** which has a 16C stone altarpiece portraying Jesus with the 12 Apostles.

▶ *Return to Bissy; take D 82 S to Azé.*

Site préhistorique d'Azé

8.5km/5.3mi SW of Lugny via Bissy. ◐*Open Apr-Oct.* ✎*Guided tours (1hr30min) daily 10am-noon, 2-7pm (Oct Sun only).* ✆*6€ (children 4€).* ✆ *03 85 33 32 23.*

The **museum** has over 2 000 artefacts found locally. The first of the **caves** (208m/682ft long) was a refuge for bears, prehistoric man, the Aedui, the Gallo-Romans and so on; the second cave has an underground river which can be followed (800m/2 625ft).

▶ *Take D 15 E then D 103 SE to Clessé.*

Clessé

This wine-growers' village (cooperative) has a late-11C **church** with a spire clad with varnished tiles.

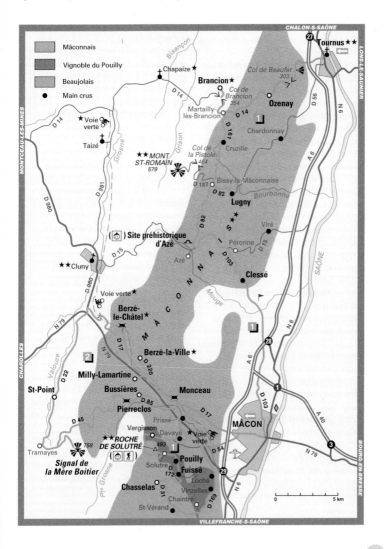

Address Book

🪙 *For coin ranges, see the Legend on the cover flap.*

WHERE TO STAY

🛏 **Camping municipal** – *25160 St-Point-Lac.* ☎03 81 69 61 64. *Open May–Sep. 84 sites. Reservations suggested.* Lovely campsite on the shore of Lac St-Point. Swimming and fishing nearby. Playground for kids.

🛏 **Chambre d'Hôte Domaine de l'Arfentière** – *rte. de Chardonnay, 71700 Uchizy, 10 km/6.2mi S of Tournus by N 6 then D 163.* ☎03 85 40 50 46. 🛌 *4 rooms.* Take advantage of your stay here to taste or buy some of the wines made on the estate. The bright rooms are decorated in a modern style. Two of them look out onto the vineyards.

🛏 **Chambre d'Hôte de Rizerolles** – *In Rizerolles, 71260 Azé, 8.5km/5.3mi SW of Lugny by D 82.* ☎03 85 33 33 26. *r.barry. aze@infonie.fr. Closed Dec-Jan.* 🛌 *5 rooms.* An old stone house in a tiny village at the foot of vineyards. You will love the flower-filled balcony and shaded courtyard. The décor of the rooms is unusual; the welcome is friendly.

🛏 **Chambre d'Hôte Mme Noblet** – *Les Cochets, 71260 Viré, 4km/2.5mi N of Clessé by D 403bis then D 15.* ☎03 85 33 92 54. *Closed 1 Nov-15 Mar.* 🛌 *3 rooms.* This old house in the village offers bright, comfortable rooms sparsely appointed with pine furniture. Note the smith's sign on the lintel above the door. Garden.

🛏 **Chambre d'Hôte Le Château d'Escolles** – *71960 Verzé, 2km/1.2mi N of Roche-Vineuse by D 85.* ☎03 85 33 44 52. *www.gite-escolles.com. 4 rooms.* Pretty outbuilding belonging to a 17C château on the edge of a park. The round windows and Virginia creeper lend it a charming appearance. The rooms under the eaves are old-fashioned in style and overlook the vineyards.

🛏 **Château de Messey** – *rte de Cluny, on D 14, 71700 Ozenay.* ☎03 85 51 16 11. *www.demessey.com. Closed Jan.3 rooms.* In the heart of a small estate, the château and its outbuildings welcomes guests to its comfortable and character-ful rooms. The meals are excellent, and

made more memorable by the wines from the property. Gîtes available.

WHERE TO EAT

🍴 **Le Moustier** – *71960 Berzé-la-Ville,* ☎03 85 37 77 41. *dhoquet@aol.com. Closed Sun evening, Tue evening except Jul-Aug, Wed.* Handsome 18C house with shaded terrace and views of the Mâconnais heights. The stone walls, beams and fireplace convey a cosy atmosphere. Tasty cuisine, with excellent homemade specialities.

🍴 **Chez Jack** – *Le Bourg, 71960 Milly-Lamartine, N 79 exit 6.* ☎03 85 36 63 72. *Closed a fortnight in Aug, Sun and Tue evening and Mon.* This residence-turned auberge is famed as the birthplace of Lamartine. Old cinema posters and photographs embellish the rustic interior. Make yourself at home and sample Mâconnais and Lyonnais regional specialties.

🍴 **Auberge la Pierre Sauvage** – *Col des Enceints, 71520 Bourgvilain, 7km/ 4.3mi E of Milly-Lamartine by D 45 toward Pierreclos, and D 212 rte. de St-Point, then take the rte. Lamartine.* ☎03 85 35 70 03. *www.la-pierre-sauvage. com. Closed 10 Jan-10 Feb, Sun evening, Tue lnch and Mon; winter open Fri-Sun. Reservations suggested.* Saved from near-ruin 20 years ago, this stone residence radiates a certain charm. Three dining rooms share a rustic stone and wood décor where diners enjoy savoury traditional French dishes.

SHOPPING

Château de Fuissé – *Plan, Exit A 6, Mâcon-Sud, toward Vinzelles, 71960 Fuissé.* ☎03 85 35 61 44 or 03 85 27 05 90. *www. chateau-fuisse.com. Open Mon-Thu 8.30am-noon, 1.30-5.30pm (Fri to 6.30pm), Sat-Sun and public holidays by appointment. Closed 1 week in Aug, 1 week at Christmas, Sat-Sun.* At the heart of a vineyard, this cellar is in an elegant family residence flanked by a pentagonal tower dating from the 15C, next to two yew trees trimmed in the shape of wine bottles. Cellar tours and tastings of Pouilly Fuissés originating from this domaine (le Clos, les Combettes, les Brûlés).

▶ *Continue S on D 103 to Mâcon.*

Mâcon
See MÂCON.

▶ *From Mâcon drive west on D 17, turn left through Prissé, and take D 209 to Davayé. Then take D 177 toward Vergisson.*

Roche de Solutré★★
This superb limestone escarpment with a distinctive profile can be seen from miles away. There is a 🥾footpath to the top (*45min there and back*), with views to the Alps in clear weather. At the foot of the rock is the **Musée départemental de Préhistoire** (🕐*open Apr-Sep 10am-6pm; Feb-Mar and Oct-Nov daily except Tue 10am-noon, 2-5pm; 🕐closed Dec-Jan, 1 May; 3.50€; ☎03 85 35 85 24*), devoted to the prehistoric archaeology of the south Mâconnais, including the important hunting grounds at Solutré.

Pouilly
This hamlet gives its name to various wines: Pouilly-Fuissé, Pouilly-Loché and Pouilly-Vinzelles. These wines are highly appreciated and go well with certain Burgundian specialities. Beyond this village the patterns of the vineyards spread over the gentle curves of the hillsides.

Fuissé
This is one of the communes (Chaintré, Fuissé, Solutré, Pouilly and Vergisson) producing Pouilly-Fuissé, classed as one of the world's great white wines.

Chasselas
3.5km/2mi W of Fuissé.
This village has developed a vine that produces a well-known dessert grape. In the background appear the valley of the Saône, the Bresse countryside and the Jura mountains.

▶ *Backtrack, then turn right on D 31 toward St-Vérand. Return to Mâcon by way of Chânes and Vinzelles (D 169).*

Lamartine Heritage Trail
70km/44mi – about 3hr

Roche de Solutré

This countryside inspired the poet and statesman Alphonse de Lamartine.

Mâcon
See MÂCON.

▶ *Head W on D 17 for 9km/5.6mi.*

Château de Monceau
🕐*Park, garden and chapel open daily.*
This château (now a home for the elderly) was one of Lamartine's favourites, where he lived the life of a vineyard owner and wrote his *Histoire des Girondins*.

Milly-Lamartine
3km/2mi further on.
An ironwork grille stands before the **Maison d'Enfance de Lamartine** (🕐*open year round; guided tours (1hr) May-Sep Wed-Sun at 11am, 4pm and 5pm. Apr and Oct Sun and public holidays only. Rest of the year public holidays only. 6€; ☎03 85 37 70 33*) where the poet spent his holidays as a child, free to enjoy the beautiful countryside nearby. It was at Milly that Lamartine composed his first meditation, *L'Isolement*.

Berzé-la-Ville★
2.5km/1.5mi N.
Towards the end of his life St Hugh of Cluny lived in the Château des Moines, a country house near the priory in Berzé owned by the abbey of Cluny.

Chapelle des Moines
🕐*Open Apr-Oct 9am-noon, 2-6pm (Apr and Oct 5.30pm). 3€. ☎03 85 38 81 18.*

This 12C Romanesque chapel, built at first floor level in an earlier (11C) building, was decorated with Romanesque **frescoes**★★; only those in the chancel are well preserved. The clear Byzantine influence is probably due to the fact that the Cluniac artists who worked here were directed by Benedictine painters from Monte Cassino in Latium, where the eastern Roman Empire's influence lasted to the 11C.

▷ *Continue along D 17 until the imposing mass of Berzé-le-Châtel comes into view.*

Château de Berzé-le-Châtel★

🕔*Open Jun-Sep.* 👣*Guided tour (45min) Jul-Aug 10am-6pm; Jun and Sep daily except Thu 2-6pm.* 🎫*6.50€.* ☎*03 85 36 60 83.*

This feudal castle was once the principal seat of the most important barony in the Mâconnais. It protected the southern approaches to Cluny from its attractive site on the vineyard-covered slopes.

▷ *Drive up the Valouze Valley to St-Point (12km/7.5mi SW of Berzé-le-Chatel).*

St-Point

The church, in the style of Cluny, has a fresco of Christ in Majesty in the apse. To the left of the church, a small door opens on to the park of the **château**★ (🕔 *open Apr-Oct;* 👣 *guided tours (45min) Jul-Aug 10am-noon, 2-6pm; Apr-Jun and Sep-Oct weekends and public holidays only;* 🎫*6€;* ☎*03 85 50 50 30;www.chateaulamartine.com),* which was given to Lamartine on his marriage in 1820. The study, bedroom and salon are much as they were in the days of Lamartine, who invited many famous guests there.

South of St-Point beside the road (D 22) lies an artificial lake which is used as a leisure and water sports centre. East of Tramayes wide views open up from the roadway.

Signal de la Mère-Boitier★

A steep road leads up to a car park. 15min round trip on foot.

🚶From the signal station (758m/2 487ft), the highest point of the Mâconnais region, there is a fine **panorama** *(viewing table)* of the Butte de Suin to the north-west, St-Cyr mountain to the west and the Bresse and Jura to the east.

▷ *Continue north-east along the D 45 for 13km/8mi.*

Château de Pierreclos

🕔*Open Easter to late Oct 9am-6pm; rest of the year Mon-Fri only.* 🎫*7€.* ☎*03 85 35 73 73. www.chateaudepierreclos.com.*

Dating from the 12C (keep) to the 17C, the château has had a troubled existence: devastated several times during the Wars of Religion, it was abandoned in 1950 and saved from imminent destruction in 1986. The château is associated with Mlle de Milly, depicted as the character Laurence in Lamartine's epic poem *Joce-*

Château de Berzé

Ph. Gajic-MICHELIN

lyn, and with Nina de Pierreclos, her sister-in-law and the poet's lover. Inside, note the elegant **spiral stairway**, the Renaissance chimney-piece in the guard-room, the kitchen with its 12C fireplace, and the bakery, which used to make bread for the whole village.

▷ *Return to Mâcon along D 85 and D 17.*

MALBUISSON★

POPULATION 400
MICHELIN MAP 321: H-6

This scenic small resort is on the east bank of the Lac de St-Point in the Upper Doubs Valley, enclosed at both ends by mountains.

▫ **Information**: 33 Grande Rue, 25160 Malbuisson.
☏03 81 69 31 21. www.malbuisson.com.
▷ **Orient Yourself**: There is a path running all round the lake (23km/16mi; *allow 6hrs*); the best views are from Chaon at the north end or from above the village of St-Point-Lac itself.

Driving Tour

▷ *Leave Malbuisson heading for Mouthe.*

Lac de Remoray-Boujeons
5km/3mi S along D 437, D 49 to the right then D 46 to the left.
This picturesque lake is separated from St-Point Lake by a strip of marshland.

Découverte de la Réserve Naturelle du Lac de Remoray
At an altitude of almost 1 000m/3 281ft, this nature reserve offers nature lovers a wealth of different ecosystems (lake, marshland, peat bog, meadow, forest) inhabited by numerous species of birds including a colony of herons. The flora is equally rich with some 400 species.

Maison de la Réserve★
♿ ◷ *Open daily 2-6pm (Jul-Aug 7pm). ◷Closed 20 Nov-3 Dec, 25 Dec and 1 Jan. ☞ 5.50€ (5-14 years 3€). ☏03 81 69 35 99. www.maisondelareserve.fr.*
Located on the way out of Laberge-ment-Ste-Marie towards Mouthe, this new centre offers information about the safeguard of the environment as well as the flora and fauna of the Haut-Doubs

Lac de St-Point

region. There are displays of stuffed animals in their natural habitat (reconstituted), aquariums and collections of fossils.

Belvédère des Deux Lacs★

As you reach the end of the Remoray-Boujeons Lake on your way to Mouthe, turn right onto a minor road towards Boujeons. The small car park past the crossroads is the start of the path to the viewpoint. There is a beautiful panoramic view of the whole valley and the two lakes.

Val de Mouthe

The area between La Chapelle-des-Bois and Mouthe, which enjoys a microclimate ensuring regular snow coverage throughout the winter, is sought after by cross-country skiers.

Source du Doubs

The road *(signposted – 2km/1.2mi)* which leaves from the war memorial in **Mouthe** leads to the river's source. The Mouthe Valley, where the Doubs rises, has a mixed landscape of meadows and fir trees. The spring gurgles from a cave at the foot of a steep slope in the forest of Noirmont.

Chaux-Neuve

This ski resort is famous for its ski jumps and is particularly suitable for Nordic skiing and dog-sledging.

Le Parc Polaire

Along D 46 left towards Chapelle-des-Bois. ⚬Open Dec-Jan 10am-5pm; Jul-Aug 10am-7pm. Rest of the year times vary. ⚬7€ (4-11 years 5.40€). ☎03 81 69 20 20. www.parcduchienpolaire.com. Here you can see one of the largest packs of huskies in Europe (guided tour, exhibition, film) and lead your own team on 15km/9mi to 30km/22mi off-piste treks across wide snow-covered areas. Possibility of sleeping in tepees.

Address Book

⚬*For coin ranges, see the Legend on the cover flap.*

WHERE TO STAY

⚬**Camping Les Fuvettes** – ☎03 81 69 31 50. www.camping-fuvettes.com. Open Apr-Sep. ⚬. Large campground with cabins and mobile homes for rent. In addition to aquatic facilities at the water's edge, there is a putt-putt course, archery ground, playground, bar, grocery store...

⚬**La Poste** – ☎03 81 69 79 34. www.lelac-hotel.com. Closed 3-15 Jan, Sun evenings and Mon. 10 rooms. ⚬9€. Restaurant⚬. Pleasant, brightly coloured rooms; those facing the lake are quieter. Traditional cuisine in the light-filled dining room.

WHERE TO EAT

⚬⚬**Le Restaurant du Fromage** – 11 Grande-Rue. ☎03 81 69 34 80. www.lelec-hotel.com. Closed Mon-Fri 13 Nov-21 Dec. With its sculpted wooden décor, this place seems to have come straight out of a fairy tale. A warm, convivial setting for light meals consisting of cheese platters and other regional specialities. Homemade bread and pastries.

⚬⚬**Auberge du Coude** – 1 r. du Coude. ☎03 81 69 31 57. www.aubergedu-coude.com. Closed Sun evening and Wed out of season. This former private home between two lakes offers updated guestrooms and a pretty garden with a pond. Regional cuisine in the rustic dining room.

SHOPPING

Atelier Bernardet – 12 r. Clos-du-Château, 25370 Touillon-et-Loutelet. ☎03 81 49 11 50. Open school holidays daily 2-7pm; rest of the year Fri-Sat 2-7pm. Mr and Madame Bernardet share their passion for fine craftsmanship by showing you round their workshop, where clocks are made according to the Franche-Comté tradition.

SARL Fonderie de Cloches Obertino Charles – 15 rte de Mouthe, 25160 Labergement-Ste-Marie. ☎03 81 69 30 72. Open (exhibition/shop) Mon-Sat 9am-noon, 2-6.30pm; tour of workshop Jul-Aug Sat 10am-noon; casting of bells enquire for information. Closed Sun and public holidays. This foundry set up in 1834 is one of the last of its kind in France. The shop offers a wide range of items made on the premises: bronze and steel bells, small spherical bells, chimes, key rings, clocks...

▶ *Continue along D 46 which runs through the Combe des Cives.*

Chapelle-des-Bois

This simple mountain village (alt 1 100m/ 3 609ft) surrounded by meadows in the heart of the Haut-Jura national park, has become a major centre for cross-country skiing. In summer, the surrounding countryside is ideal for long rambles. Take D 46 along the Combe des Cives to the **Écomusée Maison Michaud** (Kids ⏲

open Jul-Aug daily 2-6pm (Fri also 10am-12.30pm); rest of the year times vary; ☞4.90€, children 2.60€; ☎03 81 69 27 42; www.ecomusee- jura.fr), based in a 17C farmhouse. The museum gives a good impression of what life in such an isolated dwelling would have been like and the importance of the chimney, which occupies virtually a room of its own, where the family would have cooked bread, cured meats and made cheese. *Bread and cakes on sale.*

MÉTABIEF-MONT D'OR☀
19KM/11MI S OF PONTARLIER
POPULATION 691
MICHELIN MAP 321: I-6

Métabief-Mont d'Or is a winter sports resort encompassing six villages: Jougne, Les Hôpitaux-Neufs, Les Hôpitaux-Vieux, Métabief, Les Longevilles-Mont d'Or and Rochejean. In summer, mountain biking is the main activity.

🛈 **Information**: 1 pl. de la Mairie, 25370 Les Hôpitaux-Neufs. ☎03 81 49 13 81. www.metabief-tourisme.com.

▶ **Orient Yourself**: The Swiss border is just 5km/3mi away, so be adventurous...

Sight

Église Sainte-Catherine

The unassuming church in the village of Les Hôpitaux-Neufs contains a real treasure, one of the finest **Baroque interiors**☆ in the whole region (central altarpiece, side chapels, carved furniture).

Activities

Alpine skiing

Runs for downhill skiing cover some 40km/25mi and include a red run lit for night-time skiing; 40 snowmaking machines make up for the unpredictable weather conditions; 7 chair-lifts and 15 drag-lifts take skiers to the long runs suitable for all levels. Main access points are: Métabief (X Authier car park), Jougne (Piquemiette-les-Tavins) and Super-Longevilles. The Métabief drag-lift leads to almost all the runs.

Cross-country skiing

Cross-country fans can glide over 130km/80mi of tracks, as well as 24km/

15mi of cross-Jura trails; double tracks are provided to suit both styles of cross-country skiing.

Snowshoeing

The area also offers guided snowshoeing tours along marked trails.

Summer sports

The village is popular in the summer for the nearby Saint-Point Lake and for its mountain biking facilities, with multi-level permanent tracks for downhill, cross-country and trial practice. In addition, there are two 600m/1 968ft toboggan hills and a climbing wall (70 routes to the top, using 900 possible holds). Karting on grass is another option and guided hikes are organised for those who wish to explore the area.

Excursions

Le Mont d'Or★★

About 10km/6mi, then 30min round trip on foot. Leave Métabief on D 45. At Lon-

CHÂTEAU DE **MONCLEY**★
14KM/9MI NW OF BESANÇON
MICHELIN MAP 321: F-3

This rare example of neo-Classical architecture in the Franche-Comté region has an unusual concave façade and a wealth of interior decoration.

Information: ☎03 81 80 92 55. www.besancon-tourisme.com.
Don't Miss: The vegetable garden, officially classed as an historic monument.

Visit

Open Apr-Oct. Guided tours (1hr30min) by request at Besancon tourist office. 6€.

The château was built in the 18C by Bertrand, on the site of an ancient feudal fortress, in a pleasant spot overlooking the Ognon Valley. The C-shaped façade is decorated with a group of four Ionic columns supporting a triangular pediment at its centre. The side facing the garden is embellished with a rotunda topped with a dome.

Inside, the vestibule is interesting. A dozen Corinthian columns elegantly support a balustraded tribune, which is reached by taking the majestic double staircase. The first floor houses a number of admirable family portraits and Louis XVI furniture, as well as hunting trophies and various stuffed animals.

Château de Moncley

Address Book

For coin ranges, see the Legend on the cover flap.

WHERE TO STAY AND EAT

La Vieille Auberge – pl. de l'Église, 25870 Cussey-sur-l'Ognon, 7km/4.3mi NE of Moncley by D 14 then D 230. ☎03 81 48 51 70. www.la-vieille-auberge.fr. Closed 23 Aug-6 Sep, 27 Dec-3 Jan, Mon, Fri evenings out of season and Sun evenings. This fine residence covered with Virginia creeper has a dining room with wood panelling and cosy, comfortable guestrooms. The hostess will treat you to regional specialities.

Chambre d'Hôte Les Égrignes – rte. d'Hugier, Le Château, 70150 Cult, 4km/2.4mi E off Marnay. ☎03 84 31 92 06. 3 rooms. Meals. This lovely residence (1854) is a listed historic site. Tastefully decorated rooms, elegant dining room featuring an 18C faïence stove, extensive grounds and a charming welcome.

MONTARGIS

POPULATION 15 030
MICHELIN MAP 318: N-4

Montargis, capital of the Gâtinais, a region on the western fringes of Burgundy known for shooting and fishing, is a pleasant town on the banks of the Loing. Its main claim to fame is the invention of pralines, grilled almonds with a sugar coating, first produced in the 17C by the Duke of Plessis-Praslin's cook

🛈 **Information**: 1 r. du Port, 45202 Montargis. ☎02 38 98 00 87. www.montargis.fr.

▶ **Orient yourself**: The old part of Montargis is crisscrossed by waterways – the Briare Canal, smaller canals and branches of the three rivers that meet here – which are spanned by 127 road and foot bridges.

Walking Tour

▶ *Park in place du 18-Juin-1940. Follow rue du Port, boulevard du Rempart then take boulevard Durzy along the east bank of the canal from the bridge level with the Girodet Museum.*

Musée Girodet
🕐*Open Wed-Sun 9am-noon, 1.30-5.30pm (Fri 5pm).* 🚫*Closed public holidays.* ⊜*3€.* ☎*02 38 98 07 81.*
The museum is devoted to the painter **Anne-Louis Girodet-Trioson** (1767-1824), a native of Montargis, who was a pupil of David and a leading light of both Neoclassicism and Romanticism; among his 20 paintings are the extraordinary *Flood* on which the painter spent four years of study, various portraits and the replica, painted by Girodet himself, of his most famous work (now in the Louvre), *The Entombment of Atala*, inspired by Chateaubriand's novel.

Boulevard Durzy
Shaded by plane trees the boulevard is bordered on one side by the Briare canal and on the other by the Durzy garden. At the southern end is an elegant metal humpback footbridge over the canal.

▶ *Cross the canal by the footbridge and carry straight on.*

Boulevard Belles-Manières
The boulevard runs parallel to a narrow canal with footbridges giving access to the houses, built on the foundations of the rampart towers.

▶ *From the east end of boulevard Belles-Manières (retrace your steps) turn left on rue du Moulin-à-Tan; leave place de la République on the left and take rue Raymond-Laforge.*

Rue Raymond-Laforge
The bridges over the two canals provide views of the old houses and the wash-houses lining their banks and of the decorative barges, acting as large window boxes, which are tied up to the quays.

▶ *Return several yards to take rue de l'Ancien-Palais up the spit of land.*

At the end of rue de l'Ancien-Palais turn right into an alleyway which is prolonged by a bridge offering a perspective along the second canal.

Small canal in the center of town

S. Sauvignier/MICHELIN

Address Book

⚘*For coin ranges, see the Legend on the cover flap.*

WHERE TO STAY

⊜⊜⊜⊜**Chambre d'Hôte du Domaine de Bel-Ébat** – *45200 Paucourt, 6.5km/4mi NE of Montargis by the forest road of Paucourt.* ☎02 38 98 38 47. *belebat@wanadoo.fr.* 🖘 *5 rooms. Meals*⊜⊜⊜. A fine manor house nestled in Montargis ForestThe owners will share their passion for horses with you, as well as their love of tradition, including that of dressing for dinner...

WHERE TO EAT

⊜⊜**Les Dominicaines** – *6 r. du Devidet.* ☎02 38 98 10 22. *www. restaurant-lesdominicaines.com. Closed Sun and 2nd fortnight in Aug. Reserva-tions recommended.* Provençal decor of bright yellow and lavender provides a backdrop for traditional cuisine with home-made bread.

⊜⊜⊜**Mademoiselle Blanche** – *5 r. du Loing.* ☎02 38 89 00 87. *Closed 2 weeks in winter, 3 weeks in August, Sun and Mon.* This central restaurant has a pleasant dining room with stone walls, furnished with old-fashioned charm. Superb cuisine with fresh regional produce.

SHOPPING

Mazet – *43 r. du Gén.-Leclerc.* ☎03 38 98 63 55. www.mazetconfiseur.com. *Open daily 9.15am-12.15pm, 2.15-7.15 pm.* Don't leave the region without sampling the pralines: Mazet's are the most authentic.

▶ *Turn right again on rue de la Pêcherie.*

The half-timbered houses in this district have been restored. From place Jules-Ferry, rue Raymond-Tellier leads to a bridge providing another **canal landscape** which stretches as far as the Briare Canal.

▶ *Take the third turning left, continue along rue du Général-Leclerc which skirts the south side of the Église Ste-Madeleine.*

Musée du Gâtinais

🕐*Open Wed and Sat-Sun 9am-noon, 1.30-5.30pm.* 🕐*Closed public holidays.* ⊜*2.80€.* ☎02 38 93 45 63.

The archaeological museum is housed in a 15C tannery. The ground floor is devoted to the Gallo-Roman sites at Sceaux-en-Gâtinais and Les Closiers where excavations uncovered a necropolis and a cult complex near a theatre. Another section contains articles from Merovingian burial sites at Grand Bezout.

Musée des Tanneurs

🕐*Open Sat 2.30-5.30pm.* 🕐*Closed 1 Jan, Easter and 25 Dec.* ⊜*2€.* ☎02 38 98 00 87.

Across the street from the Musée du Gâti-nais, the old tannery neighbourhood (*Îlot des Tanneurs*) has been restored, and this museum explains the craft, tools and techniques involved in this arduous business over the 19C. Upstairs, note the women's headdresses, from the simple *fanchon* (checked kerchief) to the elaborate *coiffe brodée* for special occasions.

Excursion

Ferrières-en-Gâtinais

18km/11mi N along D 315 through Mon-targis Forest.

The Benedictine abbey of Ferrières, which was deconsecrated during the French Revolution, was an important monastic centre and fount of learning during the Carolingian period. Its Gothic **Eglise St-Pierre-St-Paul** has an unusual **transept crossing**★ in the form of a rotunda rising from eight tall columns. It was built in the 12C and is thought to have been inspired by an earlier (9C) Carolingian building. The 13C chancel is illuminated through five Renaissance stained-glass windows. In the north transept there is a collection of 14C-17C statues and a curious baroque liturgical object, a gilt palm tree interlaced with vine tendrils used to display the Holy Sacrament.

MONTBARD

POPULATION 6 300

MICHELIN MAP 320: G-4

Montbard rises up the slope of a hill that impedes the course of the River Brenne. Its most famous former resident is the great 18C naturalist Buffon, who has left his mark on the town of his birth.

- **Information**: pl. Henri-Vincenot, 21501 Montbard. ☎03 80 92 53 81. www.ot-montbard.fr.
- **Orient Yourself**: This part of the Côte d'Or is rich in ancient and not-so-ancient sites, including the famous abbey at Fontenay and the Gallo-Roman site at Mont Auxois.

A Bit of History

Georges-Louis Leclerc de Buffon – Born at Montbard in 1707, Buffon showed a passionate interest in science and nature from an early age. In 1733, he entered the Académie des Sciences, where he succeeded the botanist Jussieu. Six years later he became Administrator of the King's Garden (Jardin du Roi) and museum, now the Jardin des Plantes. Helped by the naturalist Daubenton (1716-99), Buffon reorganised the Jardin du Roi, extending it as far as the Seine, adding avenues of lime trees, a maze, and considerably augmenting the collections of the Natural History Museum. He also began the gigantic task of writing the history of nature. The first three volumes of his *Histoire naturelle (Natural History)*, written mostly in Montbard, were published in 1749 and the other 33 volumes followed over the next 40 years.

Sights

Parc Buffon★

Open year round daily (garden). Guided tours (1hr30min; 2.50€) of Tour de l'Aubespin and Cabinet Jun-Aug daily except Tue 10am-noon, 2-7pm; Apr-Jun and Sep-Oct daily except Tue 9am-noon, 2-6pm, Sat-Sun 10am-noon, 2-6pm. Closed 1 Jan, 1 May, 25 Dec. ☎03 80 92 50 42. www.montbard.com.

In 1735 Buffon bought the Château de Montbard, which dates from before the 10C and was by then in ruins; he demolished all but two towers and the fortified

Address Book

For coin ranges, see the Legend on the cover flap.

WHERE TO STAY

Chambre d'Hôte Mme Bacchieri – *La Forge, 21500 Rougemont, 10km/6.2mi NW of Montbard by D 905. ☎03 80 92 35 99. Closed Christmas, 31 Dec, 1 Jan. 3 rooms.* This small house facing the Burgundy Canal has cosy, tidy and carefully kept rooms, where nothing will interrupt your peaceful nights. There is a small garden near the lock and a cycling trail along the tow path.

WHERE TO EAT

Le Marronnier – *21500 Buffon, 6km/3.7mi N of Montbard by D 905. ☎03 80 92 33 65. Closed 15 Jan-5 Feb.* This house enjoys a fine location opposite the Burgundy Canal. Meals are served in a pretty dining room with stone walls and ornamental fireplace. In summer, relax out on the terrace while admiring the fountain. Traditional cooking.

L'Écu – *7 r. A.-Carré. ☎03 80 92 11 66. www.hotel-de-l-ecu.fr.* Family establishment where you can choose between three dining rooms: one vaulted room, one with huge beams and the latest one, with a modern touch. Traditional cuisine. A few renovated rooms.

Grande Forge

Ph. Gajic-MICHELIN

wall of enclosure. The gardens which he laid out, slightly altered over the years, now form the Parc Buffon. The paths and alleys provide a number of pleasant walks.

Tour de l'Aubespin – Buffon used the height of this tower (40m/131ft) to conduct experiments on the wind. From the top there is a fine view of the town.

Tour St-Louis – Buffon used the ancient tower as his library.

Cabinet de travail de Buffon (D) – It was in this small pavilion with the walls covered with 18C coloured engravings of various bird species that Buffon wrote most of his *Natural History*.

L'Ancienne Orangerie (Musée Buffon)

Open daily except Tue 10am-noon, 2-6pm (Nov-Apr 5pm). Closed 1 Jan, 1 May, 25 Dec. 2.50€. 03 80 92 50 42. www.montbard.com.

Buffon's stables now house a museum devoted to the great naturalist and his place in the history of Montbard and of 18C science.

Musée des Beaux-Arts

Open Jun-Sep daily except Tue 10am-noon, 2-6pm. 2.50€. 03 80 92 50 42. www.montbard.com.

The fine arts museum contains a magnificent wooden triptych (*Adoration of the Shepherds*) by André Ménassier (1599) and 19C and 20C art. Three of the artists represented are natives of Montbard: the sculptor Eugène Guillaume and the painters Chantal Queneville and Ernest Boguet.

Excursions

Grande Forge de Buffon

7km/5mi NW. Open Apr-Sep daily except Tue 10am-noon, 2.30-6pm (last admission 60min before closing). 6€. 03 80 92 10 35.

In 1768, when Buffon was 60 years old, he built a forge for the commercial exploitation of his discoveries about iron and steel and to continue his experiments with minerals on a large scale.

His industrial complex was on two levels: on the lower level were the production shops beside a channel containing water diverted from the River Armançon; on the upper level above the flood line were the houses and other facilities.

The **workshops** consist of three buildings separated by water channels which supplied hydraulic energy to the bellows and trip hammers. The blast-furnace was reached from the upper level by a huge internal staircase; next came the refinery, the forge itself, where the iron was recast and beaten with the trip hammer into bars, and the slitting mill where the bars could be reworked. Further on is the basin where the raw mineral was washed before being smelted.

Château de Nuits

18km/11mi NW. Open Apr-Oct. Guided tours (1hr) 11am, 3.15pm, 4.15pm. 6€. 03 86 55 71 80. www.chateau-de-nuits.com.

The castle was built in 1560 during the Wars of Religion. The attractive Renaissance façade of pediments and pilasters was formerly screened by a fortified wall. The east façade, facing the Armançon (the old border between Burgundy and Champagne), has retained its austere defensive appearance. The vaulted cellars leading to the east terrace contain a kitchen with an indoor well which enabled the castle to hold out against a siege. A large stone stairway leads to the living quarters above, with its high fireplace in pure Renaissance style and 18C wood panelling. Visitors should also see the buildings occupied by the influential Order of St-Mark (**Commanderie de St-Marc),** overlooking the River Armaçon, especially the late-12C chapel.

MONTBÉLIARD ★

CONURBATION 113 059
MICHELIN MAP 321: K-1

The majestic castle high above Montbéliard testifies to this city's rich past. The flower-decked old town with its colourful architecture betrays a distinctly Germanic influence, the result of its unusual history.

- **Information**: 1 r. Henri-Mouhot, 25200 Montbéliard. ☎03 81 94 45 60. www.ot-pays-de-montbeliard.fr.
- **Orient Yourself:** Montbeliard lies just north of the A36 between Belfort and Besançon, along the northernmost curve of the Doubs River. The historic town, where many shops and restaurants may be found, is mostly closed to vehicles. The industrial suburb of Sochaux, home to the Peugeot factory, is to the east.

A Bit of History

A German principality – For four centuries the principality of Montbéliard was a small German enclave, known as **Mömpelgard**, within the borders of France. The princes and dukes of Württemberg, who divided their time between the castle here and their palaces at Stuttgart and later Ludwigsburg, drew many German artists and craftsmen to the town. Although French continued to be the language spoken, German influence was soon evident in economic, cultural and religious fields. Under the rule of **Friedrich I of Württemberg** (1581-1608), the town blossomed into an elegant Protestant city worthy of its princely residents, imbued with the style of the Renaissance. The influx of Huguenot refugees meant that the town had to be extended beyond the medieval fortifications, resulting in the construction of the Neuve Ville. During the French Revolution, Montbéliard was besieged and finally succumbed to the French Republic on 10 October 1793.

Walking Tour ★

- *Walk up the steep rue du Château leading to the castle.*

Château des Ducs de Wurtemberg

⏱Open daily except Tue 10am-noon, 2-6pm. ⏱Closed 1 Jan, 1 May, 1 Nov, 25 Dec. ☞1.50€. ☎03 81 99 22 61.

The **Logis des Gentilhommes** stands on the Esplanade du Château and has an elegant scrolled gable of Swabian influence.

All that remains of the castle built in the 15C and 16C are two massive round towers surmounted by lantern turrets, the Tour Henriette (1422-24) and the Tour Frédéric (1575-95). The rest of the castle was demolished in the mid-18C to make way for Classical-style buildings. A beautiful contemporary wrought-iron gate by Jean Messagier closes off the doorway leading to the Tour Henriette.

The castle museum is still being restored, following a fire which damaged the towers in 1999. Currently, the former vaulted kitchens house a **historical exhibition**; 🔲 the **Cuvier natural history gallery**

Christmas lights

M Paygnard-MICHELIN

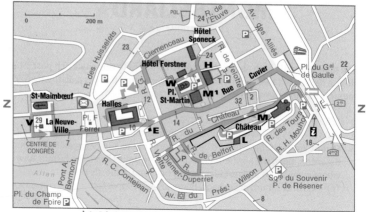

and the archaeology department contain interesting collections (in particular stuffed animals) and extensive contemporary exhibitions are held on the ground floor.

▶ *Walk down rue du Château and turn left onto rue A.-Thomas, then left again onto rue Cuvier to rue de l'Hôtel-de-Ville leading to place St-Martin.*

Place Saint-Martin

This square at the heart of old Montbéliard hosts most of the town's major events, such as the **Lumières de Noël**, a Christmas market in true German tradition (with pretzels, mulled wine and Christmas trees (*see Calendar of Events*). Many of the city's most important monuments are to be found on this square.

Musée d'Art et d'Histoire

1.50€. ☎03 81 99 24 93. Erected in 1773 by the architect Philippe de la

Guépière, the Hôtel Beurnier-Rossel is a typical 18C town mansion. Beurnier-Rossel's private rooms are especially characteristic of the era. Family portraits and period furnishings give them warmth: note the wood inlays by local craftsman Couleru, the ceramic stove by Jacob Frey and the encyclopaedic library, a must in the Age of Enlightenment. The two upper floors are devoted to the history of the town and the region. The collections are varied: popular illustrations by the Deckherr brothers, religious items from Lutheran churches, a room full of music boxes.

Temple St-Martin★

Open 25 Nov-24 Dec 4.30-7pm, weekends 2-7pm. Rest of the year Sun 10am. This is the oldest Protestant church in France (built between 1601 and 1607). The architecture of the façade draws its inspiration from the Tuscan Renaissance. The inside would be quite plain were it

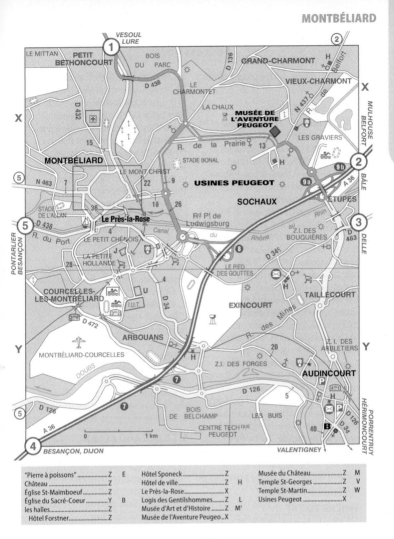

not for the original polychrome decoration, only rediscovered recently, on the mid-18C **organ** and the gallery.

Hôtel Forstner

This town house (probably from the late 16C) now houses a branch of the Banque de France. The building is named after its former occupant, the Chancellor of Friedrich I of Württemberg. The stately Renaissance façade features four storeys of superposed columns.

Hôtel de ville

The elegant pink-sandstone town hall was built from 1776 to 1778. There is a commemorative statue of Cuvier by David d'Angers in front of the building.

Hôtel Sponeck

Located near the town hall, this 18C mansion is now the home of the Scène nationale de Montbéliard.

▸ *Walk round the mansion along rue du Général-Leclerc, turn left onto rue Georges-Clemenceau and follow the street which turns to the left and joins rue des Febvres. Turn right to reach the covered market.*

Halles

The 16C-17C **covered market** has a distinctive roof and long façades with large windows with double mullions. The enormous building was the meeting hall for the town council prior to 1793; it was

Address Book

For coin ranges, see the Legend on the cover flap.

WHERE TO STAY

Hôtel Bristol – *2 r. Velotte.* ☎*03 81 94 43 17. www.hotel-bristol-montbeliard. com. Closed 31 Jul-21 Aug. 43 rooms. 7€.* This 1930s hotel is located near the château and the lively pedestrian district. Most of the guestrooms facing the rear are relatively quiet.

Hôtel Vieille Grange – *25310 Blamont, 18km/11.2mi S of Montbéliard by D 35.* ☎*03 81 35 19 00. Closed 20-26 Dec, Sat lunchtime, Mon lunchtime and Sun. 10 rooms. 5.50€. Restaurant.* As you leave the village, you will come to this 18C farmhouse which has retained all its country charm. The sober bedrooms have been set up in a modern building. Take your meals in the rustic-style dining room with its two fireplaces. Regional cooking.

Hôtel de la Balance – *40 r. de Belfort.* ☎*03 81 96 77 41. www.hotel-la-balance.com. 44 rooms. 9€. Restaurant.* This former residence lying at the foot of the château has been converted into a charming hotel with a pretty pastel façade. The bedrooms are at the top of a splendid staircase carved in wood. The dining room, with its parquet flooring and wood panelling, is warm and inviting.

WHERE TO EAT

La Porte Étroite – *4 r. du Château.* ☎*03 81 91 27 58. Closed Aug, Sun and Mon.* The warm welcome, combined with the small size of the dining room, makes this Italian restaurant a cosy refuge. Don't be shy... open the bottle on the table and get ready to sample house specialities incorporating fresh pastas, fish and seafood.

Baltica – *8 r. Belfort.* ☎*03 81 91 43 75. Closed Aug, Sun and Mon.* Voyage to the Baltic fjords without ever leaving Montbéliard via the Scandinavian specialities served here. Try the Baltica (marinated herring with potatoes) or the Royal Stockholm (three types of salmon with potatoes), and don't forget to stop in the shop for salmon or sturgeon to take home.

Le St-Martin – *1 r. du Gén.-Leclerc.* ☎*03 81 91 18 37. Closed 13-20 Feb, 1-23 Aug, Sat-Sun and public holidays.* This lovely old house with stone walls has a cosy dining room reminiscent of a brasserie. The meals are traditional, made with good fresh produce.

Sur les Rives du Doubs – *25190 Villars-sous-Dampjoux, 2km/1.2mi W of Noirefontaine by D 36 then D 312.* ☎*03 81 96 93 82. Closed 2-31 Jan, Mon evenings, Tue evenings and Wed.* This rustic-style inn on the banks of the Doubs is the perfect place for a country lunch. The regional specialities are served in one of the two dining rooms or, weather permitting, out on the terrace.

SIT BACK AND RELAX

Café de la Paix – *12 r. des Febvres.* ☎*03 81 91 03 62. Open daily 7.30am-11pm.* This small, unpretentious café is the only one in town to offer organised activities on Saturday evenings: philosophical discussions from October to April, jazz concerts from May to September.

Gourmandise – *10 r. Clemenceau.* ☎*03 81 91 09 55. Open Tue-Sat 9am-noon, 2-7pm. Closed public holidays.* This confectioners shop is paradise on earth for those who have a sweet tooth. Among the numerous delicious specialities, try the *mont-béliardes* (chocolate-coated almonds), the *cailloux du Doubs* (almond, nougatine and chocolate) and the *clarines* (chocolates with a praline filling).

then used as a store for the town's grain, as a market and as a customs post. In place Denfert-Rochereau, a 15C flagstone can be seen, which is known in Montbéliard as the **pierre à poissons**; the stone was used by fishmongers on market day. In 1524, Swiss reformer Guillaume Farel is said to have used it as a pulpit, to preach the Reformation to the people of Montbéliard.

▶ *Walk to place F.-Ferrer and continue along faubourg de Besançon to the Temple St-Georges.*

You are now in the suburb known as the Neuve Ville. Friedrich I commissioned Schickhardt to build this suburb in 1598, to accommodate the waves of Huguenot refugees fleeing France.

Temple Saint-Georges
The church was built between 1674 and 1676 when the Temple Saint-Martin could no longer accommodate all those wishing to attend services; it is now a conference centre.

Église St-Maimbœuf
The lofty mid-19C church with its exaggerated ornamentation offers a striking contrast to the nearby church and is a physical reminder of the Roman Catholic church's reconquest of this bastion of Lutheranism after Montbéliard was reclaimed by France. The interior of St-Maimbœuf is lavish: monumental tribune with Corinthian columns, extravagant wooden stucco ornamentation, Baroque style altarpieces and so on.

▶ *Instead of returning to the town centre, return to place Ferrer, follow rue Ch.-Lalance, walk across the Pont A.-Bermont and follow the Allan to a flight of steps leading down.*

Pavillon des Sciences
 🅦🕙*Open Jul-Aug Mon-Fri 10am-7pm, Sat-Sun 2-7pm. Rest of the year times vary.* 🕙*Closed Sep, 25 Dec, 1 Jan, 1 May.* *4.50€ (children 3€).* ☎*03 81 91 46 83. www.pavillon-sciences.com.*
🄺🄸🄳🅂 This centre offers the young and not so young a good introduction to scientific and technical culture by means of various activities and demonstrations.

▶ *A footbridge spans the Allan and leads to rue des Blancheries. Turn left onto avenue du Président-Wilson then right onto rue de la Chapelle.*

Sochaux

The first Peugeot car – In the 18C, Jean-Pierre Peugeot was a weaver in Hérimoncourt. When his two oldest sons, Jean-Pierre and Jean-Frédéric, founded a steelworks in the mill at Sous-Cratet in 1810, no one dreamed that this small enterprise would be a huge international industrial concern by the 20C. Soon more factories were founded at Terre-Blanche, in the Gland Valley, Valentigney and Pont-de-Roide, producing laminated steel, saw blades, tools, domestic appliances and so on, while a factory in the old mill at Beaulieu turned out various types of velocipede and later bicycles. Finally, in 1891, Peugeot produced its first automobile with a combustion engine, called the Vis-à-Vis (face-to-face) because its passengers had to sit facing one another.

Musée de l'Aventure Peugeot★★
 🕙*Open year round daily 10am-6pm.* 🕙*Closed 1 Jan and 25 Dec.* *7€ (children 10-18 3.50€, under 10 free).* ☎*03 81 99 42 03. www.musee-peugeot.com.*
🄺🄸🄳🅂 The Peugeot museum houses an extensive collection of cars, cycles, tools and other objects illustrating the Peugeot firm's output from the early days to the present. About 75 models are on show, including the elegantly decorated vis-à-vis made for the Bey of Tunis (1892), the small car designed in 1911 by Ettore Bugatti and the Peugeot 402 Limousine equipped with a gas generator and a coal box, a sign of the extreme shortage of fuel in 1941.

Tour of the Peugeot factories
🕙*Guided tours (2hr30min) Mon-Fri 8.30am by appointment.* 🕙*Closed 3 weeks in Aug and public holidays.* ☎*03 81 33 27 46.*
Sochaux is the largest Peugeot automobile production centre and the factory is still expanding. The Peugeot 307, 406 and 607 are the main models manufactured at Sochaux.

MONTBENOÎT★

POPULATION 219

MICHELIN MAP 321: I-5

This village, in a picturesque setting on a hillside overlooking the Doubs, is the tiny capital of the Saugeais Valley. The old abbey of Montbenoît is among the Jura's most beautiful architectural monuments and draws many visitors.

Information: 8 r. du Val-Saugeais, 25650 Montbenoît.
☎03 81 38 10 32. www.otcm25.org.

Orient Yourself: The border with Switzerland is not far away, and many of the surrounding villages have a distinct Swiss flavour.

A Bit of History

The rise and fall of the abbey

Montbenoît Abbey was founded in the 12C after the hermit Benedict (Br Benoît) came to live here, drawing crowds of followers with him. It was held in *commendam* from 1508 onwards; the abbots drew on the abbey's profits without having to either oversee the general administration of the abbey or even take part in the religious life of the abbey. The two most famous abbots were the Cardinal of Granvelle and Ferry Carondelet. The latter joined the order after being widowed, and became counsellor to Emperor Charles V. He was a luxury loving patron who had the church chancel rebuilt and filled it with the most beautiful works of art. He also made generous donations to the cathedral of St-Jean in Besançon, where he was canon and where he is buried. During the Revolution, the abbey of Montbenoît was declared the property of the French State and its lands were sold.

Ancienne Abbaye★

🕐*Open year round.* 🚶 *Guided tours Jul-Aug 10-11.30am, 2-5pm; rest of the year unaccompanied visit with written guide sheet (available at the tourist office).* 🎫*3€* ☎*03 81 38 10 32.*

Ancienne église abbatiale

The nave of the abbey church dates from the 12C and the chancel from the 16C. The bell-tower was rebuilt in 1903.

Nave – Against the first pillar on the south side is a monument (1522) to a local girl, Parnette Mesnier, who met her death while attempting to resist the unwelcome advances of a young man. Pretty Parnette fled him by clambering up the scaffolding above the chancel, which was under construction at the time. The young man was about to catch up with her at the top, whereupon Parnette threw herself to the ground below. Kind-hearted Ferry Carondelet donated the monument in memory of the young girl's defence of her virtue.

In the Chapelle Ferrée north of the chancel there is a 16C statue of St Jerome and a stone Pietà on the altar. The sculpted doors at the entrance to the Chapelle des Trois-Rois to the south of the chancel were part of the original 16C rood screen.

Chancel – Abbot Ferry Carondelet had travelled all over Italy as ambassador to the court of Rome for the government of the Netherlands and Flanders and sought to re-create at Montbenoît some of the magnificence and refinement of the Italian Renaissance. He personally chose the craftsmen who took just two years to create this harmonious group of sculpture and stained glass, one of the great successes of the early Renaissance in the Franche-Comté. The brilliant colours of the ornamental foliage and arabesques are still visible on the pendentive vaulting, which is decorated with a delicate network of ribs.

The decoration on the magnificent **stalls**★★, dating from 1525 to 1527, is clearly the result of both a lively wit and great artistic talent; unfortunately, very few motifs have survived intact. Note the delicacy and variety of the ornamentation on

Cloisters

the upper part between the pinnacles. One or two cleverly sculpted scenes contribute to the richness of the whole (such as *Women Fighting,* symbolising the triumph of Truth over Error) and illustrate ideas taken from the Middle Ages (*Lay of Aristotle*, representing Science being punished by Truth).

There is a beautiful marble **abbatial recess**★★ to the right of the altar; a 1526 piscina, also in marble, is next to it. Above the sacristy door is a low relief commissioned by Ferry Carondelet in memory of the Joux landlords. The sculpted man's head sticking out of the socle is probably a representation of Ferry Carondelet.

Cloisters

The architectural indecisiveness of the Franche-Comté is in evidence in the 15C cloisters. Round arches are still used, whereas the corner doors are surmounted by Flamboyant Gothic ogee arches and sculpted tympanums: the twin colonettes have archaic style capitals.

Chapter-house

This chapter-house, which opens onto the cloisters, has diagonal groined arches springing from the door.

Note the 16C painted and gilt wood statuettes of the Virgin holding Jesus as well as of the Three Kings.

Kitchen

Note a Louis XIV clock with one hand, a beautiful Louis XIII armoire and an enormous mantelpiece.

Excursion

Défilé d'Entre-Roche

17km/11mi NE along D 437.

Downstream of Montbenoît, the charming Saugeais Valley becomes a twisting gorge extending almost all the way to Morteau, known for the smoked sausage of the same name. At the Défilé d'Entre-Roche the road cuts between breathtaking limestone cliffs, in which there are two caves: the **Grotte du Trésor,** with an incredibly high entrance arch (*5min from D 437 on the rock face a little above road level*) and the cave of **Notre-Dame de Remonot,** which has been converted into a chapel and place of pilgrimage, in which the water is said to heal eye afflictions. The opening is at road level; a grille protects the entrance.

MONTS JURA✳

MICHELIN MAP 328: I-3

In 1999, the pretty mountain villages of Mijoux and Lélex in the upper Valserine Valley in southern Jura joined forces to form, with the Col de la Faucille, the region's most southerly winter sports resort, named Monts Jura.

🛈 **Information**: 01410 Mijoux. ☎04 50 20 91 43. www.monts-jura.com.

▸ **Orient Yourself**: Grab a gondola ride to the highest peaks for some breathtaking mountain views.

Activities

Alpine skiing

The two Alpine ski areas comprise 35 runs (50km/30mi) for all levels of proficiency and a difference in height of 800m/2 625ft (max height 1 680m/ 5 512ft); 28 ski lifts, including 3 gondolas, are available.

Lélex-Crozet

900m to 1 700m/2 953ft to 5 577ft.
The village has a kindergarden where youngsters can enjoy the pleasures of sliding on the snow. The Lélex gondola leads to Catheline giving access to various runs and the resort's highest point, Monthoisey (1 680m/ 5 315ft).

Mijoux-La Faucille

1 000-1 550m/3 281-5 085ft.
A chairlift links Mijoux and the Col de la Faucille. From there, a gondola and chairlift go to the top of Mont-Rond (1 534m/ 5 033ft); most runs are red. Long runs (blue and green) to Mijoux.

Cross-country skiing

The Vattay and Valserine cross-country ski areas rank among the best in the Jura mountains.

La Vattay

1 300-1 500m/4 264-4 920ft.
The area's international renown is fully justified by its extensive facilities (restaurant, bar, equipment hire service, Nordic-

B. Kaufmann-MICHELIN

The Vattay ski area is popular with beginners and champions

skiing school…) and by the quality of its 80km/50mi of pisted-down double tracks and competition tracks.

La Valserine
900m to 1 080m/2 953ft to 3 543ft.
Less popular, less challenging but pleasant even so, this area reveals the charm of this yet unspoilt valley. The 60km/37mi of tracks are also pisted down for both styles of cross-country skiing.

Other sports
When the snow goes, there is still plenty to do: fishing, canyoning, climbing, hang-gliding, walking and mountain biking are all popular in summer.

Excursions

Ascent of Crêt de la Neige★★
Alt 1 717m/5 633ft. ⏰*Open Jul-Aug and ski season 9am-1pm, 2.15-5.30pm.* ⊛*6€.*
☎ *08 36 68 39 01.*
🚶In Lélex, take the Catheline gondola *(10min one way).* On arrival, start walking right towards the Crêt de la Neige along a safe but slippery path *(allow 3hr there and back; hiking boots recommended).*
Beyond the Grand Crêt, to the east, there are views of the Jura mountains, Lake Geneva, and Geneva. The summit reveals a panoramic view of the Alps.
Between Lélex and Mijoux is the restful Valmijoux countryside with the River Valserine flowing through pastures.

Mont-Rond★★
500m/547yd from the pass where the access road to the Mont-Rond gondola branches off N 5.

The Petit and the Grand Mont-Rond peaks constitute one of the Jura's most famous viewpoints. The view from Petit Mont-Rond is the more interesting. The usual way of reaching Petit Mont-Rond is from the Col de la Faucille. Follow the wide road which leads southwards from the pass. After about 500m/550yd, leave the car in the car park and take the gondola *(télécabine).*
Another option is to take the chairlift *(télésiège)* from Mijoux to the lower gondola station at the Col de la Faucille (⏰*open Jul-Aug and ski season 9.45am-12.30pm, 2-6pm)* and continue to the summit in the gondola (⏰*open Jul-Aug and ski season 10am-6pm, 15min).*
The sweeping view from the viewing table is breathtaking. Beyond the rift valley in which Lake Geneva lies tower the Alps, extending over an area 250km/155mi wide and 150km/93mi deep, as well as the Jura and Dôle (in Switzerland) chains.
In spring the summit is carpeted with blue gentians, anemones and white crocuses, in summer and autumn with alpine asters and mountain thistles.

Colomby de Gex★★★
Accessible from the Col de la Faucille; 500m/550yd to the car park, then about 4hr on foot to the peak. To cut down the length of the walk, take the gondola to the Petit-Mont-Rond, then follow the GR 9 footpath (signposted) along the ridge.
🚶At 1 689m/5 545ft, the Colomby de Gex is one of the highest points in the Jura range, and offer an extensive **view**★ of the valley of Lake Geneva, and beyond it the Alps stretching 250km/155mi.

Address Book

WHERE TO STAY

😊😊**Chambre d'Hôte Le Crêt l'Agneau** – 25650 La Longeville, 5.5km/3.5mi N of Montbenoît by D 131 to La Longeville-Auberge. ☎03 81 38 12 51. www.lecret-lagneau.com. Closed Jul. 🛏 7 rooms. Meals 😊😊. Cosy, comfortable bedrooms await you in this delightful 17C Franche-Comté farmhouse standing amid pine trees and pastures. The meals are copious with homemade bread and jams. A perfect base for rambling and cross-country skiing excursions.

😊😊**La Petite Chaumière** – At the pass, 01170 Col de la Faucille. ☎04 50 41 30 22. www.petitechaumiere.com. Closed 3-24 Apr and 9 Oct-20 Dec. 34 rooms. 😊9.50€. Restaurant😊😊. A quiet, peaceful stay is guaranteed at this Jura chalet nestled at the foot of the slopes. The rustic-style bedrooms with wainscoting and white walls are simply charming. The dining room is extended by a large terrace that you can enjoy in all seasons.

😊😊**Chambre d'Hôte Le Boulu** – 01410 Mijoux, 4km/2.5mi SW of Mijoux by D 991 to Lélex. ☎04 50 41 31 47. Open Christmas to Easter and Jul-Sep. 🛏 5 rooms. Meals 😊😊. Stately 18C farmhouse with simple guestrooms looking out into the garden, where ducks and geese roam freely, or the forest, traversed by the peaceful River Valserine. The owner will extend a warm welcome and treat you to delicious meals. For non-smokers.

😊😊**Hôtel La Mainaz** – rte de Gex, 01170 Col de la Faucille. ☎04 50 41 31 10. www.la-mainaz.com. Closed 25 Oct-10 Dec, Sun evenings, Tue lunchtime and Mon except school holidays. 22 rooms. 😊12€. Restaurant😊😊. In fine weather this huge wooden chalet overlooking the Col de la Faucille offers breathtaking vistas of the Alpine range, Mont Blanc and Lake Geneva. The cosy rooms have pretty wainscoting. The dining room boasts a lovely wooden ceiling and a fireplace made in red brick.

SHOPPING

Le Tuyé du Papy Gaby – 25650 Gilley. ☎03 81 43 33 03. Open 9am-noon, 1.30-6pm. Closed Sun Nov-Apr. This farm boasts an impressive tuyé (Comtoise fireplace) and is widely known for the quality of its Morteau sausage. Animated figures take you through the various stages of sausage production.

Driving Tour

From La Cure To Gex 27km/17mi – allow 30min

▶ *Leave La Cure on N 5 heading towards the Col de la Faucilles.*

The road leaves the forest of Massacre to the right, beyond the dip where the Valserine flows.

Col de la Faucilles★★

At an altitude of 1 323m/4 341ft, the pass cuts a passage through the great mountainous Jura spine separating the Rhône Valley and Lake Geneva to the east from the Valserine Valley to the west. The pass is one of the main routes through the Jura mountains. The descent to Gex offers unforgettable **views**★ of Mont Blanc directly ahead and, from the end of the pass road, down into the Valserine Valley from over 300m/984ft.

Descent to Gex★★

Having crossed the pass, the road leads through pine forest. It opens up after the La Mainaz hotel, making a great hairpin meander round the green fields and houses of Le Pailly. Leave the car on the roadside where it widens to enjoy the splendid **panorama**★★. Lake Geneva appears in a sort of mist, sometimes even disappearing entirely under a sea of clouds, whereas the peaks of the Alps stand out quite sharply.

The Fontaine Napoléon comes into sight further down, on the side of the road as it makes a tight hairpin bend around a house. The countryside around Gex appears shortly afterwards, spread out at the bottom of the slopes, with its chessboard landscape of fields.

LE MORVAN ★★
MICHELIN MAP 319: G-8 TO H-10

The Morvan – from the Celtic for black mountain – is a distinct natural region between the Nivernais and Burgundy, distinguished by its vast and sombre forests. It receives an ever-growing number of visitors who are attracted by the dramatic unspoilt scenery.

- **Information**: Maison du Parc, Parc naturel régional du Morvan, 58230 Saint-Brisson. ☎03 86 78 79 00. www.parcdumorvan.org.
- ▶ **Orient Yourself:** The Morvan (70km/44mi long, 50km/31mi wide) stretches from Avallon to St-Léger-sous-Beuvray and from Corbigny to Saulieu. There are no main roads through the area.
- **Kids:** Youngsters will love the Écomusée du Morvan, with its fun exhibits on life in the Morvan of yesteryear.

A Bit of Geography

A land of water and forest

Seen from the north the Morvan appears as a vast, slightly undulating plateau, which rises slowly towards the south. The northern section (maximum altitude 600m/2 000ft) descends in terraces to the Paris basin; this is Le Bas Morvan (Lower Morvan). The southern section, Le Haut Morvan (Upper Morvan), south of Montsauche, contains the higher peaks, including the Massif du-Bois-du Roi or Haut-Folin (901m/2 956ft).

The Morvan is subject to heavy rain and snow fall because of its geographical location and altitude; it rains or snows for 180 days in an average year on the peaks. As the ground is composed of non-porous rock covered with a layer of granitic gravel (a sort of coarse sand), the rivers – Yonne, Cure, Cousin and their tributaries – can quickly become turbulent. The characteristic feature of the Morvan massif is the forest which covers between a third and a half of the surface area; beeches and oaks are being replaced gradually by fir trees.

Parc Naturel Régional

Most of the Morvan region was designated a Regional Nature Park in 1970, helping to attract visitors interested in activities such as hiking, canoeing, cycling, riding or fishing. The park's headquarters at St-Brisson, set in 40ha/ 99-acre grounds, are not only home to an information centre, but also an aboretum,

herbarium and one branch of the **Ecomusée du Morvan** (○open Apr to mid-Nov; May-Sep daily except Tue (Jul-Aug daily), 10am-1pm, 2-6pm; rest of the year 5pm; ☞3€, children 1.50€), the Maison des Hommes et des Paysages, about life in the Morvan from earliest times to the present.

Driving Tours

1 Le Bas Morvan from Vézelay

73km/45mi – allow one day
This route enters the Morvan from the north as far as Lormes, returning via the Chaumeçon and Crescent lakes.

Vézelay★★★
See VÉZELAY.

▶ *Leave Vézelay E towards Avallon.*

Vézelay and its basilica, set high on their rocky outcrop, are still visible from St-Père.

St-Père★
The village of St-Père, at the foot of the hill of Vézelay on the banks of the River Cure, has a beautiful Gothic church.

Église Notre-Dame★
The church, begun in about 1200 and completed in 1455, shows all the stages in the development of the Gothic style between the 13C and 15C. In the 16C it

became the parish church in place of the church of St-Pierre (from which the name St-Père is derived) which burned down in 1567 in the Wars of Religion. The porch added at the end of the 13C and restored by Viollet-le-Duc (1814-79) has three doorways. The central one, which has a trefoiled archway, depicts the Last Judgement.

Rebuilt in the 15C the choir is encircled by an ambulatory with five radiating chapels. The vaulting of the nave has painted bosses and corbels carved in the form of expressive faces.

In a chapel on the south side of the choir is a 10C stone altar which probably belonged to the original church. As you leave, note the curious painted baptismal font from the Carolingian period.

Musée Archéologique Régional

Open Apr to mid-Nov 10am-12.30pm, 1.30-6.30pm. ≈4€. ☎03 86 33 37 31.
This archaeological museum contains objects excavated at Fontaines-Salées, in particular sections of a water conduit made from tree trunks hollowed out by fire to carry mineral water from a spring; it dates from the Hallstatt period (First Iron Age). Also on display are a 4C Gallo-Roman weighing device, enamelled bronze fibulae in the form of sea horses or wild ducks, Merovingian weapons and jewellery found in the tombs at Vaudonjon near Vézelay, and Gratteloup near Pierre-Perthuis. The medieval room contains sculpture from the 12C to the 16C from the Vézelay region.

▶ *Drive S out of St-Père.*

The road follows the upper valley of the River Cure through a wooded gorge.

Fouilles des Fontaines-Salées

1.5km/1mi. Open Apr to mid-Nov 10am-12.30pm, 1.30-6.30pm. ≈4€. ☎03 86 33 37 31.
These excavations have unearthed Gallo-Roman baths, built on to what was once a Gaulish sanctuary within a vast precinct dedicated to the gods of the springs. These saline springs, which were used in the Iron Age, by the Romans and again in the Middle Ages, were filled in by the salt tax authorities in the 17C. Nineteen wooden casings dating from the first millennium BC have been preserved by the water's high mineral content. A stone duct from the Roman period gives access to the waters of a spring which is once again being used for treating arthritic complaints.

Pierre-Perthuis★

4km/2.5mi along D 958.
This tiny village in its picturesque **site**★ is named after a rocky spur, **Roche Percée,** which can be seen from the modern bridge spanning the Cure.

▶ *Continue S towards Lormes.*

Bazoches★

See VÉZELAY Excursions.

▶ *Drive 13.5km/8mi S on D 42 to Lormes.*

Lormes

This small town is an ideal departure point for trips to the nearby reservoirs.

Morvan landscape

Ph. Gajic-MICHELIN

Address Book

For coin ranges, see the Legend on the cover flap.

WHERE TO STAY

Camping Les Genêts – *58230 Ouroux-en-Morvan.* ☎*03 86 78 22 88. josette.guyallot@wanadoo.fr. Open May-Sep. 70 sites. Reservations recommended.* This site looking out onto rolling countryside is extremely pleasant. The sites and terraces are marked out by hedges and bushes.

Camping La Plage des Settons – *58230 Les Settons.* ☎*03 86 84 51 99. www.settons-camping.com. Open May-15 Sep. 68 sites. Reservations recommended.* At this peaceful lakeside site the lazy can rest on the beach while the more energetic use the nearby tennis court. Playing area for children.

Chambres d'Hôte Mme Berthier – *1 r. du Gén.-Leclerc, 89230 Rouvray.* ☎*03 80 64 74 61. Closed 15 Nov-15 Mar. 3 rooms.* This rustic farmhouse is creatively decorated with everyday objects used in unusual ways, and with souvenirs collected during the owners' travels. Warm welcome and thoughtful service.

Chambre d'Hôte L'Eau Vive – *71990 St-Prix, 4.5km/2.8mi NW of St-Léger by D 179.* ☎*03 85 82 59 34. redenis@club-internet.fr. Closed Nov-Mar and 15-30 Jun. 4 rooms. Meals.* A stone's throw from Mont Beuvray, this house is the perfect starting point for long, bracing walks. The drawing room and the bedrooms are pleasantly decorated with holiday mementoes. Table d'hôte meals are served in the dining room with exposed beams, blue pottery and old farming tools on the walls.

Chambre d'Hôte Le Château – *58120 Chaumard.* ☎*03 86 78 03 33. Closed 28 Dec-10 Mar. 6 rooms. Meals.* With its 2ha/5-acre park, this large 18C house is a haven of comfort and tranquillity. In summer, have breakfast on the terrace facing Pannessière Lake. Two self-catering *gîtes* are available. Riding enthusiasts are welcome.

WHERE TO EAT

L'Auberge Ensoleillée – *58230 Dun-les-Places.* ☎*03 86 84 62 76. Closed 25 Dec. Reservations needed.* On Wednesdays you can sample famed regional dishes such as *tête de veau* (boiled calf's head), *œufs en meurette* (poached eggs served in red wine sauce with lardoons) and *crapiaux* (thick pancakes cooked with pork fat). The accommodation is unpretentious.

Le Morvan – *89630 Quarré-les-Tombes.* ☎*03 86 32 29 29. www.le-morvan.fr. Closed 4-12 Oct, 22 Dec-24 Feb.* This family restaurant offers lovingly prepared regional specialities at reasonable prices. Meals are served in the restored traditional dining room. A few rooms are available.

SHOPPING

Ferme de l'Abbaye de la Pierre-qui-Vire – *1 Huis-Saint-Benoît, 89630 St-Léger-Vauban.* ☎*03 86 33 03 73. www.abbaye-pierrequivire.asso.fr. Open Mon-Sat 10.45am-noon and 3-5.30pm (Mon 5pm), Sun 11.30am-12.15pm and 3-5pm.* "La Pierre-que-Vire" is a soft, cow's milk cheese, for sale in the shop near the monastery of the same name.

Les Tombelines – *24 pl. de l'Église, 89630 Quarré-les-Tombes.* ☎*03 86 32 22 21. Open daily except Wed 7am-1pm, 2-7.30pm. Closed Jun.* This special shop sells no less than 200 kinds of jam made with old-fashioned recipes, including one made with dandelions (cramaillote) and another with lavender-flavoured apple. The shop also makes chocolates.

Rue du Panorama leads up to the lookout point by the cemetery, from where there is a **panorama** of the wooded heights of the Morvan (to the south-east), and the farmland of the Bazois and Nivernais regions dotted with little villages and woods (to the south-west).

Mont de la Justice
1.5km/1mi NW; viewing table.
The summit (470m/1 542ft) affords a fine **panorama** encompassing Vézelay (N), the Yonne Valley and Montenoison hill (W), the Bazois region (SW) and the Morvan ridge (SE).

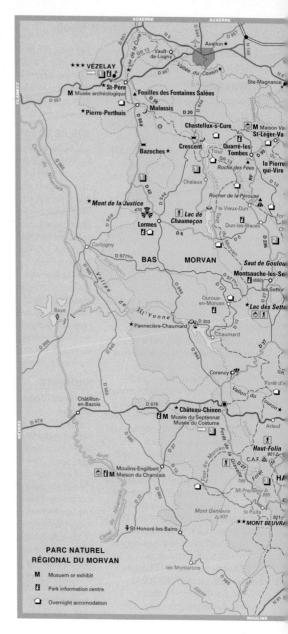

M   Musuem or exhibit

ⓘ   Park information centre

⌂   Overnight accomodation

PARC NATUREL
RÉGIONAL DU MORVAN

▶ *D 6 towards Dun-les-Places.*

Lac de Chaumeçon

The twisting road runs across undulating woodland dotted with rocks then across pastoral open country.

▶ *Drive over the dyke and turn immediately left; a short section of road (800m/875yd) leads to D 235.*

The road overlooks the Chaumeçon reservoir hemmed in by wooded heights. Beyond Vaussegrois, the road plunges

Barrage du Crescent

Built between 1930 and 1933 this dam retains the accumulated waters of the Cure and the Chalaux. It has a maximum height of 37m/ 122ft and a total length of 330m/1 083ft. The reservoir is used by the Bois-de- Cure power station to generate electricity and to help to regulate the flow of the Seine.

▸ *Take D 944 towards Avallon.*

Château de Chastellux-sur-Cure

This château was altered in the 13C and restored in 1825 and has been the seat of the Chastellux family for over 1 000 years. The best view of the château is from the viaduct which carries D 944 across the Cure. The building clings to a rocky slope amid much greenery.

▸ *Return to Vézelay along D 20 and D 36.*

2 Le Bas Morvan from Saulieu

80km/50mi – allow one day.
The route affords charming views over Les Settons reservoir and the upper valley of the Cure and includes visits to a remote abbey and the Musée Vauban.

▸ *From Saulieu, head W on the D 977.*

The road runs across a plateau dotted with woods and ponds, then through a forested area.

Maison du Parc

See above Parc Naturel Régional du Morvan.

▸ *From St-Brisson continue along the D 20 to St-Agnan.*

Lac de St-Agnan

5km/3mi N.
From the village, the road runs across the southern end of the lake, the granite-built dam being at the other end.

▸ *At Les Michaux, follow a minor road on the left towards St-Léger-en-Vauban.*

towards the lake shore and follows it closely before running over the crest of the dam towering 42m/138ft above the gorge of the River Chalaux.

▸ *Continue to Plainefas and turn right towards Chalaux.*

Abbaye de la Pierre-qui-Vire

&⊕*Open 10.15am-12.15pm, 2.30-5.30pm, Sun and public holidays 11.15am-12.15pm, 2.30-5.30pm.* ⊕*Closed Jan.* ⊕*2.30€.* ⊕*03 86 32 19 20. www.abbaye-pierrequi-vire.asso.fr.*

This monastery is in a wild and lonely part of the Morvan, on a hilly bank of the Trinquelin, the local name for the River Cousin, flowing at the foot of granite rocks in the middle of thick woods.

iIn 1850 **Father Muard** laid the foundations of his monastery on land donated by the Chastellux family. It took its name of Pierre-Qui-Vire (the Rocking Stone) from a druidic monument, an enormous block of granite, placed on another rock, which rocks with a push of the hand.

Father Muard's death in 1854 did not stop the development of the community, which joined the Benedictine Order in 1859. On the contrary, it grew so fast that the buildings put up between 1850 and 1953 were not big enough to accommodate the 85 monks and many guests. An architectural competition was launched in 1988; the winning project, completed in 1995, unified the group of buildings which had gone up over time. Other parts of the abbey, including the cloisters, have been restored but are closed to tourists.

Although the rules of monastic enclosure forbid tours of the monastery, the **salle d'exposition** is always open to visitors interested in the life of the monks and their work *(audio-visual presentation on the life of the monastery).* The church is open for **services** (&⊕*mass at 9.15am, Sun and public holidays 10am, vespers at 6pm.* ⊕*03 86 33 19 20)* and one can visit the **druidic stone** *(pierre plate)* which is outside the monastery walls.

St-Léger-Vauban

Sébastien le Prestre, who under the name of the **Marquis de Vauban** became one of the outstanding figures of the Grand Siècle (as the 17C is known in France), was born in 1633 in this little village which was then called St-Léger-de-Foucheret. The **Église St-Léger** where Vauban was baptised was originally built to a cruciform plan in the Renaissance period; it was transformed in the 19C and boasts some interesting modern additions by the sculptor Marc Hénard: carved wooden panels in the south door; the sculptures and stained-glass window in the chapel of Notre-Dame-du-Bien-Mourir (1625), left of the chancel; the beautiful blue and pink ceramic **tiles**★ (1973) which surround the high altar and depict the planets, animals, tools and so on round the triangle of the Holy Trinity.

Maison Vauban

&⊕*Open Jul-Aug daily except Tue 10am-12.30pm, 7pm. Rest of the year days and times vary.* ⊕*5€.* ⊕*03 86 32 26 30. www.vaubanecomusee.org.*

In a small room information panels and an audio-visual presentation (20min) retrace the life and work of this great Frenchman (⊕*see box below).*

Quarré-les-Tombes

About 5.5km/3.2mi via D 55.

This village owes its name to the numerous limestone sarcophagi dating from the 7C to the 10C found near the church. It is thought there must have been a sanctuary to St George in Quarré, near which knights and other people of rank were buried.

▶ *Follow D 10 towards Saulieu, then 3.5km/2.2mi past the path leading to* **La Roche des Fées** *(rock-climbing site), take the forest track towards Dun. Turn right just before Vieux-Dun onto a forest track and drive 1.6km/1mi to a signposted parking area 200m/218yd from* **Rocher de la Pérouse**.

🚶A steep footpath climbs to the rocky summit *(30min round trip on foot).* From the top there is an interesting **view** over the isolated Cure Valley and the rounded summits of the massif.

▶ *Return to the road leading to Dun-les-Places then continue S on D 236.*

Montsauche-les-Settons

This village is the highest resort (650m/2 133ft) in the massif, at the centre of the Parc Naturel du Morvan, and was rebuilt after almost total destruction in 1944.

Saut de Gouloux
6km/3.7mi NE then 15min round trip on foot. Access by a path (right) from the first bend in the road after the bridge over the Cure.
🧍Just upstream from its confluence with the Cure, the Caillot flows over an attractive waterfall.

Base Nautique des Settons
♿🕐*Open May-Sep daily 9am-7pm; Oct-Apr Mon-Fri 9am-noon, 2-6pm. 🕐Closed public holidays Oct-Apr, 25 Dec-1 Jan.* ☎*03 86 84 51 98. www.activital.net.*
The Settons sports centre is near the lake at an altitude of 600m/ 1 969ft. It offers facilities for watersports (sailing, canoeing, water-skiing, wake-board) and outdoor activities (hiking, cycling)

Lac des Settons★
S of Montsauche along D 193.
The reservoir was created originally to aid logging on the River Cure but is now used to regulate the flow of the Yonne.

▸ *After crossing the River Cure, the road follows the north shore of the reservoir, offering pretty views over the lake and its wooded islands, and leads to the charming resort of Les Settons.*

The reservoir of Les Settons, covering an area of 359ha/887 acres (alt 573m/1 880ft) is a peaceful place, surrounded by fir and larch woods, where wildfowl congregate in the autumn. Footpaths and a lakeside road provide easy access for walking, fishing and water sports.

▸ *The road continues through forests and across a plateau, dotted with woods and ponds, before reaching Saulieu via Moux, Alligny and Chamboux Lake.*

③ Le Haut Morvan from Château-Chinon

84km/52mi – allow one day
This drive crosses several forested massifs and offers far-reaching views.

Château-Chinon★
🕐*See CHÂTEAU-CHINON.*

▸ *Leave Château-Chinon by D 27 going S.*

A view opens out towards the west of a landscape of meadows, arable fields and woods. The road then rises steeply before entering the **Forêt de la Gravelle.** It follows the ridge between the basins of the Seine and the Loire.
At one point near the summit (766m/2 513ft) there is a view to the right of bleak broom-covered moorland. The road then leaves the forest. Another good view opens out southwards over a small dam nestling at the bottom of a green hollow dominated by the wooded crests which mark the limit of the Morvan.

▸ *The road leads (18km/11mi) to D 18; turn left to Mont Beuvray.*

Mont Beuvray★★
🕐*See Mont BEUVRAY.*

▸ *Take D 274 right round and back to D 18 then drive N to Glux-en-Glenne and the Forêt de St-Prix via D 300 and D 500 (very steep). The Bois-du-Roi forest track leads close to Haut-Folin.*

Haut-Folin
The Haut-Folin (901m/2 956ft), the highest peak in the Morvan, is crowned by a telecommunications mast. The slopes of this peak have been developed for skiing by the French Alpine Club.
The Bois-du-Roi forest track continues through the **Forêt de St-Prix**, a magnificent stand of spruce and fir trees with immense trunks and joins D 179 at La Croisette.

Gorges de la Canche
4km/2.5mi NE.
The road follows the gorge along the side of a hill in a wild landscape of rocks and trees. There is a fine viewpoint in a bend to the right (partly screened by trees).

▸ *Turn left onto D 978 towards Château-Chinon then right 1km/0.6mi further onto D 388 to Anost.*

Anost
8km/5mi NE.

Vauban, "the most decent man of his century"

Sébastien le Prestre was left a penniless orphan early in life, and at the age of 17 joined the army of the Prince of Condé, then in revolt against the court, and was taken prisoner by the royal forces.

Thereafter, he entered the service of Louis XIV. As a military engineer, from the youthful age of 22, he worked on 300 ancient fortified places and built 33 new ones; he successfully directed 53 sieges, justifying the saying: "a town defended by Vauban is an impregnable town: a town besieged by Vauban is a captured town". Appointed Brigadier General of the royal armies and then Commissioner General of fortifications, he was made a Field Marshal in 1704. He was extremely inventive in thinking up tactics for breaking into fortresses and designed a number of weapons and other instruments of war which were revolutionary for his period. He also systematically fortified the north and east borders of France with a belt of fortresses entirely new in conception (Verdun, Metz, Strasbourg, Neuf-Brisach).

Saint-Simon (1675-1755), a writer not known for his kind remarks, wrote of Vauban: "A man of medium height, rather squat, who had a very warlike air, but at the same time an appearance that was loutish and coarse, not to say brutal and ferocious. Nothing could be further from the truth; never was there a gentler man, more compassionate, more obliging, more respectful, and more courteous, and most sparing in the use of men's lives, a man of great worth capable of giving himself in the service of others...". The last years of Vauban's life were unhappy. Deeply affected by the misery of the common people, he sent his *Projet d'une dîme royale* (Plan for a Royal Tithe) to the king, in which he proposed ways of bettering the living conditions of the lower classes. The work was banned and Vauban, relegated virtually to disgrace by Louis XIV, died of grief on 30 March 1707.

In 1808 Vauban's heart was placed in the Invalides in Paris by Napoleon I; the rest of his body lies in the church in **Bazoches** *(20km/12mi SW of Avallon)*, near the château which was largely reconstructed by his efforts.

Anost offers tourists a choice of numerous walks, especially in the forest *(signposted forest trails)* as well as outdoor swimming. The village of **Bussy** used to be the centre of the *galvache* trade (transport by ox-drawn carts) practised in the area until the First World War.

Maison des Galvachers

🕐 *Open Jul -Aug daily except Tue 2-6pm; Jun and Sep Sat-Sun 2-6pm.* 🎫 *2€.* ☎03 85 82 73 26. www.anost.com.
Kids The museum is devoted to the men who practised this ancient trade: they would leave home for six months, from May to November, and go as far as the Ardennes in Belgium.

Notre-Dame-de-l'Aillant

NW of Anost: 15min round trip on foot.
From the statue there is a semicircular **panorama**★ over the Anost basin and the hills of the Autun depression.

▸ Drive through Anost Forest (wild boar in an enclosure) to Planchez then return to Château-Chinon via the twisting D 37; note the picturesque hilltop village of Corancy on the way.

MOUTHIER-HAUTE-PIERRE ★

POPULATION 343
MICHELIN MAP 321: H-4

This charming village set in a rocky amphitheatre is, along with Ornans, one of the prettiest spots in the Loue Valley. It grew up around an old Benedictine priory, first recorded in 870 and deconsecrated during the French Revolution.

Information: 7 r. Pierre Vernier, 25290 Ornans. ☎03 81 62 21 50.

Don't Miss: The whole area around Mouthier-Haute-Pierre is at its loveliest in late April and May, when the slopes are white with cherry blossom. The cherries themselves are used to make a famous kirsch, something else not to be missed!

Gorge de la Loue Driving Tour

40km/25mi – about 4hr 30min.

From Mouthier-Haute-Pierre, the Loue winds along the bottom of a deep and wooded gorge to its confluence with the Doubs, a popular trip with canoeists.

▷ *Head SE on D 67 towards Pontarlier.*

Cascade de Syratu

Visitors climbing back up the valley will see Syratu waterfall, just at the exit to Mouthier-Haute-Pierre, tumbling from a high cliff.

Source du Pontet and Grotte des Faux-Monnayeurs

45min there and back on foot from D 67.
The walk is mostly through woods, climbing up slopes that are sometimes quite steep. Iron ladders lead to two caves; that of the Faux-Monnayeurs is not recommended to visitors with no head for heights. The source of the Le Pontet is a resurgent spring welling up in a cave at the bottom of a wooded hollow. The Faux-Monnayeurs Cave (Counterfeiters' Cave, so named as it is said that counterfeit money was made here in the 17C) is about 30m/98ft higher up; this was the river's original source.

Belvédères★★

Two viewpoints come one after the other along D 67, from which one of the most beautiful meanders in the river can be seen, from a height of 150m/492ft.

There is another viewpoint, known as the **Belvédère de Mouthier**, 300m/330yd further on. The **view**★ is remarkable, taking in not only Mouthier but also the upper Loue Valley at the end of the Nouailles gorge.

Gorges de Nouailles★

There is a walk (1hr 30min there and back on foot) from the Café La Creuse to the source of the Loue; take the path along the gorge which branches off from D 67. This path twists along the steep cliff.
The path gives beautiful **glimpses**★ of the gorge, which is over 200m/656ft deep. It goes to the bottom of the cirque in which the Loue rises. A footbridge leads to the cave from which the river springs. This gorge was the favoured haunt of the Vouivre, the winged serpent of Franche-Comté legend which flew as fast as lightning.

Address Book

For coin ranges, see the Legend on the cover flap.

WHERE TO STAY

Hôtel des Sources de la Loue – 25520 Ouhans, 10km/6.2mi S of Mouthier-Haute-Pierre by D 67 and D 41. ☎03 81 69 90 06. hotel-des-sources-loue@wanadoo.fr. Closed 20 Dec-31 Jan, Fri evenings and Sat lunchtime Oct-Apr. 15 rooms. 7.50€. Restaurant. This unpretentious hotel is in a building typical of the region. The bar is a popular meeting place for local residents. Simple guestrooms with wood panelling. Regional specialities.

Hôtel de la Cascade – 2 rte. des Gorges de Nouailles. ☎03 81 60 95 30. Closed 3 Nov-2 Mar. 19 rooms. 8.50€. Restaurant. The Loue Valley is on the doorstep. The rooms are equipped with all modern amenities and some of them have balconies. Settle in the

WHERE TO EAT

Hôtel de France – 25930 Lods. ☎03 81 60 95 29. Closed 25 Dec-1 Jan. Three nice surprises in this village restaurant: the terrace, the serene room at the back and the simple, carefully prepared dishes.

Ferme-Auberge du Rondeau – 25580 Lavans-Vuillafans, 15km/9.3mi N of Mouthier-Haute-Pierre by D 67 heading for Vuillafans then D 27. ☎03 81 59 25 84. Closed Dec to mid-Jan and Mon out of season. Reservations recommended. This typical Franche-Comté farmhouse is in a tranquil setting in the middle of fields. The meals include homemade bread, vegetarian fare, organic produce, and goat and boar reared on the property. The eight comfortable rooms are embellished with wood from floor to ceiling.

restaurant (for non-smokers) and enjoy tasty, imaginative dishes.

▶ *After leaving Ouhans, head for the river's source along D 443, which climbs steeply uphill.*

Source de la Loue★★★

Leave the car in the car park next to the little refreshment stall, Chalet de la Loue, and go down the path (30min there and back on foot) to the valley bottom.

This spot is one of the most beautiful in the Jura. A bend in the path suddenly reveals the Loue rising up from a steep-walled basin. It has been proved that the Loue draws its waters from the Doubs. It is also fed by infiltrations from the Drugeon and by rainwater draining off the plateau, with the result that the river's flow never falls very low. As a general rule the water is very clear, except after heavy rains.

The river rises from a vast cave at the bottom of a tall cliff about 100m/328ft high. From the cave entrance, there is a good view of the sheer power and size of the Loue's source.

▶ *Return to Ouhans and take D 41 on the right towards Levier, then take D 376*

on the right shortly afterwards. On leaving Renédale, park the car near the entrance gate of the path leading to the viewpoint.

Belvédère de Renédale★

15min there and back on foot.

This pleasant path overlooks the Nouailles gorge from a height of 350m/ 1 148ft. It leads to a platform from which there is virtually a **bird's-eye view** down into the gorge; directly opposite are the cliffs with D 67 winding along them.

▶ *Take D 376 again to head N; after 2.5km/ 1.5mi the road ends at the foot of a television broadcasting station, at a viewpoint.*

Belvédère du Moine-de-la-Vallée★★

There is a superb panorama of the Loue Valley north-west to Vuillafans, Roche mountain and the village of Mouthier-Haute-Pierre.

▶ *Take the road back to Ouhans and return to Mouthier.*

NANS-SOUS-SAINTE-ANNE

POPULATION 125
MICHELIN MAP 321: G-5

This charming and tiny village near the source of the Lison is blessed with plenty of natural sights in the surrounding area.

- **Information**: 7 r. Pierre Vernier, 25290 Ornans. ☎03 81 62 21 50.
- **Orient Yourself**: Get your walking boots on: there are some excellent walks close by.

A Bit of Geography

Underground, overground

The River Lison, a tributary of the Loue, actually rises on the slopes of the forest of Scay. Its course on its upper reaches, the Lison-du-Haut, is quite irregular. It will vanish underground for a short distance, only to reappear for a little while, then disappear once more into a gully or crevice. The underground course of the river can be seen at ground level in the largely dry, at times strangely shaped valley which follows it. The valley sides become steeper and steeper, forming a gorge which is spanned by the **Pont du Diable** (devil's bridge) over which D 229 from Crouzet-Migette to Sainte-Anne runs. After heavy rainfall, the river becomes a gushing torrent, filling the valley, before it cascades into the pool known as the Creux Billard.

Taillanderie★

○Open Mar-Nov. ⟶Guided tour (1hr) Jul-Aug daily 10am-7pm; rest of the year daily 2-6pm (Mar and Nov weekends). ⊚5€ (children 4€). ☎03 81 86 64 18. www.musees-des-techniques.org.

Just outside the village (follow the signposts) is the 19C edge-tool workshop which turned out agricultural tools until 1969. Working to capacity, it employed 25 workers, most of whom lived on the premises. Hydraulic power was provided by the Arcange, a tributary of the Lison. During the 1hr visit, the process of making a scythe is explained and the large hydraulic wheel (5m/16ft in diameter), dating from 1891, is seen operating; in summer, tools are even made before your eyes.

Hike

Grotte Sarrazine★★
30min there and back on foot.

A gigantic natural porch in the steep wooded rockface marks the opening to this vast cave (90m/295ft high). Its sheer size is best appreciated in summer when the spring is dry. During rainy periods the resurgent spring, fed by an underground stretch of the Lison, flows out of the cave as a swollen torrent.

> Go back to the road on the right and after 200m/220yd take the footpath which climbs up to the source of the Lison.

Source du Lison★★
1hr there and back on foot.

The abundant fresh green foliage which surrounds this relatively large pool, going right down to the water's edge, makes a pretty scene. This is the second largest river source in the Jura after the Loue, and even when the water level is low, it flows at 600l/132gal per second. It is possible to enter the cave through a small tunnel in the rock (*take a torch; slippery underfoot*) which ends at a pulpit-shaped rocky platform (chaire à prêcher).

> Retrace your steps along the path and turn right onto a signposted footpath which twists its way up through the woods. The climb down to the Creux Billard can be a bit tricky.

Creux Billard★★
30min there and back on foot.

This deep rocky cirque (over 50m/164ft) is characterised by unusually subtle light. The water in the pool is part of the Lison's underwater course, although the river rises officially further downstream in a nearby cave. The discovery that the Creux Billard is linked with the Lison's source was made after a tragic accident: in 1899 a young girl drowned in the depths of the pool and three months later her body was found downstream of the river's source.

NANTUA★

POPULATION 3 902

MICHELIN MAP 328: G-4

Nantua, tucked in a steep-sided, evergreen-forested **cluse**★★ on the shores of a glacial lake, is a charming resort known for its freshwater crayfish (écrevisses) and a type of very light dumpling (quenelles à la Nantua).

- **Information**: pl. de la Déportation, 01130 Nantua. ☎04 74 75 00 05. www.ville-nantua.com.
- ▶ **Orient Yourself**: Nantua is a good base from which to explore both the Ain Valley and the Haut-Bugey.

A Bit of History

Within these walls

Nantua grew up around a Benedictine abbey founded in the 8C. In the Middle Àges it was a free town surrounded by solid ramparts, which it certainly needed, as it was continually caught up in the turbulent religious and political disputes between the Bugey, the Franche-Comté, Savoy and Geneva, not to mention between France and the Germanic Empire. Henri IV finally annexed Nantua to the kingdom of France in 1601.

Sights

Église St-Michel★

This church is the last trace of a 12C abbey destroyed during the Revolution. The beautiful Romanesque portal is unfortunately badly damaged, but the Last Supper can nonetheless be discerned on the lintel. The chancel contains some beautiful carved woodwork and kneeling angels either side of the altar (17C and 18C). Note the **Martyrdom of St Sebastian**★★ (1836) by Delacroix on the north wall (*light switch in the crossing opposite*).

Lac de Sylans

G. Magnin-MICHELIN

Musée Départemental d'Histoire de la Résistance et de la Déportation de l'Ain et du Haut-Jura★

Open May-Sep daily except Mon 10am-1pm, 2-6pm. 4€. 04 74 75 07 50. www.ain.fr.

The museum traces the rise of Fascism and Nazism and recalls the Vichy administration, the Occupation, the Resistance, the Maquis and deportation. Numerous documents and a film testify to the struggle between the Nazis and the Maquis in the Bugey region. The **audio-guide**★ includes the voices of former French *maquisards* and a British soldier.

Driving Tours

Haut Bugey

Allow one day.

▶ *Leave Nantua to the N on the picturesque N 84, which runs alongside the Lac de Nantua. Turn left at Montréal-la-Cluse; 2km/1.2mi after Ceignes, turn right on a road leading off N 84 and follow it for about 300m/328yd.*

Grotte du Cerdon

Open Apr-Sep. Guided tours (1hr15min) Jul-Aug10am-6pm; Apr-Jun; rest of the year times vary. 6€. 04 74 37 36 79. www.grotte-cerdon.com.

This cave was hollowed out by a subterranean river which has now dried up. The tour takes you past beautiful stalactites and stalagmites into an immense cavern in which a 30m/98ft-high arch is open to the sky. In the past, cheese was left to mature in the cave.

▶ *Continue along N 84.*

Cerdon★

Cerdon produces renowned sparkling rosé wines. The picturesque narrow streets are decorated with fountains and stone bridges spanning mountain streams..

La Cuivrerie★

Open year round. Guided tours (1hr) Jul-Aug daily 9.30am-noon, 2-6.30pm; rest of the year weekends and public holidays 2-6pm. Closed 1 Jan, 25 Dec. 5€. 04 74 39 96 44. www.cuivreriedecerdon.com.

Learn all about copper at these works, set up in 1854, and still in operation.

▶ *Continue along N 84 towards Pont-d'Ain; 6km/3.7mi further on, turn left onto D 36 towards Ambronnay.*

Jujurieux

This village, boasting 13 castles, enjoyed an extraordinary boom in the 19C on account of its weaving industry.

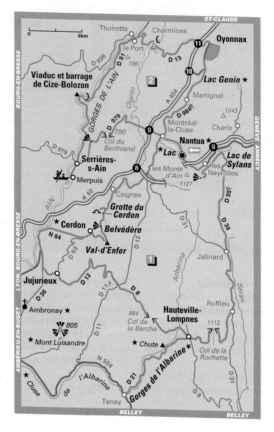

Soieries Bonnet

♿ ⏰ *Open mid-Jun to mid-Sep.* 🎧 *Guided tours (1hr15) daily except Tue 10am-noon, 2-6pm.* 💶 *4.50€.* ☎ *04 74 37 23 14.*

In 1835, CJ Bonnet, a silk manufacturer from Lyon, set up this factory. Today, the works specialise in high-quality silk velvet. There is a small museum and the workshops can be visited with the possibility of buying luxury fabrics.

▸ *Follow D 12 to Hauteville-Lompnès.*

Hauteville-Lompnès

The town, on a high plateau (850-1 200m/2 789-3 937ft), is a popular holiday resort, known for the quality of the air.

▸ *Take D 21 on the right.*

Gorges de l'Albarine★

As the River Albarine flows south-west, it has cut many impressive gorges along its course. As the road leaves the gorge, you can see the **Cascade de Charabotte**★, formed as the Albarine cascades down a 150m/ 492ft drop on the edge of the Hauteville plateau.

▸ *Return to Hauteville-Lompnès and take D 9 over the Col de la Rochette, altitude 1 112m/3 648ft, as far as Ruffieu; take D 31 N, D 31F at the Jalinard junction, D 39 on the left and D 55C on the right. Then take D 55D through Granges-du-Poizat to reach Les Neyrolles. From here, take D 39 on the left.*

After a few sharp turns in the road there is a remarkable **view**★★ of the steep slopes of the Nantua cluse and of the lake; this is a magnificent sight at sunset.

▸ *Return to the village of Neyrolles, from where D 39 leads to N 84, which leads off to the left back to Nantua.*

Address Book

(For coin ranges, see the Legend on the cover flap.

WHERE TO STAY

Lac Hôtel – 22 av. de Bresse. ☎04 74 76 29 68. www.lac-hotel.com. Closed 26 Dec-1 Jan. 28 rooms. ☐6€. Clean, basic rooms soundproofed against nearby traffic noise, and internet access, all at a very reasonable price.

L'Embarcadère – av. du Lac. ☎04 74 75 22 88. www.hotelembarcadere.com. Closed 20 Dec-5 Jan. 49 rooms. ☐9€. Restaurant☐☐. Pleasant menus and comfortable rooms a stone's throw from pretty Nantua Lake.

WHERE TO EAT

Auberge du Lac Genin – 01130 Charix, 16km/9.9mi NE of Nantua by D 74 until you reach Molet then D 95 up to the lake. ☎04 74 75 52 50. lacgenin.free.fr. Closed 17 Oct-3 Dec, Sun evenings and Mon. Enjoy the blissful quiet of this mountain inn on the edge of a lake in the heart of woodland... The bedrooms are decorated in the rustic style. Grilled meat is the speciality of the house.

Auberge Les Gentianes – 01130 Lalleyriat, 12km/7.5mi E of Nantua by N 84 and D 55B. ☎04 74 75 31 80. Closed 5-31 Jan, Sun evenings, Mon and Tue. This house is a charming sight with its façade overflowing with flowers. Fine stone fireplace and small terrace for the summer season. Thoughtful cooking with deliciously fresh produce.

Gorges de L'Ain and Plastics Vallée

Allow one day.

▷ Leave Nantua along N 84 to Cluse then drive straight on along D 979 towards Bourg-en-Bresse. Turn right before the bridge onto D 91C to Serrières.

Serrières-sur-Ain

Superb scenery round a one-arch bridge spanning the River Ain.

▷ Follow D 91 towards Merpuis and turn right towards the Merpuis site 2km/1.2mi beyond the bridge then take the steep road down to the Allement reservoir.

Boat trips on the River Ain

(Open May-Sep. Trips (1hr15 or 3hr) at 3pm and 5pm. ☐8€. ☎04 74 37 24 35. www.ile-chambod.com. Take a trip aboard a flat-bottomed boat; hydroelectric installations have considerably modified the valley's landscapes.

▷ Return to Serrières and continue along D 91 which follows the gorge N to Thoirette, with splendid river views.

Barrage de Cize-Bolozon

Built between 1928 and 1931, the 156m/170yd-long dam is surmounted by a crane. The valley progressively widens yet re-mains hemmed in by impressive heights.

▷ At Le Port, do not cross the bridge, but follow D 18 and D 13 to Oyonnax.

Oyonnax

Once famous for its wooden combs, Oyonnax now produces a wide variety of plastic objects. The association Plastics Vallée was created in 1986, bringing together businesses within a 50km/31mi radius.

Musée du Peigne et de la Plasturgie

(Open Jul-Sep Mon-Sat 2-6pm; Oct-Jun Tue-Sat 2-6pm. (Closed public holidays. ☐3.80€. ☎04 74 81 96 82. The museum's collections give a good overview of the evolution and variety of products manufactured in Oyonnax. Exhibits include combs made of boxwood, horn and celluloid, and the machines that made them.

▷ As you leave the museum car park, turn right towards A 404 then S towards Martignat and Montréal-la-Cluse (D 984D).

NEVERS★

CONURBATION 58 915
MICHELIN MAP 319: B-10

Lying in terraces above the River Loire not far from where it meets the Allier, Nevers is the capital of the Nivernais region, known for its fine pottery.

🛈 **Information**: Palais Ducal, r. Sabatier, 58000 Nevers.
☎03 86 68 46 00. www.nevers-tourisme.com.
▶ **Orient Yourself**: There is an excellent view of the old town, dominated by the tower of the cathedral and the graceful silhouette of the ducal palace, from the sandstone bridge that spans the River Loire. The best shopping is along rue St-Étienne, rue François-Mitterrand and rue St-Martin., or at the market on place Carnot on Tuesday, Wednesday and Saturday.

A Bit of History

Pottery and spun glass

Luigi di Gonzaga, the Duke of Mantua's third son who became Duke of Nevers in 1565, brought artists and artisans from Italy.He introduced artistic earthenware in Nevers between 1575 and 1585. The three Italian brothers Conrade, master potters in white and other colours, taught their art to a group of local artisans. Little by little, the shape, the colours and the decorative motifs, which at first reproduced only the Italian models and methods, evolved into a very distinctive local style. At the same time, he developed the glass industry as well as the art of enamelling, which became very fashionable. The town's products – spun glass was generally used in the composition of religious scenes – were sent by boat on the Loire to Orléans and Angers.

By about 1650 the pottery industry was at its height with 12 workshops and 1 800 workers. Today, four workshops continue this traditional craft.

Town Walk

▶ *Start from the Porte du Croux.*

Cathédrale St-Cyr-et-Ste-Julitte★★

This vast basilica displays all the architectural styles from the 10C to the 16C The plan is characterised by two apses at opposite ends of the nave: Romanesque to the west and Gothic to the east. This arrangement, common in the Carolingian period and found in some cathedrals on the banks of the Rhine, is rare in France.

The exterior bristles with buttresses, pillars, flying buttresses and pinnacles; the square tower (52m/171ft high) standing against the south arm of the transept, is flanked by polygonal buttresses.

Inside, the most striking feature is the sheer size of the 13C nave with its triforium and clerestory and the choir encircled by the ambulatory. The Romanesque apse, raised by 13 steps and with oven vaulting, is decorated with a 12C fresco representing Christ surrounded by the symbols of the Evangelists. The stained-glass windows are the work of

Porte du Croux

Ph. Gajic-MICEHLIN

Address Book

🕭 *For coin ranges, see the Legend on the cover flap.*

WHERE TO STAY

🛏🛏**Clos Ste-Marie** – *25 r. Petit-Mouësse.* ☎*03 86 71 94 50. www.clos-sainte-marie.fr. 17 rooms.* ⊐*9€. This building once housed a post office; today you can relax in one of the large, rustic rooms. Good soundproofing. Garden terrace.*

🛏🛏🛏**La Renaissance** – *58470 Magny-Cours, 12km/7.5mi S of Nevers by N 7.* ☎*03 86 58 10 40. www.hotel-la-renaissance.com. Closed 3 Feb-5 Mar, 10-18 Aug, Sun evenings and Mon. 9 rooms.* ⊐*7€. Restaurant*🍴🍴🍴*. In a quiet setting, this hotel has a cosy bar-lounge and a bright dining room extended by a terrace. Comfortable rooms with modern furniture. Traditional cuisine.*

🛏🛏🛏**Holiday Inn** – *58470 Magny-Cours, 12km/7.5mi S of Nevers by N 7.* ☎*03 86 21 22 33. www.ichotelsgroup.com. 70 rooms.* ⊐*10€. Restaurant*🍴🍴*. Close to the Magny-Cours racing circuit, this modern hotel adjoins an old farmhouse where you will find the reception. Large, bright rooms. The restaurant is built around the terrace with its pool.*

WHERE TO EAT

🍴🍴**La Cour Saint-Étienne** – *33 r. St-Étienne.* ☎*03 86 36 74 57. Closed 1-24 Aug, 1-5 Jan, 6-15 Feb, Sun and Mon. The chef of this charming restaurant makes good use of fresh ingredients from the local market to create dishes such as cannellonis of Nivernais goat cheese, knuckles of veal with raisins and so on.*

🍴🍴**Le Morvan** – *28 r. du Petit-Mouësse.* ☎*03 86 61 14 16. Closed 19 Jul-10Aug, 23 Dec-11 Jan, Sat lunchtime and Sun evening. Enjoy a glimpse of the tranquil side of Nivernois life. Food here showcases local ingredients in traditional recipes from the region, such as escargots à la bourguignonne (snails in the Burgundian tradition) and jambon persillé (ham with parsley).*

🍴🍴**La Botte de Nevers** – *r. du Petit-Château.* ☎*03 86 61 16 93. labottede nevers@wanadoo.fr. Closed Sun evenings and Mon. This restaurant close to the Palais Ducal has a traditional décor: tapestries, sturdy beams, stone walls and imposing fireplace. Traditional cooking.*

🍴🍴**La Gabare** – *58000 Challuy, 3km/ 1.9mi S of Nevers by N 7.* ☎*03 86 37 54 23. gabare@chez.com. Closed 15-22 Feb, 15-22 Apr, 26 Jul-17 Aug, Sun, Mon and public holidays. This restaurant has old-fashioned charm with its beams and fireplace. Simple, unpretentious cuisine with fresh ingredients.*

🍴🍴**Jean-Michel Couron** – *21 r. St-Étienne.* ☎*03 86 61 19 28. www.jm-couron.com. Closed 2-17 Jan, 12 Jul-3 Aug, Sun (except evenings Mar-Oct), Tue (except evenings Aug-Feb), Mon. Reservations required. This discreet restaurant has three dining rooms, one of which is crowned by the arches of a former chapel. The inventive cuisine is very popular among gourmets.*

SPORT

Karting de Nevers / Magny-Cours – *Technopôle, 58470 Magny-Cours.* ☎*03 86 21 26 18. Open until dusk.* Try the excitement of motor racing by jumping into a go-kart or something more sophisticated, or go for a spin with an experienced racing driver.

SHOPPING

Au Négus – *96 r. François-Mitterrand.* ☎*03 86 61 06 85. Open Mon-Sat 9am-noon, 2-7pm. Closed public holidays except Easter and Christmas mornings.* This shop is named after the négus, a delicious sweet made with soft caramel coated with crystallised sugar.

Édé– *75 r. François-Mitterrand.* ☎*03 86 61 02 97. Open Tue-Sat 8.45am-12.15pm and 2-7pm, Sun 8.45am-12.15pm.* The famed Nougatine de Nevers was created in this shop, established in 1840. Other sweet temptations include chocolates flavoured with orange, rum or jasmine.

SIT BACK AND RELAX

Au Bistro Gourmand – *sq. de la Résistance.* ☎*03 86 61 45 09. www.au-bistro-gourmand.com. Open noon-2.30pm and 7pm-midnight. Closed Sun evening and Mon.* This smart café's unusual décor includes colourful clowns' portraits on the walls. Jazz concerts twice a month.

five contemporary artists. In 1944, allied bombing damaged the Gothic apse and at the same time revealed a 6C baptistery *(open to visitors)*.

Palais Ducal★

The former home of the dukes of Nevers was begun in the second half of the 15C by Jean de Clamecy, Count of Nevers. It was completed at the end of the 16C by the Clèves and Gonzagasand is a beautiful example of early civil Renaissance architecture. The great round towers at the rear give on to a courtyard that overlooks rue des Ouches. The ochre façade is surmounted by a slate roof and flanked by twin turrets; the canted tower in the centre rising to a small belfry contains the grand staircase; a graceful effect is created by the placing of the windows which follow the spiralling of the stairs. The dormer windows are flanked by caryatids and the chimneys resemble organ pipes. On the left turret a plaque recalls that several princesses of the Nivernais became queens of Poland.

▸ *Pass place Mancini, turn left on rue François-Mitterrand.*

Beffroi

The vast 15C belfry, dominated by a pointed bell-tower, once housed the covered markets and council chamber.

▸ *Right on place Guy-Coquille; then rue du Fer to rue de Nièvre; Turn left.*

Hôtel des Bordes et Rue Creuse

At the top of rue Creuse, the Hôtel des Bordes (17C) was, at the time of its construction, at the edge of the city. The widow of Jean Sobieski, King of Poland, visited here. Along rue Creuse, note the monumental structure of the Mutuelle de la Nievre (19C) and the Hotel Marmigny (15-16C).

▸ *At the corner of rue des Francs-Bourgeois, turn right.*

Église St-Étienne★

This beautiful Romanesque church, which once belonged to a priory of Cluny, has a remarkable purity of style. It was built from 1063 to 1097 at the behest of Guil-laume I, Count of Nevers. The chevet, best seen from rue du Charnier, has a magnificent tiered arrangement of apse and apsidals. The transept tower, of which only the base remains, was destroyed together with the two towers surmounting the façade, at the time of the French Revolution.

Apart from the capitals in the ambulatory, the interior is devoid of sculpture but its attraction lies in its fine proportions and the golden colour of the stone. The six bays of the nave are covered by barrel vaulting with transverse arches; there is groined vaulting in the aisles. A Romanesque altar stands in the chancel *(restored)*. The row of windows beneath the vault is of impressive boldness.

Église St-Pierre and Porte de Paris

This 17C church houses a fine altar; the frescoes await restoration. The monumental portal dates from 1676.

The triumphal Porte de Paris was built in the 18C to commemorate the victory of Fontenoy; verses by Voltaire in praise of Louis XV are engraved on it.

▸ *Retrace your steps to get back to rue François-Mitterrand, the turn right on place St-Sébastien.*

Hôtel Flamen d'Assigny

Note at number 1 one of the loveliest hôtels particuliers in Nevers (18C), with its rococo-style facade.

▸ *Continue along rue St-Martin.*

Chapelle Ste-Marie

This is the former chapel, now deconsecrated, of the 7th convent of the Visitandines founded in France. The **façade**★, of Louis XIII style, is covered with Italian-type ornamentation: niches, entablatures, columns and pilasters.

▸ *Rue St-Martin (Maison du Prieur at no 5), rue du 14-Juillet and rue de la Porte-du-Croux lead back to the Porte du Croux.*

Porte du Croux★

This handsome square tower gateway, built in 1393, is one of the last remnants of the town's fortifications. It houses the **Musée Archéologique du Nivernais**

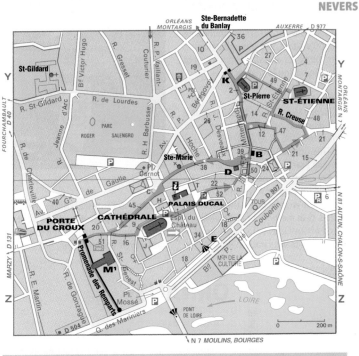

(*open by request only*) which has Greek, Roman and Romanesque sculptures.

▶ *Follow the rampart walk.*

Promenade des Remparts

A well-conserved section of the town walls, built by Pierre de Courtenay in the 12C, stretches from the Porte du Croux southwards to the Loire. Several of the original towers (Tours du Hâvre, St-Révérien and Gogin) are still standing. From quai des Mariniers, there is a fine view of the Pont de Loire.

Musée Municipal Frédéric-Blandin

Closed to 2008 for renovation work. The museum, in an old abbey, has a fine collection of Nevers pottery★, as well delicate enamels and spun glass.

▶ *Return to the crossroads and turn right onto rue des Jacobins.*

Excursion

Circuit de Nevers-Magny-Cours

13km/8mi S. ⏱*Open daily 8am-8pm except during race meetings.* ☎*03 86 21 80 00. www.magnyf1.com.*
Between Magny-Cours and St-Parize-le-Châtel, this race track inaugurated in 1960 is the stage for many spectacular automobile and motorcycle races, including the prestigious Grand Prix de France Formula 1 and the Grand Prix de France

Moto. The site, which can accommodate 110 000 visitors, has been developing over the years and offers a variety of recreational and tourist facilities.

Musée Ligier F1★

♿ ⏱ *Open May-Oct 2-6pm. Times liable to modification, call for information.* ∞7€ *(children 4€).* ☎03 86 21 80 00.
Kids This unique museum devoted to Formula 1 racing displays the cars which made history for the Ligier team. The models on exhibit have all raced and some have won trophies; they bear the initials JS in memory of Jo Schlesser, a friend of Guy Ligier who died in an accident at the Essarts track in Rouen.

Musée Ligier F1

The other section of the building is reserved for **temporary exhibits**. There is a **shop** and a **cinema**, both devoted to car and motorcycle competition.

ORNANS ★

POPULATION 4 037

MICHELIN MAP 321: G-4

Ornans' history, number of inhabitants and industrial activity justifiably make it the small capital of the Loue Valley that inspired the town's most famous native, the painter Gustave Courbet.

🄸 **Information**: 7 r. P.-Vernier, 25290 Ornans. ☎03 81 62 21 50. www.pays-ornans.com.

▶ **Orient Yourself**: The stretch of river flowing between a double row of old houses on piles is one of the prettiest scenes in the Jura. See it from the Grand Pont, the bridge just downstream of the old town.

A Bit of History

Gustave Courbet

The great painter Gustave Courbet, master of French Realism, was born in Ornans in 1819. His parents were wine-growers and wanted their son to become a notary, but he abandoned his law books for the painter's easel, teaching himself by studying the paintings in the Louvre. His work provoked a storm of both praise and criticism. He was strongly attached to Ornans and found most of his subjects in and around his birthplace. Landscapes such as *Château d'Ornans* and *Source de la Loue* capture the essence of nature in the Jura. The subjects of his portraits were friends or members of his family; *L'Après-Dînée à Ornans* and *Un enterrement à Ornans* are particularly interesting as historical documents. He excelled

at psychological portraits, especially of women, such as *L'Exilée polonaise*.

Sights

Grand Pont

This great bridge is the most famous spot in Ornans, with its picturesque **view**★ of the town's old houses reflected in the clear waters of the River Loue.

Church

The church was rebuilt in the 16C, retaining only the lower part of the 12C bell-tower from the original Romanesque building. The dome and the lantern turret date from the 17C. The church was funded by the Chancellor and the Cardinal of Granvelle, who furthermore ensured that it received a regular contribution for 30 years from the sovereign, in the

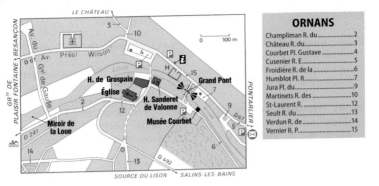

form of revenue from the sale of 10 loads of salt shipped from Salins every week.

Miroir de la Loue

The pretty stretch of water seen from the bridge downstream of the old town is known as the Loue Mirror. Church, town and cliffs are reflected in the water's silvery surface.

Musée Courbet

Open Jul-Aug 10am-12.30pm, 1.30-6pm; Sep-Jun 10am-noon, 2-6pm. Closed Tue Nov-Mar, 1 Jan, 1 May, 1 Nov, 25 Dec. 3€ (during summer exhibitions: 6€). 03 81 62 23 30. www.musee-courbet.com.

The museum is in the house where Courbet was born, a beautiful 18C building which used to be the Hôtel Hébert. There are several works by the artist on display (Jura landscapes, drawings, sculptures), as well as others by his students and friends. There are also many objects evoking 19C artistic life in Paris and in the Franche-Comté. Note in particular the *Autoportrait à Ste-Pélagie*, his famous self-portrait painted in prison after his adventures during the Paris Commune of 1871, and the beautiful landscapes *Château Chillon* and *La Papeterie d'Ornans sur le ruisseau de Bonneille*. The rooms downstairs are used for temporary exhibitions.

Muséee du Costume Comtois

Open Jul-Aug daily except Tue 2-6pm (last entrance 15min before closing); Jun and Sep Sun 2-6pm. 2.50€. 03 81 62 18 48.

Temporarily located in the former Chapel of the Visitation, this regional costume museum features an exceptional collection.

Riverside living

Excursions

Point de vue du Château★

2km/1.2mi N up a steep narrow road.

There are fine view of Ornans and the Loue Valley from this viewpoint.

Musée-Fromagerie de Trepot

Open Jun-Aug. Guided tours (45min) Jul-Aug 10.30am-noon, 2-6pm, Sun and public holidays 2-6pm; Jun Sun and public holidays 2-6pm. 3.50€. 03 81 86 71 06.

Founded in 1818, this cheesemaking facility used to turn out four types of Comté made from milk supplied by local farmers. Production stopped in 1977, but the tools and facility are now a small museum, with an interesting audiovisual presentation.

Dino-Zoo★

At Charbonnières-les-Sapins. Open May-Aug 10am-7pm (May-Jun 6pm). Rest of the year times vary. Closed Nov-Feb. 9€ (children 8€). 03 81 59 27 05. www.dino-zoo.com.

Kids Learn all about life for prehistoric man, enter the world of the dinosaurs through life-size plastic models or just enjoy a picnic in the grounds.

G. Magnin-MICHELIN

Château de Cléron

Driving Tour

35km/22mi (Ornans-Quingey) – 3hrS.

This route follows charming little roads along the banks of the Loue for the most part, but which wander away from the river in some places. The trip is at its most picturesque between Cléron and the confluence of the Loue and the Lison.

Leave Ornans on D 67 W; after 2.5km/1.5mi take D 101 to the left.

Chapelle de Notre-Dame-du-Chêne

The chapel can be seen from D 101. It was built to celebrate a miraculous revelation in 1803, when a young girl from the area claimed that there was a statue of the Virgin Mary in the trunk of a certain oak tree. The tree was opened up, and an old terracotta Madonna was indeed found inside, the tree bark having grown over it. The statuette, kept in the chapel, has drawn pilgrims ever since. A bronze Virgin stands where the oak once grew.

Miroir de Scey

This is the name given to a beautiful meander in the Loue, where the trees and plants on the river banks, and the ruins of a fortress, Châtel-St-Denis, are reflected in the river's waters (*miroir* means mirror).

Cléron

From the bridge over the Loue a well-preserved 14C-16C **château**★ (*open Jul-Aug daily except Mon, tour of the outside 2.30-6pm; armour exhibition at farm, Wed and weekends, 2.30-6pm 3€; 03 81 62 19 03*) comes into sight downstream. With its reflection in the river and surrounded by its grounds, it makes a beautiful picture. There is a pretty view of the valley upstream. There are three viewpoints (*car parks*) between Amondans and the confluence of the Loue and the Lison, all at the edge of cliffs overlooking the river valley which is narrow and deserted at this point.

Belvédère de Gouille-Noire

There is a fine view of the Amondans stream directly below. This small Loue tributary lows between two spurs.

Address Book

⚲For coin ranges, see the Legend on the cover flap.

WHERE TO STAY AND EAT

⊜**L'Auberge paysanne** – *25580 Vernierfontaine, 18 km W of Ornans by D 492 Rte. de Saules then D 392 and D 27E. ☏03 81 60 05 21. www.auberge-paysanne.fr. Closed Dec-Jan, Wed and Thu, Mon-Fri lunch Nov-Mar. Reservations recommended.* Pleasant auberge with a country dining room – exposed beams, fireplace and tools figure in the décor. In summer, eat on the charming terrace in the courtyard. In addition, there are four comfortable guestrooms.

⊜**Le Courbet** – *34 r. Pierre-Vernier. ☏03 81 62 10 15. www.restaurantlecourbet.com. Closed 16 Feb-11 Mar, Sun evenings from Nov-Mar, Mon evenings except Jul-Aug and Tue.* Located near the Courbet home, this restaurant is decorated with numerous reproductions of the artist's work. In summer, a pretty terrace borders the Loue River. Contemporary cuisine incorporates fresh market ingredients.

⊜**Hôtel de France** – *r. P.-Vernier. ☏03 81 62 24 44. www.hoteldefrance-ornans.com. Closed 8-21 Nov and 20 Dec-11 Jan. 26 rooms ⊜9€. Restaurant⊜⊜⊜.* Handsome country residence standing on the slope of a hill, opposite the bridge spanning the River Loue. The rooms giving onto the garden are more peaceful. The dining room is rustic in style, with exposed beams, fireplace and wood panelling.

Belvédère de la Piquette★

15min round trip on foot from D 135.
🚶Follow a wide path for about 100m/110yd, then take the path on the right; turn right at the edge of the cliff.
There is a **view** of a meander in the Loue, as it swirls around a wooded spur between steep banks.

Belvédère du Moulin-Sapin★

Beside D 135.
There is a beautiful **view** of the peaceful Lison Valley. The bridge crosses the Lison just after it flows into the Loue, in a lovely calm **setting**★. The source of the Lison near Nans-sous-Sainte-Anne (⚲*see NANS-SOUS-SAINTE-ANNE*) is one of the most famous sights in the Jura. Soon, the old Châtillon forge comes into sight from the road. Upstream of the dam, there is a pretty view of some little wooded islands.

Quingey

A path, bordered with plane trees, runs along the south bank of the Loue; the view of the little market town on the opposite bank reflected in the water is especially enchanting in the early morning.

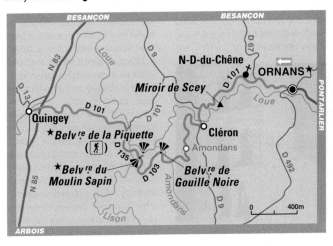

PARAY-LE-MONIAL★★

POPULATION 9 191
MICHELIN MAP 320: E-11

Paray-le-Monial, cradle of the worship of the Sacred Heart of Jesus, is a city of art: its Romanesque basilica, where a music festival is held in summer, is a magnificent example of the architecture of Cluny.

- **Information**: 25 av. Jean-Paul-II, 71600 Paray-le-Monial. ☎03 85 81 10 92. www.paraylemonial.fr.
- ▶ **Orient Yourself:** Paray-le-Monial is on the boundary between the Charollais and Brionnais regions, by the banks of the River Bourbince, a tributary of the Loire. For a good introduction to the town, take the guided tour offered by the tourist office.
- **Don't Miss:** The Basilica of the Sacred Heart, considered to be one of the finest examples of religious architecture from the Cluny period.

A Bit of History

Devotion to the Sacred Heart

The daughter of a royal notary in Veros-vres-en-Charollais, **Marguerite-Marie Alacoque** entered the convent of the Visitation at Paray-le-Monial as a novice in 1671. From 1673 onwards, Sister Marguerite-Marie received a series of visitations that continued up to her death. She wrote down the revelations made to her, thus initiating the worship of the Sacred Heart in France. She died on 17 October 1690.

In 1864, Sister Marguerite-Marie was beatified. In 1873, the first great pilgrimage in Paray-le-Monial took place in the presence of 30 000 people, and the decision was made to dedicate France to the Sacred Heart of Jesus. This event was linked to the vow made in 1870 to build a church dedicated to the Sacred Heart; this was the basilica of Sacré-Cœur

which now stands on the hill of Montmartre. Pilgrimages have been repeated each year since 1873. Sister Marguerite-Marie was canonised in 1920.

Many religious orders have communities at Paray-le-Monial which has become one of the great centres of Christianity.

Sights

Basilique du Sacré-Cœur★★

On the right bank of the Bourbince stands the church; it was originally dedicated to the Virgin Mary but in 1875 it was raised to the level of a basilica and consecrated to the Sacred Heart.

The church was built without interruption between 1092 and 1109 under the direction of St Hugues, Abbot of Cluny, and restored in the 19C and 20C; it is a model on a smaller scale of the famous Benedictine abbey at Cluny. Only the architectural style is similar; the builders eschewed decorative splendour in favour of abstract beauty, which is conducive to contemplation. The rare sculptures make use of the geometric motifs found in Islamic art, probably discovered by St Hugues during visits to Spain.

Exterior – Two buttressed square towers surmount the narthex, with four storeys of windows. The right-hand tower, built in the early 11C, has plain decoration; the other later one is more richly decorated. The octagonal tower over the transept crossing was restored in 1856.

One of the Basilica's square towers

Ph. Gajic-MICHELIN

Address Book

For coin ranges, see the Legend on the cover flap.

WHERE TO STAY AND EAT

Hôtel de la Basilique – *18 r. de la Visitation. ☎03 85 81 11 13. www. hotelbasilique.com. Open 20 Mar-31 Oct.* The same family has run this place for five generations. Meals are served in a pleasant dining room with a traditional country décor. Several simple rooms, some with a view of the basilica.

La Poste – *71600 Poisson, 8km/5mi S of Paray-le-Monial by D 34. ☎03 85 81 10 72. Closed Feb, 3-19 Oct, Mon and Tue except evenings in Jul-Aug.* This restaurant in a stone cottage consists of a dining room extended by a veranda and a summer terrace. Interesting menus. The comfortable guestroom with waxed flooring and cherry wood furniture are housed in a restored 1900 building nearby.

Chambre d'Hôte M. et Mme Mathieu – *Sermaize, 71600 Poisson, 12.5km/7.8mi SE of Paray-le-Monial by D 34 then D 458 heading for St-Julien-de-*

Civry. ☎03 85 81 06 10. mp.mathieu@ laposte.net. Closed 11 Nov-15 Mar. 5 rooms. Meals. This 14C hunting lodge stands proudly in its garden, adorned by a round turret and a square courtyard bursting with flowers. An old-fashioned spiral staircase will take you to the personalised rooms featuring parquet flooring, period furniture and a fireplace. The garden looks out over the surrounding countryside.

For coin ranges, see the Legend on the cover flap.

COUNTRY INN IN TOWN

La Gare – *79 av. du Gén.-de-Gaulle, Digoin. ☎03 85 53 03 04. www. hoteldelagare.fr. Closed Jan, Wed except Jul-Aug and Sun evenings Oct-Jun. 8 rooms. 8€.* A typical country inn extending a warm and friendly welcome. The cooking is thoughtful with a strong regional touch. As for the rooms, they are gradually being renovated to make your stay here even more agreeable.

Enter the basilica by the north arm of the transept; the beautiful Romanesque doorway is decorated with floral and geometric designs.

Interior – One is struck by the height of the building (22m/72ft in the main nave) and the simplicity of its decoration, characteristic of the art of Cluny. Huysmans (French novelist, 1848-1907) saw the symbol of the Trinity in the three naves, three bays supporting above the great arches three arcades surmounted by three windows. The choir and its ambulatory with three small apses – the Gallery of the Angels – make an elegant ensemble. The capitals of the delicate columns are a typical example of 12C Burgundian art. The oven-vaulted apse is decorated with a 14C fresco, representing a benedictory Christ in Majesty, which was brought to light only in 1935.

Musée Eucharistique du Hiéron

Open Tue-Sun 10am-noon, 2-6pm. Closed Jan to mid Mar. 4€. ☎03 85 81 36 98. www.musee-hieron.com.

This museum of sacred art houses a varied collection: 13C to 18C Italian art including works from the schools of Florence (Donatello, Bramante), Venice, Rome and Bologna; a few works from Flanders and Germany (engravings by Lucas of Leyden and Dürer); and some from from France, particularly a very beautiful 12C **tympanum**★ from the Brionnais priory at Anzy-le-Duc. In the turmoil of 1791 the doorway was taken to Château d'Arcy and then given to the museum.

Espace Saint-Jean

In the former house of the pages of Cardinal de Bouillon, this welcome centre for pilgrims has a film introduction to Paray-le-Monial, as well as several objects of convent life dating from the time of St Marguerite-Marie.

Parc des Chapelains

Open 9.30am-noon, 2-6pm; Sun 10am-6pm. Closed Jan. It is in this large park, containing Stations of the Cross, that the great pilgrimage services take place. A diorama in the park depicts the life of St Marguerite-Marie.

Chapelle des Apparitions
&. ⏱*Open 6.30am-9pm.*
It was in this little chapel that St Marguerite-Marie had her main revelations. The silver-gilt reliquary in the right-hand chapel holds the saint's relics.

Excursions

Digoin
11km/6.8mi W.
This peaceful town, on the east bank of the Loire at the junction of two canals, is popular with anglers, ramblers and boaters. The early-19C **canal-bridge** was built 50 years before the Briare Bridge.

Château de Digoine
15km/9.4mi N on D 974.
⏱*OpenJul-Aug daily 2-7pm; May-Jun and Sep-Oct weekends and public holidays only.* ⬤*6.50€ (park 3.50€).* ☎*03 85 47 96 44. www.chateaudedigoine.com.*
The main entrance to the château, built in the 18C on the site of a defensive castle, is fronted by a courtyard with a wrought-iron gate. On each side, two pavilions form the wings of the main building. The large park has a lake and there are three marked footpaths to guide you around.

PONTARLIER
POPULATION 18 360
MICHELIN MAP 321: I-5

Pontarlier, once famous for the manufacture of absinthe, an aperitif with a very high alcohol content banned in 1915, is today a popular resort both for summer holidays and winter sports.

🛈 **Information**: 14 bis r. de la Gare, 25300 Pontarlier.
☎03 81 46 48 33. www.ville-pontarlier.fr.
▶ **Orient Yourself**: Pontarlier, the capital of the Haut-Doubs, lies near the Swiss border at the foot of the Jura mountains, with forest all around.

A Bit of History

The terrors of 1639 and 1736
During the Ten Years War, mercenary troops on the French payroll spread fear and destruction throughout the Franche-Comté. On 26 January 1639, Pontarlier surrendered after a four-day siege led by Bernard de Saxe-Weimar's Swedish forces. The town was pillaged, burned, and over 400 people died. However, it didn't become became part of France until 1678, when Franche-Comté was officially annexed under the Nijmegen Treaty.
During the 18C, Pontarlier was damaged several times by fire, which caught hold quickly as the town's buildings were largely made of wood. The worst of the fires occurred on 31 August 1736, destroying half the town. Pontarlier was reconstructed to plans by Querret.

Sights

Ancienne chapelle des Annonciades
This chapel, all that remains of the Annunciade convent, was built in 1612. The **doorway**★ dates from the beginning of the 18C. The chapel, now deconsecrated, has been turned into an exhibition centre.

Porte St-Pierre
This triumphal arch was erected in 1771, based on plans by Arçon, to celebrate the reconstruction of the city; the upper section, topped with a small bell-tower, was added in the 19C. It resembles the Porte St-Martin in Paris.

Église St-Bénigne
The church was rebuilt in the 17C and then restored, but it still has an original 15C Flamboyant side doorway. This curi-

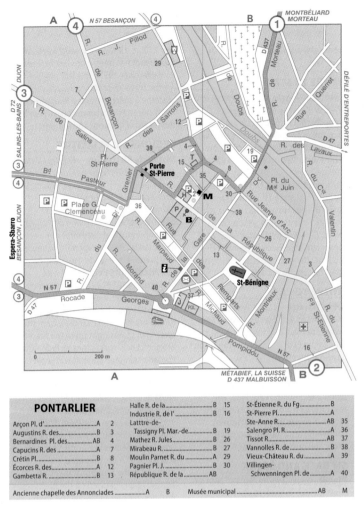

ous building has a blind façade on its right side, built after the 1736 fire to make the church blend in with the new houses round the square. The belfry-porch is in the style of mountain churches designed to withstand heavy snowfall. Inside are two particularly interesting paintings either side of the chancel: that to the left, which depicts Christ surrounded by angels bearing the instruments of the Passion; and that to the right, known as *The Miracle of Lactation* (the Virgin Mary is seen pressing her breast, from which a stream of milk flows to wet the lips of St Bernard). Note also the 1754 pulpit and 1758 organ case, skilfully carved by the Guyon brothers of Pontarlier.

Musée Municipal

 ♿ 🕐*Open daily except Tue 10am-noon, 2-6pm, Sat-Sun and public holidays 2-6pm.* 🚫*Closed 1 Jan, 1 May, 1 Nov, 25 Dec.* ♿*3.30€.* ☎ *03 81 38 82 14. www.ville-pontarlier.fr.*

The museum, housed in what was a bourgeois home, built in the 16C and later modified several times, is devoted to local history, 19C and 20C Comtois paintings (including *Autoportrait au chien* by Courbet), 18C faïence, and objects related to the history of absinthe such as posters, engravings, decorated jars and so on.

Address Book

For coin ranges, see the Legend on the cover flap.

WHERE TO STAY

Hôtel St-Pierre – 3 pl. St-Pierre. ☎03 81 46 50 80. www.hotel-st-pierre-pontarlier.fr. Closed Mon except holidays. 21 rooms. ☐6€. Restaurant☐. Newly renovated hostelry facing the Porte Saint-Pierre. Rooms come in a variety of sizes and prices, all tastefully decorated. Most face the street, but have double glazing to guard against the noise.

Villages Hôtel – 68 r. Salins. ☎03 81 46 71 78. www.villageshotel.fr. 53 rooms. ☐7.50€. Restaurant☐. A convenient base for cross-country skiers, this hotel (renovated from top to bottom) offers chic rooms in chalet-style.

WHERE TO EAT

Pic Assiette – 11 r. St-Paul. ☎03 81 39 06 42. Closed Aug, Sun and Mon. The owners of this place lived for a long time in the Pacific; shades of the tropics flavour both menu and décor.

L'Alchimie – 1 av. de l'Armée-de-l'Est. ☎03 81 46 65 89. www.lalchimie.fr. Closed 19-25 Apr, 1-15 Jul, Wed. This restaurant on a road opposite the Nestlé factories serves inventive cuisine combining regional products with exotic flavours and hints of Asia.

SIT BACK AND RELAX

Pfaadt – 23 pl. St-Pierre. ☎03 81 39 01 83. Open Tue-Sat 7am-12.30pm, 2.15-7pm, Sun 7.30am-12.30pm. Closed 2 weeks in Sep. Pfaadt has been a dessert fixture in Pontarlier since 1953. Especially popular are the three-chocolate mousse, the absinthe ganache (shaped like a green fairy) and the macaroons. Take a seat in the pleasant tearoom and indulge...

REGIONAL SPECIALITIES

Distillerie Pierre-Guy – 49 r. des Lavaux. ☎03 81 39 04 70. www.pontarlier-anis.com. Open Tue-Fri 8am-noon, 2-6pm, Sat 8am-noon; visit 9-11am, 2.30-5pm. Closed 1 week mid-Oct and 1 week beginning of Jan. This is one of the last two non-industrial distilleries remaining in Pontarlier. See how apéritifs, liqueurs and brandies are made. Fascinating.

Les Fils d'Émile Pernot – 44 r. de Besançon – ☎03 81 39 04 28. Open Mon-Fri 8.30am-noon, 2-6pm. Closed public holidays. Learn all about the manufacture of liqueurs and brandies, from the picking of plants right up to the finished product. Local specialities include Vieux Pontarlier (aniseed apéritif) and Sapin (liqueur made with pine flowers).

Fromagerie de Doubs – 1 r. de la Fruitière, 25300 Doubs. ☎03 81 39 05 21. Open Mon-Sat 8.30am-noon, 3-7pm, Sun and public holidays 9am-5pm. This cheese-making factory will show you how local cheeses like Comté, Morbier and Mont d'Or are prepared and matured in the traditional manner. Tastings are organised on the premises. And don't forget to stop at the shop.

Excursions

Cluse de Joux★★
4km/2.5mi S along N 57.
See Château de JOUX Excursions.

Grand Taureau★★
11km/7mi E. Leave Pontarlier S along N 57 and turn left onto a minor road climbing the Montagne du Larmont.
This is the highest point (1 323m/4 340ft) of the Larmont mountains, less than 1km/0.5mi from the Franco-Swiss border. The **view**★ from here stretches over Pontarlier and the Jura plateaus to the west. The Larmont is equipped with all the necessary facilities for winter sports holidays. For a full panorama, continue to the very top.

▶ *Leave the car in front of the little chalet at the end of the road. .*

Panorama★★
Climb up the slope which borders the chalet to the right and walk a little way along the ridge overlooking the Morte Valley, continuation of the Val de Travers
The all round view takes in the parallel mountain ridges of the Jura, as far as the last line of mountains looming on the other side of the Swiss border, from the Chasseral to Mont Tendre. The Berne Alps can be seen in the distance.

PONTIGNY★

POPULATION 748
MICHELIN MAP 319: F-4

This little village on the edge of the River Serein is celebrated for its former abbey, the second daughter house of Cîteaux, founded in 1114. Whereas Cîteaux is now in ruins, the abbey of Pontigny has preserved its church intact.

- **Information**: 22 r. Paul-Desjardin, 89230 Pontigny. ☎03 86 47 47 03. pontignytourisme.free.fr.
- **Orient Yourself**: As you approach the village from the north along the RN 77, the vast abbey church seems to loom out of the poplars that line the River Serein.
- **Don't Miss**: The classical concerts held here in summer and, even more magical, the occasional candlelit evening visits.

A Bit of History

The foundation

At the beginning of the year 1114 twelve monks with the Abbot Hugues de Mâcon at their head were sent from Cîteaux by St Stephen to found a monastery on the banks of the Serein, in a large clearing at a place known as Pontigny. The abbey was situated on the boundaries of three bishoprics (Auxerre, Sens and Langres) and three provinces (counties of Auxerre, Tonnerre and Champagne) and thus from its beginning benefited from the protection and the generosity of six different masters. Thibault the Great, Count of Champagne, was the abbey's most generous benefactor: in 1150 he gave the abbot the means to build a larger church than that existing at the time (the chapel of St Thomas), which had become too small for the monks. He enclosed the abbey buildings with a wall (4m/13ft high) sections of which still remain.

A refuge for archbishops

During the Middle Ages Pontigny served as a refuge for ecclesiastics fleeing from persecution in England; three archbishops of Canterbury found asylum here. **Thomas à Becket,** Primate of England, came to Pontigny in 1164 after incurring the wrath of Henry II. He returned to his country in 1170 but was murdered in his cathedral two years later.
Stephen Langton took refuge at Pontigny from 1208 to 1213 because of a disagreement with King John.

Edmund Rich, St Edmund of Abingdon, lived in Pontigny in saintly exile for several years until his death in 1240, when he was buried in the abbey church. He was canonised in 1246 and is venerated throughout the region (known locally as St Edme).

The decades of Pontigny

Abandoned during the French Revolution, the abbey served as a quarry for the nearby villages up to 1840. The ruins were then bought back by the Archbishop of Sens and put at the disposition of the Congregation of Missionary Fathers founded by Father Muard (&see *Le MORVAN Excursion, Abbaye de la Pierre-qui-Vire*) who restored the church and other buildings.

At the start of the 20C, the fathers were expelled and the property was bought by the philosopher, Paul Desjardins (1859-1940), who organised the famous Décades which brought together the most eminent personalities of the period including Thomas Mann, André Gide, TS Eliot and François Mauriac, who had lengthy literary conversations in the celebrated avenue of arbours.

Abbaye★

Opposite the War Memorial in the village, an 18C entrance flanked by small pavilions, opens into a shady avenue which leads past the conventual buildings to the abbey church.

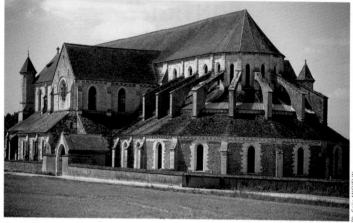

Ph. Gajic-MICHELIN

The southern façade

Church★

🕐 *Open summer 9am-7pm, winter 10am-5pm.* 🔄 *Guided tours by request.* ☎*03 86 47 54 99. abbayedepontigny.eu.*
Built in the second half of the 12C in the transitional Gothic style by Thibault, Count of Champagne, this church is austere, in conformity with the Cistercian rule. Of impressive size (108m/354ft long inside, 117m/384ft with the porch, and 52m/171ft wide at the transept), it is almost as large as Notre-Dame in Paris.

Exterior – The porch, festooned with arcades standing on consoles and small columns, takes up the whole width of the façade. Closed at the sides, it is pierced by twin, double-semicircular bays and a central doorway with a low arch. The façade, decorated with a tall lancet window and two blind arcades, ends in a pointed gable with a small oculus. The sides of the church are typically bare; no belfry breaks the long line of the roof. The transept and the aisles are of a great simplicity; flat-sided buttresses and flying buttresses support the chevet and the north side.

Interior – The long, two-storey nave has seven bays; it is the earliest Cistercian nave with pointed vaulting to have survived to the present day. The perspective of the nave is interrupted by the wooden screen of the monks' choir.

The squat side aisles of groined vaulting contrast with the more unrestricted nave. The transept, lit at either end by a rose window, is very characteristic with its six rectangular chapels opening on to each arm of the transept.

The choir, rebuilt at the end of the 12C, is very graceful with its ambulatory and its 11 apsidal chapels. The crocketed capitals of the monolithic columns are more elaborate than those of the nave where water-lily leaves, of somewhat rudimentary design, constitute the main decorative element.

At the end of the choir under a heavy baldaquin is the 18C shrine of St Edmund; the earlier Renaissance wooden shrine, is kept in one of the apsidal chapels.

The beautiful **stalls**★, the transept grille and the organ case date from the end of the 17C. The organ loft, which is heavily ornamented, the choir parclose and the altar date from the end of the 18C.

Monastery buildings

All that is left of the 12C Cistercian buildings is the wing of the lay brothers' building; the rubblestone and delicate Tonnerre stone harmonise well in the façade, which is supported by buttresses.

Of the other buildings, only the southern gallery of the cloisters, rebuilt in the 17C, remains today (*access via the church*).

POUILLY-EN-AUXOIS

POPULATION 1 502
MICHELIN MAP 320: H-6

This small town lies at the foot of Mont de Pouilly, at the exit of the tunnel through which the Canal de Bourgogne flows from the Rhône basin to the Seine basin. It is the ideal starting point for excursions in the surrounding area.

Information: Le Colombier, 21320 Pouilly-En-Auxois. ☎03 80 90 74 24. www.pouilly-auxois.com.

A Bit of Geography

Watershed line

All the water streaming down the southern slopes of Mont Pouilly runs to the Mediterranean sea; all the water streaming down the northern slopes head for the River Seine and the North sea, whereas all the water flowing on the western slopes are directed to the River Loire. Thus the relatively low Mont Pouilly (alt 559m/1 834ft) marks the watershed line between three main river basins: the Rhône, the Seine and the Loire.

Excursions

St-Thibault

17km/10.6mi NW.
The village is named after St Theobald, whose relics were presented to the local priory in the 13C. The church★ (◐*open mid-Mar to mid-Nov 9.30am-6pm; visit of*

chapel of St Gilles by request, ☎*03 80 64 66 07 or 03 80 64 62 63*) has a graceful five-sided **choir**★ and a main **doorway**★ which is considered among the most beautiful examples of 13C Burgundian architecture. Also of note are the altar **furnishings**★, including two carved wooden retables representing episodes from the life of St Theobald. The oldest part of the church is St Giles' Chapel.

Châteauneuf-en-Auxois★

12km/7.5mi SE.
This old fortified market town, in a picturesque **spot**★, is famous for its fortress, which commanded the road from Dijon to Autun and the surrounding plain. Another château open to visitors lies nearby.

Château de Châteauneuf★

◐*Open daily except Mon 10am-noon, 2-7pm (mid-Sep to mid-May 6pm). Closed 1 Jan, 1 May, 1 and 11 Nov, 25 Dec.* ⌷*5€.* ☎*03 80 49 21 89.*

Châteauneuf and the Burgundy Canal

S. Sauvignier-MICHELIN

Address Book

For coin ranges, see the Legend on the cover flap.

WHERE TO STAY

Chambre d'Hôte Mme Bagatelle – r. des Moutons, 21320 Châteauneuf-en-Auxois. ☎03 80 49 21 00. www. chezbagatelle.fr. Closed Feb school holidays. Reservations required. 4 rooms. Attractively restored sheepfold in the heart of a small village. The comfortable rooms exude great charm with their stone walls, beams and wooden furnishings. The two rooms featuring a mezzanine are particularly suitable for families. Not to be missed.

Chambre d'Hôte Péniche Lady A – Canal de Bourgogne, 21320 Vandenesse-en-Auxois, 7km/4.3mi SE of Pouilly-en-Auxois by D 970 and D 18. ☎03 80 49 26 96. www.peniche-lady-a.com. Closed Dec-Jan. 3 rooms. Meals. Three small bright cabins await you on this barge anchored along the quays of the Canal de Bourgogne. The deck has pretty views of Châteauneuf, its castle and the rolling countryside.

Hostellerie du Château Ste-Sabine – 21320 Ste-Sabine, 8km/5mi SE of Pouilly by N 81, D 977bis then D 970. ☎03 80 49 22 01. chste-sabine.ifrance.fr. Closed 3 Jan-25 Feb. 30 rooms. 10€. Restaurant. This superb 17C château of Renaissance inspiration is approached by a huge park. Inside the rooms, simplicity and sobriety are the key words. Fine vista of the lake. Summer pool. Animals roam freely on the property.

WHERE TO EAT

Le Grill du Castel – 21320 Châteauneuf-en-Auxois. ☎03 80 49 26 82. Although the fire in the chimney is extinguished during the dog days of summer, the grill produces flavourful grilled meats (with mustards made locally) for year-round enjoyment.

SHOPPING

Maison de Pays de l'Auxois Sud – Le Seuil. ☎03 80 90 75 86. Open winter Mon-Fri 10am-noon, 1.30-6pm, Sat 10am-6pm, Sun 3-6pm; summer daily 10am-7pm, Sun 3-7pm. Closed 25 Dec and 1 Jan. As its name indicates, this shop features the wonderful products of the Auxois region. You'll find a wide assortment of gourmet treats–from gingerbread and terrines to wines and liqueurs–as well as the work of local artisans.

In the 12C, the lord of Chaudenay, whose ruined castle is on an attractive site in Chaudenay-le-Château *(6km/3.5mi S),* built this fortress for his son. It was enlarged and refurbished at the end of the 15C in the Flamboyant Gothic style. The impressive structure, enclosed by thick walls flanked by massive towers, is separated from the village by a moat. There used to be two fortified gates; now a single drawbridge, flanked by huge round towers, gives access to the courtyard and the two main buildings.

Although partially ruined, the **guest pavilion** has retained its handsome ogee-mullioned windows. The **grand logis** in the other wing with its high dormer windows has been restored: the guard-room is impressive for its size as well as its huge chimney with a coat of arms. The chapel (1481) has been carefully restored to the advantage of the frescoes and the replica of Philippe Pot's tomb (the original is in the Louvre). The rooms upstairs were decorated in the 17C and 18C. Next to the Charles I of Vienna (1597-1659) room, in the keep, is a room which has kept its original brick partition (15C). From the round room, there is a view over the Morvan foothills and the Burgundy Canal.

The vast guard-room, the chapel (1481) and several rooms decorated in the 17C and 18C are open to visitors. From the circular chamber there is a panoramic view of the Morvan plain.

Château de Commarin★

8km/5mi N of Châteauneuf along D 977bis. Open Apr-Nov daily. Guided tours (30min) 10am-noon, 2-6pm. 6.50€. ☎03 80 49 23 67. www.commarin.com. This graceful building, a 14C castle remodelled in the 17C and 18C, contains some fine 16C **tapestries**★ with incredibly well-preserved colours..

LA PUISAYE

MICHELIN MAP 319: B-5
INTRODUCTION REMANIÉE

The Puisaye region has a reputation for being monotonous and even austere. The uniformity is however only superficial and the visitor will find a variety of scenery: forests dotted with ponds, wooded hills and meadows graced with the silhouettes of the many châteaux (Ratilly, St-Fargeau, St-Sauveur and St-Amand) in the area.

🛈 **Information**: pl. du Château, 89520 Saint-Sauveur-en-Puisaye.
☎ 03 86 45 61 31. www.cc-stsauveur.fr.

▸ **Orient Yourself**: The books of Colette (&see below) are rich in poetic descriptions of this area, her birthplace.

A Bit of History

Pottery in the Puisaye

The soil of the Puisaye contains uncrushed flint coated with white or red clays which were used in the Middle Ages by the potters of St-Amand, Treigny, St-Vérain and Myennes.

It was in the 17C that the pottery trade really began to develop; the fine pieces of pottery, known as the *Bleu de St-Verain* (Blue of St Verain), were followed in the next century by utility products.

Pottery making is now concentrated in **St-Amand-en-Puisaye**, where there is a training centre, and where, on the outskirts of the town, several potters' shops produce first-rate stoneware. Moutiers, near St-Sauveur, is known for the earthenware and stoneware produced at La Batisse. At the Château de Ratilly (&see below) those interested in ceramic art can observe the different stages of the potter's craft: casting, moulding and throwing on the wheel.

Driving Tour

Château de St-Fargeau★

&See SAINT-FARGEAU.

▸ *From the castle, drive 3km/1.7mi SE along D 185.*

Lac de Bourdon

This 220ha/544-acre reservoir feeds the Briare Canal and offers leisure activities (boat trips, sailing, fishing, swimming).

Parc Naturel de Boutissaint

🕘 *Open Feb to mid-Nov 8am-8pm (last entrance 6.30pm). 8€ (children 5€).* ☎ *03 86 74 07 08. www.boutissaint.com*

🅺 Created in 1968, this park of 400ha/988 acres of pastures, ponds and woods is home to over 400 large animals (deer, bison, wild boars, moufflons) and a multitude of smaller ones (squirrels, rabbits, weasels, stoats) as well as birds. Visitors can walk, ride or cycle along 100km/62mi of waymarked trails. Picnics are allowed.

▸ *A little further on, turn left onto D 955 towards St-Sauveur-en-Puisaye.*

Chantier Médiéval de Guédelon★★

🕘 *Open Jul -Aug 10am-7pm (last admission 1hr before closing). Rest of the year not Wed, times vary.* 🕘 *Closed Nov to mid-Mar.* ⊙ *9€ (children 7€).* ☎ *03 86 45 66 66. www.guedelon.fr.*

Guédelon work site

A. de Valroger-MICHELIN

Colette

Sidonie Gabrielle, daughter of Jules Colette, was born in **St-Sauveur-en-Puysaye** on 28 January 1873 and spent her first 19 years there. During her marriage to Henry Gauthier-Villars, she wrote the four novels in the Claudine series, which her husband, under his pen name of Willy, took credit (and cash) for. Blazing the trail of independent womanhood, she obtained a divorce and took to the stage (inspiration for La Vagabonde). After a failed second marriage, she finally found happiness with author Maurice Goudeket, whom she married in 1935. They set up house, with Colette's legendary cats, in an apartment overlooking the elegant Palais Royal gardens in Paris, where she died, much admired and honoured, in 1954.

Collection André de Jouvenel

Colette's novels, concerned with the pleasures and pain of love, are rich in sensory evocation of the natural environment in her native Burgundy. She brought a great sensitivity to her descriptions of the animal world (The Cat, Creatures Comfort) and childhood (My Mother's House, Sido). Her masterpieces also include post-First World War works steeped in the troubling ambivalence of those times (Chéri and The Last of Chéri); Gigi (1944) was adapted for stage and screen, a popular musical comedy.

Kids Learn more about the medieval way of life at this unusual site in a disused quarry. In 1998, the owner of St-Fargeau and the association of master builders of the Puisaye region decided to build a medieval castle using only the means available in the 13C; the project is due to last 25 years. Pottery made on the premises are on sale. There is also a workshop which introduces visitors to the art of illuminating manuscripts.

▶ *Continue along D 955 towards St-Amand-en-Puisaye; left on D 185.*

Château de Ratilly★

🕐*Open mid-Jun to mid-Sep 10am-6pm. Rest of the year call for information.* 🌐*4€.* ☎*03 86 74 79 54.*

The first sight of this large 13C castle, surrounded by magnificent trees, will charm visitors. Massive towers and high walls of an austere appearance overlook the dry moat surrounding the castle, which is built in fine ochre-coloured stone that time has mellowed.

The left wing now houses a stoneware workshop *(courses available)*. Both the workshop and the showroom, with its small exhibition on the original Puisaye stoneware, are open to the public. Other premises have been refurbished to house temporary art exhibitions.

▶ *Drive back down towards the village.*

Treigny

This village boasts an unusually vast Flamboyant-Gothic church dating from the 15C. Note the massive buttresses supporting the edifice and the two crucifix inside; the one in the aisle is the work of a 16C leper.

▶ *Follow D 66 to Moutiers.*

Moutiers-en-Puisaye

The parish church once belonged to a priory dependent on the Abbaye d'Auxerre. Note the 13C carvings decorating the narthex and, in the nave, the medieval frescoes dating from two successive periods: 12C frescoes on the north wall (Annunciation, Nativity, Christ surrounded by angels…), on the west wall (large figures) and on part of the south wall; Gothic frescoes (c 1300) on the remainder of the south wall depicting a procession (top), scenes from Genesis (centre) and the story of John-the-Baptist and Noah's Ark (bottom).

Saint-Sauveur-en-Puisaye

On Colette's namesake street, a red-marble medallion on the façade of her former home simply states, *Ici Colette est née* (Colette was born here).

Address Book

For coin ranges, see the Legend on the cover flap.

WHERE TO STAY

Chambre d'Hôte La Bruère – *La Bruère, 89130 Fontaines, 9km/5.6mi SW of Toucy by D 955, Rte. de St-Sauveur. 03 86 74 30 83. 5 rooms. Meals.* This farmhouse is the perfect place to come to for a relaxing break in the country. The spacious rooms have been set up in the former granary. The chef uses fresh organic ingredients grown on the property.

WHERE TO EAT

Le Lion d'Or – *37 r. Lucile-Cormier, 89130 Toucy. 03 86 44 00 76. Closed 1-20 Dec, Sun evenings and Mon.* The dining room is in the stables of this former post house; access is through the bar. Simple, unpretentious cooking with a traditional touch. Family atmosphere.

La Mare aux Fées – *1 pl. Lucien Gaubert, 89130 Mézilles, 11km/6.8mi NE of St-Fargeau by D 965. 03 86 45 40 43. Closed Feb, Mon evenings except Jul-Aug, Tue evenings and Wed.* Behind the attractive façade overgrown with ivy are two rustic-style dining rooms with beams, stone walls and tiled floors, one of which has a fireplace. Enjoy the warm welcome and generous helpings of traditional food.

Housed in one of the pavilions of the Château de St-Sauveur, close to the unusual 12C ironstone-built Tour Sarrasine, the **Musée Colette★** (*open Apr-Oct daily except Tue 10am-6pm; 5€; 03 86 45 61 95*) contains a collection of photographs, objects, furniture, manuscripts and books illustrating Colette's life and career. There is also a recording of some of her writings. Her drawing room and bedroom in Paris, where she spent the last years of her life, have been reconstructed with her own furniture. The visit ends in the library.

Return to St-Fargeau via D 85 (11km/ 7mi).

RONCHAMP

POPULATION 2 965

MICHELIN MAP 314: H-6

Until 1958, when the last colliery was closed down, Ronchamp was a mining town. Since the 1950s, however, it has been better known for its chapel of Notre-Dame-du-Haut, designed by Swiss architect Le Corbusier in 1955 to replace one destroyed during the Second World War.

- **Information**: 14 pl. du 14 Juillet, 70250 Ronchamp. 03 84 63 50 82. www.tourisme-ronchamp.fr.
- **Orient Yourself**: Ronchamp is inside the southern edge of the Vogses natural park.

Sights

Notre-Dame-du-Haut★★

1.5km/1mi N of town via a steep uphill road. Open Apr-Sep daily 9.30am-6.30pm. Rest of the year 10am-5pm (Nov-Feb 4pm). 03 84 20 65 13. www.chapelle-deronchamp.fr.

Le Corbusier's comment on this chapel, which is one of the most important works of contemporary religious architecture, was that he had intended his design to create a place of silence, prayer, peace and inner joy. The chapel was constructed on a hill overlooking the industrial town of Ronchamp, which had been dedicated to the worship of the Virgin Mary since the Middle Ages. It is built entirely of concrete; the brightness of its white-washed walls looks dazzling against the

Notre-Dame-du-Haut

dark grey untreated concrete of the roof. The rigid geometric lines of the walls contrast strikingly with the softer curves of the roof, which sweeps upwards in a graceful motion, and the rounded towers. In his conception of this chapel, Le Corbusier broke with the rationalist movement and its inflexible designs, creating a work which has been described as architectural sculpture. Inside, despite sloping walls and its relatively small size, the chapel seems spacious. The nave widens out towards the altar of white Burgundy stone, and the floor of the chapel follows the slope of the hill it is built on. The image of the Virgin Mary stands bathed in light in a niche in the wall. Light in the church filters through numerous different tiny windows randomly cut in the walls, allowing for a subtle interplay of light and shadow in the half darkness which softens the effect of the bare concrete walls. The three small chapels inside the three towers seen outside contribute to this subdued lighting effect.

Musée de la Mine

Open Jun-Aug daily except Tue 10am-noon, 2-7pm. Rest of the year 2-6pm only. Closed 1 Jan, 1 and 8 May, 14 Jul, Christmas holidays. 3.05€. 03 84 20 70 50. This museum retraces two centuries of mining in the region. The first gallery contains a display on coal mining – equipment, mining lamps, collections of fossils – and reproductions of common underground catastrophes in the mines.
The second gallery is given over to the life of the miners themselves, both pleasant aspects such as festivals, sports and musical activities, and the ever-present threat of illnesses such as miners' silicosis.

Address Book

For coin ranges, see the Legend on the cover flap.

FRESH FISH, FINE WINE

Restaurant Marchal – *26 r. des Mineurs. 03 84 20 64 86. Closed 20 Jun-1 Jul, 20 Dec-14 Jan, Wed evenings and Mon from 1 May to 1 Nov; Mon, Tue and Wed from 1 Nov to 30 Apr.* This restaurant has earned a reputation as the place to come to for fish specialities, notably its fried carp. Fresh fish are supplied daily. Generous portions, warm and friendly ambience.

Hostellerie des Sources – *4 r. Grand-Bois, 70200 Froideterre, 14km/8.7mi W of Ronchamp by N 19 and D 72. 03 84 30 34 72. Closed 5-24 Jan, Sun evenings, Mon and Tue except public holidays. Reservations required.* This old-stone farmhouse converted into a restaurant offers succulent food with an inventive touch. The owner is a dedicated oenologist who will share his passion for wine with you.

LES ROUSSES ✳ ✳

POPULATION 2 927
MICHELIN MAP 321: G-8

This resort, on a plateau a stone's throw from Switzerland, is renowned for its skiing, high-quality leisure activities and convivial atmosphere. In summer, it is popular with ramblers and mountain bikers, while watersports enthusiasts head for the nearby lake. The resort includes four villages: Les Rousses, Prémanon, Lamoura and Bois-d'Amont.

🛈 **Information**: r. Pasteur, 39220 Les Rousses. ☎03 84 60 02 55. www.lesrousses.com.
▶ **Orient Yourself:** The resort area lies on the French side of the Franco-Swiss border; its four villages are all centres for hotels, restaurants and shopping. Free shuttles link the various villages and ski areas, making it easy for visitors to access all corners of the resort. One of the ski areas is located in Switzerland; be prepared for a border crossing to reach it.
Kids **Kids:** If you can drag them off the slopes, children will love the glimpse of Inuit and Sami life at the Centre polaire Paul-Émile-Victor in Prémanon.

Ski Area

Alpine skiing 🎿
There are four linked ski areas, including one in Switzerland, offering 40km/25mi of runs of various levels of difficulty: 16 green runs, 7 blue ones, 16 red ones and 4 black ones; these are accessible via 40 ski lifts. There is a choice of ski passes combining several ski areas.

Les Jouvencelles 🎿
This area, ideal for beginners and families, has runs for children, very long green runs and two red runs. Halfway down (or up!) skiers can pause in the restaurant-bar Le Beauregard. Maximum altitude 1 420m/4 659ft. Snowboarding can be practised here or at Le Noirmont.

La Serra 🎿
The level here is higher: one beautiful green run but mostly blue and red runs. Maximum altitude 1 495m/4 905ft.

Le Noirmont 🎿
Beginners should avoid this area; even the long green run accessible by chairlift requires a minimum of self-confidence. The red and black runs are the favourite haunt of snowboarders who speed down the often icy slopes. Maximum altitude 1 560m/5 118ft.

La Dôle 🎿
The highest point of the massif (1 680m/5 512ft) is in Switzerland. In fair weather, the view of Lake Geneva and of the Alps is unforgettable. Competent skiers will appreciate the blue, red and black runs; there are also a few short green runs.

Cross-country skiing 🎿
There are 250km/155mi of double tracks suitable for both styles of cross-country skiing; 35 trails varying in difficulty (from green to black). The 76km/47mi Trans-Jurassienne race has been starting from Lamoura ever since 1979.

On the slopes

B. Kaufmann/MICHELIN

Address Book

For coin ranges, see the Legend on the cover flap.

WHERE TO STAY

Hôtel La Redoute – *357 rte. Blanche.* *03 84 60 00 40. www.hotellaredoute. com. Closed 5 Nov-15 Dec. 25 rooms.* *6.50€. Restaurant*. This family house stands at the entrance to the skiing resort. The accommodation consists of simply decorated but carefully kept bedrooms. Meals are served in a large rustic-style dining room. Good selection of affordable menus, including one for children.

Hôtel de France – *323 r. Pasteur.* *03 84 60 01 45. Closed 18 Apr-8 May, 18 Nov-18 Dec, Sun evening, Mon lunchtime out of season except public holidays. 30 rooms.* *11,50€. Restaurant*. A large building, typical of the region, with panelled interiors. There is 1980s décor in the guest rooms; several have balconies. Rustic dining room serving appetising French cuisine, and a good selection of Jura wines on the wine list.

WHERE TO EAT

Arbez Franco-Suisse – *2.5km/1.6mi S of Les Rousses by N 5.* *03 84 60 02 20. hotel.arbez@netgdi.com. Closed Nov, Mon and Tue out of season.* This bilingual hotel is located on the border between France and Switzerland. As regards meals, you can choose between the informal Brasserie and the dining room with its wooden decor.

L'Atelier – *1867 r. de Franche-Comté, 39220 Bois-d'Amont.* *03 84 60 94 15. restolatelier@wanadoo.fr. Closed Easter holidays, 12-28 Jul, November school holidays, Sun evening, Wed lunchtime, Mon and Tue.* This former carpenter's workshop is now a restaurant with traditional food and a rustic interior. On Thursday evenings, forget about menus, it's pizzas all round.

SHOPPING

Boissellerie du Hérisson – *101 r. Pasteur.* *03 84 60 30 84. Open daily 9.30am-noon, 2-7pm; out of season Tue-Sun 9.30am-noon, 2-7pm.* This shop offers an incredible range of fine, beautifully crafted wooden objects (old-fashioned toys, board games, chests) made for the most part by local artisans.

Fromagerie des Rousses – *137 r. Pasteur.* *03 84 60 02 62.* Delicious cheeses for sampling and for sale here include Comté, Tomme de Jura, raw-milk raclette and Morbier. You'll also find fine dairy products (butter, *crème fraiche*, *fromage blanc*) as well as seasonings, mushrooms, jams, and wines and liqueurs of the region.

Snowshoeing

Accessible to all, this activity still requires a minimum of fitness, so practice on the few waymarked trails around the resort before embarking on long excursions. There are guided tours with a member of the École du Ski Français (ESF).

Sights

Les Rousses

The village developed round its church during the 18C. The former wooden houses were replaced by housing estates and hotels. From the terrace in front of the church, there is a fine view of the Lac des Rousses and the Risoux mountain range in the background.

Lac des Rousses

2km/1.2mi N.

Covering almost 100ha/247 acres, this lake is very lively in summer, its swimming and watersports facilities attracting many holidaymakers.

Fort des Rousses

This fort, built in the 19C, is one of the largest in France; there is a vast network of underground galleries which could house up to 3 000 men. One part is now the **Caves Juraflore** (*guided tours (1hr30min) with film by reservation through the tourist office,* *5€,* *03 84 60 02 55, www.fort-des-rousses.com),* where there are more than 55 000 Comté cheeses at any one time maturing in the cool tunnels. The tour also includes an explanation of how the cheese are made. In another part is the [Kids] **Parc Aventure** (⊙ *call ☎03 84 60 02 55 for times*), with three adventure trails for children graded according to their level of difficulty and including suspended footbridges, via ferrata and so on. The courses are supervised by qualified instructors.

Prémanon

Overlooked by Mont Fier (1 282m/4 206ft), this village and the nearby hamlets rise in terraces from the banks of the Bienne to the small Dappes Valley which marks the border with Switzerland. In one of its more unusual-looking buildings is the [Kids] **Centre polaire Paul-Émile-Victor** (⊙ *open daily except Tue 10am-noon, 2-6pm;* ⊙ *closed 15 Nov-20 Dec, 1 Jan and 1 May;* ☜*5.10€ (children 2.50€);* ☎*03 84 60 77 71; www.centrepev.com*), a museum about the life of the Inuit and Sami people (traditional objects) as well as Nordic fauna. Don't miss the magnificent 3.10m/10ft-high stuffed white bear.

Bois d'Amont

The village has a long woodworking tradition; learn more about it at the **Musée de la Boissellerie** (⊙ *open daily mid-Jul to Aug 10am-noon, 2-6pm; rest of year Wed-Sun 2.30-6pm;* ⊙ *closed Nov to mid-Dec;* ☜*5€;* ☎*03 84 60 98 79; www.museedelaboissellerie.com*), in a former saw-mill. Demonstrations and audio-visual presentations illustrate the various crafts connected with wood, such as making boxes for cheese.

Lamoura

In this pretty village with its typical architecture, the town hall also contains the **Musée du Lapidaire** (♿ ⊙ *open 20 Dec-10 Apr, Jun-Sep;* ☞*guided tours (45min) daily except Sat 2.30pm-6pm; Jun and Sep Sun 2.30-6pm.* ☜*3.50€.* ☎*03 84 41 22 17*) devoted to the traditional craft of gem-cutting, once widely practised in this region. The museum, which contains a collection of gems and tools, illustrate this precision activity by means of a video film and a demonstration.

ST-CLAUDE ★

POPULATION 12 303
MICHELIN MAP 321: F-8

The town of St-Claude, tucked amid delightful countryside between the River Bienne and River Tacon, is the most important tourist centre in the Haut-Jura. It has always been famed for its charming setting and for the abbey that was once here. Sadly, the town has been destroyed several times by fire, most notably in 1799, so the cathedral is the only surviving building of any note.

🛈 **Information**: 1 av. de Belfort, 39203 St-Claude. ☎03 84 45 34 24. www.haut-jura.fr.
▶ **Orient Yourself:** The town is in the middle of the Parc Naturel Régional du Haut-Jura not far from the Franco-Swiss border, perched on a narrow terrace between two mountain rivers, the Bienne and the Tacon.

A Bit of History

A lawyer's paradise

From the 15C to the 18C, armies of lawyers made a living from settling the numerous, incredibly petty disputes between the town of St-Claude and its abbey. The question whether the bell in the monastery or that in the parish church should ring more loudly is just one example of the kind of issue which would provoke a lengthy legal wrangle – in this case 40 years, until the problem was solved by the personal intervention of Emperor Charles V.

The end of Serfdom

The lordly canons, distinctly lacking the moral tone of their saintly predecessors, were regarded by the 14 000 inhabitants of the abbey lands as a handful of utterly shameless layabouts. In 1770, six Haut-

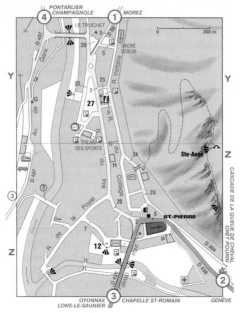

ST-CLAUDE

9-Avril-1944 Pl. du	Y	27
Abbaye Pl. de l'	Z	2
Belfort Av. de	Y	3
Christin Pl.	Y	5
Gambetta R.	Z	6
Janvier R. A.	Z	7
Lamartine R.	Y	9
Louis-XI Pl.	Z	12
Marché R. du	Z	20
Pré R. du	YZ	
République Bd de la	Z	23
Rosset R.	Z	24
Victor-Hugo R.	Y	25
Voltaire Pl.	Y	26

| Exposition de pipes de diamants et pierres fines | Z | E |

Jura villages took out a lawsuit against the chapter to win their freedom. Their case made a tremendous impact; even Voltaire, living at Ferney at the time, came to the aid of the villagers by writing pamphlets. After a court case lasting five years, the canons, who refused point-blank to give any ground, emerged victorious. The bishop suggested that, as their rights had been officially recognised, they might like to make the generous gesture of liberating their serfs on their own initiative, but the monks refused. The bishop appealed to the king, Louis XVI, but even he did not dare intervene. Finally, the problem was settled by the outbreak of the Revolution: the religious principality of St-Claude was abolished, its goods and lands confiscated and sold, and its serfs freed.

Sights

Town Setting★★
In order to fully appreciate the originality of St-Claude's setting, stand on the bridge (Grand Pont) spanning the Tacon, from where there is an overall view of the town and the Cirque des Foules. Then head to place Louis-XI, from where there is a beautiful **view**★ above the old ramparts.

Other views – There is a view of the Tacon Valley from the bottom of the steep, picturesque rue de la Poyat. This street was once an important link between the upper district (around the abbey) and the suburb inhabited by workers and craftsmen. Before the modern bridges were built, it was also one of the routes taken by pilgrims on their way to revere the relics of St Claudius.

There is a beautiful view from the **Grotte de Ste-Anne,** a cave which overlooks the town from a height of 200m/656ft. Another good viewpoint is to be found on place du 9-Avril-1944. Finally, from the middle of the viaduct the view shows clearly how the lack of level ground has made it necessary to expand the town upwards instead of outwards.

Cathédrale St-Pierre★
This cathedral church, originally dedicated to saints Peter, Paul and Andrew, was once the heart of the abbey community. The present building, originally built in the Gothic style in the 14C and 15C, was finished in the 18C with the addition of a Classical façade. The 15C tower was extended higher in the 18C. The most interesting part of the exterior is the east end, with its watch-turrets topped with spires.

Address Book

For coin ranges, see the Legend on the cover flap.

WHERE TO STAY

Hôtel du Commerce – *01410 Chézery-Forens.* ☎*04 50 56 90 67. www.hotelduco-mmerce-blanc.fr. Open 5 Feb-30 Sep. Closed Tue evenings and Wed except school holidays. 8 rooms.* ⛌*7€. Restaurant. A pleasant family hotel, whose terrace gives onto the Valserine. A smart dining room and simple, carefully kept rooms are available at extremely reasonable prices.*

Jura – *40 av. de la Gare.* ☎*03 84 45 24 04. 35 rooms.* ⛌*6.50€. Restaurant. You may prefer one of the 12 larger bedrooms; the other ones are smaller and rustic in style but all are impeccably kept.*

WHERE TO EAT

L'Écrin – *12 rte. de Genève.* ☎*03 84 45 70 00. Two small, rustic dining rooms showcase excellent traditional cuisine. Frogs' legs are a house speciality.*

Ferme-Auberge La Combe aux Bisons – *39370 La Pesse, 1.5km/0.8mi N of La Pesse by D 25 heading for L'Embossieux.* ☎*03 84 42 71 60. Closed 1-28 Dec, Mon and Tue except school holidays. Reservations required. The decor of this welcoming inn evokes the North American plains. The chef serves tasty bison meat dishes with local wines.*

SIT BACK AND RELAX

Bernard Puget – *33 r. du Pré.* ☎ *03 84 45 00 05. Open Tue-Sat 8am-7.30pm, Sun 8am-6.30pm; daily Jul-Aug. Closed 2 weeks in Jun and 1 week in Sep. Chocolate bonbons share the limelight with eight sorts of petits fours and other sweet creations. Have a seat in the tearoom and indulge!*

SHOPPING

Marché – *pl. du 9-Avril. Thu morning.* The weekly market is the place to find regional specialities, such as cheeses, as well as other tempting food stalls.

Jean-Masson – *24 rte. de la Faucille, l'Essard.* ☎*03 84 45 24 09. Open 8am-8pm.* This artisan sculpts pipes that resemble famous personalities, but also produces more classic models. Visitors are treated to a mini-course on the art of carving.

The beautiful rectangular interior is plain, even austere, and is supported by 14 massive octagonal pillars. Left of the entrance, an **altarpiece**★★ stands against the wall of the nave. It was donated in 1533 by Pierre de la Baume, the last bishop of the Franche-Comté, who lived in Geneva, in gratitude to St Peter for protecting him through all the political and religious disturbances.

The chancel is lit by **stained-glass windows**★ restored in 1999 and contains magnificent sculpted **wooden stalls**★★ which were begun before 1449 and finished in 1465 by the Geneva craftsman Jehan de Vitry. The Apostles and the Prophets are depicted alternately on the backrests, then the former abbots of the monastery; scenes from the abbey's history with the founders St Romanus and St Lupicinus, are represented on the large and small cheekpieces; the 19C restorers added scenes of everyday life to the elbow rests and misericords.

St Claudius' tomb drew crowds of pilgrims until 1794. Emperors, kings and lords all came to venerate him. Anne of Brittany had been unable to conceive until her pilgrimage to the Jura, after which she bore a daughter to Louis XII and named her Claude (the future wife of François I and

St-Pierre's Cathedral

G. Magnin-MICHELIN

Carved pipe

Queen of France). The shrine was burned during the Revolution, and the remaining relics of the saint are kept in a reliquary in the chapel south of the chancel.

Exposition de Pipes, de Diamants et de Pierres Fines

♿ ⏰ *Open May-Sep 9.30am-noon, 2-6.30pm; 20 Dec-30 Apr and Oct daily except Sun 2-6pm* ⏰ *Closed All Saints to Christmas.* 🎫 *4.50€.* ☎ *03 84 45 17 00. www.musee-pipe-diamant.com.*
This collection of 18C and 19C pipes, some artistically decorated, is very varied, as you would expect in the town that was once the capital of pipe-making and remains an important centre. The Chancellerie displays a collection of pipes marked with the names of those admitted into the famous pipe makers' guild of St-Claude.

Parc Naturel Régional du Haut-Jura

The Haut-Jura Regional Nature Park was inaugurated in 1986 and extended in 1998 to preserve the beautiful local forests and cultural heritage and create a new source of income for the region's inhabitants. The park's administration centre, **Maison du Parc du Haut-Jura** (*www.parc-haut-jura.fr*) is located in

Lajoux, a small town east of St-Claude. It also serves as an information centre for those wishing to go on walking tours or enjoy other activities in the park.
The park covers 145 000ha/358 310 acres and encompasses 96 communities *(communes)*, including St-Claude and Morez. The Crêt Pela (alt 1 495m/4 905ft), the highest summit in the Jura, offers plenty of opportunities for ski enthusiasts in winter, and for nature ramblers and mountain bikers in summer.
There are several museums which give an insight into the development of crafts and industry in the region, which range from independent artisans and cottage-industries to factories. Besides the pipe-making and diamond-cutting workshops of St-Claude, activities include spectacle making in Morez, the manufacture of earthenware in Bois-d'Amont and toys in Moirans-en-Montagne, and traditional cheesemaking at Les Moussières.
The tourist offices in St-Claude and Les Rousses and the Maison du Haut-Jura in Lajoux give information on the park itself and the accommodation and leisure facilities it has to offer visitors.

Driving tour

▷ *Drive E out of Saint-Claude on D 304 to Chaumont. On your way out of Chaumont, leave the car in the parking area.*

Cascade de la Queue de Cheval★
5km/3mi and 1hr on foot there and back.
🚶The footpath to the right leads to the foot of the narrow 50m/164ft-high waterfall, in a pretty setting, which tumbles down the rock face in two stages.

▷ *Continue along D 304. Leave the car beyond a bridge in the hamlet of La Main-Morte and follow the path (way-marked in red) leading to Crêt Pourri.*

Crêt Pourri★
🚶*30min on foot there and back.*
There is a fine **panorama**a from the viewing table (alt 1 025m/ 3 362ft).

▷ *Follow D 304 to Lamoura, go through the village and continue to Lajoux.*

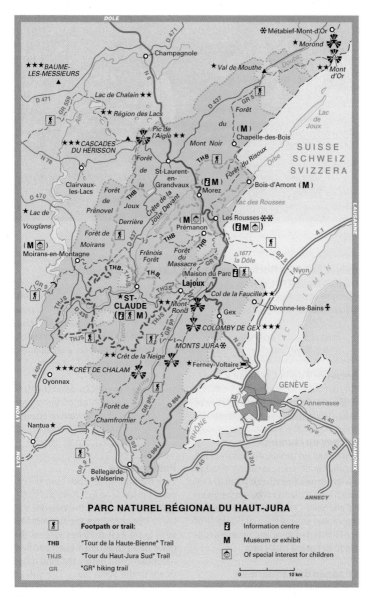

PARC NATUREL RÉGIONAL DU HAUT-JURA

	Footpath or trail:			Information centre
THB	"Tour de la Haute-Bienne" Trail		**M**	Museum or exhibit
THJS	"Tour du Haut-Jura Sud" Trail			Of special interest for children
GR	"GR" hiking trail		0 10 km	

Lajoux

The Maison du Parc is here, in the heart of the park, where a few craftsmen try to keep ancient crafts alive; note the strong barn, a free-standing construction where farmers used to keep precious goods and valuables.

▶ *Drive along D 292 to Les Molunes then on to Moussières.*

At the **Coopérative fromagère de Moussières** (○ *open 8.30am-12.30pm, 2.30-7.30pm, ☎03 84 41 60 96)*, you can watch the making of several local AOC cheeses (Comté, Morbier and Bleu de Gex) through a plate-glass window, and buy some to take home, too.

▶ *Drive N towards Saint-Claude on D 25. Take the first left to the belvedere.*

Chapeau de Gendarme

Belvédère de la Roche Blanche
From 1 139m/3 737ft, there is an extensive view of the Flumen Valley, of Saint-Claude and Septmoncel.

▸ *There is another belvedere 700m/765yd further on.*

Belvédère de la Cernaise★
This overhanging promontory offers a bird's-eye **view** of the Flumen Valley, of Saint-Claude and the Septmoncel plateau.

Gorges du Flumen★
This mountain stream, a tributary of the Tacon, can be seen cascading through a wild **gorge**★ from the cliff road (D 436) which follows the river between Septmoncel and Saint-Claude. The road offers an impressive view of the main cascade of the Flumen before going through a tunnel to get past a rocky spur.

Chapeau de Gendarme★
This natural site is interesting from a geological point of view: it consists of originally horizontal layers of rock, which were compressed and lifted during the Tertiary Era and became twisted without breaking.

▸ *Return to St-Claude.*

Cret de Chalam★★★

This is the highest peak (1 545m/5 069ft) in the range overlooking the Valserine from the west, in the south of the Haut-Jura regional park. It is easily accessible to ramblers looking for a challenging change of scenery.

▸ *Drive E from St-Claude on D 436. At Lajoux, turn right onto a minor road to La Pesse, the take the road opposite the church. After 4km/2.4mi you come to a crossroads (car park nearby).*

Panorama★★
Take the right-hand path from the car park; 1hr 30min on foot there and back.
The entire length of the Valserine Valley can be seen from the summit. The view to the east stretches as far as the great **Jura range**, the highest and final mountain chain before the land drops down to the Swiss plain. The gullied slopes of Roche Franche can be seen right in front of you; to your left are the Reculet and the Crêt de la Neige (1 717m/5 633ft); to your right is the Grand Crêt d'Eau, beyond the Sac pass. In clear weather, even Mont Blanc is visible. There is an extensive view to the west of the Jura mountains and plateaux.

ST-FARGEAU

POPULATION 1 814
MICHELIN MAP 319: B-6

St-Fargeau, chief town of the Puisaye, has a fine château filled with memories of Anne-Marie-Louise d'Orléans, cousin of Louis XIV, better known under the name of Mademoiselle de Montpensier or La Grande Mademoiselle, a supporter of the Fronde, a rising of the aristocracy and Parliament from 1648 to 1653.

- **Information**: 3 pl. de la République, 89170 St-Fargeau. ☎03 86 74 10 07. www.tourisme.ccpf.fr.
- **Don't Miss**: The amazing "Spectacles Historiques" which take place on Friday and Saturday evenings in summer at the château: 600 actors, 60 horsemen, lights and sounds all help bring the past to gloriously entertaining life.

A Bit of History

A romantic castle

The **château**★ is on the site of a fortress erected at the end of the 10C. The present building was begun in the Renaissance period and was built in several stages. However, it is **La Grande Mademoiselle** who can claim the honour of completely changing the appearance of the buildings. Mademoiselle de Montpensier was exiled to St-Fargeau for several years on the orders of Louis XIV as punishment for her attitude during the uprising of the Fronde. When she arrived in 1652 she had "to wade through knee-high grass in the courtyard" and found a dilapidated building. To make her place of exile more comfortable, she called in Le Vau, the king's architect, who laid out the inner courtyard and complete-ly refurbished the interior of the château.

In 1681, Mademoiselle de Montpensier made a gift of St-Fargeau to the Duc de Lauzun, whom she later married in a secret ceremony.

In 1715 the property was bought by Le Pelletier des Forts. His great-grandson, **Louis-Michel Le Pelletier de St-Fargeau,** became deputy to the National Convention in 1793 and voted for the death of Louis XVI. He was assassinated on the eve of the king's execution and was the revolutionaries first martyr.

Address Book

♿For coin ranges, see the Legend on the cover flap.

WHERE TO STAY

🛏🛏**Chambre d'Hôte Moulin de la Forge** – 89350 Tannerre-en-Puisaye, 11km/6.8mi NE of St-Fargeau by D 18 then D 160. ☎03 86 45 40 25. renegag-not@aol.com. 🍽 5 rooms. You will love this 14C mill surrounded by a park with a landscaped garden, a pool and a pond teeming with fish. Comfortable rooms with beams furnished in 1930s style.

WHERE TO EAT

🍽🍽**Ferme-Auberge Les Perriaux** – 89350 Champignelles, 3km/1.9mi NW of Champignelles by D 7 (heading towards Château-Coligny) then a minor road. ☎03 86 45 13 22. www.lesperriaux.com. Reservations recommended. On this 16C farm, you can sample fresh home-grown produce: terrine, foie gras and cider made on the premises. Rustic setting with fireplace for the long winter evenings. Pleasantly arranged upstairs guest room.

🍽🍽**Auberge la Demoiselle** – 1 pl. de la République. ☎03 86 74 10 58. www.auberge-lademoiselle.com. Closed 23 Dec-31 Jan, Wed evenings and Mon except 14 Jul-31 Aug, Sun evenings. Mademoiselle de Montpensier's portrait hangs above the fireplace in the dining room. Warm, lively décor in yellow hues, and a rustic touch provided by exposed beams and tiled floors. Nice cooking.

Visit

&⏰*Open late Mar to 11 Nov 10am-noon, 2-6pm. 9€. ☎✉ 03 86 74 05 67. www. chateau-de-st-fargeau.com.*

Within the feudal enclosure is a huge courtyard of rare elegance bordered by five ranges of buildings (the most recent on the right of the entrance dates from 1735). A semicircular stair in the corner between the two main wings leads to the entrance rotunda. The chapel is housed in one of the towers: on the left is the portrait gallery which led into the apartments of the *Grande Mademoiselle* until they were burned in 1752; on the right is the 17C guardroom. A grand stair leads to the rooms on the first floor. The tour of the attic lets visitors see the vast roof area and handsome timberwork.

In the English-style park (118ha/292 acres) with its charming groves there is a large lake, fed by the small River Bourdon.

At the 🖼 **Ferme du Château (**⏰*open Apr-Aug 10am-noon, 2-6pm (Apr-Jun and Sep except Mon to 5pm, Sep weekends 2-6pm; 6€ (children 4€); ☎03 86 74 03 76; www.ferme-du-chateau.com)* some of the farm buildings have been refurbished to house an exhibit on rural life and trades 100 years ago and plenty of farmyard animals to pet.

Additional Sight

Musée de l'Aventure du Son★

⏰*Open May-Sep daily 10am-noon, 2-6pm; Mar-Apr and Oct daily except Tue 2-6pm. 5.50€. ☎03 86 74 13 06. www. aventureduson.fr.*

The former town hall is now a small museum devoted to the history of ways of reproducing music and to their inventors: Cros, Edison, Bell, Lioret, Pathé, Berliner... Early music boxes, a German calliope from 1910 with a vertical disc, an automatic orchestra dating from 1925, a Limonaire carrousel organ and more make up this charming collection. The set of phonographs, some portable, shows models in fanciful shapes. Demonstrations are provided.

ÉGLISE DE **ST-HYMETIÈRE**★

MICHELIN MAP 321: D-8

The beautiful 11C Romanesque church west of St-Hymetière, a rural village in the Revermont, depended originally on a priory in Mâcon.

🛈 **Information**: Adapemont. ☎03 84 85 47 91. www.adapement.assoc.fr.

Visit

⏰*Open summer 7am-7pm.*

The curch has several striking external features: old tombstones as flagstones on the floor of the porch; massive buttresses and narrow archaic windows on the south side of the church; tall pilaster strips; a protruding apse and a tall octagonal tower. Inside, the oven-vaulted chancel enclosed by plain arcading and the south aisle recall the original Romanesque building, whereas the main vault and north aisle bear signs of the 17C reworking of the masonry.

Montfleur (Excursion)

16km/10mi SE. At the **Écomusée Vivant du Moulin de Pont des Vents (**⏰*open Mar-Dec. 3.50; ☎03 84 44 33 51; moulin.ecomusee.jura.free.fr)* you can tour a 19C watermill in working order and try your hand at baking bread.

G. Magnin-MICHELIN

One of the rare Romanesque churches still standing in the region

SALINS-LES-BAINS ⚓

POPULATION 3 333
MICHELIN MAP 321: F-5

The spa town of Salins lies in a remarkable **setting**★ along the pretty, narrow valley of the Furieuse, beneath the fortresses of Belin and St-André. It still has some traces of its medieval fortifications and one or two towers.

- ℹ **Information**: pl. des Salines, 39110 Salins-les-Bains.
  ☎03 84 73 01 34. www.salins-les-bains.com.
- ▶ **Orient Yourself**: Make to time to visit one of Salins' fortresses for the best views over the resort.

A Bit of History

White gold

In the past, salt was indispensable for preserving food. However, primitive mining methods made it so scarce and so costly that a salt mine was a real gold mine. Jean l'Antique, the most famous member of the Chalon family, seized the salt mine at Salins early in the 13C. The sale of the salt brought him huge sums of cash, which he was able to put to astute use, buying fiefs, vassals and the goodwill of bishops, monks, soldiers and wealthy merchants. Delighted with his increased power, he bestowed a charter on the home town of the salt mine, source of his wealth, in 1249, according it a fair degree of autonomy.

The timber trade

Huge quantities of wood were needed to heat the cauldrons used to evaporate water in the salt extraction process, with the result that the timber trade became almost as important for Salins as its salt mine. As many as 60 000 horse-drawn carts loaded with wood came into the town each year. The waters of the Furieuse were harnessed to drive 12 great sawmills. Salins soon developed a reputation for producing the best masts on the market, and became supplier to the French Navy. By the 17C Salins, with 5 700 inhabitants, was the second largest community in the Franche-Comté after Besançon, which had 11 500.

Address Book

🌜*For coin ranges, see the Legend on the cover flap.*

WHERE TO EAT AND STAY

🍽🍽**Les Bains** – *1 pl. des Alliés.* ☎*03 84 73 07 54. www.restaurant-les-bains.com. Closed 1-16 Jan, Tue lunchtime, Sun evening and Mon.* The " morillette" and the "comtine" are just two of the imaginative creations from the stove of chef Maurice Marchand. Classical French cuisine served in the dining room; regional specialities in the brasserie.
🍽🍽**Le Relais de Pont-d'Héry** – *rte. de Champagnole.* ☎*03 84 73 06 54. www. relaispontdhery.com. Closed 18 Oct-4 Nov, 15 Feb-3 Mar, Tue from Sep-May, and Mon.* Behind the facade of this

small house, you'll find two dining rooms serving appetizing traditional French cuisine: quail sauteed with hazelnuts, roast anglerfish with herbs; crayfish gratin, and so on.
🍽🍽**Grand Hôtel des Bains** – *1 pl. des Alliés.* ☎*03 84 37 90 50. www.hotel-des-bains.fr. Closed 2-23 Jan. 31 rooms.* 🛏*9€. Restaurant*🍽🍽*.* This hotel in the heart of the town provides direct access to the thermal baths, the swimming pool and the fitness centre; ask about special accommodation and spa packages. Functional bedrooms with white walls; the ones giving onto the back are quieter.

The former saltworks

Walking Tour

▶ *Start at the tourist office.*

Salines★

🕐*Open year round.* ╌*Guided tour (1hr) Jul-Aug 10am-noon, 2.30-5pm; rest of the year times vary. Dress warmly.* ╌*4.50€ (under 12 free).* ☎*03 84 73 10 92. www. salinesdesalins.com.*

Kids Salins is the only salt mine where visitors can see how salt water was once pumped out of the Jura soil. It is interesting to visit the underground galleries, up to 200m/656ft long, where good lighting shows off the magnificent 13C vaults. The salt water was pumped up from the salt seams, 250m/820ft underground, through boreholes 30cm/15in in diameter. A system using a long beam and a hydraulic wheel activated the pump which drew up the water, which had a high salt content of 33kg/71lb of salt per 100l/22gal. Enormous cauldrons (one of which is on display) were heated over coal fires to evaporate the water and obtain the salt.

▶ *Cross the car park to the left toward the Hôtel-Dieu.*

Hôtel-Dieu

♿🕐*Open year round.* ╌*Guided tours (30min) Jul-Aug 9am-12.30pm, 1.30-6pm (Sun 5.30pm). Rest of the year times vary.*

Book at the tourist office. ╌*4.40€.* ☎*03 84 73 01 34.*

This hospice dates from the 17C. The pharmacy has some beautiful woodwork as well as a collection of pots in Moustiers faïence.

▶ *Turn left on rue du Dr-Germain, then right on Rue de la République.*

Rue de la République

At no. 79, the Maison des Carmélites (13C), with half-timbers, is one of the few to have survived the fire of 1825. A Carmelite convent was housed here from the 17C-18C. At no. 105, the Hotel Moreau displays a grey stone facade (18C). Continue to the Tour Oudin (13C-15C), at the entrance to the city.

▶ *Retrace your steps and turn right up the Escalier St-Anatoile. Alternatively, return to the swan fountain on rue de la République and climb via rue d'Orgemont and rue des Clarisses.*

The charming **St-Anatoile staircase** twists between stone walls. Fort Belin (19C) is visible in the distance.

Église St-Anatoile

This is the most interesting church in Salins, and one of the best examples of 13C Cistercian architecture in the Franche-Comté, in which there is nonetheless

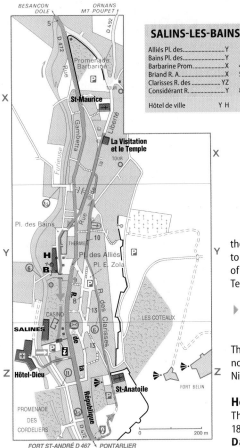

the entry, climb rue du Temple to view the handsome portal★ of marble and alabaster. The Temple (15C) is behind.

▶ *Return along rue de la Liberté.*

The monumental **doorway**★ of no. 13 is attributed to Claude-Nicolas Ledoux.

Hôtel de Ville

The town hall dates from the 18C. The 17C **chapel of Notre-Dame-de-la-Libératrice,** crowned by a dome, is in the town hall complex.

▶ *Return to the tourist office.*

Excursions

Fort St-André

4km/2.5mi S along D 472 then right on D 94, right on D 271 and right again.
This is an excellent example of 17C military architecture, designed by Vauban in 1674. On the right, beneath the ramparts, there is a fine **view**★ of Salins.

Mont Poupet★

10km/6mi N on D 492 then left on D 273 and left again (parking area near the cross). 15min on foot there and back.
From the top there is an impressive **view**★ of Mont Blanc, the Jura plateau and the Bresse plain.

evidence of the local architects' predilection for round arches.

Two protruding Flamboyant Gothic style chapels frame the beautiful Romanesque doorway. Inside, pretty round-arched arcades run along above the pointed Gothic arches separating the nave from the side aisles. Note the 17C pulpit, the 16C choir stalls decorated with striking medallions and woodwork and the carved wooden organ case from 1737.

▶ *Go down rue des Clarisses, cross place Émile-Zola and continue along rue Charles-Magnin. Turn right on rue de la Liberté.*

La Visitation et le Temple

The former Visitandines convent (1710) was converted to flats in 1960. Once past

ROUTE DES **SAPINS**★★

MICHELIN MAP 321: F TO G-6

The beautiful 50km/31mi stretch of road known as the Route des Sapins (Fir Forest Route) runs between Champagnole and Levier, through the forests of La Fresse, Chapois, La Loux and Levier. The itinerary below follows the most interesting stretch with the best facilities.

▸ **Orient Yourself:** The route is interspersed with parking spots, playgrounds, picnic areas, nature trails, viewpoints and education centres to help you make the most of your visit.

☺ **Don't Miss:** Sapin Président de la Joux, a giant tree over two hundred years old.

Driving Tour

55km/34mi from Champignole to Levier– allow 3hr .

Champagnole
☺*See CHAMPAGNOLE.*

▸ *Take D 471 NE. At a crossroads on the outskirts of Equevillon, leave D 471 and follow the Route des Sapins.*

The road climbs through the **Forêt de la Fresse**, offering glimpses of Champagnole to the left.

▸ *Turn right on D 21, leaving the Route des Sapins to the left, heading for the D 288 junction, where you turn left.*

The road follows the line of the hillside, about halfway up, along the coombe through which the Angillon has cut its river bed. To the east of the road are the magnificent stands of the forest of La Joux, and to the west the 1 153ha/2 849 acres of conifers which make up the forest of La Fresse. Just before the village of Les Nans, turn left onto the forest road known as Larderet aux Nans, which gives a good view of Les Nans and the Angillon coombe. The road rejoins the Route des Sapins at the crossroads, Carrefour des Baumes, then runs through the northern part of the forest of La Fresse, through the village of Chapois and into the La Joux forest, climbing as it goes.

Forêt de la Joux★★
This is one of France's most beautiful evergreen forests. This area, covering 2

652ha/ 6 550 acres, is separated from the Fresse Forest by the Angillion rapids to the south; it borders Levier Forest to the north. Whereas most of the trees are conifers, a few deciduous species can be found. Some of the firs are of exceptional size: up to 45m/148ft tall.

The Administration has divided the forest into five cantons, known as series. The most striking trees are in the cantons of La Glacière and Aux Sources.

▸ *Leave the Route des Sapins to take the road to the Belvédère de Garde-Bois, which is near a chapel.*

Belvédère de Garde-Bois
There is a pretty view of the deep Angillon Valley as well as the forest of La Fresse in the distance.

▸ *Carry on east along the road that led to the viewpoint to rejoin the Route des Sapins.*

The stretch of road from the Rond-du-Sauget crossroads is especially pretty.

Sapins de la Glacière
30min round trip on foot. Take the path which leads off to the right from the Route des Sapins as you come from Champagnole. This canton got its name from being the area where snow lies longest. Magnificent conifers, as straight as arrows, grow around a deep hollow in the canton's centre. There is a particularly tall, splendid tree next to the footpath. The quiet in the forest and subdued quality of the light filtered by the trees creates a soothing, meditative atmosphere.

Address Book

For coin ranges, see the Legend on the cover flap.

CHARMS OF THE FOREST

Maison Forestière du Chevreuil – 39300 Supt, 3.5km/2.3mi N of Chapois by D 251 take the D 107 toward Censeau, and the Rte. des Sapins, following the arrows. ☎03 84 51 40 85. Closed 16 Sep-15 Jun. Reservations suggested. In a pretty clearing surrounded by pine trees, this unusual house offers simple but delicious meals. Fondue and grilled beef on request. Playing area for children.

In bad weather, the restaurant may be closed; it is best to check beforehand.

Chambre d'Hôte Bourgeois-Bousson – Grande-Rue, 39110 Andelot-en-Montagne. 2.5km/1.6mi NW of Chapois by D 250. ☎03 84 51 43 77. Closed Nov to Easter. 6 rooms. Meals. This family house near the forest has a quaint, slightly old-fashioned atmosphere. Your hosts are two sisters who extend a warm welcome. The rooms are simple but comfortable. Traditional cuisine.

Épicéas d'élite

The Route de la Marine leads to this stand of spruces. Alternatively, there is a signposted footpath leading off D 473; the start is indicated about 1km/0.5mi S of the level crossing at Boujailles station (30min there and back on foot). These are the most beautiful trees in the Esserval-Tartre spruce forest, hence their name.

Maison Forestière du Chevreuil

The clearing by this forester's lodge is a major tourist attraction in the region. Those interested in forestry will be able to visit the **Arboretum**, a test planting area for trees not native to the region. Where the Route des Sapins divides into two, take the right fork, signposted Route des Sapins par les Crêtes.

Belvédère des Chérards

There is a glimpse from here of wooded plateaux.

Sapin Président de la Joux★

This fir, the most famous tree in the Chérards canton, is over two centuries old. It has a diameter of 3.85m/13ft at a height of 1.30m/4ft from the ground, and is 45m/148ft tall.

The Route des Sapins carries on through the forest, offering a pretty view of the Chalamont dip to the left.

Forêt de Levier

This forest was once the possession of the Chalon family until it was confiscated in 1562 by Philippe II, King of Spain. It became the property of the King of France after Louis XIV's conquest of Franche-Comté in 1674. At that time the forest was used to provide timber for naval construction and for the Salins salt works. Local people also came here for firewood, so large areas were planted entirely with deciduous trees, in keeping with the forest's role as a useful resource. The modern forest, at an altitude of between 670m/2 198ft and 900m/2 953ft, covers an area of 2 725ha/6 733 acres and consists almost exclusively of coniferous trees (60% fir, 12% spruce). The forest area is managed in three blocks (the séries of Jura, Arc and Scay).

Route forestière de Scay

This slightly bumpy road, which crosses the forest of Levier through the so-called quiet zone (zone de silence) of Scay, offers some beautiful views of the surrounding area. At the **Belvédère de la Roche** there is a view over the forest of Levier and the clearing in which the village of Villers-sous-Chalamont lies.

Passage taillé de Chalamont

Shortly before D 49, a footpath leads off to the right (30min there and back on foot), along what was once a Celtic, then a Roman path. Note the steps cut into the sloping or slippery sections and the grooves which guided chariot wheels. At the point where the path leaves the forest, by the ruins of the medieval tower of Chalamont, it passes through a kind of trench, a technique which was imitated

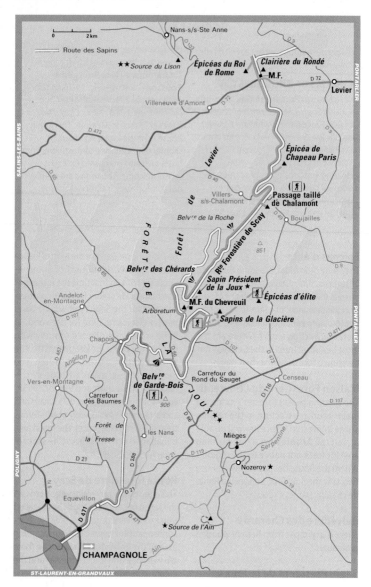

in the building of the nearby modern Boujailles/Villers-sous-Chalamont road.

Épicéa de Chapeau-Paris

This tree is to the forest of Levier what the Sapin Président is to the forest of La Joux. It is 45m/148ft tall with a diameter of 4m/13ft and represents an equivalent volume of timber of about 20m3/706cu ft.

▶ *Take Route forestière de Ravonnet; then Route du Pont de la Marine (right).*

Clairière du Rondé

This clearing contains an enclosure containing Sika deer and a forester's lodge (*maison forestière – exhibitions in summer*).

Épicéas du Roi de Rome

These trees are over 180 years old; some are more than 50m/ 164ft tall.

▶ *Turn back to take D 72 on the left towards Levier.*

SAULIEU★

POPULATION 2 837
MICHELIN MAP 320: F-6
LOCAL MAP SEE LE MORVAN

Saulieu has a long-standing gastronomic renown with a string of fine restaurants. Art lovers will find interest in the basilica of St-Andoche and in the works of François Pompon, a sculptor who was born at Saulieu in 1855.

- **Information**: 24 r. d'Argentine, 21210 Saulieu. ☎03 80 64 00 21.
- ▶ **Orient Yourself**: Saulieu is pleasantly situated on the boundaries of the Morvan and the Auxois, making it a convenient base for a variety of excursions.

A Bit of History

A gastronomic centre

The gastronomic reputation of Saulieu goes back to the 17C. In 1651 the Burgundian states decided to restore the old Paris-Lyon road, which passed along the eastern edge of the Morvan, to the importance that it had before the Middle Ages. Saulieu set about increasing its prosperity by developing local industry and fairs. The town became a post house

Ph. Gajic-MICHELIN

Le Taureau, François Pompon

Address Book

☝For coin ranges, see the Legend on the cover flap.

WHERE TO EAT AND STAY

◎**La Vieille Auberge** – 15 r. Grillot. ☎03 80 64 13 74. Closed 4-29 Jan, 29 Jun-9 Jul, Tue evenings and Wed except 14 Jul-31 Aug. This country inn at the entrance to Saulieu has a pleasant dining room. Good choice of reasonably priced menus combining traditional cuisine with a regional touch. Functional guest rooms.

◎**La Guinguette** – Moulin de la Serrée, 58230 Alligny-en-Morvan, 7km/4.3mi S of Saulieu by D 26. ☎03 86 76 15 79. Open Sat pm and Sun lunch Easter-Oct and daily Jul-Aug. This welcoming cabin is the delight of Sunday afternoon strollers. Fish farm on the property. Trout and salmon can be eaten on the premises or bought to be taken away. Fishing rods available.

◎◎◎◎**La Côte d'Or** – 2 r. d'Argentine. ☎03 80 90 53 53. www.bernard-loiseau. ☐18€. Restaurant◎◎◎◎. the wife of illustrious chef Bernard

Loiseau, with the help of a team of dedicated chefs, offers palate-pleasing meals to the gourmet diners who come from afar to this temple of gastronomy. Refined atmosphere and smart setting in a former coach inn.

SHOPPING

La Fouchale – 4 pl. de la République. ☎03 80 64 02 23. Open Tue-Sat 9am-12.30pm, 3-7pm; Easter to Oct Sun 10am-12.30pm. An astonishing variety of cheeses and other dairy products: goats cheese (chèvre), magnificent Vacherines, Époisses and Saint-Marcellins, yogurts, crème fraîche... In addition, there are several local wines.

Poulizac – 4 r. des Fours. ☎03 80 64 18 52. Open Tue-Sat 8.30am-12.30pm and 3-7pm. Closed 3 weeks in June. Having practised his art for more than 30 years, M. Poulizac truly knows his bread. A dozen varieties appear daily, including the country bread with dried figs that appears on the tables of local inns.

on the route and obliged itself to treat travellers well. Rabelais had already praised Saulieu and its excellent meals. **Madame de Sévigné** stopped in the town on her way to Vichy on 26 August 1677, and she avowed later that for the first time in her life she was a little tipsy.

Sights

Basilique St-Andoche★

🕐*Open Easter-Oct Tue-Sat 9am-noon, 1.30-6.30pm, Sun 2-6.30pm; rest of the year Tue-Sat 9am-noon, 1.30-4.30pm.* ☎*03 80 64 00 21.*

The church, which dates from the early 12C, was influenced by St-Lazare in Autun of which it was a sister house.

The main point of interest is the series of historiated or decorated **capitals**★★, inspired by those in Autun. After its restoration, the tomb of St Andoche was placed in the last chapel in the right aisle. In the north aisle is a handsome tombstone and Pietà, presented, it is said, by Madame de Sévigné as a penance for over-indulgence.

Musée Municipal François-Pompon

🕐*Open Mar-Dec daily except Tue 10am-12.30, 2-5.30pm (Apr-Sep 6pm), Sun and public holidays 10.30am-noon, 2.30-5pm.* 🕐*Closed Mon pm, Jan-Feb, 1 May and 25 Dec.* ⊚*4€.* ☎*03 80 64 19 51.*

On the ground floor of this new museum are Gallo-Roman tombstones, religious statuary, milestones and so on. The first floor is devoted to sculptor **François Pompon**, born in Saulieu in 1855. A student of Rodin, he is best known for his representations of animals;. **le Taureau**★ (Bull), one of his greatest works, was erected on a square at the town's northern entrance in 1948.

Excursion

Butte de Thil★

18km/11mi N along D 980.
The hill, visible from afar, is crowned with the ruins of a former 14C **collegiate church** and a **medieval castle** (9C-14C) dismantled by Richelieu.

SEMUR-EN-AUXOIS ★

POPULATION 4 543
MAP P000 AND MICHELIN MAP 320: G-5
LOCAL MAP SEE LE MORVAN

The **setting**★ and the town of Semur, main centre of the Auxois agricultural and stock-raising region, form a picturesque scene. A tightly packed mass of small light-coloured houses, with the great towers of the castle and the slender spire of the church of Notre-Dame rising above, stands on top of a rose-tinted granite cliff, overlooking a deep ravine with the River Armançon at the bottom.

🛈 **Information**: 2 pl. Gaveau, 21140 Semur-En-Auxois.
☎ 03 80 97 05 96. www.ville-semur-en-auxois.fr.

▶ **Orient Yourself**: Try to arrive along the Paris road, from where there is a good view of the ramparts and the town during the downhill run to the Joly Bridge.

A Bit of History

A stronghold

Semur became the strong point of the duchy in the 14C when the citadel was reinforced by ramparts and 18 towers. The town was divided into three parts each with a perimeter wall. Occupying

the whole width of the rock spur and towering above all else was the keep, a citadel in itself and reputedly impregnable. It had a sheer drop both to the north and the south to the Armançon Valley and was flanked by four enormous round towers: the Tour de l'Orle-d'Or, the Tour de la Gehenne, the Tour de la Prison and the Tour Margot. The château stood to the west, on the upper part of the peninsula, encircled by a bend in the river – the ramparts can still be seen. To the east was the town, still the most densely populated district, although the town has spread on to the west bank.

Town Walk

Porte Sauvigny
This 15C gateway, preceded by a postern, marked the main entrance to the district known as the Bourg Notre-Dame.

▷ *Follow rue Buffon.*

Collégiale Notre-Dame
The church is in place Notre-Dame, flanked by old houses. It was founded in the 11C, rebuilt in the 13C and 14C, altered in the 15C and 16C, extended by the addition of chapels to the north aisle and restored by Viollet-le-Duc.
Exterior – The 14C façade, dominated by two square towers, is preceded by a vast porch. In rue Notre-Dame, the 13C door in the north transept (Porte des Bleds) has a beautiful tympanum depicting Doubting Thomas and the bringing of the Gospel to the West Indies.
Interior – There are several interesting chapels opening off the north aisle. In the second chapel (1) is a polychrome Entombment from the late 15C with monumental figures typical of Claus Sluter. The third chapel (2) vaulting has 16C stained glass illustrating the legend of Ste Barbara. The last two chapels contain panels of stained glass given in the 15C by local guilds – the butchers (3) and eight panels from the **drapers**★ (4).
Behind the pulpit is a 15C stone canopy (5), remarkably carved with a 5m/16ft-high pinnacle.
In the last chapel of the outer north aisle is a painted retable (6) dating from 1554, representing the Tree of Jesse. The retable is surmounted by a Gothic canopy of carved wood. The Lady Chapel (7) is lit by very beautiful stained-glass windows of the 13C restored by Viollet-le-Duc. In the south aisle there is a late-15C polychrome statue (8) of Christ bearing the Five Wounds.

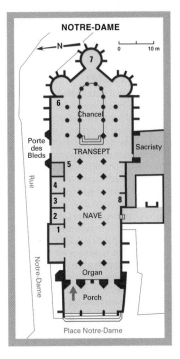

▷ *Continue along rue Fevret.*

Tour de l'Orle-d'Or and Musée
Closed to the public. This tower was part of the keep (razed in 1602).

Pont Joly
From the Joly Bridge there is an overall **view**★ of the medieval city. The bridge crosses the Armançon at the foot of the castle keep which once guarded the narrow isthmus joining the rose-coloured cliff, where the city started, to the granite plateau onto which it has spread.

Promenade des Remparts
The former ramparts along the edge of the granite spur have been converted into a promenade shaded by lime trees overlooking the valley of the Armançon. To reach the promenade, go past the hospital, a pleasant 18C building.
Rue Basse-du-Rempart skirts the foot of the ramparts. Their grandeur is emphasised by the enormous blocks of red granite, sparkling with mica and quartz, which serve as the foundations of the keep.

▷ *Walk back along rue Collenot.*

Address Book

For coin ranges, see the Legend on the cover flap.

WHERE TO STAY

⊜**Chambre d'Hôte La Maison du Canal** – *At Pont-Royal, 21390 Clamerey, 16km/ 10mi SE of Semur-en-Auxois by D 970 then D 70 (heading for Vitteaux). ☎03 80 64 62 65. ⊭ 6 rooms. Meals⊜ ⊜.* This early 19C building,on the quays of the Burgundy Canal opposite a marina, has carefully kept rooms looking out onto peaceful Auxois countryside. Information on boating available.

⊜**Chambre d'Hôte Les Langrons** – *21140 Villars-Villenotte, 5.5km/3.5mi NW of Semur-en-Auxois by D 954 then D 9A. ☎03 80 96 65 11. Closed Dec. ⊭ 3 rooms.* This beautifully restored farmhouse is near the village of Villars. The large, comfortable rooms feature exposed beams. The curtains and bedspreads have an unmistakable British touch, which is understandable because the owners come from England. Scrumpti-

ous breakfasts. Pretty, self-catering gîte at the entrance to the farm.

⊜**Cymaises** – *7 r. Renaudot. ☎03 80 97 21 44. www.hotelcymaises.com. Closed 10 Feb-3 Mar and 4-24 Nov. 18 rooms. � 6.50€.* In the heart of the medieval city, this lovely auberge has renovated, soundproofed rooms. Take breakfast on the veranda. The garden is a riot of flowers.

WHERE TO EAT

⊜**Le Calibressan** – *16 r. Févret. ☎03 80 97 32 40. le.calibressan@wanadoo.fr. Closed Jan.* She comes from California, he is from Bresse, hence the name. The same combination is echoed in the decoration and in the fusion cooking.

SHOPPING

Pellé – *1 r. de la Liberté. ☎03 80 97 08 94. Open Tue-Sun 7am-7pm.* This famed chocolatier, open for 30 years, is full of temptations. Specialities not to miss are the Granité Rose de L'Auxois, made of chocolate, almonds and orange. Also on offer: some 25 types of cake.

Museum Municipal

🕐*Open Apr-Sep daily except Tue 2-6pm; Oct-Apr Mon-Fri 2-5pm.* 🕐*Closed 1 Jan, 1 and 8 May, 14 Jul, 15 Aug, 1 and 11 Nov, 25 Dec. ⊚3.25€. ☎03 80 97 24 25.*

The ground floor displays a collection of 13C to 19C sculpture, including many original plaster figures. The first floor houses a collection on natural science, particularly zoology and geology (such as rare fish fossils and mineral samples). The second floor has articles found during the excavation of prehistoric, Gallo-Roman and Merovingian sites and a small gallery of paintings.

Excursion

Époisses

12km/7.5mi W.

This pleasant village, on the plateau of Auxois, is known for its castle and its soft, strong-flavoured cheese.

Château d'Époisses★

🕐*Open Jul-Aug daily except Tue 10am-noon, 2-6pm. Park year round daily 9am-7pm. ⊚6€ (park 2€). ☎03 80 96 40 56. www.chateaudepoisses.com.*

The château is enclosed by two fortified precincts ringed by dry moats. The buildings in the outer courtyard form a small village clustered round the church, once part of a 12C abbey, and a robust 16C dovecot. The château was remodelled in the 16C and 17C and partly demolished during the Revolution. The Guitaut family, owners of the château since the 17C, have preserved many mementoes of famous people who have stayed here. In the entrance hall, Renaissance portraits are set into the panelled walls. The small room beyond has a richly painted ceiling. The salon's Louis XIV furniture includes chairs covered with Gobelins tapestries. On the first floor the portrait gallery is hung with paintings of 17C and 18C personalities.

SENS★★

POPULATION 26 904

MICHELIN MAP 319: C-2

Now a simple sub-prefecture in the *département* of Yonne, Sens is the seat of an archbishopric, proof of its past grandeur. The attractive old town is encircled by boulevards and promenades that have replaced the ancient ramparts.

- **Information**: pl. Jean-Jaurès, 89100 Sens.
  ☎03 86 65 19 49. www.office-de-tourisme-sens.com.
- ▸ **Orient Yourself**: If possible, approach Sens from the west for scenic views as you enter the city. There are nice shops along the pedestrian Grande-Rue, and cafés with terraces line the place de la République.
- **Don't Miss:** The Cathédrale St-Étienne, the first of France's great Gothic cathedrals.

A Bit of History

An Important Diocese

During the residence in Sens of Pope Alexander III in 1163-64 the city became the temporary capital of Christianity. The church council that condemned Abélard was also held at Sens and the marriage of St Louis and Marguerite of Provence was celebrated in the cathedral in 1234. With the elevation of Paris to the rank of an archbishopric in 1622, the diocese of Sens lost the bishoprics of Meaux, Chartres and Orléans.

Cathédrale St-Étienne★★

✏Guided tours; ☎03 86 65 19 49.

The cathedral, started c 1130 by Archbishop Henri Sanglier, was the first of the great Gothic cathedrals in France. Many other buildings have borrowed largely from the design (the layout, the alternating pillars, the triforium); William of Sens, architect, used it as his model when reconstructing the chancel of Canterbury Cathedral (1175-92).

Exterior

The west front, despite the loss of a tower, has preserved its imposing majesty and harmony of balance. The north tower (*tour de plomb* or Lead Tower), built at the end of the 12C, used to be surmounted by a timbered belfry covered in lead, which was destroyed during the 19C.

The south tower (*tour de pierre* or Stone Tower), which collapsed at the end of the 13C, was rebuilt in the following century and completed in the 16C. It is topped by a graceful campanile.

The tympanum of the 12C north doorway doorway recalls the history of St John the Baptist. The central doorway has a beautiful statue of St Stephen, dating from the end of the 12C, which marks the transition period between the sculptures of Chartres and Bourges and those of Paris and Amiens. The tympanum of the right-hand doorway (early 14C) is devoted to the Virgin.

▸ *Go round the cathedral to the N and take the passage (14C St-Denis doorway) to the Maison de l'Œuvre, the 16C chapter library. Carry on to impasse Abraham.*

North transept

From impasse Abraham admire the magnificent Flamboyant-style façade built by Martin Chambiges and his son between 1500 and 1513. The sculpted decoration is very graceful.

▸ *Go back to the west front of the cathedral and enter by the south doorway.*

Interior

The nave is impressive for its size and unity; it is divided from the aisles by magnificent arches surmounted by a triforium and roofed with sexpartite vaulting. The alternating stout and slender pillars are characteristic of the Early Gothic style.

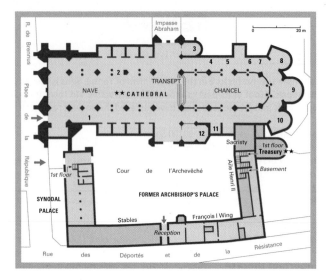

The **stained-glass windows**★★, dating from the 12C to the 17C, are magnificent. In the third bay of the south aisle is a window (1) by Jean Cousin, dating from 1530. On the north side of the nave is a Renaissance retable and a monument (2) given by Archbishop de Salazar in memory of his parents.

The stained-glass windows of the south transept (1500-02) were made in Troyes – those portraying the Tree of Jesse and Legend of St Nicholas are outstanding; the rose window represents the Last Judgement. Those in the north transept were made between 1516 and 1517 by Jean Hympe and his son, glaziers from Sens; the rose window represents Paradise.

The Good Samaritan

The choir is enclosed by handsome bronze screens (1762) bearing the arms of the Cardinal de Luynes. The large high altar is 18C by Servandoni and the stained glass of the clerestory dates from the 13C. Both St John's Chapel, which contains a fine 13C calvary (3), and the blind arcade round the ambulatory are part of the original building. The oldest stained glass, dating from the late 12C, is in the four windows overlooking the ambulatory: the story of Thomas à Becket (4), the story of St Eustache (5) and the parables of the Prodigal Son (6) and the Good Samaritan (7). The tomb (8) of the dauphin, father of Louis XVI, by Guillaume Coustou is placed in the next chapel. The 13C apsidal chapel has stained-glass windows (9) of the same period. In the chapel of the Sacré-Cœur (10) one of the windows is attributed to Jean Cousin. In summer, a 13C staircase leads up to the cathedral treasury *(in winter, go via the museum, as the staircase is closed)*.

In the chapel beyond the sacristy is a Renaissance retable (11). The Lady Chapel contains a 14C seated statue of the Virgin (12) above the altar.

▶ *Leave by the south transept.*

South transept

This was built by Martin Chambiges, master mason, who had worked at both Beauvais and Troyes. It is a fine example

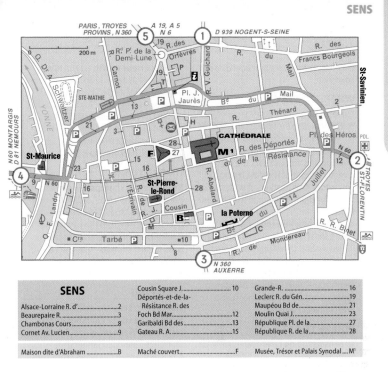

of the Flamboyant style (1490-1500); the Moses doorway is quite remarkable.

Museum, Treasury and Palais Synodal★

Open Jul-Aug except Tue 10am-6pm; Jun and Sep except Tue 10am-noon, 2-6pm; rest of the year times vary. Closed 1 Jan and 25 Dec. 5€. 03 86 64 46 22.
The Musées de Sens are housed in the **ancien archevêché** (16C-18C) and the Palais Synodal which stand on the south side of the cathedral.

François I and Henri II wings
These 16C galleries are devoted to the history of Sens and the Sens district. The first rooms display prehistoric and proto-historic articles: Paleolithic stone tools, Neolithic house and burials (7 500 to 2 500 BC), Bronze Age objects (2 500 to 750 BC) including the treasure of Villethierry (jeweller's stock), many Iron Age weapons and ornaments.
The basement contains pieces of **Gallo-Roman stonework**★ reused in the building of the town walls of Sens: architectural pieces, sculptures, tombstones.

Excavations under the courtyard have revealed the foundations of a 4C bath-house and a collection of bone combs. Sculpture from the 18C is displayed on the first floor: reliefs from the Porte Dauphine erected in memory of the dauphin, Louis XV's son, and of the dauphin's wife, and parts of a rood screen removed from the cathedral in the 19C. The second floor has 17C to 19C paintings.

Cathedral treasury (Trésor)★
Access via the museum.
This treasure house is one of the richest in France. It contains a magnificent collection of materials and liturgical vestments: the shroud of St Victor, a 13C white silk mitre embroidered with gold thread, St Thomas à Becket's alb; handsome 15C high warp tapestries (*Adoration of the Magi* and *Coronation of the Virgin*); ivories (5C and 6C pyx, the 7C liturgical comb of St Lupus, an 11C Byzantine coffret and a 12C Islamic one) as well as gold plate (late-12C ciborium).

Palais Synodal
This beautiful 13C palace was restored by Viollet-le-Duc. The great vaulted chamber on the ground floor was the

Address Book

For coin ranges, see the Legend on the cover flap.

WHERE TO STAY

Hôtel Virginia – *3km/1.9mi E of Sens by N 60 heading for Troyes. ℡03 86 64 66 66. 100 rooms. ⬜6€. Restaurant.* This motel is comprised of several buildings, so you can park the car directly in front of the door leading to your room. Grill-restaurant with special menu for children. Lounge with billiard table.

Relais de Villeroy – *89100 Villeroy, 7km/4.3mi W of Sens by D 81. ℡03 86 88 81 77. www.relais-de-villeroy.com. 8 rooms. ⬜8€. Restaurant.* This chic building outside the village offers small, comfortable guest rooms. Two dining rooms, one formal, the other rustic. Pretty flower garden.

WHERE TO EAT

Auberge de la Vanne – *176 av. de Senigallia. ℡03 86 65 13 63. Closed 12-30 Nov, Sun evening, Wed evening and Tue.* A typical Sens residence renovated as an auberge offers a cheerful refuge. Pleasant dining room; terrace overlooking the water. Classical French menu.

Au Crieur de Vin – *1 r. d'Alsace-Lorraine. ℡03 86 65 92 80. Closed 27 Jun-6 Jul, 8-24 Aug, 19 Dec-4 Jan, Sun and Mon and Tue lunchtime.* Traditional dishes like *tête de veau* (boiled calf's head) and roasted meat (poultry, lamb, pork) are the specialities of this restaurant, along with wines from the Yonne area.

ON THE TOWN

Brasserie des champs – *In the Parc d'Activité "Les Prunelliers", 89100 St-Martin-du-Tertre. ℡03 86 65 19 89.* Four types of beer issue forth from the vats of this small artisan brewery in a village near Sens. Try the summer "blanche", the aromatic blonde varieties or the amber, with hints of caramel flavour.

SHOPPING

Marché – In Sens, the market days are Monday and Friday mornings (town centre) and Wednesday and Sunday mornings (Champs-Plaisants).
À la Renommée des Bons Fromages G. Parret – *37 Grande-Rue. ℡03 86 65 11 54. Open Mon 7.30am-3pm, Fri-Sat 8am-12.30pm. Closed Feb holidays and 3 weeks in Aug.* A small dairy offering many local cheeses: Époisses, Chaource, Soumaintrain. There is an interesting choice of wines stored in the cellar.

seat of the ecclesiastical tribunal *(officialité)*. In the 13C two bays were converted into a prison and there are still traces of graffiti on the walls.

The magnificent hall on the first floor was where the bishops deliberated. The archaeological collection on the ground floor and the collections of the adjoining treasury (Lemoine paintings, tapestries...) will be rearranged once the rooms of the new museum are ready.

Additional Sights

Marché couvert

The metal framework filled with pink brick of the covered market standing opposite the cathedral is typical of the architectural style of the latter half of the 19C. The conspicuous pitched roof is ornamented with pinnacle turrets.

Around St-Pierre-le-Rond

Beside the **church** is the bell-tower (1728) and a building which in 1927 was faced with the 13C façade of the Sens charity hospital (Hôtel-Dieu).

At the corner of rue de la République and rue Jean-Cousin, stands a 16C house, the **Maison dite d'Abraham**. The carved corner post is decorated with a Tree of Jesse. The house next door, at no 50 rue Jean-Cousin, known as the House of the Pillar (Maison du Pilier) (16C), has a curious porch. Further along, at no 8, the Maison Jean-Cousin with a garden façade overlooking rue Jossey also dates from the 16C. The pedestrian shopping street, Grande Rue, has numerous half-timbered houses along it.

La Poterne

Traces of the Gallo-Roman walls are visible on boulevard du 14-Juillet.

CHÂTEAU DE **TANLAY**★★

MICHELIN MAP 319: H-4

The château of Tanlay, built about 1550, is a magnificent architectural composition and an unexpected surprise in this small village on the banks of the Canal de Bourgogne. The château is a fine monument to French Renaissance architecture at a time when it had broken away from the Italian influence.

- **Information**: ☎03 86 75 70 61.
- ▶ **Orient Yourself**: Approaching Tanlay from the east by D 965, there is a good view of this handsome residence and its park, which is particularly attractive in the evening light.

Visit

🕐*Open Apr to mid-Nov. Guided tours (1hr) daily except Tue 10am, 11.30am, 2.15pm, 3.15pm, 4.15pm, 5.15pm. 8.50€.*

Exterior

The small château (the Portal), an elegant building of Louis XIII style, leads into the Cour Verte (Green Courtyard), which is surrounded by arches except on the left where a bridge crosses the moat and leads to the great doorway opening onto the main courtyard of the large château.

The architect Pierre Le Muet, who oversaw work on the château between 1642 and 1648, designed the pyramidal obelisks at the entrance to the bridge.

The main living quarters are joined by two staircase towers to two lower wings at right angles to the main building. Each wing ends in a round domed tower.

Interior

On the ground floor, the hallway (Vestibule des Césars) is closed off by a handsome 16C wrought-iron doorway leading to the gardens. Go through the great hall and the antechamber.

Dining room – The dining room features an eye-catching monumental white-stone Renaissance chimney-piece. Interesting items of furniture include a French Renaissance cabinet and a Burgundian chest.

Drawing room – The 17C woodwork bears the mark of sculptor Michel Porticelli d'Hémery. The pair of sphinxes with women's faces on the chimney-piece are supposed to be Catherine de' Medici.

Bedchamber of the Marquis de Tanlay – Note the late-16C German School painting on copper.

Great Gallery★ – The old ballroom on the first floor is decorated with *trompe-l'œil* frescoes.

Ph. Gajic-MICHELIN

Château de Tanlay

Tour de la Ligue★ – The circular room on the top floor of this turret was used for Huguenot meetings during the Wars of Religion. Like his brother Gaspard de Châtillon, François d'Andelot had embraced the Reformation, after which Tanlay became one of the country's two main centres of Protestantism.

The domed ceiling is decorated with a painting (Fontainebleau School) depicting major 16C Roman Catholic and Protestant protagonists in the somewhat frivolous guise of gods and goddesses.

Gardens

Only partly open to visitors. These lie either side of the long canal (526m/ 1726ft) built by Particelli, which is lined with ancient trees.

TONNERRE

POPULATION 5 979

MICHELIN MAP 319: G-4

Tonnerre is a pleasant little town, terraced on one of the hills that form the west bank of the Armançon and surrounded by vineyards and greenery. Its old hospital and the beautiful sepulchre it contains are among the treasures of Burgundy.

- **Information**: pl Marguerite-de-Bourgogne, 89700 Tonnerre.
  ☎03 86 55 14 48. www.tonnerre.fr.
- **Orient Yourself**: The old town and the newer districts are dominated by the tower of Notre-Dame and church of St-Pierre, from whose terrace there is a good view of the town and its surroundings.

A Bit of History

The Knight of Éon

It was at Tonnerre that Charles-Geneviève-Louise-Auguste-Andrée-Timothée Éon de Beaumont, known as the knight or the lady-knight of Éon, was born in 1728. After a brilliant military and diplomatic career, during which he sometimes had to wear women's clothes, he met with reversals of fortune and was forced to flee to London. He was refused permission to return to France except dressed as a woman. Returning to England, he died there in 1810. To the end of his life, there was widespread speculation as to his

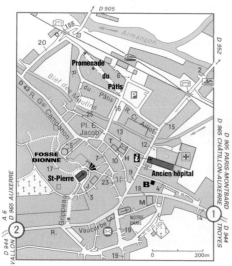

S. Sauvignier-MICHELIN

La Fosse Dionne

gender. The news of his death gave rise to a wave of curiosity ended only by an autopsy. Charles d'Éon was unquestionably a man.

Town Walk

▸ *Start from place de la Gare.*

Promenade du Pâtis
This is a pleasant shady walk.

▸ *Walk across place de la République to rue de la Fosse-Dionne.*

Fosse Dionne★
This circular basin, filled with blue-green water, was used as a wash-house. It is fed by an underground river that flows through a steeply inclined rock gallery (45m/148yd long) to emerge in the centre of the pool; its flow varies considerably according to season and rainfall. The pool overflows into the Armançon by way of a small stream.

▸ *Follow chemin des Roches.*

Église St-Pierre
○┅*Closed for restoration.*
With the exception of the 14C chancel and the 15C square tower, the church was rebuilt in 1556 after the fire that ravaged the town. There is a handsome doorway on the south side with a statue of St Peter on the pier.

▸ *Walk along rue St-Pierre to see the unusual west front of Notre-Dame then follow rue de l'Hôpital leading to the former hospital; however, before you reach it, turn right onto rue des Fontenilles.*

Hôtel d'Uzès
A savings bank occupies this Renaissance dwelling, birthplace of the Knight of Éon; note the design on the doors.

Hôtel-Dieu

○*Open Apr-Sep 9.30am-noon (Jul-Aug 12.30pm), 1.30-6pm, Sun and public holidays 10am-12.30pm, 2-6pm; Oct-Mar daily except Wed and Sun 9-noon, 2-6pm. Closed 25 Dec-1 Jan, 1 May. 4.50€. ☎03 86 55 14 48. www.tonnerre.fr.*
This beautiful old hospital, erected between 1293 and 1295 by Margaret of Burgundy, widow of Charles d'Anjou, King of Naples and Sicily and brother of St Louis, has survived intact, apart from minor modifications. From the outside, the walls of the hall, despite their buttresses, seem to be crushed by the tall roof which covers an area of 4 500m²/5 382 sq yd. The west front was changed in the 18C.

Interior
Although shortened in the 18C, the great hall is of an impressive size (90m/295ft long and 18.2m/60ft wide). The broken-barrel vaulting and the **oak timbering** are remarkable. The 40 beds for the sick

Address Book

For coin ranges, see the Legend on the cover flap.

WHERE TO STAY

⊜**Gîte d'Étape La Gravière du Moulin** – 7 rte. de Frangey, 89160 Lézinnes, 11km/6.8mi SE of Tonnerre by D 905. ☎03 86 75 68 67. ⊐32 guests per night. This 19C mill over the Armançon offers accommodation for families and groups of friends. There are rooms with two, six or 12 beds. Library, lab for developing photographs.

⊜**Chambre d'Hôte M. et Mme Piedallu** – 5 av. de la Gare, 89160 Lézinnes, 11km/6.8mi SE of Tonnerre by D 905. ☎03 86 75 68 23. ⊐3 rooms. This charming modern house with a round tower has been built in accordance with local tradition. The rooms under the eaves are spacious and comfortable with period furniture. Breakfast is served on the veranda.

WHERE TO EAT

⊜**Le Saint Père** – 2 av. G.-Pompidou. ☎03 86 55 12 84. Closed 29 Dec-20 Jan, Sun pm and Wed. This modest restaurant serves traditional cooking in a simple but well-kept dining room. Attractive choice of menus at affordable prices. Note the collection of coffee grinders.

SHOPPING

Caveau de Fontenilles – pl. Marguerite-de-Bourgogne. ☎03 86 55 06 33. Open Tue-Sat 9.30am-noon, 2.30-7pm; Sun 10am-12.30pm. This winery has won several medals: recent prizewinners include the Pinot Noir and Chardonnay. Another star is the Cuvée Marguerite-des-Fontenilles, aged in oak and dedicated to the founder of the local hospital.

were set in wooden alcoves built in lines along the walls as at Beaune, which was built 150 years later.

The walls themselves were pierced by high semicircular bays, divided by pointed arches. From 1650, the hall was put to many different uses and often served as the parish church. Many citizens of Tonnerre were buried there, which explains the numerous tombstones. Note the gnomon (sundial) on the paving, designed in the 18C by a Benedictine monk and the astronomer Lalande (1732-1807).

The chapel opens off the end of the hall. The tomb of Margaret of Burgundy, rebuilt in 1826, is in the centre of the choir. Above the altar is a 14C stone statue of the Virgin Mary. To the right of the high altar, a little door leads to the sacristy which contains a carved **Entombment**★, presented to the church in the 15C by a rich merchant of the town. The figures of this Holy Sepulchre make up a scene of dramatic intensity reminiscent of Claus Sluter's style. In the north side chapel is the monumental tomb of the French statesman Louvois, who acquired the county of Tonnerre in 1684 and served as Minister of War under Louis XIV.

Among the objects on view in the Salle du Conseil (consultation room) of the hospital is a great golden cross in which is mounted a piece of wood reputed to be part of the True Cross.

Musée

In the 18C hospital buildings, the collection includes several objects and manuscripts linked to its history: an 18C silver reliquary; the hospital's founding Charter (1293); the Last Will and Testament of Marguerite de Bourgogne, dated 1305. From the more recent past, a ward (1850) and operating theatre (1908) have been re-created for visitors.

TOURNUS ★

POPULATION 6 231

MICHELIN MAP 320: J-10 LOCAL MAP SEE LE MÂCONNAIS

This small town on the right bank of the Saône between Chalon and Mâcon, is one of the oldest and most important of the monastic centres in France owing to the architectural beauty and the harmonious proportions of the church and the conventual buildings, which date from the 10C.

- **Information**: 2 pl. de l'Abbaye, 71700 Tournus. ☎03 85 27 00 20. www.tournugeois.fr.
- ▶ **Orient Yourself:** Tournus sits on the unofficial boundary between northern France and the Midi, about halfway between Chalon-sur-Sâone and Mâcon.

A Bit of History

Monastic centre

When St Valerian, a Christian from Asia Minor, escaped from persecution in Lyon in 177, he travelled to Tournus to convert the people but was martyred on a hillside above the Saône; a sanctuary was built beside his tomb. In the Merovingian period it was converted into an abbey and dedicated first to St Valerian, and later St Philibert. A Hungarian invasion in 937 checked the prosperity of the abbey which was destroyed by fire and rebuilt. In about 945 the monastery was abandoned by the monks, but in 949 Abbot Stephen, formerly prior of St Philibert, was ordered to return to Tournus with a group of monks. The reconstruction which he set in motion was completed in the 12C; it produced one of the most beautiful parts of the church.

Over the centuries the building underwent damage, repair and modification; in 1562 it was sacked by the Huguenots. The abbey became a collegiate church in 1627 and in 1790 a parish church, avoiding irrevocable damage in the Revolution.

Ancienne Abbaye ★★

The Church

Église St-Philibert

The façade, dating from the 10C and 11C and built of beautifully cut stone, has almost the appearance of a castle keep with the dark loophole slits emphasising the warm colour of the stone. The crenellated parapet with machicolations linking the two towers accentuates the military appearance of the building. Both this gallery and the porch are the work of Questel in the 19C.

The right tower is topped by a saddle-back roof; the other was heightened at the end of the 11C by the addition of a two-storey belfry surmounted by a tall spire.

▶ *Enter the church by the doorway to the right of the main façade.*

Chapelle St-Michel(a)

The chapel occupies the upper room in the narthex which was built before the nave (*access via a spiral staircase*). In plan, it is identical with the ground floor but the astonishing height of the central section and the amount of light give it an entirely different feel. The great arched bay opening into the organ loft was once the entrance to a small oven-vaulted apsidal chapel which was suppressed when the organ loft was built in 1629. The ancient sculpture on the capitals and the blocks which they support have survived from the Carolingian period.

Narthex

This is the place of transition from the outer world to the house of God, where reflection and preparation for prayer are encouraged by the half-light. Its rugged and simple architecture achieves a singular grandeur. Four enormous circular abacus pillars divide it into a nave and two aisles, each of three bays.

One bay of the vault is painted in a black and white chequered pattern, the arms

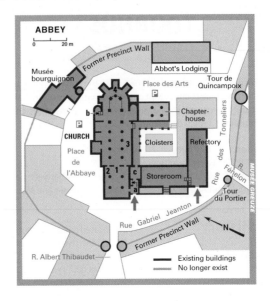

ABBEY

0   20 m

Former Precinct Wall

Musée bourguignon

Abbot's Lodging

Tour de Quincampoix

Place des Arts

Chapter-house

CHURCH

Cloisters

Refectory

Place de l'Abbaye

Storeroom

Tour du Portier

Rue Gabriel Jeanton

Former Precinct Wall

N

R. Albert Thibaudet

━━ Existing buildings
━━ No longer exist

of Digoine, an old and powerful Mâcon family. On the wall above the entrance to the nave is a 14C fresco of Christ in Majesty (**1**); the end wall of the north aisle carries another 14C fresco portraying the Crucifixion (**2**). The round tombstones are peculiar to this region.

The nave

The nave, which dates from the beginning of the 11C, is now devoid of decoration. Magnificently tall cylindrical pillars made from the rose-coloured stone of Préty (a small place near Tournus) are surmounted by ordinary flat capitals,

St-Philibert's nave

B. Kaufmann-MICHELIN

like those in the narthex; they divide the five bays of the nave from the aisles.

A most unusual feature is the central vault which consists of five transverse barrel vaults resting on transverse arches with alternating white and pink arch stones; great columns surmounted by slim columns support the arches, which obscure the clerestory, through which light enters the nave.

The side chapels in the north aisle date from the 14C and 15C.

A 15C niche in the south aisle contains a 12C statue-reliquary of the Virgin (**3**), Notre-Dame-de-la-Brune, which shows the artistic influence of the Auvergne. The statue, which is made of painted cedar wood (regilded in the 19C) retains an aura of calm and majestic beauty.

Transept and choir

Built at the start of the 12C, the transept and choir contrast strongly with the rest of the building in the whiteness of the stonework; they show the rapid evolution of Romanesque art.

In the transept the contrast can be seen between the spaciousness of the nave and the narrowness of the choir which the architect restricted to the dimensions of the existing crypt.

The oven-vaulted apse is supported by six columns with capitals, surmounted by semicircular windows framed by

Address Book

For coin ranges, see the Legend on the cover flap.

WHERE TO STAY

⬭**Camping Château de l'Épervière** – *In Épervière, 71240 Gigny-sur-Saône, 12 km/7.5mi N of Tournus by D 271. ☎ 03 85 94 16 90 – domaine-de-leperviere@wanadoo.fr. Open Apr-Sep. Reservations recommended. 100 sites. Meals available evenings.* This campsite is clustered around a 14C and 18C château amid wooded parkland on the edge of a lake. Shaded sites. Swimming pool with shallow basin for children. Tennis court nearby. Self-catering accommodation available.

⬭ **Chambre d'Hôte Manoir de Champvent** – *In Champvent, 71700 Chardonnay, 11km/6.8mi SW of Tournus by D 56 then D 463. ☎03 85 40 50 23. Closed Nov-Feb. 5 rooms.* The rooms in the outbuildings of this manor house have old-fashioned furniture; some of them are under the eaves. Theatrical performances are held on the premises. Large meadow and courtyard bursting with flowers.

WHERE TO EAT

⬭⬭**Le Terminus** – *21 av. Gambetta. ☎03 85 51 05 54. www.leterminustournus. com. Closed Wed.* Before the era of the motorway, Tournus was a popular stopping place for travellers. With its contemporary dining room, this place is a tribute to those early days. Renovated rooms.

⬭⬭**Aux Terrasses** – *18 av. du 23-Janvier. ☎03 85 51 01 74. www.aux-terrasses.com. Closed 2 Jan-2 Feb, 6-14 Jun, 16-22 Nov, Sun evenings, Tue lunch and Mon.* This well-known restaurant serves carefully prepared traditional dishes, some at extremely reasonable prices, in a pretty dining room.

⬭⬭⬭⬭**Restaurant Greuze** – *1 r. A.-Thibaudet. ☎03 85 51 13 52. www.restaurant-greuze.com. Closed 14 Nov-5 Dec.* Housed in a handsome stone building, this restaurant near Tournus Abbey is a temple of French gastronomy. The vast dining hall is sparsely furnished and enhanced by light walls, dark panelling and white tablecloths. First-rate cuisine served in grand style.

SHOPPING

La Cave des vignerons de Mancey – *N 6. ☎03 85 51 00 83. www.cave-mancey. com. Open daily 8am-noon, 2-6pm.* This cooperative association showcases wines from some 80 regional winegrowers. The selection is diverse and of high quality. Try the Essentielles, including remarkable Mâcon-Villages, Mâcon-Mancey and Burgundy Pinot Noir.

---

delicately sculpted decoration. The barrel-vaulted ambulatory built at the beginning of the 11C has three radiating chapels and two oriented chapels; the axial chapel contains the shrine of St Philibert (4). The modern stained-glass windows blend well with the rest.

Crypt★ (b)

Access by steps in the north transept. The crypt with its thick walls was built by Abbot Stephen at the end of the 10C and restored by Questel in the 19C. The height (3.5m/12ft) is quite exceptional. The central part, flanked by two rows of slender columns (some have a typical archaic bulge) with delightful foliated capitals, is surrounded by an ambulatory with radiating chapels. The 12C fresco,

decorating the chapel on the right and representing a Virgin and Child and a Christ in Majesty, is the best preserved in the church.

Conventual Buildings

To reach the cloisters one passes through the old alms room (c) or warming room (13C) adjoining the south wall of the narthex. It contains a lapidary collection including the column-statues and capitals from the north tower as well as a few sculptures from the cloisters.

Cloisters

Only the north gallery remains; at the end, a 13C doorway leads into the aisle of the church. The buildings on the south side, which hide the refectory, now house both the public and abbey libraries (many illuminated medieval manuscripts). They are dominated by the square Prieuré Tower.

Chapter-house

This was rebuilt by Abbot Bérard following a fire in 1239 and now houses temporary exhibitions. The pointed vaulting is visible through the Romanesque apertures overlooking the cloisters.

▷ *Leave by place des Arts.*

Admire the east end with its five chapels and the 12C belfry over the transept crossing. This fine tower was inspired by Cluny.

Abbot's Lodging

This is a charming late-15C building. In rue des Tonneliers stands the Quincampoix Tower which was built after the Hungarian invasion in 937; it was part of the wall of enclosure of the old abbey as was the neighbouring tower, called the Tour du Portier.

Refectory

This magnificent 12C chamber has no transverse arches but is vaulted with slightly broken barrel vaulting. When the abbey was secularised in 1627 the hall was used for tennis matches and was called the Ballon (ball). It is now used for temporary exhibitions.

Storeroom

The storeroom, also 12C, has broken barrel vaulting resting on transverse arches. It is lit by two small windows set high up. The vast cellars below are now occupied by various craftsmen.

Additional Sights

Musée Bourguignon

◐*Open Apr-Oct Wed-Sun 10am-1pm, 2-5pm.* ◉ *2.50€.* ☎*03 85 51 29 68.*
Wax models in Burgundian costume re-create scenes from daily life of past centuries (about 40 figures in eight rooms). The scenes include the interior of a Bresse farm, a local Tournus interior with nine variations of the regional costume, the large room of the Burgundian spinners, collections of headdresses, costumes, and, in the basement, the reconstruction of a Burgundian cellar.

Hôtel-Dieu★

♿◐*Open late Mar-early Nov daily except Tue 10am-6pm.* ◉*5.25€.* ☎*03 85 51 23 50.*
After three centuries of providing health care to the poor, this historic hospital closed in 1982. The traditional curtained beds in oak wood are still lined up in three vast rooms set around the chapel: one for men, one for women and one for soldiers. The **apothecary**★ displays typical 17C Nevers ceramic jars used to store powders and herbs.

Excursion

Chapaize★

16km /10mi W.
On the River Bisançon, to the west of the magnificent forest of Chapaize, this little village is dominated by the high belfry of its **Romanesque church**★, all that remains of a Benedictine priory founded in the 11C. There are clear Lombard influences in the architecture; Italian stonemasons almost certainly worked on it. The interior has a stark beauty.

VESOUL

POPULATION 17 168
MICHELIN MAP 314: E-7

Vesoul boasts an interesting old town and a pleasant lake offering a choice of outdoor activities.

🛈 **Information**: 2 r. Gevrey, 70002 Vesoul. ☎03 84 97 10 85. www.ot-vesoul.fr.
▷ **Orient Yourself**: The town is in the delightful valley of the Durgeon, a tributary of the Saône, not far from the Jura border with the southern part of Lorraine.

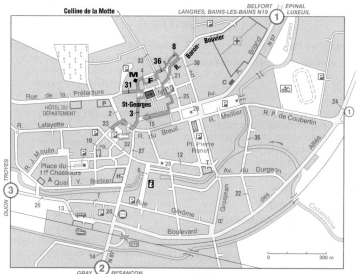

A Bit of History

Birth of a capital

Prehistoric man first settled on the La Motte outcrop overlooking the town to the north. This settlement was replaced by a Roman military camp intended to guard the road between Luxeuil and Besançon. A small market town grew up in the 13C under the sheltering walls of the fort on the plateau. Then the inhabitants moved down into the plain, and Vesoul became an active commercial, religious and military centre. The fort was attacked several times and was finally razed in 1595.

Town Walk

▸ *Start from the car park on rue des Tanneurs.*

Rue d'Alsace-Lorraine boasts several fine structures, particularly no. 22.

Église St-Georges

⚷ *Closed for restoration.*

This church is a beautiful 18C Classical building with Rhenish Gothic influence. Outside, note at no. 2 the **Maison Baressois** (15-16C), with its mullioned windows. The contemporary fountain, by Aline Bienfait, is titled *La Rencontre*.

▸ *Turn left to look down rue Salengro.*

Rue Salengro

At no. 11 note the **Hôtel Thomassin** (15C), its doors, windows and gutters graced with twist moulding. A few steps farther, peek to the right to see a flowered courtyard and a 15C tower.

▸ *Retrace your steps; take rue des Ursulines to Musée Georges-Garret.*

Musée Georges-Garret

🕐 *Open daily except Tue 2-6pm.* 🚫 *Closed 1 Jan, 1 May, 14 Jul, 1 and 25 Nov, 25 Dec.* ☎03 84 76 51 54.

Address Book

WHERE TO STAY

⌂**Camping International du Lac** – *2.5km/1.5mi W of Vesoul.* ☎*03 84 76 22 86. Open Mar-Oct.* ✉ *Reservations recommended. 160 sites.* If you are keen on sporting activities, this is the place for you. Spread out over a huge recreational area on the edge of a lake, it offers facilities for swimming, sailing, fishing, archery, tennis, table-tennis and basketball, and there are hiking trails and cycling paths.

WHERE TO EAT

⊜⊜**Le Caveau du Grand Puits** – *r. Mailly.* ☎*03 84 76 66 12. Closed 15 Aug-1 Sep, 24 Dec-3 Jan, Wed lunchtime, Sat lunchtime, Sun and public holidays.* Walk down a few steps and enter a lovely vaulted cellar with stone walls that serves as a setting to this family restaurant. Traditional bill of fare. Terrace giving onto the courtyard. Highly popular among local residents.

SIT BACK AND RELAX

Azouz Mickaël – *22 r. d'Alsace-Lorraine.* ☎*03 84 75 05 93. www.azouz.com. Open Tue-Sat 8.30am-7pm, Sun 9am-12.30pm.* Do not miss the chance to taste the house specialities of this award-winning chocolatier and cake-maker: the "Élégantes de Vesoul", the "Franc-Comtois", or any of 25 different flavoured chocolates. Make your selection (or selections) and have a seat in the pleasant tearoom which also serves as an art gallery.

The lower floor houses temporary exhibitions and an archaeological department with an interesting collection of Gallo-Roman **funerary steles.** The upper floor is devoted to painting and sculpture, including a large collection of work by local artist Gérome.

▶ *Turn right on rue des Annonciades.*

Les "traiges"★

Here you'll get a glimpse into the "hidden" corner of old Vesoul, with secret courtyards and gardens tucked between houses from the 16C and 17C. The path ends at rue Paul-Petitclerc *(turn right).* Note the fine ironwork along rue Vendémiaire.

In the Musée Georges-Garret

Rue de Mailly

The Hôtel de Magnoncourta (1530) maintains its handsome staircase. Further on, you'll see two more buildings from the same period.

Rues du Châtelet et Baron-Bouvier

The path leads to the former site of the entrance-gate into the old city. *(Turn right).* The rue du Baron-Bouvier here is lined with market stalls. Note at no. 2 the elegant **Hôtel de Montgenet** (1549), and facing it, the **Maison Cariage** (15C).

▶ *Turn left.*

18C buildings

The 18C was a time of prolific construction in Vesoul, particularly in this area, distinguished by the many buildings with harmonious and symmetrical lines: **Hôtel Lyautey de Colombe**★, Hôtel Raillard de Granvelle (place du Grand-Puits) and Palais de Justice (place du Palais).

▶ *Walk along the right side of the palais, and turn onto rue des Boucheries.*

Note, at no. 14, a handsome structure (1525), with tower, gargoyles and Gothic doorway.

▶ *Return to your car via rue Georges-Genoux.*

VÉZELAY★★★

POPULATION 492

MICHELIN MAP 319: F-7

LOCAL MAP SEE LE MORVAN

In a beautiful setting on a hill overlooking the Cure Valley on the edge of the Morvan, Vézelay with its old houses and ramparts is one of the treasures of Burgundy and France.

- **Information**: 12 r. St-Étienne, 89450 Vézelay.
  ☎03 86 33 23 69. www.vezelaytourisme.com.
- ▶ **Orient Yourself:** The 11C basilica, heart of Vézelay, overlooks the town from its tall hill. The Promenade des Fossés and the Grande-Rue both lead from the place du Champ-de-Foire at the lower end of town to the basilica.

A Bit of History

The call of St Bernard

Vézelay's abbey, founded in the middle of the 9C, was at the height of its glory when St Bernard preached the Second Crusade there on 31 March 1146. For a century the church had sheltered the relics of Mary Magdalene, and Vézelay was one of the great places of pilgrimage and the start of one of four routes that led pilgrims and merchants across France to Santiago de Compostela.

St Bernard launched his vibrant call for the Crusade in the presence of King Louis VII of France and his family as well as a crowd of powerful barons. His call was received with great enthusiasm by all those present.

Although the Third Crusade, undertaken in 1190, was not preached at Vézelay, it was there that King Philippe-Auguste of France and King Richard the Lionheart of England met before their departure.

Basilique Ste-Marie-Madeleine★★★

🕐 *Open 7am-8pm.* 🚶*Guided tours Jul-Aug 2.30pm; rest of the year on request.* ☎*03 86 33 39 50. vezelay.cef.fr.*

The monastery founded in the 9C was dedicated to Mary Magdalene. The miracles that happened at her tomb soon drew so great a number of penitents and pilgrims that it became necessary to enlarge the Carolingian church (1096-1104); in 1120 a fire broke out on the eve of 22 July, day of the great pilgrimage, destroying the whole nave and engulfing more than 1 000 pilgrims.

Vézelay

J. Damase-MICHELIN

The work of rebuilding was immediately begun, the nave was soon finished and, about 1150, the pre-nave or narthex was added. In 1215 the Romanesque-Gothic choir and transept were completed.

After the discovery at the end of the 13C of other relics of Mary Magdalene at St-Maximin in Provence, pilgrimages became fewer and the fairs and market lost much of their importance. The religious struggles caused the decline of the abbey, which was transformed into a collegiate church in 1538, pillaged by Huguenots in 1569 and finally partially razed during the French Revolution.

In the 19C **Prosper Mérimée** (novelist, 1803-70), in his capacity as Inspector of Historical Monuments, drew the attention of the public works' authorities to the building, which was on the point of collapsing. In 1840 Viollet-le-Duc, who was then less than 30 years old, undertook the work, which he finally finished in 1859.

Exterior

The façade

This was reconstructed by Viollet-le-Duc according to plans contained in the ancient documents. Rebuilt about 1150 in pure Romanesque style it was given a vast Gothic gable in the 13C, with five narrow bays decorated with statues. The upper part forms a tympanum decorated with arcades framing the statues of Christ Crowned, accompanied by the Virgin Mary, Mary Magdalene and two angels. The tower on the right – Tour Saint-Michel – was surmounted by a storey of tall twin bays in the 13C; the octagonal wooden spire was destroyed by lightning in 1819. The other tower remained unfinished.

Three Romanesque doorways open into the narthex; the tympanum of the central doorway on the outside was remade in 1856 by Viollet-le-Duc, who took the mutilated original tympanum as his inspiration: the archivolt, decorated with plant designs, is authentic, but the rest of the arches and the capitals are modern.

Tour of the exterior

Walk round the building counterclockwise to appreciate its length and the flying buttresses which support it. This side of the church is dominated by the 13C tower of St-Antoine (30m/98ft high) which rises above the junction of the nave and the transept; the two storeys of round-headed bays were originally intended to be surmounted by a stone spire.

The chapter-house, built at the end of the 12C, abuts the south transept. The gallery of the cloisters was entirely rebuilt by Viollet-le-Duc.

Château Terrace

Access by rue du Château. From this terrace, shaded by handsome trees, situated behind the church on the site of the old Abbot's Palace, there is a fine **panorama**★ *(viewing table)* of the valley of the River Cure and the northern part of the Morvan.

Continue round the basilica past the attractive houses built by the canons of the chapter in the 18C.

Interior

▶ *Enter the basilica by the door on the south side of the narthex.*

Narthex

This pre-nave, consecrated in 1132 by Pope Innocent II, is later than the nave and the interior façade. Unlike the rib-vaulted church, the Romanesque narthex is roofed with pointed arches and ogival vaulting. The narthex is so large it seems like a church in its own right. The nave is divided into three bays flanked by aisles surmounted by galleries. The four cruciform pillars of engaged columns decorated with historiated capitals are extremely graceful. The capitals portray scenes from both the Old and New Testaments.

Three doorways in the narthex open into the nave and the aisles of the church. When the central door is open, there is a marvellous perspective along the full length of the nave and choir.

Tympanum of the central doorway★★★

This is a masterpiece of Burgundian-Romanesque art, ranking with that of St-Lazare at Autun. At the centre of the composition a mandorla surrounds an immense figure of Christ Enthroned (1) extending his hands to his Apostles (2) assembled round him; the Holy Ghost is

Address Book

🪙 *For coin ranges, see the Legend on the cover flap.*

WHERE TO EAT

🍽 **Les Glycines** – *r. St-Pierre.* ☎*03 86 32 35 30. Closed 4 Jan-15 Mar, 11 Nov-20 Dec.* Stop for a snack or light meal on the wisteria-shaded terrace of this charming café.

🍽🍽 **L'Entre-Vignes** – *89450 St-Père.* ☎*03 86 33 33 33. www.marcmeneau.org. Closed 25 Jan-5 Mar, Tue lunchtime from Easter-Oct, Tue-Fri lunctime in winter, Sun evening and Mon.* Step into this warm, cheerful bistrot and make your selections from a menu of traditional fare. Sunday brunch.

A MEAL AND A BED

🛏 **Cabalus, l'Ancienne Hôtellerie de l'Abbaye** – *r. St-Pierre.* ☎*03 86 33 20 66. www.cabalus.com. Closed Mon in low season and Tue. 4 rooms.* 🛏*8.80€. Meals*🍽🍽. This former 12C hostelry attached to Vézelay Abbey has been converted into a tea shop. The vaulted room is full of sculptures, paintings and pottery pieces. Soup and different spreads for open sandwiches are on offer. Four guestrooms are available.

🛏🛏 **Les Aquarelles** – *89450 Fontette.* ☎*03 86 33 34 35. Closed 12 Nov-5 Dec, 26 Dec-12 Mar, Mon and Tue in Nov-Dec. 10 rooms.* 🛏*6€. Meals*🍽🍽. At this old farmhouse in a peaceful hamlet, you'll be welcomed as an old friend. Small, but well-kept rooms. Simple meals make use of fresh local ingredients. Wine tasting.

🛏🛏 **Hôtel La Palombière** – *pl. du Champ-de-Foire.* ☎*03 86 33 28 50. www. lapalombierevezelay.com. Closed Jan-Feb, Mon in low season. 10 rooms.*

🛏*10€.* This 18C mansion overgrown with Virginia creeper has tremendous character. The rooms are cosy and charming, with satin bedspreads, old-fashioned bathrooms and Louis XIII, Louis XV and Empire furniture. Enjoy breakfast on the veranda.

🛏🛏 **Hôtel Crispol** – *rte. d'Avallon, 89450 Fontette, 5km/3.1mi E of Vézelay by D 957.* ☎*03 86 33 26 25. www.crispol. com. Closed 10 Jan to end of Feb, Tue lunchtime and Mon. 12 rooms.* 🛏*9€. Restaurant*🍽🍽. The elegant, carefully kept rooms of this hotel are furnished in contemporary style and have lovely bathrooms. The big, bright dining room affords pretty views of Vézelay hill. Delicious meals with fresh produce.

FARM INN

🍽🍽 **Ferme-Auberge de Bazoches** – *Domaine de Rousseau.* ☎*03 86 22 16 30. www.auberge-bazoches.com.* ✍ *Reservations recommended.* Pigs and Charolais cows are reared at this imposing 18C farmhouse opposite the château. The attic guest rooms with exposed beams and sloping roofs have old-fashioned furniture. Tuck into the succulent homemade pies, chicken and guinea fowl dishes, and the pork roasted with honey.

SHOPPING

Les Caves du Pèlerin – *32 r. St-Étienne.* ☎*03 86 33 30 84. Open 16 Mar-31 Dec Thu-Mon 9.30am-noon, 2-6pm.* Traditional village house transformed into the "wine museum" of Vézelay. Shop and tastings.

---

shown radiating from the stigmata to touch the head of each of the Twelve. All around, on the arch stones and the lintel, are crowded the converts to be received at the feet of Christ by St Peter and St Paul (**3**), symbols of the universal Church. People of every sort are called: on the lintel are *(left)* archers (**4**), fishermen (**5**), farmers (**6**), and *(right)* distant and legendary people – giants (**7**), pygmies (climbing a ladder to mount a horse (**8**), men with huge ears (one with a

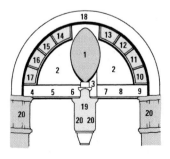

Central doorway

Ph. Gajic-MICHELIN

humorous interpretations of his contemporaries at work.

Tympana of the side doors

Two recessed arches with ornamental foliage and rosettes frame the historiated tympana on the side doors.

The one on the right represents the Childhood of Christ: on the lintel are the Annunciation, the Visitation and the Nativity; on the tympanum is the Adoration of the Magi. The one on the left represents the apparitions of Christ after His Resurrection; on the tympanum is the apparition to the Apostles; on the lintel is the apparition to the disciples at Emmaus.

Nave

Rebuilt between 1120 and 1135, this Romanesque nave is noteworthy for its huge size (62m/203ft long), the use of different coloured limestone, the lighting and the fine series of capitals.

The nave is much higher than the side aisles and is divided into 10 bays of groined vaulting separated by transverse arches with alternating light and dark stones. These do much to mitigate the severity of the lines.

The great semicircular arches, surmounted by windows, rest on cruciform pillars ornamented with four engaged columns decorated with capitals. A graceful decoration of convex quarter-section mouldings, rosettes and pleated ribbons goes round the arches, the main arches and the string course that runs between the windows and the arches.

The capitals★★★

As they are more beautiful than those in the narthex they deserve to be examined in detail (see plan).

The sculptors – five different hands have been detected in the work – must have had an astonishing knowledge of composition and movement.

Right side

1) A duel.
2) Lust and Despair.
3) Legend of St Hubert.
4) Sign of the Zodiac: Libra.
5) The mystical mill.
6) The death of Dives and Lazarus.
7) Lamach kills Cain.

feather-covered body (9). The arch stones show Armenians (wearing clogs (10), Byzantines perhaps (11), Phrygians (12) and Ethiopians (13); immediately next to Christ are men with dogs' heads (the cynocephalics converted by St Thomas in India (14). The next two panels show the miracles that accompanied the divine word preached by the Apostles: two lepers show their regenerated limbs (15) and two paralytics their healthy arms (16). Lastly two Evangelists record all that they have seen (17).

The large-scale composition seeks to demonstrate that the word of God is intended for the whole world. The signs of the zodiac which alternate with the labours of the months on the outer arch stone (18) introduce the notion of time: the Apostles' mission must also be transmitted from generation to generation. On the central pier John the Baptist (19) carrying the paschal lamb (unfortunately missing) is shown at the feet of Christ as if supporting Him and introducing Him to His rightful place in the centre. Below Him and on the flanking piers are more Apostles (20).

The power of the Holy Ghost which fills the 12 Apostles is symbolised by a strong wind which ruffles the garments and sways the bodies. The linear skill, which is the dominant feature of this masterly work, suggests that in the principal scene the sculptor was following the work of a calligrapher, whereas in the medallions, showing the signs of the zodiac and the months of the year, he felt free to carve

8) The four winds of the year.

9) David astride a lion.

10) St Martin avoids a tree about to fall on him.

11) Daniel subdues the lions.

12) An angel wrestling with Jacob.

13) Isaac blessing Jacob.

Left side

14) St Peter delivered from prison.

15) Adam and Eve.

16) Legend of St Anthony.

17) The execution of Agag.

18) Legend of St Eugenia.

19) Death of St Paul the hermit.

20) Moses and the Golden Calf.

21) Death of Absalom.

22) David and Goliath.

23) Killing of the Egyptian by Moses.

24) Judith and Holophernes.

25) Calumny and Greed.

Transept and choir

Built in 1096, when the Carolingian church was enlarged, the Romanesque transept and choir were demolished at the end of the 12C and replaced by this beautiful Gothic ensemble completed in 1215. The relics of Mary Magdalene (a), preserved in the base of a column surmounted by a modern statue, are in the south transept. A vast ambulatory, with radiating chapels, surrounds the choir.

Crypt

The Carolingian crypt was completely altered in the second half of the 12C. It used to contain Mary Magdalene's tomb and still houses part of her relics. The painting on the vaulting is 13C.

Chapter-house and cloisters

Built at the end of the 12C, shortly before the choir of the basilica, the chapter-house has pointed vaulting. It was completely restored by Viollet-le-Duc. The cloisters were razed during the French Revolution; Viollet-le-Duc rebuilt one gallery in Romanesque style.

Excursion

Château de Bazoches★

10km/6mi S. ◷ *Open Jul-Aug 9.30am-6pm; 25 Mar-Jun and Sep-5 Nov 9.30am-noon,*

2.15-6pm (Oct-5 Nov 5pm). ⊜*7€.* ☎*03 86 22 10 22. www.chateau-bazoches.com.*

This 12C château was once the favoured dwelling of the famous military engineer and marshal of France, **Vauban** (1633-1707). Visitors are reminded that he was an author as well, and mementoes recall his family life and work habits. The Grand Gallery built by Vauban was used as a design and drafting office; parts of it have been set up to look as they must have when the engineer was at work there. Vauban would have easily recognised his own **room**★, with its well-crafted bed and six armchairs (17C). On the ground floor, more memorabilia is exhibited in his wife's room; she lived here until her death in 1705.

Vauban's tomb is in the church in Bazoches (12C-16C), whereas his heart has been laid to rest in the cenotaph erected in his memory in the Invalides, in Paris.

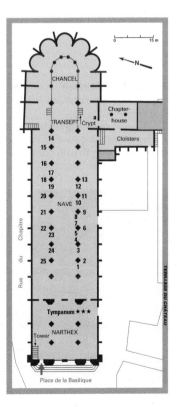

VILLERS-LE-LAC★

POPULATION 4 196

MICHELIN MAP 321: K-4

This small town in the Doubs Valley, where the river spreads to form the Chaillexon Lake★, is the starting point of excursions to the **Saut du Doubs** waterfall.

- **Information:** R. Berçot, 25130 Villers-le-Lac.
  ☎03 81 68 00 98. www.villers-le-lac-info.org.
- **Orient Yourself**: The most relaxing way to enjoy the scenery is on a boat trip.

A Bit of Geography

Lac de Chaillexon

The two slopes on either side of the River Doubs crumbled in here and blocked a part of the valley, creating a natural dam which in turn formed the lake. There are two principal parts to it: in the first, the water is a single open stretch between the gentle slopes of the valley; in the second, it lies between abrupt limestone cliffs which divide this part of the lake into a number of basins. The serpentine lake is 3.5km/2.1mi long, and on average about 200m/220yd wide.

Sight

Musée de la Montre★

&. ⊙Open school holidays daily. ☜5.50€.
☎03 81 68 44 53.
This museum celebrates the history of watch-making, a long-standing tradition of the Jura region on both sides of the Franco-Swiss border. There are watches of all shapes, depicting a variety of themes from the religious to the suggestive, along with precision tools.

Excursion

Saut du Doubs★★★

⊙This is less interesting during periods of drought, when the Saut du Doubs tends to dry up. From the raised level of the lake, the Doubs tumbles to its natural level in a magnificent cascade.

There is a **boat service** (⊙open daily Apr-Oct, Mar and Nov limited departures; ☜11.80€; ☎03 81 68 13 25, www.sautdu-doubs.fr) from Villers-le-Lac to the Saut du Doubs. The boats follow the river's meanders as they gradually open up to form the Chaillexon Lake; then they take their passengers through a gorge, the most picturesque part of the trip. From the landing-stage, take the path (30min round trip on foot) which leads to the two viewpoints overlooking the Saut du Doubs (height: 27m/88.5ft).

Le Saut du Doubs

LAC DE **VOUGLANS**★

MICHELIN MAP 321: D-8

This long manmade lake follows part of the Ain gorge; the finest viewpoints are on the east shore, but the best way to enjoy the scenery is on a boat trip.

🛈 **Information**: 2 pl. Robert-Monnier, 39260 Moirans-en-Montagne.
☎03 84 42 31 57. www.jurasud.net.
Kids **Especially For Kids**: Spend a few hours in the fun Toy Museum in Moirans-en-Montagne.

A Bit of Geography

From gorges to lakes

The Ain once flowed through striking gorges after the Cluse de la Pyle; the walls of the gorges now rise up on either side of several broad lakes created along the river's course by a series of dams. The confluence of the Bienne and the Ain divides the valley into two sections. To the north is the plateau through which the Ain has carved a course, to the south, the Bugey mountain range.

Driving Tour★

The Vouglans dam flooded 35km/22mi of the Ain gorge, forming the Lac de Vouglans. There's no road all the way round but the itinerary below often gets close to shore and offers superb views of the lake.

Pont-de-Poitte

There is a view of the River Ain from the bridge. When the water is low the giants' cauldrons are very much visible. When it is high, the rocky bed disappears under an impressive foaming torrent.

▷ Leave Pont-de-Poitte on D 49. 6km/4mi further on, take D 60 to the left, then turn left again towards St-Christophe.

St-Christophe

This little village is set against a high cliff, overlooked by the remaining walls of a château as well as the pilgrimage **church of St-Christophe** (🕑open mid-Jun to mid-Sep 9am-noon, 3-6pm; rest of the year: by prior appointment, ask at the presbytery; ☎03 84 25 42 58). This was built in the 12C and 15C and contains interesting works of art and wooden statues.

▷ Go down to the village of Tour-du-Meix and take D 470 to the left. From the Pyle Bridge, follow D 301 to the right (200m/220yd after crossing the bridge).

As you turn, there is a lovely **view**★ of the whole stretch of water contained by the dam. More **glimpses**★ of the reservoir appear between the oaks and evergreens which line the twisting road.

Maisod

1hr there and back on foot.
🚶There is a signposted footpath in Maisod by the château entrance, which leads to the cliff overlooking the reservoir, and then continues along its edge.

▷ Carry on along D 301. A road leading to the edge of the lake leads off 1.5km/1mi beyond Maisod. Turn right on D 470 towards Moirans.

Belvédère du Regardoir★

15min round trip on foot.
🚶There is a superb view from the platform overlooking the crescent-shaped section of reservoir.

Moirans-en-Montagne

This small town is a centre for crafts and toy manufacture.

Musée du jouet★

♿🕑*Open Jul-Aug 10am-6.30pm; Sep-Jun 10am-12.30pm, 2-6pm, Sat-Sun 2-6pm. Closed Mon 15 Sep-15 Apr, mornings Jan, Mar, Oct-Nov, 1 Jan and 25 Dec.* ✺*5€*

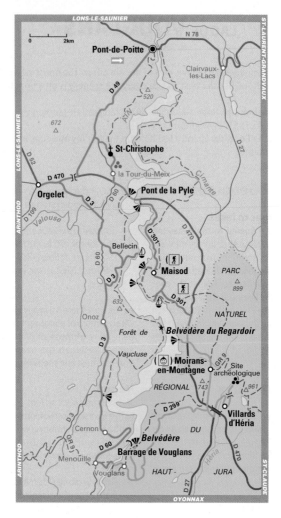

(children 2.50€). ☎03 84 42 38 64. www.
musee-du-jouet.com.

Kids This toy museum is inviting and colourful. The collections fill two storeys,
with more than 5 000 toys, organised by
themes. There is a play area and plenty
of child-friendly activities.

▶ Take D 470 S.

Villards d'Héria

▶ On the left, a small, steep road leads
to the excavations.

Archaeological site

🕑Open Jul-Aug Mon-Fri. ✎Guided
tours (1hr) 10.30am, 2pm, 3.30pm and
5pm. ◉3€. ☎ 03 84 47 12 13.
Recently protected by huge, high-tech
structures, the Gallo-Roman site was

Moirans-en-Montagne – Play time!

G.B. à la Guillaume-Musée du Jouet, Moirans

Address Book

🖢 *For coin ranges, see the Legend on the cover flap.*

WHERE TO STAY

🛏 **Camping Trelachaume** – *39260 Maisod, 2km/1.2mi S of Maisod by D 301.* ☎*03 84 42 03 26. www.camping-trelachaume.com. Open 21 Apr-8 Sep. Reservations recommended. 180 sites.* Pleasant campground with outstanding views over Vouglans Lake, the mountains and the leafy forests. Many sporting facilities including sailing, volley ball, bathing and hiking.

🛏 **Camping Surchauffant** – *At Pont de la Pyle, 39270 La Tour-du-Meix.* ☎*03 84 25 41 08. www.camping-surchauffant.com. Open May-11 Sep. Reservations recommended.180 sites.* Those keen on bathing, water-skiing and fishing will be able to indulge in their favourite sport in Vouglans Lake, a few steps away from the camp site. There is also a childrens play area.

🛏🛏 **Chambre d'Hôte La Baratte** – *39270 Présilly, 5km/3.1mi N of Orgelet by D 52 then D 175.* ☎*03 84 35 55 18. www. labaratte.fr. 🍴 4 rooms. Meals 🛏🛏.*

The former barn and stables of this old farmhouse have been converted into a series of impeccably kept rooms with all modern conveniences. The menu focuses on regional dishes from the Franche-Comté area.

WHERE TO EAT

🍴**Ferme-Auberge La Bergerie** – *39260 Crenans, 3km/1.9mi N of Moirans-en-Montagne by D 296.* ☎*03 84 42 00 50. www.bergerie.com. Closed Nov.* Charming farmouse in a tiny village. Rooms are smart and carefully kept. Eat kid, rabbit, organic lamb and cheese in the old living room, the stables or on the terrace. Interesting choice of good Jura wines.

🍴 **Le Regardoir** – *At the Moirans-en-Montagne Belvedere, 39260 Moirans-en-Montagne.* ☎*03 84 42 01 15. www. leregardoir.com. Closed mid-Dec to mid-Mar. Reservations recommended.* Book a table under the oak trees or on the terrace for a traditional lunch or pizza from an open oven. Superb views over the lake and the rolling countryside.

---

used for worship; two temples and the baths were a place for pilgrimage for the Sequani resident here in the 1C.

Belvédère du Barrage de Vouglans

2km/1.2mi from D 299. Platform and shelter. View of the Vouglans dam.

▷ *At Menouille take D 60 right, which leads to the level of the top of the dam.*

Barrage de Vouglans

The 103m/338ft-high and 420m/1 378ft-long arch dam, which was first put in service in 1968, is only 6m/20ft thick at the top. Containing 600 million m^3/2 119 million cu ft, it is the third largest reservoir in France.

▷ *Drive N along D 60.*

One of the most beautiful meanders of the flooded valley can be seen after Cernon, shortly before the intersection with D 3. There is a **view**★★ of a wild landscape, including the wooded peninsula which extends to the middle of the lake (*car park right of the road*).

Vaucluse Forest (named after the Carthusian monastery flooded when the dam was built) stretches a little further to the right. On the way to Orgelet, the road runs past the Bellecin water sports centre which includes an artificial beach.

▷ *Left to Orgelet at the D 3 intersection.*

The road climbs, with views towards the wooded heights of Haut-Jura.

Orgelet

To the west of the church lies a large, grassy square with beautiful plane trees. The interior of the **church** is surprisingly spacious, with a tall Gothic vault and wide galleries across the west end of the nave and above the first arches of the aisles on either side of the nave.

▷ *From Orgelet, return to Point-de-Poitte along D 470 and D 49.*

A

INDEX

INDEX

INDEX

WHERE TO EAT

INDEX

WHERE TO STAY

INDEX

MAPS AND PLANS

LIST OF MAPS

COMPANION PUBLICATIONS

REGIONAL AND LOCAL MAPS

- To make the most of your journey, travel with Michelin maps at a scale of 1:250 000 - 300 000: Regional maps nos 519, 514, 515, 520 and 523 and the new local maps, which are illustrated on the map of France below. For each of the sites listed in this guide, map references are indicated to help you find your location on these maps.
- In addition to identifying the nature of the main and secondary roads, Michelin maps show castles, churches, scenic view points, megalithic monuments, swimming beaches, golf courses, race tracks and more.

MAPS OF FRANCE

- And remember to travel with the latest edition of the map of France no 721, which gives an overall view of the region of Burgundy-Jura, and the main access roads which connect it to the rest

of France. The entire country is mapped at a 1:1 000 000 scale and clearly shows the main road network. Convenient Atlas formats (spiral, hard cover, "mini" and motorways) are also available.

INTERNET

- Michelin is pleased to offer a route-planning service on the Internet: www. ViaMichelin.com. Choose the shortest route, a route without tolls, or the Michelin recommended route to your destination; you can also access information about hotels and restaurants from The Red Guide, and tourist sites from The Green Guide.
- There are a number of useful maps and plans in the guide, listed in the table of contents.

Bon voyage!

LEGEND

	Sight	Seaside resort	Winter sports resort	Spa
Highly recommended ★★★		♨♨♨	❋❋❋	⚕⚕⚕
Recommended ★★		♨♨	❋❋	⚕⚕
Interesting ★		♨	❋	⚕

Additional symbols

🛈		Tourist information
═══ ═══		Motorway or other primary route
❶	❶	Junction: complete, limited
⊨═══⊨	═══	Pedestrian street
ɪ══════ɪ		Unsuitable for traffic, street subject to restrictions
⊞⊞⊞⊞	- - - -	Steps – Footpath
🚉	🚉	Train station – Auto-train station
🚌	🚌 SNCF	Coach (bus) station
⊷——⊷		Tram
🚇		Metro, underground
P R		Park-and-Ride
♿		Access for the disabled
✉		Post office
☏		Telephone
⬚		Covered market
×ᕽ×		Barracks
△		Drawbridge
℧		Quarry
✗		Mine
B	F	Car ferry (river or lake)
🚢		Ferry service: cars and passengers
⛴		Foot passengers only
③		Access route number common to Michelin maps and town plans
Bert (R.)...		Main shopping street
AZ **B**		Map co-ordinates

Sports and recreation

🏇		Racecourse
⛸		Skating rink
♨	⊞	Outdoor, indoor swimming pool
🎬		Multiplex Cinema
⛵		Marina, sailing centre
⛺		Trail refuge hut
⊐-■-■-⊐		Cable cars, gondolas
⊏+++++⊐		Funicular, rack railway
🚂		Tourist train
◇		Recreation area, park
🎢		Theme, amusement park
⋎		Wildlife park, zoo
✿		Gardens, park, arboretum
◔		Bird sanctuary, aviary
🚶		Walking tour, footpath
👶		Of special interest to children

381

Selected monuments and sights

	Tour - Departure point
	Catholic church
	Protestant church, other temple
	Synagogue - Mosque
	Building
	Statue, small building
	Calvary, wayside cross
	Fountain
	Rampart - Tower - Gate
	Château, castle, historic house
	Ruins
	Dam
	Factory, power plant
	Fort
	Cave
	Troglodyte dwelling
	Prehistoric site
	Viewing table
	Viewpoint
	Other place of interest

Abbreviations

A	Agricultural office (Chambre d'agriculture)
C	Chamber of Commerce (Chambre de commerce)
H	Town hall (Hôtel de ville)
J	Law courts (Palais de justice)
M	Museum (Musée)
P	Local authority offices (Préfecture, sous-préfecture)
POL.	Police station (Police)
	Police station (Gendarmerie)
T	Theatre (Théâtre)
U	University (Université)

Special symbols

	Water park
	Beach
	Boat trips departure
	Fortified town (bastide): in southwest France, a new town built in the 13-14C and typified by a geometrical layout.